ALPHA - ANYBODY CAN CODE

OPTIMUM

PYTHON POWER

SERIES V

UNLEASHING THE POTENTIAL OF DATA SCIENCE

FROM LOGIC TO PREDICTION

Unlocking the Power of Data Science:
Mastering Models, Algorithms, and Core Intuition!

SHREE SHAMBAV

OPTIMUM – PYTHON POWER – Series V

UNLEASHING THE POTENTIAL OF DATA SCIENCE

FROM LOGIC TO PREDICTION

Shree Shambav

Published by Shree Shambav, Tamil Nadu, India
Shree Shambav Ink & Imagination "Where Words Breathe and Imagination Soars"

First Edition, 2025

ISBN: 978-93-5592-543-5

Email:shreeshambav@gmail.com

Web:www.shambav.org

DEDICATION

"Isavasyam idam sarvam yat kim ca jagatyam jagat, tena tyaktena bhunjitha, ma gridhah kasyasvid dhanam"

To the Almighty,

the Divine Masters,

the family who listens,

and my parents who see –

your presence shapes the pages of my life's journey.

"Isavasyam idam sarvam yat kim ca jagatyam jagat"

Meaning: "God encompasses everything you perceive, see, or touch with your sense organs."

DISCLAIMER

The material presented in this book is intended solely for educational and informational purposes. While every effort has been made to ensure the accuracy, clarity, and applicability of the concepts, methods, examples, and code snippets included, the author and publisher make no representations or warranties—express or implied—regarding their completeness, reliability, or suitability for any specific purpose.

This book is designed for readers with a foundational understanding of Python and basic programming principles. Prior exposure to data analysis, statistics, and introductory machine learning will significantly enhance comprehension and practical application.

The techniques, algorithms, and frameworks discussed are provided as general guidance and inspiration for data science, machine learning, and deep learning projects. Actual results and outcomes may differ depending on implementation choices, data characteristics, software versions, computational environments, and the rapidly evolving nature of AI technologies.

The author and publisher disclaim any liability for direct, indirect, incidental, or consequential damages arising from the use, misuse, or interpretation of the information provided. All trademarks, service marks, product names, and brand names referenced in this work remain the property of their respective owners. Their inclusion is for identification and educational purposes only and does not imply endorsement, affiliation, or sponsorship.

Readers are strongly encouraged to verify critical information, consult official documentation, and adapt any techniques responsibly to meet their specific requirements and constraints. Continued learning, critical thinking, and thoughtful experimentation are essential when applying the concepts presented in this book.Mastery in data science is not forged by algorithms alone, but by the curiosity to explore, the discipline to learn, and the courage to build. Every line of Python becomes a step toward shaping intelligent systems that redefine possibility."

Note - If any part of the book, in any sequence, hurts the reader's sentiments, it would be just out of a sheer accident, not intentional

EPIGRAM

"Mastery in data science is not forged by algorithms alone, but by the curiosity to explore, the discipline to learn, and the courage to build. Every line of Python becomes a step toward shaping intelligent systems that redefine possibility."

– Shree Shambav

Suggested Reads

FROM BEST-SELLING AUTHOR

Suggested Reads

Endorsements

"Optimum: Python Power Series V is a masterfully structured guide for serious learners and professionals. It unifies machine learning, probabilistic models, time series, and reinforcement learning into a clear, practical blueprint. A powerhouse resource for anyone committed to building intelligent, scalable, and future-ready AI systems."

"A comprehensive, brilliantly written roadmap for modern data science. This book demystifies complex concepts—from Bayesian reasoning to actor–critic RL—with clarity, depth, and hands-on practicality. Optimum: Python Power Series V is essential reading for learners who want to move beyond theory and build real-world, high-impact AI solutions."

About the Author

Shree Shambhav's journey embodies the harmony of creativity, purpose, and transformation. A world record holder, he is an acclaimed author, inspirational speaker, artist, philanthropist, life coach, and entrepreneur. His deep passion for music has given rise to ten soul-stirring albums available across major platforms, each inspired by his acclaimed poetry collection *Whispers of Eternity*. With a rare fusion of grace, wisdom, and authenticity, Shree Shambhav continues to touch countless lives—guiding individuals toward self-discovery, transformation, and excellence through his profound teachings, insightful counselling, and impactful literary works.

▪ LITERARY EXCELLENCE

Shree Shambav is a 100x best-selling author celebrated for his groundbreaking works across multiple genres, including Non-Fiction, Self-Help, Technology, Short Stories, Anthologies, and Poetry. His thought-provoking articles have also graced the pages of prominent magazines, solidifying his influence as a literary force.

His journey as an author took flight with the acclaimed "Journey of Soul – Karma", a masterpiece that explores the profound interplay of human experience, karma, and spiritual evolution. This seminal work earned him recognition and accolades in the literary world, marking the beginning of a legacy that continues to inspire.

▪ TECHNOLOGY AND INNOVATION

Shree Shambav's contributions extend beyond the realm of literature. A graduate of the prestigious Indian Institute of Management (IIM) and the National Institute of Technology (NIT), he combines academic brilliance with real-world expertise. Throughout his illustrious career, he has held leadership positions in renowned multinational corporations, excelling in strategy, performance improvement, change management, and human capital development.

His technical acumen shines through his acclaimed "Optimum – Python Power Series", a comprehensive collection of books that serve as an invaluable resource for aspiring and seasoned technologists.

- Optimum - Python Series I: Ultimate Guide for Beginners laid the foundation for mastering Python.
- Optimum - Python Series II: Exploring Data Structures and Algorithms elevated readers' understanding of coding efficiency and problem-solving.
- Optimum – Python Power Series III: Unleashing the Potential of Data Science with Libraries stands as a crowning achievement, delving deep into essential libraries for data science and equipping readers with tools to thrive in this ever-evolving domain.
- Optimum – Python Power Series IV: From Logic to Libraries serves as a comprehensive and practical guide, empowering readers to harness the full potential of Python for real-world data science applications. Rooted in Shree Shambhav's rich consulting experience and deep cross-industry insights, this volume bridges theory and practice—helping learners master models, algorithms, and the intuition behind intelligent data-driven solutions.

His latest endeavour, **Optimum Python Power Series V – Unleashing The Potential Of Data Science, From Logic To Prediction** explores the quantitative backbone of analytics—covering the Role of Mathematics, Probability Laws, Sampling, Regression, Bayesian Models, Reinforcement Learning, and Time Series Analysis. With clarity and precision, Shree Shambhav transforms complex statistical foundations into accessible, applicable knowledge, guiding readers to uncover structure, logic, and meaning within data.

Shree Shambav's writing is enriched by his extensive consulting background and a profound comprehension of diverse industries, providing readers with invaluable insights and practical knowledge.

Each book is a testament to Shree Shambav's deep understanding of technology and his ability to make complex concepts accessible, actionable, and transformative.

☐ DRIVING INNOVATION ACROSS INDUSTRIES

Beyond his literary works, Shree Shambav's professional expertise has left an indelible mark across diverse industries, including banking, insurance, retail, and hospitality. He has architected and developed systems that are not only robust and resilient but also revolutionary:

Forecasting Engines and Predictive Models: For pricing, customer churn prediction, and risk portfolio management.

Data-Driven Systems: Web-based architectures, rule engines, ETL frameworks, and BI systems that streamline data flow, enhance accessibility, and support strategic decision-making.

Analytical Dashboards: Insightful tools that deliver powerful visualizations, enabling businesses to navigate challenges and optimize performance.

His work also extends to creating structured practice intellectual properties (IPs), KPI frameworks, and maturity models, empowering organizations to achieve sustainable growth and innovation.

☐ A PHILANTHROPIC SPIRIT AND ADVOCATE FOR CHANGE

Shree Shambav's vision transcends personal success. As a philanthropist and life coach, he remains deeply committed to societal well-being, working to uplift individuals and communities. Through the Ayur Rakshita Foundation (www.shambav-ayurrakshita.org), he leads initiatives that promote health, education, and holistic living, reflecting his belief in creating a harmonious and purposeful world.

☐ A LIFE DEDICATED TO LEARNING AND TRANSFORMATION

Shree Shambav's journey is a testament to his unwavering pursuit of knowledge, innovation, and service. Whether through his books, technical expertise, or philanthropic efforts, he continues to empower others to unlock their potential and live with greater meaning.

During his leisure time, he remains devoted to innovation, channelling his expertise into developing prediction models and exploring emerging fields—an embodiment of lifelong learning and curiosity.

☐ CONNECT WITH SHREE SHAMBAV

Shree Shambav extends his heartfelt gratitude to all those who have shown interest in his works. To explore his books, teachings, and initiatives:

Website: www.shambav.org

Foundation: www.shambav-ayurrakshita.org

LinkedIn: https://www.linkedin.com/in/shreeshambav/

Blog: https://blog.shambav.org/

Instagram: https://www.instagram.com/shreeshambav/

YouTube: https://www.youtube.com/@shreeshambav

Amazon: https://www.amazon.com/author/shreeshambav

Goodreads: https://www.goodreads.com/author/show/22367436.Shree_Shambav

Follow Him on Social Media: @shreeshambav

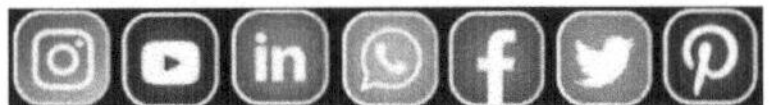

Technical Support and Reviewer

Apeksha Prabhu is a talented technology graduate who specialises in Computer Science and Technology. She has gained extensive experience in the field through her work as a full-stack developer and currently holds a position at Nokia.

Apeksha has completed many outstanding projects during her academic and professional careers. Her outstanding academic achievements match her outstanding practical experience. She has published research papers in prestigious technical journals such as IJERT and IJSCE. Her contributions to different publications show a deep understanding of complex technical concepts, meticulous attention to detail, and a dedication to the advancement of open-source Python.

Apeksha's work is filled with passion and an unwavering dedication to pushing the boundaries of what is possible in her field. She constantly strives to innovate and expand her knowledge, ensuring her work is always at the cutting edge of technological advancement.

Author's Note

Optimum Python Power Series V – Unleashing The Potential Of Data Science, From Logic To Prediction represents a significant milestone in my journey as both a learner and a teacher of advanced analytics and intelligent systems. This book was written with one purpose: to make complex ideas accessible without diluting their depth. As the fields of machine learning, probabilistic reasoning, time series forecasting, and reinforcement learning expand at an extraordinary pace, the need for clarity, structure, and practical intuition becomes increasingly vital.

Throughout this book, I have aimed to bridge the gap between theory and practice, offering readers not only explanations but also guiding principles, code templates, and thought processes that empower real-world application. Each chapter has been crafted to help you build confidence, strengthen your analytical mindset, and develop the ability to navigate the rapidly evolving landscape of data-driven intelligence.

Whether you are a beginner stepping into the world of machine learning or an experienced practitioner seeking deeper insight, I hope this book becomes a trusted companion on your learning journey. May it inspire curiosity, encourage experimentation, and spark the joy of discovery that lies at the heart of every scientific endeavour.

With curiosity and conviction,

Shree Shambav

PREFACE

In a world where data shapes decisions, behaviours, and breakthroughs, the ability to harness its potential has become a defining skill. *Optimum Python Power Series V – Unleashing The Potential Of Data Science, From Logic To Prediction* is crafted with a singular purpose—to guide learners, practitioners, and innovators toward mastering the deeper, more dynamic layers of modern artificial intelligence. This book represents a culmination of years of exploration across machine learning, probabilistic reasoning, time series forecasting, and reinforcement learning, synthesised into a structured, intuitive, and practical learning journey.

The Optimum Series has always aimed to make complex concepts accessible without compromising depth. With this fifth volume, the intention is to elevate the reader from understanding traditional data science workflows to building intelligent, adaptive, and context-aware systems. Each concept included here was chosen carefully—because it either forms a foundational pillar of AI or represents the frontier of what is shaping next-generation models.

This book is designed not only to teach but to inspire. It highlights the elegance behind algorithms, the logic within uncertainty, and the remarkable power of machines that learn from experience. By bridging theory with hands-on practices, it encourages the reader to experiment, question, and create. From probabilistic models that quantify belief to reinforcement learning agents that master complex environments, every chapter is written to cultivate both clarity and curiosity.

Readers will find this book valuable whether they are students seeking strong conceptual grounding, professionals expanding their ML toolkit, or researchers exploring advanced deep learning architectures. The inclusion of practical Python templates and real-world scenarios ensures that the knowledge gained is immediately applicable.

As technology continues to move at a breathtaking pace, the demand for thoughtful, ethical, and effective AI solutions grows. I hope that this book empowers you not just to develop intelligent systems, but to envision new possibilities—solutions that are innovative, responsible, and impactful.

May this volume serve as a trusted companion in your journey toward mastery. Let it spark ideas, refine skills, and illuminate paths you have yet to explore. The future belongs to those who can understand data deeply and use it wisely. This book is one step toward that future.

Happy coding and exploring!

Sincerely,

Shree Shambav

INTRODUCTION

Optimum Python Power Series V – Unleashing The Potential Of Data Science, From Logic To Prediction

Unlocking the Power of Deep Learning: Advancing Intelligence Through Models, Mathematics, and Modern Algorithms

Welcome to *Optimum: Python Power Series V*, a continuation of a learning journey designed to help students, professionals, and AI enthusiasts grasp the full power of data science, machine learning, probabilistic modelling, time series forecasting, and reinforcement learning. As data continues to reshape industries, the ability to understand and harness advanced models has become essential. This book stands as your guide to mastering not only the tools but also the intuition behind intelligent systems.

Python remains the backbone of all modern AI work, offering libraries that support everything from numerical computation and probability theory to neural network training and reinforcement learning pipelines. Through clear explanations and practical coding templates, this book helps you uncover the deeper mechanics that enable models to learn, reason, predict, and adapt.

Journey Overview

This book is structured as a progressive journey, beginning with advanced machine learning principles and moving toward sophisticated modelling frameworks. You will:

- Build strong conceptual grounding in ML paradigms
- Learn to quantify uncertainty through probabilistic models
- Explore time series as a dynamic, temporal data domain
- Step into the world of intelligent agents through reinforcement learning
- Develop practical coding experience using Python and PyTorch

- Strengthen both conceptual intuition and hands-on ability

Each unit builds on the previous one, creating a natural flow from foundational understanding to advanced applications. By the end of this journey, you will not only know *how* models work but also *why* they behave the way they do across different data challenges.

Why This Book?

The primary objective of this book is clarity. Modern AI is powerful but often overwhelming due to its mathematical depth and algorithmic complexity. This book breaks through that barrier by offering:

1. Conceptual Depth With Simplicity

Each chapter translates complex theory into an intuitive understanding without compromising accuracy. Models are explained through reasoning rather than memorisation.

2. Practical, Clean, and Reusable Code

You will find clean PyTorch templates, minimal examples, and implementation-ready snippets that serve as blueprints for your own projects.

3. Broad but Focused Coverage

Instead of covering hundreds of topics superficially, this book dives deep into the essential pillars of modern AI—machine learning, probabilistic modelling, time series, and reinforcement learning.

4. Real-World Thinking

Wherever relevant, concepts are linked to real-world applications: anomaly detection, forecasting, NLP, recommendation systems, autonomous agents, and more.

5. A Bridge Between Theory and Industry

Many learners either understand theory without knowing how to implement it, or can code without grasping the intuition. This book closes that gap.

In essence, this book helps you *think like a data scientist*, *reason like a statistician*, and *build like an engineer.*

Target Audience

This book is designed for a wide spectrum of learners:

Beginners and Students

Who want a clear pathway from fundamentals to advanced topics, with strong conceptual foundations and practical examples.

Intermediate Practitioners

Who understand the basics but wish to deepen their knowledge of probabilistic models, time series forecasting, and reinforcement learning.

Researchers and Developers

Who require structured explanations, mathematical clarity, and high-quality PyTorch implementations.

Domain Professionals

From finance, healthcare, marketing, and operations who need practical models for forecasting, modelling uncertainty, or automated decision-making.

Enthusiasts of AI and Deep Learning

Who wants to understand not just how to use models, but how they fundamentally function.

If you're building your expertise in data science, this book is designed to meet you where you are while pushing you to the next level.

Book Coverage

The book is organised into four major parts, each tackling an essential dimension of advanced data science:

PART ONE: Advanced Machine Learning Techniques

You begin with the deeper structures of machine learning—supervised and unsupervised learning, self-supervision, ensemble methods, reinforcement learning fundamentals, and key ML terminologies. You learn the essential machine learning pipeline: data preparation, feature engineering, model training, evaluation, and deployment.

PART TWO: Foundations of Probabilistic Models

This section explores the mathematical core of uncertainty. You will understand generative vs. discriminative models, MLE, MAP, PDFs, likelihoods, Naive Bayes variants, Gaussian Processes, LDA, QDA, Bayesian Belief Networks, Hidden Markov Models, and Gaussian Mixture Models. The unit ends with Variational Bayes and Dirichlet Process Mixtures for automatic cluster inference.

PART THREE: Time Series Modelling

This unit builds practical forecasting expertise with trend, seasonality, ACF/PACF, stationarity, ARIMA, SARIMA, SARIMAX, missing data handling, decomposition techniques, and multivariate models like VAR. Tools such as Granger causality and cointegration deepen your understanding of temporal relationships.

PART FOUR: Reinforcement Learning

The final unit reveals the mechanics of intelligent decision-making: MDPs, Bellman equations, Q-Tables, DQN, Double and Dueling DQN, PER, Rainbow DQN, Distributional RL, Policy Gradients, PPO, Actor-Critic systems, including DDPG, TD3, SAC, and an introduction to Multi-Agent RL.

By the end of this book, you will possess the knowledge and confidence to design, implement, evaluate, and optimise advanced models across multiple domains. You will be able to think in terms of probability, time, uncertainty, reward, and deep learning frameworks—all essential lenses of modern artificial intelligence.

Let this book be your companion as you unlock the deeper layers of intelligence hidden within data.

Happy coding and exploring!

☐ PROGRAMS

The table presents a detailed distribution of the programs included in this book, categorised by units within each part.

Part	Unit	Lessons covered	Program	Total Program
One	1	Getting started	1	**1**
Two	2	Foundations of Probabilistic Models	18	**18**
Three	3	Time Series Forecasting	29	**29**
Four	4	Reinforcement Learning	37	**37**
Appendix	A	Online Resources		
	B	Practice Question		**70**
	C	Quiz		**70**
		Total Programs		**85**

☐ PRACTICE QUESTIONS

The table provides a comprehensive breakdown of the practice questions featured in this book, sorted by units within each part.

Part	Practice Question	Total
One	0	**0**
Two	15	**15**
Three	25	**25**
Four	30	**30**
Total Questions	**217**	**70**

☐ ASSIGNMENT AND QUIZ

The table provides a comprehensive breakdown of the assignment featured in this book, sorted by units within each part.

Part	Unit	Assignment	Quiz
One	1		0
Two	2		20
Three	3		20
Four	4		30
Total		**0**	**70**

☐ TABLES AND ILLUSTRATIONS

Part	Tables	Illustration	Flowchart
One	2	8	0
Two	16	33	0
Three	0	31	0
Four	15	60	0
Total	**33**	**132**	

CONTENTS

Getting Started

☐ Understanding Data Science, AI, Machine Learning & Deep Learning

Data Science is a multidisciplinary field that integrates scientific methods, statistical reasoning, computational tools, and domain expertise to extract meaningful insights from data. It brings together an expansive range of techniques—including data preprocessing, visualisation, statistical modelling, machine learning, and deep learning—to uncover patterns, build predictive systems, and support informed decision-making.

While *Data Science*, *Machine Learning*, and *Artificial Intelligence (AI)* are closely connected, they each serve distinct roles within the broader ecosystem of intelligent computing.

☐ Data Science

Data Science is a comprehensive discipline focused on analysing, modelling, and interpreting data to derive actionable knowledge. It encompasses:

- **Data acquisition** from structured, semi-structured, and unstructured sources
- **Cleaning and preprocessing** to remove inconsistencies, noise, missing values, and outliers
- **Exploratory Data Analysis (EDA)** to identify patterns, trends, and correlations
- **Statistical analysis** to quantify uncertainty and validate assumptions
- **Predictive modelling and machine learning** to forecast outcomes
- **Data visualisation and storytelling** to communicate insights effectively

Data scientists use a wide array of techniques—ranging from statistical methods and data mining to machine learning and advanced analytics—to solve real-world challenges and drive strategic decisions.

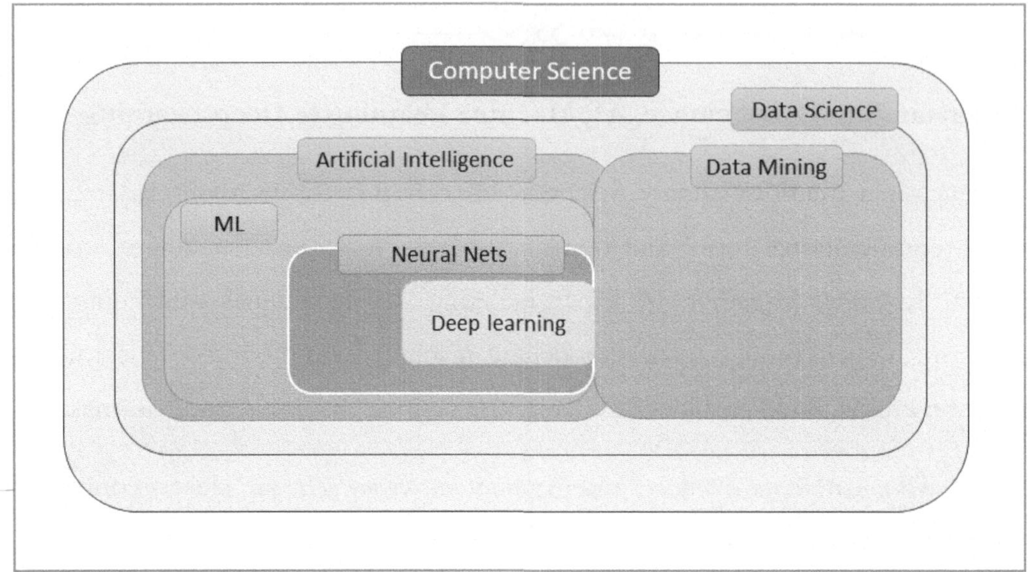

Illustration data4:

□ **Artificial Intelligence (AI)**

Artificial Intelligence refers to the development of systems capable of performing tasks that typically require human intelligence. These include:

- Reasoning and problem-solving
- Learning from experience
- Understanding natural language
- Recognising images, objects, and speech
- Autonomous decision-making

AI spans multiple subfields such as natural language processing, computer vision, robotics, expert systems, and knowledge representation. Approaches range from symbolic and rule-based systems to modern machine learning, deep learning, and neural networks.

Machine Learning (ML)

Machine Learning is a key subset of AI focused on algorithms that learn patterns from data and improve their performance over time without explicit programming. ML models are trained using historical data and then used to make decisions or predictions on new data.

Major categories include:

- **Supervised learning** (classification, regression)
- **Unsupervised learning** (clustering, association, dimensionality reduction)
- **Reinforcement learning** (learning optimal actions via rewards and penalties)

Machine learning drives a broad spectrum of applications—from fraud detection and recommendation engines to NLP, computer vision, and predictive analytics.

Deep Learning & Neural Networks

Deep Learning is a powerful extension of machine learning that uses multilayered neural networks to learn complex hierarchical representations of data. These models consist of interconnected artificial neurons arranged in layers, inspired by the structure of the human brain.

Deep learning excels in:

- Image and video processing
- Speech and audio recognition

- Natural language understanding
- Autonomous systems
- High-dimensional pattern recognition

Neural networks learn through iterative weight adjustments, enabling them to model intricate relationships that traditional algorithms often struggle to capture.

Deep learning has revolutionised modern AI by enabling systems to perform at—and sometimes beyond—human-level accuracy in many tasks.

☐ Key Features of Data Science

Data Science involves a systematic, iterative workflow that blends analytical thinking with computational efficiency. Essential components include:

1. Data Collection

Gathering relevant data from databases, APIs, sensors, logs, web scraping, or external repositories. Data may be structured, semi-structured, or unstructured.

2. Data Cleaning & Preprocessing

Removing inaccuracies, handling missing values, addressing outliers, encoding categorical data, transforming features, and preparing datasets for modelling.

3. Exploratory Data Analysis (EDA)

Using summary statistics and visualisations to understand distributions, relationships, anomalies, and trends—guiding modelling choices.

4. Statistical Analysis

Applying descriptive and inferential techniques, hypothesis testing, and regression methods to quantify patterns and validate insights.

5. Feature Engineering

Creating, transforming, and selecting meaningful features to enhance model performance. This stage blends creativity with domain knowledge.

6. Model Evaluation & Validation

Assessing predictive models using metrics such as accuracy, precision, recall, F1-score, RMSE, or AUC, along with validation strategies like cross-validation and hold-out testing.

7. Machine Learning & Modelling

Training supervised, unsupervised, and reinforcement learning models to make predictions, segment groups, or automate decision-making.

8. Data Visualisation

Communicating insights through charts, dashboards, and interactive tools for clarity and decision support.

9. Deployment & Productionisation

Integrating models into real-world applications or pipelines to generate predictions at scale, ensuring reliability, security, and performance.

10. Continuous Learning & Iteration

Refining models, updating data pipelines, retraining algorithms, and adapting to changing business needs or data patterns.

Summary

- **Data Science** is the overarching discipline that extracts insights and decisions from data.

- **Machine Learning** is a subset focused on developing predictive algorithms.
- **Deep Learning** is a further subset using neural networks to learn hierarchical representations.
- **AI** is the broader goal of building intelligent systems capable of human-like reasoning and perception.

Together, these components form the backbone of modern intelligent systems—and the foundation upon which this book builds advanced techniques in time series modelling, probabilistic reasoning, and reinforcement learning.

☐ PROGRAMMING LANGUAGES:

Various programming languages are utilised for AI and related tasks. Here are some examples:

Python: Known for its simplicity and vast ecosystem of libraries like TensorFlow, PyTorch, and scikit-learn, Python is one of the most popular languages for AI development.

R: Particularly prominent in statistical analysis and data visualisation, R is frequently used for tasks like exploratory data analysis and statistical modelling in AI applications.

Java: Although not as commonly associated with AI as Python or R, Java is still utilised for AI development, particularly in large-scale enterprise systems where performance and scalability are crucial.

Lisp: Lisp, particularly its dialects like Common Lisp and Clojure, has a rich history in AI research and development. It is known for its powerful meta-programming capabilities and is used in various AI applications.

SWI Prolog: Prolog is a logic programming language commonly used in fields like natural language processing and expert systems. SWI Prolog, in particular, is popular in medical projects and other domains where logical reasoning is essential.

Matlab: Widely used in engineering and scientific computing, Matlab provides extensive tools for numerical computing, simulation, and data analysis, making it suitable for certain AI tasks.

Julia: Julia is gaining popularity in scientific computing and AI due to its high performance and easy interoperability with other languages like Python and R. It is particularly well-suited for tasks involving numerical computation and optimization.

These languages offer diverse capabilities and are chosen based on factors like the nature of the AI problem, existing infrastructure, performance requirements, and developer expertise.

☐ THE GROWTH OF AI

1950: Alan Turing publishes "Computing Machinery and Intelligence," proposing the Turing Test as a measure of machine intelligence.

1951: Marvin Minsky and Dean Edmonds develop SNARC, the first neural network simulator, at Princeton University.

1956: The term "Artificial Intelligence" is coined at the Dartmouth Summer Research Project, marking the official birth of AI as a scientific field.

1959: Herbert Simon and Allen Newell create the Logic Theorist, the first AI program capable of proving mathematical theorems.

1960: John McCarthy develops the LISP programming language, which becomes a foundational language for AI research.

1961: The first industrial robot, Unimate, is deployed at General Motors, introducing AI applications in manufacturing.

1997: IBM's Deep Blue defeats world chess champion Garry Kasparov, demonstrating AI's ability in strategic computation and decision-making.

2005: Stanley, an autonomous vehicle from Stanford University, wins the DARPA Grand Challenge, advancing robotics and autonomous driving.

2011: IBM's Watson defeats human champions on Jeopardy!, showcasing the power of natural language understanding and question answering.

2012: AlexNet, a deep convolutional neural network, wins the ImageNet Challenge, igniting the deep learning revolution.

2015: DeepMind's AlphaGo defeats world champion Lee Sedol in the game of Go, marking a historic milestone in AI's cognitive capabilities.

2018: OpenAI's GPT (Generative Pre-trained Transformer) model demonstrates exceptional language generation and comprehension.

2019: Google's BERT (Bidirectional Encoder Representations from Transformers) revolutionises Natural Language Processing (NLP) tasks with bidirectional understanding.

2020: AI achieves widespread industrial adoption across healthcare, finance, transportation, and education, driving innovation and efficiency.

2021: Transformer-based architectures dominate machine learning research, powering breakthroughs in computer vision, speech, and multimodal AI.

2022: AI ethics, fairness, and responsible AI governance become central to discussions as AI systems influence society at scale.

2023: Continued evolution in reinforcement learning, autonomous systems, and multimodal models (seeing, hearing, and reasoning together) defines the new AI frontier.

2024–Present: The rise of Generative AI, LLMs (Large Language Models) like GPT-4 and beyond, Retrieval-Augmented Generation (RAG), and AI Agents heralds an era where AI collaborates with humans in creativity, reasoning, and decision-making—shaping the future of intelligence itself.

☐ AI SPECTRUM

Artificial intelligence (AI) encompasses a spectrum of capabilities and goals. Here's an improved breakdown of the different types of AI:

Artificial Narrow Intelligence (ANI): ANI, also known as weak AI, refers to AI systems that are designed and trained for specific tasks or narrow domains. These systems excel at performing well-defined tasks within limited contexts. Examples include virtual personal assistants like Siri or Alexa, recommendation systems, and image recognition algorithms.

Artificial General Intelligence (AGI): AGI, often referred to as strong AI, represents a hypothetical AI system with human-level cognitive abilities across a broad range of domains. AGI would possess the ability to understand, learn, and apply knowledge in a manner similar to human intelligence. AGI remains a theoretical concept, and creating such a system is a major goal of AI research.

Artificial Super Intelligence (ASI): ASI goes beyond AGI and describes an AI system that surpasses human intelligence in every aspect, including creativity, problem-solving, and social skills. ASI represents the upper limit of AI capabilities and is often associated with speculative scenarios of AI surpassing human control and comprehension.

Each type of AI represents a different level of intelligence and capability, with ANI being the most prevalent and AGI and ASI representing increasingly advanced and theoretical stages of AI development. Understanding these distinctions is crucial for discussions about the potential impact and ethical considerations surrounding AI technology.

☐ ADVANCEMENT OF AI KEY FACTORS

More Data: The proliferation of digital technologies has led to an exponential increase in the volume, variety, and velocity of data generated globally. This abundance of data provides a rich resource for AI systems to learn from and make predictions or decisions.

More Computational Power: Advances in hardware, such as GPUs (Graphics Processing Units) and specialised AI accelerators, have significantly increased computational power. This increased computational power enables the training and deployment of more complex AI models capable of processing vast amounts of data efficiently.

Better Algorithms: Ongoing research in machine learning and AI has led to the development of more sophisticated algorithms and techniques. These advancements have improved the performance and capabilities of AI systems, enabling them to tackle a wider range of tasks with greater accuracy and efficiency.

Broad Investment: There has been a surge in investment in AI research and development across various sectors, including technology, healthcare, finance, manufacturing, and transportation. This broad investment reflects the growing recognition of AI's potential to drive innovation, enhance productivity, and address complex challenges across industries.

Overall, the convergence of these factors has fuelled the rapid advancement and adoption of AI technologies, making it a central topic of discussion and a transformative force in shaping the future of society, economy, and technology.

What are Python libraries and why?

Python libraries are collections of pre-written code that provide a wide range of functionalities and tools to enhance Python programming. These libraries are developed by the Python community and serve as valuable resources for developers.

Python libraries address common programming challenges, such as data manipulation, scientific computing, machine learning, web development, and more. They offer ready-made solutions and functionalities that can be easily incorporated into projects, saving time and effort.

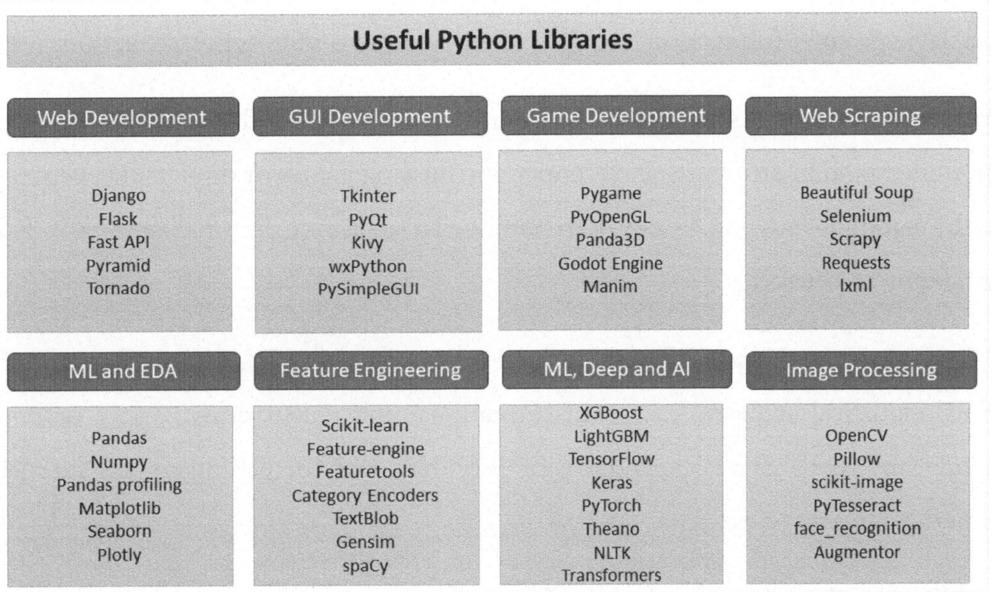

How are Python libraries useful in Data science?

Python libraries are incredibly useful in data science due to their extensive functionality and ease of use. Here are some key Python libraries and their specific contributions to data science:

☐ **HOW TO APPROACH DATA SCIENCE USING PYTHON LIBRARIES?**

To approach Data Science using Python libraries, you can follow a systematic process that typically involves the following steps:

Define the problem: Begin by articulating the problem you aim to address or the question you seek to answer through data analysis. Gain a comprehensive understanding of the goals and objectives underlying your analysis to ensure alignment with overarching objectives.

Gather data: Proceed to collect pertinent data from diverse sources, including databases, files, APIs, or through web scraping methodologies. Prioritise the acquisition of clean, comprehensive datasets that accurately reflect the nuances of the problem at hand, laying a solid foundation for subsequent analysis and insights extraction.

Explore and preprocess the data: Use libraries like pandas and NumPy to explore the data, understand its structure, and identify any missing values or outliers. Preprocess the data by handling missing values, performing data cleaning, normalization, or feature engineering as necessary.

Perform data analysis: Utilize libraries like pandas, NumPy, and SciPy to perform various statistical analyses, data transformations, and calculations. Apply descriptive statistics, inferential statistics, and exploratory data analysis techniques to gain insights and understanding of the data.

Visualize the data: Use visualization libraries such as Matplotlib and Seaborn to create informative and visually appealing charts, plots, and graphs. Visualizations can help in understanding patterns, relationships, and trends in the data.

Build predictive models: Employ machine learning libraries like Scikit-learn or deep learning libraries like TensorFlow and Keras to build predictive models. Choose appropriate algorithms based on the problem type (regression, classification, clustering) and train the models using the prepared data.

Evaluate and validate models: Assess the performance of your models using evaluation metrics, cross-validation techniques, or train-test splits. Optimize the models by fine-tuning hyperparameters and adjusting the model architecture.

Communicate results: Present your findings and insights clearly and concisely using visualisations, reports, or interactive dashboards. Use libraries like Jupyter Notebook or data storytelling tools to effectively communicate your data analysis process and results.

Iterate and refine: Continuously iterate on your analysis, models, and visualisations based on feedback, new data, or changing requirements. Refine your approach and improve the accuracy and relevance of your analysis.

Throughout this process, make use of the extensive documentation and community support available for the Python libraries you are using. Experiment with different techniques, algorithms, and parameters to find the most suitable approach for your specific problem.

☐ WHAT DO YOU HOPE TO GAIN FROM THIS BOOK?

By exploring **Optimum – Python Power Series V**, you embark on a transformative journey into the deeper architecture of data science—where mathematics, intuition, and intelligent systems converge. This volume is crafted to empower you with the clarity, precision, and practical mastery needed to tackle the next generation of data challenges.

Strengthen Your Data Science Foundation:

Gain a refined understanding of advanced data-processing techniques, probabilistic reasoning, and mathematical principles that underpin modern analytics.

Master Advanced Machine Learning & Deep Learning:

Explore algorithms that move beyond the basics—delving into probabilistic models, time series forecasting, reinforcement learning, and neural architectures that power intelligent systems.

Build Analytical Intuition:

Develop a sharper, more conceptual understanding of *why* models work, not just *how* to implement them. This book trains your mind to think like a data scientist, mathematician, and engineer—simultaneously.

Gain Practical, Real-World Experience:

Through hands-on Python and PyTorch examples, you'll apply every concept in meaningful ways—bridging theory with implementation and transforming insight into action.

Advance Your Career with Confidence:

Whether you're an aspiring data scientist or a seasoned practitioner seeking depth, this book equips you with the advanced tools, frameworks, and mindset needed to excel in a rapidly evolving AI-powered world.

☐ How to Use This Book

Start with the Foundations

If you're new to machine learning, begin with the introductory chapters that explain core concepts, key terminologies, and the role of Python in the data science ecosystem.

Explore Hands-On Examples

Every concept is accompanied by real code snippets and practical use cases. Run them, tweak them, and observe how small changes influence outcomes—because the best way to learn is by doing.

Recommended Reference:

Optimum – Python Series I: Ultimate Guide for Beginners lays the groundwork for Python mastery.

Optimum – Python Series II: Exploring Data Structures and Algorithms: A foundational guide that strengthens understanding of efficient coding, problem-solving, and algorithmic thinking. It helps readers build robust logic and optimize solutions for real-world programming challenges.

Optimum – Python Power Series III: Unleashing the Potential of Data Science with Libraries: A powerful exploration of essential data science libraries that form the backbone of modern analytics. It equips readers with tools, techniques, and confidence to excel in an ever-evolving data-driven world.

Optimum – Python Power Series IV: From Logic to Libraries: A comprehensive guide that blends industry experience with practical insights for real-world data science. It helps learners bridge theory and implementation, mastering models, algorithms, and intuitive decision-making.

Use as a Modular Reference

This volume is intentionally structured for flexible learning. Each chapter stands as a self-contained module, allowing you to dive directly into the concepts that match your current goals—whether probabilistic models, time series, or reinforcement learning.

Bridge Theory and Practice

Beyond code implementation, this book reveals the underlying logic and mathematical intuition that make each technique work. It closes the gap between "knowing the method" and "understanding the mechanism," empowering you to apply concepts with confidence and clarity.

Engage with an Evolving Field

Data Science, Machine Learning, and Deep Learning continue to advance at an extraordinary pace. Use this book as a foundation—and a launchpad—to explore emerging models, evolving libraries, and cutting-edge research as the field grows.

Apply Concepts to Real Projects

Mastery comes through practice. You are encouraged to experiment with your own datasets, run iterative tests, and adapt the techniques to real-world challenges. Every chapter equips you with actionable tools to enrich your projects and expand your expertise.

Gateway to Generative AI & Reinforcement Learning

This volume also offers a forward-looking introduction to Generative AI and a deep dive into Reinforcement Learning—two domains shaping the next frontier of intelligent systems. These sections provide you with both practical insights and a conceptual roadmap to the technologies defining the future.

☐ Who Is This Book Aimed At?

Optimum – Python Power Series V is crafted for a diverse audience of learners and professionals, including:

Beginners: Individuals stepping into the world of data science who seek a clear, structured, and practical foundation in Python, machine learning, probabilistic models, and modern analytical thinking.

Intermediate Practitioners: Readers with foundational knowledge who want to expand their expertise, strengthen intuition, and master more advanced methods—from time series forecasting to reinforcement learning—with hands-on, implementation-driven clarity.

Experienced Professionals: Data scientists, ML engineers, and analysts aiming to stay current with evolving tools, libraries, and algorithms, while deepening their ability to model uncertainty, build intelligent systems, and optimise real-world solutions.

Students and Educators: University learners in data science, computer science, AI, mathematics, and engineering, along with educators seeking a thorough, well-structured resource that blends theory, application, and conceptual depth.

Domain Experts Across Industries: Professionals in finance, healthcare, marketing, manufacturing, operations, research, and technology who rely on data-driven decision-making and want to elevate their analytical, predictive, and AI capabilities.

Reader Responses:

We highly value the feedback from our readers. It helps us improve and create titles that cater to your interests. Please share your thoughts about this book, what you found helpful, or what could be improved. You can send your general feedback to shreeshambav.optimum@gmail.com, and kindly include the book's title in the subject line. If you have knowledge or expertise on a particular subject and are interested in contributing to a book, please send your inquiries to the same email address mentioned above.

PART ONE

Getting Started

Advanced Techniques

"Every model is a mirror—imperfect, yet revealing. What we learn depends on how honestly, we look."

– Shree Shambav

PART ONE

DAY ONE

Unit 1 - Lesson One

Introduction to Machine Learning

☐ Introduction to Machine Learning:

Master said, "Arthur Samuel, an early American leader in computer gaming and artificial intelligence, introduced the term "Machine Learning" in 1959 during his tenure at IBM. He described machine learning as 'the field of study that gives computers the ability to learn without being explicitly programmed.'"

However, there is no single, universally accepted definition of machine learning. Different authors offer varied interpretations.

- Machine learning involves programming computers to optimise a performance criterion using example data or past experiences. It entails defining a model with parameters and employing a computer program to adjust these parameters based on training data or past experiences. The model may be predictive, making forecasts for the future, or descriptive, extracting insights from data.

- The field of study referred to as machine learning deals with constructing computer programs that enhance their performance with experience.

> "Machine learning is the art of empowering machines to learn and evolve from data, transforming algorithms into powerful tools that uncover patterns, make predictions, and shape the future." – Shree Shambav

Machine learning is a subset of artificial intelligence dedicated to developing algorithms and statistical models that enable computers to enhance their performance in tasks through experience. These algorithms and models are crafted to learn from data and make predictions or decisions without explicit instructions. There are various types of machine learning, including supervised learning, unsupervised learning, and reinforcement learning. Supervised learning entails training a model on labelled data, whereas unsupervised learning involves training on unlabelled data. Reinforcement learning involves training through trial and error. Machine learning finds application in diverse areas, including image and speech recognition, natural language processing, and recommender systems.

Definition of learning:

A computer program is considered to learn from experience E concerning a class of tasks T and a performance measure P if its performance at tasks T, as evaluated by P, improves with experience E.

Examples:

Handwriting recognition learning problem:

> **Task T**: Recognizing and classifying handwritten words within images.
>
> **Performance P**: Percentage of words correctly classified.
>
> **Training experience E**: A dataset of handwritten words with corresponding classifications.

Definition: A computer program that learns from experience is commonly referred to as a machine learning program or simply a learning program.

☐ Classification of Machine Learning

Master explained that the Machine learning implementations can be categorised into four major types based on the nature of the learning signal or response available to a learning system:

Supervised learning:

Supervised learning involves learning a function that maps input to output based on labelled input-output pairs. The data provided for training is labelled, and both classification and regression problems fall into this category.

Learning Algorithms

- Linear Regression
- Logistic Regression
- Decision Trees
- Random Forests
- Naïve Bayes
- KNN
- Support Vector Machines (SVM)
- Gradient Boosting

Purpose: Used for tasks with labelled examples, aiming to learn the mapping between input features and output labels.

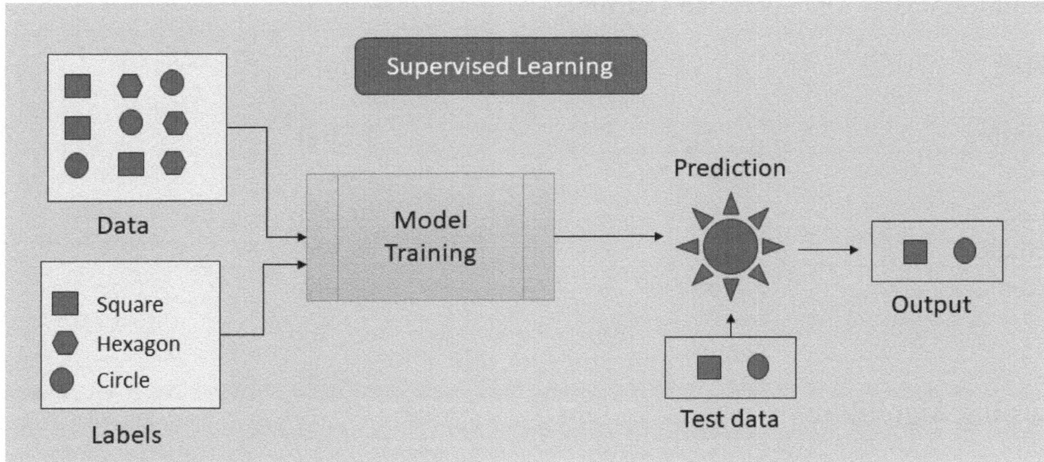

Illustration sup: Suprevised Learning

Example — Consider a dataset of patients entering a clinic, where each patient's gender, age, and health status (labelled as "healthy" or "sick") are recorded.

Unsupervised learning:

Unsupervised learning algorithms draw inferences from datasets consisting of input data without labelled responses. In this type, the data lacks explicit classification or categorisation. Example: A dataset of patients entering a clinic containing only gender and age information.

This learning method mirrors human observation-based classification, where objects or events are grouped based on similarity. Many recommendation systems and marketing automation tools use unsupervised learning.

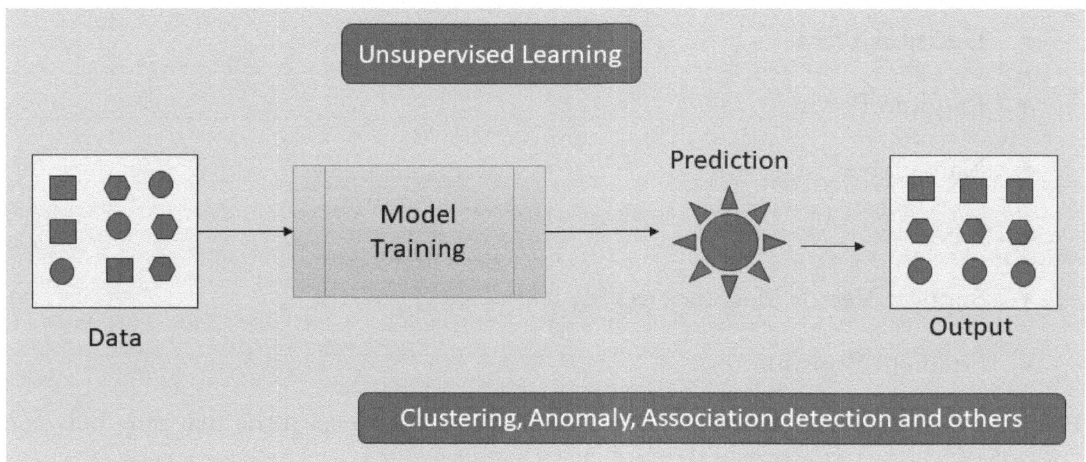

Illustration unsup: Unsupervised Learning

Table 1:

Gender	**Age**	**Label**
Male	69	sick
Male	48	healthy
Female	56	sick
Female	50	healthy

Learning Algorithm:

- K-means Clustering
- DBSCAN
- Gaussian Mixture Models (GMM)
- Principal Component Analysis (PCA)

- Independent Component Analysis (ICA)

Purpose: Applied to tasks such as clustering, dimensionality reduction, and feature extraction when labelled examples are absent, or the goal is to discover patterns in data.

Table 2:

Gender	Age
Male	69
Male	48
Female	56
Female	50

☐ Another categorisation

Another categorisation of machine learning tasks is based on the desired output:

Classification: Involves dividing inputs into two or more classes, with the model assigning unseen inputs to one or more predefined classes. This is typically accomplished through supervised learning. An example is spam filtering, where emails are classified as "spam" or "not spam."

Regression: Addresses cases where the outputs are continuous rather than discrete. Also, in a supervised problem, regression predicts numerical values based on input data.

Clustering: Involves dividing a set of inputs into groups, with the groups not known beforehand. This is typically an unsupervised task.

Learning algorithm for clustering:

- K-means
- Agglomerative Clustering
- Spectral Clustering
- DBSCAN

Purpose: Groups unlabelled data into clusters, identifying inherent structures or relationships without labelled examples.

Machine learning enables the resolution of problems that cannot be addressed using traditional approaches. By leveraging ML algorithms and modern computing technologies, scalability and efficiency can be improved. Modern ML models have applications ranging from predicting disease outbreaks to analysing stock market trends.

Need

Master explained that the need for machine learning (ML) arises from the proliferation of data sources such as cloud data, the Internet of Things (IoT), and social media. ML enables the analysis, processing, and predictive modelling of vast datasets, leveraging the abundance of data available. With ML, organisations can harness data to generate insights, improve decision-making processes, uncover patterns and trends, and solve complex problems effectively. The applications of ML span various domains, including healthcare, finance, marketing, and cybersecurity, where it plays a crucial role in optimising processes, enhancing efficiency, and driving innovation.

Terminologies of ML

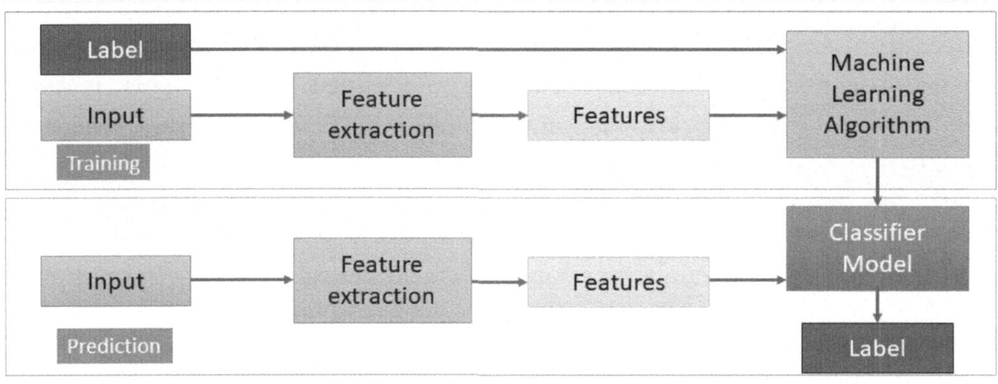

Model: A model, also known as a hypothesis, is a representation learned from data using machine learning algorithms. It encapsulates the learned patterns and relationships within the data, enabling predictions or classifications for new, unseen instances.

Feature: A feature refers to an individual measurable property or characteristic of the data. Features provide the input information to the model and are typically represented as a feature vector. These vectors encapsulate multiple features, such as colour, smell, or taste, which are essential for making predictions or classifications. Selecting informative, discriminating, and independent features is crucial for the effectiveness of machine learning algorithms. Feature extraction techniques are often employed to extract relevant features from raw data.

Target (Label): The target variable, also known as the label, is the value that the model aims to predict. In the context of the fruit example discussed earlier, the label corresponds to the name of the fruit, such as apple, orange, or banana. During training, the model learns to associate input features with the corresponding target labels.

Training: Training involves providing the model with a dataset containing input features, along with their corresponding target labels. The model learns from this labelled data to generate predictions or classifications for new instances. Through iterative optimisation processes, the model adjusts its parameters to minimise prediction errors and improve performance on the training data.

Prediction: Once trained, the model can make predictions or classifications for new input instances. Given a set of input features, the model outputs a predicted label or value. It is essential to evaluate the model's performance on unseen data to ensure its generalisation ability. A well-performing model should demonstrate robust performance in unseen instances, indicating its effectiveness in making accurate predictions.

Enhanced Machine Learning Process:

Define Objective: Clearly articulate the problem or goal that the machine learning model aims to address or achieve.

Data Gathering: Collect relevant data sources that contain information necessary for training and testing the model.

Data Preparation: Cleanse, preprocess, and format the data to ensure it is suitable for analysis and model training.

Data Exploration: Explore and analyse the data to gain insights into its characteristics, distributions, and relationships.

Building Model: Develop and train machine learning models using appropriate algorithms and techniques tailored to the defined objective.

Model Evaluation: Assess the performance of the trained models using evaluation metrics and techniques to ensure they meet the defined criteria and objectives.

Predictions: Deploy the trained models to make predictions or decisions on new or unseen data, leveraging the insights gained from the model evaluation process.

Steps to Get Started with Machine Learning:

- Define the Problem: Identify the problem you want to solve and determine if machine learning can be used to solve it.
- Collect Data: Gather and clean the data that you will use to train your model.

The quality of your model will depend on the quality of your data.

- Explore the Data: Use data visualization and statistical methods to understand the structure and relationships within your data.
- Pre-process the Data: Prepare the data for modeling by normalizing, transforming, and cleaning it as necessary.
- Split the Data: Divide the data into training and test datasets to validate your model.
- Choose a Model: Select a machine learning model that is appropriate for your problem and the data you have collected.
- Train the Model: Use the training data to train the model, adjusting its parameters to fit the data as accurately as possible.
- Evaluate the Model: Use the test data to evaluate the performance of the model and determine its accuracy.
- Fine-tune the Model: Based on the results of the evaluation, fine-tune the model by adjusting its parameters and repeating the training process until the desired level of accuracy is achieved.
- Deploy the Model: Integrate the model into your application or system, making it available for use by others.
- Monitor the Model: Continuously monitor the performance of the model to ensure that it continues to provide accurate results over time.

Approach for Weather Forecast Example:

Step 1: Define Objective

- Identify the prediction target: Will it rain? (Yes/No)
- Determine relevant input features: Humidity level, precipitation, wind speed, etc.
- Classify the problem: Binary classification

Step 2: Data Gathering

- Assess data availability and sources
- Utilise sampling techniques or access datasets from platforms like Kaggle

Step 3: Prepare Data

- Transform data into a desired format for analysis
- Perform data cleaning: Handle missing values, remove corrupted or unnecessary data

Step 4: Data Exploration

- Analyse patterns and trends in the data
- Extract insights and observe correlations between variables

Step 5: Build ML Model

- Select an appropriate predictive model
- Split data into training and testing sets
- Train the model to predict the likelihood of rain (Yes/No)
- Choose classification algorithms such as Logistic Regression, SVM, Naïve Bayes, based on problem requirements

Step 6: Model Evaluation and Optimisation

- Assess model efficiency and accuracy
- Optimise model performance using techniques like parameter tuning and hyperparameter optimisation

Step 7: Prediction

- Use the trained model to make predictions
- Output categorical predictions: e.g., "Raining: Yes" or "Raining: No"

This refined approach provides a structured framework for developing a weather forecasting model, ensuring thorough data preparation, model selection, evaluation, and prediction.

Master said, "Akshaya, here is a simple machine learning example in Python that illustrates how to train a model to predict the species of iris flowers based on their sepal and petal measurements. We'll use the popular Iris dataset for this task."

Example P1 – U1 – D1	

ML - simple machine learning	Output

# Importing necessary libraries 	
import pandas as pd
from sklearn.datasets import load_iris
from sklearn.model_selection import train_test_split
from sklearn.linear_model import LogisticRegression
from sklearn.metrics import accuracy_score
 	
# Load the Iris dataset 	
iris = load_iris()
# Creating a DataFrame from the dataset 	
df = pd.DataFrame(data=iris.data, columns=iris.feature_names)
df['target'] = iris.target
# Splitting the data into features and target 	
X = df.drop('target', axis=1)
y = df['target']
# Splitting the data into training and testing sets 	
X_train, X_test, y_train, y_test = train_test_split(X, y, test_size=0.2, random_state=42)
# Training the Logistic Regression model 	
model = LogisticRegression(max_iter=1000)
model.fit(X_train, y_train)
# Making predictions on the test data 	
y_pred = model.predict(X_test)
# Calculating the accuracy of the model 	
accuracy = accuracy_score(y_test, y_pred)
print("Accuracy:", accuracy)
	Accuracy: 1.0

This Python code demonstrates a simple machine learning example using the Iris dataset. The goal is to train a model to predict the species of iris flowers based on their sepal and petal measurements. Here's a breakdown of the code:

- **Importing Libraries:** Necessary libraries such as pandas for data manipulation, load_iris to load the Iris dataset, train_test_split for splitting the dataset, LogisticRegression for creating the model, and accuracy_score for evaluating the model's accuracy are imported.
- **Loading the Dataset:** The Iris dataset is loaded using the load_iris function from sklearn.datasets.
- **Creating DataFrame:** The dataset is converted into a DataFrame for easier manipulation and analysis.
- **Splitting Data:** The data is split into features (X) and target variable (y), where X contains the sepal and petal measurements, and y contains the target variable (species).
- **Splitting into Training and Testing Sets:** The dataset is further split into training and testing sets using train_test_split, with 80% of the data used for training and 20% for testing.
- **Training the Model:** A logistic regression model is instantiated and trained on the training data using the fit method.
- **Making Predictions:** Predictions are made on the test data using the trained model's predict method.
- **Evaluating Model Accuracy:** The accuracy of the model is calculated by comparing the predicted values with the actual values from the test set using the accuracy_score function.
- **Printing Accuracy:** Finally, the accuracy of the model is printed to assess its performance in predicting the species of iris flowers based on their measurements.

This code provides a concise demonstration of a typical machine learning workflow, including data loading, preprocessing, model training, prediction, and evaluation.

PART ONE

DAY ONE

Unit 1 - Lesson Two

Modern Paradigms of Intelligent Systems

☐ **Semi-Supervised Learning**

Master said, "Akshaya, let us understand Semi-Supervised Learning — the art of learning from what is known and what is hidden."

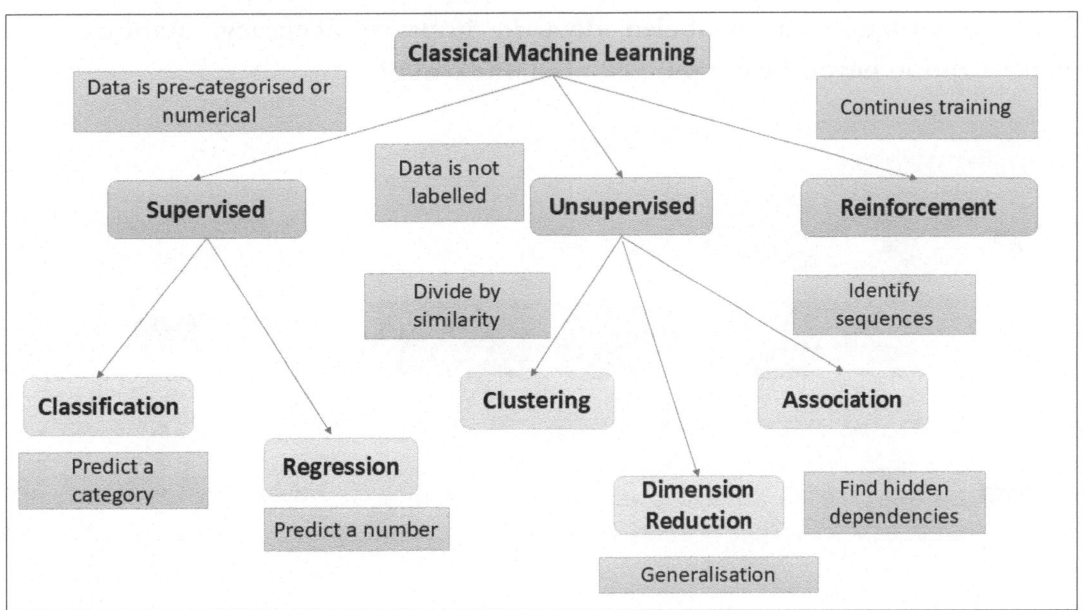

Illustration TL_0 : Classical Machine Learning

He continued, "In the world of Machine Learning, we often imagine a student who learns only when a teacher explicitly provides the answers — this is supervised learning. And then we imagine another student who learns purely from observation, without any guidance — this is unsupervised learning.

But real learning, Akshaya, rarely happens at the extremes. True mastery comes when the student receives *some* guidance, and then uses intuition, structure, and patterns from the remaining experience to teach themselves."

"This middle ground, where a small set of labeled data meets a vast ocean of unlabeled data, is what we call **Semi-Supervised Learning**. It stands as a bridge between the clearly known and the yet-to-be-understood."

The Essence of Semi-Supervised Learning

Master said, "When you have a handful of labeled examples — like a few points of light in a dark night and a massive amount of unlabeled samples — like countless stars whose stories remain silent — semi-supervised learning attempts to illuminate the entire sky using just those few clues."

Its purpose is simple but profound:

Use the structure in unlabeled data to improve accuracy, stability, and generalization beyond what pure labels alone can give.

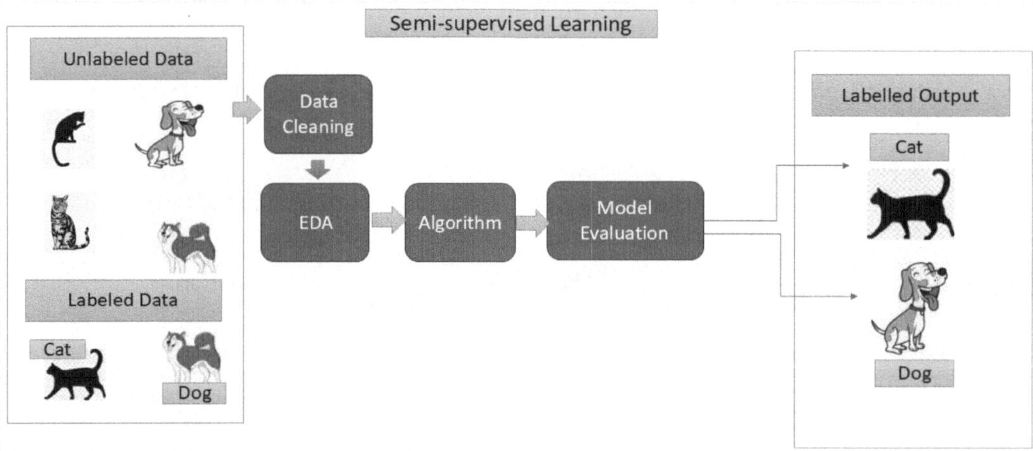

Illustration TL_1 : Self-Supervised

It is especially useful when labeling is expensive, slow, or requires expert knowledge. Medical diagnosis, satellite image recognition, speech understanding — everywhere labels are scarce but raw data is abundant.

☐ The Core Principles and Approaches

Master said, "To truly appreciate semi-supervised learning, you must understand the principles that breathe life into it."

Consistency Regularization — Learning Stability from Noise

"In nature, truth does not change simply because the light falls differently upon it.

A tree is still a tree whether you look at it from the left or the right."

Similarly, for unlabeled data:

- If you add noise, perturbations, or augmentations,
- And the model still predicts the *same class*,

then the model is demonstrating consistency — and consistency is treated as a sign of correctness.

Algorithms following this principle:

- **Π-model**
- **Temporal Ensembling**
- **Mean Teacher** (a student model learns from a slowly-updating teacher model)

This idea teaches the model that local neighborhoods in data space should share labels.

Pseudo-Labeling / Self-Training — When the Student Becomes the Teacher

Master smiled, "Sometimes the student learns enough to help teach themselves."

In pseudo-labeling:

- The model makes predictions on unlabeled data.
- If it is highly confident, these predictions become temporary labels — pseudo-labels.
- The model is then retrained using these newly labeled samples.

This works beautifully when:

- The model's confidence aligns with correctness,

- And when unlabeled data is similar to labeled data.

But Master warned, "Confidence is not always wisdom. One must guard against reinforcing mistakes."

Entropy Minimization — Seeking Confident Decisions

Entropy measures uncertainty.

- High entropy → confusion.
- Low entropy → confident prediction.

Semi-supervised learning encourages the model to make sharp, confident predictions for unlabeled samples, rather than hovering indecisively between classes.

The principle is:

A good boundary should lie in regions with fewer data points.

This is also known as the cluster or low-density separation assumption.

Graph-Based Methods — Learning Structure from Connections

Master said, "Imagine each datapoint as a node in a vast network, and each similarity as a thread connecting them. Wisdom flows through these threads."

Graph-based SSL:

- Builds a similarity graph of all samples
- Propagates labels from labeled nodes to similar unlabeled ones

This works well when data forms natural clusters or manifolds.

Generative Semi-Supervised Learning — Modeling the World Itself

Here, models learn the joint distribution **p(x)** and **p(y|x)**.

By understanding how data is generated, unlabeled samples contribute to shaping the learned representation.

VAEs, GAN-based SSL models, and other generative frameworks often use this idea.

Master said, "When you understand the nature of data itself, labels become only one piece of the truth."

Modern Practical Frameworks — MixMatch, FixMatch, UDA

These modern algorithms combine multiple principles:

- Data augmentations
- Consistency under transformations
- Confidence-based pseudo-labeling
- Sharpening of predictions
- Strong vs weak augmentations

FixMatch, in particular, has become widely used for its efficiency and simplicity:

- Generate a weakly augmented version → get a pseudo-label
- Apply strong augmentation → enforce consistency
- Use only high-confidence predictions (> threshold)

Master said, "These methods embody wisdom — simplicity on the surface, but profound regularization beneath."

Why Semi-Supervised Learning Matters

Master explained, "In many areas of life, guidance is precious and scarce — but experience is abundant."

Likewise:

- Labeled data is expensive (medical images, legal documents, expert annotations).
- Unlabeled data is everywhere (raw images, text, logs, signals).

Semi-supervised learning taps into the vast reservoir of unlabeled data to:

- Boost accuracy
- Improve robustness
- Reduce annotation cost
- Enable learning from real-world distributions

It is heavily used in:

- Medical imaging
- Remote sensing
- Industrial inspection
- Speech processing
- NLP for low-resource languages

Pitfalls, Warnings, and Wisdom

Master's voice softened: "With great power comes great responsibility."

Confirmation Bias

Erroneous pseudo-labels can snowball into bigger mistakes.

Remedy:

Use confidence thresholds, data augmentation, teacher–student consistency.

Domain Mismatch

If unlabeled data differ in distribution, performance collapses.

Overconfidence and Calibration

Modern neural networks often produce overconfident predictions.

Calibration techniques or conservative use of pseudo-labels are essential.

Compute Costs

Some SSL methods require multiple augmentations, ensembles, or heavy training loops.

Evaluation — The Honest Measure

Master said, "Never assume improvement unless measured."

Evaluation should include:

- A supervised baseline (trained with only labeled samples)
- A semi-supervised model
- A validation set drawn from labeled data
- Metrics tracked as labeled sample size changes

This reveals how much unlabeled data truly contributes.

Master looked at Akshaya and said, "When you understand Semi-Supervised Learning, you understand a deeper truth of intelligence —that knowledge is not only taught, but also discovered."

"Learning is not merely receiving answers —it is the art of letting data speak."

☐ Self-Supervised Learning

Master said, "Nikash, today we shall understand Self-Supervised Learning — the discipline of learning without labels, the art of discovering structure where no teacher exists."

He paused, letting the weight of the statement settle.

The Essence of Self-Supervised Learning

Master said, "In the world of human learning, not every lesson is taught by a teacher. A child learns language not by being told the grammar rules, but by listening, imitating, and discovering patterns.

A bird learns to fly not through instruction, but through instinct, practice, and feedback from the world."

"In the same way, Self-Supervised Learning (SSL) allows a model to learn **directly from raw data**, without human-annotated labels.

It creates *its own supervision* — by hiding part of the data, transforming it, reordering it, or pairing it, and then learning to recover what was changed."

It is learning from what *is* present to understand what *is not* explicitly given.

Why Self-Supervision Matters

Master said:

"Labels are precious, costly, and slow — but raw data is infinite.

Images, text, audio, and video flow endlessly in the real world.

To rely only on labeled samples is to limit intelligence."

Self-supervised learning matters because:

- It unlocks the hidden structure in massive unlabeled datasets.
- It reduces the need for human labeling, often requiring far fewer labeled examples later.
- It leads to representations that transfer across tasks, meaning the features learned through SSL can be reused for classification, detection, retrieval, and more.

He looked at Nikash and said, "Think of SSL as building a foundation of understanding before the real exam even begins."

□ Core Ideas: The Pretext Tasks

Master said, "To teach without labels, we invent tasks that force the model to understand meaning, context, and structure. These are called *pretext tasks* — simple tasks that reveal deep patterns."

Contrastive Learning — Bringing the Similar Together, Pushing the Dissimilar Apart

"This is the discipline of comparison," Master said.

- Take an image
- Create two different versions of it (crop, colour change, blur, rotate)
- These two views are **positive pairs**

- Different images are **negative pairs**

The model must:

- Pull positive pairs closer in representation space
- Push negative pairs apart

Methods:

- SimCLR
- MoCo
- BYOL, SimSiam (variants without explicit negatives)

Contrastive learning teaches invariances — what properties of the data remain stable under transformation.

Masked Modeling — Learning by Predicting the Missing

Master said:

"In language, what you do not hear is as important as what you do hear."

In masked modeling:

- Hide part of the input
- Ask the model to reconstruct it

Examples:

- **BERT** predicts masked tokens in text
- **MAE (Masked Autoencoders)** predict masked patches in images
- **Wav2Vec** predicts masked segments in speech

This forces the model to understand global context, relationships, and structure.

Context & Prediction Tasks — Understanding Order and Flow

Master explained:

"Life unfolds in sequences — words, frames, movements.

Predicting the next piece teaches the rhythm of the world."

Examples:

- Predict the next word (GPT style)
- Predict the next video frame
- Solve a jigsaw puzzle of shuffled image patches
- Predict temporal order

Such tasks teach understanding of:

- Spatial structure
- Temporal consistency
- Causality

Generative Modeling — Learning by Reconstructing the Whole

Autoencoders and VAEs compress input into a meaningful latent representation and reconstruct it.

Master said, "This method teaches the model what must be remembered to recreate reality."

It learns:

- Object shape
- Texture
- High-level structure
- Variations and patterns

Clustering and Self-Labeling — Discovering Natural Groups

Here, the model:

- Computes embeddings
- Clusters them

- Uses cluster IDs as pseudo-labels
- Trains itself on these labels
- Recomputes embeddings and repeats

Example: **DeepCluster**

"This is learning by grouping similar ideas together, without knowing the names of the groups," Master said.

What SSL Representations Capture

Self-supervised models learn the statistical regularities of the world:

- **Language:** grammar, syntax, semantics
- **Vision:** shapes, textures, edges, objects
- **Speech:** phonetics, tone, rhythm
- **Video:** movement, temporal order

These representations transfer exceptionally well to downstream tasks with minimal fine-tuning.

Master said, "A mind that understands structure can adapt to any test."

Strengths and Limitations

Advantages

- Learns from massive unlabeled data
- Greatly reduces the need for manual labels
- Improves sample efficiency and generalization
- Enables large-scale pretraining
- Useful across NLP, vision, speech, and multimodal domains

Limitations

- Poorly chosen pretext tasks → poor representations

- Contrastive methods can be computationally expensive
- Masked modeling reduces negatives but requires reconstruction capacity
- Models may inherit biases from unlabeled datasets

Master warned, "When you learn from the world, you also learn its imperfections."

Practical Wisdom for Using SSL

Master outlined the key practices:

Match pretext tasks to the domain:

Predicting masked words for text, masked patches for images, and temporal tasks for video.

Use strong + weak augmentations wisely in contrastive learning.

Measure representation quality using:

- Linear probes
- Fine-tuning
- Transfer tasks

Evaluate robustness to ensure learned features are stable and general.

Where SSL Is Used

- **NLP:** BERT, RoBERTa, GPT pretraining
- **Computer Vision:** MAE, SimCLR, MoCo
- **Speech:** Wav2Vec, HuBERT
- **Multimodal:** CLIP (text–image contrastive learning)
- **Foundational models:** Most modern AI systems rely heavily on SSL pretraining

Master said, "Self-Supervised Learning is the path of awakening without a teacher. It is the ability to transform raw experience into understanding."

He looked at Nikash and added, "When you grasp the principles of SSL, you understand that intelligence need not always be instructed — sometimes, it must *discover itself*."

☐ Ensemble Learning

Master said, "Apeksha, let us speak briefly about Ensemble Learning. This topic has already been explored deeply in *Optimum Python Power – Series IV*, yet its essence is so profound that it deserves to be revisited. Sometimes even a familiar truth becomes new when seen from a higher vantage point."

Ensemble Learning — Strength in Numbers

Ensemble learning is the art of letting **many minds think together**.

In machine learning, it means **combining multiple models** so that their collective wisdom outperforms any individual model working alone.

Think of it like a **council of sages**.

Each sage brings a different perspective, a different intuition, and even different blind spots.
But when their voices are blended—when their insights are averaged or weighed—what emerges is a decision far more stable, reliable, and intelligent than the opinion of any single sage.

This is the philosophy behind ensemble learning.

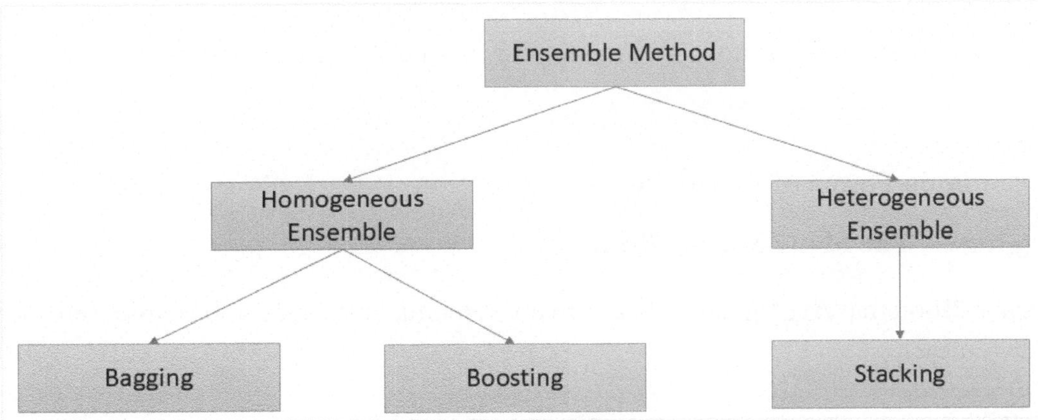

Illustration TL_4 : Self-Supervised

Why Ensembles Work — The Deeper Truth

Master continued,

"Every model is like a single traveller walking through a dense forest.

It may lose its way, stumble on rocks, or misinterpret the shadows.

But when many travellers walk together, their shared observations cancel out errors.

One sees what another misses. One stumbles where another stands."

This balancing out of mistakes is the heart of ensemble learning.

Bias–Variance Harmony

- **Bagging lowers variance**

Like asking 100 people the same question and taking their average—you minimize random errors.

- **Boosting lowers bias**

Like training a group of students where each new student focuses on the questions the previous ones got wrong.

- **Stacking balances both**

By letting a "master expert" (meta-learner) learn how to best combine the judgments of all others.

The diversity of models is not a weakness—it is the *source of strength.*

☐ **Common Forms of Ensemble Learning**

Bagging — The Many Mirrors Principle

Bagging (Bootstrap Aggregating) creates many versions of the data and trains a separate model on each.

Analogy:

Imagine holding a gemstone under different lights. Each angle reveals a new reflection, a new truth. By combining all reflections, you see the gem as it truly is.

Random Forest is simply a forest of such mirrored trees—each seeing the world from a slightly different angle.

Effect: Reduces variance, stabilises noisy models.

Boosting — The Wise Teacher Method

Boosting trains models sequentially.

Each new model focuses on mistakes made by previous ones.

Analogy:

A teacher first gives a student a test. The student errs.

The next lesson focuses only on those errors.

With each iteration, the student becomes sharper, more precise.

AdaBoost, Gradient Boosting, XGBoost, and LightGBM follow this philosophy.

Effect: Reduces bias and variance by addressing weaknesses step-by-step.

Stacking — The Council of Masters

Stacking puts many expert models together—each giving its prediction—and then trains a meta-learner to interpret their collective voice.

Analogy:

A council of astrologers may predict a child's future.

But the king appoints one grand astrologer to listen to them all and derive the final judgement.

Effect: Flexibly learns the best combination of model predictions.

Simple Voting/Averaging — The Democracy of Models

Sometimes the simplest methods are surprisingly powerful.

Analogy:

When villagers vote on the best time to plant seeds, their collective, time-tested wisdom often surpasses any individual's guess.

In machine learning, voting and averaging work the same way.

Practical Considerations — The Hidden Costs of a Large Council

Master warned, "Even a council of sages consumes time, resources, and attention. The goal is wisdom, not unnecessary noise."

Considerations:

- **Inference cost increases**

Many models → more memory + slower predictions

→ use *model distillation* to compress into a single learner.

- **Overfitting risk**

If models are too similar, they reinforce each other's biases instead of correcting them.

- **Interpretability drops**

A single tree is easy to explain; a forest is not.

→ use SHAP or feature importance to understand decisions.

- **Calibration**

Ensembles often give better probability estimates, but this must be verified.

Use-Cases — Were Ensembles Rule Supreme

- **Tabular data**

XGBoost and LightGBM dominate competitions like Kaggle.

- **High-reliability systems**

Banks, healthcare systems, and fraud-detection modules often deploy ensembles.

- **Situations where performance matters more than simplicity**

When a 1–2% accuracy improvement is worth millions.

Master said, "Apeksha, remember this:

A single lamp shows a fragment of the night.

A thousand lamps turn darkness into day.

Ensemble learning is the science of many lamps—each illuminating what the others cannot."

☐ Unsupervised Learning

Master said, "Roopa, let us learn how to see hidden order where no instruction has been given."

Unsupervised Learning — finding structure with no labels

Master continued, "In the wilderness of data, there are no signposts. Unsupervised learning is the explorer's craft — it maps the land, discovers rivers and mountains, and draws a useful map without anyone telling it what anything is called."

At its heart, unsupervised learning asks: *What structure lives inside these examples if I do not impose names upon them?* It does not seek to predict a teacher's labels; it seeks to reveal latent form, compress reality, detect the strange, and suggest hypotheses.

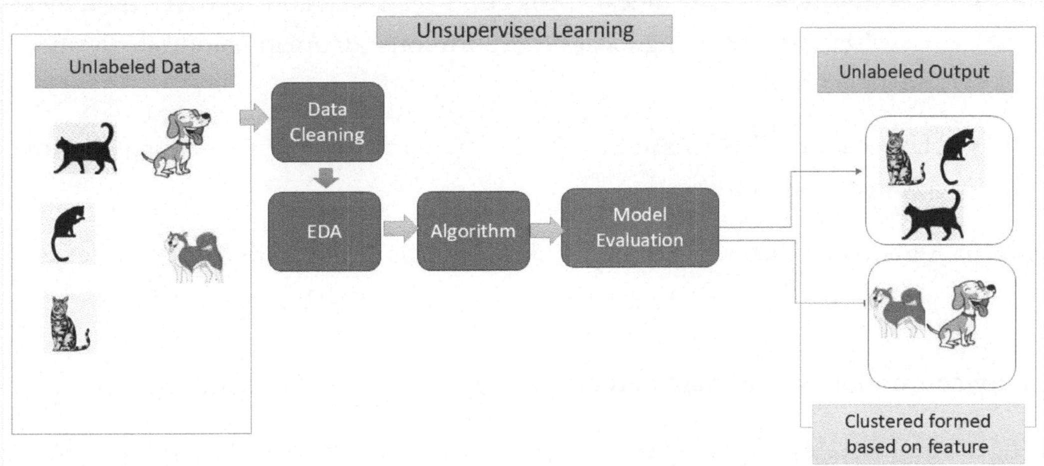

Illustration TL_2: Unsupervised

Major tasks

Clustering — grouping the village

Analogy: Imagine a valley with people scattered about. Clustering is the process of seeing natural villages form where people tend to live near each other.

- **What it does:** Groups similar points into clusters.
- **Algorithms:** K-means (simple, assumes spherical clusters), hierarchical clustering (tree of groups), DBSCAN (finds dense regions, handles noise), spectral clustering (uses graph structure).
- **Use-cases:** Customer segmentation, image segmentation, and discovering cell types in biology.

Wisdom: Clusters reveal *cohesion* — items inside a cluster are close — but cluster *names* must be added by a human.

Dimensionality reduction / manifold learning — drawing the map

Analogy: You have a globe (high-dimensional data). Dimensionality reduction is flattening it into a map that preserves important relationships so travellers can navigate.

- **What it does:** Compresses data to fewer dimensions while preserving structure.
- **Techniques:** PCA (linear projection), t-SNE and UMAP (nonlinear visualization preserving local neighborhoods), Isomap (geodesic distances on a manifold).
- **Use-cases:** Visualization, noise reduction, pre-processing before clustering or classification.

Wisdom: A good low-dimensional map makes patterns visible; a poor one misleads.

Density estimation & anomaly detection — sensing the shoreline

Analogy: Imagine a shoreline of everyday life. Density estimation tells you where the sea of normal data is; anomalies are the foreign ships in the mist.

- **What it does:** Estimates p(x) or identifies points in low-density regions.
- **Methods:** Gaussian Mixture Models, Kernel Density Estimation, Isolation Forests, One-Class SVMs, reconstruction-error from autoencoders.
- **Use-cases:** Fraud detection, manufacturing defect detection, rare-event discovery.

Wisdom: "Rare" ≠ "important" — anomalies need human verification.

Representation learning/embeddings — learning the language of the data

Analogy: Find a compact alphabet to write lengthy poems; embeddings are that alphabet — compact codes that retain meaning.

- **What it does:** Learns lower-dimensional features (embeddings) that capture semantic or structural relations.
- **Models:** Autoencoders, Variational Autoencoders (VAEs), contrastive embeddings.
- **Use-cases:** Feature inputs for downstream supervised tasks, similarity search, transfer learning.

Wisdom: A powerful representation can make downstream tasks simpler and more sample-efficient.

Generative models — the artist of the domain

Analogy: An artist who studies a village until they can paint a new, believable street scene that never existed.

- **What it does:** Learns to sample new data resembling the training set.
- **Architectures:** GANs (adversary learns realism), VAEs (probabilistic latent codes), autoregressive models.
- **Use-cases:** Data augmentation, synthesis, creative generation, simulation for training.

Wisdom: Generators can create useful synthetic data — but they can also replicate biases.

Topic modeling — the librarian's sorting

Analogy: From a pile of books, infer the main topics so a librarian can shelve them without reading each page.

- **What it does:** Finds latent topics in text (e.g., LDA, neural topic models).
- **Use-cases:** Document clustering, search, exploratory analysis of large corpora.

Wisdom: Topics are soft and overlapping — interpret with care.

Why unsupervised matters — the deeper value

Master said:

Exploration & discovery: When we lack labels, unsupervised methods reveal hypotheses and patterns worthy of human attention.

- **Preprocessing & representation:** They produce features and compressions that improve supervised learning.
- **Anomaly detection & monitoring:** They detect the unexpected before labels exist.
- **Synthesis & simulation:** Generative models help create realistic data for training, creativity, or stress-testing systems.

In short: unsupervised learning turns raw experience into structure, and structure into opportunity.

Limitations

Master warned:

- **No single objective:** There's no universal "good" — usefulness depends on your goal. A visualization that looks pretty may not be useful for prediction.
- **Arbitrariness of labels:** Clusters or dimensions need a human meaning attached; the algorithm does not name them.

- **Evaluation difficulty:** Internal metrics (silhouette, reconstruction error) do not always align with downstream value. Always validate with the task you care about.
- **Sensitivity:** Results depend heavily on preprocessing (scaling, normalization), hyperparameters, and distance measures.
- **Bias and modes:** Generative models can miss rare modes or amplify dataset biases.

Practical advice

- **Visualize first:** Use PCA, UMAP, or t-SNE to get intuition; plots often reveal gross issues.
- **Preprocess carefully:** Standardize, remove outliers, and consider feature engineering before applying algorithms.
- **Try multiple methods:** Different algorithms reveal different facets; compare and triangulate insights.
- **Human-in-the-loop:** Combine unsupervised outputs with expert labeling or curation to validate and refine groupings.
- **Use downstream tasks as the judge:** Ultimately, measure how unsupervised features help real tasks (classification accuracy, retrieval quality, detection rate).
- **Beware scale and distance:** High-dimensional distances can be misleading — consider cosine similarity or learned metrics for embeddings.

How to evaluate

Master advised:

- Create small labeled test sets if possible to check clustering/embeddings.
- Use reconstruction error, likelihoods, or proxy metrics, but always correlate them with downstream performance.
- Test sensitivity to seeds and hyperparameters; robust patterns persist across

reasonable variations.

Master said, "Roopa, unsupervised learning is the art of listening to the data when no teacher speaks. It does not hand you answers — it hands you questions worth asking."

"If you seek patterns, be ready to interpret, validate, and refine them. The map is only as useful as the journey it enables."

☐ Reinforcement Learning

Master said, "Akshatha, let us understand Reinforcement Learning — the art of learning by trial, reward, and consequence."

Reinforcement Learning — learning by trial and reward

Master began:

"Imagine a gardener teaching a sapling to climb a trellis. The gardener does not tell the plant each precise movement. Instead, the gardener arranges conditions — light, support, pruning — and rewards growth that moves toward the trellis. Over time the plant 'learns' the path of least resistance to the sun. Reinforcement Learning (RL) is similar: an **agent** acts, the **environment** responds, and sparse signals — rewards — guide behaviour."

At its heart, RL is **sequential decision-making under uncertainty**. Actions now influence not only immediate outcomes but the shape of all future possibilities.

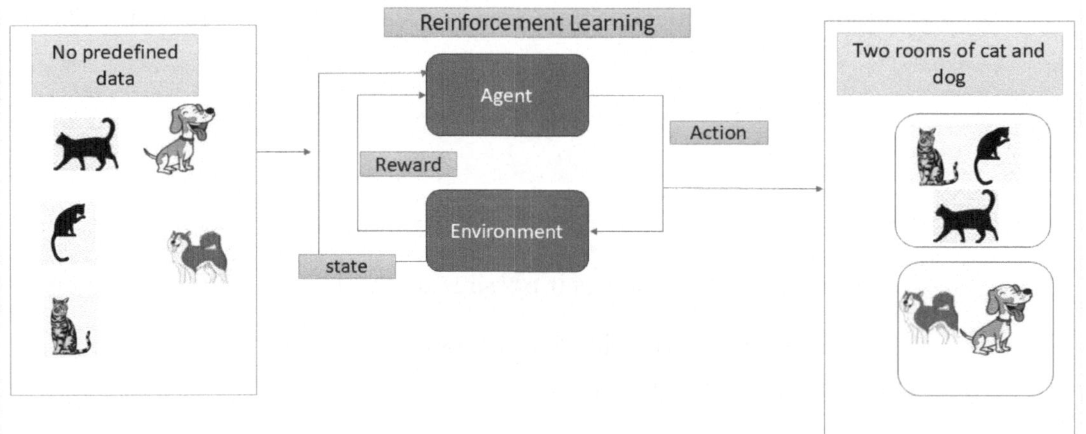

Illustration TL_3: Reinforcement

The Formal Scaffold — MDP as the Playground

Master explained the formal world the agent inhabits:

- **S (States):** the gardener's field at a moment — soil moisture, sapling height.
- **A (Actions):** prune, water, move a support — the choices available.
- **P (Transition probabilities):** how the world reacts to actions (uncertain weather, growth rates).
- **R (Reward):** scalar feedback — a flourish, a wilt, a bloom.
- **γ (Discount factor):** how much the gardener values today's bloom vs tomorrow's forest.

Objective: maximize expected cumulative (discounted) reward

E $\sum_{t=0}^{\infty} \gamma^t\ r^t$ choose actions that yield the best long-run harvest.

Policy (π): the agent's temperament — a mapping from states to action choices (probabilistic or deterministic).

Value functions (V, Q): the agent's foresight — estimates of future returns from states or state-action pairs.

Families of Methods — how the learner can train

Master said, "There are many schools of thought; each trades off sample use, bias, and stability."

Model-free vs Model-based — Planner vs Trial-and-Error

- **Model-free**: Like a child learning to ride a bicycle by falling and correcting — learns policy or value directly from experience (Q-learning, SARSA, DQN, Policy Gradients).

Pros: Simple to implement in many domains.

Cons: Often sample-inefficient.

- **Model-based**: Like a navigator building a map of the terrain and planning routes — the agent learns or uses a model of environment dynamics P and plans within it.

Pros: More sample-efficient if the model is accurate.

Cons: Model errors can mislead planning.

Value-based methods — Learning the worth of actions

- **Q-learning, DQN:** Learn Q(s,a) and act greedily. Think of keeping a diary that scores each action in each situation and choosing the highest-scoring entry.

Policy-gradient methods — Sculpting the policy directly

- **REINFORCE, Actor-Critic:** Directly optimize the policy by nudging it toward actions that produced larger returns.

Actor (policy) + Critic (value estimator) is a powerful hybrid — the critic judges, the actor acts.

Modern stable algorithms

- **PPO, A3C/A2C, SAC:** Practical recipes that tame instability — clipping updates, entropy regularization, off-policy corrections. These are the contemporary tools of choice for many continuous-control problems.

Core Challenges

Exploration vs. Exploitation — the eternal tension

Master compared it to foraging:

"A forager must decide whether to harvest known berries or risk a new path for a richer patch."

- **Exploration**: discover new, possibly better strategies (ε-greedy, UCB, intrinsic curiosity, Thompson sampling).
- **Exploitation**: use the best-known action to maximize reward now.

Balancing these is central — too little exploration traps you in suboptimal habits; too much wastes precious trials.

Credit Assignment — which act sowed the harvest?

Rewards can be delayed. Which past choices deserve credit when the field finally yields fruit? This is the **credit-assignment problem** — solved by temporal-difference learning, eligibility traces, or policy gradients that aggregate returns.

Sample Efficiency — the cost of real-world trials

In real systems (robots, clinical trials), every action costs. Simulators, model-based methods, demonstrations, and off-policy learning are ways to reduce required real-world interactions.

Stability & Convergence — neural nets complicate things

Using function approximators (deep nets) introduces instability. Tricks that help: replay buffers, target networks, clipped objectives, normalization, careful hyperparameter tuning, and multiple seeds.

Reward Design / Shaping — the silent saboteur

Bad reward functions produce clever but useless behaviours (reward hacking). Shaping helps learning speed but can bias solutions. Preferred pattern: sparse true reward + well-chosen auxiliary tasks.

Practical Advice — how to train an RL agent

- **Start in simulation**: iterate quickly, then transfer via domain randomization or sim2real techniques.
- **Curriculum learning**: begin with easy tasks and increase difficulty gradually.
- **Use demonstrations**: imitation learning or initializing a policy with expert

data speeds learning.

- **Hybridize**: combine model-based planning with model-free fine-tuning for efficiency and robustness.
- **Evaluate rigorously**: report mean and variance across seeds; track sample efficiency, asymptotic performance, robustness to perturbations.
- **Safeguard with constraints**: safety guards, constrained RL, and conservative policy updates for real-world deployments.

Common Applications

- **Games:** chess, Go, Atari — clear reward structure and fast simulators.
- **Robotics & control:** locomotion, manipulation — continuous actions and physics-based dynamics.
- **Recommendation as sequential decisions:** treat user interaction as a long-term engagement optimization.
- **Autonomous vehicles, operations research, finance, and adaptive systems.**

Analogies to Fix Understanding

- **Gardener & Sapling:** rewards shape gradual policy (care over seasons → mature behaviour).
- **Explorer mapping unknown islands:** model-based planning builds maps; model-free explorers learn paths by travel.
- **Student solving puzzles:** policy gradients are like students updating strategies from exam scores; actor-critic is a student (actor) guided by a tutor (critic).

Master said, "An agent optimizes rewards — if rewards are mis-specified, the agent will optimize the wrong objective. In real-world domains, prioritise safety constraints, fairness, and interpretability. Test for reward hacking and adversarial exploits."

☐ Representation

Master said, "Let us now understand the cross-cutting themes that quietly bind all learning paradigms — the invisible threads that weave coherence across the entire landscape of machine intelligence."

Representation is the foundation.

"Whether we supervise, partially supervise, or avoid labels altogether, one truth remains unchanged:

A model is only as powerful as the representation it learns.

Self-supervised and unsupervised learning *exist* to sculpt these representations; semi-supervised learning builds upon them; reinforcement learning dramatically benefits from them."

Master compared representations to the **roots of a tree**:

"You may admire the branches, flowers, and fruits (predictions, rewards, decisions), but it is the hidden root system — the representation — that determines the health of the entire organism."

The distribution defines the world.

"All learning quietly assumes a world with certain rules:

- supervised/semi-supervised assume data is IID,
- semi-supervised assumes unlabeled data follows the same distribution,
- RL assumes stationarity in the environment's dynamics.

Break these assumptions, and even the most sophisticated model stumbles."

Master continued, "It is like navigating a city using an old map — the streets may have changed, and your knowledge becomes unreliable."

Evaluation is more than accuracy.

Master said:

"Do not be hypnotized by a single metric.

Evaluate with both **intrinsic measures** (loss, clustering scores) and **real-world outcomes** (downstream task performance)."

He added:

"Track the subtler qualities too —

- sample efficiency,
- training stability,
- fairness and bias, for these are the true signs of maturity in a system."

Combine approaches — the future is hybrid.

"Modern ML is no longer a single-path journey.

Real systems blend techniques like spices in a well-balanced dish."

Examples:

- self-supervised pretraining → supervised fine-tuning → ensemble for production
- RL agents enriched with self-supervised representation learning
- model-based RL mixed with model-free fine-tuning
- unsupervised clustering to bootstrap labeling pipelines

Master said, "Do not cling to rigid boundaries. Intelligence emerges when methods complement each other."

Compute vs. Benefit

"Advanced methods often demand more compute, more memory, and more time. Choose wisely. A simple model delivered today may be more valuable than a perfect model delivered too late."

Master smiled, "Power is not in complexity — it is in **proportion**."

A Simple Decision Guide — When to Use What

Master drew five paths on the whiteboard:

- **When you have no labels but want general, transferable features**

  → *Choose Self-Supervised or Unsupervised Learning.*

- **When you have a few labels but abundant unlabeled data**

  → *Choose Semi-Supervised Learning (FixMatch, MixMatch, pseudo-labeling).*

- **When you need the highest predictive performance and robustness**

  → *Choose Ensemble Methods (bagging, boosting, stacking).*

- **When actions influence the future and feedback comes as rewards**

  → *Choose Reinforcement Learning.*

- **When the goal is anomaly detection, structure discovery, or data compression**

  → *Choose Unsupervised Learning (density estimation, autoencoders, clustering).*

Master said, "Machine learning is not many disjoint islands. It is one vast continent — and these themes are the rivers that run through it, nourishing every method."

Summary

In this unit, we explored the foundational concepts of machine learning, establishing a clear understanding of the different learning paradigms and essential terminologies. We began with the three primary types of machine learning—**supervised learning**, where models learn from labeled examples; **unsupervised learning**, which uncovers hidden patterns without labels; and **reinforcement learning**, where agents learn through rewards and interactions. We also introduced **semi-supervised learning**, **self-supervision**, and **ensemble learning**, expanding the perspective on how hybrid and collective methods enhance performance.

Beyond the learning categories, we examined the fundamental building blocks of any machine learning project. Key terms such as **features**, **labels**, **training data**, **testing data**, and **validation sets** were discussed to establish how data flows through a model.

We also reviewed essential **evaluation metrics** that measure performance and guide model improvement. This chapter laid a strong foundation for understanding how machine learning models are developed, trained, and assessed.

Whats Next

In the next part, we move from classical probabilistic foundations into **modern advanced machine learning models** that build on these principles. We will explore **latent variable models**, **Bayesian deep learning**, and **probabilistic graphical models** with richer structures. This includes **Variational Autoencoders (VAEs)**, **normalizing flows**, and **advanced inference techniques** such as variational inference and Markov Chain Monte Carlo (MCMC). We will also study how probabilistic reasoning integrates with neural networks, enabling models that not only make predictions but also estimate uncertainty. This transition prepares us for cutting-edge applications in vision, language, and decision-making systems.

PART TWO

MACHINE LEARNING

Foundations of Probabilistic Models

"Probability does not eliminate doubt—it refines it. In every distribution lies a quiet negotiation between what we know, what we assume, and what reality permits."

– Shree Shambav

PART TWO

DAY TWO

Unit 2 - Lesson One

The Probabilistic Approach

☐ Probabilistic Models in Machine Learning

In the real world, certainty is a luxury. Every measurement contains noise, every observation is incomplete, and every decision must be made amid ambiguity. Probabilistic models embrace this truth. Instead of demanding perfect information, they **model uncertainty itself**, turning ambiguity into structured reasoning.

Think of them as the **science of informed guessing**—not blind guesses, but disciplined, mathematically grounded predictions based on what is known and what *could* be true.

What Are Probabilistic Models?

Master said, "A deterministic mind sees the world as fixed. A probabilistic mind sees the world as unfolding."

Probabilistic models do not try to say, *"This IS the truth."*

Instead, they say, *"This is LIKELY the truth, given the evidence we have."*

They treat data not as absolute commands but as **samples from a deeper, hidden process**—a process that we wish to understand.

Analogy: The Foggy Forest

Imagine walking through a forest covered in thick fog.

You cannot see the entire path, but you notice footprints, broken twigs, the direction of the wind, and distant sounds.

From these clues, you estimate:

- *Where you are*
- *Where the path might lead*
- *What dangers or opportunities lie ahead*

You don't know with certainty, but you make the **best possible decision given incomplete information**.

This is exactly what probabilistic models do.

Why Probabilistic Models Matter

- They **handle noisy, imperfect data**
- They **generalize better**, especially with limited samples
- They **provide confidence levels**, not just answers
- They allow reasoning under uncertainty
- They form the foundation of Bayesian thinking—where *knowledge evolves with evidence*

Foundational Approaches in Probabilistic Modeling

1. Bayesian Inference – Learning Through Belief Updates

Master said, **"A wise man does not discard his past understanding; he refines it with new evidence."**

Bayesian inference combines:

- **Prior belief** (what we know)

- **Likelihood** (what the new data suggests)
- **Posterior belief** (updated understanding)

Analogy: The Weather-Wise Farmer

A farmer knows that *usually* it doesn't rain in January (prior).

But today the sky is unusually dark (new evidence).

He updates his belief and predicts rain (posterior).

Bayesian models learn exactly like this—through continuous refinement.

2. Maximum Likelihood Estimation (MLE) – Finding the Best Explanation

MLE chooses the model parameters that **make the observed data most probable**.

Analogy:

Imagine tuning a musical instrument to match a reference note.

MLE is like adjusting the strings until the resonance matches the sample sound as closely as possible.

Categories of Probabilistic Models

1. Generative Models – The Storytellers of Data

Master said, **"To know a phenomenon fully, you must be able to recreate it."**

Generative models learn the **joint probability distribution**:

P(X, Y) — how data *and* labels arise together.

They can:

- Generate realistic images
- Produce human-like text
- Create synthetic voices
- Simulate environments

Analogy:

A skilled painter doesn't just identify art; he can **create** it.

Generative models do the same—learning the essence of data so deeply that they can generate new, believable samples.

Examples:

- Variational Autoencoders (VAEs)
- Generative Adversarial Networks (GANs)
- Hidden Markov Models (HMMs)

2. Discriminative Models – The Decision Makers

Master said, **"Some do not tell stories—they draw boundaries."**

Discriminative models learn the **conditional probability**:

P(Y | X) — given the features, what is the predicted class?

They don't try to recreate data; they try to classify or separate it.

Analogy:

A judge does not recreate a crime scene; he decides guilt or innocence based on evidence.

His purpose is **perfect classification**, not storytelling.

Examples:

- Logistic Regression
- Support Vector Machines
- Conditional Random Fields (CRFs)

3. Graphical Models – Maps of Dependencies

Graphical models combine probability theory with graph structure.

They show *how* variables influence each other through visual structure.

Master said, "Understanding the web of relationships is more powerful than understanding nodes in isolation."

Analogy:

A city map helps you understand how roads connect, where traffic flows, and how one area influences another.

Graphical models do the same for variables.

Examples:

- Bayesian Networks
- Markov Random Fields
- Factor Graphs

The Essence of Probabilistic Models

Probabilistic models encourage:

- Thinking in terms of uncertainty
- Updating beliefs with new information
- Understanding relationships between variables
- Generating and evaluating possibilities

They teach machines to behave more like humans—adaptive, uncertain, yet intelligent.

Master said, "Sam, certainty is brittle.

But probability—when understood deeply—gives you strength to navigate the unknown."

Master said, "Nikash, come — let us peer into how probability and deep nets walk together.

Probabilistic models in deep learning are not an ornament; they are the lanterns we carry when the path is foggy."

☐ Probabilistic Models in Deep Learning

Deep learning builds very flexible function approximators — neural networks with millions (or billions) of parameters. But flexibility without humility is dangerous: when data is scarce, noisy, or out-of-distribution, a deterministic network can be **overconfident** and brittle. Probabilistic modeling brings *humility*: it lets the network say **"I don't know"**, quantify uncertainty, and reason under ambiguity.

At the heart of probabilistic deep learning is the **predictive distribution**:

$$p(y|x, D) = \int p(y \mid x, \theta)\, p(\theta \mid D)\, d\theta$$

where $p(\theta|D)$ is the posterior over neural network parameters given data D. These integral expresses that predictions should average over plausible models, not rely on a single point estimate.

Why adopt probabilistic views in deep learning?

Master said:

- **Uncertainty quantification:** Not just "what" the model predicts, but **how confident** it is. Vital in medicine, autonomous driving, and safety-critical systems.
- **Robustness & generalization:** Averaging over plausible parameter settings reduces overfitting and can improve out-of-distribution behavior.
- **Principled decision-making:** When actions have costs, expected-utility calculations require predictive distributions.
- **Active learning & exploration:** Uncertainty guides which examples to label or which actions to try.
- **Better calibration:** Probabilistic methods often produce better-calibrated probabilities — forecasts that match observed frequencies.

Analogy: A single deep network is like a lone navigator with one map; a probabilistic deep learner is a council of navigators, each with slightly different maps and assumptions — together they give a range of plausible routes and how confident they are in each.

Two faces of uncertainty

Master whispered, "Not all ignorance is the same."

- **Aleatoric uncertainty (data uncertainty):** Irreducible noise in the observations (e.g., sensor noise, inherent ambiguity). Even a perfect model can't remove it. Can be *homoscedastic* (constant) or *heteroscedastic* (input-dependent).
- **Epistemic uncertainty (model uncertainty):** Due to lack of knowledge, limited data, or extrapolation. This is reducible by collecting more data.

Analogy: Aleatoric = fog that always blurs the view. Epistemic = missing map tiles that you can fill by exploring.

Probabilistic deep learning aims primarily at measuring epistemic uncertainty (but often models aleatoric too).

How to build probabilistic deep models

1. Bayesian Neural Networks (BNNs)

Place a prior $p(\theta)$ on network weights and perform Bayesian inference to obtain the posterior $p(\theta|D)$. The predictive distribution is the posterior-weighted average.

Exact Bayesian inference is intractable for large nets, so approximations follow.

2. Variational Inference (VI) — approximate the posterior

VI chooses a simpler family $q\phi(\theta)$ and optimizes it to be close to the true posterior by maximizing the Evidence Lower Bound (ELBO):

$$ELBO(\phi) = E_{q}\phi(\theta)[\log p(D|\theta)] - KL(q\phi(\theta) \| p(\theta))$$

- **Amortized VI** scales this idea by learning ϕ with gradient-based optimization (reparameterization trick for continuous weights).
- **Pros:** Scalable, compatible with SGD and minibatches.
- **Cons:** Approximation gap depends on chosen family q; mean-field approximations can be too crude.

Analogy: VI is like approximating a complex mountain range with a simpler silhouette that's easy to carry — useful but not a perfect map.

3. Monte Carlo (MCMC) methods

Draw samples from the posterior (e.g., Hamiltonian Monte Carlo). MCMC is asymptotically exact but usually too expensive for very deep nets.

Analogy: MCMC explores the full landscape carefully — accurate but slow.

4. Laplace approximation

Fit a Gaussian around the MAP estimate using the Hessian (or its approximation). Useful as a local, cheap approximation.

5. Deep Ensembles

Train multiple networks from different random initializations (and possibly different subsets of data or architectures). Predictions average across ensemble members.

- **Why it works:** Ensembles empirically capture epistemic uncertainty well and often outperform many Bayesian approximations in practice.
- **Tradeoff:** Multiply compute and memory by the number of members (but easy to implement).

Analogy: Ensembles are like consulting multiple doctors; even if none is perfectly Bayesian, the consensus is often reliable.

6. MC Dropout (approximate Bayesian)

Use dropout at test time and average several stochastic forward passes. Interpreted as approximate variational inference under certain conditions.

- **Pros:** Cheap to add to existing networks.
- **Cons:** Approximation assumptions are limited.

7. Deterministic approaches + calibration

Train deterministic networks but calibrate outputs (temperature scaling), or use explicit predictive models for aleatoric uncertainty (e.g., output mean and variance with a heteroscedastic loss).

8. Score-based & flow-based generative models

For density estimation and uncertainty (estimating p(x)), use normalizing flows, autoregressive models, or score-based models. These help detect low-density (anomalous) inputs.

Modern - what practitioners actually do

- **Deep ensembles** are often the go-to for reliable epistemic uncertainty and strong predictive performance.
- **VI with expressive posterior families** (e.g., normalizing flows for $q(\theta)$ can help reduce the approximation gap.
- **Combine aleatoric + epistemic:** Predict observation noise (heteroscedastic variance) while using BNN/ensemble for model uncertainty.
- **Use temperature scaling or isotonic regression** to calibrate probabilities for deployment.
- **Evaluate with proper scoring rules**: Negative log-likelihood (NLL), Brier score, expected calibration error (ECE), and sharpness metrics. Don't trust accuracy alone.

The reparameterization trick & amortized inference

To back-propagate through stochastic nodes (e.g., sampling $\theta \sim q_\phi(\theta)$, we rewrite sampling as a deterministic transformation of noise: $\theta = g_\phi(\epsilon)$ where $\epsilon \sim p(\epsilon)$. This enables gradient-based optimization of ELBO — foundational to modern VI for deep nets.

Analogy: Instead of tossing coins inside a sealed box, you control the random seed externally and can thus learn how the coin outcomes depend on your choices.

Diagnostics & evaluation — how to trust uncertainty estimates

Master said, "Merit all claims by tests."

- **Calibration plots & ECE**: do predicted probabilities match observed frequencies?
- **NLL & Brier**: penalize overconfident wrong answers.
- **Predictive intervals / coverage**: do 95% intervals actually contain ~95% of true values?
- **Out-of-distribution (OOD) detection**: does the model assign low confidence or low density to OOD inputs?
- **Robustness across seeds & datasets**: ensure uncertainty estimates are stable.

Applications where probabilistic deep learning shines

- **Healthcare:** quantify diagnostic uncertainty; guide additional tests.
- **Autonomy & robotics:** safe decision-making, exploration in unknown environments.
- **Active learning:** choose examples where model uncertainty is highest to label next.
- **Forecasting & weather:** probabilistic forecasts are core to decision-making.
- **Anomaly detection & monitoring:** identify inputs that the model should not trust.

Practical caveats & trade-offs

- **Compute & engineering cost:** BNNs, VI and ensembles add training and inference overhead. Choose methods proportional to the risk/cost of wrong decisions.

- **Approximation gaps:** VI families or MC-dropout approximations can understate uncertainty. Validate thoroughly.
- **Misleading density:** Some likelihood models assign high likelihood to OOD data — be cautious with raw density as an OOD signal.
- **Priors matter:** In low-data regimes, priors strongly influence posteriors. Encode domain knowledge when possible.
- **Robust evaluation:** Calibration and predictive performance may vary with domain — run realistic deployment tests.

Practical checklist — how to add probabilistic rigour to a deep learning project

1. Decide what uncertainty matters: aleatoric, epistemic, or both.
2. Pick a method aligned to budget & risk: ensembles for reliability, VI or Laplace for parameter uncertainty, MC-dropout for lightweight Bayesian behaviour.
3. Model aleatoric noise where relevant: regress both mean and variance when outputs are noisy.
4. Calibrate predictions for deployment.
5. Evaluate with proper scores (NLL, ECE, Brier) and OOD tests.
6. If safety-critical, combine methods (ensemble + heteroscedastic model + calibration).
7. Document assumptions and priors.

Master closed his eyes and said, **"Imagine a lighthouse.** A single bright lamp (standard deep net) can guide ships on a clear night — but when fog thickens, one lamp can mislead. A probabilistic approach is like a lighthouse with multiple beams, each sweeping slightly different angles, reporting visibility and fog density. Mariners do not ask for a single direction; they want **a probability map** of safe passages. That is how we must build intelligent systems — not with one deterministic signal, but with many voices that say how certain they are."

☐ Probabilistic Reasoning in AI

Master said, "When the world is foggy, wisdom does not walk with certainty — it walks with probabilities."

This is the essence of Probabilistic Reasoning in Artificial Intelligence (AI).

Probabilistic Reasoning in AI — Seeing Clearly in an Uncertain World

In the natural world, nothing arrives perfectly labeled or fully known.

Sensors are noisy, humans speak ambiguously, environments shift unpredictably, and data often hides more than it reveals.

Traditional rule-based AI assumed the world was crisp and logical:

If A happens, then B must follow.

But reality rarely behaves so cleanly.

Probabilistic reasoning recognises this. It does not search for *certainty* — it searches for *likelihood.* Instead of asking:

"What is the answer?"

it asks:

"What is the most probable answer given the evidence?"

It accepts uncertainty, models it, and *uses it* to guide decision-making.

The Foggy Harbor

Master said,

"Imagine a ship entering a harbor covered in thick fog.

Visibility is low. The captain cannot see the rocks or coastline clearly.

Should the ship stop still? Should it continue? Which direction is safest?"

A deterministic system would panic: *"I must know exactly where the rocks are!"* But a probabilistic system reasons:

- With 80% probability, the coastline lies ahead.
- With 15% probability, a rock is on the left.
- With 5% probability, the path on the right is risky.

The ship steers where the **risk is lowest** — not where certainty exists, but where **probability favours safety**.

This is exactly how modern AI works under uncertainty.

What Is Probabilistic Reasoning?

Probabilistic reasoning is an AI approach that uses **probability theory** to quantify uncertainty in observations, decisions, and predictions.

Rather than saying:

- "This is definitely true,"

it says:

- "This is true with 70% probability,"
- "This outcome is less likely,"
- "This decision carries a higher risk."

It integrates **evidence**, updates **beliefs**, and revises predictions as new information arrives.

This mirrors how humans naturally think:

We rarely know things with 100% certainty — we approximate, evaluate likelihoods, and act accordingly.

Why AI Needs Probabilistic Reasoning

Master explained, "AI must survive in the same uncertain world humans do. It cannot demand perfect clarity — it must reason with imperfect shadows."

Here's why probabilistic reasoning is essential across major AI domains:

1. Machine Learning — Learning from Imperfect Data

Real-world datasets are messy:

- Missing values
- Noisy sensors
- Outliers
- Ambiguity

Probabilistic reasoning allows ML models to:

- Estimate likelihoods instead of hard truths
- Make predictions even when some information is missing
- Quantify uncertainty in predictions
- Update beliefs as more data is seen (Bayesian updating)

Analogy:

A weather forecaster never says, "It will rain."

They say, "There is a 70% chance of rain."

Machine learning uses the same mindset.

2. Robotics — Navigating a Dynamic, Unpredictable World

Robots operate in environments full of uncertainty:

- Objects move
- Sensors give incomplete information
- Maps are imperfect
- Humans behave unpredictably

Probabilistic tools (like Kalman Filters, Particle Filters, and POMDPs) help robots:

- Estimate their position
- Predict dangers
- Plan safe actions

- Adapt when environments change

Analogy:
A robot is like a blindfolded traveller using sound, touch, and memory to guess where it is — probabilities help it refine its guess.

3. Natural Language Processing (NLP) — Understanding Ambiguous Language

Human language is ambiguous by nature.

Consider:

"I saw the man with the telescope."

Who has the telescope — you or the man?

Deterministic systems fail here.

Probabilistic models evaluate:

- Meaning A: 65%
- Meaning B: 35%

And choose the more likely interpretation.

Modern NLP systems like BERT, GPT, and translation engines all rely on probabilistic concepts such as:

- Word distributions
- Attention probabilities
- Likelihood-based token prediction

Analogy:

Understanding language is like reading a blurred text — probabilities fill the missing letters.

4. Decision Making — Choosing Wisely Under Uncertainty

AI often must choose between multiple actions:

- Should a self-driving car turn left or brake?
- Should a medical AI recommend treatment A or B?
- Should a trading bot buy, hold, or sell?

Probabilistic reasoning enables:

- Evaluation of all possible outcomes
- Assessment of risks
- Approximation of expected rewards
- Planning under uncertainty

This is foundational to:

- Bayesian decision theory
- Markov decision processes
- Reinforcement learning

Analogy:

Good decision-makers are not those who know the future, but those who evaluate all futures and choose the most favourable one.

A Deeper Insight: Probabilistic Reasoning Mirrors Human Intelligence

Human intelligence evolved to operate under uncertainty.

Our ancestors tracked prey, predicted weather, and avoided danger — all without complete information.

AI now follows the same evolutionary path.

- **Probabilistic reasoning = AI's intuition**
- **Bayesian updating = AI's way of learning from experience**
- **Probabilistic prediction = AI's foresight**

It is the foundation behind:

- Bayesian networks
- Hidden Markov Models
- Probabilistic graphical models
- Variational inference
- Modern uncertainty-aware deep learning

The Mind as a Probability Engine

Master said,

"The mind is not a machine of certainties. It is a river of shifting probabilities, continually updated by experience.

When AI learns to reason this way, it stops being rigid machinery— it becomes an intelligent companion capable of navigating the world's uncertainty."

Key Concepts in Probabilistic Reasoning

Master said, "Sam, certainty is a luxury of perfect worlds. But intelligence is born in imperfect ones."

Probabilistic reasoning gives AI the ability to think clearly even when the world is blurry.

It teaches machines to **measure uncertainty**, **update beliefs**, and **choose wisely** when information is incomplete.

To understand this art, you must understand its essential tools.

1. Probability — The Language of Uncertainty

Probability is the foundation of all probabilistic reasoning.

It measures how likely something is, expressed between 0 and 1.

Master explained with an analogy:

"Imagine you are standing at the entrance of a dark forest.

You cannot see what lies inside.

But you hear a faint sound — maybe a river, maybe wind.

Probability is your intuition quantifying the uncertainty:

'There is a 70% chance that sound is flowing water.'

It does not give perfect truth —it gives *likely truth*."

In AI, probability allows models to:

- Predict with confidence levels
- Handle missing data
- Incorporate noise and randomness
- Quantify risk instead of ignoring it

Probability is not just a number —It is how intelligence survives the unknown.

2. Bayes' Theorem — The Art of Updating Beliefs

Bayes' theorem is the heart of probabilistic reasoning. It teaches AI how to update beliefs when new evidence appears.

The formula:

$$P(A|B) = \frac{P(B|A) \cdot P(A)}{P(B)}$$

Master said:

"Imagine a detective who starts with a suspicion (prior belief).

Then new clues emerge — footprints, fingerprints, a witness report.

The detective does not throw away old beliefs.

Instead, he **updates** them.

The more evidence supports the theory, the stronger his belief becomes.

This is Bayes' theorem —the mathematics of changing the mind wisely."

In AI, Bayes' theorem allows systems to:

- Refine predictions with new data
- Correct old assumptions
- Combine prior knowledge with fresh evidence
- Handle sequential or streaming information

It is the formula that turns learning into reasoning.

3. Conditional Probability — When One Event Depends on Another

Conditional probability answers: "What is the chance of A happening given that B has already happened?"

Master explained:

"If you hear thunder, the probability of rain increases.

The events are not independent — one influences the other.

Conditional probability captures this dependency."

In AI, this concept is crucial for:

- Speech recognition ("If the previous word is *I*, the next is more likely *am*")
- Medical diagnosis ("If test A is positive, disease B becomes more likely")
- Fraud detection ("If a transaction is abroad and at midnight, risk increases")

AI uses conditional probabilities to understand **how events shape each other**.

4. Random Variables — Quantifying Uncertainty

A random variable is a value that changes based on chance.

Master said:

"A random variable is like a leaf floating in the wind.

Its path is uncertain — yet governed by underlying forces.

We cannot predict each movement, but we can model the probability of where it may land."

Random variables allow AI to:

- Represent uncertain quantities
- Build probabilistic models
- Describe distributions (Gaussian, Bernoulli, etc.)
- Perform inference and prediction

They are the building blocks of uncertainty.

Techniques in Probabilistic Reasoning

Understanding the concepts is only the beginning.

AI must also *use* these concepts to infer, learn, and decide.

1. Inference — Discovering the Invisible from the Visible

Inference means computing probabilities of hidden or unknown events using known evidence.

Master illustrated:

"When you see ripples in a pond, you infer that something disturbed the water — a stone, a fish, or the wind.

You cannot see the cause directly, but probabilistic inference reveals the unseen."

In AI:

- **Exact inference** uses methods like variable elimination
- **Approximate inference** uses methods like MCMC or sampling
- It helps compute hidden variables in Bayesian networks
- It allows AI to reason about missing or uncertain data

Inference is the process of **seeing through the fog** using logic and probability.

2. Learning — Refining the Model with Evidence

Learning updates the parameters of probabilistic models as new data arrives.

Master said:

"A wise person does not cling to outdated beliefs.

Each new experience reshapes their understanding.

So must an intelligent machine learn."

AI uses:

Maximum Likelihood Estimation (MLE)

Choosing parameters that best explain the data.

Bayesian Estimation

Updating distributions instead of fixed values, incorporating prior knowledge.

This allows models to:

- Adapt to new environments
- Improve their predictions
- Capture uncertainty in parameters
- Learn robustly even with noisy data

Learning transforms probabilities from guesses into wisdom.

3. Decision Making — Choosing Wisely Under Uncertainty

Decision-making combines probabilities with rewards to select the best action.

Master shared another analogy:

"A traveler sees three paths:

one short but dangerous,

one long but safe,

and one mysterious.

Probabilistic reasoning evaluates the risks and rewards — choosing the path with the highest *expected* return, not the highest certainty."

AI uses concepts like:

- **Expected Utility**
- **Markov Decision Processes (MDPs)**
- **POMDPs** (when some information is hidden)
- **Reinforcement Learning**

These help AI choose actions that maximize long-term benefits even when the environment is unpredictable.

Master said, "To think probabilistically is to accept humility.

It is the art of navigating life with incomplete maps, imperfect signals, and evolving evidence.

An intelligent system — like an intelligent human — does not seek absolute truth, but **the most reasonable truth given what is known.**"

Master said, "Niaksh, let us revisit our discussion on Probabilistic Models and Probabilistic Reasoning."

"Though they walk together, their purposes are distinct. One builds the world; the other learns to move through it."

Probabilistic Models — The Structure of Uncertainty

Master continued, "A probabilistic model is the *architecture* in which uncertainty lives."

It defines:

- What variables exist
- How they relate and depend on one another
- What probability distributions govern them
- How information flows between events

Examples include:

- Bayesian Networks
- Hidden Markov Models
- Gaussian Mixture Models
- Markov Random Fields

"Think of the probabilistic model as the *map*: the nodes, edges, distributions, and structural relationships that describe the terrain of uncertainty."

Probabilistic Reasoning — The Process of Understanding

Master then said, "Probabilistic reasoning is the act of *using* that map."

It answers:

- Given the model, what can we infer?
- What is the probability of X when Y is known?
- How does evidence reshape our belief?

Examples include:

- Bayes' rule updates
- Belief propagation
- MAP (Maximum A Posteriori) estimation
- Predicting hidden states
- Marginalization and inference

"Reasoning is navigation—drawing conclusions, updating beliefs, and making predictions as new information appears."

The Simple Analogy

Master summarized gently:

- Probabilistic Model = the *blueprint* of a house
- Probabilistic Reasoning = how you *live* inside that house—how you move, decide, and adapt with experience

The essence

"Niaksh, remember this," the Master said:

- Probabilistic Models define *how uncertainty is structured.*
- Probabilistic Reasoning defines *how we think, infer, and evolve* within that structure.

☐ MLE and MAP

Master said, "Apeksha, let us now explore the subtle difference between *Maximum Likelihood Estimation (MLE)* and *Maximum A Posteriori Estimation (MAP).*

Both seek the truth hidden behind data — but they walk different paths to reach it."

1. **Maximum Likelihood Estimation (MLE) — Truth Seen Only Through Data**

Master continued, "Imagine you are standing in a valley, surrounded by echoes. MLE listens *only* to the echoes.

It trusts nothing except what the data reveals."

In MLE:

- We choose the parameter that **makes the observed data most probable.**
- No assumptions, no prior beliefs.

- Purely data-driven.

Mathematically:
It finds the parameter θ that maximizes **P(Data | θ)**.

Master said, "MLE is like a traveller surveying a land for the first time. He carries no maps, no memories, no prior wisdom. He decides the shape of the land *only* from what he sees before him."

Strengths:

- Objective
- Works well with large datasets
- Simple and widely used

Limitations:

- Blind to prior knowledge
- Can overfit when data is limited

2. Maximum A Posteriori (MAP) Estimation — Truth Guided by Belief and Data

Master then said, "MAP estimation is the same traveler…

but this time he carries a map — perhaps incomplete, perhaps old — yet it is still useful."

MAP combines:

- Prior beliefs (before seeing the data)
- Observed data

It finds the parameter θ maximizing P(θ | Data), which is proportional to:

```
P(Data | θ) × P(θ)
```

"MAP is the art of blending experience with observation," the Master said.

Strengths:

- Useful when data is scarce
- Helps avoid extreme or unreasonable estimates
- Allows domain knowledge to guide the solution

Limitations:

- Depends on the choice of prior
- If prior is biased, inference may shift

Two Ways of Finding the True Path

Master smiled and said, **"Apeksha, imagine you are trying to predict tomorrow's weather."**

1. MLE Approach

You look only at **today's sky**.

- If it is cloudy today, you predict rain.
- If it is sunny, you predict sunshine.

"You use no historical wisdom — only the present evidence."

2. MAP Approach

You look at:

- Today's sky
- The season
- Your past experience

If today is cloudy but it's *summer*, MAP might still lean toward sunshine.

"MAP blends the moment with memory. MLE hears only the moment."

The Essence

Master said:

- MLE = *What does the data alone suggest?*
- MAP = *What does the data suggest, guided by prior wisdom?*

"MLE is pure perception. MAP is perception refined by belief."

"One is the voice of the present. The other is the dialogue between past and present."

Master said, "John, come sit — let us open the doors of Bayesian probability and the quiet law called conditional independence. These are the two pillars on which much of sensible reasoning is built."

1. Bayesian Probability — Belief as a Living Thing

Master spoke slowly.

"Think of probability not as a cold frequency alone, but as a **degree of belief** — how strongly you trust a hypothesis given what you know. Bayesian probability treats knowledge as dynamic: every piece of evidence shifts what you should believe, just as wind shifts the sailboat's course."

At its heart sits Bayes' theorem, a simple formula with profound implications:

$$P(H|D) = P(D|H)\,P(H)/P(D)$$

Read it as a sentence:

- P(H) - the **prior**: what you believed about hypothesis H before seeing data.
- P(D|H) - the **likelihood**: how well hypothesis H explains the new data D.
- P(D) - the **evidence**: the total probability of seeing D under all hypotheses.
- P(H|D) - the **posterior**: your updated belief in H after seeing D.

Analogy:

"Imagine you are a farmer watching the sky," Master said. "The prior is your memory of the season — perhaps monsoon months make rain more likely. The likelihood is what you see today: dark clouds. The evidence is how often you have seen such clouds produce rain. Combine these, and you update your belief: will it rain today? That updated belief is the posterior."

Why is this powerful?

Because Bayesian inference formalizes *learning*: you start with prior knowledge, observe data, and update gracefully. It gives a principled way to fold experience into decision-making.

Example: **Bayesian Probability**

Situation:

A disease affects **2%** of the population.

A test detects the disease with:

- **Sensitivity (True Positive Rate):** 90%
- **False Positive Rate:** 5%

John asked: "Master, if my test is positive, what is the probability I actually have the disease?"

Step 1 — Define the terms

Let:

- H = having the disease
- D = test result is positive

Given:

$P(H) = 0.02$ (prior)

$P(\neg H) = 0.98$

$P(D|H) = 0.90$ (likelihood for true positive)

$P(D|\neg H) = 0.05$ (false positive)

Step 2 — Compute the evidence

$P(D) = P(D|H)\ P(H) + P(D|\neg H)\ P(\neg H)$

$P(D) = (0.90)\ (0.02) + (0.05)\ (0.98)$

$P(D)=0.018+0.049=0.067$

Step 3 — Compute the Posterior Using Bayes' Rule

$P(H|D) = P(D|H)\ P(H)/P(D)$

$P(H|D) = 0.90\times 0.02/0.067$

$P(H|D) = 0.018/0.067 \approx 0.268$

Result:

Even if the test is positive, the chance of actually having the disease is only 26.8%.

2. Conditional Independence — The Quiet Shortcuts

Master leaned in. "But John, the world is complex. Every variable may, in principle, influence every other. We cannot reason if every dependency is considered — the combinatorial web overwhelms us. Here, *conditional independence* is a mercy."

Definition: Two variables A and B are **conditionally independent** given C if, once you know C, learning about A gives you no additional information about B. Symbolically:

$$P(A,B|C) = P(A|C)\ P(B|C)$$

Analogy:

"Suppose you and I are two messengers in different towns. Each may receive news from the same central postmaster. Once we both have the postmaster's message C, knowledge of my news A adds nothing to your understanding of yours B — they're independent *given* the postmaster's letter."

Practical use: Conditional independence lets us **factor** joint probabilities into simpler pieces. The joint distribution of many variables becomes tractable by exploiting conditional independences.

Example: Conditional Independence

Now, Master continued, **"Let us take another example to understand conditional independence."**

Scenario:

A sprinkler (S) and rain (R) can both make the grass wet (G).

But **sprinkler and rain are independent causes** unless we observe the effect (wet grass).

Let's assign real probabilities.

Given:

- $P(R=1) = 0.30 \rightarrow 30\%$ chance of rain
- $P(S=1) = 0.40 \rightarrow 40\%$ chance sprinkler is on
- Rain and sprinkler are **independent** initially

Grass becomes wet if:

- Rain makes it wet with probability 0.9
- Sprinkler makes it wet with probability 0.8
- If both occur, grass is certainly wet (≈ 1)

Conditional Independence BEFORE seeing the grass

Since rain and sprinklers don't influence each other:

$P(R|S) = P(R) = 0.30$

They are **independent.**

Now suppose the grass *is wet.*

John asked, "Master, does the sprinkler tell us something about rain now?"

Master replied, "Yes, John — when the effect is known, the causes become dependent. This is *explaining away.*"

Let us calculate it.

Step 1: Probability grass is wet

Let's compute:

$P(G=1) = P(R=1)\ P(G|R) + P(R=0, S=1)\ P(G|S) + P(R=1,S=1)P(G|R,S)$

Approximation:

- Only rain → $0.30 \times 0.9 =$ **0.27**
- Only sprinkler → $0.70 \times 0.40 \times 0.8 =$ **0.224**
- Both → $0.30 \times 0.40 \times 1 =$ **0.12**

$P(G=1) = 0.27+0.224+0.12=0.614$

Step 2: Compute P(R = 1 | G = 1)

"Given grass is wet, what is the probability it rained?"

$P(R=1|G=1) = P(G=1|R=1)\ P(R=1)/P(G=1)$

Where:

- $P(G=1|R=1) \approx 0.9+(0.4)\ (0.1) = 0.94$

$P(R=1|G=1) = 0.94\times0.30/0.614$

$P(R=1 \mid G=1) = 0.282/0.614 \approx 0.459$

Result:

Given the grass is wet, the chance of rain rises from 30% to ~46%.

Step 3: Conditional dependence appears

Now calculate:

$P(R=1|S=1, G=1)$

Compute numerator:

- If the sprinkler is on AND the grass is wet, rain was LESS needed.

Approx:

Grass can be wet via sprinkler alone with probability 0.8.

Using Bayes' rule:

$P(R=1|S=1, G=1) = P(G=1|R=1,S=1)P(R=1)P(S=1) / P(G=1,S=1)$

Skipping algebra, the value becomes:

≈ 0.32

Interpretation:

Without observing grass:

Sprinkler and rain are independent.

After observing the wet grass:

Knowing the sprinkler is ON **reduces belief in rain**

(46% → 32%) because sprinkler "explains" the wetness.

This is **explaining away** — the heart of conditional independence.

Master said, "John, imagine two students who might have solved a riddle: Meera and Arjun.

Before seeing the solution, whether Meera solved it doesn't affect whether Arjun did.

But once you see the riddle is solved…if you learn Meera solved it, your belief that Arjun also solved it drops.

The effect ties the causes together."

3. Chain Rule and Factorization

Master continued: "The chain rule expresses any joint distribution as a product of conditionals."

$$P(X_1, X_2,\ldots,X_n) = \prod_{i=1}^{n} P(X_i \mid X_{1:i-1})$$

"But if we know some conditional independences," he said, "many of those conditionals reduce to simpler terms. This is the algebraic key behind Bayesian Networks."

Example: In a simple Bayesian network A→C←B (a "V-structure"), A and B are independent, but become dependent when we condition on C - a surprising fact captured by *explaining away.*

Graphical Models — Maps of Dependence

Master drew an invisible diagram. "Graphical models — Bayesian networks and Markov random fields — are maps of dependencies. Nodes are variables; edges show direct probabilistic influence. The graph encodes conditional independences visually. From it, we read factorization: the joint distribution equals the product over nodes of each node's conditional probability given its parents."

Analogy:
"If a town map shows which roads connect directly, you know where traffic can flow. Those road connections tell you which places influence travel times directly; others only influence indirectly through intermediate links."

This representation is both **intuitive** and **computationally useful**: inference algorithms (exact or approximate) exploit graph structure to propagate beliefs efficiently.

Examples to Ground the Ideas

1. **Medical diagnosis (Bayes):**
    - Prior: prevalence of disease.
    - Likelihood: probability of symptoms given disease.
    - Posterior: updated chance patient has the disease given the symptoms. Bayes helps avoid surprises like false alarms from rare diseases.
2. **Naive Bayes classifier (Conditional independence):**
    - Assumes features $X_1,\ldots, X_n$ are independent given class Y.
    - Factorizes $P(X|Y)$ into product of $P(X_i|Y)$.

   - It's a crude assumption, yet often remarkably effective — a practical lesson in how useful simple conditional independences can be.

3. **Explaining away:**

   - Two independent causes (A and B) both can produce effect C. If C is observed, learning A is true, reduces belief in B (they become dependent given C). This is a quintessential Bayesian phenomenon.

Why This Matters —

Master's voice softened: "Probability is humility formalized. It admits we are seldom certain. Bayesian thinking models how humans and intelligent systems should *update* — not cling to old maps when new terrain appears. Conditional independence is practically formalized: it allows us to simplify without losing essential truth."

He said, "In practice, we build models (the maps), assume some conditional independences to reduce complexity, and then use Bayes to update beliefs as evidence arrives. As you craft these models, remember: the better your structural assumptions (independences), and the more honest your priors, the more faithful will be your conclusions."

PART TWO

DAY THREE

Unit 2 - Lesson Two

Naïve Bayes

Task: Classification

- Description: Probabilistic algorithm based on applying Bayes' theorem; assumes that features are conditionally independent given the class.
- Algorithm: Naive Bayes is a probabilistic algorithm based on Bayes' theorem.
- Application: Email spam filtering, sentiment analysis, and document classification.

Master explained that the Naïve Bayes algorithm is a supervised learning method grounded in Bayes' theorem, utilised predominantly for classification tasks. Particularly prominent in text classification due to its efficacy with high-dimensional datasets, it stands out for its simplicity and rapid predictive capabilities.

Key Features:

- Simplicity and Efficiency: Naïve Bayes Classifier is lauded for its simplicity, making it computationally efficient and suitable for large-scale applications.
- Probabilistic Approach: It operates on the principle of probability, predicting outcomes based on the likelihood of occurrence.
- Versatility: Widely employed across various domains, including spam

filtering, sentiment analysis, and article categorisation.

Origins of "Naïve" and "Bayes":

Naïve: The term "Naïve" stems from the algorithm's assumption of feature independence. Each feature is considered in isolation, disregarding potential interdependencies. For instance, in fruit classification based on colour, shape, and taste, the algorithm treats each feature independently, facilitating swift identification without considering their correlations.

Example: Regardless of order, treat all features equally. It has high bias and low variance.

Score for Shape and Colour p(N) x p(shape | F) x p(colour | F) = 0.57

Score for Colour and Shape p(N) x p(colour | F) x p(shape | F) = 0.57

Bayes: Named after Reverend Thomas Bayes, the algorithm relies on Bayes' theorem, a fundamental principle in probability theory, to make predictions.

Bayes' Theorem:

Bayes' theorem, also known as Bayes' Rule or Bayes' law, calculates the probability of a hypothesis given prior knowledge.

It is expressed as:

$$P(A|B) = P(B|A) \times P(A) / P(B)$$

Where:

- **P(A | B)** is the probability of event **A** occurring given that event **B** has occurred.
- **P(B | A)** is the probability of event **B** occurring given that event **A** has occurred.
- **P(A)** is the probability of event **A** occurring.
- **P(B)** is the probability of event **B** occurring.

Components:

- Posterior Probability (P(A|B)): Probability of hypothesis A given the observed event B.
- Likelihood Probability (P(B|A)): Probability of evidence given the hypothesis is true.
- Prior Probability (P(A)): Probability of the hypothesis before considering the evidence.
- Marginal Probability (P(B)): Overall probability of the evidence.

Case 1: Probability of Drawing a King Given It's a Face Card

We want to find the probability of randomly picking a King (denoted as **K**) from a deck of cards, given that the card is a face card (denoted as **F**).

Total number of cards in a deck: 52

Number of Kings in the deck: 4

Therefore, the probability of drawing a King: P(K) = 4/52 = 1/13

Number of face cards in each suit: 3 (Jack, Queen, King)

- Total number of face cards in the deck: 3 face cards per suit * 4 suits = 12 face cards
- Therefore, the probability of drawing a face card: P(F) = 12/52 = 3/13

Probability of drawing a face card given that it is a King:

Since all Kings are face cards: **P(F|K) = 1**

Using Bayes' Theorem:

P(K|F) = (P(F|K) * P(K)) / P(F) = (1 * (1/13)) / (3/13) = 1/3

Conclusion

The probability of drawing a King given that the card is a face card is:

P(K|F) = 1/3

This result aligns with our intuitive understanding since there are three types of face cards (Jack, Queen, King), and each type has an equal probability of being drawn if we know the card is a face card.

Case 2: A game of golf

Master said, "Roopa, iIn a fictional dataset, we capture the weather conditions tailored for a game of golf. Each entry in this dataset categorises the prevailing weather as either suitable ('Yes') or unsuitable ('No') for playing golf. This binary classification enables us to assess the compatibility of weather conditions with the game."

	Outlook	Temperature	Humidity	Windy	Play Golf
0	Rainy	Hot	High	False	No
1	Rainy	Hot	High	True	No
2	Overcast	Hot	High	False	Yes
3	Sunny	Mild	High	False	Yes
4	Sunny	Cool	Normal	False	Yes
5	Sunny	Cool	Normal	True	No
6	Overcast	Cool	Normal	True	Yes
7	Rainy	Mild	High	False	No
8	Rainy	Cool	Normal	False	Yes
9	Sunny	Mild	Normal	False	Yes
10	Rainy	Mild	Normal	True	Yes
11	Overcast	Mild	High	True	Yes
12	Overcast	Hot	Normal	False	Yes
13	Sunny	Mild	High	True	No

Illustration Naive_1: Naïve Bayes

Let's assess a new set of features for today's weather: (Sunny, Hot, Normal Humidity, No Wind). We want to determine the probability of playing golf (Yes) or not playing golf (No) given these weather conditions.

We start by calculating the probabilities using Bayes' theorem. For instance, to find P(Yes|today), we multiply the individual probabilities of each feature given the outcome "Yes" (playing golf) and then normalise.

$$P(Yes|today)=P(SunnyOutlook|Y)\times P(HotTemperature|Y)\times P(Normal\ Humidity|Y)\times P(NoWind|Y)\times P(Y)/P(today)$$

Similarly, the probability of not playing golf P(No|today) is calculated in the same manner but considering the features given the outcome "No" (not playing golf).

Naïve Bayes

Outlook	Y	N	P(Y)	P(N)
Sunny	3	2	2/9	3/5
Overcast	4	0	4/9	0/5
Rainy	3	2	3/9	3/5
Total	9	5	100%	

Temp	Y	N	P(Y)	P(N)
Hot	2	2	2/9	2/5
Mild	4	2	4/9	2/5
Cool	3	1	3/9	1/5
Total	9	5	100%	

Calculate P(xi|yi) for each xi in X and y

P(temp. = cool | play golf = Y) = 3/9

Humidity	Y	N	P(Y)	P(N)
High	3	4	3/9	4/5
Normal	6	1	6/9	1/5
Total	9	5	100%	

Windy	Y	N	P(Y)	P(N)
False	6	2	6/9	2/5
True	3	3	3/9	3/5
Total	9	5	100%	

Play		P(Y)/P(N)
Y	9	9/14
N	5	5/14
Total	14	100%

P(play golf = Y) = 9/14

Illustration Naive_2: Naïve Bayes

Since P(today) is common in both probabilities, we can ignore it and find the proportional probabilities.

$$P(Yes|today) \propto (3/9) \times (2/9) \times (6/9) \times (6/9) \times (9/14) \approx 0.06375$$

$P(No|today) \propto (2/5)\times(2/5)\times(1/5)\times(2/9)\times(5/14) \approx 0.012698$

To convert these proportional probabilities into actual probabilities, we normalize them by dividing each by the sum of the probabilities.

$P(Yes|today) = [0.06375]/[0.06375+0.012698] \approx 0.8341$

$P(No|today) = [0.012698]/[0.06375+0.012698] \approx 0.1659$

Predict:

Since P(Yes|today) is greater than P(No|today), we predict that golf will be played (Yes).

It's worth noting that this method is applicable to discrete data. For continuous data, we need to make assumptions about the distribution of feature values. Different Naïve Bayes classifiers vary based on these assumptions.

Case 3: Analysing Word Frequency and Probabilities in Spam Detection

Master said, "Let us begin by creating a histogram to analyse the word frequencies in the messages. Our dataset included 8 normal messages and 4 spam messages. The next step was to calculate the probability of each word appearing in normal and spam messages."

Here's a step-by-step outline of the process:

Word Histogram: We started by examining the occurrence of each word in both normal and spam messages. This provided us with the word frequency distribution.

Probability Calculation: For each word, we calculated its probability of appearing in normal messages and in spam messages.

$p(Dear | Normal)$

Initial Probability Guess: We made an initial guess about the probability of encountering a normal message. This guess can be any value between 0 and 1. We also made a similar guess for the probability of encountering a spam message.

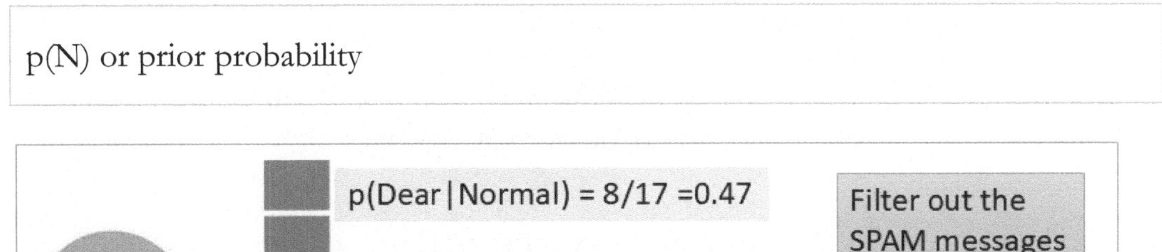

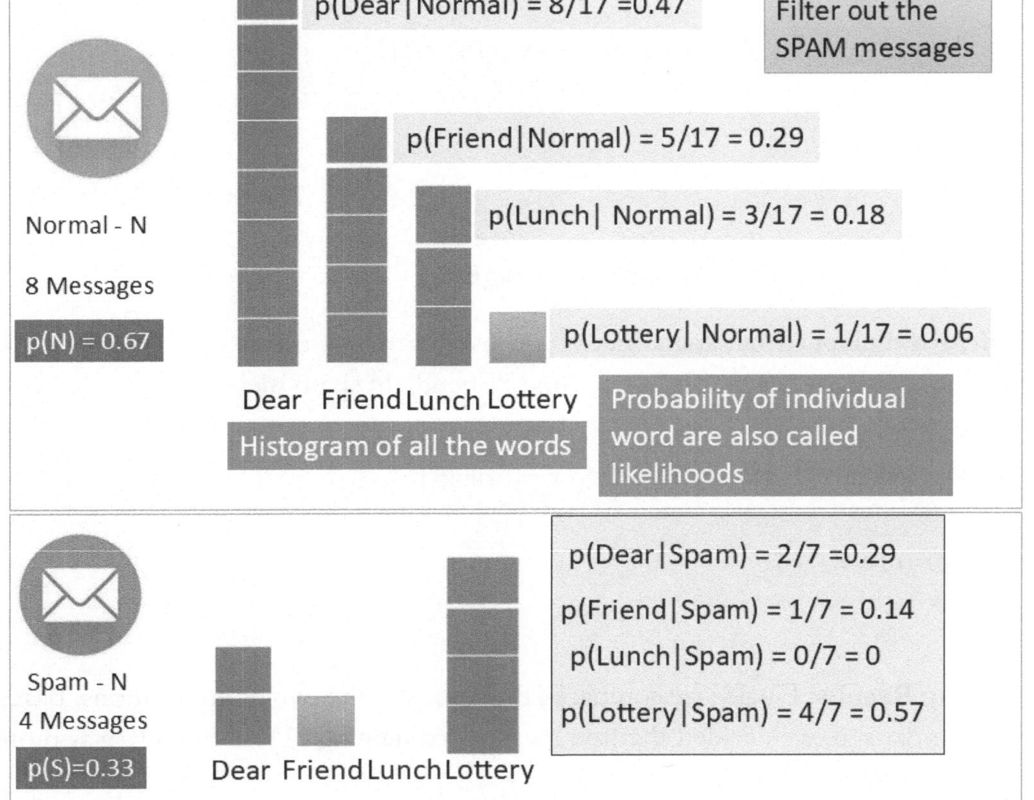

Illustration Naive_3: Naïve Bayes

Classify a new message containing the words 'Dear Friend' as either Normal or Spam.

From the training data — Normal class:

p(N), the prior probability of a message being *Normal*, is 8/(8+4) =0.67

From the training data — Spam class:

p(S), the prior probability of a message being *Spam*, is 4/(4+8) =0.33

Probability Multiplication for Normal Messages:

We multiplied our initial guess (probability that a message is normal) by the probabilities of seeing the words "Dear" and "Friend" in normal messages.

p(N| Dear Friend) = p(N) x p(Dear| N) x p(Friend|N)

= 0.67*0.47*0.29 = 0.09

Probability Multiplication for Spam Messages:

Similarly, we multiplied our initial guess (probability that a message is spam) by the probabilities of seeing the words "Dear" and "Friend" in spam messages.

p(S| Dear Friend) = p(S) x p(Dear| S) x p(Friend|S)

= 0.33*0.29*0.14 = 0.01

Comparing Results: Finally, we compared the results of the two multiplications. Based on this comparison, we decided that the message containing "Dear Friend" was more likely to be a normal message.

Normal message 0.09 > 0.01

This approach uses Bayesian inference to classify messages based on word probabilities. By calculating and comparing the probabilities, we can determine whether a given message is likely to be normal or spam.

Case 4: Handling Zero Probabilities in Spam Detection

Let's consider a more complex problem with the message "Lunch, Lottery, Lottery, Lottery, Lottery." It seems reasonable to predict that this message will be classified as spam. Let's go through the calculations to understand why and how we can refine our approach to improve classification accuracy.

Master said, "Apeksha, look closely at this illustration. It reveals a profound lesson hidden within the mechanics of learning.

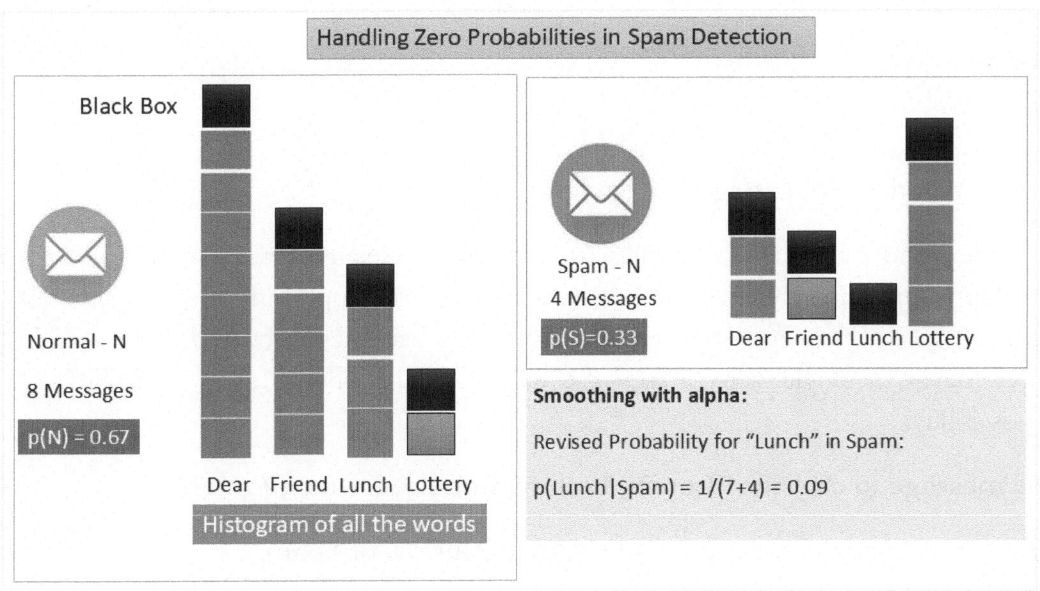

Illustration Naive_4: Naïve Bayes

Here, we have two kinds of messages—Normal and Spam—each carrying its own history, its own patterns, its own likelihood of appearing. From these patterns, we calculate their prior probabilities. Most messages lean toward the Normal class, while fewer fall into Spam. This becomes our first insight.

Two categories of messages

Normal messages (N) → 8 messages

Prior probability: **p(N) = 0.67**

Spam messages (S) → 4 messages

Prior probability: **p(S) = 0.33**

Word histograms for each class

The bars show how often each word appears in:

- Normal messages
- Spam messages

Words shown: *Dear, Friend, Lunch, Lottery*

This helps calculate **likelihood probabilities** such as

p(Lunch|N) or p(Lottery|S).

Then comes the new message: *'Lunch, Lottery, Lottery, Lottery, Lottery.'*

To understand whether it is harmless or harmful, we examine the likelihood of each word appearing in each category. But notice something important: in the Spam class, the word *'Lunch'* has never appeared. Its probability becomes zero. And in the world of Naive Bayes, a single zero erases the entire calculation—turning possibility into impossibility.

The message to classify: "Lunch, Lottery, Lottery, Lottery, Lottery."

We want to determine whether this message is **Normal** or **Spam**.

Initial Naive Bayes Calculation

Normal Message Probability: $p(N) \times p(Lunch | N) \times p(Lottery | N)^4 = 0.000002$

Spam Message Probability: $p(S) \times p(Lunch | S) \times p(Lottery | S)^4 = 0$

Why zero?

Because the word **"Lunch" never appears in spam messages →**

p(Lunch|S) = 0

One zero makes the entire multiplication **zero**, which is a major problem.

"But here is the problem," Master said. "In the Spam messages, the word *'Lunch'* never appears. So its probability becomes zero. And Apeksha, in Naive Bayes, if even one word has zero probability, the entire calculation collapses to zero. That means the model would completely reject the Spam possibility—even if everything else points strongly toward Spam."

"So what do we do?" the Master asked gently. "We use a technique called *smoothing*—a small adjustment that prevents any word from having zero probability. It says: 'Even if we haven't seen this word before, let us assign it a tiny chance.' With smoothing, the probability of 'Lunch' in Spam becomes a small number instead of zero."

Problem with Zero Probabilities:

To resolve this, we need to avoid zero probabilities. This is achieved by adding a count (typically referred to as alpha) to each word in our histogram. Here, we set alpha to one.

Smoothing with Alpha:

Revised Probability for "Lunch" in Spam: p(Lunch | Spam) = 1/(7+4) = 0.09

Recalculating Probabilities:

The addition of counts (alpha) ensures we never get a zero probability for any word. This smoothing does not change our initial guesses for p(N) and p(S).

Revised Normal Message Probability: p(N) x p(Lunch | N) x p(Lottery | N)^4 = 0.00001

Revised Spam Message Probability: p(S) x p(Lunch | S) x p(Lottery | S)^4 = 0.00122

Final Classification:

Master said, "With these revised probabilities, we now get a non-zero value for the message being spam, which is greater than the probability of it being normal. - Therefore, the message "Lunch, Lottery, Lottery, Lottery, Lottery" is classified as spam. By incorporating smoothing (adding counts to each word), we ensure that no word has a zero probability, thus improving the robustness of our classification and allowing the model to make more accurate predictions."

Master said, "We learnt how zero probabilities can mislead the model, and how smoothing helps restore balance. It is a reminder that in learning—whether by machines or humans—we must avoid absolute judgments. A small allowance for the unseen keeps our understanding whole."

☐ Types of Naïve Bayes Model:

Gaussian Naive Bayes Classifier:

- Assumes that continuous feature values follow a Gaussian (normal) distribution.
- Feature distributions are represented by bell-shaped curves symmetric around the mean.
- Suitable for datasets with continuous features exhibiting Gaussian distributions.

Multinomial Naive Bayes:

- Utilizes feature vectors to capture the frequencies of events generated by a multinomial distribution.
- Commonly employed in document classification tasks where features represent word counts or frequencies.
- Effective for text classification tasks where features are discrete and represent occurrences of words or terms.

Bernoulli Naive Bayes:

- Assumes that features are independent binary variables, typically representing the presence or absence of specific features.
- Well-suited for datasets where features are binary or Boolean, such as document classification based on the presence of specific keywords.
- Particularly useful for tasks involving binary feature representations, such as spam detection or sentiment analysis.

These three variants of Naive Bayes models cater to different types of data and feature distributions, allowing for versatile applications across various classification tasks. Whether dealing with continuous Gaussian distributions, discrete multinomial feature representations, or binary Bernoulli features, Naive Bayes provides a simple yet effective approach to probabilistic classification.

☐ Normal Distribution

Sam asked, "What is Mean?"

Master said, "The mean is the average of a set of values. In a normal distribution, it is the central value around which the data points are symmetrically distributed."

Mathematically, the mean μ of a dataset is calculated by summing all the data points and then dividing by the number of data points:

$$\text{Mean}(\mu) = \frac{\sum_{i=1}^{n} x_i}{n}$$

Where N is the number of data points, and x_i represents each individual data point.

Apeksha asked, "What is Standard Deviation?"

Master continued, the standard deviation is a measure of the amount of variation or dispersion in a set of values. In a normal distribution, it indicates how to spread out the data points are around the mean. A low standard deviation means that the data points tend to be close to the mean, while a high standard deviation indicates that the data points are spread out over a wider range.

Mathematically, the standard deviation σ is calculated as:

$$\text{Variance}(\sigma^2) = \frac{\sum_{i=1}^{n} (xi - \mu)^2}{n}$$

$$\text{Standard Deviation}(\sigma) = \sqrt{Variance}$$

Normal Density vs. Gaussian Density:

Normal Density: Refers to the probability density function (PDF) of a normal distribution, which describes the likelihood of a continuous random variable taking on a particular value.

Gaussian Density: Another name for the normal density function. Named after Carl Friedrich Gauss, who contributed significantly to the mathematical description of this distribution.

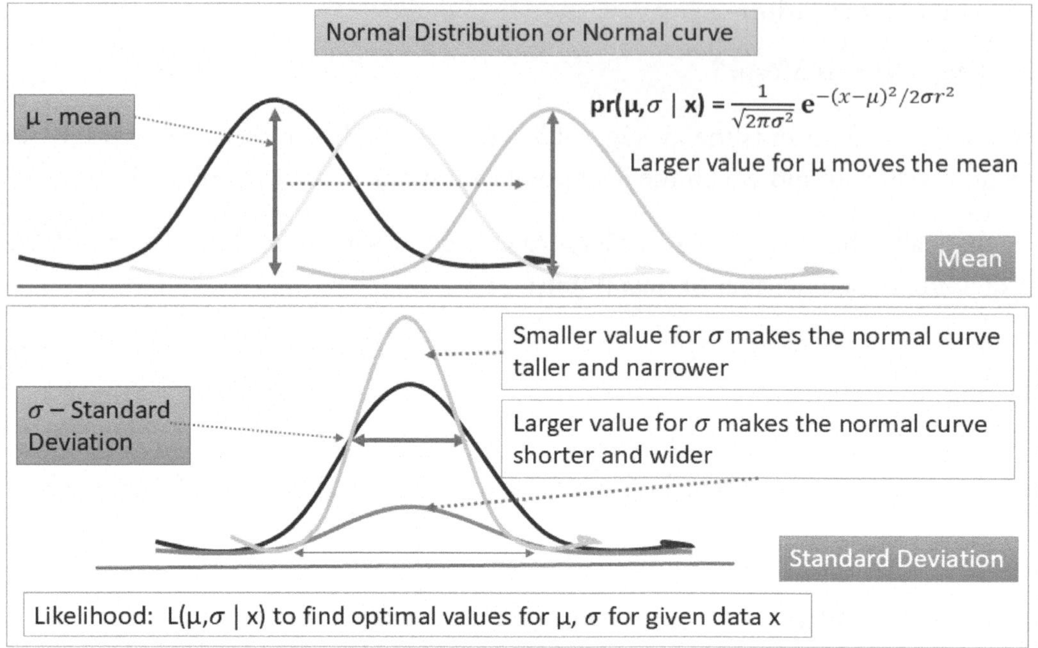

Illustration ND_1: Normal Distrubution

The probability density function (PDF) is bell-shaped and follows the formula:

$$pr(\mu,\sigma \mid x) = \frac{1}{\sqrt{2\pi\sigma^2}} e^{-(x-\mu)^2/2\sigma x^2}$$

Normal and Gaussian distribution:

Master said, "Sam, a *normal distribution*—also called the *Gaussian distribution*—is a continuous probability distribution perfectly symmetric around its mean (μ). Its shape forms the well-known 'bell curve.' It carries several important properties:

The **mean**, **median**, and **mode** are all equal, sitting at the center of the curve.

The distribution is fully defined by just **two parameters**: the **mean (μ)**, which determines its center, and the **standard deviation (σ)**, which determines its spread or width.

Visualizing Normal Distributions:

Normal distributions can vary in shape and size depending on their standard deviations. Here's a Python code snippet to visualize normal distributions with different standard deviations using Matplotlib:

Example P2 – U2 – D2	
Normal Distribution	**Output**

```
import numpy as np
import matplotlib.pyplot as plt
# Parameters for the normal distributions
mean = 0
std_devs = [0.5, 1.0, 2.0]  # Narrow, medium, and wide
distributions

# Define x range for plotting
x = np.linspace(-10, 10, 1000)
# Create the plot
plt.figure(figsize=(10, 6))
# Plot each distribution
for std_dev in std_devs:
    y = (1 / (np.sqrt(2 * np.pi) * std_dev)) * np.exp(-0.5 *
((x - mean) / std_dev)**2)
    plt.plot(x, y, label=f'Standard Deviation = {std_dev}')

# Add titles and labels
plt.title('Normal Distributions with Different Standard
Deviations')
plt.xlabel('Value')
plt.ylabel('Probability Density')
plt.legend()
# Show the plot
plt.grid(True)
plt.show()
```

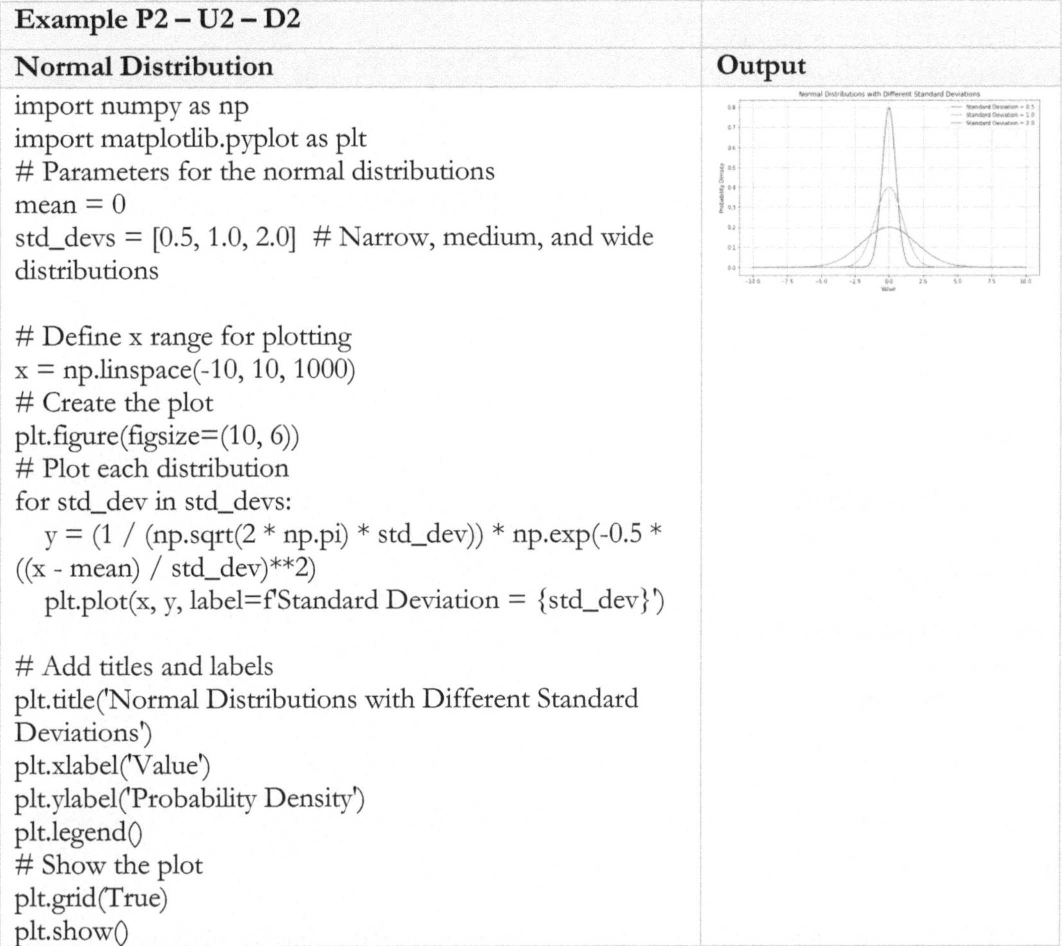

This code will demonstrate how the distributions shift along the x-axis while also showing variations in shape due to different standard deviations.

Example P2 – U2 – D3	
Normal Distribution – Mean and Standard Deviation	**Output**

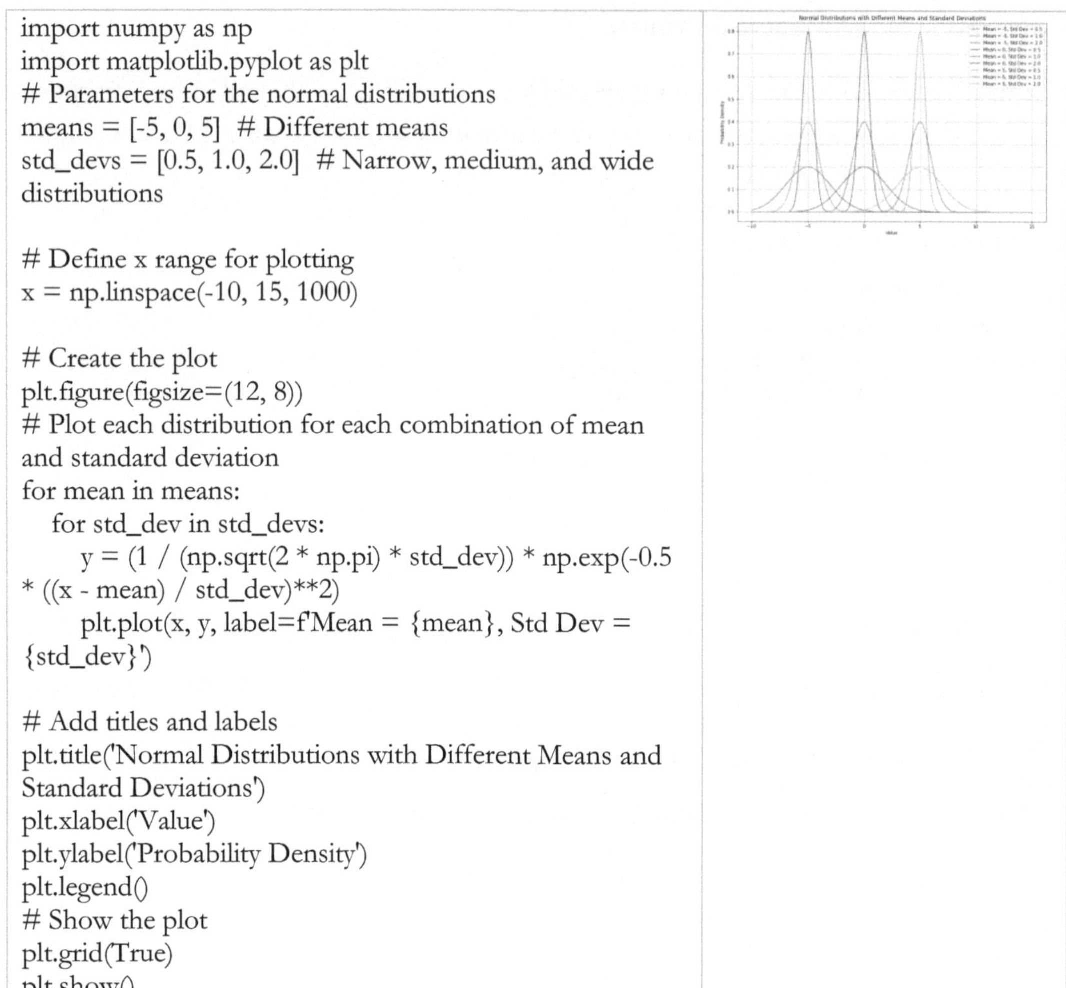

```
import numpy as np
import matplotlib.pyplot as plt
# Parameters for the normal distributions
means = [-5, 0, 5]  # Different means
std_devs = [0.5, 1.0, 2.0]  # Narrow, medium, and wide
distributions

# Define x range for plotting
x = np.linspace(-10, 15, 1000)

# Create the plot
plt.figure(figsize=(12, 8))
# Plot each distribution for each combination of mean
and standard deviation
for mean in means:
    for std_dev in std_devs:
        y = (1 / (np.sqrt(2 * np.pi) * std_dev)) * np.exp(-0.5
* ((x - mean) / std_dev)**2)
        plt.plot(x, y, label=f'Mean = {mean}, Std Dev =
{std_dev}')

# Add titles and labels
plt.title('Normal Distributions with Different Means and
Standard Deviations')
plt.xlabel('Value')
plt.ylabel('Probability Density')
plt.legend()
# Show the plot
plt.grid(True)
plt.show()
```

In a normal distribution:

- Approximately 68% of the data falls within one standard deviation ($\mu \pm \sigma$) from the mean.
- Approximately 95% of the data falls within two standard deviations ($\mu \pm 2\sigma$) from the mean.
- Approximately 99.7% of the data falls within three standard deviations ($\mu \pm 3\sigma$) from the mean.

Master said, “Let us visualize how data naturally spreads around the mean in a normal distribution. Observe how values fall within one, two, and three standard deviations from the center using the following code.”

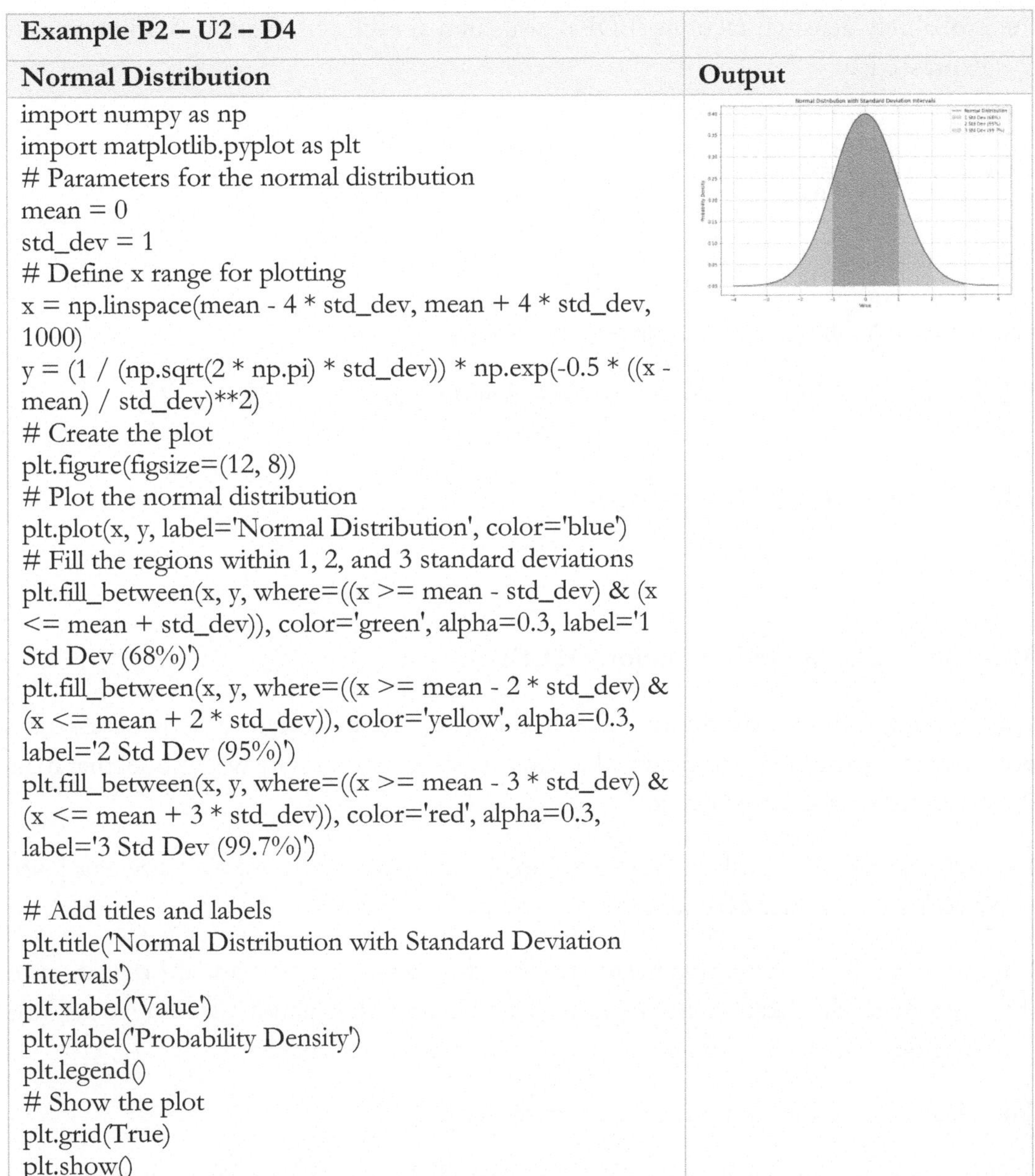

Example P2 – U2 – D4	
Normal Distribution	**Output**

```
import numpy as np
import matplotlib.pyplot as plt
# Parameters for the normal distribution
mean = 0
std_dev = 1
# Define x range for plotting
x = np.linspace(mean - 4 * std_dev, mean + 4 * std_dev,
1000)
y = (1 / (np.sqrt(2 * np.pi) * std_dev)) * np.exp(-0.5 * ((x -
mean) / std_dev)**2)
# Create the plot
plt.figure(figsize=(12, 8))
# Plot the normal distribution
plt.plot(x, y, label='Normal Distribution', color='blue')
# Fill the regions within 1, 2, and 3 standard deviations
plt.fill_between(x, y, where=((x >= mean - std_dev) & (x
<= mean + std_dev)), color='green', alpha=0.3, label='1
Std Dev (68%)')
plt.fill_between(x, y, where=((x >= mean - 2 * std_dev) &
(x <= mean + 2 * std_dev)), color='yellow', alpha=0.3,
label='2 Std Dev (95%)')
plt.fill_between(x, y, where=((x >= mean - 3 * std_dev) &
(x <= mean + 3 * std_dev)), color='red', alpha=0.3,
label='3 Std Dev (99.7%)')

# Add titles and labels
plt.title('Normal Distribution with Standard Deviation
Intervals')
plt.xlabel('Value')
plt.ylabel('Probability Density')
plt.legend()
# Show the plot
plt.grid(True)
plt.show()
```

☐ Likelihood

Master said, "Sam, likelihood is the measure of how probable a given set of observations is, assuming certain model parameters. Simply put, it tells us how likely it is to see the data we observed if the model's parameters are true."

He continued, "For a normal distribution with mean μ and standard deviation σ, and given a set of observations $x_1,x_2,\ldots,x_n$ the likelihood function $L(\mu,\sigma)$ is the product of the probability density functions (PDFs) evaluated at each observation. Mathematically, it is expressed as:"

$$L(\mu,\sigma|x) = \frac{1}{\sqrt{2\pi\sigma^2}} e^{-(x-\mu)^2/2\sigma x^2}$$

Example: Likelihood of selecting apple of weight 32 grams.

When Mean =28 and standard deviation = 2 and weight of an apple is 32

$$L(\mu = 28,\sigma = 2|x = 32) = \frac{1}{\sqrt{2\pi 2*2}} e^{-(32-28)^2/2*2*2*2} = 0.03$$

Maximum Likelihood Estimation (MLE)

Master said, "Jhon, Maximum Likelihood Estimation—often called MLE—is a powerful method used to determine the parameter values of a statistical model that make the observed data most probable.

In simple words, MLE asks a very direct question: *'Given the data I have, which parameter values make this data most likely to occur?'*

For a normal distribution, this means finding the mean (μ) and standard deviation (σ) that maximize the likelihood function. The likelihood function itself tells us how probable our observed values are under specific parameter choices."

The Master paused for a moment, then continued:

"When we have observations $x_1, x_2, \ldots, x_n$, the likelihood for a normal distribution is constructed by multiplying the probability density of each observation. MLE then seeks the parameter values where this likelihood reaches its peak.

To understand this intuitively, let us explore two scenarios—starting with the simplest one."

Scenario 1: Varying the Mean While Keeping the Standard Deviation Fixed

Master said, "Imagine we hold the standard deviation, σ, constant. Now we vary the mean, μ, to see how well each possible mean explains the data.

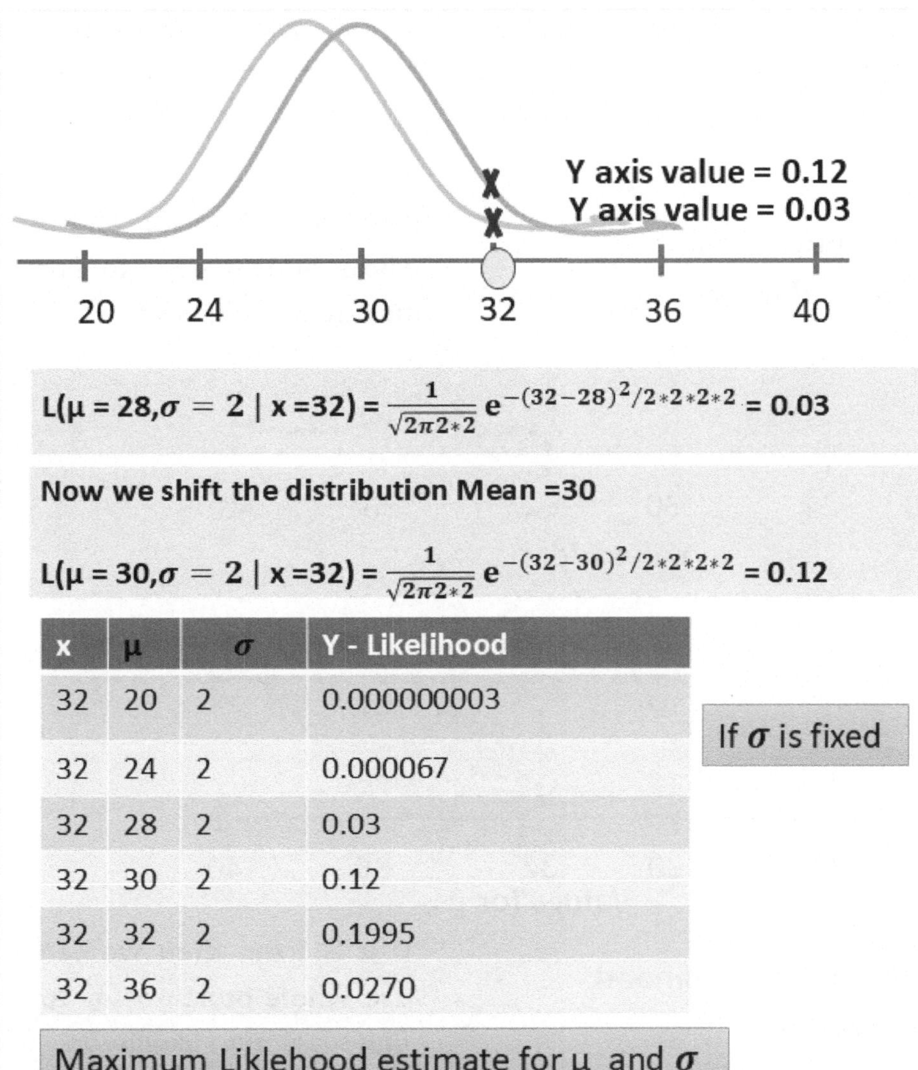

x	μ	σ	Y - Likelihood
32	20	2	0.000000003
32	24	2	0.000067
32	28	2	0.03
32	30	2	0.12
32	32	2	0.1995
32	36	2	0.0270

Illustration MLE_1A: Maximum Likelihood Estimation

If we plot the likelihood as a function of the mean:

- **The x-axis** represents different possible values of the mean.
- **The y-axis** represents the likelihood of the observed data for each of those mean values.

As we sweep through these possible means, the likelihood rises and falls, forming a smooth curve. The highest point of this curve—the peak—is the maximum likelihood estimate (MLE) of the mean."

Master said, "At that peak, the slope becomes zero. This is the value of μ where the data feels most 'at home.' In other words, it is the mean that best explains the observations according to the model."

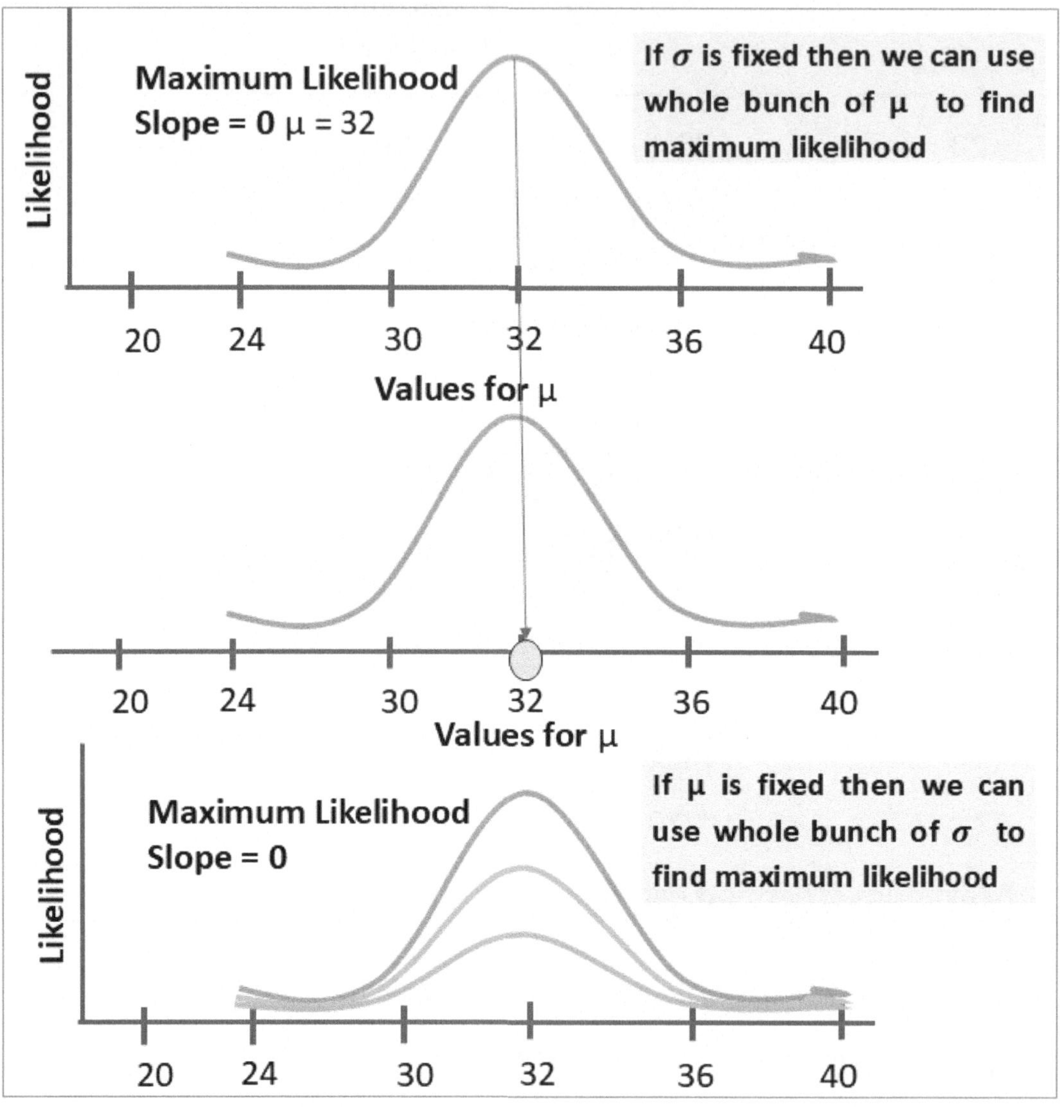

Illustration MLE_1B: Maximum Likelihood Estimation

Scenario 2: Varying the Standard Deviation While Keeping the Mean Fixed

Master said, "Now, John, let us consider the opposite situation. Suppose we keep the mean μ fixed. This time, we allow the standard deviation σ to vary.

Just as before, we evaluate how the likelihood changes—but now as a function of σ."

John listened carefully, and the Master continued:

"When we plot the likelihood against different values of σ:

- **The x-axis** shows the possible values of the standard deviation.
- **The y-axis** shows the likelihood of the observed data for each of those choices.

As we adjust σ, the likelihood will rise and fall, forming another curve—different from the one we saw when varying the mean.

Here too, the peak of this curve represents the maximum likelihood estimate of the standard deviation."

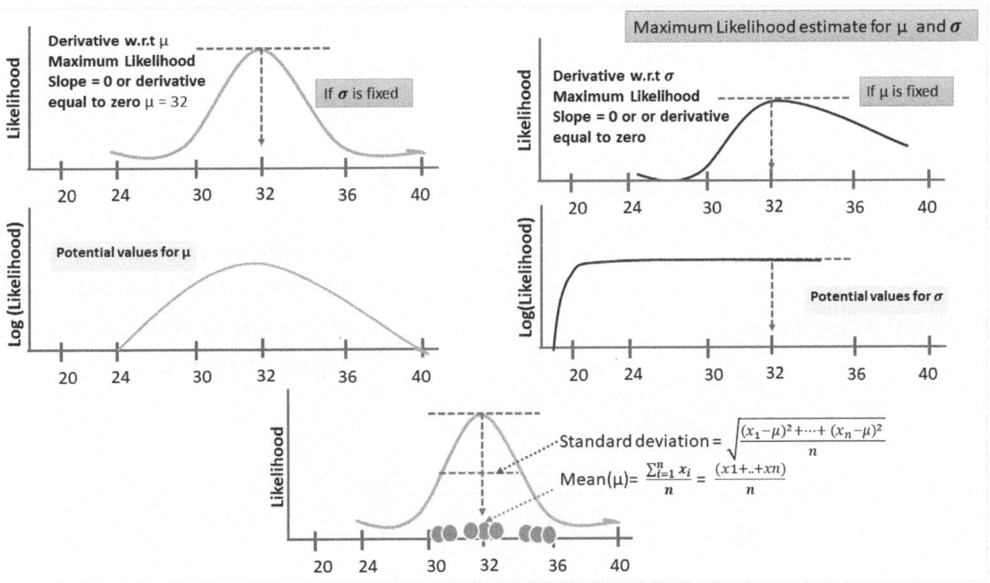

The Master leaned forward and explained the intuition:

Master said, "Why does this happen?

Because the standard deviation controls the *spread.*

- If σ is very small, the distribution becomes too narrow, and it cannot accommodate the natural variability in your data.

- If σ is very large, the distribution spreads too widely, giving too much 'room' and lowering precision.

MLE finds the perfect balance—the value of σ that best fits the natural dispersion of your observations."

Master, after a pause, said, "At the peak of the likelihood curve, the slope becomes zero. That value of σ is the one that most faithfully represents the true spread in the data—according to the model."

Finding the Maximum Likelihood Estimate for the Mean (μ)

(when **σ is fixed**)

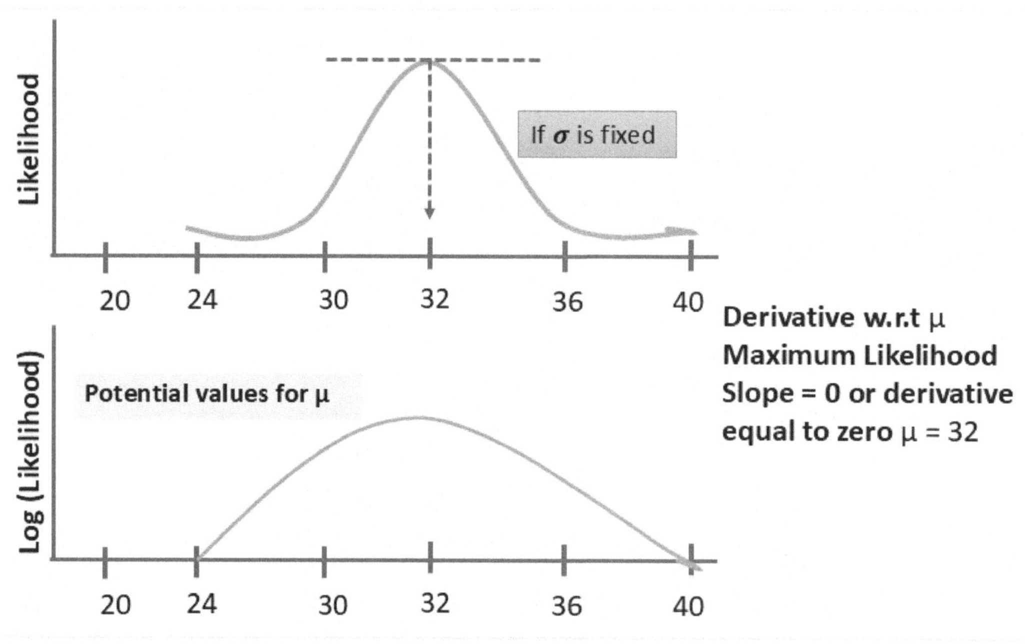

Illustration MLE_2A: Maximum Likelihood Estimation

- The top and bottom plots show how the **likelihood** (and log-likelihood) changes when we test different possible values of μ.
- The curve reaches its **highest point** at $\mu = 32$.
- This peak occurs where the **derivative of the likelihood w.r.t μ is zero**, indicating the **maximum likelihood**.

Conclusion: **The MLE for μ is the sample mean.**

Finding the Maximum Likelihood Estimate for Standard Deviation (σ)

(when **μ is fixed**)

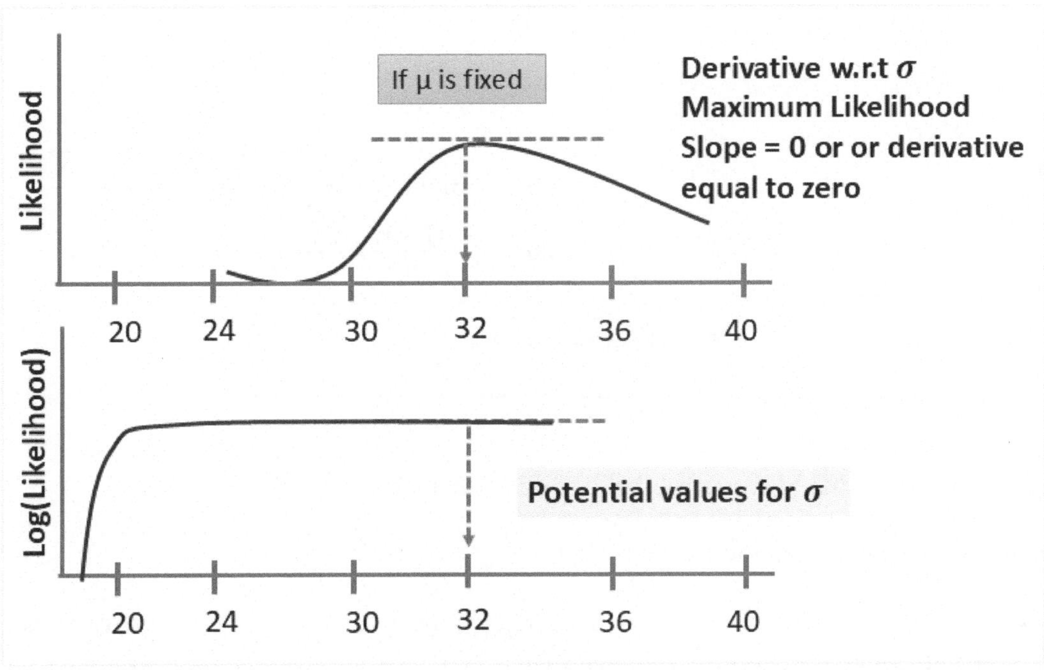

Illustration MLE_2A: Maximum Likelihood Estimation

- The top and bottom plots show how the likelihood behaves for different σ values.
- The likelihood increases initially and then peaks at a particular σ value.
- The maximum point occurs where the **derivative of the likelihood w.r.t σ is zero.**

Conclusion: **The MLE for σ is the square root of the average squared deviation from the mean** (i.e., the sample standard deviation).

Combined Interpretation

Observed data points clustered around a center.

- A normal curve adjusted to:
    - **Mean = sample mean**
    - **Standard deviation = sample standard deviation**

These are the *MLE values* that best fit the data.

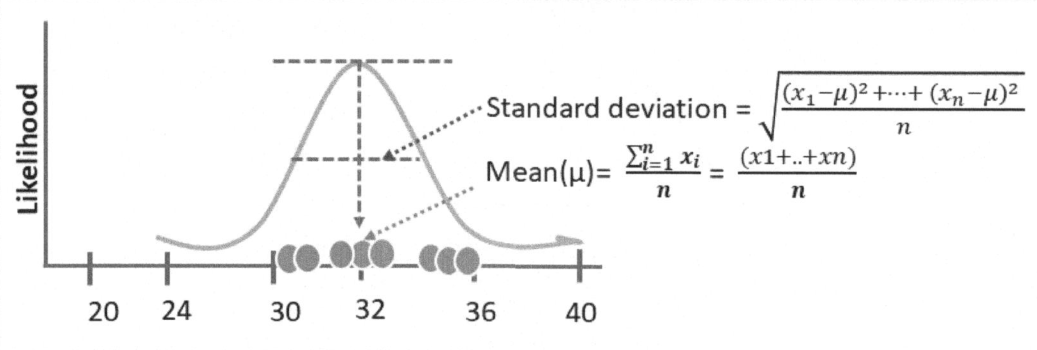

Illustration MLE_2C: Maximum Likelihood Estimation

Master said, "The illustration explains that,

- To fit a normal distribution to data, we find μ and σ that **maximize the likelihood** of observing the given data.
- This is done by:
    - Varying μ (with σ fixed)
    - Varying σ (with μ fixed)
- The "peak" of each likelihood curve gives the **maximum likelihood estimate.**

In simple terms, **MLE chooses the mean and standard deviation for which the observed data is most probable.**

☐ **Mathematical Intuition**

Let's understand the math behind calculating the likelihood and maximum likelihood for a normal distribution using two datasets: an apple weighing 32 grams and an apple weighing 34 grams.

Master said, "Sam, this expression describes how we compute the likelihood of observing two data points when we assume they come from a normal distribution with mean μ=28 and standard deviation σ=2.

It means this:

Each data point has its own likelihood.

The likelihood of observing x1 = 32 under the model is:

L (μ=28, σ=2 | x1=32)

Similarly, the likelihood of observing x2=34 is:

L (μ=28, σ=2 | x2=34)

If the data points are independent, the combined likelihood is the product of the individual likelihoods.

So,

First, we calculate the likelihood for each data point individually and then combine them:

$$L(\mu = 28, \sigma = 2|x1 = 32 \text{ and } x2 = 34) = L(\mu = 28, \sigma = 2|\ x1 = 32) * L(\mu = 28, \sigma = 2|x2 = 34)$$

Master said, "This equation simply says: *To find how likely it is to observe both values together, multiply how likely the first point is by how likely the second point is—because they are independent observations.*"

The likelihood of a normal distribution for multiple measurements is the product of individual likelihoods:

$$L(\mu,\sigma|x1, x2 \ldots xn) = L(\mu ,\sigma|\ x1) * L(\mu ,\sigma|\ x2) = \frac{1}{\sqrt{2\pi\sigma^2}}\, e^{-(x1-\mu)^2/2\sigma r^2} * \frac{1}{\sqrt{2\pi\sigma^2}}\, e^{-(x2-\mu)^2/2\sigma r^2}$$

Taking the natural logarithm of the likelihood function simplifies it:

Ln[L(μ,σ|x1, x2 … xn)] = ln [L(μ ,σ| x1) +..+ L(μ ,σ| xn)] = ln [$\frac{1}{\sqrt{2\pi\sigma^2}}$ $e^{-(x1-\mu)^2/2\sigma x^2}$ +..+ $\frac{1}{\sqrt{2\pi\sigma^2}}$ $e^{-(xn-\mu)^2/2\sigma x^2}$]

Step 1: ln [$\frac{1}{\sqrt{2\pi\sigma^2}}$ $e^{-(x1-\mu)^2/2\sigma x^2}$]

Step 2: ln [$\frac{1}{\sqrt{2\pi\sigma^2}}$] + ln [$e^{-(x1-\mu)^2/2\sigma x^2}$]

Step 3: $-\frac{1}{2}(\ln 2\pi]$ - ln $\sigma - \frac{(x_i-\mu)^2}{2\sigma^2}$

L(μ,σ|x1, x2 … xn) = $-\frac{1}{2}(\ln 2\pi]$ - ln $\sigma - \frac{(x_i-\mu)^2}{2\sigma^2}$ - .. - - $\frac{1}{2}(\ln 2\pi]$ - ln $\sigma - \frac{(x_n-\mu)^2}{2\sigma^2}$

L(μ,σ|x1, x2 … xn) = $-\frac{n}{2}(\ln 2\pi] - n \ln \sigma - \frac{(x_i-\mu)^2}{2\sigma^2}$ - .. - $\frac{(x_1-\mu)^2}{2\sigma^2}$ - .. - $\frac{(x_n-\mu)^2}{2\sigma^2}$

Derivative:

$\frac{dL(\mu,\sigma|\ x1,x2\ ...\ xn)}{dy} = 0 - 0 - \frac{(x_1-\mu)}{\sigma^2} + \ldots + \frac{(x_n-\mu)}{\sigma^2}$

Apply chain rule for $\frac{(x_1-\mu)^2}{2\sigma^2} = \frac{(x_1-\mu)}{\sigma^2}$

Now simplified: Derivative of log-likelihood function w.r.t to Mean(μ)

$\frac{dL(\mu,\sigma|\ x1,x2\ ...\ xn)}{dy} = \frac{1}{\sigma}$ [(x_1 + …+ x_n) - n μ - A

Now simplified: Derivative of log-likelihood function w.r.t to std(σ)

$\frac{dL(\mu,\sigma|\ x1,x2\ ...\ xn)}{dy} = 0 - \frac{n}{\sigma} + \frac{(x_i-\mu)^2}{2\sigma^3} + .. + \frac{(x_n-\mu)^2}{2\sigma^3} = \frac{n}{\sigma} + \frac{1}{\sigma^3}$ [(x_1 - μ $)^2$ + .. + (x_n - μ$)^2$] -B

Master said, "To obtain the maximum likelihood estimates of μ and σ, we work with the *log-likelihood function*. We differentiate it with respect to each parameter and set those derivatives equal to zero.

From this procedure, two elegant results emerge:

- **The MLE for the mean μ** becomes the **sample mean.**

- **The MLE for the standard deviation σ** becomes the **square root of the sample variance.**

Thus, the data itself reveals the most likely parameters of the normal distribution."

$$\text{Mean}(\mu) = \frac{\sum_{i=1}^{n} x_i}{n} = \frac{(x1+..+xn)}{n}$$

$$\text{Standard deviation} = \sqrt{\frac{(x_1-\mu)^2+\cdots+(x_n-\mu)^2}{n}}$$

Data Normally Distributed

Master said, "When data follows a normal distribution, we expect most observations to cluster around the mean, with fewer values appearing as we move away from it. Such data appears balanced—neither leaning heavily to the left nor right. And remember, normal distributions themselves can take many forms: narrow, medium, or wide, depending on their variance."

He continued, "Once we understand the *shape* of the distribution, the next question is: *Where should its center be?* How do we judge whether one center is more suitable than another?

Before diving into deeper calculations, let us start with a simple idea. Imagine selecting a standard normal distribution and asking, 'How well do you match our data?' This distribution essentially claims: *Most measured values should lie close to my average.*"

"If our actual measurements lie far from that average, the fit is clearly poor. The distribution is not aligned with reality. To improve the fit, we shift the normal curve so that its mean matches the average of our observed values. Once this alignment happens, the likelihood—the probability of observing our data under that distribution—becomes notably higher."

$$\text{pr}(x \mid \mu,\sigma) = \frac{1}{\sqrt{2\pi\sigma^2}} e^{-(x-\mu)^2/2\sigma r^2}$$

Shifting the Distribution

When we shift the normal distribution away from the true mean, the likelihood of observing our actual measurements decreases. By plotting the likelihood of the data against different possible locations of the distribution's center, we can identify the point where the curve reaches its peak. This highest point represents the **maximum likelihood estimate (MLE)** for the mean—the value of the mean that makes the observed data most probable.

Determining the Standard Deviation

After finding the best center, we turn our attention to the spread. To determine the **MLE for the standard deviation**, we analyze how likely the data is under various possible standard deviations. By plotting these likelihoods, we again look for the peak—the value of the standard deviation that maximizes the probability of observing our measured weights.

Fitting the Normal Distribution

The normal distribution that best fits the data is the one constructed using both of these MLEs:

- the mean that maximizes likelihood, and
- the standard deviation that maximizes likelihood.

When someone says they have obtained the MLE for the mean or the standard deviation, they mean they have found the parameters that make the observed data *most probable* under the assumed normal model.

In summary, fitting a normal distribution involves:

- **Centering the distribution:** Adjust the mean so it aligns with the data.
- **Maximizing likelihood:** Find the standard deviation that best explains the variability in the data.
- **Using MLE:** Estimate both parameters by identifying the values that maximize the likelihood of observing the data.

This process ensures that the chosen normal distribution reflects the observed data as accurately as possible, creating a strong foundation for further statistical analysis and reliable predictions.

Gaussian Naïve Bayes:

Exercise P2 – U2 – D5	
Naïve Bayes - Gaussian Naive Bayes Classifier	**Output**

from sklearn.datasets import load_iris
iris = load_iris()
# Store the feature matrix (X) and response vector (y) 	
X = iris.data
y = iris.target
 	
# Splitting X and y into training and testing sets 	
from sklearn.model_selection import train_test_split
X_train, X_test, y_train, y_test = train_test_split(X, y, test_size=0.4, random_state=1)
 	
# Training the model on the training set 	
from sklearn.naive_bayes import GaussianNB
gnb = GaussianNB()
gnb.fit(X_train, y_train)
 	
# Making predictions on the testing set 	
y_pred = gnb.predict(X_test)
 	
# Comparing actual response values (y_test) with predicted response values (y_pred) 	
from sklearn import metrics
accuracy = metrics.accuracy_score(y_test, y_pred)
print("Gaussian Naive Bayes model accuracy (in %):", accuracy * 100)
# Generating the confusion matrix 	
from sklearn.metrics import confusion_matrix
conf_matrix = confusion_matrix(y_test, y_pred)
print("Confusion Matrix:")
print(conf_matrix)
	Gaussian Naive Bayes model accuracy (in %): 95.0
	Confusion Matrix:
	[[19 0 0]
	 [0 19 2]
	 [0 1 19]]

This code snippet demonstrates how to apply the Gaussian Naive Bayes classifier to the classic Iris dataset for a simple and effective classification task. It walks through loading the data, training the model, making predictions, and evaluating performance. In essence, it provides a clear, hands-on example of how Gaussian Naive Bayes works in practice—showing how continuous features can be modeled using a normal distribution to produce fast, interpretable results.

- Loading the Iris Dataset: The Iris dataset is loaded using load_iris() from sklearn.datasets, and the feature matrix X and target vector y are extracted.

- Splitting Dataset: The dataset is split into training and testing sets using train_test_split() from sklearn.model_selection, with a 60-40 split ratio and a fixed random state for reproducibility.

- Training the Model: A Gaussian Naive Bayes classifier object (gnb) is created using GaussianNB() from sklearn.naive_bayes, and it is trained on the training set using gnb.fit(X_train, y_train).

- Making Predictions: Predictions are made on the testing set (X_test) using gnb.predict(X_test).

- Evaluating Model Accuracy: The accuracy of the model is computed using accuracy_score() from sklearn.metrics, comparing the actual response values (y_test) with the predicted response values (y_pred). The accuracy is printed to the console.

- Generating Confusion Matrix: The confusion matrix is generated using confusion_matrix() from sklearn.metrics, which provides insights into the performance of the classifier by showing the count of true positive, true negative, false positive, and false negative predictions.

Overall, this code snippet showcases the complete workflow of training a Gaussian Naive Bayes classifier on the Iris dataset, evaluating its performance, and generating a confusion matrix for further analysis.

Advantages

Easy Implementation and Efficiency: Naive Bayes classifiers are straightforward to implement and are computationally efficient, making them suitable for large-scale applications.

Effective in High-Dimensional Data: Particularly adept in scenarios with numerous features, where other algorithms might struggle due to the curse of dimensionality.

Robustness with Limited Training Data: Performs admirably even when training data is scarce, making it a valuable tool in scenarios where collecting extensive datasets is challenging.

Handling Categorical Features: Excellently suited for datasets with categorical features, showcasing its versatility across different data types.

Assumption on Numerical Data: While it assumes normal distributions for numerical features, this can be advantageous in many cases and can be adjusted or complemented with preprocessing techniques for non-normal data.

Disadvantages

Independence Assumption: Relies on the strong assumption of feature independence, which may not always hold in real-world data, potentially leading to suboptimal performance.

Sensitivity to Irrelevant Attributes: Like many other classifiers, Naive Bayes can be influenced by irrelevant attributes, necessitating careful feature selection or preprocessing.

Zero Probability for Unseen Events: May assign zero probability to events not present in the training data, which can lead to poor generalisation and handling of novel instances.

Applications

Spam Email Filtering: Naive Bayes classifiers are widely used to classify emails as spam or non-spam, based on various features extracted from the email content.

Text Classification: In sentiment analysis, document categorisation, and topic classification, Naive Bayes classifiers are instrumental in organising and understanding large volumes of textual data.

Medical Diagnosis: By analysing symptoms and patient data, Naive Bayes classifiers aid in predicting the likelihood of diseases, supporting medical professionals in decision-making processes.

Credit Scoring: Utilised in assessing the creditworthiness of individuals, Naive Bayes classifiers assist financial institutions in making informed decisions regarding loan approvals.

Weather Prediction: Naive Bayes classifiers are employed to classify weather conditions based on various factors, such as temperature, humidity, and atmospheric pressure, facilitating accurate weather forecasting.

PART TWO

DAY FOUR

Unit 2 - Lesson Three

Multinomial Naïve Bayes

Master said, "Akshaya, let us go deeper — Multinomial Naive Bayes is not just an algorithm, it is a storyteller of words."

Applying Multinomial Naive Bayes to NLP Problems

Master continued, "Multinomial Naive Bayes (MNB) is one of the simplest yet most effective models for text classification. It treats text as counts of words — like a merchant counting goods — and uses probability to decide which 'category' a document most likely belongs to. It is built on Bayes' Theorem and the assumption that every word contributes independently to the class, once the class is known."

To understand how MNB works in NLP, imagine you are sorting letters in a post office.

Even without reading the full letter, the *frequency of certain words* (like *buy*, *offer*, *discount*) quickly tells you it's a marketing message, while words like *dear*, *family*, *remembrance* hint toward a personal note.

MNB behaves exactly like this—using word counts to infer the underlying class.

1. Preprocessing the Text Data — Preparing the Raw Material

Before the model can understand text, the raw text must be cleaned, organized, and reduced to its essence.

Master said, "Just as a sculptor removes impurities before carving the statue, text too must be purified."

This purification involves:

- **Tokenization:** Breaking the text into individual words or symbols.
- **Stop-word Removal:** Removing frequent but trivial words like "the," "and," "is"—they are the noise in the song.
- **Stemming:** Cutting words down to their stem (e.g., *running* → *run*), reducing variations.
- **Lemmatization:** Converting words to their correct dictionary form using grammar (e.g., *better* → *good*).

Each step makes the text more structured, reducing confusion for the model.

2. Feature Extraction — Turning Words Into Numbers

Master said, "Akshaya, a machine cannot understand poetry or prose, but it can count."

Here, the text is transformed into numeric vectors:

- **Bag-of-Words Model:** Each document becomes a vector representing how many times each word appears.

  It ignores grammar and order — much like a shopkeeper counting the number of each item without caring about the arrangement.

This step translates language into mathematics.

3. Splitting the Data — Training vs. Testing

The dataset is divided into:

- **Training Set:** The teacher — it teaches the model how words relate to classes.
- **Testing Set:** The exam — it checks how well the model has learned.

Master said, "Knowledge must always be tested. A sword's strength is known only after the strike."

4. Training the MNB Model — Learning From Word Frequencies

The model learns two things:

- **Prior Probabilities:** The general probability of each class (e.g., how many emails are spam vs. ham).
- **Likelihoods:** The probability of each word appearing within each class (e.g., how likely is "offer" in spam?).

This forms the mathematical backbone of prediction.

5. Evaluating the Model — Measuring Understanding

Using the testing set, the model's performance is judged through:

- **Accuracy:** Overall correctness.
- **Precision:** Out of predicted positives, how many were correct?
- **Recall:** Out of actual positives, how many did the model catch?
- **F1-Score:** A balanced score when precision and recall conflict.

Master said, "A model must not only be knowledgeable but wise — precision and recall measure its wisdom."

6. Making Predictions — Applying the Learned Knowledge

When new text arrives:

1. It is preprocessed like before.
2. Converted into its Bag-of-Words representation.
3. Fed into the trained model, which computes the most probable class.

Master said, "Thus, the Multinomial Naive Bayes model reads the world not by understanding the meaning of each sentence, but by counting the whispers of words. In those counts lie the hidden probabilities, and in those probabilities lies the truth."

Advantages and Limitations

- Advantages: MNB is simple, efficient, and often works well for many NLP problems such as sentiment analysis, spam detection, and topic classification.

- Limitations: The assumption of independence between features may not hold true in some cases, potentially impacting the model's performance. It's crucial to evaluate the model thoroughly before deploying it in real-world applications.

By following these steps, Multinomial Naive Bayes can be effectively applied to various NLP tasks, providing a robust solution for text classification challenges.

Example:

Master said, "The purpose of the code is to show how the Naive Bayes algorithm—specifically the Multinomial Naive Bayes model—can be applied to text classification. In this example, it is used to perform sentiment analysis on movie reviews, teaching the system to distinguish between positive and negative emotions expressed in text."

Example P2 – U2 – D6	
Multinomial Naïve Bayes - NLP	**Output**

# Step 1: Import necessary libraries 	
import pandas as pd
import re
import nltk
from nltk.corpus import stopwords
from nltk.stem.porter import PorterStemmer
from sklearn.feature_extraction.text import CountVectorizer
from sklearn.model_selection import train_test_split
from sklearn.naive_bayes import GaussianNB
from sklearn.metrics import confusion_matrix
 	
# Step 2: Load the dataset 	
path = r'C:\Users\User\mraj4\Documents\Optimum\Py-lib\scikit\movie_reviews_nlp.csv'
dataset = pd.read_csv(path)
 	
# Step 3: Download NLTK resources 	
nltk.download('stopwords')
 	
# Step 4: Initialize Porter Stemmer and CountVectorizer 	
ps = PorterStemmer()
cv = CountVectorizer(max_features=1500)
 	
# Step 5: Initialize list to store preprocessed texts 	
corpus = []
 	
# Step 6: Clean and preprocess each review text 	
for text in dataset['Text']:
	Confusion Matrix:
	[[0 0]
	 [1 1]]

```
    # Convert to lowercase
    text = text.lower()
    # Remove non-alphabetic characters and tokenize
    text = re.sub('[^a-zA-Z]', ' ', text).split()
    # Remove stopwords and perform stemming
    text = [ps.stem(word) for word in text if word not in
set(stopwords.words('english'))]
    # Join the words back into sentences
    text = ' '.join(text)
    corpus.append(text)

# Step 7: Create Bag of Words model
X = cv.fit_transform(corpus).toarray()
y = dataset['Sentiment']

# Step 8: Splitting the dataset into training set and test set
X_train, X_test, y_train, y_test = train_test_split(X, y,
test_size=0.25, random_state=0)

# Step 9: Fitting Naive Bayes Model to the training set
classifier = GaussianNB()
classifier.fit(X_train, y_train)

# Step 10: Predicting test set results
y_pred = classifier.predict(X_test)

# Step 11: Evaluating the model with confusion matrix
cm = confusion_matrix(y_test, y_pred)
print("Confusion Matrix:")
print(cm)
```

Here's a breakdown of the code's purpose and steps:

- Import Libraries: Import necessary libraries such as Pandas for data manipulation, NLTK for text preprocessing, CountVectorizer for converting text into numerical features, and scikit-learn for machine learning tasks like train-test splitting, building the Naive Bayes model, and evaluating its performance.

- Load Dataset: Load the movie review dataset from a CSV file containing two columns: "Text" (review text) and "Sentiment" (positive or negative sentiment label).

- Preprocessing Text: Clean and preprocess each review text by converting it to lowercase, removing non-alphabetic characters, tokenizing, removing stopwords, performing stemming, and joining the words back into sentences.

- Feature Extraction: Convert preprocessed text data into numerical feature vectors using the Bag of Words model created with CountVectorizer.
- Splitting Dataset: Split the dataset into training and testing sets to train the model on one portion and evaluate its performance on another.
- Training Naive Bayes Model: Fit a Multinomial Naive Bayes model to the training set to learn the relationships between features (words) and sentiments.
- Predicting Sentiments: Use the trained model to predict sentiment labels (positive or negative) for the test set.
- Evaluating Model Performance: Calculate and print the confusion matrix, a performance metric showing the number of correct and incorrect predictions made by the model on the test set.

In summary, the confusion matrix suggests that the model has correctly identified one positive sentiment but has incorrectly identified one negative sentiment.

□ NLP: Steps Involved

Master said, "Akshatha, NLP—Natural Language Processing—is the field that enables computers to understand, interpret, and generate human language. It is the bridge through which machines learn to read, listen, and communicate with us."

To make this possible, NLP follows a series of structured steps:

Step 1: Text Normalization

Text normalization prepares raw text so that it becomes clean, consistent, and meaningful for machine learning models. Think of it as *sweeping the floor before drawing a rangoli*—you must prepare the surface before creating patterns.

1. Sentence Tokenization

Breaking the corpus into sentences.

Example:

"This is amazing! I won the competition."

→ ['This is amazing!', 'I won the competition']

2. Word Tokenization

Splitting each sentence into words or tokens.

Example:

"This is an example sentence."

→ ['This', 'is', 'an', 'example', 'sentence']

3. Stopword Removal

Removing very common words that add grammatical structure but little meaning.

Example:

"Shree likes to read books, and he is not too fond of movies."

→ ['Shree', 'likes', 'read', 'books', 'fond', 'movies']

4. Converting Text to Common Case (Lowercasing)

Standardizing word form so the model treats "WORLD", "world", and "World" as the same word.

Example:

"WORLD", "WORld", "world" → "world"

5. Stemming

Reducing words to their crude root form.

Example:

"Affected" → "Affect"

"Troubling" → "Troubl"

6. Lemmatization

Reducing words to their meaningful dictionary base form.

Example:

"Troubled" → "Trouble"

"Changes" → "Change"

Step 2: Bag of Words (BoW)

Bag of Words is a feature extraction technique used in Natural Language Processing (NLP) to convert text data into numerical vectors. It treats each document as a collection of words and represents them as numerical features.

Key Concepts:

Convert Tokens into Numbers: Each unique word in the corpus is assigned a unique number.

Feature Extraction: BoW explains the occurrence of each word using a number, disregarding the word's position in the text.

Frequency Table: A frequency table is created to count the occurrences of each word in the document.

Example:

Step 2A:

Consider three sample documents:

- Doc 1: "Shree and Akshaya are happy."
- Doc 2: "Shree went to Bangalore"
- Doc 3: "Raj went to Chennai"

Step 2B:

List all unique words and create a vocabulary:

Shree, and, Akshaya, are, happy, went, to, Bangalore, Raj, Chennai

Step 2C:

Create a document vector:

Each document is represented as a vector with binary values indicating the presence (1) or absence (0) of each word from the vocabulary.

- **Doc 1 vector:** 1, 1, 1, 1, 1, 0, 0, 0, 0, 0
- **Doc 2 vector:** 1, 0, 0, 0, 0, 1, 1, 1, 0, 0
- **Doc 3 vector:** 0, 0, 0, 0, 0, 1, 1, 0, 1, 1

Document	Shree	and	Akshaya	are	happy	went	to	Bangalore	Raj	Chennai
Doc 1	1	1	1	1	1	0	0	0	0	0
Doc 2	1	0	0	0	0	1	1	1	0	0
Doc 3	0	0	0	0	0	1	1	0	1	1

Master said, "Akshaya, Step 3 takes us deeper into understanding which words truly matter in a document."

Step 3: Term Frequency-Inverse Document Frequency (TF-IDF):

TF-IDF is one of the most powerful techniques in NLP for identifying meaningful words in a collection of documents.

While the Bag-of-Words model captures *whether* a word appears, TF-IDF captures *how important* that word is.

Master smiled and said, "Think of each document as a classroom discussion. TF tells you **how often** a student speaks in that class, while IDF tells you **how rare or special** that student's ideas are across all classes. A student who speaks rarely but says something unique becomes more important."

1. Term Frequency (TF)

Definition:

TF measures how frequently a word occurs in a single document.

Formula:

$$TF = \frac{Number\ of\ times\ the\ word\ appears\ in\ the\ document}{Total\ number\ of\ words\ in\ the\ document}$$

Documents

- **Doc 1:** "Shree and Akshaya are happy" (5 tokens)
- **Doc 2:** "Shree went to Bangalore" (4 tokens)
- **Doc 3:** "Raj went to Chennai" (4 tokens)

Vocabulary (order): **Shree, and, Akshaya, are, happy, went, to, Bangalore, Raj, Chennai.**

Total documents N=3. IDF uses natural log: IDF= $\ln \frac{N}{DF}$

Term Frequency (TF) — normalized (term count / total tokens in document)

Term	TF (Doc1 = /5)	TF (Doc2 = /4)	TF (Doc3 = /4)
Shree	0.200000	0.250000	0.000000
and	0.200000	0.000000	0.000000
Akshaya	0.200000	0.000000	0.000000
are	0.200000	0.000000	0.000000
happy	0.200000	0.000000	0.000000
went	0.000000	0.250000	0.250000
to	0.000000	0.250000	0.250000
Bangalore	0.000000	0.250000	0.000000
Raj	0.000000	0.000000	0.250000
Chennai	0.000000	0.000000	0.250000

Master said, "TF tells us how loud a word speaks *within its own document*, but it does not tell us whether this word is special or common across all documents."

2. Inverse Document Frequency (IDF)

Definition:

IDF measures how rare or informative a word is in the entire corpus.

Formula:

$$\text{IDF} = \log \frac{\textit{Total number of documents}}{\textit{Number of documents containing the word}}$$

IDF Table (3 Documents Total)

Document Frequency (DF) and Inverse Document Frequency (IDF)

Term	DF (how many docs contain the term)	IDF = ln(N/DF)
Shree	2	0.405465
and	1	1.098612
Akshaya	1	1.098612
are	1	1.098612
happy	1	1.098612
went	2	0.405465
to	2	0.405465
Bangalore	1	1.098612
Raj	1	1.098612
Chennai	1	1.098612

Master explained, "A word like **'and'** appears in only **one** document, so its IDF is high — it carries unique information. But a word like **'went'** appears in **two** documents — so it is less unique, and its IDF is lower."

3. TF-IDF Score

The final weight of a word combines both ideas:

How frequently it appears in a document × How unique it is across all documents

Formula:

TF–IDF = TF × IDF (per document)

TF-IDF Score

Term	**TF–IDF (Doc1)**	**TF–IDF (Doc2)**	**TF–IDF (Doc3)**
Shree	0.081093	0.101366	0.000000
and	0.219722	0.000000	0.000000
Akshaya	0.219722	0.000000	0.000000
are	0.219722	0.000000	0.000000
happy	0.219722	0.000000	0.000000
went	0.000000	0.101366	0.101366
to	0.000000	0.101366	0.101366
Bangalore	0.000000	0.274653	0.000000
Raj	0.000000	0.000000	0.274653
Chennai	0.000000	0.000000	0.274653

(Values rounded to six decimal places; IDF uses natural log.)

Master said:

"TF tells us the volume of a word's voice within a document.

IDF tells us whether that voice is common gossip or rare wisdom.

TF-IDF brings them together, allowing the system to highlight words that truly matter."

Why TF-IDF Matters in NLP

TF-IDF transforms natural language into numerical form — but not just numbers, **meaningful weights** that reveal importance.

This weighting is essential for:

- Sentiment analysis
- Document classification
- Search engines
- Information retrieval
- Keyword extraction

In summary, TF and IDF are crucial components in the TF-IDF weighting scheme, allowing us to identify the significance of words within documents and across the entire corpus.

TF - IDF(W) = TF(W) * log(IDF(W))

Using nltk: The nltk library provides tools for performing TF-IDF calculations.

Gaussian process classification (GPC)

Master continued, "Nikash, we will watch how Gaussian Processes think, and why a small toy like XOR can teach us much about learning with uncertainty."

Gaussian Process Classification

A **Gaussian Process (GP)** is not a single function but a *family* of smoothly related functions — a distribution over possible functions that could have produced the data. In classification, we do not observe functions directly; we observe class labels that arise from an underlying latent function. **Gaussian Process Classification (GPC)** places a GP prior on that latent function and converts its values into class probabilities with a squashing (link) function (e.g., logistic or probit).

Analogy — the council of landscape-painters

Imagine a studio of many painters asked to depict the same hillside. Each painter draws a slightly different landscape (a different smooth function). You haven't chosen a single painting; instead, you keep the whole gallery of plausible paintings. When asked what colour the hill is at a particular point, you look across all paintings and estimate a distribution of colours (a mean and an uncertainty). That ensemble-of-paintings is the

GP; its curator — the **kernel** — governs how similar paintings are between nearby points (smoothness, wiggliness, scale).

Key pieces that make a GPC

1. **Latent function f(x)** — an unobserved continuous score over inputs (the painters' sketches).
2. **GP prior**: $f(x) \sim GP(m(x), k(x, x'))$ where
   - m(x) is the mean function (often zero),
   - k(x, x') is the kernel/covariance (measures similarity).
3. **Link (squash) function** — transforms real-valued latent f(x) into probabilities $p(y=1|x) = \sigma(f(x))$.
4. **Approximate inference** — because the Bernoulli likelihood breaks Gaussian conjugacy, we approximate the posterior over functions (Laplace, EP, or variational methods) and then compute predictive probabilities.

The kernel — the creed of similarity

The **kernel** is the GP's philosophy: it says how correlation decays with distance, whether functions should be smooth or allow roughness, whether certain input dimensions matter more (ARD), or whether patterns repeat (periodic kernel).

- **RBF (Gaussian) kernel**: favours very smooth functions; nearby inputs produce similar latent values.
- **Matern**: allows rougher functions if needed.
- **Composed kernels** (sums/products): encode richer structure.

Analogy: The kernel is the fabric the painters paint on — a taut silk yields smooth hills, a rough canvas yields craggy cliffs.

Why GPC is probabilistic and why that matters

Unlike hard classifiers that spit a label, GPC returns a **predictive distribution**: a mean probability plus uncertainty (variance) about that probability. This is critical when data is sparse, noisy, or when we must know how much to trust a decision (medicine, robotics, safety-critical systems).

Analogy: A doctor not only names a likely diagnosis but also says, "I am 70% confident" — that honesty helps decide whether to request more tests.

Why XOR is an instructive toy

The XOR problem (four points in 2D with labels that are not linearly separable) is a classic minimal test of nonlinearity. A linear model cannot separate classes, but a kernel-based method can implicitly map inputs into a function space where separation is possible. With an RBF kernel, the GP can shape a smooth latent surface that assigns high latent values to one class's points and low to the other — after squashing, those become near-certain class probabilities.

Caveat: Perfect classification on the four training points is expected — GPs interpolate small datasets well. The real test is the behaviour between and beyond training points (predictive uncertainty and generalization), not just training accuracy.

Purpose of the code — what the script demonstrates

1. **Generate XOR dataset:** create four 2-D inputs and their binary labels — a small nonlinearly separable problem.
2. **Instantiate GPC:** build a GaussianProcessClassifier (scikit-learn) with a chosen kernel (e.g., RBF) and default approximate inference.
3. **Fit the model:** learn kernel hyperparameters (lengthscale, variance) by maximizing marginal likelihood (evidence) under the approximate posterior.
4. **Predict & evaluate:** compute predicted class labels and predictive probabilities on the same XOR points; print accuracy and confusion matrix.
5. **Interpret result:** if the confusion matrix shows perfect classification, it demonstrates that GPC can model nonlinearity and interpolate the training set, and you can inspect predictive variance to see where the model is uncertain.

Example P2 – U2 – D7

GaussianProcessClassifier

```
import numpy as np
import matplotlib.pyplot as plt
from sklearn.gaussian_process import GaussianProcessClassifier
from sklearn.gaussian_process.kernels import RBF
from sklearn.metrics import accuracy_score, confusion_matrix
```

```
# XOR dataset
X = np.array([[0, 0], [0, 1],
              [1, 0], [1, 1]])
y = np.array([0, 1, 1, 0])

# Gaussian Process Classifier
gpc = GaussianProcessClassifier(kernel=RBF(length_scale=1.0))
gpc.fit(X, y)

# ---- PREDICTIONS ----
y_pred = gpc.predict(X)

print("Predictions:", y_pred)
print("Accuracy:", accuracy_score(y, y_pred))
print("Confusion Matrix:")
print(confusion_matrix(y, y_pred))

# ---- PLOT ----

# Create a grid of points
xx, yy = np.meshgrid(
    np.linspace(-0.5, 1.5, 200),
    np.linspace(-0.5, 1.5, 200)
)
grid = np.c_[xx.ravel(), yy.ravel()]

# Probabilities for class 1
probs = gpc.predict_proba(grid)[:, 1].reshape(xx.shape)

# Plot heatmap
plt.figure(figsize=(8, 7))
plt.contourf(xx, yy, probs, cmap='coolwarm', alpha=0.85)

# Decision boundary line
contour = plt.contour(xx, yy, probs, levels=[0.5], colors='black', linewidths=2)
plt.clabel(contour, fmt={0.5: 'Decision Boundary'}, fontsize=10)

# Training points
plt.scatter(X[y == 1, 0], X[y == 1, 1], c='red', edgecolor='black', s=120, label='Class 1')
plt.scatter(X[y == 0, 0], X[y == 0, 1], c='blue', edgecolor='black', s=120, label='Class
0')

plt.title("Gaussian Process Classification on XOR\nDecision Boundary (p = 0.5)")
plt.xlabel("X1")
plt.ylabel("X2")
plt.legend()
plt.colorbar(label="P(class = 1)")
plt.show()
```

Output:

```
Output
Predictions: [0 1 1 0]
Accuracy: 1.0
Confusion Matrix:
[[2 0]
 [0 2]]
```

The code demonstrates **Gaussian Process Classification (GPC)** applied to the classic **XOR dataset** — a simple but nonlinearly separable problem. A Gaussian Process is a probabilistic model that predicts outputs *along with uncertainty*, using a kernel function to define similarity between points.

Key Steps in the Code

Create XOR dataset

- Input points: (0,0), (0,1), (1,0), (1,1)
- Labels follow XOR logic: 0, 1, 1, 0

Define a Gaussian Process Classifier

- Uses an **RBF kernel** (Radial Basis Function), which creates a smooth function and handles nonlinear boundaries.

Fit the GPC model

- The model learns how similar each point is based on the kernel.
- It builds a probability distribution over possible classification functions.

Predict and evaluate

- Predictions are made on the same input points.
- Accuracy and confusion matrix confirm perfect classification on the dataset.

Uncertainty Visualization (Probability Heatmap)

- A grid is created around the XOR points.
- predict_proba() gives the probability that each grid point belongs to class 1.

- This probability forms a heatmap showing decision boundaries and uncertainty.

What to inspect beyond "perfect accuracy"

- **Predictive probabilities:** Are predictions confident (≈0 or 1) or soft? High confidence far from the data is worrying.
- **Predictive variance/uncertainty map:** Visualize the latent mean and variance across a grid to see where the GP is confident vs uncertain.
- **Decision boundary plot:** See the smooth boundary that separates classes.
- **Hyperparameter values:** Lengthscale tells you how quickly the function varies; very small/large values can indicate overfit/underfit.
- **Robustness tests:** Add noisy or held-out points to see generalization.
- **Cross-validation / multiple restarts:** Avoid local optima in hyperparameter tuning.

Plot:

This plot is a **visual map of the classifier's belief** across the input space.

Color Interpretation

- **Red regions (near probability = 1.0)**

  The model is *highly confident* that the area belongs to **class 1**.

- **Blue regions (near probability = 0.0)**

  The model is *highly confident* that the area belongs to **class 0**.

- **White / Pale regions (around probability = 0.5)**

  These represent **uncertainty** — the decision boundary where the model is unsure.

Points on the Plot

The four training data points are shown as large dots:

- Two **red** points → class 1: (0,1) and (1,0)
- Two **blue** points → class 0: (0,0) and (1,1)

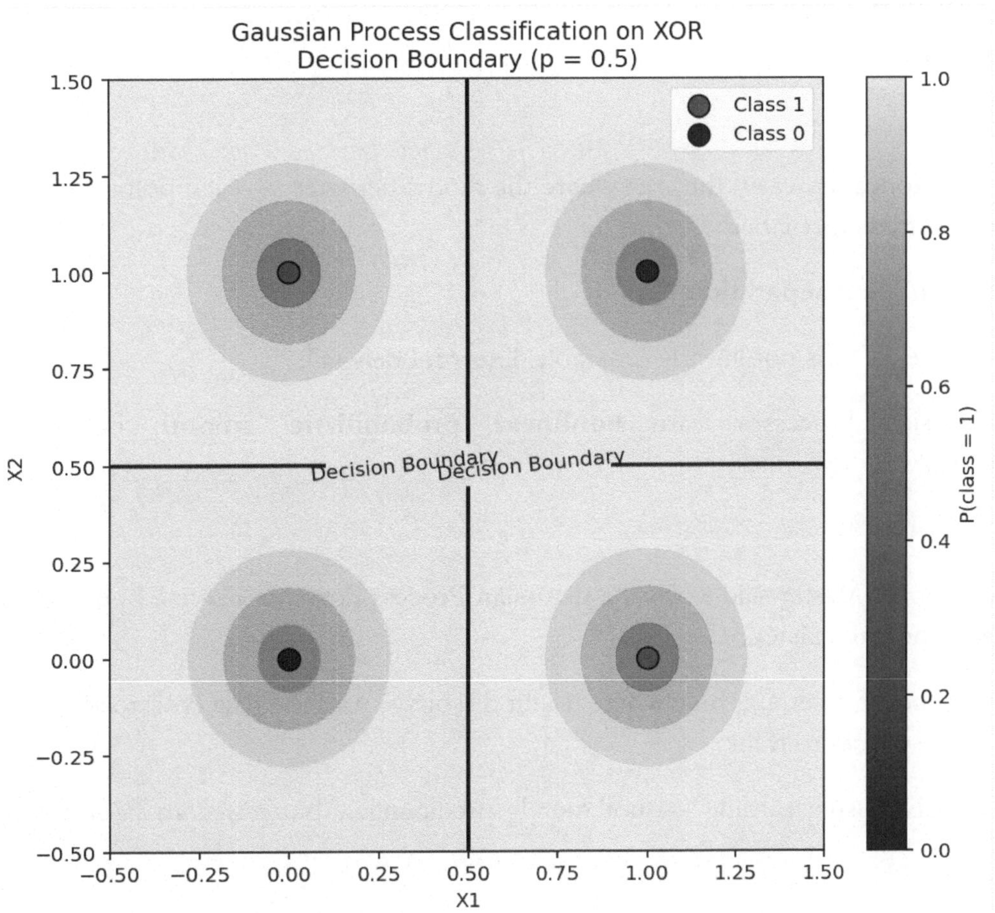

Illustration GPC_1: Gaussian Process Classification

What the Plot Shows

1. **Smooth decision regions**
2. Because Gaussian Processes create *smooth function priors*, the boundary between red and blue is gentle and curved.
3. **Perfect classification near training points**
4. The regions around datapoints are pure red or pure blue — the model is absolutely

confident around what it has seen.

5. **Uncertainty Along the Middle Lines**

It shows **vertical and horizontal uncertainty boundaries at x=0.5 and y=0.5**

because the GP classifier learned a **cross-shaped decision boundary**, not a circular or diagonal one.

These pale zones represent the area where the model hesitates — each point is equally close to contradictory labels.

1. **Nonlinear separation**
2. Since XOR is not linearly separable, linear models fail.

But Gaussian Processes learn **nonlinear**, **probabilistic**, **smooth** boundaries automatically.

"Notice, John," Master said softly, "a Gaussian Process does not carve a boundary. It **breathes** one into existence.

Red where belief is certain, Blue where doubt dissolves, And the pale crossroads where the universe pauses to think.

This is probabilistic learning — not merely predicting… but *understanding uncertainty itself.*"

Master said, "Sam, this code reveals how a Gaussian Process understands a nonlinear world."

It begins by letting you choose between three kernels—RBF, Matern, or Rational Quadratic—each shaping how the model interprets smoothness and variation. The XOR dataset, a classic nonlinear puzzle, is then used to train the Gaussian Process Classifier. After fitting, the code prints predictions, accuracy, and the confusion matrix, confirming how well the model learns this challenging pattern.

A dense grid is created to compute probabilities across the input space, allowing a detailed visualization. The 2D plot shows soft uncertainty shading, crisp decision boundaries, and confidence contours. Finally, a 3D probability surface reveals how the model forms a smooth landscape of belief over class-1 probability—bringing clarity to complex decision structures.

Example P2 – U2 – D8
GaussianProcessClassifier

```
import numpy as np
import matplotlib.pyplot as plt
from sklearn.gaussian_process import GaussianProcessClassifier
from sklearn.gaussian_process.kernels import RBF, Matern, RationalQuadratic
from sklearn.metrics import accuracy_score, confusion_matrix
from mpl_toolkits.mplot3d import Axes3D

# ======================
# 1. SELECT KERNEL HERE
# ======================
# kernel = 1.0 * RBF(length_scale=1.0)
# kernel = 1.0 * Matern(length_scale=1.0, nu=1.5)
kernel = 1.0 * RationalQuadratic(length_scale=1.0, alpha=1.0)

print("Using Kernel:", kernel)

# XOR dataset
X = np.array([
    [0, 0],
    [0, 1],
    [1, 0],
    [1, 1]
])
y = np.array([0, 1, 1, 0])

# Train GPC
gpc = GaussianProcessClassifier(kernel=kernel)
gpc.fit(X, y)

# Predictions
y_pred = gpc.predict(X)
print("Predictions:", y_pred)
print("Accuracy:", accuracy_score(y, y_pred))
print("Confusion Matrix:\n", confusion_matrix(y, y_pred))

# ===== GRID FOR VISUALIZATIONS =====
xx, yy = np.meshgrid(np.linspace(-0.5, 1.5, 200),
                     np.linspace(-0.5, 1.5, 200))

grid_points = np.c_[xx.ravel(), yy.ravel()]
Z = gpc.predict_proba(grid_points)[:, 1]  # class-1 probability
```

```
Z = Z.reshape(xx.shape)

# ==========================================
# 2. MAIN 2D PLOT — DECISION + CONFIDENCE
# ==========================================
plt.figure(figsize=(7, 6))

# Soft uncertainty shading
plt.contourf(xx, yy, Z, levels=50, cmap="coolwarm", alpha=0.6)

# Crisp decision boundary (0.5)
plt.contour(xx, yy, Z, levels=[0.5], colors='black', linewidths=2)

# Confidence contour lines
conf_levels = [0.2, 0.5, 0.8]
plt.contour(xx, yy, Z, levels=conf_levels, colors='k', linewidths=1, linestyles='--')

# Training points
plt.scatter(X[y == 0][:, 0], X[y == 0][:, 1], c='red', edgecolor='k', s=90, label="Class 0")
plt.scatter(X[y == 1][:, 0], X[y == 1][:, 1], c='blue', edgecolor='k', s=90, label="Class 1")

plt.title("Gaussian Process Classification — Decision Boundary & Confidence")
plt.xlabel("X1"); plt.ylabel("X2")
plt.legend()
plt.grid(True)
plt.show()

# ==================================
# 3. 3D PROBABILITY SURFACE PLOT
# ==================================
fig = plt.figure(figsize=(8, 7))
ax = fig.add_subplot(111, projection='3d')

ax.plot_surface(xx, yy, Z, cmap="coolwarm", edgecolor='none', alpha=0.9)
ax.set_title("3D Probability Surface — P(Class = 1)")
ax.set_xlabel("X1"); ax.set_ylabel("X2"); ax.set_zlabel("P(class=1)")
plt.show()
```

Output:

```
Output
Using Kernel: 1**2 * RationalQuadratic(alpha=1, length_scale=1)
Predictions: [0 1 1 0]
Accuracy: 1.0
Confusion Matrix:
 [[2 0]
 [0 2]]
```

Plots:

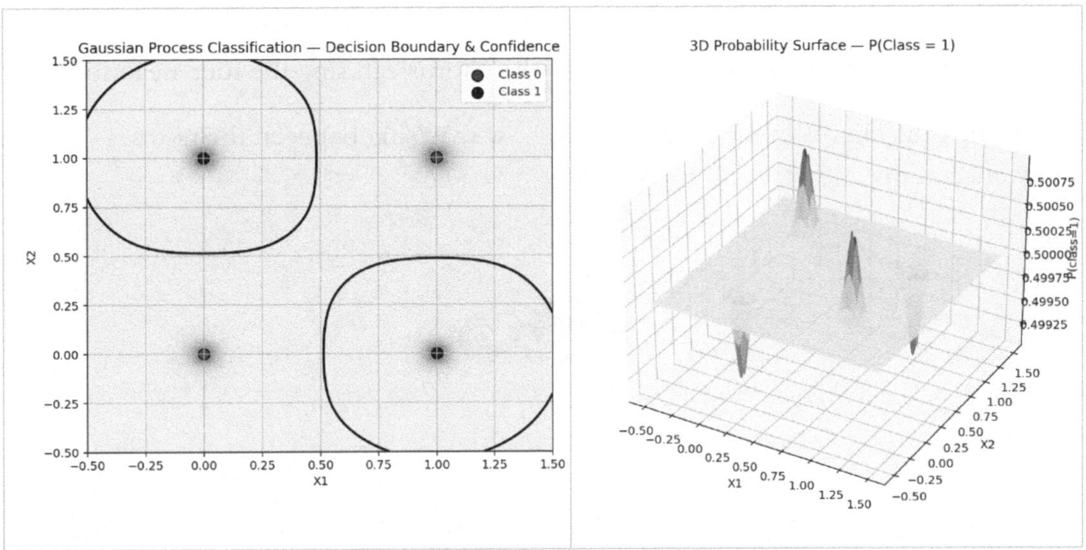

Illustration GPC_2 and GPC_3: Gaussian Process Classification

Strengths and limitations

Strengths

- Principled uncertainty estimates.
- Flexibility through kernels.
- Strong performance on small-to-moderate datasets.

Limitations

- Naive computational cost O(n3) — not suitable for very large datasets without sparse approximations.
- Classification needs approximation — quality depends on the method.
- Can overfit tiny datasets if hyperparameters are poorly constrained — always check uncertainty and test behavior.

Master said:

"A Gaussian Process is like consulting a chorus rather than a single oracle.

The chorus gives you not only the song (the predicted class) but also how certain each line is sung.

The XOR code is a small verse — it shows the chorus can sing the tune beautifully.

But to trust the chorus in the wild, listen to how they sing between the notes — that is, study uncertainty and generalization."

PART TWO

DAY FIVE

Unit 2 - Lesson Four

Discriminant Analysis

Master said, "Roopa, imagine the world of data as a vast landscape filled with patterns, shapes, and hidden boundaries.

Discriminant Analysis is the art of discovering these boundaries— not by force, but by understanding how different groups naturally spread themselves across the land."

Discriminant analysis is a statistical and machine-learning technique used to classify observations into predefined groups. Rather than merely drawing a line between classes, it seeks something deeper:

It discovers the combination of features that maximally separates the classes.

It models how each class generates its data.

And then it uses this knowledge to classify new observations.

It is a **generative technique**, meaning it tries to answer:

"How does each class produce its data?"

Once that is understood, classification becomes a simple matter of comparing probabilities.

What does discriminant analysis do?

Discriminant analysis builds statistical models of each class's distribution and uses those models to decide where a new observation most likely belongs. It **seeks directions (linear or curved) in feature space that best separate classes**, then classifies by where a point falls in that transformed space.

Analogy — tribes on hills

Imagine several tribes living on different hills. Each tribe spreads its tents in a particular pattern (shape, spread, orientation). Discriminant analysis studies the hills' shapes and centers.

- **LDA** assumes every tribe's tent pattern is the same shape and orientation (same covariance) but centered at different places.
- **QDA** allows each tribe a unique tent pattern (different covariance), so boundaries between tribes curve to follow individual spreads.

A newcomer's footprints are matched against these patterns to decide which tribe they most likely belong to.

Types of Discriminant Analysis:

1. Linear Discriminant Analysis (LDA) — The Straight Road

Master continued: "LDA assumes that different classes breathe the same air — that they spread with the same shape, the same variance, the same covariance. Only their centers differ."

Assumptions:

- Each class is generated from a **Gaussian distribution**.
- All classes share the **same covariance matrix**.
- Means differ, but the "shape" of each class is identical.
- The decision boundary must be **linear**.

What LDA Does

- Finds a **linear combination of features** that maximizes class separation.

- Reduces dimensionality.
- Works well for **multi-class** problems.
- Projects high-dimensional data onto a line that best separates classes.

Mathematical Heart of LDA

The discriminant function:

Equation: $\delta_k(x) = x^T\Sigma^{-1}\mu_{k} - 1/2\, \mu_k^T\ \Sigma^{-1}\mu_k + \log(\pi_k)$

Here:

- x = input
- μ_k is class mean
- Σ is the shared covariance
- π_k is prior class probability

Optimization View (Fisher's Criterion)

LDA maximizes:

$J(w) = \ w^T S_B w / w^T S_W w$

- SB: **between-class scatter**
- SW: **within-class scatter**

This equation expresses a profound idea:

"Separate the class means as far as possible, while keeping each class tight and compact along the projected direction."

Analogy

LDA is like shining a flashlight through a cloud of mixed particles.

The direction where the shadows of the two clouds separate the most is the direction LDA chooses.

2. Quadratic Discriminant Analysis (QDA) — The Curved Path

Master said, **"But, Roopa, what if the classes do *not* share the same shape?**

What if one class spreads like a sphere and another like an ellipse?

Then a straight road is too crude.

You must follow the curves of the land."

This is where QDA comes.

Assumptions:

- Each class is Gaussian.
- But each class has its **own covariance matrix**.

Consequences:

- Decision boundaries become **quadratic**, not linear.
- More flexible.
- Can capture curved, nonlinear separation.

Equation:

Equation: $\delta_k(x) = -1/2 \log|\Sigma_k| - 1/2(x-\mu_k)^T \ \Sigma_k^{-1} \ (x-\mu_k) + \log(\pi_k)$

You can see:

- Class-specific covariance → nonlinear terms.
- Model becomes more expressive but also more complex.

Analogy

If LDA draws a straight fence between two farms, QDA draws a fence that bends with the terrain.

3. Gaussian Discriminant Analysis (GDA) – The Umbrella Framework

Master smiled and said:

"Roopa, both LDA and QDA are children of a larger philosophy —

Gaussian Discriminant Analysis.

GDA says: 'Assume classes are Gaussian.

Everything else depends on how you model their covariance.'"

GDA models the class-conditional densities:

$p(x|y=k)$

as Gaussian.

GDA's Flexibility

Depending on the covariance assumption:

- **Shared covariance → becomes LDA**
- **Class-specific covariance → becomes QDA**

Thus:

Feature	LDA	QDA	GDA
Covariance	Shared	Class-specific	Either
Boundary	Linear	Quadratic	Depends
Complexity	Low	High	Variable
Best For	Linearly separable data	Curved boundaries	Gaussian data in general

Analogy

GDA is like learning the shape of clouds in the sky.

- If all clouds have the same softness → LDA.
- If each cloud has a distinct texture → QDA.
- GDA simply says, "Clouds are Gaussian; what shape they take is your choice."

Comparison: LDA vs QDA vs GDA vs Logistic Regression

Overall Perspective

- **LDA** and **QDA** belong to the **generative** family:

They model how each class *generates* data: p(x|y) and priors p(y).

Bayes' rule then gives p(y|x).

- **GDA** is the **umbrella framework** that includes both LDA and QDA, depending on whether covariance is shared or class-specific.
- **Logistic Regression** is **discriminative**:

It does *not* model class-conditional densities.

It directly models the boundary through p(y|x), without Gaussian assumptions.

Geometric Interpretation

- **LDA:**

  Assumes all classes share a common covariance → boundaries are **straight hyperplanes**.

- **QDA:**

  Allows each class its own covariance → boundaries become **curved**, bending to fit each class's shape.

- **Logistic Regression:**

  Also produces **linear boundaries**, but through a *different philosophy* — not via Gaussian distributions, but by optimizing the log-likelihood of class labels.

- **GDA:**

Produces **linear or quadratic boundaries** depending on covariance assumptions.

Key Mathematical Intuitions

1. Class Means μ_k

Think of them as the centers of tribes, marking where each group tends to live.

2. Covariance Σ or Σk

Encodes:

- Spread
- Orientation
- Feature correlations
- Shape of each class cloud

If covariance differs across classes, the boundary must curve (QDA).

3. Priors p(y=k)

Shift the boundary toward smaller or larger tribes.

Essential when class imbalance exists.

4. Discriminant Score

Classification = choosing the class with the highest "score":

$score_k = \log p(x \mid y=k) + \log p(y=k)$

Higher score ⇒ more evidence for class k.

Assumptions and Their Consequences

1. Gaussianity

- If data truly follows Gaussian clusters → LDA/QDA are powerful and elegant.
- If strongly non-Gaussian (skewed, multimodal), they may mislead.

Remedies:

- Transform features
- Use nonparametric methods (kNN, trees)
- Or use discriminative models like Logistic Regression or SVM

2. Equal Covariances (LDA)

- If classes truly share covariance → LDA is optimal and stable.
- If incorrect → boundaries become oversimplified.

Alternatives:

- QDA
- Regularized LDA
- Shrinkage estimators

3. Linearity of Decision Boundaries (for LDA)

If classes need curved or complex separation:

- Use QDA
- Kernel LDA
- Nonlinear methods (SVM with kernels, neural networks)

4. Sample Size Requirements

- **QDA** must estimate a full covariance matrix for each class → requires *many more samples.*

- When data is limited:
    - Prefer **LDA**
    - Or **Regularized LDA**
    - Or **shrinkage covariance estimates**

Comparison: Table 1:

Method	Type	Boundary	Assumptions
LDA	Generative	Linear	Gaussian + shared covariance
QDA	Generative	Quadratic	Gaussian + class-specific covariance
GDA	Generative (general)	Linear or quadratic	Gaussian
Logistic Regression	Discriminative	Linear	No Gaussian assumptions

Comparison: Table 2:

Method	Strength	Weakness
LDA	Stable, low-variance	Fails if covariances differ
QDA	Flexible	High variance, needs more data
GDA	Unifying framework	Still assumes Gaussianity
Logistic Regression	Robust, works well in practice	Linear boundary only, unless kernelized

Practical Tips & Diagnostics

Visualize projections:

Plot the first one or two discriminant directions to see how well classes separate. Good separation indicates LDA/QDA assumptions are reasonable.

Check covariance equality:

LDA assumes all classes share the same covariance. Compare class covariance matrices to the pooled one (via Box's M test or simple visual inspection). Large differences suggest QDA or regularized LDA.

Regularize when data is limited:

If the number of samples is small relative to features, covariance estimates become unstable. Use shrinkage LDA (Ledoit–Wolf, James–Stein) or penalized covariance estimators.

Use priors intentionally:

Set class priors based on class frequencies or domain importance. Priors shift the decision boundary toward more common classes — crucial for imbalanced datasets.

Cross-validate thoroughly:

Generative models can perform exceptionally well when their assumptions hold, but can degrade sharply when assumptions fail. Use cross-validation to evaluate real predictive performance.

Preprocess features wisely:

Centering and scaling help prevent domination by features with large numerical ranges. When features are highly correlated, applying PCA before LDA often improves stability and reduces noise.

Extensions & Related Ideas

Kernel Fisher Discriminant (KFD):

Maps data into a nonlinear feature space using kernels, then applies the Fisher criterion. Produces nonlinear decision boundaries while retaining LDA's interpretability essence.

Regularized Discriminant Analysis (RDA):

Smoothly interpolates between LDA and QDA by shrinking class-specific covariances toward the pooled covariance. Controls bias–variance trade-off.

Sparse LDA:

Applies sparsity penalties to produce discriminant vectors with fewer nonzero coefficients. Useful in high-dimensional data like genomics or text.

Relation to PCA:

PCA finds directions capturing maximum overall variance; LDA finds directions that best separate class means. They solve different problems but complement each other—PCA reduces noise, LDA maximizes discrimination.

Interpretability & Use-Cases

Discriminant analysis is valued for clear, interpretable feature contributions. The discriminant coefficients reveal how features drive class separation. Common use-cases include:

- **Medical diagnostics:** classify disease subtypes
- **Credit scoring:** accept/reject decisions
- **Face recognition (Fisherfaces):** LDA applied to image vectors
- **Marketing segmentation:** classify customers into behavioural groups

□ Linear Discriminant Analysis (LDA)

LDA is a supervised machine learning approach used for multi-class classification problems. It reduces data dimensionality while separating multiple classes with multiple features. Also known as Normal Discriminant Analysis (NDA) or Discriminant Function Analysis (DFA), LDA follows a generative model framework, modelling the data distribution for each class and utilizing Bayes' theorem to calculate conditional probabilities. This allows LDA to predict the probability of an input data set belonging to a particular class.

LDA identifies a linear combination of features that best separates or characterises two or more classes. It projects data with multiple dimensions into a single dimension to facilitate classification, a technique referred to as dimensionality reduction. Unlike logistic regression, which is limited to binary classification, LDA is versatile and can handle multi-class classification problems. It is often used to enhance the performance of other classification algorithms such as decision trees, random forests, or support vector machines (SVM).

For instance, consider a scenario where we have two classes to separate, each with multiple features. If we attempt to classify these classes using only a single feature, we might encounter overlap between them. To achieve proper classification, we can increase the number of features considered, which helps in distinguishing the classes more effectively.

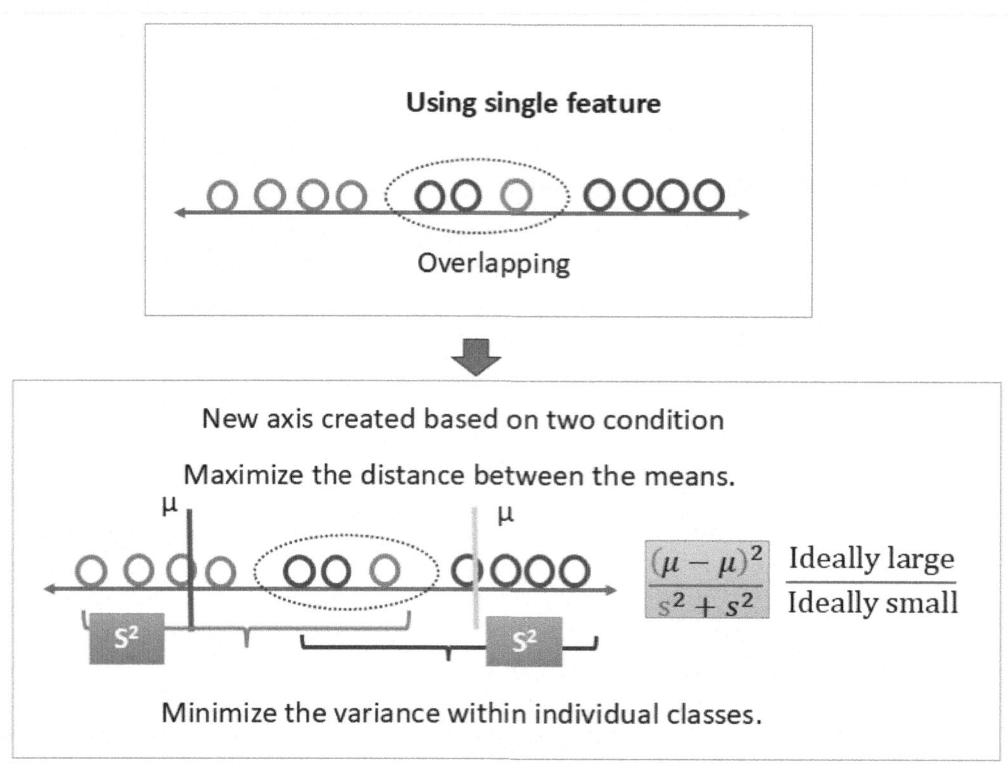

Illustration LDA_3: Discriminant analysis

Assumptions of LDA:

- Gaussian Distribution: LDA assumes that the data follows a Gaussian (normal) distribution.
- Equal Covariance Matrices: It assumes that the covariance matrices of the

different classes are equal.

- Linear Separability: LDA assumes that the data is linearly separable, meaning that a linear decision boundary can effectively classify the different classes.

Scenario:

Suppose we have two sets of data points belonging to two different classes that we want to classify. When these data points are plotted on a 2D plane, there might not be a straight line that can completely separate the two classes. In such cases, LDA can be used to transform the data in a way that maximises the separability between the classes.

How LDA Transforms the Data

A. Dimensionality Reduction

LDA reduces the dimensionality of the data — for example, from **2D to 1D** — but does so in a way that preserves *maximum class separation*. This is different from PCA, which preserves variance but ignores class labels.

B. Creating a New Axis

LDA forms a **new axis** by taking a weighted combination of the original features (X and Y).

All data points are **projected** onto this new line.

The orientation of this line is chosen to **maximize the differences between classes**.

The Optimization Criteria Used by LDA

LDA chooses the projection direction by optimizing two opposing objectives:

Maximize Between-Class Separation

The distance between **class means** should be as large as possible. This spreads the class centers apart on the new axis.

Minimize Within-Class Variance

The spread of points **within each class** should be as small as possible. This tightens each class cluster on the new axis.

Together, these criteria ensure the classes are pushed farther apart and made more compact — improving separability.

Illustration: In the given 2D graph, a new axis is generated in such a way that it maximises the distance between the means of the two classes and minimises the within-class variance. This newly generated axis increases the separation between the data points of the two classes. Once the new axis is created, all data points from the two classes are projected onto this axis, effectively reducing the problem from 2D to 1D while maximising class separability.

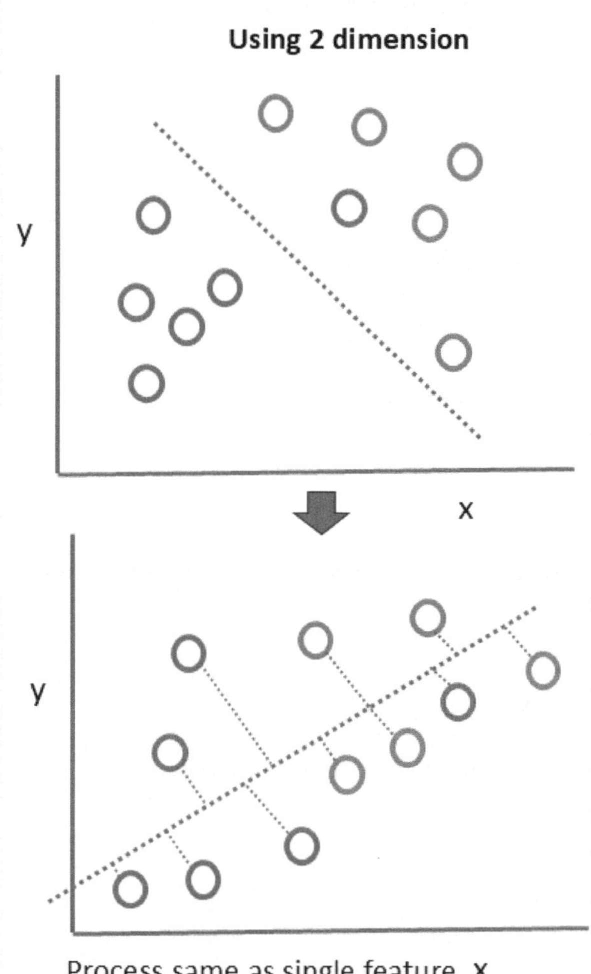

Illustration LDA_4: Discriminant analysis

When LDA Fails

LDA cannot create a separating axis if:

- Class means are identical, or
- Linear separation does not exist even after projection.

In such cases, nonlinear techniques are preferred:

- Kernel LDA
- QDA (Quadratic Discriminant Analysis)
- SVM with nonlinear kernels

These methods capture curved or complex boundaries that LDA cannot.

Summary:

LDA is a powerful tool for reducing the dimensionality of data while maximising the separability of classes. By projecting the data onto a new axis, LDA makes it easier to distinguish between different classes, provided that the assumptions of Gaussian distribution, equal covariance matrices, and linear separability hold true.

Implementing LDA effectively involves several preparatory steps:

- Preprocessing the data by normalizing and centering.
- Choosing the appropriate number of dimensions using the n_components parameter.
- Regularizing the model to prevent overfitting.
- Evaluating the model performance using cross-validation.

☐ Difference between LDA and PCA

Linear Discriminant Analysis (LDA) and Principal Component Analysis (PCA) are both techniques used for dimensionality reduction, but they have different goals and applications. Here’s a clear comparison:

Objective:

- LDA: Aims to find a feature space that best separates the classes in a dataset. It focuses on maximizing the separability among known categories.
- PCA: Seeks to find a new set of orthogonal axes (principal components) that capture the maximum variance in the data, regardless of the class labels.

Supervision:

- LDA: Supervised learning technique. It uses class labels to find the axes that maximize the separation between multiple classes.
- PCA: Unsupervised learning technique. It does not use class labels and focuses only on the variance in the data.

Methodology:

- LDA: Projects the data onto a lower-dimensional space by maximizing the ratio of between-class variance to within-class variance, enhancing class separability.
- PCA: Projects the data onto a new coordinate system where the greatest variances by any projection of the data come to lie on the first coordinates (principal components).

Usage:

- LDA: Primarily used when the primary goal is to improve class separability and enhance the performance of classification algorithms.
- PCA: Used when the goal is to reduce the dimensionality of the data while preserving as much variability as possible, often as a preprocessing step before other analyses.

Dimensionality:

- LDA: The number of dimensions it can reduce to is at most $c-1$, where c is the number of classes.
- PCA: Can reduce to any number of dimensions, up to the number of original features.

Example Applications:

- LDA: Face recognition, spam detection, medical diagnosis, and other applications where classification is key.
- PCA: Image compression, noise reduction, exploratory data analysis, and as a preprocessing step for clustering or other machine learning algorithms.

Mathematical Formulation:

- LDA: Focuses on the scatter matrices (between-class scatter and within-class scatter) to find the linear discriminants.
- PCA: Focuses on the covariance matrix to find the eigenvectors (principal components).

Summary:

- LDA: Best for enhancing class separability using class labels.
- PCA: Best for reducing dimensionality while retaining the most variance without considering class labels.

Understanding these differences helps in choosing the right technique based on the specific requirements of the analysis or the machine learning task at hand.

Master said, "Roopa, remember— Discriminant Analysis is not simply mathematics. It is the art of finding boundaries by listening to how each class speaks through its patterns."

"LDA listens when classes speak with the same accent.

QDA listens when each class speaks its own dialect.

GDA listens to all truths, absorbing them without judgment."

"When you learn to hear these voices, classification becomes effortless."

Master said, "This code demonstrates how Linear Discriminant Analysis (LDA) and Quadratic Discriminant Analysis (QDA) classify data and how their decision boundaries appear visually. The Iris dataset is loaded, and only the first two features—sepal length and sepal width—are used to allow 2D plotting. The data is split into training and test sets using a 70–30 ratio. LDA and QDA models are then trained on the training subset. Since LDA and QDA are special cases of Gaussian Discriminant Analysis (GDA), they serve as representative models for visual comparison."

Example P2 – U2 – D9

LDA, QDA

```
import numpy as np
import matplotlib.pyplot as plt
from sklearn import datasets
from sklearn.discriminant_analysis import LinearDiscriminantAnalysis,
QuadraticDiscriminantAnalysis
from sklearn.model_selection import train_test_split

# Load the Iris dataset
iris = datasets.load_iris()
X = iris.data[:, :2]  # We only take the first two features for easy plotting
y = iris.target

# Split the dataset into training and test sets
X_train, X_test, y_train, y_test = train_test_split(X, y, test_size=0.3, random_state=42)

# Train LDA, QDA models
lda = LinearDiscriminantAnalysis()
lda.fit(X_train, y_train)

qda = QuadraticDiscriminantAnalysis()
qda.fit(X_train, y_train)

# For Gaussian Discriminant Analysis, use LDA and QDA as they are special cases of
GDA
models = [("LDA", lda), ("QDA", qda)]

# Create a mesh to plot the decision boundaries
x_min, x_max = X[:, 0].min() - 1, X[:, 0].max() + 1
y_min, y_max = X[:, 1].min() - 1, X[:, 1].max() + 1
xx, yy = np.meshgrid(np.arange(x_min, x_max, 0.02),
                     np.arange(y_min, y_max, 0.02))

# Plotting
fig, axes = plt.subplots(1, 2, figsize=(12, 6))

for ax, (name, model) in zip(axes.ravel(), models):
    Z = model.predict(np.c_[xx.ravel(), yy.ravel()])
    Z = Z.reshape(xx.shape)
    ax.contourf(xx, yy, Z, alpha=0.4)
```

```
    scatter = ax.scatter(X[:, 0], X[:, 1], c=y, edgecolor='k', s=20)
    ax.set_title(name)
    ax.set_xlabel('Sepal length')
    ax.set_ylabel('Sepal width')

# Adding the legend
legend1 = axes[0].legend(*scatter.legend_elements(), title="Classes")
axes[0].add_artist(legend1)
plt.show()
```

A mesh grid covering the feature space is created to generate predicted class labels across the plane. These predictions are reshaped and plotted as filled contour regions, showing how each model separates the classes. The original Iris samples are then overlaid on the plots. Finally, legends are added for clarity, and both LDA and QDA decision boundaries are displayed side by side for comparison.

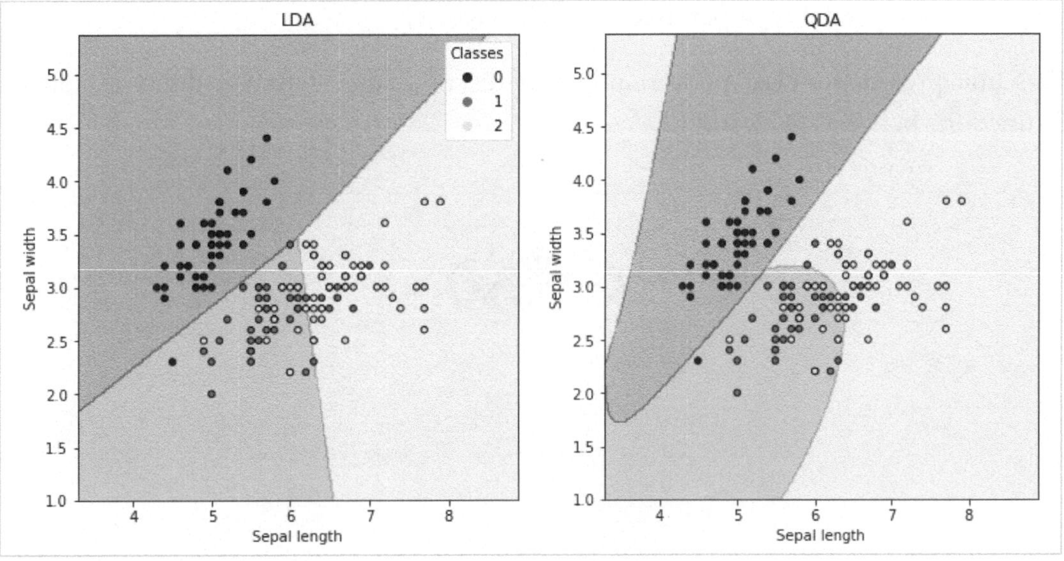

Illustration LDA_QDA: Plot

Summary:

In this unit, we covered Discriminant Analysis and its types, as well as the differences between PCA and LDA:

Discriminant Analysis:

- Linear Discriminant Analysis (LDA): Assumes normally distributed classes with the same covariance matrix, used for classification and dimensionality reduction.

- Quadratic Discriminant Analysis (QDA): Similar to LDA but allows different covariance matrices for each class, suitable for more complex datasets.
- Generalized Discriminant Analysis (GDA): Extends LDA to non-linear relationships using kernel functions.

PCA vs. LDA:

- PCA (Principal Component Analysis): Reduces dimensionality by maximising variance along principal components, unsupervised, does not consider class labels.
- LDA (Linear Discriminant Analysis): Reduces dimensionality by maximising class separability, supervised, uses class labels.

This unit provided a clear understanding of discriminant analysis techniques and the distinctions between PCA and LDA.

PART TWO

DAY FIVE

Unit 2 - Lesson Four

Bayesian

☐ **Bayesian Belief Network**

A **Bayesian Belief Network (BBN)** - also called a **Bayesian Network (BN)**—is a powerful probabilistic model designed to capture uncertainty, causality, and the interdependencies among multiple variables. At its core, it is a structured way of representing how different pieces of information influence one another and how beliefs should be updated when new evidence arrives. It does not simply classify data; it reasons under uncertainty by combining probability theory with graph-based structure.

What a Bayesian Network Truly Represents

A Bayesian Network expresses the **joint probability distribution** of a set of random variables, but does so **efficiently** by leveraging **conditional independence**. Instead of storing an exponentially large table of all possible combinations, it decomposes the joint distribution using local relationships of the form:

$$P(\text{all variables}) = \Pi_i P(X_i | \text{Parents}(X_i))$$

This factorization lies at the heart of Bayesian reasoning: **each node only depends on its parents**, not on every variable in the system. As a result, even complex systems with dozens of variables become computationally manageable.

Structure: The Directed Acyclic Graph (DAG)

A Bayesian Network is built upon a **Directed Acyclic Graph (DAG)**:

1. Nodes — The Variables

Each node represents a random variable:

- medical symptoms
- sensor readings
- weather conditions
- financial indicators
- or any event with uncertainty

Nodes can be **discrete** (e.g., yes/no, colors) or **continuous** (temperature, price).

2. Directed Arcs — The Dependencies

Arrows indicate **causal or influential relationships**.

If there is an arrow from A to B, it means:

- A directly influences B, or
- knowing A changes the belief about B.

This does **not** require strict physical causation; it requires only statistical dependency.

Conditional Probability Tables (CPTs): The Heart of Inference

Each node has an associated **Conditional Probability Table** that describes:

$$P(X|Parents(X))$$

For example, a CPT might show how the probability of a disease changes based on symptoms or test results. These tables encode **the strength and nature of the relationships**.

In continuous BNs, CPTs are replaced by **parametric distributions**, such as Gaussians.

Why Bayesian Networks Are Powerful

A. They Model Uncertainty Naturally

Unlike rigid rule-based systems, Bayesian networks treat every relationship probabilistically. This allows them to handle noise, missing data, and incomplete knowledge gracefully.

B. They Support Inference

Given new evidence, a Bayesian Network can update beliefs about all related variables through **Bayes' theorem**.

This allows reasoning such as:

- "Given the symptoms, what is the most likely disease?"
- "If the sensor fails, what is the probability the system will still succeed?"
- "How does seeing event X change the probability of Y?"

C. They Exploit Conditional Independence

This drastically simplifies learning and inference in high-dimensional domains.

Influence Diagrams: Decision-Making with Bayesian Networks

A **Bayesian Network** describes uncertainty.

An **Influence Diagram** extends this framework to include:

- **Decision nodes** – choices available to the decision-maker
- **Utility nodes** – rewards, risks, or costs

This allows the model not only to reason about uncertainty but to identify **optimal decisions** under that uncertainty.

Influence diagrams are widely used in:

- medical decision systems
- risk analysis
- finance and investment models

- strategic planning
- robotics and autonomous control

Summary

A Bayesian Belief Network is far more than a classification tool. It is a full probabilistic reasoning framework that:

- represents uncertainty in a structured graphical form
- expresses complex joint distributions efficiently
- allows belief updates when new data arrives
- captures causal and statistical dependencies
- supports decision-making under uncertainty through influence diagrams

It unifies probability, graphs, and reasoning—making it one of the most elegant and powerful tools in modern machine learning and AI.

Joint Probability Distribution

Master said, "A Bayesian network is a beautiful way to express how the world arranges itself through dependencies. Consider a set of variables X1,X2,…,Xn. The joint probability distribution of all these variables can be written as a product of conditional probabilities:

$$P(X_1,X_2,\ldots,X_n) = P(X_1| X_2, X_3,\ldots, X_n)\, P(X_2,X_3,\ldots, X_n) = P(X_1| X_1,X_2,\ldots,X_n) , P(X_2| X_3,X_4,\ldots,Xn) \ldots P(Xn-1 | Xn)$$

$$P(X_1,X_2,\ldots,X_n) = \prod_{i=1}^{n} P(Xi|X_1,X_2,\ldots,X_{i-1})$$

Master said, "A Bayesian network is a beautiful way to express how the world arranges itself through dependencies. Consider a set of variables X1,X2,…,Xn. The joint probability distribution of all these variables can be written as a product of conditional probabilities:

$$P(X_i|X_{i-1},\ldots, X_1) = P(X_i |Parents(X_i))$$

But a Bayesian network simplifies this further. Instead of conditioning each variable on all those that came before it, we condition each variable only on its **parents**—the variables that directly influence it:

$$P(X_1, X_2, \ldots, X_n) = \Pi_{i=1}^{n} P(Xi| \text{ Parents } (Xi))$$

This is the essence: **dependence only flows along meaningful relationships, not everywhere at once.**

Now, let us apply this Bayesian approach to a simple and practical question:

'Is the mobile phone in the bedroom (R1) or in the study room (R2), given the noise we hear?'

To clarify the process, let us walk through the steps with greater detail."

To improve the Bayesian approach for predicting whether the mobile phone is in the bedroom (R1) or the study room (R2) based on the noise, let's clarify and detail the steps involved:

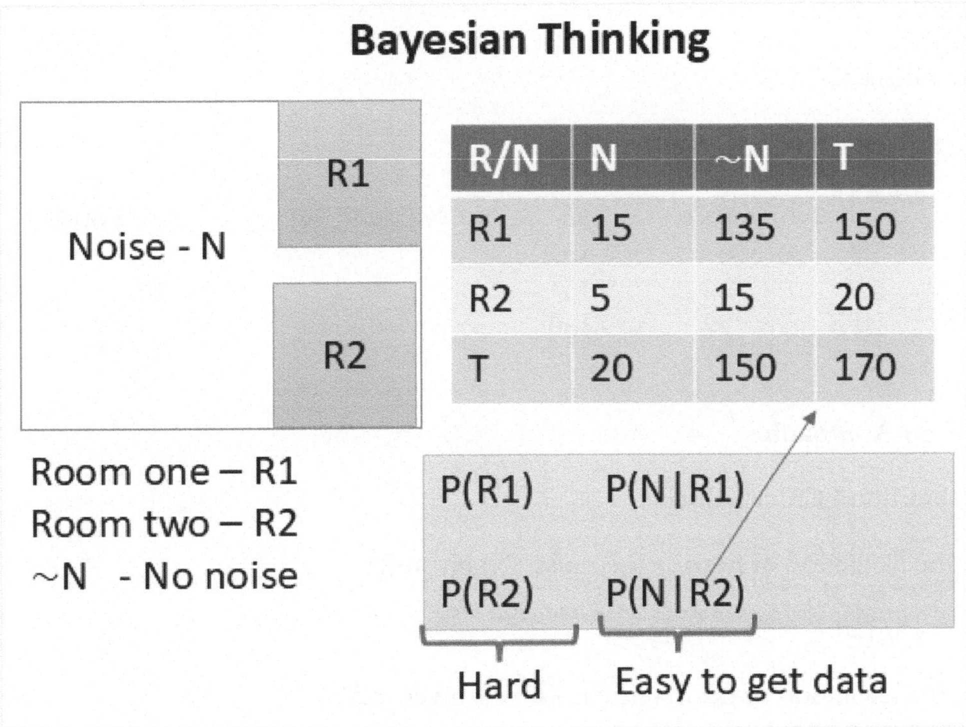

R/N	N	~N	T
R1	15	135	150
R2	5	15	20
T	20	150	170

Illustration Bay_1: Plot

Bayesian Thinking

Approach One
P(N|R1) = 15/150 = 10%
P(N|R2 = 5/20 = 25%

Prior – P(R1) P(R2)
Likelihood - P(N|R1) P(N|R2)
Posteriors – P(R1|N) P(R2|N)

Approach Two Bayesian
P(R1|N) = 15/20 = 75%
P(R2|N) = 5/20 = 25%

Prior beliefs get updated with new data

P(R1|N) = P(R1&N) = P(R1)P(N|R1)/P(N)
P(R2|N) = P(R2&N) = P(R2)P(N|R2)/P(N)

How do you get Prior?

Illustration Bay_2: Plot

Bayesian Thinking

Given the following probability matrix:

	Noise (N)	No Noise (~N)	Total
R1	15	135	150
R2	5	15	20
Total	20	150	170

Step-by-Step Approach

Step 1: Likelihood Calculation

Calculate the likelihood of hearing the noise (N) given R1:

P(N|R1) = 15/150 = 10%

Calculate the likelihood of hearing the noise (N) given R2:

P(N|R2 = 5/20 = 25%

Step 2: Prior Calculation

To use Bayesian inference, we need the prior probabilities P(R1) and P(R2). These are the probabilities of the mobile being in R1 or R2 before hearing the noise.

$P(R1) = \text{Total cases}/\text{Total cases in R1} = 150/170 \approx 0.882$

$P(R2) = \text{Total cases}/\text{Total cases in R2} = 20/170 \approx 0.118$

Step 3: Marginal Probability of Noise

The marginal probability of hearing the noise, P(N), is the total number of cases with noise divided by the total number of cases:

$P(N) = 20170 \approx 0.118$

Step 4: Posterior Calculation using Bayes' Theorem

Using Bayes' theorem to calculate the posterior probabilities P(R1|N) and P(R2|N):

Posterior probability of R1 given N:

$P(R1|N) = P(R1) \cdot P(N|R1) \ / \ P(N) = (0.882)*(0.10)/(0.118) \approx 0.748$

Posterior probability of R2 given N:

$P(R2|N) = P(R2) \cdot P(N|R2)/P(N) = (0.118)*(0.25)/(0.118) \approx 0.252$

Summary of Steps

- Calculate the likelihood P(N|R1) and P(N|R2).
- Determine the prior probabilities P(R1) and P(R2) from the total cases.
- Compute the marginal probability P(N).
- Apply Bayes' theorem to find the posterior probabilities P(R1|N) and P(R2|N).

Given the noise, the probability that the mobile is in the bedroom (R1) is approximately 74.8%, and the probability that it is in the study room (R2) is approximately 25.2%. This Bayesian approach effectively combines the prior information and the likelihood to provide a more accurate prediction.

☐ **Example Scenario: Bayesian Network**

Master said, "**Nikash**, imagine a simple house equipped with an alarm system.

Consider an alarm system 'A' installed in a house. The alarm rings due to two events: burglary 'B' and fire 'F'. These events are parent nodes of the alarm 'A'. The alarm, in turn, is a parent node to two other events: calls from person 'P1' and 'P2'.

- Alarm 'A': Rings due to burglary 'B' and fire 'F'.
- Person 'P1': Calls person 'X' when the alarm 'A' rings, but may forget.
- Person 'P2': Calls person 'X' when the alarm 'A' rings, but may fail to hear the alarm from a distance.

Bayesian Network Description

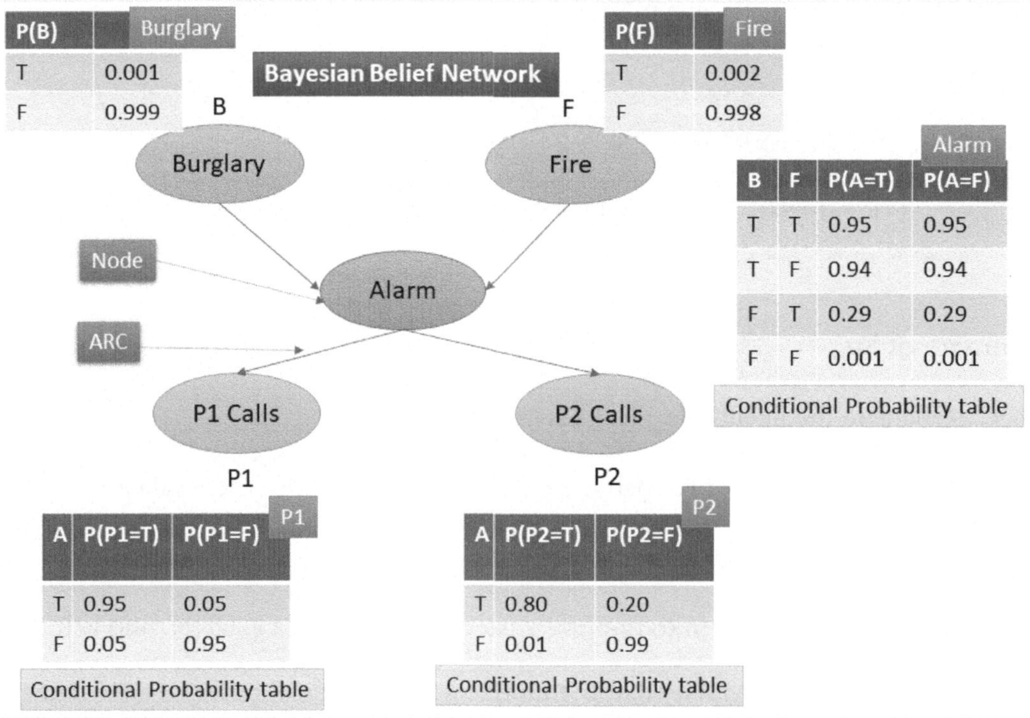

Illustration Bay_3:

- **Alarm A**

Triggered by **burglary (B)** or **fire (F)**.

- **Person P1**

  Calls person **X** if the alarm rings, though sometimes **he forgets.**

- **Person P2**

  Calls person **X** if the alarm rings, though sometimes **she does not hear it** from far away.

Thus, the dependency chain is:

B,F⟶A⟶P1,P2

Probability Calculation

We want to find the probability that 'P1' and 'P2' call person 'X' when the alarm 'A' rings, given no burglary 'B' and no fire 'F'.

That is:

$$P\ (P1{=}T,\ P2{=}T|B{=}F,\ F{=}F)$$

Given Probabilities

1. **Burglary and Fire Priors:**

Burglary 'B'	**Fire 'F'**
P(B=T) = 0.00 1	P(F=T) = 0.002
P(B=F) = 0.999	P(F=F) = 0.998

2. **Alarm A Conditional Probabilities**

$$P(A|B,F)$$

Alarm 'A'	
P(A=T|B=T, F=T) = 0.95	P(A = F | B = T, F = T) = 0.05
P(A=T|B=T, F=F) = 0.94	P(A = F | B = T, F = F) = 0.06
P(A=T|B=F, F=T) = 0.29	P(A = F | B = F, F = T) = 0.71
P(A=T|B=F,F=F) =0.001	P(A = F|B = F, F = F) = 0.999

3. **Person P1 and P2 Conditional Probabilities**

Person 'P1'	Person 'P2'
P(P1=T|A=T) = 0.95	P(P2=T|A=T) = 0.80
P(P1=F|A=T) = 0.05	P(P2=F|A=T) = 0.20
P(P1=T|A=F) = 0.05	P(P2=T|A=F) = 0.01
P(P1=F|A=F) = 0.95	P(P2=F|A=F) = 0.99

4. Calculation

To compute the probability that both P1 and P2 call and the alarm rings, given that there is no burglary and no fire, we evaluate:

$P(P1=T, P2=T, A=T|B=F, F=F)$:

Using the conditional independence assumptions of the Bayesian network:

$$P(P1,P2,A,\neg B,\neg F) = P(P1|A) \times P(P2|A) \times P(A|\neg B,\neg F) \times P(\neg B) \times P(\neg F)$$

Now substitute the given probabilities:

- $P(P1=T|A=T)=0.95$
- $P(P2=T|A=T)=0.80$
- $P(A=T|B=F, F=F)=0.001$
- $P(B=F)=0.999$
- $P(F=F)=0.998$

Thus:

$P(P1=T, P2=T, A=T|B=F, F=F) = 0.95 \times 0.80 \times 0.001 \times 0.999 \times 0.998 \approx 0.00075772152$

Example P2 – U2 – D10	
Bayesian Network	**Output**

# Define the probabilities 	
P_B_true = 0.001
P_B_false = 0.999
 	
P_F_true = 0.002
P_F_false = 0.998
	Probability P(P1=T, P2=T, A=T | B=F, F=F): 0.00075772152

```
P_A_given_BF = {
    (True, True): 0.95,
    (True, False): 0.94,
    (False, True): 0.29,
    (False, False): 0.001
}

P_P1_given_A = {
    True: 0.95,
    False: 0.05
}

P_P2_given_A = {
    True: 0.80,
    False: 0.01
}

# Given no burglary (B=False) and no fire (F=False)
B = False
F = False

# Probability that alarm (A) rings given no burglary and no fire
P_A = P_A_given_BF[(B, F)]

# Probability that person P1 calls given alarm rings
P_P1 = P_P1_given_A[True]

# Probability that person P2 calls given alarm rings
P_P2 = P_P2_given_A[True]

# Calculate the joint probability P(P1, P2, A, ~B, ~F)
joint_probability = P_P1 * P_P2 * P_A * P_B_false * P_F_false
print("Probability P(P1=T, P2=T, A=T | B=F, F=F):",
joint_probability)
```

Example:

Master said, "Let us consider a simple example. The purpose of this code is to build and query a Bayesian Belief Network (BBN) to determine the probability that a person has heart disease, given that they suffer from high blood pressure. The network models how different factors—such as exercise habits, diet quality, heartburn, and chest pain—interact and influence the likelihood of heart disease. By encoding these relationships as conditional probabilities, the BBN allows us to reason under uncertainty and compute how observing one condition (like high blood pressure) updates the probability of another outcome (like heart disease)."

Example P2 – U2 – D11

Bayesian Network

```
from pgmpy.models import BayesianNetwork
from pgmpy.factors.discrete import TabularCPD
from pgmpy.inference import VariableElimination

# Define the structure of the Bayesian Network
model = BayesianNetwork([
    ('Exercise', 'BloodPressure'),
    ('Diet', 'BloodPressure'),
    ('Heartburn', 'HeartDisease'),
    ('BloodPressure', 'HeartDisease'),
    ('HeartDisease', 'ChestPain')
])

# Define the CPDs (Conditional Probability Distributions)
cpd_exercise = TabularCPD(variable='Exercise', variable_card=2, values=[[0.7], [0.3]])
cpd_diet = TabularCPD(variable='Diet', variable_card=2, values=[[0.6], [0.4]])
cpd_heartburn = TabularCPD(variable='Heartburn', variable_card=2, values=[[0.8],
[0.2]])

cpd_blood_pressure = TabularCPD(variable='BloodPressure', variable_card=2,
                        values=[[0.9, 0.7, 0.6, 0.4],
                                [0.1, 0.3, 0.4, 0.6]],
                        evidence=['Exercise', 'Diet'],
                        evidence_card=[2, 2])

cpd_heart_disease = TabularCPD(variable='HeartDisease', variable_card=2,
                        values=[[0.99, 0.85, 0.75, 0.5],
                                [0.01, 0.15, 0.25, 0.5]],
                        evidence=['BloodPressure', 'Heartburn'],
                        evidence_card=[2, 2])

# Corrected CPD for ChestPain
cpd_chest_pain = TabularCPD(variable='ChestPain', variable_card=2,
                        values=[[0.95, 0.2],
                                [0.05, 0.8]],
                        evidence=['HeartDisease'],
                        evidence_card=[2])

# Add CPDs to the model
model.add_cpds(cpd_exercise, cpd_diet, cpd_heartburn, cpd_blood_pressure,
cpd_heart_disease, cpd_chest_pain)
```

```
# Check if the model is valid
assert model.check_model()

# Perform inference
inference = VariableElimination(model)

# Query the probability of having heart disease given high blood pressure
query_result = inference.query(variables=['HeartDisease'], evidence={'BloodPressure': 1})

print(query_result)
```

Output:

```
| HeartDisease    | phi(HeartDisease) |
| HeartDisease(0) |       0.7000      |
| HeartDisease(1) |       0.3000      |
```

Here's a step-by-step explanation of the code's purpose and functionality:

Define the Structure of the Bayesian Network

The Bayesian Network structure is defined using the BayesianNetwork class. The network includes the following nodes and their relationships:

- Exercise and Diet influence BloodPressure.
- BloodPressure and Heartburn influence HeartDisease.
- HeartDisease influences ChestPain.

Define the Conditional Probability Distributions (CPDs)

For each node, a Conditional Probability Distribution (CPD) is defined to represent the probabilities of different outcomes given their parent nodes:

- Exercise, Diet, and Heartburn are root nodes with their respective probabilities.
- BloodPressure is influenced by Exercise and Diet.
- HeartDisease is influenced by BloodPressure and Heartburn.
- ChestPain is influenced by HeartDisease.

Add CPDs to the Model and Validate the Model

The CPDs are added to the model, and the model's validity is checked using model.check_model(). This ensures that the network structure and CPDs are correctly specified.

Perform Inference

Using the VariableElimination class, probabilistic inference is performed on the network. Specifically, the code queries the probability of having HeartDisease given that the individual has high BloodPressure.

PART TWO

DAY SIX

Unit 2 - Lesson Five

HMM

Master said, "Apeksha, imagine life as a journey through a series of rooms. Each room represents a *state*—a moment, a condition, a circumstance. Now, when you stand in any one room, the door through which you will exit next does not depend on how you arrived there, nor on the twists and turns that brought you to this moment. It depends only on where you are *now*.

This, in essence, is a **Markov Chain**—a mathematical model where the next step relies only on the present step, not on the entire history. This powerful simplicity is what we call the **Markov property**."

Key Features of a Markov Chain

1. States — The Rooms of Experience

A Markov chain is built on the idea of **states**, each representing a distinct condition or situation the system can be in.

- In **weather prediction**, states may be *Sunny*, *Rainy*, or *Cloudy*.
- In a **board game** like Snakes and Ladders, every square is a state the player can occupy.
- In **human behaviour**, moods like *joy*, *fear*, and *calm* can be modeled as states.

Analogy:
Imagine each state as a **room in a long corridor**. Today, you may wake up in the *Sunny Room*, wander into the *Cloudy Room* tomorrow, and later return to the *Sunny Room* again.

Each room defines your current experience, and at any moment, you can only be in one room.

But the corridor doesn't remember where you came from. It only knows the room you're standing in right now.

This captures the essence of the Markov property.

2. Transition Probabilities — The Rules Hidden Behind the Doors

Between these rooms are doors—some wide open, some narrow, some rarely used. These doors represent **transition probabilities**, describing how likely it is to move from one state to another. They are organized in what we call a **transition matrix**, where:

- Each **row** is your current room,
- Each **column** is the room you might enter next.

Analogy:
If you currently stand inside the *Sunny Room*, there are several doors in front of you:

- A **wide door** (70% chance) that leads back into another *Sunny* day,
- A **medium door** (20% chance) opening toward a *Cloudy* day,
- A **small door** (10% chance) leading to *Rain.*

You don't choose the door consciously—the system follows the probability rules.

The future depends only on *where you stand now*, not on the path that brought you here.

The transitions encode the behavior of the entire system: they decide how the story unfolds, step by step, room by room.

3. Memorylessness — The Corridor That Forgets Your Footsteps

Master said, "Apeksha, the deepest essence of a Markov chain lies in its **memorylessness**.
This means the future depends only on the **present state**, not on the entire journey you took to reach here."

Think of it this way:

You may have walked through ten different rooms before arriving at the **Cloudy Room**, but the corridor holds **no memory** of those steps.

The doors available to you now—and the chances of each door opening—depend **only** on the room you stand in at this moment.

Analogy:
You could have reached *Cloudy* from *Sunny*, from *Rainy*, or from ten other paths. But once inside the *Cloudy Room*, every past route collapses into irrelevance. The corridor whispers only one truth:

"Where you are now is all that matters."

This is the **Markov property**.

4. Transition Matrix — The Map of Invisible Rules

Master continued, "To navigate this corridor of rooms, you must study the hidden mathematical map called the **transition matrix**."

This matrix is like the sacred blueprint of the corridor:

- **Rows** represent your current room.
- **Columns** represent the room you may enter next.
- Each number is the **probability** that a specific door will open.

The transition probabilities can be represented in a matrix form, where each element Pij represents the probability of moving from state i to state j.

$$P = \begin{pmatrix} P11\ P12 \ldots\ P1n \\ P21\ P22 \ldots P2n \\ \ldots\ldots\ldots\ldots\ldots\ldots.. \\ Pn1\ Pn2 \ldots Pnn \end{pmatrix}$$

Analogy:

Imagine holding a scroll that lists every room and every door:

- In the *Sunny Row*, the scroll says:
  - 0.7 chance to stay in the *Sunny Room*
  - 0.2 chance to move to *Cloudy*
  - 0.1 chance to drift into *Rain*
- In the *Rain Row*, the scroll might say:
  - 0.5 chance of staying in *Rain*
  - 0.5 chance of rolling into *Cloudy*

This matrix is the **law of the corridor**—the silent architect of all movements, the invisible force that shapes every step taken, every door opened, every future that unfolds.

5. Steady States — The Room Where the Journey Settles

Master smiled softly, "Now, Apeksha, imagine walking through the corridor for a very long time.

At first, you may jump unpredictably between rooms. But eventually, a pattern emerges."

In many Markov chains, no matter where you start, your **long-term presence** settles into a stable distribution. This is called the **steady state**.

Analogy:

You might begin your journey in the *Sunny Room*.

You may wander into *Rain*, drift back to *Sunny*, tumble into *Cloudy*, and continue this dance endlessly.

Yet, after thousands of steps, you might realize:

- You spend **60%** of the time in *Sunny*,
- **30%** in *Cloudy*,
- **10%** in *Rain*.

This long-run pattern does not depend on where you began. It is the natural rhythm of the corridor itself.

Master said:

"The steady state is the **true personality of the chain**, the destiny toward which all journeys converge.

It reveals the long-term behaviour, the equilibrium hidden beneath the short-term fluctuations."

The Philosophy Behind Markov Chains

A Markov chain mirrors a profound truth:

Not all systems carry their past with them. Some evolve purely from their present reality.

- A stock's next movement often depends only on its current price—not the path of prices before.
- Your next emotional reaction sometimes depends only on how you feel now—not on last month's memories.
- In genetics, the next mutation depends only on the current DNA state—not the past sequence of changes.

The Markov chain teaches us both mathematically and metaphorically: **What matters is where you stand now, not how you arrived here.**

☐ Types of Markov Chains

1. Discrete-Time Markov Chain (DTMC)

Master said, *"When time moves in steps—tick, pause, tick—every transition happens at those fixed moments."*

A discrete-time Markov chain changes states only at specific, separated time intervals.

Think of it like walking on stepping stones—you move only when your foot reaches the next stone.

2. Continuous-Time Markov Chain (CTMC)

Master continued, *"But life does not always wait for a step. Sometimes changes flow like a river—smooth, uninterrupted."*

A continuous-time Markov chain allows transitions at any moment, not restricted by fixed time steps.

Imagine water flowing between interconnected pools; movement happens whenever nature decides.

Example of a Markov Chain

Master said, *"Let us look at the sky—it teaches Markov chains every day."*

Suppose we model weather with three states:

Sunny, **Cloudy**, and **Rainy**.

The transition matrix is:

$$P = \begin{pmatrix} 0.6 & 0.3 & 0.1 \\ 0.2 & 0.5 & 0.3 \\ 0.1 & 0.3 & 0.6 \end{pmatrix}$$

This matrix means that:

Master explained:

- **If today is Sunny**

  "There is a 60% chance the light remains tomorrow, a 30% chance the sky softens to cloud, and a 10% chance the heavens weep."

- **If today is Cloudy**

  "There is a 20% chance the clouds part for sunlight, a 50% chance they remain, and a 30% chance they grow heavy into rain."

- **If today is Rainy**

  "There is a 10% chance the rain clears to sunshine, a 30% chance it calms to cloud, and a 60% chance the rain endures."

Master said, *"This is the dance of probability—the world shifting from one state to another, step by step, guided by the quiet mathematics beneath existence."*

☐ Applications of Markov Chains

Markov chains are used in various fields, including:

- Economics: Modelling economic systems and stock prices.
- Game Theory: Analysing board games and decision-making processes.
- Genetics: Studying the evolution of gene sequences.
- Queueing Theory: Understanding and predicting the behaviour of queues in systems like telecommunications.

Markov chains provide a robust framework for modelling systems where the future state depends only on the current state, making them a powerful tool in stochastic processes and probability theory.

☐ Hidden Markov Model (HMM)

Master said, "Akshaya, the Hidden Markov Model is not merely a mathematical structure… it is a mirror of life itself."

He continued:

"A Hidden Markov Model (HMM) describes a world where the truth is concealed behind a veil.

We do not see the real states directly.

We only see their reflections—symbols, signals, hints—emitted into the world.

From these scattered observations, we attempt to infer the unseen dance beneath."

Just like:

- You hear someone's voice but cannot see their emotions.
- You observe the market price but cannot see the hidden sentiment driving it.
- You hear spoken words but cannot perceive the neural states forming them.

This is the essence of HMM:

A system with *hidden internal states* that move over time, and *visible outputs* that reveal glimpses of those hidden states.

Why HMM is Powerful

Master said, "The world rarely shows its inner mechanism openly. Life is full of hidden causes and visible effects. HMMs model exactly this."

- They capture **uncertainty**, because we never know the true state for sure.
- They capture **temporal dependency**, because the next hidden state depends on the previous one.
- They capture **probabilistic emission**, because one hidden state may produce many possible observations.

That is why HMMs rule fields like:

- **Speech recognition** – where sounds are visible but phonemes are hidden.
- **Finance** – where prices are visible, but market regimes are hidden.
- **Bioinformatics** – where DNA sequences are visible but evolutionary states are hidden.
- **Human emotions** – where behaviour is visible but inner feelings remain hidden.

Master said, **"To understand the seen, you must first model the unseen."** This is the philosophy of the Hidden Markov Model.

Components of a Hidden Markov Model

Master unfolded the five pillars of HMM, each glowing like a lamp illuminating the darkness within the model:

A. Hidden States — The Unseen Rooms of Reality

"These are the secret chambers where the real process unfolds," the Master said.

You cannot enter these rooms.

You cannot see what happens inside.

But their presence influences everything.

Examples of hidden states:

- The emotion behind a person's tone
- The underlying market condition
- The phoneme being spoken
- The biological state of a cell

They follow a **Markov process — the next hidden state depends only on the current hidden state.**

Master said, "Even when truth is hidden, it still moves with its own internal logic."

B. Observations — The Footprints of the Invisible

"These," Master explained, "are the clues left behind by the hidden states."

You cannot see the hidden cause, but you can observe the effect.

Examples:

- A sound wave produced by a phoneme
- A stock price produced by a hidden market regime
- A DNA letter produced by a hidden evolutionary step
- A facial expression produced by a hidden emotion

Observations are the **visible outputs**.

They are the shadows cast by invisible states.

C. Initial Probabilities — The First Breath of the System

Master said softly, **"Every journey begins somewhere."**

The initial probabilities describe:

- Where the system *likely* starts
- Which hidden state is most probable at time t = 0

Sometimes the beginning is clear.

Often, it is uncertain.

But the model assigns probabilities to each possible starting point.

D. Transition Probabilities — The Flow of Hidden States

"These," Master said, "are the secret pathways between the unseen rooms."

They define:

- How likely the system is to move from one hidden state to another
- How the internal truth evolves over time
- The rhythm and movement of the invisible process

Just like:

- Emotions shifting from joy → calm → worry
- Market regimes moving from bullish → neutral → bearish
- Speech moving from one phoneme to the next

Master said, **"Even unseen, the inner world has its own pattern."**

E. Emission Probabilities — The Language of the Hidden World

"These probabilities," Master explained, "describe how hidden states speak to us through observable signals."

Given a hidden state, what is the likelihood of each possible observation?

Examples:

- The probability that a phoneme produces a certain sound pattern

- The probability that a bullish regime produces an upward price movement
- The probability that sadness produces a particular facial expression

Emission probabilities form the bridge between the invisible cause and the visible effect.

Master said, "The hidden world emits signs.

To read them is to understand the model.

To understand the model is to unveil the truth that lies beneath the surface."

Mathematical Formulation

Initial Probability Distribution (π): The probability of starting in each hidden state i.

$$\pi_i = P(Q_1 = S_i)$$

Where Q_1 is the initial state, and S_i represents the hidden states.

Transition Probability Matrix (A): The probability of transitioning from hidden state i to hidden state j.

$$Aij = P(Q_{t+1} = S_j \mid Q_t = S_i)$$

where Qt and Q_{t+1} are the hidden states at time t and t+1 respectively.

Emission Probability Matrix (B): The probability of observing o_t given the hidden state S_i .

$$Bi(o_t) = P(O_t = o_t \mid Q_t = S_i)$$

Where O_t is the observed output at time t.

The Hidden Markov Model (HMM) algorithm can be implemented using the following steps

- Define the state space and observation space.
- Initialize the state distribution (π).

- Define the state transition matrix (A).
- Define the observation likelihood (Emission) matrix (B).
- Train the model using the Baum-Welch or forward-backward algorithm.
- Decode the hidden states using the Viterbi algorithm.
- Evaluate the model's performance using appropriate metrics.

This improved structure provides a clear and detailed overview of implementing and understanding the Hidden Markov Model algorithm.

Example:

Consider an HMM used for weather prediction where the hidden states are the weather conditions (Cloudy, Sunny, Rainy) and the observations are the activities (Umbrella, Normal, Raincoat).

Hidden States

Weather: Cloudy, Sunny, Rainy

Observations

Activities: Umbrella, Normal, Raincoat

Initial Probability Distribution

Cloudy	**Sunny**	**Rainy**
Cloudy	0.5	0.2

Transition Probability Matrix

	Cloudy	**Sunny**	**Rainy**
Cloudy	0.5	0.2	0.3
Sunny	0.4	0.4	0.2
Rainy	0.3	0.2	0.5

Emission Probability Matrix

	Umbrella	Normal	Raincoat
Cloudy	0.7	0.2	0.1
Sunny	0.3	0.6	0.1
Rainy	0.5	0.1	0.4

☐ Example: Problems

What is the probability of the following weather sequence?

Cloudy → Sunny → Cloudy → Rainy

Solution

A. Probability of the Sequence Cloudy → Sunny → Cloudy → Rainy

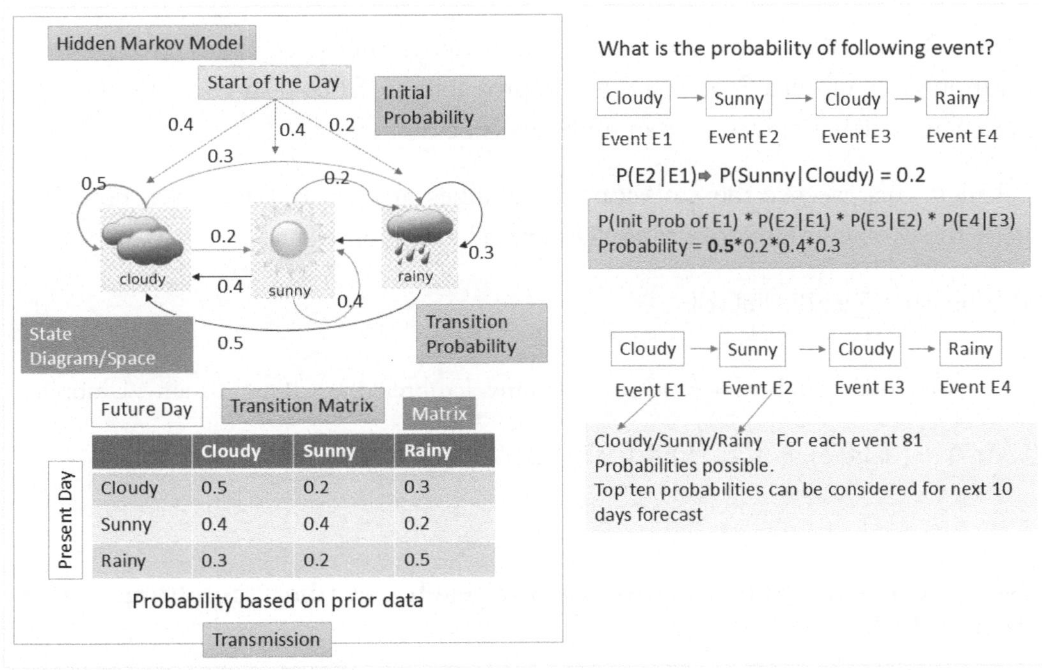

Illustration HMM_1: HMM

To find the probability of the sequence "Cloudy → Sunny → Cloudy → Rainy", we multiply the initial probability of starting in the first state by the transition probabilities between the states in the sequence.

P(Cloudy → Sunny → Cloudy → Rainy) = π(Cloudy) × A(Sunny|Cloudy) x A(Cloudy|Sunny) × A(Rainy|Cloudy)

P(Cloudy → Sunny → Cloudy → Rainy) = π(Cloudy) × A(Sunny|Cloudy) x A(Cloudy|Sunny) × A(Rainy|Cloudy)

Using the provided probabilities:

P(Cloudy → Sunny → Cloudy → Rainy) = 0.5×0.2×0.4×0.3=0.012

The probability of the sequence "Cloudy -> Sunny -> Cloudy -> Rainy" is 0.012.

B. Probability of Weather Condition Given an Observation

Question: What is the probability of it being Cloudy, Sunny, or Rainy given that the observation is "Umbrella"? or What is the probability of being in each weather state (Cloudy, Sunny, Rainy) given that an umbrella is being carried?

To calculate this, we use the emission probabilities and apply Bayes' theorem. First, calculate the probability of observing "Umbrella" across all states.

P(Umbrella) = $\sum i\pi i \cdot$Bi,Umbrella

= (πCloudy·BCloudy, Umbrella) + (πSunny·BSunny, Umbrella) + (πRainy·BRainy, Umbrella)

= (0.5·0.7) + (0.3·0.3) + (0.2·0.5) = 0.35 + 0.09 + 0.1 = 0.54

C. Now, calculate the probability for each weather condition given "Umbrella":

P(Cloudy|Umbrella) = (πCloudy·BCloudy, Umbrella) / P(Umbrella) = (0.5·0.7) / 0.54 = 0.35 / 0.54 ≈ 0.648

P(Sunny|Umbrella) = (πSunny·BSunny, Umbrella) / P(Umbrella)

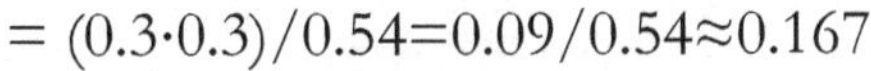

$= (0.3 \cdot 0.3)/0.54 = 0.09/0.54 \approx 0.167$

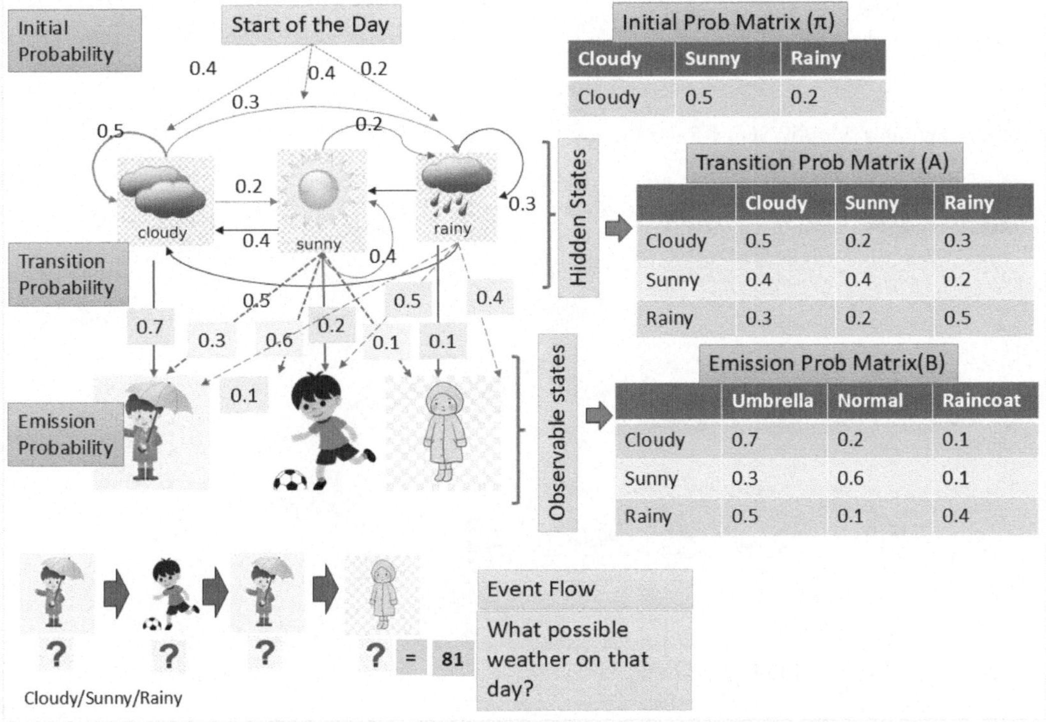

Illustration HMM_2: HMM

P(Rainy|Umbrella) = (πRainy·BRainy, Umbrella) / P(Umbrella) = (0.2·0.5) / 0.54 = 0.1 / 0.54 ≈ 0.185

The probabilities of it being Cloudy, Sunny, or Rainy given that the observation is "Umbrella" are approximately 0.648, 0.167, and 0.185, respectively.

To calculate all possible events, we use both Emission probabilities and transmission probabilities for all 81 events.

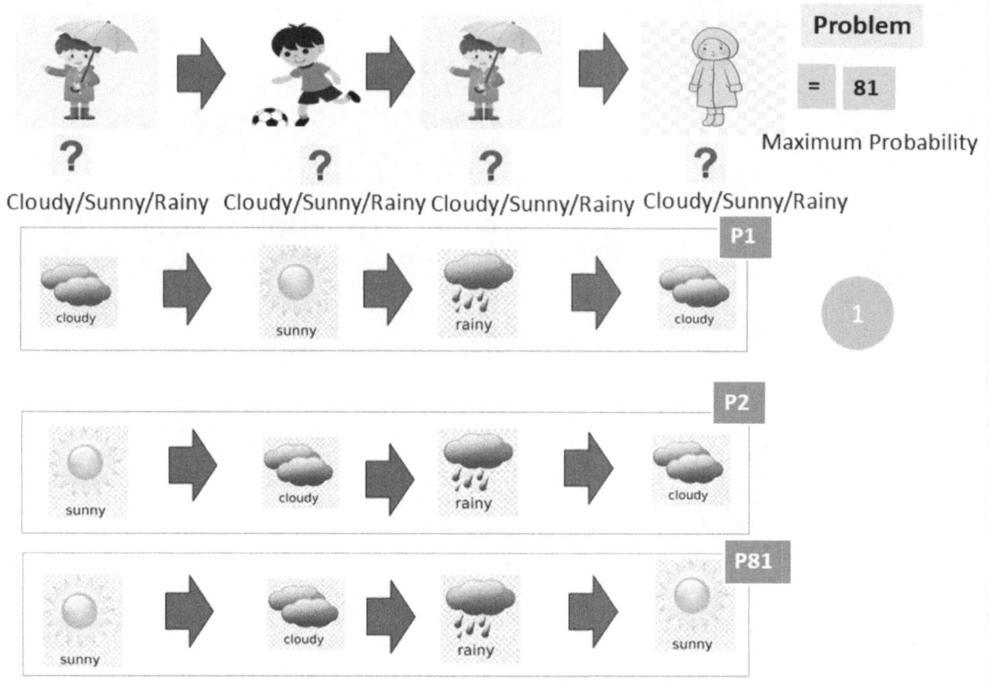

Illustration HMM_3: HMM

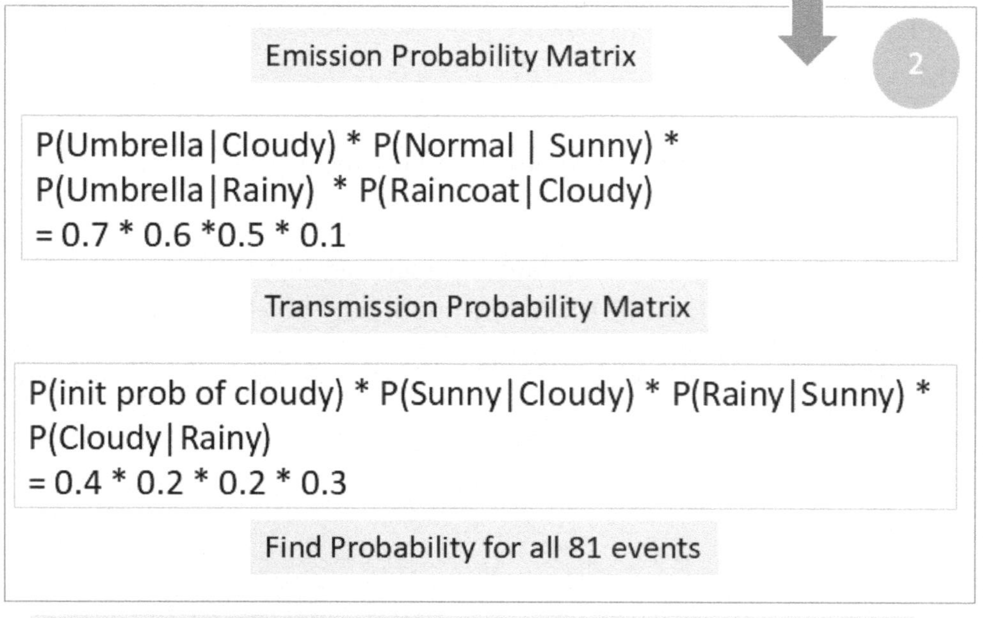

Illustration HMM_4: HMM

Conclusion

Using these components, HMMs can effectively model sequences of observations to predict the underlying hidden states and future observations. This example illustrates how to calculate the probability of a specific sequence of hidden states and the probability of hidden states given an observation.

The purpose of the code is to demonstrate how to model a Hidden Markov Model (HMM) for weather prediction, where the states (weather conditions) are hidden, and the observations (activities) are visible.

Example P2 – U2 – D12

Hidden Markov

```
import numpy as np

# Define the number of hidden states and observed states
n_states = 3
n_observations = 3

# Define the HMM parameters
start_prob = np.array([0.5, 0.3, 0.2])  # Initial probabilities: Cloudy, Sunny, Rainy

trans_prob = np.array([
    [0.5, 0.2, 0.3],  # Transition probabilities from Cloudy
    [0.4, 0.4, 0.2],  # Transition probabilities from Sunny
    [0.3, 0.2, 0.5]   # Transition probabilities from Rainy
])

emit_prob = np.array([
    [0.7, 0.2, 0.1],  # Emission probabilities for Cloudy: Umbrella, Normal, Raincoat
    [0.3, 0.6, 0.1],  # Emission probabilities for Sunny: Umbrella, Normal, Raincoat
    [0.5, 0.1, 0.4]   # Emission probabilities for Rainy: Umbrella, Normal, Raincoat
])

# Define a function to compute the probability of a given sequence of states
def compute_sequence_probability(start_prob, trans_prob, sequence):
    prob = start_prob[sequence[0]]
    for i in range(1, len(sequence)):
        prob *= trans_prob[sequence[i-1], sequence[i]]
    return prob

# Calculate the probability of the sequence: Cloudy -> Sunny -> Cloudy -> Rainy
sequence = [0, 1, 0, 2]  # 0: Cloudy, 1: Sunny, 2: Rainy
sequence_prob = compute_sequence_probability(start_prob, trans_prob, sequence)
```

```
print(f"Probability of the sequence Cloudy -> Sunny -> Cloudy -> Rainy:
{sequence_prob}")

# Define all possible sequences of length 4 with 3 possible states each
all_sequences = np.array([[a, b, c, d] for a in range(n_states) for b in range(n_states) for
c in range(n_states) for d in range(n_states)])

# Calculate the probabilities for all sequences
all_sequence_probs = [compute_sequence_probability(start_prob, trans_prob, seq) for
seq in all_sequences]

# Print the probabilities for all 81 sequences
for sequence, prob in zip(all_sequences, all_sequence_probs):
    print(f"Sequence: {sequence}, Probability: {prob}")

# Calculate the probability of each state given the observation 'Umbrella'
obs = 0  # 0: Umbrella
obs_prob = start_prob * emit_prob[:, obs]
obs_prob /= obs_prob.sum()
print(f"Probability of being in each state given 'Umbrella': {obs_prob}")
```

Output:

```
Output

Probability of the sequence Cloudy -> Sunny -> Cloudy -> Rainy: 0.012000000000000002

Probability of being in each state given 'Umbrella': [0.64814815 0.16666667 0.18518519]
```

The code performs the following tasks:

Define HMM Parameters:

- **Initial Probabilities** (start_prob): The probability of starting in each state (Cloudy, Sunny, Rainy).
- **Transition Probabilities** (trans_prob): The probability of transitioning from one state to another.
- **Emission Probabilities** (emit_prob): The probability of observing each possible observation (Umbrella, Normal, Raincoat) given the current state.

Calculate Probability of a Specific Sequence:

Computes the probability of a given sequence of weather conditions (e.g., Cloudy -> Sunny -> Cloudy -> Rainy).

Calculate Probabilities for All Possible Sequences:

Generates all possible sequences of weather conditions of a certain length (4 in this case) and computes their probabilities.

Calculate Probability Given an Observation:

Determines the probability of each weather condition given a specific observation (e.g., observing an Umbrella).

☐ Applications of Hidden Markov Models

- Speech Recognition: HMMs are used to model the sequence of spoken words, where the hidden states represent the phonemes or words and the observations are the acoustic signals.
- Bioinformatics: In gene prediction and sequence alignment, HMMs help in identifying the regions of DNA sequences by modelling the hidden biological states.
- Finance: HMMs are applied to model the hidden market conditions and predict future stock prices based on observed financial indicators.

PART TWO

DAY SIX

Unit 2 - Lesson Five

GMM

☐ **Gaussian Mixture Model**

Master said, "Apeksha, let us look deeply into the nature of a Gaussian Mixture Model."

A **Gaussian Mixture Model (GMM)** is not merely a statistical tool—it is a meditation on complexity. It recognises that life, like data, rarely belongs to a single identity. Every point carries shades of multiple possibilities, just as every person holds many roles, emotions, and potentials simultaneously.

Where **K-Means demands a rigid identity -**"You belong here and nowhere else."

GMM honours subtlety, saying: *"You may belong a little here, a little there; life is not binary but blended."*

Example of Hidden Tribes Within a Forest

"Imagine," the Master said, "a vast ancient forest inhabited by many hidden tribes.

Each tribe has its own way of living—its own *rhythm*, *patterns*, *temperatures*, *sounds*, and *footsteps.*

A traveller walking through the forest hears a rustle.

Is it from the River Tribe?

Or the Wind Tribe?

Or the Shade Tribe?

The sound does not reveal its tribe directly. It only carries *hints*, *patterns*, and *probabilities*.

GMM is the art of listening to these subtle sounds."

In this forest:

- Each **tribe** = a **Gaussian distribution**
- Each **tribe's lifestyle** (its mean μ and covariance Σ) = the **shape of the Gaussian**
- The **influence or size of each tribe** = the **mixing weight** π
- The **traveller's observation** (the sound they hear) = a **data point**
- The **true tribe behind the sound** = a **latent variable z**

But the tribes are hidden.

The forest doesn't say: "Sound belongs to Tribe A with certainty."

Instead, it whispers:

"There is a 70% chance it is the River Tribe, 20% the Wind Tribe, 10% the Shade Tribe."

This is **soft clustering**—gentle probabilities instead of strict boundaries.

Working of GMM

The Probability of a Point Belonging to Each Tribe (Cluster)

For a sound (data point) x_n, GMM calculates:

$$P(z_n = k|x_n) = \pi_k \cdot N(x_n|\mu_k, \Sigma_k) / \sum_{k=1}^{K} \pi_k \cdot N(x_n | \mu_k, \Sigma_k)$$

Meaning:

- $z_n = k$ - which tribe produced the sound
- π_k - how large or influential the tribe is
- $N(x_n | \mu_k, \Sigma_k)$ - how well the sound matches the tribe's characteristics
- The denominator — total credibility of all tribes combined

The forest listens not to one tribe, but to all—each adding its voice to the final probability.

The Overall Likelihood of a Data Point

$$P(x_n) = \sum_{k=1}^{K} \pi_k \cdot N(x_n | \mu_k, \Sigma_k)$$

This expresses the **total chance of hearing that sound**, considering all tribes.

If many tribes can produce that sound, the likelihood is high.

If few can, it is low.

Apeksha asked, "Master, why is this approach so powerful?"

Master replied, "Because GMM captures the truth of life: There is rarely one cause for anything. Most things arise from a mixture of influences."

- A person's personality is a mixture of traits.
- A city's culture is a mixture of communities.
- A voice is a mixture of tones.
- A color is a mixture of frequencies.

GMM does not simplify life—it **honours its complexity**.

A. Example: The Symphony Hall

Master continued, "Imagine an orchestra rehearsal.

You hear a single note.

Is it the violin?

The flute?

The clarinet?

Each instrument contributes to the note with certain probabilities.

GMM listens to that note and says:

- 60% violin
- 30% flute
- 10% clarinet

It recognises that the note is born from a *mixture of voices*, not from a single rigid identity."

Master said, "A Gaussian Mixture Model is more than mathematics.

It is a philosophy of perception.

It teaches us to see the world not as sharply divided, but as beautifully blended.

To understand GMM is to understand the subtle whispers of reality."

Master said, "Let me give you a deeper analogy, Apeksha."

B. Example: The Symphony of Colors in a Sunrise

Imagine you watch a sunrise.

You see:

- Orange
- Yellow
- Light pink
- Faint purple

But the sky does not label them:

- "This is purely orange."
- "This is purely pink."

Instead, every streak of colour is a **mixture**.

Perhaps:

- 40% orange
- 30% yellow
- 20% red
- 10% violet

This is how GMM sees the world.

Every point is: **a mixture of possibilities, not a single definitive identity.**

Each Gaussian is a **colour component**.

The mixing weight π_k is how strongly that colour contributes to the sunrise.

The Gaussian density describes the *shape and spread* of that colour in the sky.

And the sunrise you witness is the **sum of all Gaussians**, just as:

$$P(x_n) = \sum_k \pi_k \cdot N(x_n \mid \mu_k, \Sigma_k)$$

is the sum of all contributions to each data point.

Why GMM is Powerful

Master concluded:

- It adapts to *non-circular* clusters via covariance
- It handles overlapping categories

- It provides probabilities, not rigid assignments
- It uncovers hidden structure beneath apparent randomness
- It forms the foundation of advanced techniques like EM Algorithm, HMMs, and density estimation

"GMM does not ask, 'Which single cluster does this point belong to?'

Instead it asks, 'With what grace and proportion do all hidden sources contribute to the truth we observe?'"

☐ Covariance

Master said, "Apeksha, listen closely. The heart of a Gaussian Mixture Model lies not only in its means but in its covariances.

For it is the covariance that gives each cluster its soul — its posture, its spread, its direction, its uniqueness."

1. Quick Recap — What Covariance Truly Does

In every Gaussian component of a GMM, we have a mean **μ** (the center) and a covariance **Σ** (the shape-shaper).

Σ determines:

- **Shape** — whether the cluster looks stretched, round, tilted, or flat
- **Size** — how wide or narrow the cluster spreads
- **Orientation** — the direction the cluster leans toward

Interpretation via eigenvalues & eigenvectors:

- **Large eigenvalue** → wide spread along that direction
- **Small eigenvalue** → tight compression
- **Non-zero off-diagonal terms** → correlation, causing rotation or tilt

Analogy:

Imagine each Gaussian as a dancer on a stage. The mean μ is where the dancer stands. The covariance Σ is how the dancer moves — wide arcs, sharp turns, gentle circles, or straight lines. The dance style defines the shape of the cluster itself.

2. Four Covariance Types — Intuition, Geometry & Proper Use

A. Full Covariance

What:

Each Gaussian component gets its **own full** Σ_k , a complete D×D covariance matrix.

Geometry:

Any possible ellipse or ellipsoid — different size, shape, and orientation for every cluster.

Flexibility:

Most expressive. Captures correlations and complex patterns.

Cost / Risk:

Highest number of parameters ($O(K \cdot D^2)$) → expensive, data-hungry, prone to overfitting.

Use When:

- Clusters are irregular, oriented differently
- Low- to medium-dimensional data
- You have enough samples per cluster

Insight:

"Full covariance is like allowing every dancer to craft their own choreography — beautiful when you have skilled performers, chaotic when you do not."

B. Tied Covariance

What:

All components **share a single full covariance** Σ.

Geometry:

Clusters differ in location (means) but not in overall shape or orientation.

Flexibility:

Moderate. Better than diagonal; more restrictive than full.

Cost / Risk:

Reduced parameter count; suitable when spreads are similar.

Use When:

- Data suggests uniform noise or uniform variance
- Clusters differ mainly by centre, not behaviour

Insight:

"Tied covariance is like giving many dancers the same set of movements but allowing them to begin at different positions on stage."

C. Diagonal Covariance

What:

Each component has its own diagonal Σ_k (variances only — no correlations).

Geometry:

Axis-aligned ellipses — each dimension scaled differently but no tilt.

Flexibility:

Good balance — captures independent variations, fails when correlations matter.

Cost / Risk:

Efficient: $O(K \cdot D)$ parameters.

Use When:

- High-dimensional data
- Features uncorrelated or pre-decorrelated (PCA/whitening)

Insight:

"Diagonal covariance is like a dancer allowed to stretch differently in each direction but unable to rotate — movements are controlled yet expressive."

D. Spherical Covariance

What:

Each component has a **single variance value** σ^2_k.

Geometry:

Perfect spheres — identical spread in every direction.

Flexibility:
Most restrictive.

Cost / Risk:

Very efficient: O(K) parameters, but rarely fits real-world clusters well.

Use When:

- Baselines
- Very noisy or isotropic data
- Low data, need a simple model

Insight:

"Spherical covariance is like dancers confined to small circular movements. Simple, elegant — yet unable to express complexity."

3. Parameter Scale — Why Covariance Type Matters

Per component:

- **Full:** D(D+1)/2 parameters
- **Tied:** same number as Full, but shared
- **Diagonal:** D
- **Spherical:** 1

Full grows quadratically (O(D^2)), quickly dominating computation.

4. How to Choose

Master said, "Models fail not because they are wrong, but because we choose them without understanding the data's nature."

a) Start simple

Use **diagonal** or **spherical** to establish a baseline.

b) Inspect the data

Plot if dimension ≤ 3, or analyze eigenvectors/eigenvalues.

c) Compare using BIC/AIC

BIC is especially useful — penalizes unnecessary complexity.

d) Preprocess wisely

Standardize features; consider PCA or whitening.

e) Watch your data size

Fewer samples → avoid full covariance.

f) Ensure stability

Use n_init > 1 to avoid poor local maxima.

5. Pitfalls and Remedies

Singular Covariance Matrix

- Increase reg_covar
- Reduce components
- Choose diagonal/tied

Local Optima

- Increase n_init

Overfitting (Full Covariance)

- Compare BIC: if high, step down to tied/diagonal

Strong Feature Correlation

- Use full covariance

  or

- Perform PCA before diagonal/spherical

Master said, "This code demonstrates how different covariance structures shape the behaviour of a Gaussian Mixture Model."

The script begins by loading the Wine dataset and selecting the first two features to keep the visualization simple. The data is standardized using **StandardScaler** so all features contribute fairly to clustering. Four covariance types—**full, tied, diagonal, spherical**—are tested. For each type, a **GaussianMixture** model with three components is created, trained using EM, and evaluated. The code prints how many iterations the algorithm needed to converge and the **BIC score**, helping compare model complexity versus goodness of fit.

All fitted models are stored, and their **covariances_** attribute is examined. This reveals the internal structure of each model: full covariances produce 3 matrices, tied produces one shared matrix, diagonal gives per-component variances, and spherical yields one variance per component.

Thus, this code highlights how covariance choices directly affect model shape, flexibility, and performance.

Example P2 – U2 – D13
GMM Covariance

```
from sklearn import datasets
from sklearn.mixture import GaussianMixture
from sklearn.preprocessing import StandardScaler
import numpy as np

# Load Wine dataset, use first 2 features for visualization
X = datasets.load_wine().data[:, :2]
X = StandardScaler().fit_transform(X)

cov_types = ['full', 'tied', 'diag', 'spherical']
models = {}
for cov in cov_types:
    gmm = GaussianMixture(n_components=3, covariance_type=cov,
                    reg_covar=1e-6, n_init=5, random_state=0)
    gmm.fit(X)
    models[cov] = gmm
    print(cov, 'converged in', gmm.n_iter_, 'iters, BIC=', gmm.bic(X))

# Access covariances_
for cov, gmm in models.items():
    print('---', cov)
    print(gmm.covariances_.shape)
    # e.g. full: (K, D, D); tied: (D, D); diag: (K, D); spherical: (K,)
```

Output:

Output

```
full converged in 12 iters, BIC= 936.8859297668
tied converged in 4 iters, BIC= 989.3034568136236
diag converged in 10 iters, BIC= 927.3713087879365
spherical converged in 8 iters, BIC= 965.0164001812852
--- full
(3, 2, 2)
--- tied
(2, 2)
--- diag
(3, 2)
--- spherical
(3,)
```

Master said, This code demonstrates how different covariance structures influence Gaussian Mixture Models (GMMs) and their geometric interpretation. First, the Wine dataset is loaded and standardized to ensure all features share a common scale. Four GMM variants—full, tied, diagonal, and spherical—are trained using three components each, and their convergence and BIC values are printed for comparison.

Example P2 – U2 – D14

GMM Covariance

```
# =================================
# 1. Import Libraries
# =================================
from sklearn import datasets
from sklearn.mixture import GaussianMixture
from sklearn.preprocessing import StandardScaler
import numpy as np
import matplotlib.pyplot as plt
from matplotlib.patches import Ellipse


# =================================
# 2. Load & Preprocess Data
# =================================
X = datasets.load_wine().data[:, :2]
X = StandardScaler().fit_transform(X)


# =================================
# 3. Fit GMM Models for All Covariance Types
# =================================
cov_types = ['full', 'tied', 'diag', 'spherical']
models = {}

for cov in cov_types:
    gmm = GaussianMixture(
        n_components=3,
        covariance_type=cov,
        reg_covar=1e-6,
        n_init=5,
        random_state=0
    )
    gmm.fit(X)
    models[cov] = gmm
    print(f"{cov} model converged in {gmm.n_iter_} iterations, BIC={gmm.bic(X)}")


# =================================
```

```
# 4. Ellipse Plotting Function
# ================================
def plot_gmm_ellipses(gmm, X, title):
    plt.figure(figsize=(6, 5))
    plt.scatter(X[:, 0], X[:, 1], s=10)

    for i, mean in enumerate(gmm.means_):

        # Select proper covariance matrix for component i
        if gmm.covariance_type == "full":
            cov_matrix = gmm.covariances_[i]

        elif gmm.covariance_type == "tied":
            cov_matrix = gmm.covariances_

        elif gmm.covariance_type == "diag":
            cov_matrix = np.diag(gmm.covariances_[i])

        elif gmm.covariance_type == "spherical":
            cov_matrix = np.eye(X.shape[1]) * gmm.covariances_[i]

        # Eigen decomposition
        eigvals, eigvecs = np.linalg.eigh(cov_matrix)
        order = eigvals.argsort()[::-1]
        eigvals, eigvecs = eigvals[order], eigvecs[:, order]

        angle = np.degrees(np.arctan2(*eigvecs[:, 0][::-1]))
        width, height = 2 * np.sqrt(eigvals)

        ellipse = Ellipse(
            xy=mean,
            width=width,
            height=height,
            angle=angle,
            fill=False,
            linewidth=2
        )

        plt.gca().add_patch(ellipse)

    plt.title(title)
    plt.xlabel("Feature 1")
    plt.ylabel("Feature 2")
    plt.grid(True)
    plt.show()


# ================================
```

```
# 5. Generate Plots for All Models
# ================================
for cov, gmm in models.items():
    plot_gmm_ellipses(gmm, X, f"GMM Ellipses – Covariance Type: {cov}")
```

Output:

```
Output
full model converged in 12 iterations, BIC=936.8859297668
tied model converged in 4 iterations, BIC=989.3034568136236
diag model converged in 10 iterations, BIC=927.3713087879365
spherical model converged in 8 iterations, BIC=965.0164001812852
```

Full and Tied:

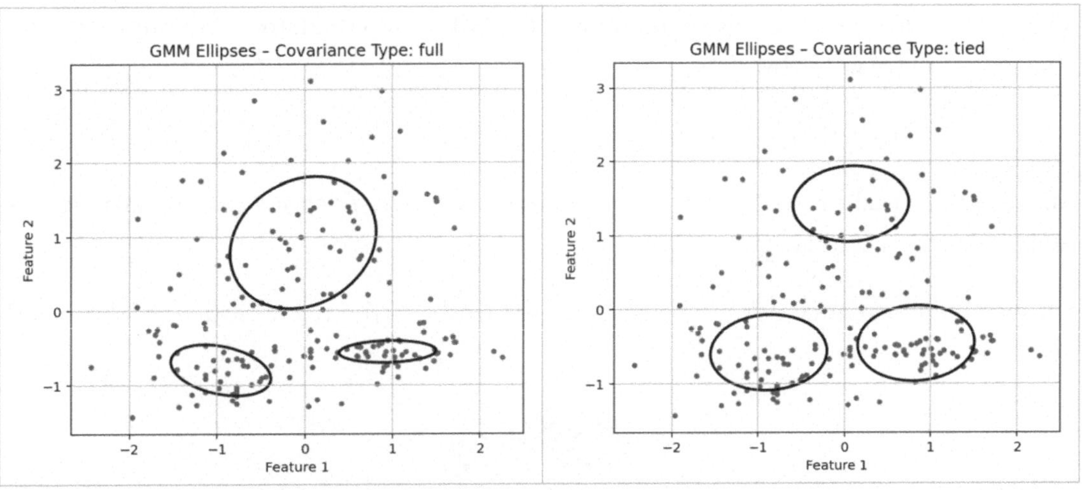

A dedicated function then visualizes each model by plotting covariance ellipses, which show the shape, orientation, and spread of each Gaussian component. Depending on the covariance type, the code extracts the appropriate covariance matrix, performs eigen decomposition to compute ellipse axes and rotation, and overlays these ellipses on a scatter plot of the data.

Diagnol and Spherical

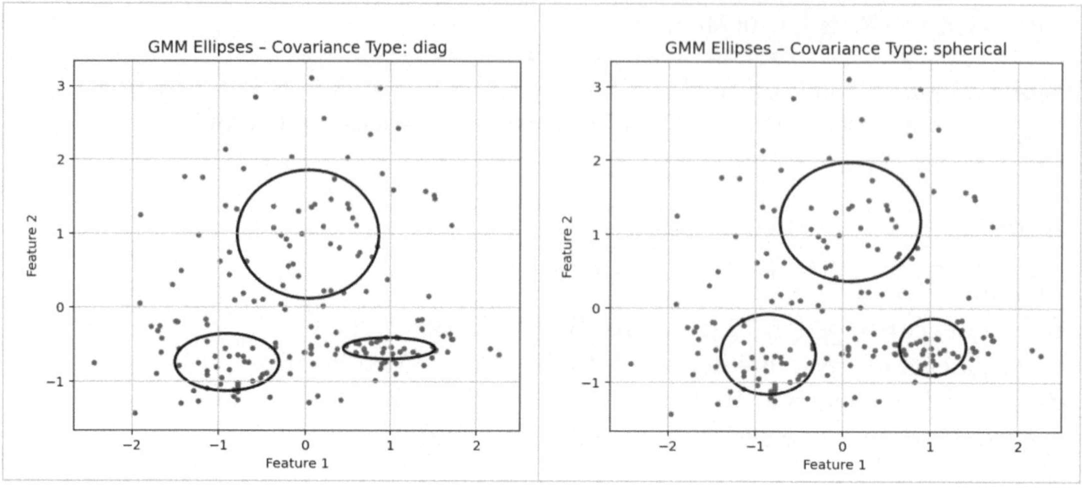

Finally, the script loops through all models and renders their respective ellipse plots. This provides a clear, intuitive understanding of how covariance assumptions alter cluster geometry in GMMs.

Master said, "Full offers freedom, Tied offers discipline, Diagonal offers balance, and Spherical offers simplicity.

Choose the covariance not for beauty, but for truth — the truth hidden in your data's geometry."

PART TWO

DAY SEVEN

Unit 2 - Lesson Six

EM

☐ **Expectation–Maximization (EM)**

Master said, "Sam, the Expectation–Maximization (EM) algorithm is the quiet ritual by which hidden structure reveals itself."

1. What EM seeks to do

EM finds parameter values that **maximize the likelihood** of observed data when the model contains **latent (unobserved) variables**.

Instead of optimizing directly over incomplete-data likelihood (difficult), EM alternates between **estimating the missing data** (softly) and **optimizing parameters** as if those estimates were real.

Analogy:

Imagine reconstructing a faded mosaic made by several hidden artisans.

- **E-step:** estimate each artisan's contribution to each tile (soft credit).
- **M-step:** adjust each artisan's palette and technique to better explain the tiles.

  Repeat until the mosaic and the artisan hypotheses agree.

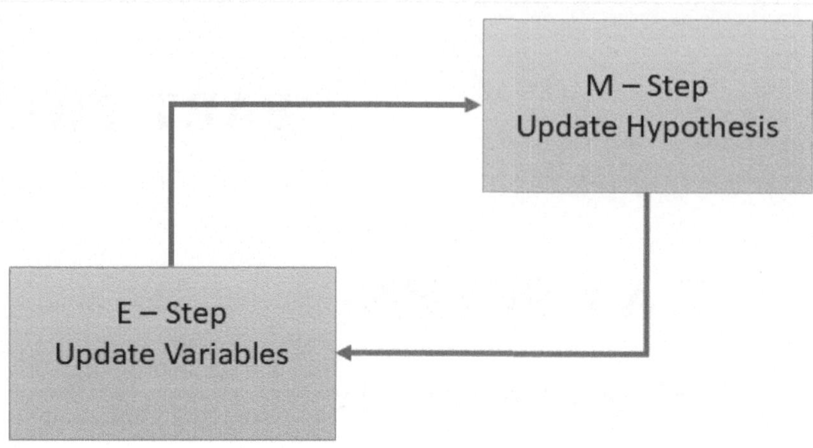

Illustration EM_1: EM

2. EM in the GMM context — mathematical core

Data: $\{x_n\}_{n=1}^{N}$

Latent variables: cluster indicators $z_n \in \{1,\ldots,K\}$.

Parameters: $\Theta = \{\pi_k, \mu_k, \Sigma_k\}_{k=1}^{K}\}$ (weights, means, covariances).

A. E-step (responsibilities)

3. Compute the posterior probability (responsibility) that component k generated x_n:

$$\gamma_{nk} \equiv P(z_n = k | x_n, \Theta^{(t)}) = \pi_k^{(t)} N(x_n | \mu_k^{(t)}, \Sigma_k^t) / \Sigma_{j=1}^{K} \pi_j^{(t)} N(x_n | \mu_j^{(t)}, \Sigma_j^t)$$

Interpretation: soft assignment of points to clusters.

B. M-step (parameter updates)

Compute effective counts $N_k = \sum_n \gamma_{nk}$. Then update:

$$\pi_k^{(t+1)} = N_k/N$$

$$\mu_k^{(t+1)} = \frac{1}{N_k}(\sum_{n=1}^{N} (\gamma_{nk}\, x_n)$$

$$\Sigma_k^{t+1} = \frac{1}{N_k}(\sum_{n=1}^{N} \gamma_{nk}\, (x_n - \mu_k^{(t+1)})\, (x_n - \mu_k^{(t+1)})^T$$

These maximize the expected complete-data log-likelihood given current responsibilities.

C. Log-likelihood monitoring

4. Observed-data log-likelihood:

$$L(\Theta) = \Sigma_{n=1}^{N} \, log \, (\Sigma_{k=1}^{K} \, \pi_k \, N(x_n \,|\, \mu_k, \Sigma_k)$$

EM guarantees $L(\Theta^{(t+1)}) \geq L(\Theta^{(t)})$; monitor this for convergence.

5. Why EM converges (intuition)

EM maximizes a lower bound on L - the **Q-function** (expected complete-data log-likelihood).

E-step constructs the bound (via posterior over latent variables); M-step maximizes the bound with respect to parameters. This coordinate ascent on the lower bound yields monotone improvement until a (usually local) maximum.

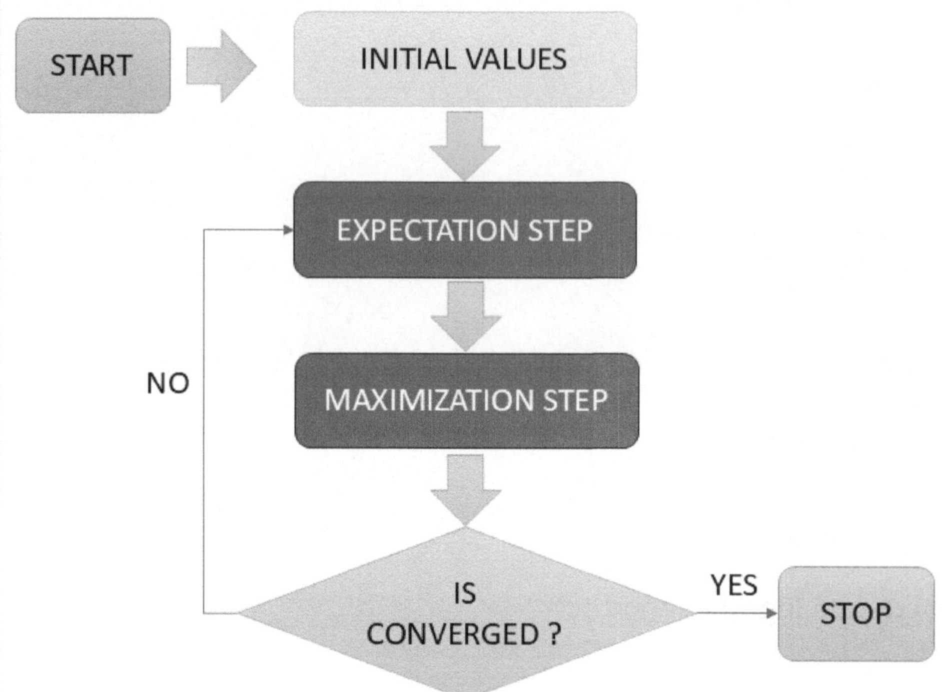

Illustration EM_2: EM

6. Pseudocode

```
Initialize Θ(0) (means, covariances, weights)
for t = 0,1,2,... until convergence:
   # E-step
   for n,k: compute γ_nk = P(z_n=k | x_n, Θ(t))
   # M-step
   for k:
      N_k = sum_n γ_nk
      π_k <- N_k / N
      μ_k <- (1/N_k) * sum_n γ_nk * x_n
      Σ_k <- (1/N_k) * sum_n γ_nk * (x_n-μ_k)(x_n-μ_k)^T
   compute log-likelihood L(Θ(t+1)); stop if improvement < tol
```

7. Practical guidance & diagnostics

Initialization

- Crucial. EM finds *local* maxima. Common choices: k-means centroids, random sub-samples, or multiple random restarts (n_init) and pick the best log-likelihood.

Regularization

- Addreg_covar = I to covariances to avoid singular matrices and numerical instability.

Stopping criteria

- Small relative increase in log-likelihood (e.g., tol=1e-6) or max iterations.
- Also inspect parameter changes and cluster stability.

Model selection

- Use **BIC** or **AIC** for choosing K and covariance type (penalize complexity).
- Visualize clusters, check residuals, or use held-out likelihood.

Scaling & preprocessing

- Standardize features; for diagonal/spherical covariances consider PCA/whitening.

Monitoring

- Plot log-likelihood curve — smooth increase suggests healthy EM; jumps or plateaus might indicate issues.

8. Common pitfalls and remedies

Singularities/component collapse

- A Gaussian may collapse onto a single data point → covariance → 0, likelihood → ∞.
- **Fixes:** reg_covar, remove/merge tiny components, limit responsibilities floor, or use Bayesian priors (MAP/Variational).

Overfitting

- Full covariance + large K can overfit. Use BIC/AIC, tied/diagonal covariances, or increase regularization.

Local optima

- Use k-means init, multiple restarts, and choose the best likelihood.

Slow convergence

- Smart initialization, smaller tol, or use Accelerated EM variants (e.g., EM with conjugate-gradient in M-step) or stochastic/online EM for large datasets.

9. Complexity & scalability

Per EM iteration (full covariance): roughly $O(NKD^2)$ due to Mahalanobis computations and covariance updates.

Diagonal/spherical reduces cost to O(NKD). For very large N, use minibatch/online EM.

10. Variants and extensions

MAP-EM / Bayesian EM

- Place priors on parameters to avoid overfitting; perform Maximum A Posteriori updates.

Variational Inference (VI)

- Approximate Bayesian posteriors; provides model selection and component pruning.

Stochastic / Online EM

- Update parameters with mini-batches for streaming/large-data scenarios.

Robust EM

- Use heavy-tailed components (Student's t) or outlier models to reduce sensitivity to anomalies.

11. Visualization & interpretation

- Plot responsibilities as soft colour blends to see ambiguous points.
- Draw covariance ellipses to inspect shapes (full/tied/diag/spherical).
- Project high-D data via PCA for visualization of cluster structure.

Master said, "EM is humble and iterative: it never claims certainty, only gradual refinement.

Treat it with care: initialize well, regularize, watch the likelihood, and choose model complexity to match your data. Use EM not as a hammer, but as a patient artisan — estimate what is hidden, then refine the machines that made the observations, until the hidden patterns stand revealed."

Master said, This code demonstrates the complete implementation of the Expectation–Maximization (EM) algorithm for estimating a Gaussian Mixture Model with two components. It begins by generating a synthetic dataset from two Gaussian distributions and combines them into a single dataset. Initial guesses are made for the means, standard deviations, and mixing proportions. The EM algorithm then runs for 20 iterations: the **E-step** computes the responsibilities (probabilities of each point belonging to each Gaussian), and the **M-step** updates the parameters based on these responsibilities. The code tracks the log-likelihood to monitor convergence.

Example P2 – U2 – D16

EM

```
import numpy as np
import matplotlib.pyplot as plt
from scipy.stats import norm

# -------------------------------------------
# Step 1: Generate Dataset (Two Gaussian Sources)
# -------------------------------------------

np.random.seed(42)

# True parameters (unknown to EM)
true_mu1, true_sigma1, true_size1 = 0, 1.0, 400
true_mu2, true_sigma2, true_size2 = 5, 1.5, 600

# Sample from two Gaussians
data1 = np.random.normal(true_mu1, true_sigma1, true_size1)
```

```
data2 = np.random.normal(true_mu2, true_sigma2, true_size2)

# Combined dataset
X = np.hstack([data1, data2])


# ------------------------------------------
# Step 2: Initialize Parameters for EM
# ------------------------------------------

# Random initial guesses
mu1, mu2 = -1.0, 4.0
sigma1, sigma2 = 1.2, 2.0
pi1, pi2 = 0.5, 0.5   # mixing proportions

# Store log-likelihood history
log_likelihoods = []

# ------------------------------------------
# Step 3: EM Algorithm
# ------------------------------------------

for epoch in range(20):

    # --------- E-step: Compute responsibilities ----------
    gamma1 = pi1 * norm.pdf(X, mu1, sigma1)
    gamma2 = pi2 * norm.pdf(X, mu2, sigma2)

    # Normalize
    total = gamma1 + gamma2
    gamma1 /= total
    gamma2 /= total

    # --------- M-step: Update parameters ----------
    N1 = gamma1.sum()
    N2 = gamma2.sum()

    # Update means
    mu1 = np.sum(gamma1 * X) / N1
    mu2 = np.sum(gamma2 * X) / N2

    # Update standard deviations
    sigma1 = np.sqrt(np.sum(gamma1 * (X - mu1)**2) / N1)
    sigma2 = np.sqrt(np.sum(gamma2 * (X - mu2)**2) / N2)

    # Update mixing proportions
    pi1 = N1 / len(X)
    pi2 = N2 / len(X)
```

```
    # --------- Compute log-likelihood for monitoring ----------
    ll = np.sum(np.log(pi1 * norm.pdf(X, mu1, sigma1) +
                       pi2 * norm.pdf(X, mu2, sigma2)))
    log_likelihoods.append(ll)

    print(f"Epoch {epoch+1:02d}: Log-likelihood = {ll:.4f}")


# ------------------------------------------
# Step 4: Plot Final Result
# ------------------------------------------

# Plot histogram of data
plt.hist(X, bins=50, density=True, alpha=0.5, label="Data distribution")

# Plot estimated Gaussians
x_vals = np.linspace(min(X), max(X), 500)

estimated_pdf = (pi1 * norm.pdf(x_vals, mu1, sigma1) +
                 pi2 * norm.pdf(x_vals, mu2, sigma2))

plt.plot(x_vals, estimated_pdf, linewidth=2, color='red',
         label="Estimated GMM (EM result)")

plt.title("Final EM Estimated Gaussian Mixture Model")
plt.xlabel("x")
plt.ylabel("Density")
plt.legend()
plt.grid(True)
plt.show()


# ------------------------------------------
# Step 5: Plot Log-Likelihood Curve
# ------------------------------------------

plt.plot(log_likelihoods, marker='o')
plt.title("Log-Likelihood Over EM Iterations")
plt.xlabel("Iteration")
plt.ylabel("Log-Likelihood")
plt.grid(True)
plt.show()
```

Output:

```
Output
```

Epoch 17: Log-likelihood = -2256.5856

Epoch 18: Log-likelihood = -2256.5855

Epoch 19: Log-likelihood = -2256.5855

Epoch 20: Log-likelihood = -2256.5854

Finally, it visualizes both the estimated mixture model over the data distribution and the log-likelihood curve showing the improvement across iterations.

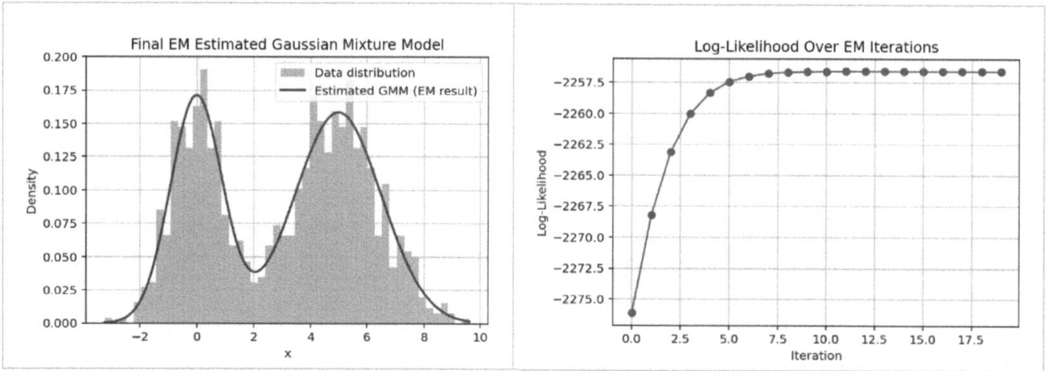

Illustration EM_3 EM_4: EM

Master said, "John, to understand Gaussian Mixture Models, you must first understand the shapes of clusters—because in GMM, clusters are not mere groups of points, but living geometries shaped by probability itself."

☐ Cluster Shapes in Gaussian Mixture Models (GMM)

In GMM, each cluster emerges from an underlying **Gaussian distribution**, and the nature of that distribution profoundly shapes the cluster's geometry.

A. Mean (μ): The Heart of the Cluster

The mean is the gravitational center toward which the points tend.

It is not just a numerical average; it is the **anchor point** of the Gaussian.

Shift the mean, and the whole cluster migrates across the feature space.

Each Gaussian component in a GMM has its own unique mean, allowing clusters to reside in entirely different regions.

B. Covariance (Σ): The Soul that Defines Shape

Unlike K-Means—which assumes every cluster is a perfect sphere—GMM allows clusters to breathe, stretch, rotate, and tilt.

The covariance matrix tells us:

- How wide or narrow the cluster is
- Whether it spreads equally or disproportionately along dimensions
- How variables move together (their co-dependence)
- The orientation (tilt) of the ellipse

Thus, every Gaussian cluster becomes an **ellipse**, not a circle, shaped uniquely by its covariance.

This is the greatest philosophical difference between K-Means and GMM:

K-Means sees clusters as rigid and equal.

GMM sees clusters as organic, adaptive, and inherently probabilistic.

Visual Understanding

Imagine two sets of data:

- One Gaussian wide and horizontal
- Another narrow and tilted diagonally

Scatter plots reveal clusters around their means, but **the true personality of each cluster** emerges through:

- KDE contours that trace smooth probability boundaries

- Elliptical shapes of the Gaussian distributions

This visualization shows how GMMs can gracefully fit real-world data that rarely forms neat, spherical groups.

Where GMM Excels (Use-Cases)

Clustering:

In marketing, biology, or customer segmentation, real data rarely forms round clusters. GMM captures natural variation.

Anomaly Detection:

Points with low likelihood under the mixture distribution are anomalies—useful in fraud detection or medical alert systems.

Image Segmentation:

GMM can distinguish textures, tissues, or regions in images—vital in medical scans and satellite imaging.

Density Estimation:

When we need a smooth probabilistic model for generative tasks, GMM serves as a flexible distribution estimator.

Advantages of GMM

- **Flexible Cluster Shapes**

  Elliptical, overlapping, rotated, unequal—GMM models reality, not idealised symmetry.

- **Soft Assignments**

  Every point gets probabilities instead of strict labels, reflecting uncertainty realistically.

- **Handles Missing Data**

The EM algorithm naturally accommodates incomplete observations.

- **Interpretability**

  Means, covariances, and mixing weights offer deep insights into the data's structure.

Limitations of GMM

- **Sensitive to Initialization**

  Poor starting values may trap EM in local minima.

- **Computationally Heavy**

  High-dimensional covariance estimation is expensive.

- **Assumes Gaussian Shape**

  If clusters are non-Gaussian (spiral, crescent), GMM struggles.

- **Must Predefine Number of Clusters**

  Unlike density-based methods, GMM requires setting "K" upfront.

Master said, "John, K-Means draws circles. GMM paints ellipses.

But more importantly—GMM does not merely assign points;

it *believes* in them with probability.

And that is why it understands data more deeply."

☐ **Variational Bayes**

Master said, "Apeksha — when the world is noisy, and the truth hides in many small voices, Variational Bayesian Inference gives us a wise, probabilistic way to listen."

Why Variational Bayes for GMM?

A classical GMM fits parameters by maximum likelihood (EM). EM finds point estimates and needs the user to firmly commit to the number of components. **Variational Bayesian (VB) inference** treats parameters as *random variables with priors*, and computes an approximate posterior over them. This gives:

- **Uncertainty estimates** for parameters (means, covariances, mixture weights).
- **Automatic complexity control**: with a generous upper bound on components, VB often *prunes* unnecessary components (Automatic Relevance Determination).
- **Regularization via priors**, reducing overfitting when data are limited.

Analogy: instead of forcing each artist to claim a stroke (hard assignment), we let each artist maintain a *confidence distribution* over how much they contributed. Over time, artists with near-zero confidence are quietly ignored.

Core concepts

The probabilistic model

We place priors on mixture parameters, for example:

- A Dirichlet prior (or Dirichlet Process-like prior) on mixing weights π.
- Normal-Wishart (or Normal-Inverse-Wishart) priors on component means μ_k and covariances Σ_k.

The posterior $p(\pi, \mu, \Sigma, Z \mid X)$ is intractable. Variational Bayes approximates it with a factorized variational distribution (mean-field):

$$q(\pi,\mu,\Sigma,Z) \approx q(\pi) \prod_k q(\mu_k, \Sigma_k) \prod_k q(z_n)$$

We then minimize the KL divergence $KL(q \parallel p)$, which is equivalent to maximizing the Evidence Lower BOund (ELBO):

$$\text{ELBO}(q) = E_q[\log p(X,Z,\pi,\mu,\Sigma)] - E_q[\log q(\pi,\mu,\Sigma,Z)]$$

EM performs coordinate ascent on parameters; VB performs coordinate ascent on *distributions* (the factors q(·). Updates are analytic for conjugate priors (hence closed-form variational updates for GMM with conjugate priors).

Weight sparsity (ARD / Dirichlet process style)

If you choose a Dirichlet-process-like prior (in sklearn:

weight_concentration_prior_type='dirichlet_process' with small

weight_concentration_prior), the posterior tends to concentrate mass on a few components — unused components get tiny expected weights. This is how VB **automatically selects** the effective number of clusters.

Intuition: the learning story

- **E-like step:** compute expected cluster responsibilities under the current variational posterior over parameters. Responsibilities are softer (distributions over assignments).
- **M-like step:** update the posterior factors for parameters (weights, means, covariances) based on responsibilities. These updates incorporate prior strength (regularization).

Thus VB blends prior knowledge and observed data to produce a tempered posterior belief.

Practical recipe & sklearn implementation notes

Key sklearn class

```
from sklearn.mixture import BayesianGaussianMixture
```

Important parameters

- n_components: upper bound on components (choose generously, VB will prune).

- covariance_type: 'full', 'tied', 'diag', 'spherical'.
- weight_concentration_prior_type: 'dirichlet_distribution' (finite Dirichlet) or 'dirichlet_process' (encourages sparsity).
- weight_concentration_prior: lower values (≪1) encourage sparsity (fewer active components); larger values lead to more uniform weights.
- max_iter, tol, n_init, init_params: same pragmatics as EM.
- mean_precision_prior, mean_prior, degrees_of_freedom_prior, covariance_prior: advanced priors if you want stronger regularization.

Example:

Master said, "This code implements Variational Bayesian Gaussian Mixture Modeling (VB-GMM) to cluster credit-card transaction data. It begins by importing essential libraries for preprocessing, dimensionality reduction, clustering, and visualization. The creditcard.csv dataset is loaded and cleaned by removing non-informative features such as Time, Amount, and the target label Class, since this is an unsupervised task. The remaining features are standardized using StandardScaler to ensure all variables contribute equally. PCA reduces the data to two dimensions to allow meaningful visualization.

A Variational Bayesian Gaussian Mixture model is then fitted to the scaled data. Unlike traditional GMM, this method automatically determines the effective number of clusters using a Dirichlet Process prior, making it robust for high-dimensional datasets. The model assigns cluster labels and identifies active components. Finally, the code visualizes the clusters in PCA space, highlights cluster centers, and prints key VB-GMM parameters for interpretation.

Example P2 – U2 – D17

Variational Bayes

```
# ---------------------------------------------------------
# Step 1: Import Necessary Libraries
# ---------------------------------------------------------
import pandas as pd
import numpy as np
from sklearn.preprocessing import StandardScaler
```

```
from sklearn.decomposition import PCA
from sklearn.mixture import BayesianGaussianMixture
import matplotlib.pyplot as plt

# -----------------------------------------------------------
# Step 2: Load the Dataset (Download from Kaggle)
# -----------------------------------------------------------
# Make sure creditcard.csv is in your working directory
X_raw = pd.read_csv("C:\\Users\\User\\mraj4\\Documents\\data\\creditcard.csv")
print("Dataset Loaded:", X_raw.shape)

# -----------------------------------------------------------
# Step 3: Data Cleaning
# -----------------------------------------------------------

# Drop unnecessary columns for clustering
# Keeping only features V1..V28
X = X_raw.drop(['Time', 'Amount'], axis=1)

# Remove target column (Unsupervised Clustering)
if 'Class' in X.columns:
    X = X.drop('Class', axis=1)

print("Data after cleaning:", X.shape)

# -----------------------------------------------------------
# Step 4: Preprocessing (Standard Scaling)
# -----------------------------------------------------------
scaler = StandardScaler()
X_scaled = scaler.fit_transform(X)

# -----------------------------------------------------------
# Step 5: Dimensionality Reduction for Visualization
# -----------------------------------------------------------
pca = PCA(n_components=2)
X_2D = pca.fit_transform(X_scaled)

# -----------------------------------------------------------
# Step 6: Variational Bayesian Gaussian Mixture Model
# -----------------------------------------------------------

vbgmm = BayesianGaussianMixture(
    n_components=10,   # VB will automatically shrink irrelevant clusters
    covariance_type='full',  # full covariance structure
    weight_concentration_prior_type='dirichlet_process',  # DP Prior
    max_iter=500,
    random_state=42
)
```

```
vbgmm.fit(X_scaled)

# Predict labels
labels = vbgmm.predict(X_scaled)

# Number of effective clusters
unique_clusters = np.unique(labels)
print("Clusters found:", len(unique_clusters))

# ---------------------------------------------------------
# Step 7: Visualize Clustering Results
# ---------------------------------------------------------
plt.figure(figsize=(10, 6))
plt.scatter(X_2D[:, 0], X_2D[:, 1], c=labels, cmap='viridis', s=3)
plt.title("Variational Bayesian GMM Clustering (PCA 2D View)")
plt.xlabel("PC1")
plt.ylabel("PC2")
plt.colorbar(label="Cluster ID")
plt.grid(True)
plt.show()

# ---------------------------------------------------------
# Step 8: Plot Component Means in PCA Space
# ---------------------------------------------------------
means_2D = pca.transform(vbgmm.means_)

plt.figure(figsize=(10, 6))
plt.scatter(X_2D[:, 0], X_2D[:, 1], c=labels, cmap='viridis', s=3, alpha=0.3)
plt.scatter(means_2D[:, 0], means_2D[:, 1],
        color='red', s=200, marker='X', label='Cluster Means')
plt.title("Cluster Means (VB-GMM in PCA space)")
plt.xlabel("PC1")
plt.ylabel("PC2")
plt.legend()
plt.grid(True)
plt.show()

# ---------------------------------------------------------
# Step 9: Print Model Parameters (Optional for Interpretation)
# ---------------------------------------------------------
print("\n=== VB-GMM Model Parameters ===")
print("Effective Cluster Weights:", vbgmm.weights_)
print("\nMeans Shape:", vbgmm.means_.shape)
print("\nCovariance Type:", vbgmm.covariance_type)
```

Output:

```
Output
Dataset Loaded: (284807, 31)
Data after cleaning: (284807, 28)
Clusters found: 10
=== VB-GMM Model Parameters ===
Effective Cluster Weights: [0.07786652 0.08962775 0.02914778 0.07270998 0.11741061 0.03043584
 0.20018851 0.03386031 0.05060739 0.29814531]
Means Shape: (10, 28)
Covariance Type: full
```

Visualization and diagnostics

Use PCA or t-SNE to reduce dimensionality for plotting means and contours.

Inspect bgmm.weights_, bgmm.means_, bgmm.covariances_, and bgmm.lower_bound_ (ELBO).

Components with near-zero weights_ are effectively pruned.

When to use VB-GMM (use-cases & benefits)

- **Unknown number of clusters**: set a generous n_components and let VB prune.
- **Small samples / heavy regularization needed**: priors stabilize estimates.
- **Need uncertainty quantification**: VB gives posterior distributions (approximate) not just point estimates.
- **Automatic complexity control**: useful as a Bayesian alternative to choosing K via cross-validation.

Comparisons: VB vs EM (MLE-GMM)

- **VB** produces posterior distributions and can prune components; **EM** finds point estimates and can overfit.

- **VB** is more robust with priors and small data; **EM** is often faster per iteration and simpler.
- **Both** rely on iterative coordinate ascent and can get stuck in local optima; use multiple inits.

Pitfalls, cautions & practical tips

- Initialization matters: use init_params='kmeans' or multiple n_init.
- Priors matter: overly strong priors bias results; too weak priors mimic EM. Tune weight_concentration_prior.
- Convergence: monitor lower_bound_ (ELBO) for monotone increase. If it stalls or oscillates, try different initialization or smaller learning goals.
- Computation: VB is heavier than EM; limit n_components and prefer diagonal/tied covariances in high-D.
- Interpretation: VB's 'effective' number of components depends on prior choices; report both n_components and the number of components with significant weight.

Extended ideas & variants

- Variational Bayes with full Dirichlet Process GMM (infinite mixtures) — conceptually elegant; sklearn's dirichlet_process option approximates this behavior.
- Hierarchical priors or informative priors for domain knowledge (e.g., known cluster centers).
- Stochastic Variational Inference (SVI) for large-scale datasets (mini-batches).

Practical checklist before running VB-GMM

- Standardize features (StandardScaler).

- If D is large, reduce it with PCA to a few principal components for modeling/visualization.
- Choose n_components generously but not absurdly large (e.g., 10–50).
- Start with weight_concentration_prior_type='dirichlet_process' and weight_concentration_prior ≈ 0.1.
- Use n_init≥3, max_iter≥200, watch lower_bound_.
- Inspect weights_ and prune components with tiny mass.
- Visualize results and run sensitivity checks (vary priors).

Master said, "If EM is a committee choosing a single leader for each task, Variational Bayes is a council that keeps a distribution of trusted advisors — measuring not only who leads, but how confident we are that they belong. It lets weak voices fade, and strong ones persist — and tells you how certain it is of every whisper."

PART TWO

DAY SEVEN

Unit 2 - Lesson Six

DPPMs

☐ Dirichlet

Master said, "Sam, the Expectation–Maximization (EM) algorithm is the quiet ritual by which hidden structure reveals itself."

Master said, "Apeksha, some truths cannot be forced into fixed boxes. They must be allowed to reveal themselves. That is the spirit of the Dirichlet Process and its mixtures."

Big idea — flexible clustering without fixing K

A **Dirichlet Process Mixture Model (DPMM)** is a Bayesian, nonparametric extension of mixture models (e.g., Gaussian Mixtures) that **lets the data decide how many clusters are needed**. Instead of choosing a fixed number of components K, DPMM places a prior over infinitely many components, but only a finite number are used for any finite dataset. The model grows in complexity with the data.

Analogy: imagine a market with infinitely many stalls. Customers arrive and choose stalls — popular stalls get more customers, and new stalls can appear when needed. Over time, the market's active stalls reflect real demand. DPMM is that market.

Core ingredients

- **Base distribution G0** — prior over component parameters (e.g., mean & covariance for Gaussians). It is the *template* for new clusters.

- **Concentration parameter α** - controls the tendency to create new clusters (higher α → more clusters).
- **Dirichlet Process DP(α, G_0)** - a distribution over distributions; draws from it are discrete with probability mass on countably many atoms (cluster parameters).

Two constructive views

Stick-Breaking Construction (Sethuraman)

Generate mixture weights $\{\pi_k\}$:

- Draw vk∼Beta(1, α)
- Let π1=v1, π2=v2(1−v1), π3=v3(1−v1) (1−v2), etc.

  Each component k gets a parameter $\theta_k \sim G_0$. The mixture is $\sum_{k=1}^{\infty} \pi_k \delta \theta_k$.

  This shows explicit weights summing to 1, produced by successive "stick breaks".

Chinese Restaurant Process (CRP) — predictive view

Imagine customers (data points) enter a restaurant with infinite tables (clusters). Customer nnn sits at:

- existing table k with probability proportional to n_k (current customers there), or
- a new table with probability proportional to α.

Formally, for data point i:

$$P(z_i = k | z_{-i}) \propto \begin{cases} n_k & \text{existing cluster} \\ \alpha & \text{new cluster} \end{cases}$$

This gives a simple, exchangeable predictive rule that naturally favours rich-get-richer behaviour.

DPMM as a mixture model — how it generalises GMM

Instead of a finite mixture $\sum_{k=1}^{K} f(x|\theta_k)$, DPMM uses an (infinite) random measure $G \sim DP(\alpha, G_0)$ and observations $x_n \sim \int f(x|\theta)\, dG(\theta)$. Practically, only a finite set of θ_k (clusters) receives data.

How inference works (algorithms)

a) Gibbs sampling (collapsed or conditional)

- **Collapsed Gibbs (Polya urn/CRP):** integrate out G and sample cluster assignments z_i directly using the CRP predictive probabilities multiplied by the likelihood of data under cluster. When assigning to a new cluster, draw its parameter from G_0. Repeat until mixing.
- **Conditional Gibbs (stick-breaking):** explicitly represent weights π_k and parameters θ_k, sample conditional on them.

b) Variational Inference

- Truncate the infinite mixture at large Ktrunc (truncated stick-breaking) and optimize variational distributions for weights and assignments. Faster and scalable, but requires a truncation choice.

c) Sequential / SMC / MAP approximations

- Sequential Monte Carlo or MAP-based approximations exist for streaming or large data.

Assignment probabilities (intuition & formula)

When considering a point x_i, the posterior probability of joining the existing cluster k is proportional to:

$$P(z_i = k|z_{-i}, X) \propto n_{k,-i}\, p(x_i|X_{k,-i})$$

For a new cluster:

$$P(z_i = new|z_{-i}, X) \propto \alpha \int p(x_i|\theta)\, dG_0(\theta)$$

where $p(x_i | X_{k,-i})$ is the predictive (marginal) likelihood given cluster k's data; for conjugate priors, this has a closed form.

Role of the concentration parameter α

- **Small α:** few clusters; data tends to clump into larger groups.
- **Large α:** many small clusters; new clusters are easier to form.

  One usually places a hyperprior on α (e.g., Gamma) and infers it, giving adaptive cluster complexity.

Base distribution G_0 matters

G_0 encodes prior belief about cluster parameters (e.g., Normal–Inverse-Wishart for Gaussian components). If G_0 is broad, new clusters are varied; if narrow, new clusters are similar to the prior center.

Practical recipe & tips

- **Conjugacy:** Choose conjugate priors (e.g., Normal–Inverse-Wishart for Gaussian likelihood) so predictive distributions and Gibbs updates are closed-form — vastly simpler and faster.
- **Initialization:** random or k-means seeding helps mixing.
- **Truncation for VI:** choose a truncation level larger than the expected number of clusters. Monitor active components.
- **Hyperpriors:** place a hyperprior on α to let data determine richness.
- **Scaling:** DPMMs scale well conceptually, but naive Gibbs can be slow for large N; use minibatch VI or collapsed samplers with clever data structures.
- **Diagnostics:** trace number of clusters, posterior of α, cluster sizes, and predictive likelihood.

Advantages & Applications

Advantages

- Automatically infers the number of clusters.
- Principled Bayesian uncertainty quantification.
- Rich, flexible clustering adapts with data size.

Applications

- Topic modeling (mixture of topics; e.g., HDP for hierarchical topics)
- Genomics (discovering cell types)
- Anomaly detection (small clusters)
- Time series segmentation (with extensions)
- Clustering when the natural number of groups is unknown

Limitations & pitfalls

- **Computational cost:** MCMC may be slow on large datasets.
- **Sensitivity to priors:** G_0 and α influence results; use sensible defaults or infer hyperparameters.
- **Label switching:** as with other mixtures, component labels are arbitrary — use predictive checks or cluster matching for interpretation.
- **Over-fragmentation:** overly flexible priors (very large α) can produce many tiny clusters; guard with hyperpriors or model checks.
- **Non-Gaussian clusters:** choose an appropriate likelihood (mixture of t-distributions, kernels) if Gaussian is inadequate.

Master said, "Think of data as arriving in a library of stories. The Dirichlet Process hands you an infinite shelf. When a new manuscript arrives, the librarian either places it on an existing shelf (if it fits the theme) or creates a new shelf. Popular shelves grow; rare tales get their own niche. Over time, the library's layout mirrors the world's diversity."

Example P2 – U2 – D18

DPMM

```
import os
import numpy as np
import pandas as pd
import matplotlib.pyplot as plt
from sklearn.preprocessing import StandardScaler
from sklearn.decomposition import PCA
from sklearn.mixture import BayesianGaussianMixture

# ----------------------------------------------------------
# Step 1: Load dataset from user-provided path
# ----------------------------------------------------------

csv_path = r"C:\Users\User\mraj4\Documents\data\Mall_Customers.csv"

def load_mall_dataset():
    if os.path.exists(csv_path):
        print(f"Loading dataset from: {csv_path}")
        return pd.read_csv(csv_path)
    else:
        print(f"File NOT FOUND at: {csv_path}")
        print("Generating synthetic dataset instead...\n")
        return generate_synthetic_mall()

def generate_synthetic_mall(seed=42, n=400):
    """Generate synthetic mall-customer-like dataset."""
    rng = np.random.RandomState(seed)
    segments = []
    segments.append(rng.normal(loc=[25, 30, 70], scale=[4, 6, 8], size=(int(n*0.25),3)))
    segments.append(rng.normal(loc=[45, 60, 40], scale=[6, 8, 10], size=(int(n*0.25),3)))
    segments.append(rng.normal(loc=[35, 85, 20], scale=[5, 7, 6], size=(int(n*0.25),3)))
    segments.append(rng.normal(loc=[55, 40, 50], scale=[5, 6, 9], size=(n -
3*int(n*0.25),3)))

    data = np.vstack(segments)
    df = pd.DataFrame(data, columns=["Age","Annual Income (k$)","Spending Score (1-
100)"])

    df["Age"] = df["Age"].clip(18, 70).round().astype(int)
    df["Annual Income (k$)"] = df["Annual Income (k$)"].clip(10, 200).round(1)
    df["Spending Score (1-100)"] = df["Spending Score (1-100)"].clip(1,
100).round().astype(int)

    print("Synthetic dataset created.")
    return df
```

```
df = load_mall_dataset()

print("Dataset shape:", df.shape)
print("Columns:", list(df.columns))

# ------------------------------------------------------------
# Step 2: Select features
# ------------------------------------------------------------

preferred_cols = ["Age", "Annual Income (k$)", "Spending Score (1-100)"]
available = [c for c in preferred_cols if c in df.columns]

if len(available) < 2:
    numeric = df.select_dtypes(include=[np.number]).columns.tolist()
    numeric = [c for c in numeric if "id" not in c.lower()]
    available = numeric[:3]
    print("Using fallback numeric columns:", available)
else:
    print("Using features:", available)

X = df[available].values

# ------------------------------------------------------------
# Step 3: Preprocess & PCA (2D)
# ------------------------------------------------------------

scaler = StandardScaler()
X_scaled = scaler.fit_transform(X)

pca = PCA(n_components=2, random_state=0)
X_2d = pca.fit_transform(X_scaled)

# ------------------------------------------------------------
# Step 4: Fit the Dirichlet Process Mixture Model
# ------------------------------------------------------------

bgmm = BayesianGaussianMixture(
    n_components=12,
    covariance_type='full',
    weight_concentration_prior_type='dirichlet_process',
    weight_concentration_prior=0.5,
    max_iter=500,
    n_init=5,
    random_state=0
)

bgmm.fit(X_scaled)
labels = bgmm.predict(X_scaled)
```

```
weights = bgmm.weights_
active = np.sum(weights > 1e-3)

print(f"\nActive Clusters (weight > 0.001): {active}")
print("Top Component Weights:", np.round(np.sort(weights)[-6:], 4))

# -----------------------------------------------------------
# Step 5: Visualization
# -----------------------------------------------------------

plt.figure(figsize=(10, 6))
scatter = plt.scatter(X_2d[:,0], X_2d[:,1], c=labels, cmap='tab10', s=20, alpha=0.7)
plt.title("DPMM Clustering — Mall Customers (PCA 2D)")
plt.xlabel("PC1")
plt.ylabel("PC2")
plt.grid(alpha=0.3)
plt.colorbar(scatter, label="Cluster ID")
plt.show()

# Plot cluster means
means_scaled = scaler.transform(bgmm.means_)
means_2d = pca.transform(means_scaled)

plt.figure(figsize=(10, 6))
plt.scatter(X_2d[:,0], X_2d[:,1], c=labels, s=20, cmap='tab10', alpha=0.3)

for i, (m, w) in enumerate(zip(means_2d, weights)):
    if w < 1e-3:
        continue
    plt.scatter(m[0], m[1], marker='X', s=250*np.sqrt(w), edgecolor='black',
            linewidth=1.2, label=f"Cluster {i} (w={w:.3f})")

plt.title("Cluster Means (Only Active Clusters)")
plt.xlabel("PC1")
plt.ylabel("PC2")
plt.legend(bbox_to_anchor=(1.05, 1), loc='upper left')
plt.grid(alpha=0.3)
plt.show()

# -----------------------------------------------------------
# Optional: Print Cluster Counts
# -----------------------------------------------------------

cluster_ids, counts = np.unique(labels, return_counts=True)
print("\nCluster Distribution:")
print(pd.DataFrame({"Cluster": cluster_ids, "Count": counts}))
```

Master said, This program demonstrates how to apply a Dirichlet Process Mixture Model (DPMM) using the Bayesian Gaussian Mixture approach from scikit-learn for clustering mall customer data. The code begins by importing essential libraries for data handling, preprocessing, visualization, and modeling. It attempts to load the dataset from a specified file path. If the file is not found, it automatically generates a synthetic dataset resembling mall customer profiles, ensuring the workflow continues smoothly.

Next, the script selects key customer features such as Age, Annual Income, and Spending Score, or falls back to available numerical columns if necessary. The selected data is standardized using StandardScaler to prepare it for modeling. Dimensionality reduction is then performed using PCA, projecting the data into two components to enable easier visualization of clustering patterns.

The core of the program fits a Bayesian Gaussian Mixture Model using a Dirichlet process prior, allowing the model to automatically infer the number of meaningful clusters without manual specification. After training, cluster labels and component weights are extracted to determine active clusters. Finally, the results are visualized: first the clusters in PCA space, then the cluster centers represented by weighted markers. A detailed cluster count summary is also provided for interpretation.

Output
Dataset shape: (200, 5) Columns: ['CustomerID', 'Genre', 'Age', 'Annual Income (k$)', 'Spending Score (1-100)'] Using features: ['Age', 'Annual Income (k$)', 'Spending Score (1-100)'] Active Clusters (weight > 0.001): 9 Top Component Weights: [0.1024 0.1247 0.1315 0.1428 0.1996 0.2461]

Collapsed Gibbs steps for the conjugate Gaussian case

1. Remove data point i from its cluster, decrement counts.
2. For each existing cluster k, compute: $w_k = n_{k,-i} \cdot p(x_i | X_{k,-i})$.
3. For a new cluster: $w_{new} = \alpha \cdot p(x_i | G_0)$.
4. Normalize w's → sample new assignment for z_i.
5. If assigned to a new cluster, sample its parameter θ_{new} from the posterior given x_i.

6. Repeat for many sweeps, optionally resampling α.

Master said, "DPMMs teach humility: do not force a fixed structure on nature. Let models grow where needed, shrink where redundant, and always keep a prior as a gentle guide. Combine conjugacy for tractability, hyperpriors for adaptivity, and diagnostics for wisdom — then let the data speak."

Applications of DPMMs

- **Customer Segmentation:**

  Automatically discover natural customer groups without pre-defining how many clusters should exist, making it ideal for evolving markets.

- **Topic Modeling:**

  Identify latent topics in text corpora when the number of underlying themes is unknown or varies across datasets.

- **Image Segmentation:**

  Partition images into meaningful regions for tasks such as medical imaging, object detection, and scene understanding.

- **Speaker Clustering:**

  Distinguish between multiple speakers in audio recordings, even when the number of speakers is not known beforehand.

- **Bioinformatics:**

  Cluster genes, proteins, or single cells where biological structures are complex and the number of groups cannot be predetermined.

Summary:

Foundations of Probabilistic Models

Part Two introduces the essential principles of probabilistic modeling—approaches that embrace uncertainty and variability as core elements of intelligent decision-making. We began with an overview of **probabilistic models**, distinguishing between **generative models**, which learn how data is produced, and **discriminative models**, which focus directly on predicting outcomes. Foundational estimation techniques such as **Maximum Likelihood Estimation (MLE)** and **Maximum A Posteriori (MAP)** were discussed, setting the stage for a deeper understanding.

A central focus of the unit was **Naive Bayes**, a fast and elegant algorithm grounded in **Bayes' theorem**. We reviewed the conditional independence assumption, which simplifies probability computation while retaining strong predictive power. The major variants—**Gaussian**, **Multinomial**, and **Bernoulli**—were examined in relation to the types of data they model. Key statistical ideas such as probability density functions, likelihood, and normal distributions were explored to support practical application.

We studied **Multinomial Naive Bayes** in depth, especially in the context of **Natural Language Processing (NLP)**. Steps such as data preprocessing, tokenization, and feature extraction were explained to show how raw text is transformed into model-ready representations.

The unit then introduced **Gaussian Process Classification (GPC)**, a non-parametric Bayesian framework known for modelling uncertainty explicitly. Its flexibility and ability to provide confidence estimates make it particularly valuable in sensitive decision-making environments.

We continued with classical probabilistic classifiers—**LDA**, **QDA**, and **GDA**—highlighting how different covariance assumptions influence decision boundaries.

Next, we explored **Bayesian Belief Networks (BBNs)**, using directed acyclic graphs to represent conditional dependencies. Concepts such as conditional and joint probabilities were demonstrated as the mathematical backbone of inference in BBNs.

Sequential data modeling was introduced through **Hidden Markov Models (HMMs)**, covering their components and essential algorithms including Forward-Backward, Baum-Welch, and Viterbi.

Finally, we examined **Gaussian Mixture Models (GMMs)**, covariance structures, and the **Expectation–Maximization (EM)** algorithm. Advanced Bayesian clustering methods—**Variational Bayes** and the **Dirichlet Process Mixture Model (DPMM)**—showcased how models can infer the number of clusters automatically.

Together, these topics build a strong and practical foundation in probabilistic reasoning and machine learning.

What Next:

The unit provides a comprehensive introduction to time series analysis and visualization, exploring techniques for analysing and interpreting time-dependent data. It covers the types of time series, trends, seasonality, and methods for visualising data, such as seasonal and box plots. The unit details decomposing time series into components and differentiating between multiplicative and additive models. It addresses handling missing values, stationarity concepts, and tests for stationarity using ADF and KPSS tests. Advanced topics included ARIMA, SARIMA, and SARIMAX models, along with accuracy metrics like MAPE, MAE, and RMSE. Key tests for time series analysis, including the ADF test, Granger Causality Test, and cointegration tests, were also discussed, providing a solid foundation for effective time series analysis and forecasting.

P2-U2-L1-6 - Practice Question

1. What is Naive Bayes, and how is it rooted in Bayes' theorem?
2. Explain the conditional independence assumption in Naive Bayes and its role in probability computations.
3. How does Bayes' theorem combine prior knowledge with new evidence for predictions?
4. What are the different variants of Naive Bayes, and how are they tailored for specific data types?
5. Why are statistical concepts like normal distribution, probability density function, likelihood, and maximum likelihood estimation essential for understanding Naive Bayes?
6. Describe Multinomial Naive Bayes and its effectiveness in text classification tasks in NLP.
7. Outline the steps involved in Natural Language Processing (NLP) and their significance in text analysis.
8. What is Gaussian Process Classification (GPC), and what distinguishes it from other classification models?
9. How does GPC quantify uncertainty in predictions, and why is this valuable in real-world applications?
10. Explain the difference between Linear Discriminant Analysis (LDA) and Quadratic Discriminant Analysis (QDA), highlighting their respective use cases.
11. What is Generalized Discriminant Analysis (GDA), and how does it extend LDA to handle non-linear relationships?
12. Compare Principal Component Analysis (PCA) and Linear Discriminant Analysis (LDA) in terms of their objectives and methodologies.

13. How does PCA reduce dimensionality, and what are its limitations compared to LDA?
14. Define Bayesian Belief Networks (BBNs) and explain their representation using directed acyclic graphs (DAGs).
15. Discuss the significance of conditional and joint probabilities in Bayesian Belief Networks, and how they contribute to effective probabilistic modelling.

PART THREE

DATA

Time Series

"Time series data is the heartbeat of a system—it doesn't just tell you what happened, it shows how life unfolds moment by moment."

– Shree Shambav

PART THREE

DAY EIGHT

Unit 3 - Lesson One

Unfolding Time

Master said, "Nikash, Data mining encompasses the extraction of knowledge from vast datasets, representing the convergence of science, art, and technology…"

A single guiding metaphor

Data mining is like **listening to three orchestra sections** that together play the music of a system:

- **Sequence Data** is the *melody line* — order matters.
- **Graphs** are the *score of interactions* between instruments — who influences whom.
- **Network mining** is the *acoustics and propagation* — how sound (information) travels, echoes, and amplifies.

Each section requires different listening skills, notation, and interpretation.

Sequence Data — anatomy, intuition, and practice

Sequence data are ordered records. The crucial question is: *what does the order represent?* That answer splits the category into the three you mentioned.

1. Time-series (regularly sampled numeric sequences)

Essence: A scalar or vector value measured at regular timestamps. **Common tasks:** forecasting, anomaly detection, decomposition, and change-point detection.

Mathematical intuition: Many time-series models view the current value as a function of past values + noise. ARIMA(p,d,q) formalizes this:

- AR (p): $x_t=\phi_1 x_{t-1}+\cdots+\phi_p x_{t-p}+\varepsilon_t$
- I (d): differencing to remove trend
- MA (q): moving average of past errors

Practical pattern types:

- **Trend** — slow upward or downward movement.
- **Seasonality** — repeating cycles (daily, weekly, yearly).
- **Noise** — idiosyncratic variability.

Diagnostics & best practice:

- Plot autocorrelation (ACF/PACF) to choose model orders.
- Use rolling/expanding cross-validation (time-aware splits).
- Beware structural breaks — models must be re-assessed for regime change.

Analogy: Forecasting a time-series is like predicting tides: regular forces (moon, seasons) create predictable waves, but storms (shocks) add irregularities.

2. Symbolic sequences (ordered events, no fixed sampling)

Essence: Sequences of discrete tokens: transactions, clicks, or actions. Order matters, but not regular timestamps.

Common tasks: frequent sequence mining, next-item prediction, session clustering, sequence classification.

Core algorithms:

- **Apriori / PrefixSpan / GSP:** find subsequences that occur frequently above support thresholds.

- **Markov models / n-grams:** predict next token using limited context.
- **Sequence-to-sequence models / Transformers:** capture long-range dependencies for prediction and classification.

Practical concerns: sparsity of long patterns, explosion of candidate subsequences. Use sliding windows, constraint-based mining, or probabilistic models to manage complexity.

Analogy: Symbolic sequence mining is like finding recurring refrains in folk songs — short snippets repeat across many songs and reveal structure.

3. Biological sequences (DNA/RNA/proteins)

Essence: Extremely long symbolic sequences with biochemical meaning and evolutionary history. Small changes can have big effects.

Key tasks: alignment (find similarity), motif discovery (functional subsequences), homology search, variant calling.

Core methods:

- **Dynamic programming:** Needleman–Wunsch (global alignment), Smith–Waterman (local alignment). These compute optimal alignments with substitution matrices (e.g., BLOSUM) and gap penalties.
- **Indexing/search:** BLAST speeds queries by seed-and-extend heuristics rather than full dynamic programming.
- **Probabilistic models:** HMMs for gene/family modeling; modern deep embeddings capture context and function.

Domain nuance: biological sequences are not iid — bases and amino acids follow constraints from chemistry and evolution. Interpret outputs via phylogeny and functional assays.

Analogy: Reading DNA is like comparing centuries of handwritten manuscripts: you look for copied passages, edits, and recurring motifs that reveal lineage and meaning.

4. Graphs

Essence: Data where relationships are as important as entities. Nodes + edges form irregular structures not easily linearized.

Key questions: Who are hubs? What communities exist? Which links are missing or will appear?

Foundational tools:

- **Centrality metrics:** degree, betweenness, eigenvector/PageRank.
- **Community detection:** modularity maximization (Louvain), spectral methods.
- **Link prediction & node classification:** supervised learning using graph features or embeddings (node2vec, DeepWalk, GNNs).
- **Graph Neural Networks (GNNs):** learn node/graph representations by iterative neighbor aggregation.

Pitfalls: heterogeneity (multiple node/edge types), temporal dynamics, and sensitivity to sampling bias.

Analogy: A graph is a city map — streets connect places; centrality finds the marketplaces, community detection finds neighborhoods.

Network mining - processes running on graphs

Essence: Study of dynamics over networks: diffusion, cascades, contagion, and influence.

Common models:

- **Independent cascade/threshold models** for diffusion.
- **Epidemiological models** (SIR, SEIR) adapted to network structure.
- **Influence maximization:** choose seed nodes to maximize eventual spread.

Evaluation: simulate diffusion, measure cascade size, time-to-peak, or precision for predicting spreaders.

Analogy: Network mining is traffic engineering — given the roads (graph), how will a message, virus, or product adoption flow?

Cross-cutting themes:

Typical pipeline: acquisition → cleaning → representation (features/embeddings) → model → validation → interpretation → deployment.

Universal pitfalls: mixing correlation/causation, overfitting, ignoring non-stationarity, and mismatched validation schemes.

Evaluation metrics (task-dependent): RMSE/MAE for forecasting; precision/recall/AUC for classification/link prediction; support/confidence/lift for frequent pattern mining; sequence-aware metrics for next-item prediction.

Actionable advice

- **Start from the question.** The problem defines whether you model data as a time-series, a symbolic sequence, a graph, or a process on a graph.
- **Visualize first.** Even a tiny sample plotted or a small subgraph drawn yields intuition.
- **Design validation to mirror the world.** Use time-aware splits for sequences, node/edge holdouts for graphs.
- **Combine views.** Use sequence features + graph embeddings when interactions and order both matter.
- **Keep interpretability in mind.** Domain experts trust models that map back to understandable motifs, shifts, or influential nodes.

Basic DateTime Operations

Python's built-in datetime module is a powerful tool for handling dates and times, offering several object classes each tailored to specific functionalities. Here are the main object classes along with their components:

- datetime.time: Represents time without a date. It consists of attributes like hour, minute, second, and microsecond, allowing precise time representation.
- datetime.datetime: Represents both date and time. It includes attributes such as year, month, day, hour, minute, second, and microsecond, providing a

comprehensive timestamp.

- datetime.tzinfo: An abstract base class for time zone information objects. It allows the implementation of time zone-specific behavior, enabling localization and conversion of datetime objects between different time zones.
- datetime.timedelta: Represents the difference between two datetime objects, measured in days, seconds, and microseconds. It facilitates arithmetic operations on datetime objects, such as addition, subtraction, and comparison.
- datetime.timezone: Represents a fixed offset from UTC (Coordinated Universal Time). It allows datetime objects to be associated with specific time zones, enabling accurate time zone conversions and daylight saving time adjustments.

For a comprehensive understanding and detailed discussions on these object classes and their functionalities, refer to the book "Python OPTIMUM Series II Exploring Data Structures and Algorithms" by Shree Shambav. This book provides in-depth coverage of Python's datetime module, offering insights into its usage, features, and best practices for effective date and time manipulation in Python programming.

☐ Time Series Analysis and Visualization

Master explained that **time-series data occupies a place of exceptional importance** in the universe of datasets, for it alone carries the rhythm of change across time. Unlike static snapshots, time-series sequences allow us to observe how a phenomenon *evolves*, much like watching the unfolding of a story rather than reading a single page torn from a book.

Time-Series Visualisation and Analytics

At the heart of time-series analysis lies the art of **visualisation**. Through line graphs, gauges, heatmaps, and temporal tables, we transform raw numbers into living narratives. These visual tools illuminate hidden dynamics—subtle drifts, sudden spikes, long-term cycles, and recurring seasonal patterns.

Master often said, *"To see a sequence is to understand its spirit."*

With effective visualisation, organisations gain the ability to track changes, identify emerging risks, and convert temporal behaviour into actionable intelligence. This empowers them to forecast the future with greater clarity and confidence.

Understanding Time-Series Data

Time-series data consists of observations arranged **chronologically**; each point is tied to a specific moment. This temporal structure is not incidental—it is the very essence of time-series science.

Time-series analysis gathers a set of techniques designed to extract meaning from such ordered data: revealing trends, detecting structural breaks, measuring correlations across time, and forecasting future values.

Through these methods, organisations unlock the power to study both **historical records** and **real-time streams**, gaining a panoramic view of their operational landscape. In essence, time-series analytics transforms temporal data into insight, insight into knowledge, and knowledge into foresight.

Importance of time series

Master continued, the significance of time series analysis transcends numerous industries, including finance, pharmaceuticals, social media, web services, and research. Effective comprehension of time-series data hinges on visualisation, an indispensable tool for driving meaningful insights. Indeed, any data analysis endeavour remains incomplete without compelling visualisations, as they offer profound insights into the underlying data.

Let's delve into some fundamental time series concepts:

Trend: A trend delineates the overarching direction of a time series over an extended period, indicating whether values are ascending, descending, or stable.

Seasonality: Seasonality manifests as recurring patterns or cycles at regular intervals within a time series, often aligned with specific time units like days, weeks, months, or seasons.

Moving Average: This technique smoothens short-term fluctuations in data, accentuating longer-term trends or patterns by averaging consecutive data points within a defined window.

Noise: Noise, or random fluctuations, introduces irregular and unpredictable components into a time series, contributing variability unrelated to underlying trends or seasonality.

Differencing: Differencing involves computing differences between consecutive data points within specified intervals, commonly employed to eliminate trends from the data.

Stationarity: A stationary time series maintains constant statistical properties such as mean, variance, and autocorrelation over time.

Order of Differencing: Refers to the number of differencing steps required to attain stationarity in a time series.

Autocorrelation: Autocorrelation measures the similarity between a time series and its lagged version, offering insights into temporal dependencies.

Resampling: Resampling entails altering the frequency of data observations, often transitioning from daily to monthly intervals to elucidate clearer patterns or trends.

Mastering these fundamental concepts equips analysts with the tools necessary to unlock the insights embedded within time-series data, facilitating informed decision-making and strategic planning across diverse industries.

☐ Types of Time Series Data

Time series data can be broadly categorised into two main types:

Continuous Time Series Data: Continuous time series data entails measurements or observations recorded at regular intervals, forming a seamless and uninterrupted sequence. This type of data exhibits a continuous range of possible values and finds application across diverse domains:

- Temperature Data: Continuous recordings of temperature taken at consistent intervals, such as hourly or daily measurements.
- Stock Market Data: Continuous tracking of stock prices or values throughout trading hours, providing insights into market trends and fluctuations.
- Sensor Data: Continuous measurements from sensors capturing variables like pressure, humidity, or air quality, aiding in environmental monitoring and industrial processes.

Discrete Time Series Data: Discrete time series data comprises measurements or observations that are confined to specific values or categories. Unlike continuous data, discrete data does not span a continuous range of possible values, but consists of distinct and separate data points. Common examples include:

- Count Data: Tracking the frequency or number of occurrences within a defined time frame, such as the number of website visits per day or the count of customer transactions.

- Categorical Data: Classifying data into distinct categories or classes, such as customer segments, product types, or weather conditions.

- Binary Data: Recording data with only two possible outcomes or states, such as yes/no responses, presence/absence indicators, or true/false values.

Understanding these distinctions in time series data types is essential for effectively analysing and interpreting datasets across various domains and applications.

Visualisation Approach for Different Data Types:

When visualising continuous time series data, employing line, area, or smooth plots proves highly effective. These graphical representations capture the dynamic nature of trends, enabling analysts to discern patterns and fluctuations over time with clarity and precision.

In contrast, discrete time series data benefits from visualisation techniques, such as bar charts, histograms, and stacked bar plots. These visualisations excel in showcasing patterns and distributions within the data, offering insights into the frequency and distribution of specific occurrences or categories over time.

Master said, "This code performs a complete time-series analysis workflow on stock market data using Python. It begins by loading a CSV file into a Pandas DataFrame and setting the Date column as the index. After removing an unnecessary column, it visualizes the stock's High price over time using Seaborn to observe trends. The script then examines seasonality by plotting the Autocorrelation Function (ACF) of trading volume.

To assess whether the data is stationary—a key requirement for many forecasting models—the Augmented Dickey-Fuller (ADF) test is applied to both the original and differenced series. The code also smoothens the data using two techniques: first-order differencing to remove trend components and moving averages to highlight long-term patterns. Finally, it compares original and transformed data, removes missing values, and performs a second ADF test to confirm improved stationarity, preparing the dataset for further modelling."

Example P3 – U3 – D1

Time series

```
# Step 1: Importing Libraries
import pandas as pd
import seaborn as sns
import matplotlib.pyplot as plt
from statsmodels.graphics.tsaplots import plot_acf
from statsmodels.tsa.stattools import adfuller

# Step 2: Loading Dataset
# Load the dataset from a CSV file.
path = r'C:\Users\User\mraj4\Documents\Optimum\Py-lib\scikit\stock_data.csv'
df = pd.read_csv(path, parse_dates=True, index_col="Date")  # Specify "Date" column
as index
# Displaying the first five rows of the dataset
print(df.head())

# Step 3: Dropping Unwanted Columns
# Deleting the "Unnamed: 0" column
df.drop(columns='Unnamed: 0', inplace=True)
print(df.head())

# Step 4: Plotting a Line plot for Time Series data
# Set the style to whitegrid for a clean background
sns.set(style="whitegrid")

# Create a figure with the specified size
plt.figure(figsize=(12, 6))

# Plotting the line plot for High price over time
sns.lineplot(data=df, x=df.index, y='High', label='High Price', color='blue')

# Adding labels and title
plt.xlabel('Date')
plt.ylabel('High Price')
plt.title('Share Highest Price Over Time')

plt.show()

# Step 5: Detecting Seasonality Using Auto Correlation
# Plot the ACF
plt.figure(figsize=(12, 6))
```

```
plot_acf(df['Volume'], lags=40)  # You can adjust the number of lags as needed
plt.xlabel('Lag')
plt.ylabel('Autocorrelation')
plt.title('Autocorrelation Function (ACF) Plot')
plt.show()

# Step 6: Detecting Stationarity
# Perform Augmented Dickey-Fuller test for stationarity
result = adfuller(df['High'])
print('ADF Statistic:', result[0])
print('p-value:', result[1])
print('Critical Values:', result[4])

# Step 7: Smoothening the data using Differencing and Moving Average
# Step7A - Smoothening the data using Differencing
df['high_diff'] = df['High'].diff()

# Plotting
plt.figure(figsize=(12, 6))
plt.plot(df['High'], label='Original High', color='blue')
plt.plot(df['high_diff'], label='Differenced High', linestyle='--', color='green')
plt.legend()
plt.title('Original vs Differenced High')
plt.show()

# Step 7B - Smoothening the data using  Moving Average
# Moving Average
window_size = 120
df['high_smoothed'] = df['High'].rolling(window=window_size).mean()

# Plotting
plt.figure(figsize=(12, 6))

plt.plot(df['High'], label='Original High', color='blue')
plt.plot(df['high_smoothed'], label=f'Moving Average (Window={window_size})',
linestyle='--', color='orange')

plt.xlabel('Date')
plt.ylabel('High')
plt.title('Original vs Moving Average')
plt.legend()
plt.show()

# Step 8: Original Data Vs Differenced Data
# Printing the original and differenced data side by side
# Create a DataFrame with 'high' and 'high_diff' columns side by side
df_combined = pd.concat([df['High'], df['high_diff']], axis=1)
```

```
# Display the combined DataFrame
print(df_combined.head())

# Remove rows with missing values
df.dropna(subset=['high_diff'], inplace=True)
df['high_diff'].head()

# Step 9: Let us conduct an ADF test
from statsmodels.tsa.stattools import adfuller
result = adfuller(df['high_diff'])
print('ADF Statistic:', result[0])
print('p-value:', result[1])
print('Critical Values:', result[4])
```

Output

```
Output

ADF Statistic: 0.7671404880535937

p-value: 0.9910868050318213

Critical Values: {'1%': -3.4325316347197403, '5%': -2.862503905260741, '10%': -2.5672831121111113}

            High  high_diff

Date

2006-01-03  41.22        NaN

2006-01-04  41.90       0.68

2006-01-05  41.73      -0.17

2006-01-06  43.57       1.84

2006-01-09  43.66       0.09

ADF Statistic: -12.148367478343273

p-value: 1.591276613414641e-22

Critical Values: {'1%': -3.4325316347197403, '5%': -2.862503905260741, '10%': -2.5672831121111113}
```

Plot1:

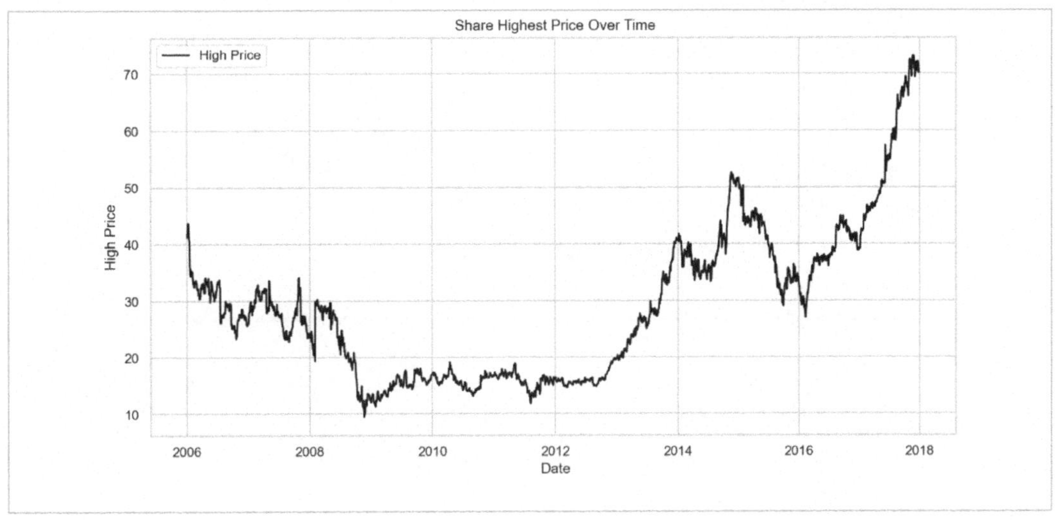

Plot2:

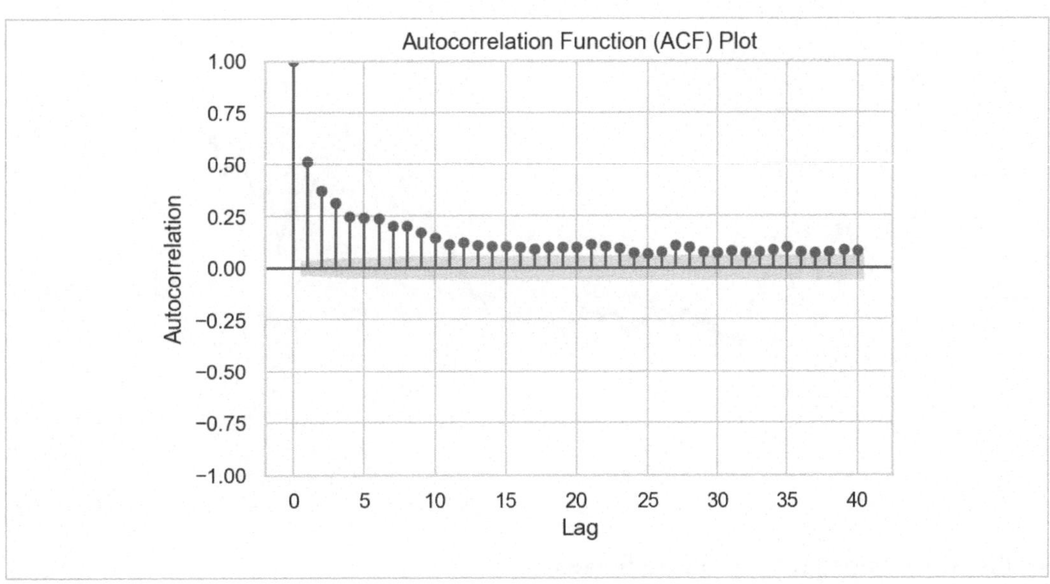

Plot3:

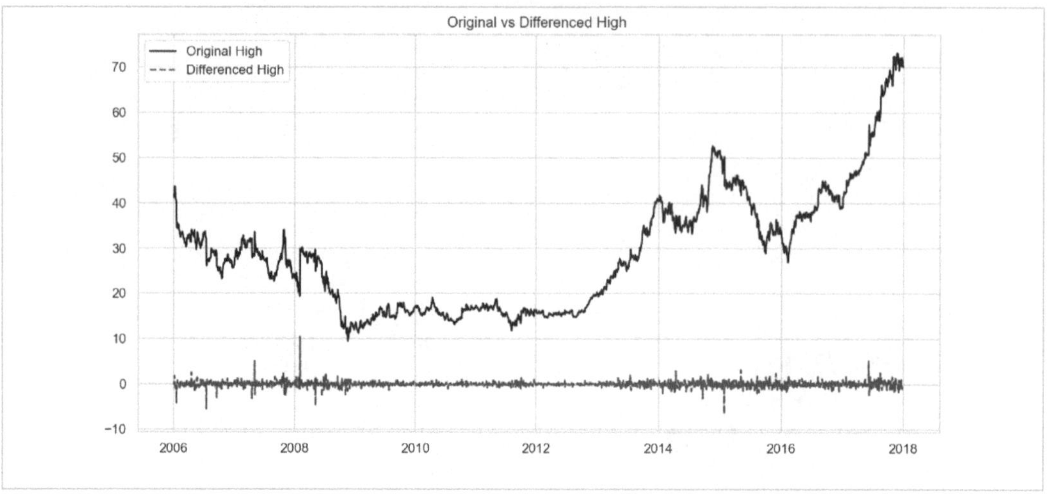

Plot4:

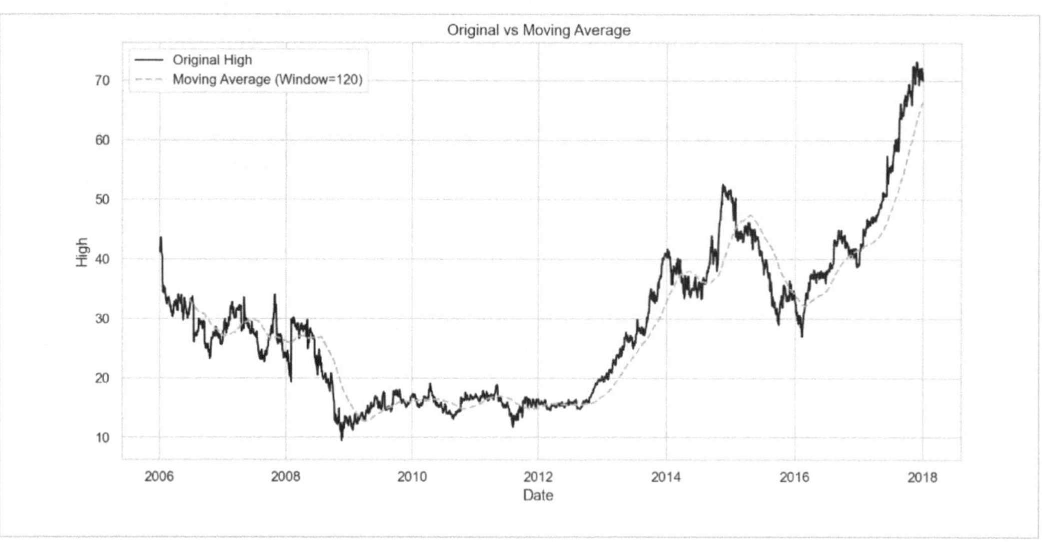

Visualisation Approach for Time Series

Seasonal Plot of a Time Series: Yearly /Monthly

Master said, "This code performs seasonal analysis and visualisation of a time-series dataset containing monthly drug sales. It begins by loading the CSV file, converting the date index to datetime, and extracting year and month components. Unique colors are generated for each year, and a seasonal line plot is created, showing month-wise sales patterns across different years. Labels and annotations enhance readability. The code then produces box plots to compare yearly trends and monthly seasonality, highlighting variations, outliers, and repeating patterns in the data. These visualisations help identify long-term trends and seasonal behaviour within the time-series."

Example P3 – U3 – D2
Time series – Seasonal Plots

```
# Importing Libraries
import pandas as pd
import matplotlib.pyplot as plt
import numpy as np
import matplotlib as mpl
import seaborn as sns
# Loading Dataset
path = r'C:\Users\User\mraj4\Documents\Optimum\Py-lib\scikit\time_One.csv'
df = pd.read_csv(path, parse_dates=True, index_col="date")
# Print the first few rows to verify the DataFrame
print(df.head())

# Convert index to datetime
df.index = pd.to_datetime(df.index)

# Prepare data
df.reset_index(inplace=True)
df['year'] = df['date'].dt.year
df['month'] = df['date'].dt.strftime('%b')

# Prep Colors
np.random.seed(100)
mycolors = np.random.choice(list(mpl.colors.XKCD_COLORS.keys()), len(df['year'].unique()),
replace=False)

# Draw Plot
plt.figure(figsize=(16, 12))
for i, year in enumerate(df['year'].unique()):
    if i > 0:
        plt.plot('month', 'value', data=df.loc[df['year'] == year], color=mycolors[i], label=str(year))
        plt.text(df.loc[df['year'] == year, :].shape[0]-0.9, df.loc[df['year'] == year, 'value'][-1:].values[0],
str(year), fontsize=12, color=mycolors[i])

# Decoration
plt.gca().set(xlim=(-0.3, 11), ylim=(2, 30), ylabel='$Drug Sales$', xlabel='$Month$')
plt.yticks(fontsize=12, alpha=0.7)
plt.title("Seasonal Plot - Drug Sales Time Series", fontsize=20)
plt.legend(title='Year', loc='upper right', fontsize=12)
plt.show()

# Draw Box Plot for Yearly and Monthly
fig, axes = plt.subplots(1, 2, figsize=(20, 7), dpi=80)
sns.boxplot(x='year', y='value', data=df, ax=axes[0])
sns.boxplot(x='month', y='value', data=df.loc[~df['year'].isin([1991, 2008]), :], ax=axes[1])
# Set Title
```

```
axes[0].set_title('Year-wise - Box Plot\n(The Trend)', fontsize=18)
axes[1].set_title('Month-wise - Box Plot\n(The Seasonality)', fontsize=18)
plt.show()
```

Output

Output
date
1991-07-01   3.526591
1991-08-01   3.180891
1991-09-01   3.252221
1991-10-01   3.611003
1991-11-01   3.565869

Plot 1:

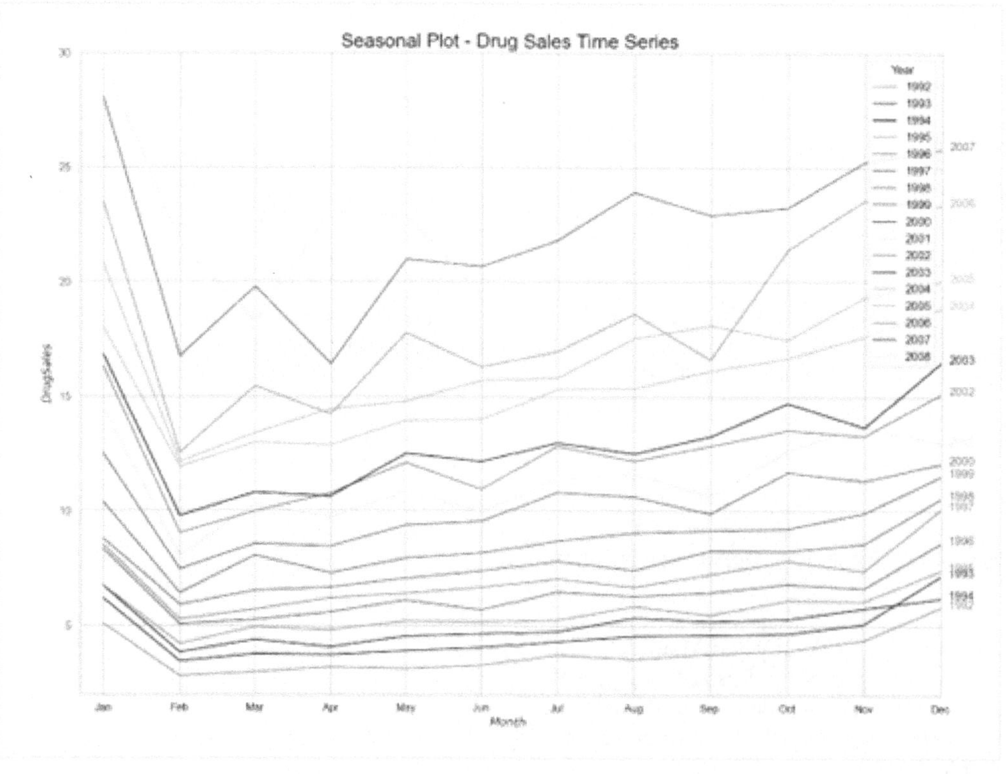

Plot 2:

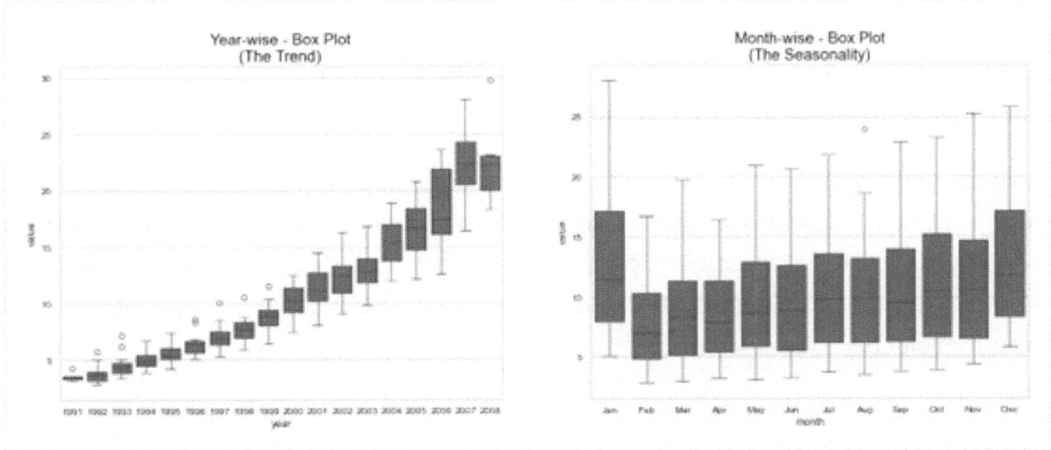

The fluctuation in drug sales exhibits a distinct cyclic pattern, characterised by a notable decline in February followed by a resurgence in March, only to decrease again in April, and so forth. This cyclical behaviour repeats consistently each year, while overall drug sales show an upward trend over time.

To gain deeper insights into this phenomenon, we employ statistical tools such as Box plots, which effectively illustrate the distribution of values within each year or month. By grouping the data into seasonal intervals, we can visually compare how these values evolve over time. Year-wise and month-wise boxplots vividly portray the distribution patterns, enabling us to discern trends and seasonal variations.

Upon closer inspection, month-wise boxplots highlight spikes in drug sales during December and January, coinciding with the holiday season and associated discounts. This observation underscores the influence of external factors on consumer behaviour and purchasing patterns.

While we have successfully identified the recurring trends, the next step is to detect any deviations from the established pattern. This involves employing statistical techniques, such as anomaly detection algorithms or time-series analysis, to identify outliers or irregularities in the data. By systematically analysing deviations from expected patterns, we can uncover potential anomalies that may warrant further investigation or intervention.

Patterns - Types of Time Series

Master said, "In time series analysis, we discern two fundamental components: trend and seasonality. A trend manifests as a consistent upward or downward movement over time, indicating a long-term pattern of growth or decline in the data. Conversely, seasonality reflects recurring patterns at regular intervals, influenced by external factors like months, days, weekdays, or even specific times of the day."

It's crucial to note that not all time series exhibit both trend and seasonality. Some may display a clear trend without distinct seasonal variations, while others may showcase seasonality without a discernible trend. Thus, a time series can be conceptualised as comprising three main elements: the underlying trend, the cyclic seasonal patterns, and the random fluctuations or error terms.

Understanding these components is essential for effectively modelling and forecasting time series data. Let's categorize time series data based on its composition before diving into imputation methods. If we use a linear regression model to break down the time series data, it can be represented as:

$$Y(t) = T(t) + S(t) + \varepsilon(t)$$

Where:

- T(t) represents the trend,
- S(t) represents seasonality, and
- ε(t) represents random variables.

Based on the presence or absence of these components, the passage identifies four types of time series data:

No trend or seasonality (Constant): Data remains relatively constant over time, showing neither trend nor seasonal fluctuations.

$$Y(t) = \varepsilon(t)$$

Trend, but no seasonality (Trendy): Data exhibits a clear long-term trend, either increasing or decreasing, but no regular seasonal patterns.

$$Y(t) = T(t) + \varepsilon(t)$$

Seasonality, but no trend (Seasonal): Data shows recurring fluctuations within a specific period, such as monthly sales cycles, but no overall trend over time.

$$Y(t) = S(t) + \varepsilon(t)$$

Both trend and seasonality (Trend-seasonal): Data exhibits both a long-term trend and recurring seasonal patterns. This is the most complex type of time series data.

$$Y(t) = T(t) + S(t) + \varepsilon(t)$$

Master said, "This code visualizes three different time-series patterns using separate datasets. It begins by importing pandas, matplotlib, and seaborn, then loads three CSV files representing distinct temporal behaviors. A figure with three side-by-side subplots is created for comparison. The first dataset is plotted to show trend-only movement over time, the second highlights pure seasonality, and the third demonstrates a combination of trend and seasonality. Each CSV is read with its date column parsed as a datetime index for accurate time-series plotting. Finally, all three graphs are displayed together, enabling clear visual comparison of different time-series components."

Example P3 – U3 – D3

Time Series - Types of Time Series

```
import pandas as pd
import matplotlib.pyplot as plt
import seaborn as sns
# Loading Dataset
path1 = r'C:\Users\User\mraj4\Documents\Optimum\Py-lib\scikit\Rice.csv'
path2 = r'C:\Users\User\mraj4\Documents\Optimum\Py-lib\scikit\sunspotarea.csv'
path3 = r'C:\Users\User\mraj4\Documents\Optimum\Py-lib\scikit\Air_Pass.csv'

# Create Subplots
fig, axes = plt.subplots(1, 3, figsize=(20, 4), dpi=100)

# Plot 1: Trend Only
pd.read_csv(path1, parse_dates=['date'], index_col='date').plot(title='Trend Only', legend=False,
ax=axes[0])

# Plot 2: Seasonality Only
pd.read_csv(path2, parse_dates=['date'], index_col='date').plot(title='Seasonality Only',
legend=False, ax=axes[1])

# Plot 3: Trend and Seasonality
pd.read_csv(path3, parse_dates=['date'], index_col='date').plot(title='Trend and Seasonality',
legend=False, ax=axes[2])
# Show the Plots
```

```
plt.show()
```

Plot

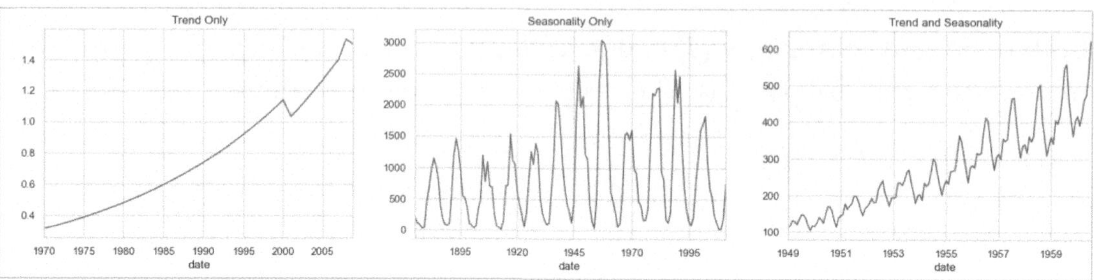

Understanding the distinction between cyclic and seasonal patterns is crucial in time series analysis. While both involve repetitive fluctuations, they differ in terms of their timing and underlying causes.

Seasonal patterns occur at fixed calendar-based intervals, such as monthly, quarterly, or yearly cycles. These patterns are driven by predictable factors like weather, holidays, or cultural events. In contrast, cyclic patterns lack this fixed periodicity and occur due to broader economic or business-related influences. Cyclic fluctuations may span irregular time frames and are typically linked to factors such as economic cycles, business cycles, or other socio-economic dynamics.

To differentiate between a cyclic and seasonal pattern, one must examine the frequency and regularity of the observed fluctuations. If the patterns occur at consistent calendar-based intervals, it is likely seasonal. Conversely, if the fluctuations do not adhere to fixed time frames and are influenced by broader economic or business factors, they are considered cyclic.

Understanding the composition of time series data is crucial for effective modelling and forecasting. Two common approaches to modelling time series are additive and multiplicative models, each offering unique insights into the underlying components.

In an additive time series model, each observation (Y(t)) is expressed as the sum of its components: trend (T(t)), seasonality (S(t)), and an error term (ε(t)). This model assumes that the influence of trend and seasonality on the data remains constant over time, with any deviation attributed to random fluctuations or noise.

$$Y(t) = T(t) + S(t) + \varepsilon(t)$$

Conversely, a multiplicative time series model represents each observation (Y(t)) as the product of its components: trend (T(t)), seasonality (S(t)), and an error term (ε(t)). This model is suitable when the magnitude of trend and seasonality varies with the level of the data, indicating a nonlinear relationship between the components.

$$Y(t) = T(t) * S(t) * \varepsilon(t)$$

☐ Decomposing a time series

Master said, "Sam, to truly understand a time series, one must first uncover the layers hidden within it. Decomposition is the art of separating a complex sequence into its core components—trend, seasonality, and residuals—so the story within the data becomes visible."

Choose a Decomposition Method:

Select an approach such as classical decomposition, moving averages, or advanced techniques like STL (Seasonal and Trend decomposition using Loess).

Identify Seasonal Periodicity:

Determine the natural cycle of the data—daily, weekly, monthly, quarterly, or yearly.

Perform Decomposition:

Apply the chosen method to split the series into:

- **Trend:** the long-term direction
- **Seasonality:** the repeating patterns
- **Residuals:** irregular fluctuations and noise

Validate the Components:

Visually inspect the outputs, conduct statistical checks, or compare model accuracy to ensure the decomposition is meaningful.

Interpret the Patterns:

Study each component to reveal trends, recurring cycles, anomalies, or subtle behaviours influencing the data.

Apply Insights for Forecasting:

Use the decomposed elements to build more accurate forecasts, detect anomalies, identify correlations, or guide decisions.

Master said, "When you decompose a time series, Sam, you don't just analyse data—you understand its rhythm, its pulse, and the truth it has been trying to tell."

Master said, "This code performs both multiplicative and additive decomposition on a time-series dataset using seasonal_decompose. After loading the data, it separates the series into trend, seasonal, residual, and observed components for each decomposition model. The results are visualised through plots to compare how both methods capture underlying patterns. The code then reconstructs the original series using the multiplicative components and displays the combined DataFrame. This helps analysts understand structure, identify seasonality, and choose the most suitable decomposition approach for further analysis.

Example P3 – U3 – D4

Time Series - Types of Time Series

```
from statsmodels.tsa.seasonal import seasonal_decompose
from dateutil.parser import parse
import pandas as pd
import matplotlib.pyplot as plt

# Loading Dataset
path = r'C:\Users\User\mraj4\Documents\Optimum\Py-lib\scikit\time_One.csv'
df = pd.read_csv(path, parse_dates=True, index_col="date")

# Multiplicative Decomposition
result_mul = seasonal_decompose(df['value'], model='multiplicative', extrapolate_trend='freq')

# Additive Decomposition
result_add = seasonal_decompose(df['value'], model='additive', extrapolate_trend='freq')

# Plot
plt.rcParams.update({'figure.figsize': (10,10)})
result_mul.plot().suptitle('Multiplicative Decomposition', fontsize=22)
result_add.plot().suptitle('Additive Decomposition', fontsize=22)
plt.show()

# Actual Values = Product of (Seasonal * Trend * Resid)
df_reconstructed = pd.concat([result_mul.seasonal, result_mul.trend, result_mul.resid,
result_mul.observed], axis=1)
df_reconstructed.columns = ['seas', 'trend', 'resid', 'actual_values']
print(df_reconstructed.head())
```

The seasonal_decompose function from statsmodels.tsa.seasonal module is utilized for decomposition, with the model parameter specifying the decomposition method ('multiplicative' or 'additive') and the extrapolate_trend parameter determining how to handle missing values in the trend component.

Setting extrapolate_trend='freq' is a useful parameter choice as it addresses any potential missing values in the trend and residual components, specifically at the inception of the time series data.

Finally, the decomposed components are plotted using Matplotlib, with separate plots for the multiplicative and additive decompositions. Each plot includes the trend, seasonal, and residual components, providing visual insights into the decomposition process and the underlying patterns within the time series data.

Plot 1:

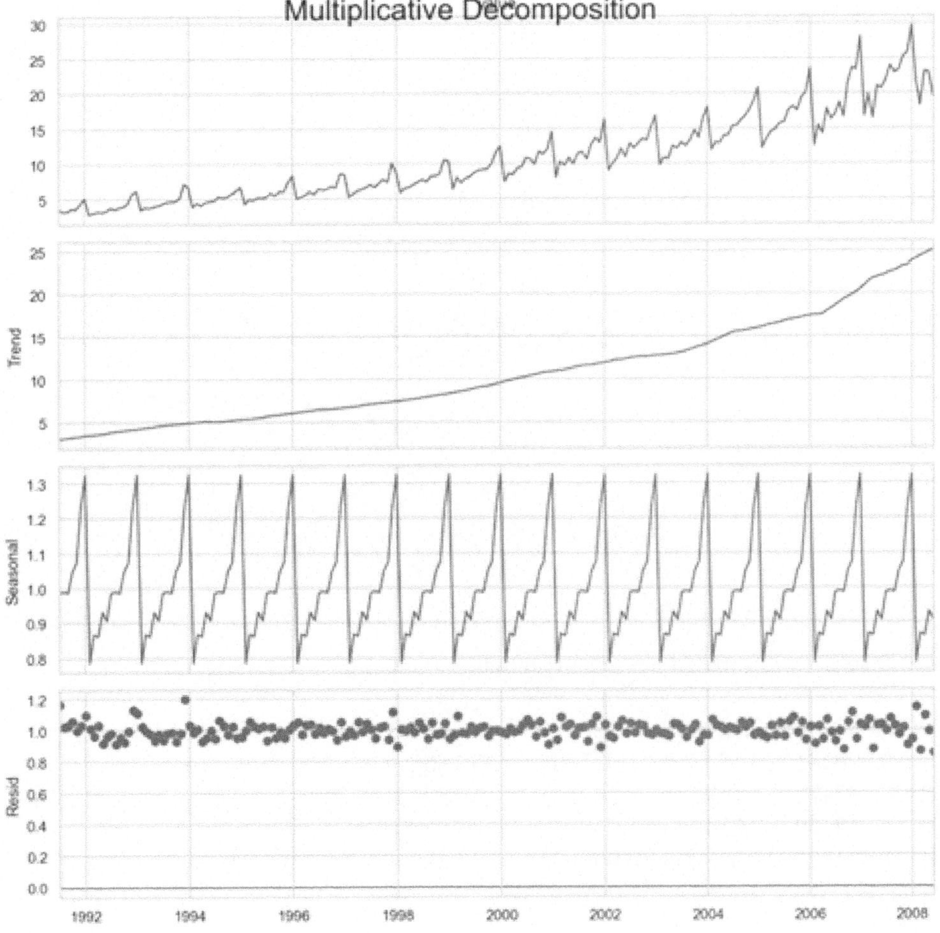

Plot 2:

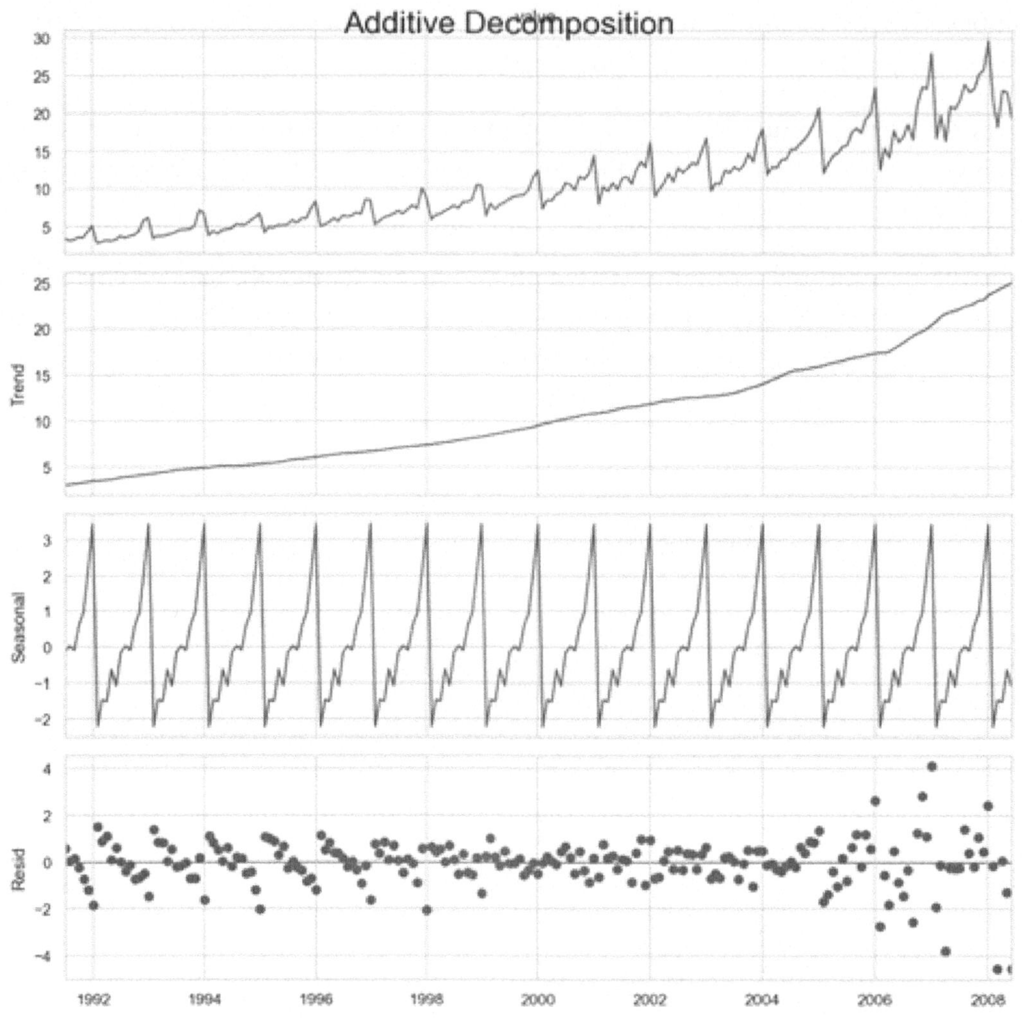

Output

Output:

date	seas	trend	resid	actual_ values
1991-07-01	0.987845	3.060085	1.166629	3.526591
1991-08-01	0.990481	3.124765	1.027745	3.180891
1991-09-01	0.987476	3.189445	1.032615	3.252221
1991-10-01	1.048329	3.254125	1.058513	3.611003
1991-11-01	1.074527	3.318805	0.999923	3.565869

☐ Stationary and Non-Stationary Time Series

John asked, "What is stationarity?"

Master replied, "Stationarity is a fundamental property of a time series. A stationary series is one where the statistical properties, such as mean, variance, and autocorrelation, remain constant over time. Additionally, a stationary time series is devoid of seasonal effects. Identifying whether a series is stationary or not is crucial for accurate modelling and forecasting."

Types of Stationary and Non-Stationary Series:

- Stationary: Consistent mean, variance, and autocorrelation over time.
- Nonconstant variance: Variances fluctuate over time.
- Seasonal components: Exhibits recurring patterns at fixed intervals.
- Nonconstant mean and seasonal components: Mean and seasonal effects change over time.
- Nonconstant mean, variance, and seasonal components: All statistical properties vary over time.

Significance of Stationarity: Stationarity is vital for time series analysis, as non-stationary series can yield unreliable predictions.

Making a Time Series Stationary: Various techniques can be employed to make a non-stationary series stationary:

- **Differencing the Series:** Subtracting consecutive values to remove trend.
- **Taking the Log:** Reducing variability and stabilizing non-constant variance.
- **Taking the nth Root:** Stabilizing non-constant variance.
- **Combination:** Employing a combination of the above methods.

The most common method to stationarize a series is by differencing the series at least once until it becomes approximately stationary.

Sam asked, "What is Differencing?"

Master said, "Differencing involves subtracting the current value from the next value. If the first difference does not induce stationarity, further differencing can be applied."

Example: Consider the series [1, 6, 2, 12, 25].

First difference: [6-1, 2-6, 12-2, 25-12] = [5, -4, 10, 13].

Second difference: [-4-5, -10-4, 13-10] = [-9, -14, 3].

Iterative differencing continues until stationarity is achieved.

☐ Why make a Non-Stationary series Stationary before Forecasting?

Forecasting a stationary series is notably more straightforward, and the resulting forecasts are generally more reliable.

One key rationale is rooted in the nature of autoregressive forecasting models, which essentially function as linear regression models using lagged values of the series as predictors.

In linear regression, optimal performance is achieved when predictors (X variables) exhibit minimal correlation among themselves. By stationarizing the series, we effectively address this issue by eliminating persistent autocorrelation, thereby rendering the predictors (lags of the series) in forecasting models nearly independent.

Now, how do we check if a given series Is Stationary or Not?

We can employ statistical tests such as the Augmented Dickey-Fuller (ADF) test and the Kwiatkowski-Phillips-Schmidt-Shin (KPSS) test to assess stationarity. These tests evaluate whether the series possesses certain statistical properties that are indicative of stationarity, such as constant mean and variance.

Apeksha asked, "How to Test for Stationarity?"

Master said, "Establishing the stationarity of a series can be initially assessed by visually inspecting its plot. However, for a more quantitative determination, statistical tests called 'Unit Root Tests' are employed. These tests examine whether a time series is non-stationary and possesses a unit root."

Variations of Unit Root Tests:

Augmented Dickey Fuller (ADF) Test: Checks for the presence of a unit root. The null hypothesis is that the series possesses a unit root and is non-stationary. If the p-value from the ADF test is less than the significance level (typically 0.05), the null hypothesis is rejected.

Kwiatkowski-Phillips-Schmidt-Shin (KPSS) Test: Specifically assesses trend stationarity. Here, the null hypothesis is the opposite of the ADF test: the series is trend stationary. A p-value less than the significance level indicates rejection of the null hypothesis.

Implementations in Python:

The most commonly used implementations of these tests are available in the statsmodels package in Python. Specifically:

- ADF Test: adfuller function
- KPSS Test: kpss function

These functions provide a convenient way to conduct these tests and interpret their results. By comparing the p-values obtained from these tests with the chosen significance level, one can make informed decisions regarding the stationarity of the time series.

Master said, "This code evaluates the stationarity of a time series using two key statistical tests: the Augmented Dickey–Fuller (ADF) and the KPSS test. After loading the dataset, the ADF test examines whether the series has a unit root, while the KPSS test checks if the series is trend-stationary. The code prints the test statistics, p-values, and critical values for both methods. Using ADF and KPSS together provides a more reliable diagnosis of stationarity, helping guide further time-series modelling and transformations."

Example P3 – U3 – D5	
Time series – Stationary Test	**Output**
from statsmodels.tsa.stattools import adfuller, kpss from dateutil.parser import parse import pandas as pd import matplotlib.pyplot as plt # Loading Dataset	ADF Test: ADF Statistic: 3.145185689306742 p-value: 1.0 Critical Values: 1%: -3.465620397124192 5%: -2.8770397560752436

path = r'C:\Users\User\mraj4\Documents\Optimum\Py-lib\scikit\time_One.csv'
df = pd.read_csv(path, parse_dates=True, index_col="date")
 	
# ADF Test 	
result_adf = adfuller(df['value'], autolag='AIC')
print('ADF Test:')
print(f'ADF Statistic: {result_adf[0]}')
print(f'p-value: {result_adf[1]}')
print('Critical Values:')
for key, value in result_adf[4].items():
    print(f'   {key}: {value}')
 	
# KPSS Test 	
result_kpss = kpss(df['value'], regression='c')
print('\nKPSS Test:')
print('KPSS Statistic: %f' % result_kpss[0])
print('p-value: %f' % result_kpss[1])
print('Critical Values:')
for key, value in result_kpss[3].items():
    print(f'   {key}: {value}')
	10%: -2.5750324547306476
	
	KPSS Test:
	KPSS Statistic: 2.013126
	p-value: 0.010000
	Critical Values:
	  10%: 0.347
	  5%: 0.463
	  2.5%: 0.574
	  1%: 0.739

☐ Difference Between White Noise and Stationary Series

While both white noise and stationary series exhibit constancy in mean and variance over time, they differ in their underlying characteristics.

Master said, "John, although white noise and a stationary series may appear similar because both maintain constant mean and variance over time, their inner nature is very different."

White Noise:

- Purely random data with a mean of 0.
- Contains no pattern, structure, or predictability.
- In real life, the static sound between FM radio channels is a perfect example.
- Mathematically, it is simply a sequence of independent, random values with zero mean.

Stationary Series:

- Also maintains a constant mean and variance across time.
- But unlike white noise, it can still exhibit structure—mild patterns, correlations, or predictable behaviour.
- Many time series models assume stationarity because its statistical properties remain stable.

Master said, "So remember, John—white noise is pure randomness, a chaotic whisper with no memory. A stationary series, however, may hold subtle patterns beneath its calm surface."

Example P3 – U3 – D6
Time series – White Noise

```
import pandas as pd
import numpy as np
import matplotlib.pyplot as plt
# Generate Random White Noise
randvals = np.random.randn(800)
# Plotting
pd.Series(randvals).plot(title='Random White Noise', color='k')
plt.xlabel('Time')
plt.ylabel('Value')
plt.grid(True)
plt.show()
```

Plot

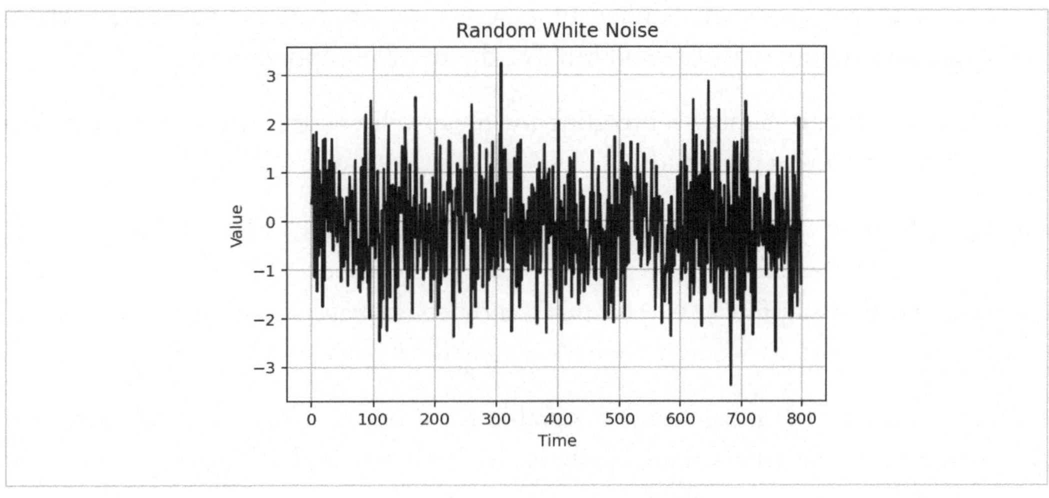

White Noise Test:

Ljung-Box Test: The Ljung-Box test evaluates the overall randomness of a time series by examining a set number of autocorrelations. It assesses whether any of a group of autocorrelations in the time series significantly deviate from zero. In essence, the test determines if the observed autocorrelations are statistically different from what would be expected in a white noise process.

Box-Pierce Test: Similar to the Ljung-Box test, the Box-Pierce test also evaluates the overall randomness of a time series using a specified number of autocorrelations. It examines whether any of the autocorrelations in the time series significantly depart from zero. This test serves as an alternative to the Ljung-Box test for assessing the randomness of a time series.

□ Detrend a Time Series:

Nikash asked, "How to Detrend a Time Series?"

Master said, "Detrending a time series involves removing the trend component from the data."

Several approaches exist for extracting the trend:

Subtracting the Line of Best Fit: This involves fitting a linear regression model to the time series data, where the time steps serve as predictors. For more complex trends, quadratic terms (x^2) can be included in the model.

Time Series Decomposition: Utilize time series decomposition methods, such as seasonal decomposition, to isolate and remove the trend component.

Subtracting the Mean: Simply subtracting the mean value of the series from each data point effectively removes the trend.

Applying Filters: Use specialized filters like the Baxter-King filter (statsmodels.tsa.filters.bkfilter) or the Hodrick-Prescott Filter (statsmodels.tsa.filters.hpfilter) to eliminate moving average trend lines or cyclical components.

Each method has its advantages and is suitable for different types of trends and data characteristics. Experimentation and analysis are often required to determine the most appropriate detrending approach for a specific time series.

Master said, "This code demonstrates detrending of a time series using SciPy's signal.detrend function. After loading the dataset and setting the date column as the index, the script removes the linear trend from the drug-sales values. Detrending helps isolate fluctuations by eliminating long-term upward or downward movement in the data. The resulting detrended series is plotted with labels and a grid, offering a clearer view of short-term variations and making further time-series analysis more accurate and insightful."

Example P3 – U3 – D7
Time series – Detrend

```
from scipy import signal
import pandas as pd
import matplotlib.pyplot as plt
# Loading Dataset
path = r'C:\Users\User\mraj4\Documents\Optimum\Py-lib\scikit\time_One.csv'
df = pd.read_csv(path, parse_dates=True, index_col="date")

# Detrending
detrended = signal.detrend(df['value'].values)
# Plotting
plt.plot(detrended)
plt.title('Detrended Drug Sales', fontsize=16)
plt.xlabel('Time')
plt.ylabel('Detrended Value')
plt.grid(True)
plt.show()
```

Plot

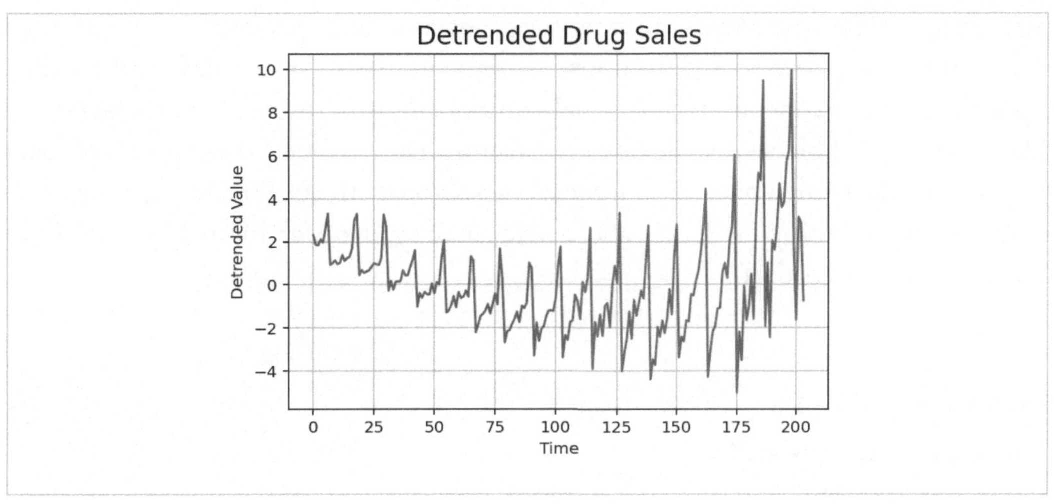

☐ **Deseasonalize:**

Akshatha asked, "How to Deseasonalize a Time Series?"

Master replied, "Deseasonalizing a time series involves removing the seasonal component from the data."

Several approaches can be employed:

- **Moving Average:** Calculate a moving average with a window length equal to the seasonal cycle. This smoothing process helps in removing the seasonal fluctuations.
- **Seasonal Differencing:** Take the difference between the current value and the corresponding value from the previous season. This approach directly removes the seasonal component from the series.
- **Dividing by Seasonal Index:** Divide the series by the seasonal index obtained from Seasonal and Trend decomposition using Loess (STL). This method normalizes the series with respect to the seasonal component.

If dividing by the seasonal index doesn't yield satisfactory results, another option is to take the logarithm of the series before deseasonalizing. Later, the original scale can be restored by taking an exponential.

Experimentation and analysis are often needed to determine the most suitable deseasonalizing approach for a specific time series.

Master said, "This code loads a time series dataset and performs multiplicative decomposition using seasonal_decompose to separate trend, seasonality, and residual components. After extracting the seasonal component, it deseasonalizes the series by dividing the original values by the seasonal factor. The resulting deseasonalized data highlights the underlying trend without recurring seasonal effects. Finally, the code plots this cleaned series with clear labels and a grid, making it easier to analyse long-term behaviour in drug sales data."

Example P3 – U3 – D8

Time series – Deseasonalize

```
import pandas as pd
import matplotlib.pyplot as plt
from statsmodels.tsa.seasonal import seasonal_decompose
```

```
# Loading Dataset
path = r'C:\Users\User\mraj4\Documents\Optimum\Py-lib\scikit\time_One.csv'
df = pd.read_csv(path, parse_dates=True, index_col="date")

# Time Series Decomposition
result_mul = seasonal_decompose(df['value'], model='multiplicative',
extrapolate_trend='freq')

# Deseasonalize
deseasonalized = df['value'].values / result_mul.seasonal
# Plot
plt.plot(deseasonalized)
plt.title('Deseasonalized Drug Sales', fontsize=16)
plt.xlabel('Time')
plt.ylabel('Deseasonalized Value')
plt.grid(True)
plt.show()
```

Plot

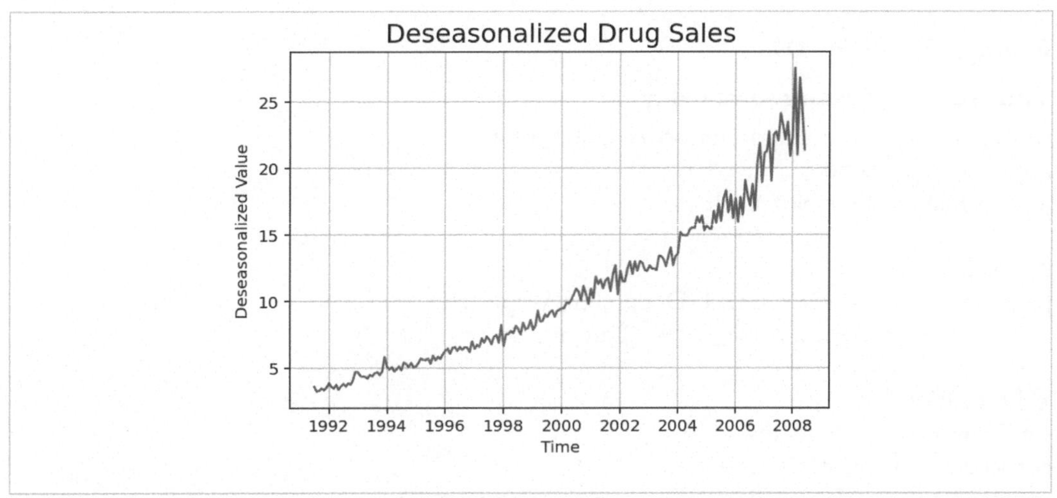

How to Test for Seasonality of a Time Series?

Seasonality in a time series can be assessed through various methods:

Visual Inspection: Plot the series and observe for repeatable patterns at fixed time intervals such as hour of day, day of month, weekly, monthly, or yearly. Seasonal patterns often manifest as regular fluctuations in the data.

Autocorrelation Function (ACF) Plot: Utilise the ACF plot to examine the correlation between observations at different time lags. In the presence of strong seasonality, the ACF plot typically reveals definitive repeated spikes at multiples of the seasonal window. For example, for a monthly series with yearly seasonality, spikes may appear at the 12th, 24th, 36th, and so on, lag lines.

It's essential to exercise caution when interpreting these patterns, especially in real-world datasets, where strong patterns may be obscured by noise. Careful observation and analysis are necessary to accurately identify and capture seasonal patterns in the data.

Master said, "This code visualises the autocorrelation of a time-series using autocorrelation_plot from pandas. After loading the dataset and setting the date column as the index, it generates an autocorrelation plot to examine how current values relate to past values at different lags. The plot helps identify repeating patterns, seasonality, or dependencies within the data. With customised figure size, labels, and grid, the visualisation provides a clear view of correlation strength across lags, supporting deeper time-series analysis and forecasting decisions."

Example P3 – U3 – D9

Time series – Test for seasonality

```
from pandas.plotting import autocorrelation_plot
import pandas as pd
import matplotlib.pyplot as plt

# Loading Dataset
path = r'C:\Users\User\mraj4\Documents\Optimum\Py-lib\scikit\time_One.csv'
df = pd.read_csv(path, parse_dates=True, index_col="date")

# Draw Plot
plt.figure(figsize=(9, 5), dpi=120)
autocorrelation_plot(df['value'])
plt.title('Autocorrelation Plot of Drug Sales', fontsize=16)
plt.xlabel('Lag')
plt.ylabel('Autocorrelation')
plt.grid(True)
plt.show()
```

Plot

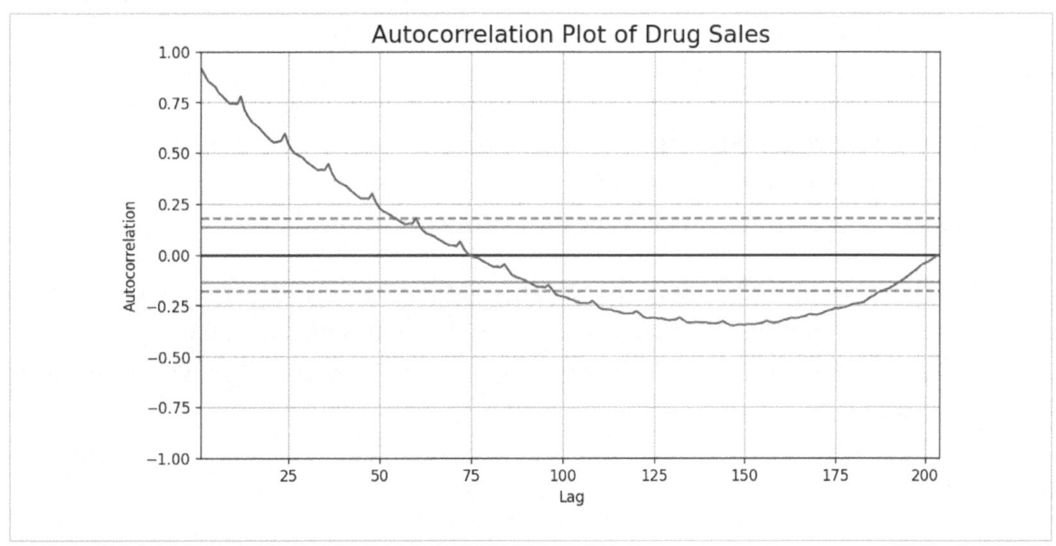

☐ Seasonality Tests

QS Test: The QS test is a variant of the Ljung-Box test computed on seasonal lags, focusing only on positive autocorrelations. It assesses whether there are significant seasonal patterns in the autocorrelations of a time series.

F Test on Seasonal Dummies: The F test on seasonal dummies examines the significance of seasonal effects by fitting seasonal dummy variables in a regression model and testing their joint significance.

Canova-Hansen Test: The Canova-Hansen test, also known as the Friedman test, is a non-parametric method for testing the presence of stable seasonality in time series data. It compares the rankings of observations across different months or quarters to determine if there are significant differences. Rejection of the null hypothesis suggests the presence of seasonality.

Kruskal-Wallis Test: The Kruskal-Wallis test is another non-parametric test used to assess whether samples originate from the same distribution. In the context of seasonality testing, it compares the median values of observations across different months or quarters. Rejection of the null hypothesis indicates significant differences in the distribution of time series values between periods.

Seasonality Test Based on Periodogram: This test assesses seasonality by analysing the periodogram of the time series, which is a graphical representation of the frequencies present in the data. Peaks in the periodogram suggest periodic behaviour, indicating the presence of seasonality.

Test Based on Autoregressive Spectrum: This test examines seasonality by analysing the autoregressive spectrum of the time series. It assesses the presence of periodic components in the spectrum, which indicate seasonality in the data.

Seasonality Test Based on Tukey Spectrum: Similar to the autoregressive spectrum test, the Tukey spectrum test evaluates seasonality by analysing the Tukey spectrum of the time series. It identifies periodic components in the spectrum, providing insights into the presence of seasonality.

PART THREE

DAY NINE

Unit 3 - Lesson Two

Rhythms in Data

☐ **Missing Values**

Master said, "Apeksha — Missing values are a natural part of time-series data, often arising from measurement errors, equipment failures, gaps in observation, or inconsistencies in data collection. These gaps can break the continuity of the series, distort underlying patterns, and lead to biased interpretations or weak predictive models. Therefore, recognising **why** data is missing and **how it affects the structure of the series** is essential. Only with this understanding can we choose the right method to handle missingness and preserve the integrity of the time-series analysis."

Types of Missingness Mechanisms:

- **Missing Completely at Random (MCAR):** Missingness is unrelated to any observed or unobserved variables. For example, random sensor failures in a weather monitoring system.
- **Missing at Random (MAR):** Missingness depends on observed variables but not on the missing data itself. For instance, missing temperature readings due to sensor malfunction during extreme weather conditions.
- **Missing Not at Random (MNAR):** Missingness depends on unobserved variables or the missing data itself. An example would be patients avoiding follow-up appointments if they experience adverse effects from a treatment.

Challenges in Time Series Data: Time series data exhibits temporal dependencies and trends, making it sensitive to missing values handling. Simply applying traditional imputation methods without considering these temporal characteristics can distort the underlying patterns and lead to biased analysis.

Avoiding Biases in Imputation: Traditional imputation methods like mean or mode imputation can introduce biases by ignoring temporal relationships and patterns in the data. Time series data often exhibits seasonality, trend, and cyclic patterns, making it inappropriate to replace missing values with global summary statistics.

- **Advanced Imputation Techniques:** Advanced imputation techniques tailored for time series data leverage temporal information to produce more accurate estimates:

- **Interpolation:** Utilizes neighboring data points to estimate missing values based on the trend or pattern of the time series.

- **Time-Based Imputation**: Considers time intervals or periodicity to impute missing values, such as using values from the same time period in previous years.

- **Model-Based Imputation:** Employs statistical models or machine learning algorithms to predict missing values based on the observed data.

Missing Values:

Roopa asked, "How to treat missing values in a Time Series?"

Master explained that in handling missing values within a time series, various strategies can be employed based on the nature of the data and the context:

Zero Fill: If the missing values represent periods where the measurement was zero, filling those periods with zero is appropriate.

Forward Fill: Forward-filling involves propagating the last observed value forward in time to fill missing data points. This approach is suitable when the time series exhibits persistence or when abrupt changes are unlikely.

Backward Fill: Backward-filling involves using the next observed value to fill missing data points. It's appropriate when future data points are more likely to resemble past observations.

Linear Interpolation: Linear interpolation estimates missing values by fitting a straight line between adjacent observed data points and assigning values along this line. It assumes a linear relationship between consecutive observations.

Quadratic Interpolation: Quadratic interpolation extends linear interpolation by fitting a quadratic curve between adjacent observed data points. It's suitable when the time series exhibits curvature between observations.

Mean of Nearest Neighbors: This method fills missing values by averaging the values of neighboring data points. It captures local trends and patterns in the time series.

Mean of Seasonal Counterparts: For seasonal time series, missing values can be replaced with the mean of corresponding seasonal periods from other years. This method preserves seasonal patterns and trends.

To assess the effectiveness of these imputation techniques, one can introduce artificial missing values into the time series, apply each imputation method, and then evaluate the imputed values against the actual data using metrics such as mean squared error (MSE). This empirical evaluation helps determine the most suitable imputation approach for the specific time series dataset.

Example P3 – U3 – D10

Time series – Imputing Missing Values

```
from scipy.interpolate import interp1d
from sklearn.metrics import mean_squared_error
import pandas as pd
import numpy as np
import matplotlib.pyplot as plt

# Loading Dataset
path = r'C:\Users\User\mraj4\Documents\Optimum\Py-lib\scikit\time_One.csv'
df_orig = pd.read_csv(path, parse_dates=True, index_col="date")
df = df_orig.copy()

fig, axes = plt.subplots(7, 1, sharex=True, figsize=(10, 12))
plt.rcParams.update({'xtick.bottom': False})

# Case One: Actual
df_orig.plot(title='Actual', ax=axes[0], label='Actual', color='red', style=".-")
df.plot(title='Actual', ax=axes[0], label='Actual', color='green', style=".-")
axes[0].legend(["Missing Data", "Available Data"])

# Forward Fill
df_ffill = df.ffill()
```

```
error = mean_squared_error(df_orig['value'], df_ffill['value'])
df_ffill['value'].plot(title='Forward Fill (MSE: {:.2f})'.format(error), ax=axes[1],
label='Forward Fill', style=".-")

# Backward Fill
df_bfill = df.bfill()
error = mean_squared_error(df_orig['value'], df_bfill['value'])
df_bfill['value'].plot(title="Backward Fill (MSE: {:.2f})".format(error), ax=axes[2],
label='Back Fill', color='firebrick', style=".-")

# Linear Interpolation
df['rownum'] = np.arange(df.shape[0])
df_nona = df.dropna(subset=['value'])
f = interp1d(df_nona['rownum'], df_nona['value'])
df['linear_fill'] = f(df['rownum'])
error = mean_squared_error(df_orig['value'], df['linear_fill'])
df['linear_fill'].plot(title="Linear Fill (MSE: {:.2f})".format(error), ax=axes[3],
label='Linear Fill', color='brown', style=".-")

# Cubic Interpolation
f2 = interp1d(df_nona['rownum'], df_nona['value'], kind='cubic')
df['cubic_fill'] = f2(df['rownum'])
error = mean_squared_error(df_orig['value'], df['cubic_fill'])
df['cubic_fill'].plot(title="Cubic Fill (MSE: {:.2f})".format(error), ax=axes[4],
label='Cubic Fill', color='red', style=".-")

# Mean of 'n' Nearest Past Neighbors
def knn_mean(ts, n):
    out = np.copy(ts)
    for i, val in enumerate(ts):
        if np.isnan(val):
            n_by_2 = np.ceil(n/2)
            lower = np.max([0, int(i-n_by_2)])
            upper = np.min([len(ts)+1, int(i+n_by_2)])
            ts_near = np.concatenate([ts[lower:i], ts[i:upper]])
            out[i] = np.nanmean(ts_near)
    return out

df['knn_mean'] = knn_mean(df['value'].values, 8)
error = mean_squared_error(df_orig['value'], df['knn_mean'])
df['knn_mean'].plot(title="KNN Mean (MSE: {:.2f})".format(error), ax=axes[5],
label='KNN Mean', color='tomato', alpha=0.5, style=".-")

# Seasonal Mean
def seasonal_mean(ts, n, lr=0.7):
    out = np.copy(ts)
    for i, val in enumerate(ts):
        if np.isnan(val):
```

```
        ts_seas = ts[i-1::-n]  # previous seasons only
        if np.isnan(np.nanmean(ts_seas)):
            ts_seas = np.concatenate([ts[i-1::-n], ts[i::n]])  # previous and forward
        out[i] = np.nanmean(ts_seas) * lr
    return out

df['seasonal_mean'] = seasonal_mean(df['value'], n=12, lr=1.25)
error = mean_squared_error(df_orig['value'], df['seasonal_mean'])
df['seasonal_mean'].plot(title="Seasonal Mean (MSE: {:.2f})".format(error), ax=axes[6], label='Seasonal Mean', color='blue', alpha=0.5, style=".-")

plt.show()
```

Plot:

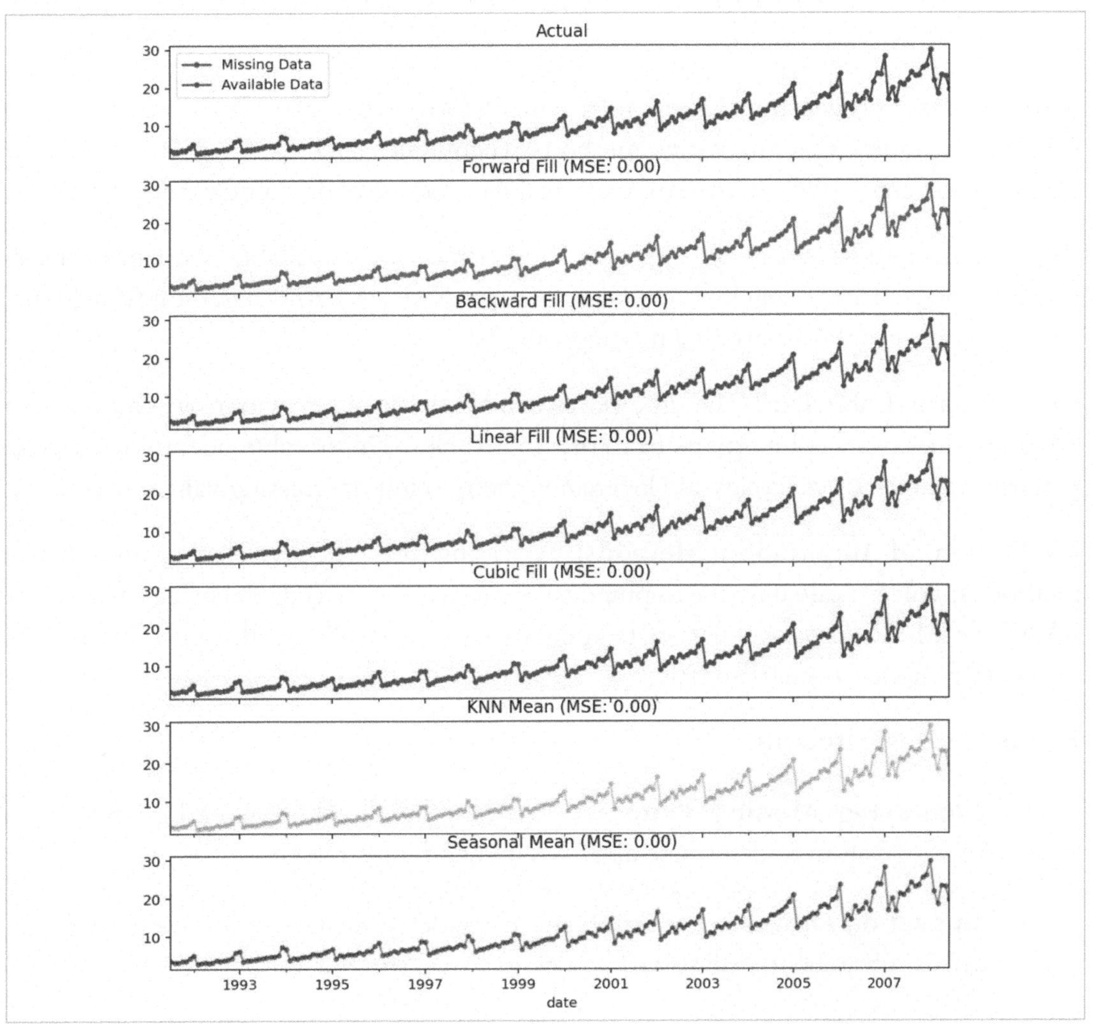

Master said, "This code compares multiple techniques for handling missing values in a time-series dataset. After loading the original data, it creates visual subplots to show how each method restores missing points. It applies common strategies such as forward fill, backward fill, and linear interpolation, and computes the Mean Squared Error (MSE) to assess accuracy. It also implements more advanced methods, including cubic interpolation, KNN-based neighbour averaging, and seasonal mean estimation. Finally, all reconstructed series are plotted together, helping evaluate which technique best matches the original data."

Master continued, "We can explore additional approaches based on the desired accuracy of imputations."

Utilise Explanatory Variables: If we possess explanatory variables, we can employ prediction models like random forests or k-Nearest Neighbors to predict missing values based on the available features.

Time Series Forecasting: Given sufficient historical data, we can forecast missing values using time series forecasting methods. Techniques such as ARIMA, Prophet, or machine learning models trained on historical data can provide accurate imputations.

Backcasting: In scenarios where future observations are available, we can backcast missing values. Backcasting involves forecasting past observations based on future data, which can be useful for imputing missing values.

Counterparts Forecast: If the time series exhibits cyclical behaviour, we can forecast missing values using counterparts from previous cycles. This involves identifying similar patterns from historical cycles and leveraging them to impute missing values effectively.

Evaluation of Imputation Methods: Assessing the effectiveness of imputation methods involves evaluating the imputed values against observed data using metrics like RMSE or MAE. Cross-validation techniques can also validate the performance of imputation models on unseen data.

Practical Considerations

- **Identifying Missing Patterns:** Analyze the distribution and patterns of missing values to determine appropriate handling strategies.
- **Impact on Downstream Analysis:** Consider how imputation methods may affect subsequent analysis tasks, such as forecasting or anomaly detection.
- **Computational Complexity vs. Accuracy:** Balance the computational

complexity of advanced imputation techniques with the accuracy improvement they offer.

Dealing with missing values in time series data requires careful consideration of temporal characteristics and patterns. By employing advanced imputation techniques that leverage temporal information, analysts can mitigate biases and preserve the integrity of time series data for meaningful analysis and modelling. Understanding the nuances of missingness mechanisms and selecting appropriate handling strategies are essential steps in ensuring the reliability of insights derived from time series data.

☐ Autocorrelation and Partial Autocorrelation

Nikash asked, "What are autocorrelation and partial autocorrelation functions?"

Master replied, "Autocorrelation and partial autocorrelation functions are essential tools in time series analysis."

Autocorrelation measures the correlation between a series and its own lagged values. It helps identify repeating patterns or dependencies within the series. For instance, a positive autocorrelation at lag 1 indicates that a high value at time t tends to be followed by another high value at time t+1.

On the other hand, partial autocorrelation captures the correlation between a series and its lag, excluding the correlation contributions from intermediate lags. It provides insights into the direct relationship between observations at different time points. For example, a significant partial autocorrelation at lag k implies that there is a direct relationship between observations k time units apart, after removing the effects of shorter lags.

Both autocorrelation and partial autocorrelation functions are vital for identifying the order of autoregressive and moving average components in time series models like ARIMA (AutoRegressive Integrated Moving Average). They help determine the appropriate lag values for constructing these models, thereby improving forecast accuracy.

Master said, "This code analyses the autocorrelation and partial autocorrelation of a time-series to understand its dependence structure. After loading the dataset, it computes the ACF and PACF values up to 50 lags using acf and pacf from statsmodels. These metrics help identify repeating patterns, seasonality, and autoregressive or moving-average behaviour. The results are visualised using plot_acf and plot_pacf in two side-by-side plots, offering clear insight into lag relationships and guiding model selection for AR, MA, or ARIMA-based forecasting."

Example P3 – U3 – D11
Time series – ACF and PACF

```
from statsmodels.tsa.stattools import acf, pacf
from statsmodels.graphics.tsaplots import plot_acf, plot_pacf
import pandas as pd
import matplotlib.pyplot as plt
# Loading Dataset
path = r'C:\Users\User\mraj4\Documents\Optimum\Py-lib\scikit\time_One.csv'
df = pd.read_csv(path, parse_dates=True, index_col="date")

# Calculate ACF and PACF upto 50 lags
acf_50 = acf(df.value, nlags=50)
pacf_50 = pacf(df.value, nlags=50)

# Draw Plot
fig, axes = plt.subplots(1, 2, figsize=(16, 3), dpi=100)
plot_acf(acf_50, ax=axes[0])
plot_pacf(pacf_50, ax=axes[1])
plt.show()
```

Plot:

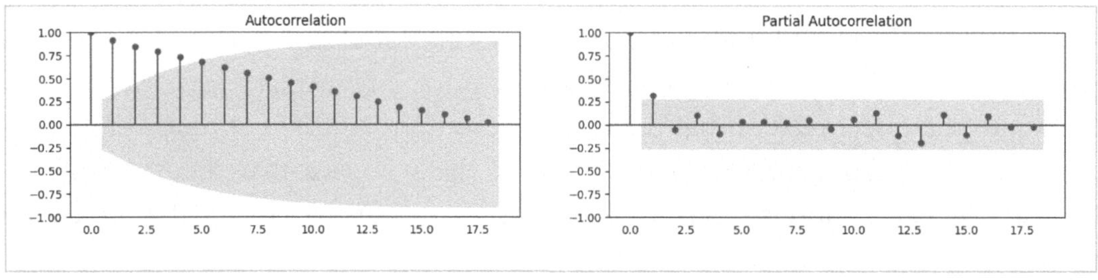

How to compute the partial autocorrelation function?

To compute the partial autocorrelation function (PACF) of a time series, follow these steps:

Fit an autoregressive (AR) model of order k to the time series.

Calculate the residuals from this model.

Compute the correlation coefficient between the original series and the lagged series, excluding the influence of the intermediate lags represented by the residuals.

The formula for the PACF of lag k is given by:

$$PACF(k) = Corr(Y_t, Y_{t-k} \mid Y_{t-1}, Y_{t-2}, \ldots, Y_{t-(k-1)})$$

Where:

- Y_t is the time series at time t.
- Y_{t-k} is the time series at time $t-k$.
- Y_{t-i} for $i = 1, 2, \ldots, k-1$ are the intermediate lags used to account for the autocorrelation structure.

LAG

Lag plots, on the other hand, are scatter plots of a time series against a lag of itself. They are useful for visualising autocorrelation in the data. If there is a discernible pattern in the lag plot, it indicates autocorrelation in the series. Conversely, if there is no clear pattern and the points are scattered randomly, the series is likely to be random white noise.

Master said, "This code visualises lag relationships in two time-series datasets—sunspot area and drug sales—using lag plots. After loading each dataset, it generates four lag plots for lags 1 to 4, showing how current values relate to past values. The plots help identify autocorrelation: tighter clusters indicate stronger correlation, while scattered points suggest weaker dependence as lag increases. Separate figure groups are created for each dataset, with consistent axis sharing for comparison. These visuals provide insight into the underlying structure, making it easier to assess predictability and time-series behaviour."

Example P3 – U3 – D12

Time series – Partial autocorrelation

```
from pandas.plotting import lag_plot

import pandas as pd

import numpy as np
import matplotlib.pyplot as plt

plt.rcParams.update({'ytick.left': False, 'axes.titlepad': 10})

# Define file paths
```

```
path1 = r'C:\Users\User\mraj4\Documents\Optimum\Py-lib\scikit\sunspotarea.csv'

path2 = r'C:\Users\User\mraj4\Documents\Optimum\Py-lib\scikit\time_One.csv'

# Plot lag plots for sun spot area

fig, axes = plt.subplots(1, 4, figsize=(10, 3), sharex=True, sharey=True, dpi=100)

for i, ax in enumerate(axes.flatten()[:4]):

    lag_plot(pd.read_csv(path1)['value'], lag=i + 1, ax=ax, c='firebrick')

    ax.set_title('Lag ' + str(i + 1))

fig.suptitle('Lag Plots of Sun Spots Area \n(Points get wide and scattered with increasing
lag -> lesser correlation)\n', y=1.15)

# Plot lag plots for drug sales

fig, axes = plt.subplots(1, 4, figsize=(10, 3), sharex=True, sharey=True, dpi=100)

for i, ax in enumerate(axes.flatten()[:4]):

    lag_plot(pd.read_csv(path2)['value'], lag=i + 1, ax=ax, c='firebrick')

    ax.set_title('Lag ' + str(i + 1))

fig.suptitle('Lag Plots of Drug Sales', y=1.05)

plt.show()
```

Plot 1

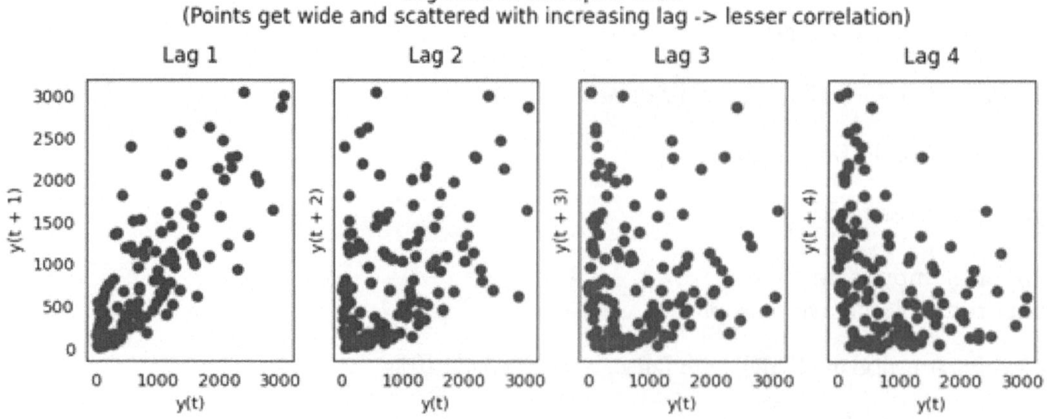

Plot 2

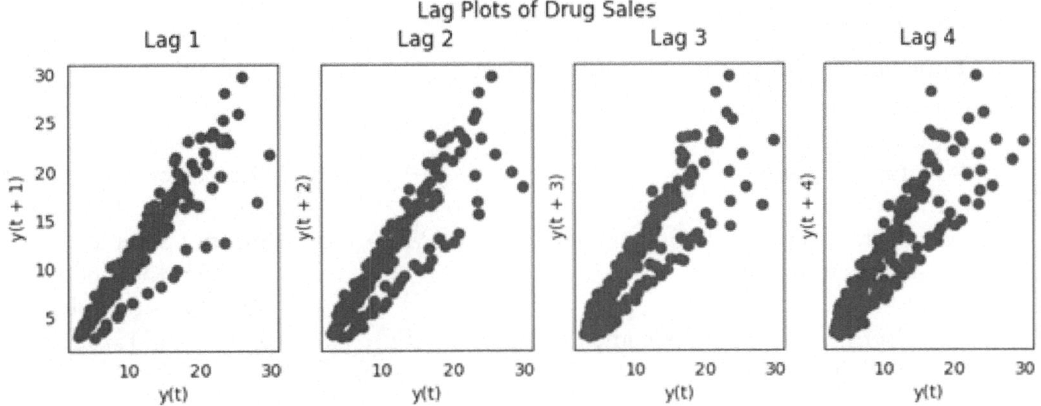

☐ Forecastability of a time series

Sam asked, "How to estimate the forecastability of a time series?"

Master replied, "To estimate the forecastability of a time series, you can use metrics such as Approximate Entropy and Sample Entropy. These metrics quantify the regularity and unpredictability of fluctuations in the time series, providing insights into its forecastability."

Approximate Entropy (ApEn): Approximate Entropy measures the unpredictability of fluctuations in a time series. It quantifies the likelihood that similar patterns of data points will repeat. Higher values of ApEn indicate greater complexity and unpredictability in the time series, making it more difficult to forecast. Lower values suggest more regular and predictable patterns, indicating higher forecastability.

Sample Entropy (SampEn): Sample Entropy is a variation of Approximate Entropy that addresses its limitations, particularly for a shorter time series. It provides a more consistent estimation of complexity, even for smaller datasets. Similar to ApEn, higher values of SampEn suggest greater unpredictability and lower forecastability.

By calculating these entropy metrics for a time series, you can gauge its forecastability. A time series with higher entropy values is likely to be more challenging to forecast due to its irregular and unpredictable fluctuations, while lower entropy values indicate more regular patterns and higher forecastability.

<table>
<tr><th>Example P3 – U3 – D13</th><th></th></tr>
<tr><th>Time series – Imputing Missing Values</th><th>Output</th></tr>
<tr><td><pre>
import pandas as pd
import numpy as np
# Define file paths
path1 =
r'C:\Users\User\mraj4\Documents\Optimum\Py-
lib\scikit\sunspotarea.csv'
path2 =
r'C:\Users\User\mraj4\Documents\Optimum\Py-
lib\scikit\time_One.csv'

rand_small = np.random.randint(0, 100, size=36)
rand_big = np.random.randint(0, 100, size=136)

# Calculate Approximate Entropy
def approximate_entropy(U, m, r):
    """Compute Approximate entropy"""
    def _maxdist(x_i, x_j):
        return max([abs(ua - va) for ua, va in zip(x_i, x_j)])

    def _phi(m):
        x = [[U[j] for j in range(i, i + m - 1 + 1)] for i in
range(N - m + 1)]
        C = [len([1 for x_j in x if _maxdist(x_i, x_j) <= r]) /
(N - m + 1.0) for x_i in x]
        return (N - m + 1.0)**(-1) * sum(np.log(C))

    N = len(U)
    return abs(_phi(m + 1) - _phi(m))

# Calculate Sample Entropy
def sample_entropy(U, m, r):
    """Compute Sample entropy"""
    def _maxdist(x_i, x_j):
        return max([abs(ua - va) for ua, va in zip(x_i, x_j)])

    def _phi(m):
        x = [[U[j] for j in range(i, i + m - 1 + 1)] for i in
range(N - m + 1)]
        C = [len([1 for j in range(len(x)) if i != j and
_maxdist(x[i], x[j]) <= r]) for i in range(len(x))]
        return sum(C)

    N = len(U)
    return -np.log(_phi(m + 1) / _phi(m))
</pre></td><td>Sunspot Approximate:
0.6514704970333534
Drug Sales Approximate:
0.5374775224973489
Sunspot Sample:
0.7853311366380039
Drug Sales Sample:
0.41887013457621214</td></tr>
</table>

```
# Load data from CSV files
data_path1 = pd.read_csv(path1).value
data_path2 = pd.read_csv(path2).value

# Calculate and print approximate entropy
print("Sunspot Approximate:",
approximate_entropy(data_path1, m=2, r=0.2 *
np.std(data_path1)))
print("Drug Sales Approximate:",
approximate_entropy(data_path2, m=2, r=0.2 *
np.std(data_path2)))

# Calculate and print sample entropy
print("Sunspot Sample:", sample_entropy(data_path1,
m=2, r=0.2 * np.std(data_path1)))
print("Drug Sales Sample:", sample_entropy(data_path2,
m=2, r=0.2 * np.std(data_path2)))
```

- **Forecast Evaluation:**

Diebold-Mariano Test: The Diebold-Mariano test is a statistical test used to compare the forecasting accuracy of the two competing models. It assesses whether one forecasting model significantly outperforms another in terms of forecast accuracy. The test examines whether the difference in forecast errors between the two models is statistically significant.

Encompassing Test: The encompassing test evaluates the performance of a new forecasting model relative to an existing model. It assesses whether the new model provides additional information beyond what is captured by the existing model. The test examines whether the new model "encompasses" the forecasting performance of the existing model by providing more accurate forecasts.

Bias Test: The bias test evaluates whether a forecasting model exhibits systematic errors or biases in its predictions. It assesses whether the forecast errors of the model are consistently positive or negative, indicating a tendency to overestimate or underestimate the true values, respectively. The bias test helps identify and correct for systematic errors in forecasting models.

Smoothing a time series can be beneficial for various reasons:

Noise Reduction: Smoothing helps in reducing the impact of noise present in the signal, allowing for a clearer understanding of the underlying patterns.

Feature Extraction: The smoothed version of a series can serve as a useful feature to explain the original series, aiding in feature engineering for predictive modelling.

Trend Visualization: Smoothing techniques help in visualising the underlying trend of the data, making it easier to identify long-term patterns and trends.

To smoothen a time series, you can employ different methods:

Moving Average: Compute the average of a rolling window of a defined width. Care must be taken to choose an appropriate window size to avoid over-smoothing.

LOESS (Localized Regression): LOESS fits multiple regressions in the local neighborhood of each point, allowing for flexible smoothing. The degree of smoothing can be controlled using parameters like the fraction of nearby data points to consider.

LOWESS (Locally Weighted Regression): Similar to LOESS, LOWESS performs locally weighted regressions to achieve smoothing. It offers flexibility in controlling the degree of smoothing by adjusting the weight assigned to each data point based on its proximity.

By applying these smoothing techniques, you can effectively reduce noise, extract meaningful features, and visualize trends in time series data.

Example P3 – U3 – D14

Time series – Smoothing

```
from statsmodels.nonparametric.smoothers_lowess import lowess
import pandas as pd
import numpy as np
import matplotlib.pyplot as plt
# Define file paths
path1 = r'C:\Users\User\mraj4\Documents\Optimum\Py-lib\scikit\elec.csv'
# Load Dataset
df_orig = pd.read_csv(path1, parse_dates=['date'], index_col='date')

# Set plot parameters
plt.rcParams.update({'xtick.bottom': False, 'axes.titlepad': 5})

# 1. Moving Average
df_ma = df_orig['value'].rolling(window=3, center=True, closed='both').mean()

# 2. Loess Smoothing (5% and 15%)
df_loess_5 = pd.DataFrame(lowess(df_orig['value'], np.arange(len(df_orig['value'])),
frac=0.05)[:, 1], index=df_orig.index, columns=['value'])
df_loess_15 = pd.DataFrame(lowess(df_orig['value'], np.arange(len(df_orig['value'])),
frac=0.15)[:, 1], index=df_orig.index, columns=['value'])
```

```
# Plot
fig, axes = plt.subplots(4, 1, figsize=(7, 7), sharex=True, dpi=120)
df_orig['value'].plot(ax=axes[0], color='k', title='Original Series')
df_loess_5['value'].plot(ax=axes[1], title='Loess Smoothed 5%')
df_loess_15['value'].plot(ax=axes[2], title='Loess Smoothed 15%')
df_ma.plot(ax=axes[3], title='Moving Average (3)')
fig.suptitle('How to Smoothen a Time Series', y=0.95, fontsize=14)
plt.show()
```

Plot

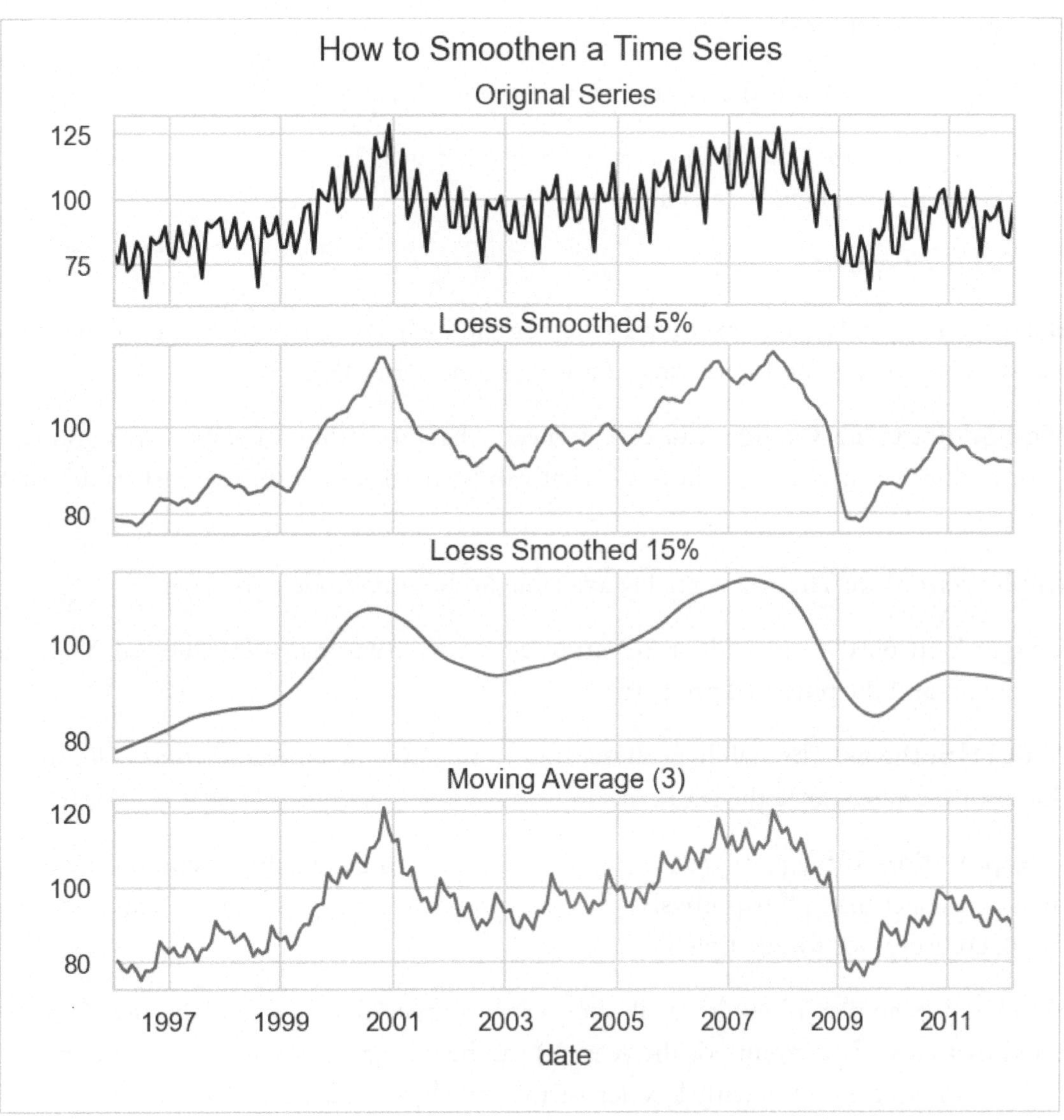

Master said, "The code demonstrates different smoothing techniques to reduce noise and reveal underlying patterns in a time-series. After loading the dataset, it applies a 3-point moving average to smooth short-term fluctuations. It then uses LOESS smoothing with two window proportions (5% and 15%), providing both fine and broader smoothing effects. Four subplots compare the original series, LOESS-smoothed outputs, and moving-average results. This visual comparison helps understand how each method balances noise reduction and trend preservation, making it useful for signal cleaning, trend extraction, and time-series preprocessing."

Granger causality test

Akshaya asked, "What is the Granger causality test?"

Master explained that the Granger causality test is a valuable tool for assessing whether one time series can help predict another.

Here's how it works:

Basic Concept: The test examines whether the inclusion of past values of one time series (X) improves the forecasting of another time series (Y).

Methodology: If X Granger-causes Y, it means that past values of X provide significant information for predicting Y beyond what can be predicted from the past values of Y alone.

Implementation: The test is readily available in the statsmodels package.

Usage: You need to provide a 2D array with two columns: the values of Y (to be predicted) and the potential predictor X.

Null Hypothesis: The null hypothesis states that the series in the second column (X) does not Granger-cause the series in the first column (Y).

Interpretation: If the p-values are below a chosen significance level (commonly 0.05), then you reject the null hypothesis. This indicates that the lag of X included in the test is indeed useful for forecasting Y.

Here's an example: If you're analysing air passenger data, you might use Granger causality to test if the month of the year (X) can help predict air passenger numbers (Y). If the p-values are consistently low across multiple lags, it suggests that the month does indeed contribute to predicting air passenger traffic.

Example P3 – U3 – D15

Time series - Granger causality test

```
from statsmodels.tsa.stattools import grangercausalitytests
import pandas as pd
# Load Dataset
path = r'C:\Users\User\mraj4\Documents\Optimum\Py-lib\scikit\time_One.csv'
df = pd.read_csv(path, parse_dates=True, index_col="date")
# Add month column
df['month'] = df.index.month

# Perform Granger causality test
granger_results = grangercausalitytests(df[['value', 'month']], maxlag=2)

# Print results
for lag in granger_results.keys():
    print(f"Lag {lag}:")
    for key, value in granger_results[lag][0].items():
        print(f"{key}: {value}")
    print()
```

Output:

```
Granger Causality
number of lags (no zero) 1
ssr based F test:         F=54.7797  , p=0.0000  , df_denom=200, df_num=1
ssr based chi2 test:   chi2=55.6014  , p=0.0000  , df=1
likelihood ratio test: chi2=49.1426  , p=0.0000  , df=1
parameter F test:         F=54.7797  , p=0.0000  , df_denom=200, df_num=1

Granger Causality
number of lags (no zero) 2
ssr based F test:         F=162.6989, p=0.0000  , df_denom=197, df_num=2
ssr based chi2 test:   chi2=333.6567, p=0.0000  , df=2
likelihood ratio test: chi2=196.9956, p=0.0000  , df=2
parameter F test:         F=162.6989, p=0.0000  , df_denom=197, df_num=2
Lag 1:
ssr_ftest: (54.77967483557363, 3.661425871353039e-12, 200.0, 1)
ssr_chi2test: (55.60136995810724, 8.876175235021315e-14, 1)
lrtest: (49.142602330049954, 2.3801430060455094e-12, 1)
params_ftest: (54.77967483557355, 3.6614258713532185e-12, 200.0, 1.0)

Lag 2:
ssr_ftest: (162.69891799873238, 1.9133235086856856e-42, 197.0, 2)
ssr_chi2test: (333.6566643222735, 3.5267600881279647e-73, 2)
lrtest: (196.99559277182198, 1.6709003499115789e-43, 2)
params_ftest: (162.6989179987326, 1.913323508685497e-42, 197.0, 2.0)
```

PART THREE

DAY TEN

Unit 3 - Lesson Three

Decoding Time

☐ Why Forecasting?

Master said, "Akshaya — Forecasting time-series data such as demand and sales carries immense commercial value, forming the backbone of intelligent business decision-making."

Accurate forecasts empower organisations to plan effectively, optimise resources, and reduce operational risks.

Business Planning: Accurate forecasts drive strategic decision-making processes, including resource allocation, capacity planning, and inventory management.

Supply Chain Management: Forecasts inform procurement, production scheduling, and logistics operations, optimising the flow of goods and minimising inventory costs.

Cost Savings: Precision in forecasting reduces overstocking and stockouts, leading to cost savings by minimising excess inventory and lost sales.

☐ Types of Time Series Forecasting

Forecasting methods can be broadly categorised into two types:

Univariate Time Series Forecasting: This approach utilises only the historical values of the target variable to predict its future values. Techniques such as autoregressive integrated moving average (ARIMA), exponential smoothing methods (e.g., Holt-Winters), and seasonal decomposition are commonly used in univariate forecasting.

Multivariate Time Series Forecasting: In this approach, predictors other than the target series, known as exogenous variables, are used alongside historical data to forecast future values. Multivariate forecasting models leverage the relationships between the target variable and other relevant factors, enabling more accurate predictions. Examples include vector autoregression (VAR), dynamic regression, and machine learning algorithms like random forests and gradient boosting.

Both univariate and multivariate forecasting techniques play vital roles in diverse business contexts, offering distinct advantages based on the availability of data and the complexity of the underlying processes.

By leveraging forecasting models effectively, organisations can enhance their operational efficiency, optimise resource utilisation, and adapt to dynamic market conditions, ultimately driving sustainable growth and competitive advantage.

☐ Understanding ARIMA Models

Sam asked, "What is an ARIMA Model?"

Master replied, "ARIMA, or AutoRegressive Integrated Moving Average, is a widely used forecasting algorithm designed to capture patterns and dependencies within a time series dataset."

It comprises three key components:

AutoRegressive (AR) Term (p): The 'AR' term represents the relationship between the current observation and its lagged values. It captures the linear dependency of the series on its own past values. The parameter 'p' denotes the number of lagged terms included in the model.

Integrated (I) Term (d): The 'I' term reflects the number of differencing operations needed to transform the time series into a stationary process. Stationarity is crucial for many time series models, as it ensures that statistical properties remain constant over time. The parameter 'd' signifies the degree of differencing applied to stabilize the series.

Moving Average (MA) Term (q): The 'MA' term accounts for the dependency between the current observation and a residual error from a moving average model. It captures the short-term fluctuations or irregularities not accounted for by the autoregressive component. The parameter ‘q’ specifies the number of lagged forecast errors considered in the model.

Non-Seasonal ARIMA Modelling

Master continued, ARIMA models are particularly effective for non-seasonal time series data, exhibiting discernible patterns or trends. By analysing the autocorrelation and partial autocorrelation functions, analysts can determine the appropriate values of ‘p’, ‘d’, and ‘q’ to construct an optimal ARIMA model.

Seasonal ARIMA (SARIMA) and SARIMAX Models:

For time series with seasonal patterns, such as monthly or quarterly data, the standard ARIMA framework may not suffice. SARIMA extends the ARIMA model to incorporate seasonal components, including seasonal autoregressive (SAR) and seasonal moving average (SMA) terms. This allows for more accurate forecasting of seasonal variations.

SARIMAX further enhances the SARIMA model by incorporating exogenous variables, such as external predictors or covariates, into the forecasting process. By integrating additional information, SARIMAX models can capture external influences and improve forecast accuracy.

In summary, ARIMA models offer a versatile framework for time series forecasting, capable of capturing both non-seasonal and seasonal patterns. By fine-tuning the model parameters and considering external factors, analysts can develop robust forecasting solutions to support decision-making in various domains.

Autoregressive (AR) Model:

In an Autoregressive (AR) model, the value of the time series at a given point is modelled as a linear combination of its own past values, also known as lags. Mathematically, an AR(p) model of order ‘p’ is represented as:

$$Yt = c + \phi_1 Y_t - 1 + \phi_2 Y_{t-2} + \ldots + \phi_p Y_{t-p} + \varepsilon_t$$

where:

- Y_t is the value of the time series at time ‘t’.
- c is a constant term.

- $\phi_1, \phi_2, \ldots, \phi_p$ are the parameters (coefficients) of the model representing the relationship between the current value and its lagged values.
- ε_t is the error term representing the random noise at time 't'.

Moving Average (MA) Model:

In a Moving Average (MA) model, the value of the time series at a given point is modelled as a linear combination of white noise terms from the previous time steps. Mathematically, an MA(q) model of order 'q' is represented as:

$$Y_t = \mu + \theta_1 \varepsilon_{t-1} + \theta_1 \varepsilon_{t-2} + \cdots + \theta_1 \varepsilon_{t-q} + \varepsilon_t$$

where:

- t is the value of the time series at time 't'.
- μ is the mean of the series.
- $\theta_1, \theta_2, \ldots, \theta_q$ are the parameters (coefficients) of the model representing the relationship between the current value and the white noise terms at previous time steps.
- ε_t is the error term representing the random noise at time 't'.

These equations illustrate the fundamental principles of AR and MA models, where the AR model captures the relationship between the current value and its own past values, while the MA model captures the relationship between the current value and past random shocks or disturbances.

Differencing

To find the optimal order of differencing (d) in an ARIMA model, you can follow these steps:

Check for Stationarity: Use the Augmented Dickey Fuller (ADF) test to determine if the time series is stationary. If the p-value of the test is less than the significance level (usually 0.05), the series is considered stationary, and no differencing is required (d=0). If the series is non-stationary (p-value > 0.05), proceed to the next step.

Plot ACF and PACF: Plot the Autocorrelation Function (ACF) and Partial Autocorrelation Function (PACF) of the differenced series. Look for significant spikes in the ACF and PACF plots, which indicate potential orders of differencing (d).

Test Different Orders of Differencing: Start with d=1 and incrementally increase the order of differencing until the series becomes stationary. For each order of differencing, use the ADF test to check for stationarity.

Select the Optimal Order: Choose the order of differencing (d) that results in a stationary series with the lowest standard deviation and a well-behaved ACF plot (autocorrelations decay to zero quickly).

Model Fitting: Once the optimal order of differencing is determined, proceed with fitting an ARIMA model using the selected order of differencing along with appropriate values for the AR (p) and MA (q) parameters.

By following these steps, you can effectively determine the optimal order of differencing for your ARIMA model, ensuring that it captures the underlying patterns in the time series data while maintaining stationarity.

Master said, "This code performs the Augmented Dickey–Fuller (ADF) test to check whether a time-series dataset is stationary. It imports the adfuller function from statsmodels and loads a CSV file using pandas. After reading the data into a DataFrame, it removes missing values from the value column and applies the ADF test. The output prints the ADF statistic and p-value, helping determine if the series has a unit root or requires differencing for further time-series modeling."

Example P3 – U3 – D16	
Time series – Order of Differencing	**Output**
from statsmodels.tsa.stattools import adfuller import pandas as pd # Load Dataset path = r'C:\Users\User\mraj4\Documents\Optimum\Py-lib\scikit\time_one.csv' df = pd.read_csv(path) result = adfuller(df.value.dropna()) print('ADF Statistic: %f' % result[0]) print('p-value: %f' % result[1])	ADF Statistic: 3.145186 p-value: 1.000000

Order of Differencing

Master said, This code demonstrates how a time series transforms through differencing to achieve stationarity. It begins by importing NumPy, pandas, matplotlib, and the ACF plotting tool from statsmodels. After loading the dataset, a figure with multiple subplots is created to compare the original series with its first and second differences. The original data is plotted alongside its autocorrelation function, revealing inherent patterns. Then, first-order and second-order differenced series are generated and visualized with their respective ACF plots. Through these visual insights, one learns how differencing removes trends and stabilizes the variance in time-series analysis.

Example P3 – U3 – D17

Time series – Imputing Missing Values

```
import numpy as np
import pandas as pd
import matplotlib.pyplot as plt
from statsmodels.graphics.tsaplots import plot_acf
plt.rcParams.update({'figure.figsize': (12, 10), 'figure.dpi': 120})
# Load Dataset
path = r'C:\Users\User\mraj4\Documents\Optimum\Py-lib\scikit\time_two.csv'
df = pd.read_csv(path, names=['value'], header=0)

# Original Series
fig, axes = plt.subplots(3, 2, sharex=True)
fig.suptitle('Original Series and Differenced Series', fontsize=16)

# Plot original series
axes[0, 0].plot(df.value)
axes[0, 0].set_title('Original Series')
axes[0, 0].set_xlabel('Time')
axes[0, 0].set_ylabel('Value')
plot_acf(df.value, ax=axes[0, 1])
axes[0, 1].set_title('ACF of Original Series')

# 1st Differencing
axes[1, 0].plot(df.value.diff())
axes[1, 0].set_title('1st Order Differencing')
axes[1, 0].set_xlabel('Time')
axes[1, 0].set_ylabel('Differenced Value')
plot_acf(df.value.diff().dropna(), ax=axes[1, 1])
axes[1, 1].set_title('ACF of 1st Order Differencing')

# 2nd Differencing
axes[2, 0].plot(df.value.diff().diff())
axes[2, 0].set_title('2nd Order Differencing')
axes[2, 0].set_xlabel('Time')
axes[2, 0].set_ylabel('Differenced Value')
plot_acf(df.value.diff().diff().dropna(), ax=axes[2, 1])
axes[2, 1].set_title('ACF of 2nd Order Differencing')

plt.tight_layout()
plt.show()
```

Plot

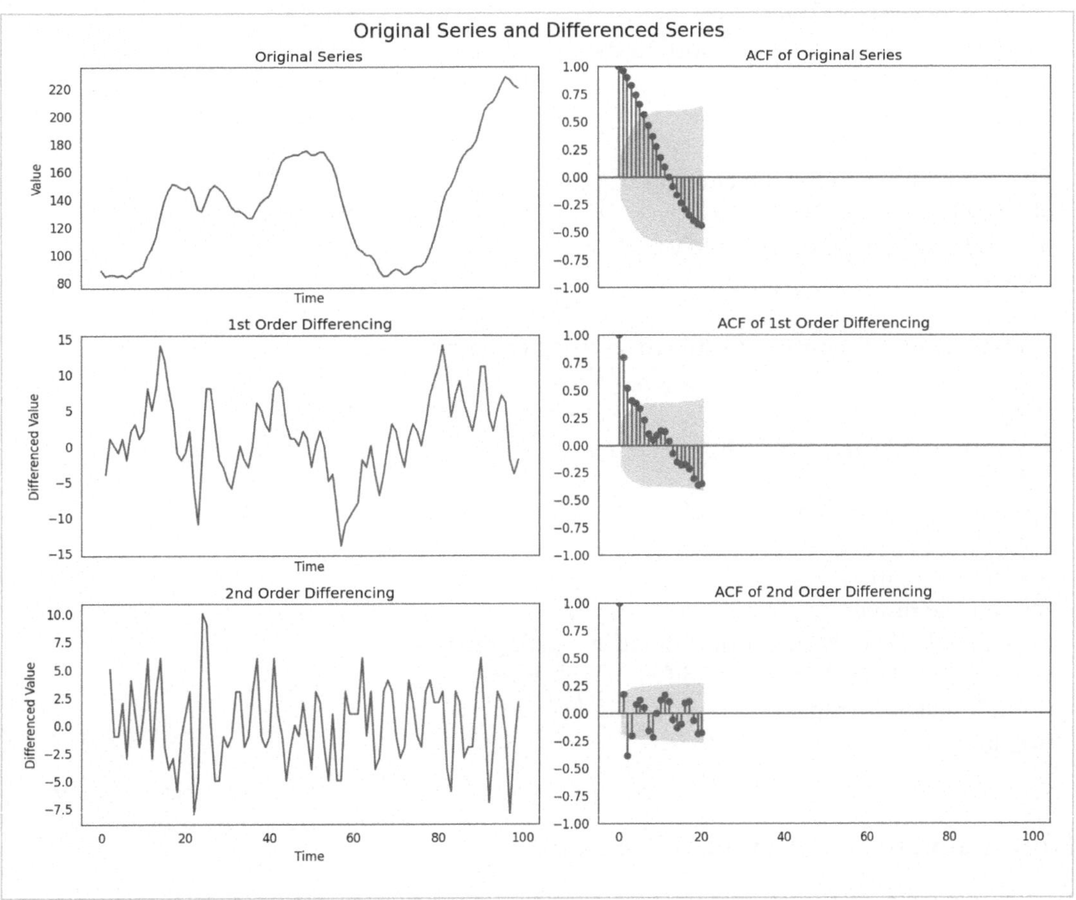

For the above series, the time series reaches quasi-stationarity with two orders of differencing. However, on examining the autocorrelation plot for the 2nd differencing, the lag quickly enters the far negative zone. This behaviour suggests that the series might have been over-differenced.

Therefore, we tentatively fix the order of differencing as 1, even though the series is not perfectly stationary. Instead, it exhibits quasi-stationarity, where differencing helps in achieving a more stable behaviour similar to a stationary series.

Master said, This code helps determine how many times a time series must be differenced to become stationary. After loading the dataset, the series is passed through three statistical tests—ADF, KPSS, and Phillips-Perron—using the ndiffs function from pmdarima. Each test suggests the minimum differencing required to remove trends and stabilize the data. The results are printed, offering guidance for ARIMA model building. This approach ensures the series is properly transformed before forecasting, improving accuracy and model reliability.

Example P3 – U3 – D18	
Time series – Different tests	**Output**

from pmdarima.arima.utils import ndiffs
import pandas as pd
# Load Dataset 	
path =
r'C:\Users\User\mraj4\Documents\Optimum\Py-lib\scikit\time_two.csv'
df = pd.read_csv(path, names=['value'], header=0)
y = df.value
 	
# Determine the number of differences using different tests 	
# ADF Test 	
adf_diffs = ndiffs(y, test='adf')
# KPSS Test 	
kpss_diffs = ndiffs(y, test='kpss')
# Phillips-Perron Test 	
pp_diffs = ndiffs(y, test='pp')
# Print the results 	
print("ADF Test - Number of differences:", adf_diffs)
print("KPSS Test - Number of differences:", kpss_diffs)
print("Phillips-Perron Test - Number of differences:", pp_diffs)
	ADF Test - Number of differences: 2
	KPSS Test - Number of differences: 0
	Phillips-Perron Test - Number of differences: 2

How to find the order of the AR term (p)

To determine the number of autoregressive (AR) terms needed in the model, we examine the Partial Autocorrelation Function (PACF) plot.

PACF:

John asked, "What is PACF?"

Master replied, "The Partial Autocorrelation Function (PACF) represents the correlation between the series and its lag, excluding the contributions from intermediate lags. Essentially, PACF provides the pure correlation between a lag and the series, helping us understand whether that lag is necessary in the AR term."

Mathematical Formula for PACF:

$$y_t = \alpha_0 + \alpha_1 y_{t-1} + \alpha_2 y_{t-2} + \alpha_3 y_{t-3}$$

The partial autocorrelation of lag *k* of a series is the coefficient of that lag in the autoregression equation of *Y*. For instance, if *Yt* is the current series and *Yt*−1 is the lag 1 of *Y*, then the partial autocorrelation of lag 3 (*Yt*−3) is represented by the coefficient *a*3 of *Yt*−3 in the autoregression equation.

Determining the Order of AR Term:

The initial order of the AR term (p) is set equal to the number of lags that cross the significance limit in the PACF plot. Any autocorrelation in a stationarized series can be corrected by adding sufficient AR terms.

Master said, this code visualizes both the ACF and PACF of a time series before and after differencing to assess stationarity and identify ARIMA model parameters. After loading the dataset, a 2×2 subplot layout is created. The top row displays the ACF and PACF of the original series, helping detect trends, seasonality, and autoregressive patterns. The bottom row plots the first-order differenced series along with its ACF and PACF, revealing how differencing impacts autocorrelation. These visual diagnostics guide the selection of AR (p) and MA (q) terms, ensuring accurate and well-structured time-series modelling.

Example P3 – U3 – D19

Time series – Find AR and MA

```
import numpy as np
import pandas as pd
import matplotlib.pyplot as plt
from statsmodels.graphics.tsaplots import plot_acf, plot_pacf
plt.rcParams.update({'figure.figsize': (12, 10), 'figure.dpi': 120})

# Load Dataset
path = r'C:\Users\User\mraj4\Documents\Optimum\Py-lib\scikit\time_two.csv'
df = pd.read_csv(path, names=['value'], header=0)

# Plot ACF and PACF
fig, axes = plt.subplots(2, 2, figsize=(12, 6))

# Plot ACF of original series
plot_acf(df.value, ax=axes[0, 0], lags=50)
axes[0, 0].set_title('Autocorrelation Function (ACF)')

# Plot PACF of original series
plot_pacf(df.value, ax=axes[0, 1], lags=30)
axes[0, 1].set_title('Partial Autocorrelation Function (PACF)')

# Plot ACF of first differenced series
```

```
axes[1, 0].plot(df.value.diff())
axes[1, 0].set_title('1st Differencing')
plot_acf(df.value.diff(), ax=axes[1, 0], lags=50)

# Plot PACF of first differenced series
axes[1, 1].plot(df.value.diff())
axes[1, 1].set_title('1st Differencing')
plot_pacf(df.value.diff().dropna(), ax=axes[1, 1], lags=30)
plt.tight_layout()
plt.show()
```

We observe that the PACF at lag 1 is notably significant, well above the significance line. Lag 2 also appears to be significant, albeit slightly crossing the significance limit (blue region). However, we adopt a conservative approach and tentatively fix the number of AR terms, denoted as p, as 1.

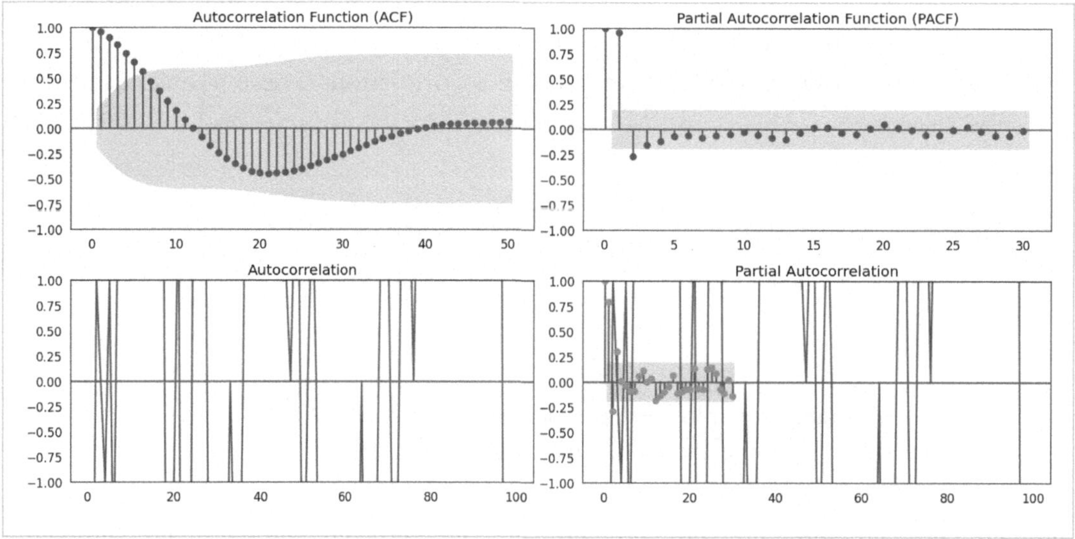

Similarly, we can utilise the ACF plot to determine the number of MA terms, denoted as q. An MA term represents the error of the lagged forecast. Upon inspecting the ACF plot, we notice that a couple of lags exceed the significance line. Therefore, we tentatively fix q as 2.

In situations of uncertainty, it's advisable to opt for the simpler model that adequately captures the underlying patterns in the data.

☐ ARIMA MODEL:

Master continued, if a time series is slightly under-differenced, adding one or more additional autoregressive (AR) terms can often rectify the issue. Conversely, if it is slightly over-differenced, consider incorporating an additional moving average (MA) term.

To build the ARIMA model, once the values of p, d, and q are determined, everything needed is in place. We can utilize the ARIMA() implementation from the statsmodels package.

Master said, This code demonstrates how to build and evaluate an ARIMA model for time series forecasting. After loading the dataset, an ARIMA model with parameters (1, 1, 2) is created—representing one autoregressive term, first-order differencing, and two moving-average terms. The model is then fitted to the data to learn underlying patterns and temporal dependencies. Finally, the summary output displays key statistical metrics, coefficients, and diagnostics, helping assess model performance and suitability for forecasting future values.

Example P3 – U3 – D20

Time series – ARIMA Model

```
from statsmodels.tsa.arima.model import ARIMA
import pandas as pd
# Load Dataset
path = r'C:\Users\User\mraj4\Documents\Optimum\Py-lib\scikit\time_two.csv'
df = pd.read_csv(path, names=['value'], header=0)
# Build ARIMA Model
model = ARIMA(df.value, order=(1, 1, 2))
model_fit = model.fit()
# Print Model Summary
print(model_fit.summary())
```

Output:

```
Output

 SARIMAX Results
Dep. Variable:              value   No. Observations:          100
Model:              ARIMA(1, 1, 2)  Log Likelihood          -254.126
Date:             Fri, 21 Nov 2025   AIC                     516.253
Time:                     10:54:37   BIC                     526.633
Sample:                          0   HQIC                    520.453
                             - 100
Covariance Type:               opg
              coef    std err       z     P>|z|    [0.025    0.975]
```

```
--------------------------------------------------------------------------------
ar.L1        0.6976     0.130     5.365      0.000      0.443      0.952
ma.L1         0.4551     0.169     2.699      0.007      0.125      0.786
ma.L2        -0.0664     0.157    -0.424      0.671     -0.373      0.241
sigma2        9.7898     1.421     6.889      0.000      7.005     12.575
===================================================================================
Ljung-Box (L1) (Q):                   0.00   Jarque-Bera (JB):                 0.09
Prob(Q):                              0.98   Prob(JB):                         0.95
Heteroskedasticity (H):               0.63   Skew:                            -0.07
Prob(H) (two-sided):                  0.19   Kurtosis:                         3.03
```

Upon examining the model summary, valuable insights can be gleaned. The coefficients table provides information about the weights of the respective terms. For instance, if a coefficient is close to zero and the p-value in the 'P>|z|' column is highly insignificant (ideally less than 0.05), it suggests that the corresponding term may not be significant.

In such cases, it's prudent to rebuild the model without the insignificant term MA2.

Example P3 – U3 – D21
Time series – Arima Model

```
import pandas as pd
from statsmodels.tsa.arima.model import ARIMA
import matplotlib.pyplot as plt
# Load Dataset
path = r'C:\Users\User\mraj4\Documents\Optimum\Py-lib\scikit\time_two.csv'
df = pd.read_csv(path, names=['value'], header=0)

# Build ARIMA Model
model = ARIMA(df.value, order=(1, 1, 1))
model_fit = model.fit()
# Print Model Summary
print(model_fit.summary())

# Plot residual errors
residuals = pd.DataFrame(model_fit.resid)
fig, ax = plt.subplots(1, 2, figsize=(12, 6))
residuals.plot(title="Residuals", ax=ax[0])
residuals.plot(kind='kde', title='Density', ax=ax[1])
plt.show()

# Forecast - Actual vs Fitted
forecast_steps = 10  # Specify the number of steps ahead for forecasting
forecast_index = pd.date_range(start=df.index[-1], periods=forecast_steps + 1)[1:]
# Generate Forecast
```

```
forecast = model_fit.forecast(steps=forecast_steps)
# Plot Forecast
plt.plot(df.index, df.value, label='Actual')
plt.plot(forecast_index, forecast, color='red', label='Forecast')
plt.title('Actual vs Forecast')
plt.xlabel('Date')
plt.ylabel('Value')
plt.legend()
plt.show()
```

The improved significance of the AR1 and MA1 terms, with p-values substantially below 0.05, is a positive indicator of model fit. Now, it's crucial to examine the residuals to verify if they exhibit any discernible patterns. Residuals should ideally be devoid of any systematic patterns, showcasing a random scatter around zero, indicating that the model has adequately captured the underlying data dynamics.

Output:

```
Ouput

SARIMAX Results
================================
Dep. Variable:            value      No. Observations:           100
Model:              ARIMA(1, 1, 1)   Log Likelihood           -254.150
Date:             Fri, 21 Nov 2025   AIC                      514.300
Time:                  11:08:15      BIC                      522.086
Sample:                       0      HQIC                      517.450
                          - 100
Covariance Type:            opg
================================
          coef    std err      z     P>|z|    [0.025     0.975]
------------------------------------------------------------------------------
ar.L1     0.6504   0.090    7.258    0.000     0.475     0.826
ma.L1     0.5256   0.088    5.994    0.000     0.354     0.697
sigma2    9.7934   1.405    6.970    0.000     7.040    12.547
====================================
Ljung-Box (L1) (Q):              0.03   Jarque-Bera (JB):         0.12
Prob(Q):                     0.86       Prob(JB):                 0.94
Heteroskedasticity (H):          0.63   Skew:                    -0.08
Prob(H) (two-sided):             0.19   Kurtosis:                 3.06
```

Let's proceed to plot the residuals and ensure they meet these criteria.

Actual vs Fitted

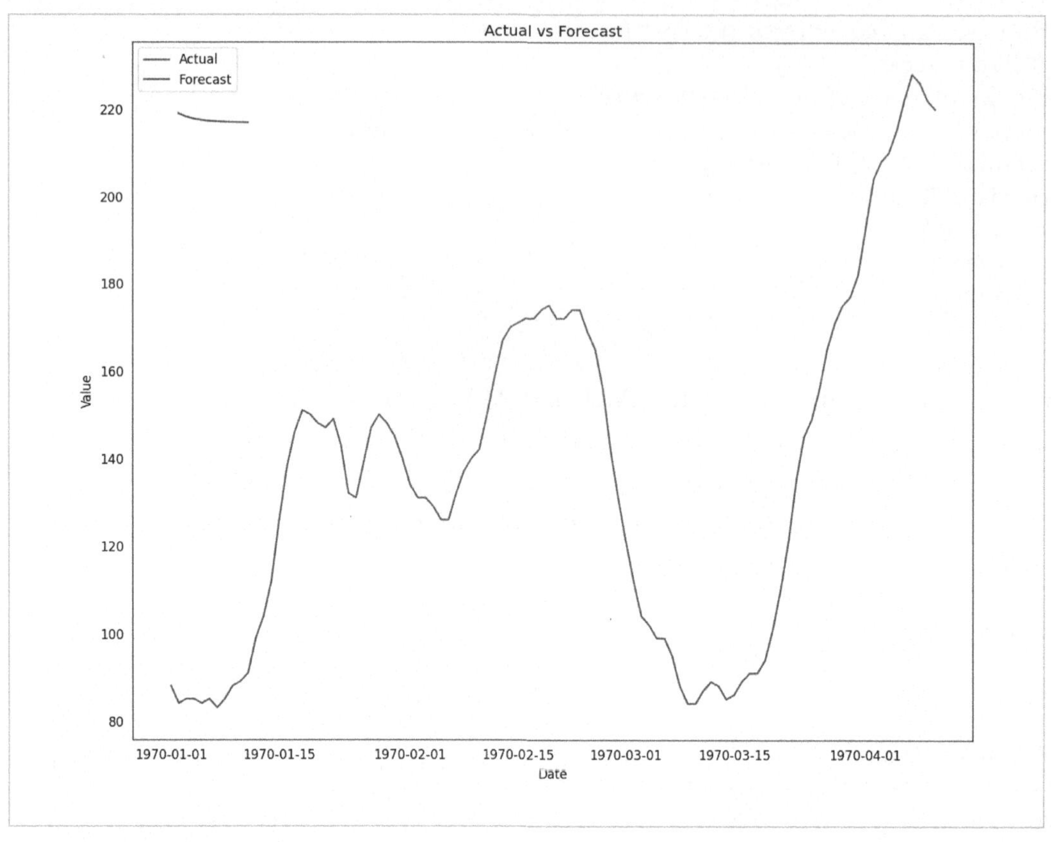

Residual Errors

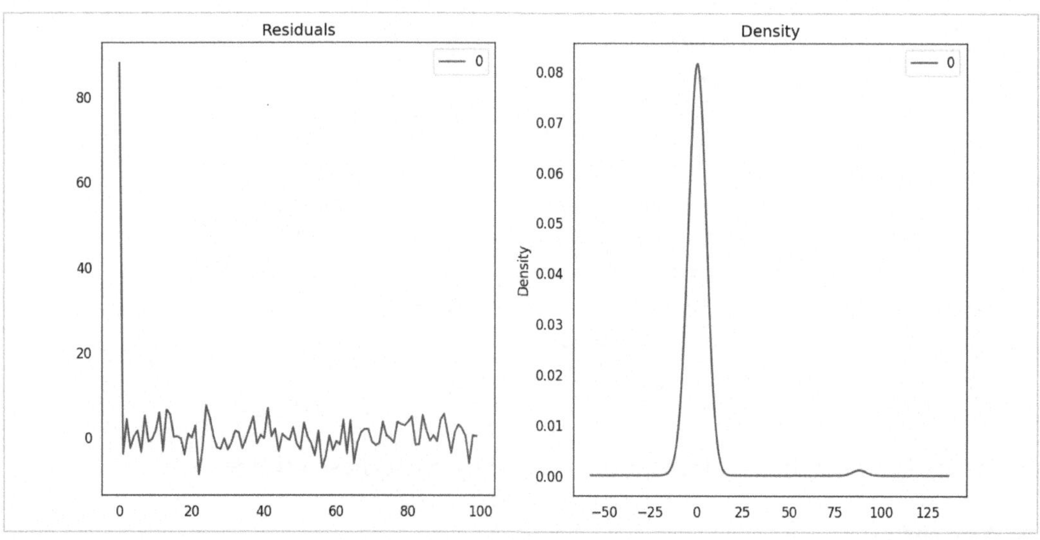

The residual errors appear satisfactory, displaying a near-zero mean and uniform variance. Now, let's visualize the relationship between the actual values and the fitted values using the plot_predict() function.

When you set dynamic=False, the model employs in-sample lagged values for prediction. In other words, the model is trained using data up until the previous value to predict the next one. This approach can sometimes make the fitted forecast appear deceptively accurate when compared to the actuals.

While it seems like we have a decent ARIMA model, we can't definitively claim it's the best yet. This is because we haven't forecasted into the future and compared those forecasts with actual performance. To achieve a more reliable validation, we need to conduct Out-of-Time cross-validation.

To manually find the optimal ARIMA model using Out-of-Time Cross Validation, follow these steps:

- Split the time series data into training and testing datasets.
- Build an ARIMA model using the training dataset.
- Forecast future values using the ARIMA model.
- Compare the forecasted values against the actual values in the testing dataset.
- Evaluate the performance of the model using appropriate metrics.
- Repeat steps 2-5 for different combinations of ARIMA parameters.
- Choose the model with the best performance based on the evaluation metrics.

Example P3 – U3 – D22

Time series – ARIMA

```
import pandas as pd
from statsmodels.tsa.arima.model import ARIMA
import matplotlib.pyplot as plt
# Load Dataset
path = r'C:\Users\User\mraj4\Documents\Optimum\Py-lib\scikit\time_two.csv'
df = pd.read_csv(path, names=['value'], header=0)

# Split into training and test sets
train_size = int(len(df) * 0.85)
train, test = df.value[:train_size], df.value[train_size:]

# Build and fit an ARIMA Model on training data
model = ARIMA(train, order=(1, 1, 1))
fitted = model.fit()
```

```
# Forecast
forecast_steps = len(test)
fc = fitted.forecast(steps=forecast_steps)
conf = fitted.get_forecast(steps=forecast_steps).conf_int(alpha=0.05)

# Convert forecasts to pandas series
fc_series = pd.Series(fc, index=test.index)
lower_series = pd.Series(conf.iloc[:, 0], index=test.index)
upper_series = pd.Series(conf.iloc[:, 1], index=test.index)

# Plot
plt.figure(figsize=(12, 5), dpi=100)
plt.plot(train, label='Training')
plt.plot(test, label='Actual')
plt.plot(fc_series, label='Forecast')
plt.fill_between(lower_series.index, lower_series, upper_series,
                 color='k', alpha=0.15)
plt.title('Forecast vs Actuals')
plt.legend(loc='upper left', fontsize=8)
plt.show()
```

In this code:

Train-Test Split: The dataset is split into training and test sets, with 85% of the data used for training.

Model Building: An ARIMA model with order (1, 1, 1) is built and fitted using the training data.

Forecasting: The model forecasts the next n steps, where n is the length of the test set. The 95% confidence intervals for the forecasts are also calculated.

Plotting: The training data, actual test data, forecasted values, and confidence intervals are plotted for comparison.

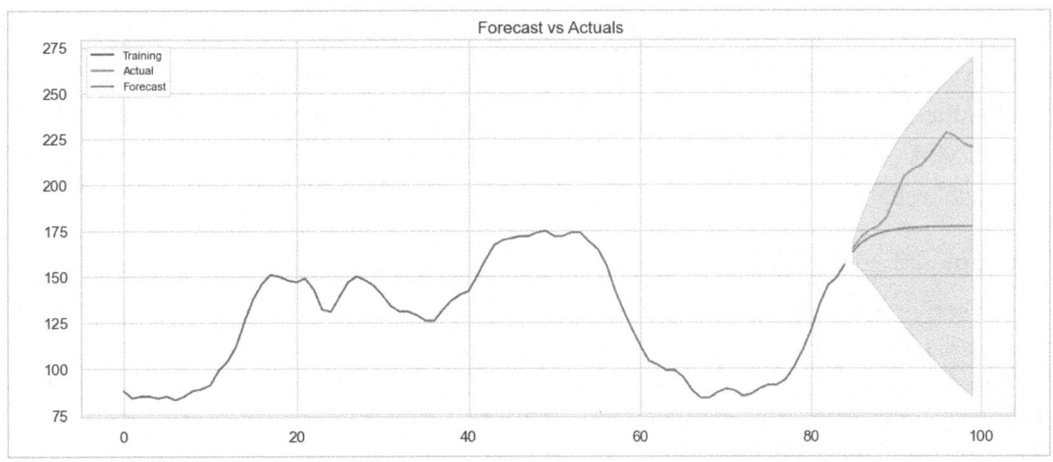

The ARIMA(1,1,1) model provides a directionally accurate forecast, with the actual observed values falling within the 95% confidence interval. This indicates the model captures the general trend of the data well.

However, the predicted values consistently fall below the actual values, suggesting a systematic bias. To correct this and improve forecast accuracy, adding a small constant to the forecasts could be beneficial.

To further refine the model, we plan to:

- Increase Differencing Order: Increase the differencing order to two (d=2) to better handle potential non-stationarity in the data.
- Iterative Model Selection: Systematically explore ARIMA models by varying the autoregressive (p) and moving average (q) orders, ranging from 0 to 5. This will help identify the model with the lowest Akaike Information Criterion (AIC), indicating the best fit.

The goal is to find a model that not only has the lowest AIC but also produces forecasts closely aligned with the actual values when plotted.

P-value Evaluation: After fitting the model, check the P-values of the AR and MA terms to ensure they are statistically significant. They should be as close to zero, ideally less than 0.05.

Master said, this code demonstrates a complete workflow for time series forecasting using an ARIMA model. The dataset is loaded and split into training (85%) and testing sets. An ARIMA(3,2,1) model is trained on the training data, and the statistical significance of AR and MA terms is checked using p-values. The model then forecasts values for the test period, generates confidence intervals, and plots the training data, actual values, and forecast results. Finally, custom accuracy metrics—including MAPE, MAE, RMSE, correlation, and ACF1—are calculated to evaluate forecast performance and model reliability.

Example P3 – U3 – D23

Time series – Arima

```
import pandas as pd
import numpy as np
from statsmodels.tsa.arima.model import ARIMA
from statsmodels.tsa.stattools import acf
import matplotlib.pyplot as plt
# Load Dataset
path = r'C:\Users\User\mraj4\Documents\Optimum\Py-lib\scikit\time_two.csv'
df = pd.read_csv(path, names=['value'], header=0)

# Split into training and test sets
train_size = int(len(df) * 0.85)
train, test = df.value[:train_size], df.value[train_size:]

# Build and fit ARIMA Model on training data
model = ARIMA(train, order=(3, 2, 1))
fitted = model.fit()
print(fitted.summary())

# Ensure the P-values of AR and MA terms are less than 0.05
ar_p_value = fitted.pvalues.get('ar.L1', None)
ma_p_value = fitted.pvalues.get('ma.L1', None)
if ar_p_value is not None and ma_p_value is not None:
    if ar_p_value < 0.05 and ma_p_value < 0.05:
        print("The AR and MA terms are statistically significant.")
    else:
        print("Consider revising the model, as some terms are not statistically significant.")
else:
    print("AR or MA terms not found in the model summary. Check model specification.")

# Forecast
forecast_steps = len(test)
forecast_result = fitted.get_forecast(steps=forecast_steps)
forecast_mean = forecast_result.predicted_mean
confidence_intervals = forecast_result.conf_int(alpha=0.05)

# Convert forecasts and confidence intervals to pandas series
fc_series = pd.Series(forecast_mean, index=test.index)
lower_series = pd.Series(confidence_intervals.iloc[:, 0], index=test.index)
```

```
upper_series = pd.Series(confidence_intervals.iloc[:, 1], index=test.index)

# Plot
plt.figure(figsize=(12, 5), dpi=100)
plt.plot(train, label='Training')
plt.plot(test, label='Actual')
plt.plot(fc_series, label='Forecast')
plt.fill_between(lower_series.index, lower_series, upper_series, color='k', alpha=0.15)
plt.title('Forecast vs Actuals')
plt.legend(loc='upper left', fontsize=8)
plt.show()

# Accuracy metrics
def forecast_accuracy(forecast, actual):
    mape = np.mean(np.abs(forecast - actual) / np.abs(actual))  # MAPE
    me = np.mean(forecast - actual)                             # ME
    mae = np.mean(np.abs(forecast - actual))                    # MAE
    mpe = np.mean((forecast - actual) / actual)                 # MPE
    rmse = np.mean((forecast - actual) ** 2) ** .5              # RMSE
    corr = np.corrcoef(forecast, actual)[0, 1]                  # Correlation
    mins = np.amin(np.vstack([forecast, actual]), axis=0)
    maxs = np.amax(np.vstack([forecast, actual]), axis=0)
    minmax = 1 - np.mean(mins / maxs)                           # Min-Max Error
    acf1 = acf(forecast - actual)[1]                            # ACF1
    return {'mape': mape, 'me': me, 'mae': mae,
            'mpe': mpe, 'rmse': rmse, 'acf1': acf1,
            'corr': corr, 'minmax': minmax}

# Calculate and print accuracy metrics
accuracy_metrics = forecast_accuracy(fc_series.values, test.values)
print("Forecast Accuracy Metrics:")
for metric, value in accuracy_metrics.items():
    print(f"{metric}: {value:.4f}")
```

Output:

Output

```
Forecast Accuracy Metrics:
mape: 0.0412
me: -7.1281
mae: 8.7817
mpe: -0.0319
rmse: 10.6912
acf1: 0.8589
corr: 0.9735
minmax: 0.0411
```

Plot:

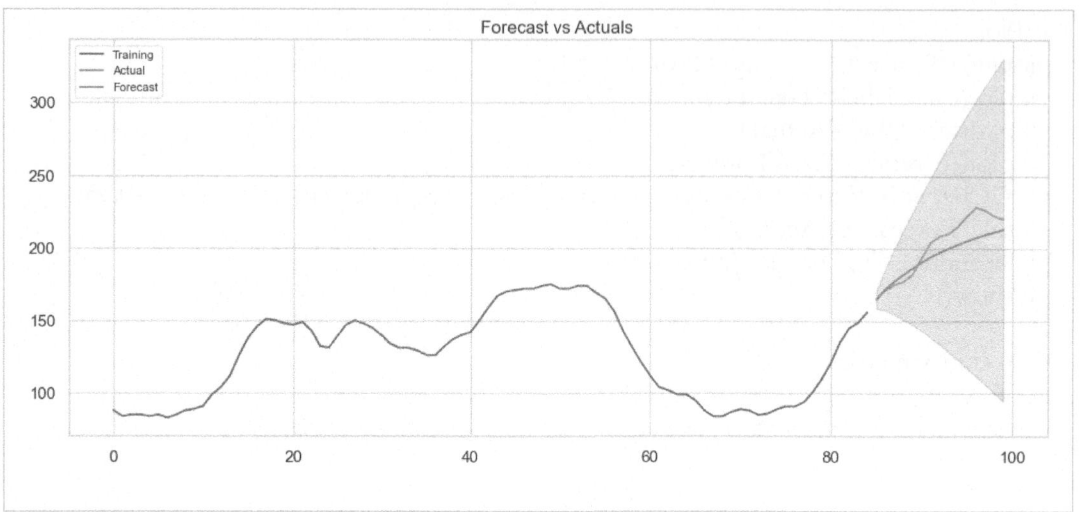

The model's Akaike Information Criterion (AIC) has decreased, indicating an improved fit. Additionally, the P-values of the AR and MA terms are both less than 0.05, which means they are statistically significant and contribute meaningfully to the model.

However, to further enhance the model's robustness and accuracy, it is advisable to experiment with multiple combinations of parameters based on the dataset's characteristics. This can involve:

Seasonal Considerations: Adjusting the model to account for different frequencies, such as monthly or quarterly data, to capture seasonal patterns.

Model Comparisons: Evaluating the performance of various ARIMA models with different (p, d, q) parameters across these periods.

Performance Metrics: Monitoring how the forecasts perform at different points in the year to ensure the model captures all underlying patterns and trends.

By exploring these combinations, you can achieve more reliable and precise forecasts that better reflect the temporal dynamics of your data.

☐ Accuracy Metrics for Time Series Forecasting

When evaluating the accuracy of time series forecasts, several metrics are commonly used:

- Mean Absolute Percentage Error (MAPE)

- Mean Error (ME)
- Mean Absolute Error (MAE)
- Mean Percentage Error (MPE)
- Root Mean Squared Error (RMSE)
- Lag 1 Autocorrelation of Error (ACF1)
- Correlation between the Actual and the Forecast (corr)
- Min-Max Error (minmax)

Forecast Accuracy Metrics: mape: 0.0411 me: -7.1163 mae: 8.7732	mpe: -0.0318 rmse: 10.6801 acf1: 0.8589 corr: 0.9735 minmax: 0.0410

Key Metrics for Comparison

When comparing forecasts of two different time series, the following metrics are particularly useful:

- MAPE (Mean Absolute Percentage Error)
- Correlation (corr)
- Min-Max Error (minmax)

Akshaya asked, "Why do we focus on these Metrics?"

Master said, "These three metrics are percentage-based errors that range between 0 and 1. This range makes them scale-independent, allowing for meaningful comparisons across different time series, regardless of their magnitude."

Limitations of Other Metrics

Other error metrics, such as RMSE, ME, and MAE, are absolute quantities. This characteristic means they are influenced by the scale of the data, making them unsuitable for comparing forecasts of differently scaled time series. For instance:

An RMSE of 100 for a series with a mean in the thousands might be considered better than an RMSE of 5 for a series with a mean in the tens.

This dependency on the scale makes it difficult to use these metrics for direct comparison across different datasets.

Summary: When comparing the accuracy of forecasts for different time series, focus on MAPE, correlation, and min-max error. These metrics provide a standardized way to judge forecast performance, ensuring meaningful comparisons irrespective of the series' scales.

☐ Model Accuracy and Automation

A MAPE (Mean Absolute Percentage Error) of around 4% implies that the model is approximately 96% accurate in its predictions. This level of accuracy is generally considered excellent in time series forecasting.

Now that you understand how to manually build an ARIMA model, it's important to consider practical applications in industrial settings. In such environments, you will often need to forecast multiple time series and perform these forecasting tasks on a regular basis. Therefore, automating the model selection process is essential to enhance efficiency and consistency.

☐ Automating the Best Model Selection Process

To handle numerous time series and ensure timely and accurate forecasts, consider the following steps to automate the model selection process:

Data Preprocessing:

- Standardize data cleaning procedures.
- Implement automated handling of missing values and outliers.

Model Selection:

- Use algorithms to automatically test multiple ARIMA configurations (varying p, d, q parameters).
- Consider incorporating other models like SARIMA for seasonal data, or machine learning models if appropriate.

Evaluation Metrics:

- Define clear criteria for model selection, such as the lowest AIC (Akaike Information Criterion) and significant p-values for AR and MA terms.
- Use cross-validation to ensure robustness.

Automation Tools:

- Utilise libraries such as pmdarima (Auto-ARIMA) that can automate the ARIMA modelling process.
- Develop scripts or use existing tools to automate model fitting, evaluation, and selection.

Regular Updates:

- Implement scheduling for regular updates of models as new data becomes available.
- Continuously monitor model performance and retrain as needed.

Scalability:

- Ensure the automation pipeline is scalable to handle an increasing number of time series efficiently.

By automating the model selection process, you can save significant time and resources, allowing for more consistent and reliable forecasting across various time series. This approach not only enhances operational efficiency but also ensures that the best possible model is used for each forecasting task, maintaining high accuracy and reliability.

☐ Performing Auto ARIMA Forecast in Python

In Python, you can easily perform Auto ARIMA forecasting using the auto_arima() function provided by the pmdarima package.

The auto_arima() function employs a stepwise approach to automatically search through various combinations of ARIMA parameters (p, d, q) and selects the best model based on the lowest Akaike Information Criterion (AIC).

Here's how you can use auto_arima() to streamline the model selection process:

Example P3 – U3 – D24

Time series – Automate ARIMA

```
import pandas as pd
import numpy as np
import matplotlib.pyplot as plt
import pmdarima as pm
```

```
# Load Dataset
path = r'C:\Users\User\mraj4\Documents\Optimum\Py-lib\scikit\time_two.csv'
df = pd.read_csv(path, names=['value'], header=0)

# Fit Auto ARIMA Model
model = pm.auto_arima(df.value,
                start_p=1, start_q=1,
                test='adf',       # Use ADF test to find optimal 'd'
                max_p=3, max_q=3, # Maximum p and q
                m=1,              # Frequency of series
                d=None,           # Let model determine 'd'
                seasonal=False,   # No Seasonality
                start_P=0,
                D=0,
                trace=True,
                error_action='ignore',
                suppress_warnings=True,
                stepwise=True)

# Print Model Summary
print(model.summary())
# Residual Plots
model.plot_diagnostics(figsize=(7, 5))
plt.show()

# Forecast
n_periods = 24
forecast, confidence_intervals = model.predict(n_periods=n_periods,
return_conf_int=True)
index_of_forecast = np.arange(len(df), len(df) + n_periods)

# Create series for plotting purpose
forecast_series = pd.Series(forecast, index=index_of_forecast)
lower_confidence_series = pd.Series(confidence_intervals[:, 0],
index=index_of_forecast)
upper_confidence_series = pd.Series(confidence_intervals[:, 1],
index=index_of_forecast)

# Plot
plt.plot(df.value, label='Actual', color='blue')
plt.plot(forecast_series, label='Forecast', color='darkgreen')
plt.fill_between(lower_confidence_series.index, lower_confidence_series,
upper_confidence_series, color='k', alpha=.15)
plt.title("Final Forecast of WWW Usage")
plt.xlabel("Time")
plt.ylabel("Usage")
plt.legend()
plt.show()
```

Output:

Output

```
ARIMA(3,2,1)(0,0,0)[0]          : AIC=inf, Time=0.15 sec

Best model:  ARIMA(2,2,0)(0,0,0)[0]
Total fit time: 0.879 seconds
                    SARIMAX Results
==========================
Dep. Variable:              y   No. Observations:         100
Model:           SARIMAX(2, 2, 0)   Log Likelihood          -252.732
Date:          Fri, 21 Nov 2025   AIC                   511.465
Time:                12:00:35   BIC                   519.220
Sample:                     0   HQIC                  514.601
                    - 100
Covariance Type:          opg
==========================
           coef    std err        z     P>|z|      [0.025     0.975]
------------------------------------------------------------------------------
ar.L1       0.2579     0.103     2.510     0.012      0.056      0.459
ar.L2      -0.4407     0.087    -5.093     0.000     -0.610     -0.271
sigma2     10.1268     1.519     6.668     0.000      7.150     13.103
==============================
Ljung-Box (L1) (Q):             0.05   Jarque-Bera (JB):          0.10
Prob(Q):                     0.82   Prob(JB):              0.95
Heteroskedasticity (H):         0.49   Skew:                  -0.07
Prob(H) (two-sided):            0.05   Kurtosis:               2.92
```

Interpreting Residual Plots in ARIMA Models

Master continued: the residual plots are essential for evaluating the goodness of fit of an ARIMA model. Here's how to interpret the plot diagnostics:

Top Left: The plot shows the residual errors over time. Ideally, the residuals should fluctuate randomly around a mean of zero, indicating that the model captures the data's underlying patterns. Additionally, the spread of residuals should remain consistent across the time series, indicating a uniform variance.

Top Right: This is a density plot of the residual errors. A bell-shaped curve with a mean of zero suggests that the residuals follow a normal distribution. Any deviations from this pattern might indicate issues, such as skewness or outliers.

Bottom Left: The Q-Q (Quantile-Quantile) plot compares the distribution of the residuals against a theoretical normal distribution. Ideally, all points should fall along the red line, indicating that the residuals are normally distributed. Significant deviations may suggest non-normality in the residuals.

Bottom Right: The correlogram, or ACF (Autocorrelation Function) plot, displays the autocorrelation of the residuals at different lag values. In a well-fitted model, the autocorrelation values should be within the confidence bands and close to zero, indicating that there is no significant pattern left in the residuals. Any spikes or patterns in the ACF plot suggest that additional predictors (X variables) may be needed to improve the model's explanatory power.

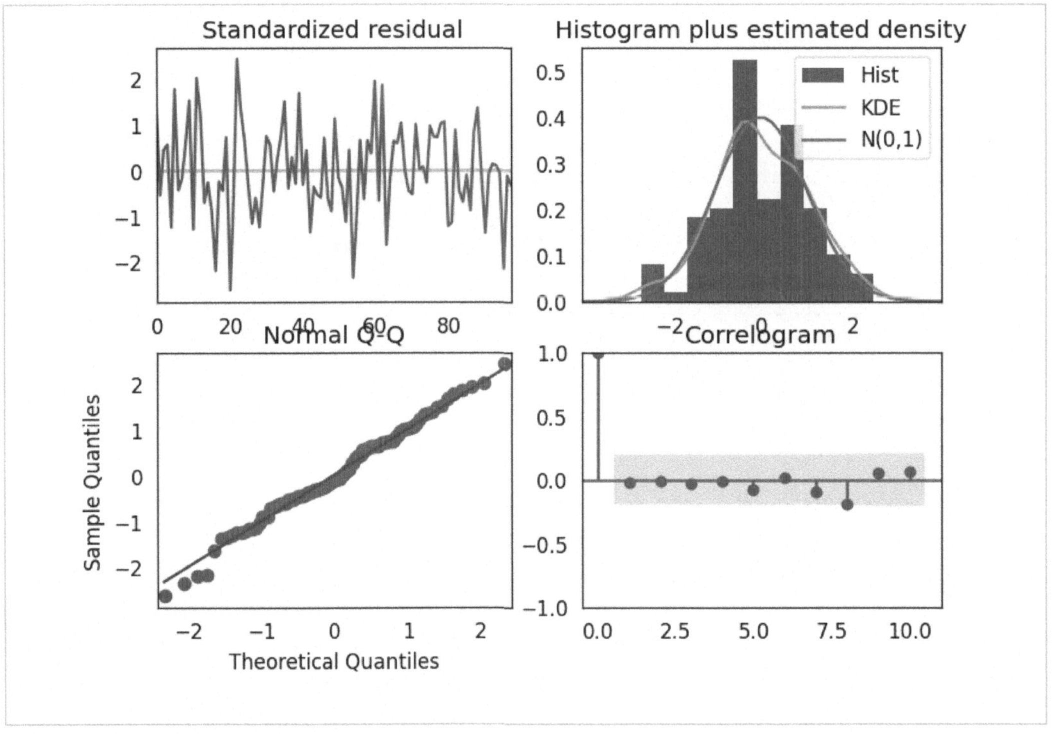

Conclusion

Based on the interpretation of the residual plots:

- The ARIMA model seems to capture the data's underlying patterns well.
- The residual errors exhibit randomness, normal distribution, and no significant autocorrelation.
- Overall, the model appears to be a good fit for the data.

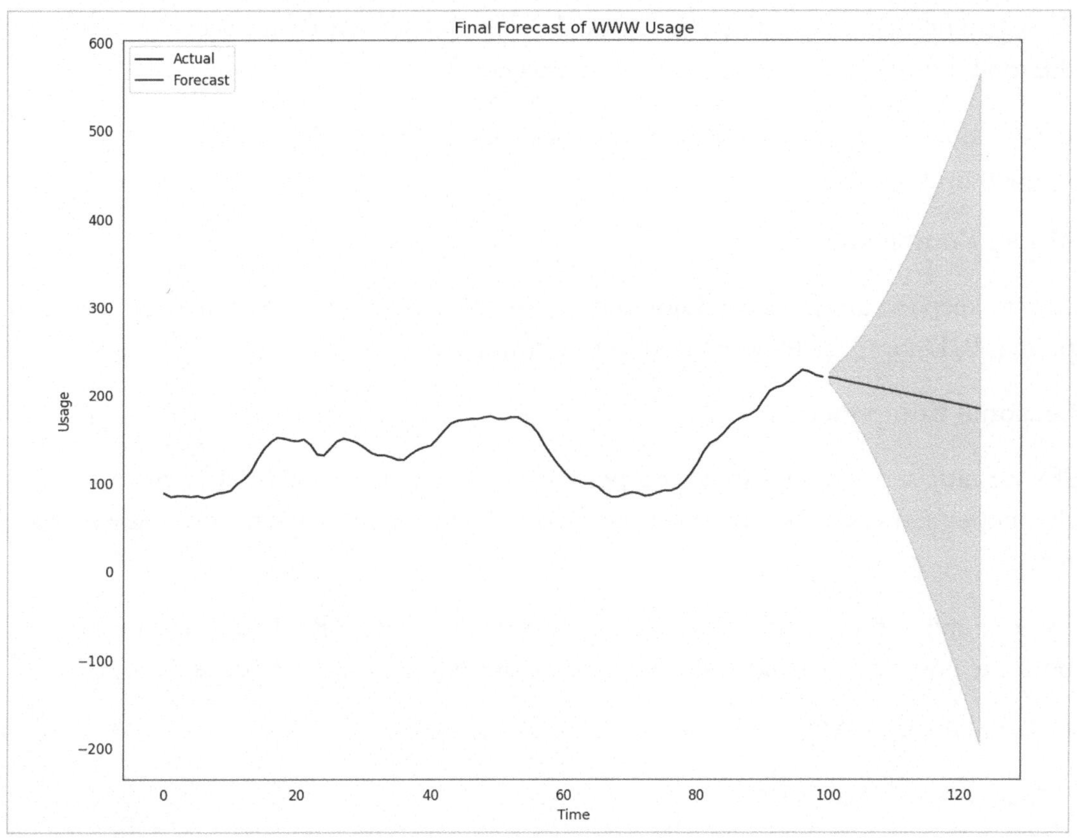

☐ Automatic SARIMA Model Building in Python

The limitation of a plain ARIMA model is its inability to handle seasonality in time series data. To address this issue, we turn to SARIMA (Seasonal ARIMA) models, which incorporate seasonal differencing.

Seasonal differencing is akin to regular differencing, but instead of subtracting consecutive terms, you subtract the value from the previous season.

A SARIMA model is represented as SARIMA(p, d, q) × (P, D, Q)_m, where:

- p, d, q: AR, differencing, and MA terms for the non-seasonal component.
- P, D, Q: Seasonal AR, seasonal differencing, and seasonal MA terms.
- m: The frequency of the time series (e.g., 12 for monthly data).

When working with SARIMA models, it's crucial to keep the following points in mind:

Setting Parameters:

As a general rule, ensure that the seasonal differencing term D never exceeds one, and the total differencing term 'd + D' never exceeds 2.

If your time series exhibits well-defined seasonal patterns, enforce D=1 for the given frequency 'm'.

Model Complexity:

Aim to keep the model as parsimonious as possible. Avoid unnecessarily high values for p, d, q, P, D, or Q, as they can lead to overfitting.

Seasonal Components:

If your time series has seasonal components, consider including SAR or SMA terms in the model. However, be cautious not to overwhelm the model with too many seasonal terms.

By adhering to these guidelines, you can effectively build SARIMA models that capture both the non-seasonal and seasonal patterns present in your time series data.

Let's build a SARIMA model on the drug sales dataset.

Example P3 – U3 – D25

Time series – Differencing and seasonal differencing

```
import pandas as pd
import matplotlib.pyplot as plt
# Load Dataset
path = r'C:\Users\User\mraj4\Documents\Optimum\Py-lib\scikit\time_one.csv'
df = pd.read_csv(path, parse_dates=['date'], index_col='date')

# Plot
fig, axes = plt.subplots(2, 1, figsize=(10, 5), dpi=100, sharex=True)

# Usual Differencing
axes[0].plot(df, label='Original Series')
axes[0].plot(df.diff(1), label='Usual Differencing')
axes[0].set_title('Usual Differencing')
axes[0].legend(loc='upper left', fontsize=10)

# Seasonal Differencing
axes[1].plot(df, label='Original Series')
axes[1].plot(df.diff(12), label='Seasonal Differencing', color='green')
axes[1].set_title('Seasonal Differencing')
axes[1].legend(loc='upper left', fontsize=10)

# Set common labels and title
```

```
plt.xlabel('Date')
plt.suptitle('Drug Sales', fontsize=16)
plt.show()
```

Now, let's examine the residual diagnostics plot to ensure the model's assumptions are met.

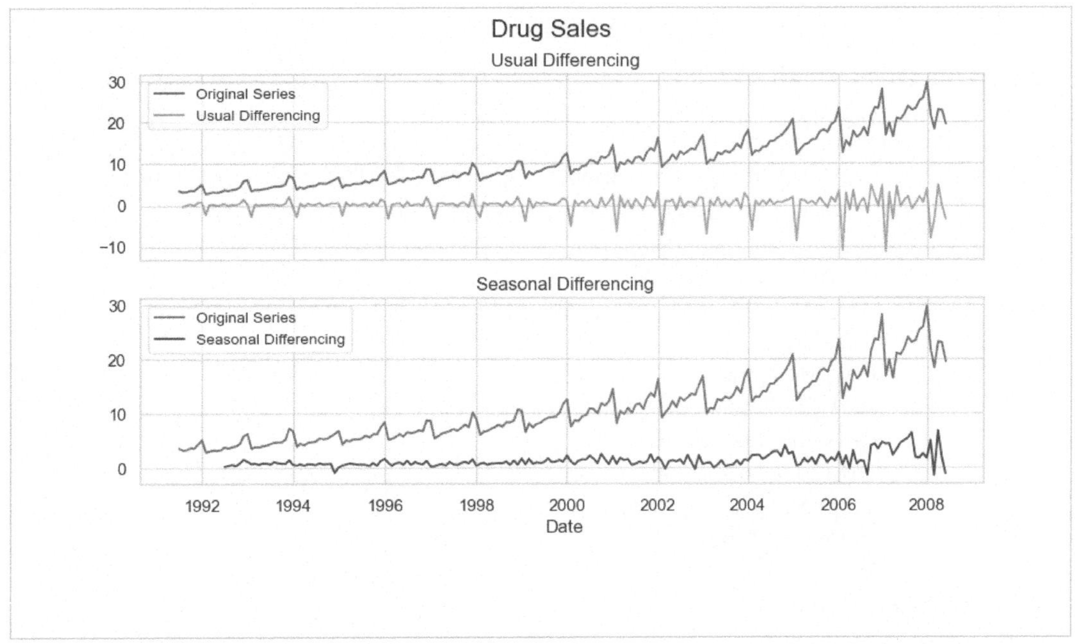

Advantages of Seasonal Differencing in SARIMA Models

Upon applying traditional differencing (lag 1), it's evident that the seasonal spikes persist in the data. However, these spikes are rectified after implementing seasonal differencing.

To harness the power of seasonal differencing and build a SARIMA model, we'll utilize auto_arima() from the pmdarima library. Here's how to proceed:

Set Seasonal Differencing Parameters:

- When invoking auto_arima(), ensure to set seasonal=True to enable seasonal modeling.
- Specify the frequency m, which corresponds to the number of periods in a season. For monthly data, m=12.
- Enforce D=1 to indicate seasonal differencing.

By incorporating these parameters, auto_arima() will automatically explore various SARIMA configurations and select the optimal model based on statistical criteria.

Let's proceed with building the SARIMA model and forecast for the next 24 months.

Example P3 – U3 – D26
Time series – Imputing Missing Values

```
import pandas as pd
import matplotlib.pyplot as plt
import pmdarima as pm

# Load Dataset
path = r'C:\Users\User\mraj4\Documents\Optimum\Py-lib\scikit\time_one.csv'
df = pd.read_csv(path, parse_dates=['date'], index_col='date')

# Seasonal - fit stepwise auto-ARIMA
smodel = pm.auto_arima(df, start_p=1, start_q=1,
                       test='adf',
                       max_p=3, max_q=3, m=12,
                       start_P=0, seasonal=True,
                       d=None, D=1, trace=True,
                       error_action='ignore',
                       suppress_warnings=True,
                       stepwise=True)

# Print SARIMA model summary
print(smodel.summary())

# Forecast
n_periods = 24
fitted, confint = smodel.predict(n_periods=n_periods, return_conf_int=True)
index_of_fc = pd.date_range(df.index[-1], periods=n_periods + 1, freq='MS')[1:]

# Create series for plotting purpose
fitted_series = pd.Series(fitted, index=index_of_fc)
lower_series = pd.Series(confint[:, 0], index=index_of_fc)
upper_series = pd.Series(confint[:, 1], index=index_of_fc)

# Plot
plt.figure(figsize=(10, 5))
plt.plot(df, label='Actual', color='blue')
plt.plot(fitted_series, label='Forecast', color='darkgreen')
plt.fill_between(lower_series.index, lower_series, upper_series, color='k', alpha=0.15)
plt.title("SARIMA - Final Forecast of Drug Sales")
plt.xlabel("Date")
plt.ylabel("Sales")
plt.legend()
```

```
plt.show()
```

Output:

```
Output
ARIMA(3,0,0)(1,1,2)[12] intercept   : AIC=inf, Time=1.68 sec
 ARIMA(3,0,0)(0,1,1)[12]            : AIC=532.348, Time=0.17 sec

Best model:  ARIMA(3,0,0)(0,1,1)[12] intercept
Total fit time: 17.421 seconds
                              SARIMAX Results
==============================================
Dep. Variable:                         y   No. Observations:              204
Model:          SARIMAX(3, 0, 0)x(0, 1, [1], 12)   Log Likelihood            -258.394
Date:                    Fri, 21 Nov 2025   AIC                        528.788
Time:                            12:23:10   BIC                        548.333
Sample:                        07-01-1991   HQIC                       536.704
                             - 06-01-2008
Covariance Type:                      opg
==============================
              coef    std err        z      P>|z|      [0.025      0.975]
------------------------------------------------------------------------------
intercept     0.1638    0.097     1.696     0.090     -0.026      0.353
ar.L1         0.0960    0.043     2.228     0.026      0.012      0.180
ar.L2         0.4148    0.035    11.921     0.000      0.347      0.483
ar.L3         0.3510    0.054     6.546     0.000      0.246      0.456
ma.S.L12     -0.4627    0.058    -7.966     0.000     -0.577     -0.349
sigma2        0.8470    0.057    14.914     0.000      0.736      0.958
======================================
Ljung-Box (L1) (Q):              0.03   Jarque-Bera (JB):            124.39
Prob(Q):                         0.86   Prob(JB):                      0.00
Heteroskedasticity (H):         12.65   Skew:                          0.30
Prob(H) (two-sided):             0.00   Kurtosis:                      6.90
```

Plot:

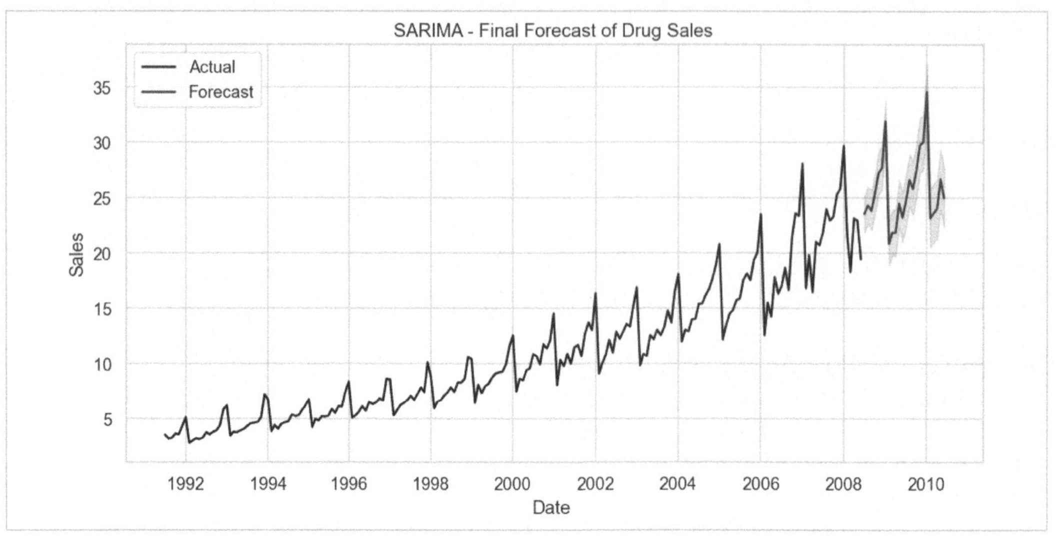

☐ How to Build a SARIMAX Model with an Exogenous Variable

Master said, "We'll demonstrate how to build a SARIMAX model by incorporating an exogenous variable. A SARIMAX model extends the SARIMA model by including external predictors, also known as exogenous variables."

The key requirement for using an exogenous variable is knowing its values during the forecast period.

For demonstration purposes, we'll use the seasonal index from the classical seasonal decomposition applied to the latest 36 months of data as our exogenous variable. This is a useful exercise as it shows how to force recent seasonality patterns into both the training and forecast phases of the model.

Why use the Seasonal Index as an Exogenous Variable?

SARIMA already models' seasonality: However, by explicitly including the recent seasonal index, we ensure that the most recent patterns are taken into account.

Demo purposes: This approach is illustrative and provides a template for incorporating any exogenous variable into your model.

Predictability: Seasonal indices repeat every frequency cycle (12 months, in this case), making it easy to predict their future values.

Example P3 – U3 – D27

Time series – Imputing Missing Values

```
import pandas as pd
import matplotlib.pyplot as plt
import pmdarima as pm
from statsmodels.tsa.seasonal import seasonal_decompose
import numpy as np

# Load Dataset
path = r'C:\Users\User\mraj4\Documents\Optimum\Py-lib\scikit\time_one.csv'
df = pd.read_csv(path, parse_dates=['date'], index_col='date')

# Compute Seasonal Index using multiplicative seasonal decomposition
result_mul = seasonal_decompose(df['value'][-36:],  # Last 3 years of data
                        model='multiplicative',
                        extrapolate_trend='freq')

seasonal_index = result_mul.seasonal[-12:].to_frame(name='seasonal_index')
seasonal_index['month'] = pd.to_datetime(seasonal_index.index).month

# Merge seasonal index with the base data
df['month'] = df.index.month
df = df.merge(seasonal_index, how='left', on='month')

# Build SARIMAX Model using auto_arima
sxmodel = pm.auto_arima(df[['value']], exogenous=df[['seasonal_index']],
                    start_p=1, start_q=1,
                    test='adf',
                    max_p=3, max_q=3, m=12,
                    start_P=0, seasonal=True,
                    d=None, D=1, trace=True,
                    error_action='ignore',
                    suppress_warnings=True,
                    stepwise=True)

# Print SARIMAX model summary
print(sxmodel.summary())

# Forecast the next 24 periods
n_periods = 24
future_exog = np.tile(seasonal_index['seasonal_index'].values, 2).reshape(-1, 1)
fitted, confint = sxmodel.predict(n_periods=n_periods,
                        exogenous=future_exog,
                        return_conf_int=True)

# Create an index for the forecasted periods
index_of_fc = pd.date_range(df.index[-1], periods=n_periods + 1, freq='MS')[1:]

# Create series for plotting purposes
```

```
fitted_series = pd.Series(fitted, index=index_of_fc)
lower_series = pd.Series(confint[:, 0], index=index_of_fc)
upper_series = pd.Series(confint[:, 1], index=index_of_fc)

# Plot the actual data and the forecast
plt.figure(figsize=(10, 5))
plt.plot(df['value'], label='Actual', color='blue')
plt.plot(fitted_series, label='Forecast', color='darkgreen')
plt.fill_between(lower_series.index, lower_series, upper_series, color='k', alpha=0.15)
plt.title("SARIMAX Forecast of Drug Sales")
plt.xlabel("Date")
plt.ylabel("Sales")
plt.legend()
plt.show()
```

Output:

Output

```
ARIMA(3,0,0)(0,1,1)[12]          : AIC=532.348, Time=0.44 sec

Best model:  ARIMA(3,0,0)(0,1,1)[12] intercept
Total fit time: 26.870 seconds
                    SARIMAX Results
=======================================
Dep. Variable:                    y   No. Observations:          204
Model:        SARIMAX(3, 0, 0)x(0, 1, [1], 12)  Log Likelihood          -258.394
Date:                 Fri, 21 Nov 2025   AIC                    528.788
Time:                       12:32:06   BIC                  548.333
Sample:                            0   HQIC                 536.704
                              - 204
Covariance Type:                 opg
=========================
            coef    std err       z     P>|z|     [0.025      0.975]
----------------------------------------------------------------------
intercept    0.1638    0.097    1.696    0.090    -0.026    0.353
ar.L1       0.0960    0.043    2.228    0.026    0.012    0.180
ar.L2       0.4148    0.035   11.921    0.000    0.347    0.483
ar.L3       0.3510    0.054    6.546    0.000    0.246    0.456
ma.S.L12    -0.4627    0.058   -7.966    0.000    -0.577    -0.349
sigma2      0.8470    0.057   14.914    0.000    0.736    0.958
==============================
Ljung-Box (L1) (Q):              0.03  Jarque-Bera (JB):         124.39
Prob(Q):                      0.86  Prob(JB):              0.00
Heteroskedasticity (H):          12.65  Skew:                   0.30
Prob(H) (two-sided):             0.00  Kurtosis:               6.90
```

Steps to Build the SARIMAX Model

Compute the Seasonal Index:

- Use the last 36 months of data to compute the seasonal index via multiplicative seasonal decomposition.
- This index will serve as our exogenous variable.

Build the SARIMAX Model:

- Incorporate the seasonal index as an exogenous variable into the SARIMAX model using pmdarima's auto_arima() function.

Forecast with the Model:

- Forecast the next 24 months, using the seasonal index values for the forecast period.

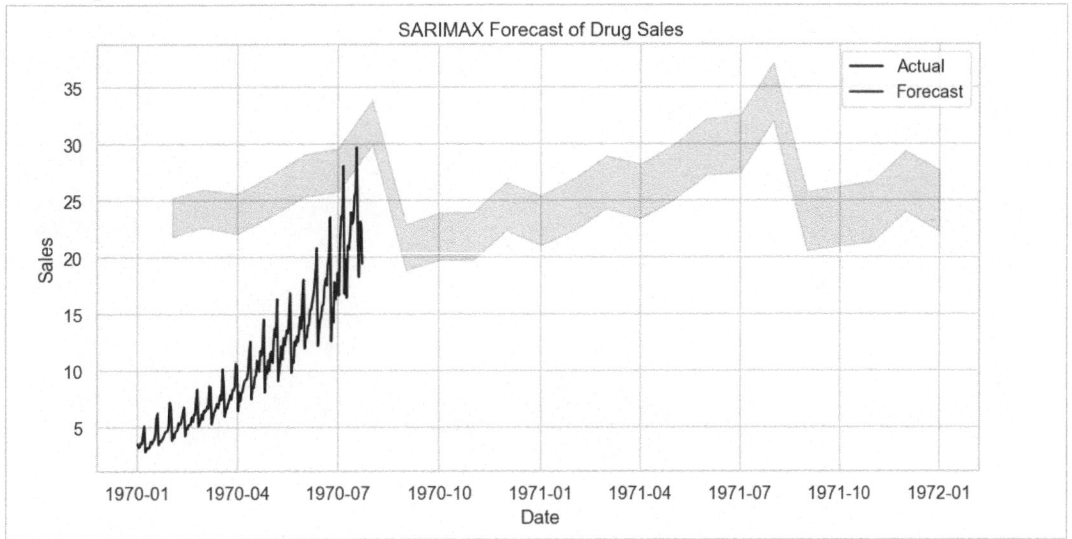

PART THREE

DAY ELEVEN

Unit 3 - Lesson Four

The Pulse of Data

☐ Augmented Dickey-Fuller (ADF) Test

Akshatha asked, "What is an ADF test?"

Master said, "The Augmented Dickey-Fuller (ADF) test is a widely used statistical test that assesses whether a given time series is stationary or not. Stationarity is a crucial property in time series analysis and forecasting, especially when using autoregressive models like ARIMA."

Here's a comprehensive overview of the ADF test, its importance, and how to interpret the results.

Purpose of the ADF Test: The primary objective of the ADF test is to determine if a time series is stationary. A stationary time series has a constant mean, variance, and autocorrelation structure over time. Stationarity is essential for building reliable ARIMA models because non-stationary data can lead to inaccurate forecasts.

Steps in ARIMA Modelling

In ARIMA (AutoRegressive Integrated Moving Average) time series forecasting, the first step is to identify the number of differencing operations required to make the series stationary. Differencing helps to remove trends and seasonality, stabilising the mean of the series.

Importance of the ADF Test

Since stationarity testing is a frequent task in autoregressive models, the ADF test, along with the KPSS (Kwiatkowski-Phillips-Schmidt-Shin) test, is a fundamental tool in time series analysis. Being proficient in these tests is crucial for analysing and modelling time series data effectively.

Hypothesis Testing in the ADF Test

The ADF test is a statistical significance test that involves hypothesis testing. The hypotheses for the ADF test are as follows:

Null Hypothesis (H0): The time series has a unit root (i.e., it is non-stationary).

Alternative Hypothesis (H1): The time series does not have a unit root (i.e., it is stationary).

The test computes a test statistic and reports p-values. The inference about stationarity is made based on the test statistic and the p-value.

Interpreting the ADF Test Results

Test Statistic: If the test statistic is less than the critical value, you reject the null hypothesis.

P-value: A p-value less than a chosen significance level (e.g., 0.05) indicates strong evidence against the null hypothesis, suggesting that the series is stationary.

Mathematical Intuition and Example

To understand the ADF test mathematically, consider the following regression model used in the test:

$$\Delta y_t = a + \beta_t + \gamma\, y_{t-1} + \delta_1\, \Delta y_{t-1} + \delta_2\, \Delta y_{t-2} + \cdots + \delta_p\, \Delta y_{t-p} + \epsilon_t$$

Where:

- Δy_t is the differenced series.
- a is a constant.
- β_t is a trend term.
- $\gamma\, y_{t-1}$ is the lagged value of the series.

- δ_i are the coefficients of the lagged differenced terms.
- ϵ_t is the error term.

The null hypothesis is that $\gamma = 0$, indicating a unit root (non-stationary). The alternative hypothesis is that $\gamma < 0$, indicating stationarity.

Example

Let's consider a time series of monthly Drug sales data. To perform the ADF test, we use statistical software or Python libraries like statsmodels.

If the p-value is less than 0.05, we reject the null hypothesis, indicating that the series is stationary.

Example P3 – U3 – D28

Time series – ADF Test

```
# Import Libraries
from statsmodels.tsa.stattools import adfuller
import pandas as pd
import matplotlib.pyplot as plt
# Load Dataset
path = r'C:\Users\User\mraj4\Documents\Optimum\Py-lib\scikit\time_one.csv'
df = pd.read_csv(path, parse_dates=['date'], index_col='date')

# Plot the time series
df.plot(figsize=(14, 8), legend=None, title='a10 - Drug Sales Series')
plt.xlabel('Date')
plt.ylabel('Sales')
plt.show()

# Extract the series for ADF Test
series = df['value'].values

# Perform ADF Test
result = adfuller(series, autolag='AIC')

# Extract and print the results
test_statistic, p_value, used_lag, n_obs, critical_values, icbest = result

print('ADF Test Statistic:', test_statistic)
print('p-value:', p_value)
print('Number of lags used:', used_lag)
print('Number of observations used:', n_obs)
print('Critical Values:')
for key, value in critical_values.items():
    print(f'   {key}: {value}')
```

Output

```
Output
ADF Test Statistic: 3.1451856893067376
p-value: 1.0
Number of lags used: 15
Number of observations used: 188
Critical Values:
   1%: -3.465620397124192
   5%: -2.8770397560752436
   10%: -2.5750324547306476
```

Conclusion

The ADF test is a critical tool for determining the stationarity of a time series. Understanding how to interpret its results is essential for building robust time series models. By mastering the ADF test and other stationarity tests, you can ensure that your time series analysis and forecasting are based on reliable and accurate models.

- **Vector Autoregression (VAR)**

Master explained that the Vector Autoregression (VAR) is a multivariate forecasting algorithm used when two or more time series influence each other. Unlike univariate models, which predict a single time series based on its past values, VAR simultaneously models the joint behaviour of multiple time series. This approach captures the interdependencies between the series, allowing for more accurate and insightful forecasts.

Key Concepts and Requirements

Multivariate Time Series:

- You need at least two time series (variables).
- The time series should influence each other bi-directionally.

Autoregressive Nature:

Each variable in the VAR model is a function of its own past values and the past values of all other variables in the system. This makes it an autoregressive model because it relies on past data to predict future values.

Difference from Univariate Models:

Unidirectional Models: AR, ARMA, and ARIMA are unidirectional models where predictors influence the response variable (Y) but not vice-versa.

Bi-directional Influence: In VAR, all variables influence each other, capturing the dynamic interplay between multiple time series.

Why do we use VAR?

- Comprehensive Forecasting: VAR can provide a more comprehensive understanding of the relationships between multiple time series, making it valuable for economic, financial, and other types of multivariate data analysis.
- Capturing Interdependencies: It can capture the interdependencies and feedback loops between the variables, leading to more accurate forecasts.

The intuition behind the VAR Model Formula

Master said, "The VAR model encapsulates the dynamic relationships among multiple time series variables by expressing each variable as a linear combination of its past values and the past values of other variables in the system."

Imagine you have a set of time series variables that influence each other's behaviour. For instance, if you're analysing economic data, these variables could represent different economic indicators like GDP, inflation rate, unemployment rate, etc. Each variable's current value is influenced not only by its past values but also by the past values of other variables.

In a VAR model, this interdependence is captured through a system of equations, where each equation represents a variable's relationship with itself and other variables. If you have, say, 5 time series variables, you'll have a system of 5 equations.

For instance, consider a VAR(1) model with two time series variables, Y1 and Y2. The equations for this model would be:

$$Y_{1t} = c_1 + \phi_{11}\, Y1_{,t-1} + \phi_{12}\, Y_{2,t-1} + \epsilon_{1t}$$

$$Y_{2t} = c_2 + \phi_{21}\, Y_{1,t-1} + \phi_{22}\, Y_{2,t-1} + \epsilon_{2t}$$

Here:

- Y_{1t} and Y_{2t} represent the current values of variables Y1 and Y2, respectively.
- c_1 and c_2 are intercept terms for each equation.
- ϕ_{ij} are coefficients representing the influence of the lagged values of variables on the current value of each variable.
- ϵ_{1t} and ϵ_{2t} are error terms representing unexplained variance or shocks in each equation.

These equations express how each variable's current value is determined by its own past values and the past values of other variables. This modelling approach captures the complex interactions and feedback mechanisms among the variables, allowing for more accurate forecasting and analysis.

Training and Forecasting with VAR in Python using statsmodels

Masters said, "Here's a step-by-step guide to training and forecasting a VAR model using the statsmodels library in Python."

Master said, "Apeksha, this code demonstrates a complete workflow for building, validating, and forecasting a Vector Autoregressive (VAR) model. It begins by importing essential libraries and loading a multivariate time-series dataset. The series are visually inspected, followed by Granger causality testing to identify directional influence among variables. Johansen cointegration testing checks long-run relationships. The data is then split into training and testing sets, and stationarity is examined using the Augmented Dickey-Fuller test. When needed, the series are differenced to achieve stationarity.

Next, the optimal VAR lag order is selected using AIC, BIC, FPE, and HQIC. The model is fitted, and residuals are tested for serial correlation using the Durbin-Watson statistic. Forecasts are generated and then inverted back to the original scale through cumulative differencing. Finally, forecast accuracy is evaluated using metrics such as MAPE, RMSE, correlation, and Min-Max error, along with visual comparison against actual values."

Example P3 – U3 – D29

Time series – VAR

```
# Step 1: Import Necessary Libraries
import pandas as pd
import numpy as np
import matplotlib.pyplot as plt
```

```
from statsmodels.tsa.api import VAR
from statsmodels.tsa.stattools import adfuller
from statsmodels.tsa.stattools import grangercausalitytests
from statsmodels.tsa.vector_ar.vecm import coint_johansen
from statsmodels.stats.stattools import durbin_watson

# Step 2: Load and Prepare the Data
# Load Dataset
path = r'C:\Users\User\mraj4\Documents\Optimum\Py-lib\scikit\var.csv'
df = pd.read_csv(path, parse_dates=['date'], index_col='date')

print(df.shape)

# Visualize Time series
fig, axes = plt.subplots(nrows=4, ncols=2, dpi=120, figsize=(10,6))
for i, ax in enumerate(axes.flatten()):
    data = df[df.columns[i]]
    ax.plot(data, color='red', linewidth=1)
    # Decorations
    ax.set_title(df.columns[i])
    ax.xaxis.set_ticks_position('none')
    ax.yaxis.set_ticks_position('none')
    ax.spines["top"].set_alpha(0)
    ax.tick_params(labelsize=6)
plt.tight_layout();

# Step 3: Testing Causation using Granger's Causality Test
maxlag=12
test = 'ssr_chi2test'
def grangers_causation_matrix(data, variables, test='ssr_chi2test', verbose=False):

    df = pd.DataFrame(np.zeros((len(variables), len(variables))), columns=variables,
index=variables)
    for c in df.columns:
        for r in df.index:
            test_result = grangercausalitytests(data[[r, c]], maxlag=maxlag, verbose=False)
            p_values = [round(test_result[i+1][0][test][1],4) for i in range(maxlag)]
            if verbose: print(f'Y = {r}, X = {c}, P Values = {p_values}')
            min_p_value = np.min(p_values)
            df.loc[r, c] = min_p_value
    df.columns = [var + '_x' for var in variables]
    df.index = [var + '_y' for var in variables]
    return df

grangers_causation_matrix(df, variables = df.columns)

# Step 4: Cointegration Test
def cointegration_test(df, alpha=0.05):
```

```
    """Perform Johanson's Cointegration Test and Report Summary"""
    out = coint_johansen(df,-1,5)
    d = {'0.90':0, '0.95':1, '0.99':2}
    traces = out.lr1
    cvts = out.cvt[:, d[str(1-alpha)]]

    # Define adjust function
    def adjust(val, length= 6): return str(val).ljust(length)

    # Summary
    print('Name  ::  Test Stat > C(95%)    =>   Signif  \n', '--'*20)
    for col, trace, cvt in zip(df.columns, traces, cvts):
        print(adjust(col), ':: ', adjust(round(trace,2), 9), ">", adjust(cvt, 8), ' =>  ' , trace > cvt)

cointegration_test(df)

# Step 5: Split the Series into Training and Testing Data
nobs = 4
df_train, df_test = df[0:-nobs], df[-nobs:]

# Check size
print(df_train.shape)
print(df_test.shape)

# Step 6: ADF test
# Check for Stationarity and Make the Time Series Stationary
def adfuller_test(series, signif=0.05, name='', verbose=False):
    """Perform ADFuller to test for Stationarity of given series and print report"""
    r = adfuller(series, autolag='AIC')
    output = {'test_statistic':round(r[0], 4), 'pvalue':round(r[1], 4), 'n_lags':round(r[2], 4),
'n_obs':r[3]}
    p_value = output['pvalue']

    # Define adjust function
    def adjust(val, length= 6): return str(val).ljust(length)

    # Print Summary
    print(f'    Augmented Dickey-Fuller Test on "{name}"', "\n   ", '-'*47)
    print(f' Null Hypothesis: Data has unit root. Non-Stationary.')
    print(f' Significance Level    = {signif}')
    print(f' Test Statistic        = {output["test_statistic"]}')
    print(f' No. Lags Chosen       = {output["n_lags"]}')

    for key,val in r[4].items():
        print(f' Critical value {adjust(key)} = {round(val, 3)}')

    if p_value <= signif:
        print(f" => P-Value = {p_value}. Rejecting Null Hypothesis.")
```

```
        print(f" => Series is Stationary.")
    else:
        print(f" => P-Value = {p_value}. Weak evidence to reject the Null Hypothesis.")
        print(f" => Series is Non-Stationary.")


# ADF Test on each column
for name, column in df_train.items():
    adfuller_test(column, name=column.name)
    print('\n')

# Step 7: Differencing
# First difference
df_differenced = df_train.diff().dropna()

# Re-run ADF test on each differenced series.
# ADF Test on each column of 1st Differences Dataframe
for name, column in df_differenced.items():
    adfuller_test(column, name=column.name)
    print('\n')

# Second Differencing
df_differenced = df_differenced.diff().dropna()
# ADF Test on each column of 2nd Differences Dataframe
for name, column in df_differenced.items():
    adfuller_test(column, name=column.name)
    print('\n')

# Step 8: Order of VAR
# How to Select the Order (P) of VAR model
model = VAR(df_differenced)
for i in [1,2,3,4,5,6,7,8,9]:
    result = model.fit(i)
    print('Lag Order =', i)
    print('AIC : ', result.aic)
    print('BIC : ', result.bic)
    print('FPE : ', result.fpe)
    print('HQIC: ', result.hqic, '\n')

# Step 9: Alternate method Order (P)
x = model.select_order(maxlags=12)
x.summary()

# Step 10: Order of Var - 4
# Train the VAR Model of Selected Order(p)
model_fitted = model.fit(4)
model_fitted.summary()
```

```
# Step 11: Check for Serial Correlation of Residuals (Errors) using Durbin Watson
Statistic
from statsmodels.stats.stattools import durbin_watson
out = durbin_watson(model_fitted.resid)

# Define adjust function
def adjust(val, length= 6): return str(val).ljust(length)

for col, val in zip(df.columns, out):
   print(adjust(col), ':', round(val, 2))

# Step 12: How to Forecast VAR model using statsmodels
# Get the lag order
lag_order = model_fitted.k_ar
print(lag_order)  #> 4

# Input data for forecasting
forecast_input = df_differenced.values[-lag_order:]

# Forecast
fc = model_fitted.forecast(y=forecast_input, steps=nobs)
df_forecast = pd.DataFrame(fc, index=df.index[-nobs:], columns=df.columns + '_2d')

# Step 13: Invert the transformation to get the real forecast
def invert_transformation(df_train, df_forecast, second_diff=False):
   """Revert back the differencing to get the forecast to the original scale."""
   df_fc = df_forecast.copy()
   columns = df_train.columns
   for col in columns:
      # Roll back 2nd Diff
      if second_diff:
         df_fc[str(col)+'_1d'] = (df_train[col].iloc[-1]-df_train[col].iloc[-2]) +
df_fc[str(col)+'_2d'].cumsum()
      # Roll back 1st Diff
      df_fc[str(col)+'_forecast'] = df_train[col].iloc[-1] + df_fc[str(col)+'_1d'].cumsum()
   return df_fc

df_results = invert_transformation(df_train, df_forecast, second_diff=True)

# Step 14: Plot of Forecast vs Actuals
fig, axes = plt.subplots(nrows=int(len(df.columns)/2), ncols=2, dpi=150, figsize=(10,10))
for i, (col,ax) in enumerate(zip(df.columns, axes.flatten())):
   df_results[col+'_forecast'].plot(legend=True, ax=ax).autoscale(axis='x',tight=True)
   df_test[col][-nobs:].plot(legend=True, ax=ax);
   ax.set_title(col + ": Forecast vs Actuals")
   ax.xaxis.set_ticks_position('none')
   ax.yaxis.set_ticks_position('none')
   ax.spines["top"].set_alpha(0)
```

```
    ax.tick_params(labelsize=6)

plt.tight_layout();

# Step 15: Evaluate the Forecasts
from statsmodels.tsa.stattools import acf
def forecast_accuracy(forecast, actual):
    mape = np.mean(np.abs(forecast - actual)/np.abs(actual))  # MAPE
    me = np.mean(forecast - actual)             # ME
    mae = np.mean(np.abs(forecast - actual))    # MAE
    mpe = np.mean((forecast - actual)/actual)   # MPE
    rmse = np.mean((forecast - actual)**2)**.5  # RMSE
    corr = np.corrcoef(forecast, actual)[0,1]   # corr

    mins = np.amin(np.hstack([np.expand_dims(forecast, axis=1), np.expand_dims(actual,
axis=1)]), axis=1)
    maxs = np.amax(np.hstack([np.expand_dims(forecast, axis=1), np.expand_dims(actual,
axis=1)]), axis=1)

    minmax = 1 - np.mean(mins/maxs)             # minmax
    return({'mape':mape, 'me':me, 'mae': mae,
            'mpe': mpe, 'rmse':rmse, 'corr':corr, 'minmax':minmax})

print('Forecast Accuracy of: rgnp')
accuracy_prod = forecast_accuracy(df_results['rgnp_forecast'].values, df_test['rgnp'])
for k, v in accuracy_prod.items():
    print(adjust(k), ': ', round(v,4))

print('\nForecast Accuracy of: pgnp')
accuracy_prod = forecast_accuracy(df_results['pgnp_forecast'].values, df_test['pgnp'])
for k, v in accuracy_prod.items():
    print(adjust(k), ': ', round(v,4))

# Repeat for other variables...
```

VAR models are powerful tools for multivariate time series forecasting, especially when the series influence each other. By capturing the bidirectional relationships between the variables, VAR models can provide more accurate and insightful forecasts compared to univariate models. Using the statsmodels library in Python, you can easily train and forecast VAR models, making it a practical choice for complex time series analysis.

Output

Output
Forecast Accuracy of: rgnp

```
mape  : 0.0192
me    : 79.1031
mae   : 79.1031
mpe   : 0.0192
rmse  : 82.0245
corr  : 0.9849
minmax : 0.0188

Forecast Accuracy of: pgnp
mape  : 0.0005
me    : 2.0432
mae   : 2.0432
mpe   : 0.0005
rmse  : 2.146
corr  : 1.0
minmax : 0.0005
```

Visualise Time series:

Plot 1:

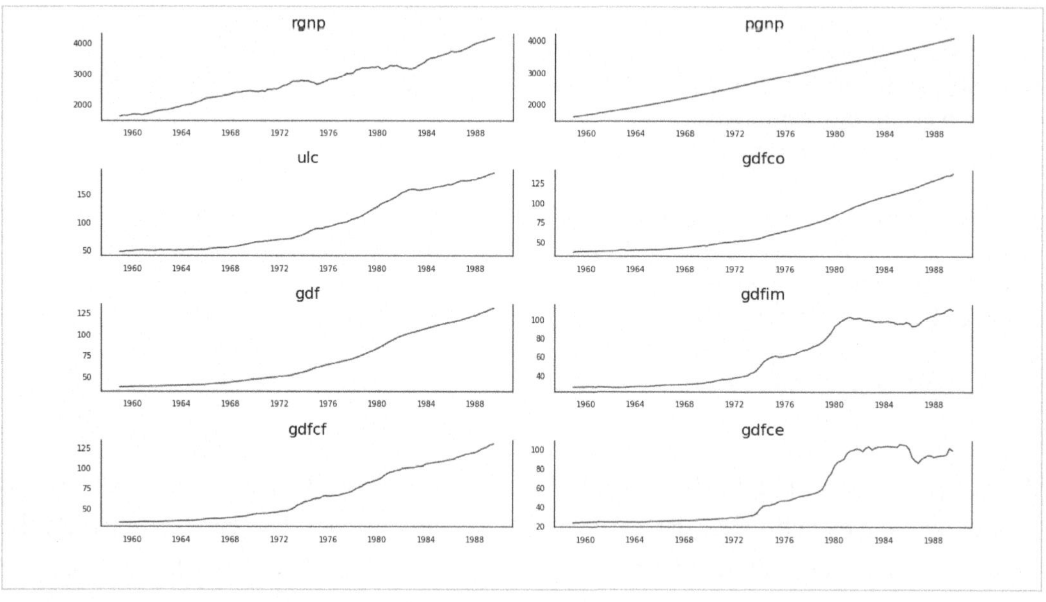

Plot 2:

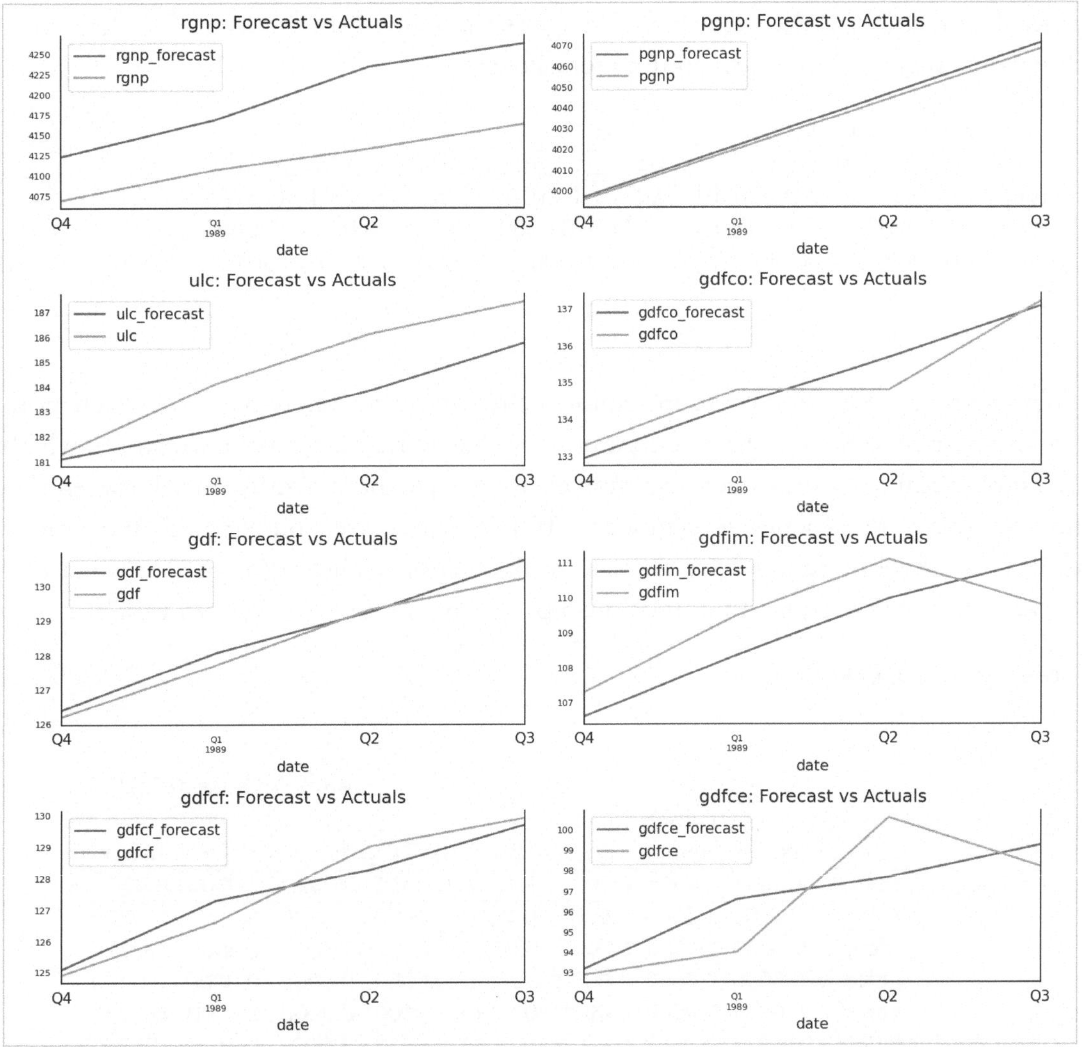

The analysis reveals that most series exhibit similar trend patterns over the years, except for gdfce and gdfim.

Testing Causation using Granger's Causality Test

Master continued that the next crucial step involves investigating potential causal relationships among these series. To achieve this, two widely used statistical tests can be employed: Granger's Causality test and the Cointegration test.

Granger's Causality Test: This test assesses whether one time series can forecast another. By examining the lagged values of the potential cause (independent variable), the test determines if they contain useful information in predicting the future values of the possible effect (dependent variable). Granger's Causality test is valuable for identifying directional relationships between time series data.

Granger's Causality Matrix:

	rgnp_x	pgnp_x	ulc_x	gdfco_x	gdf_x	gdfim_x	gdfcf_x	gdfce_x
rgnp_y	1.0000	0.0003	0.0001	0.0212	0.0014	0.0620	0.0001	0.0071
pgnp_y	0.0000	1.0000	0.0000	0.0000	0.0000	0.0000	0.0000	0.0000
ulc_y	0.0000	0.0000	1.0000	0.0002	0.0000	0.0000	0.0000	0.0041

Cointegration Test: Cointegration explores the long-term relationship between non-stationary time series that have a common stochastic trend. Unlike correlation, which measures linear association, cointegration examines whether the difference between two non-stationary time series is stationary. If two series are cointegrated, they move together in the long run, despite short-term fluctuations. This test is particularly useful for detecting stable, equilibrium relationships among multiple time series variables.

Cointegration Test:

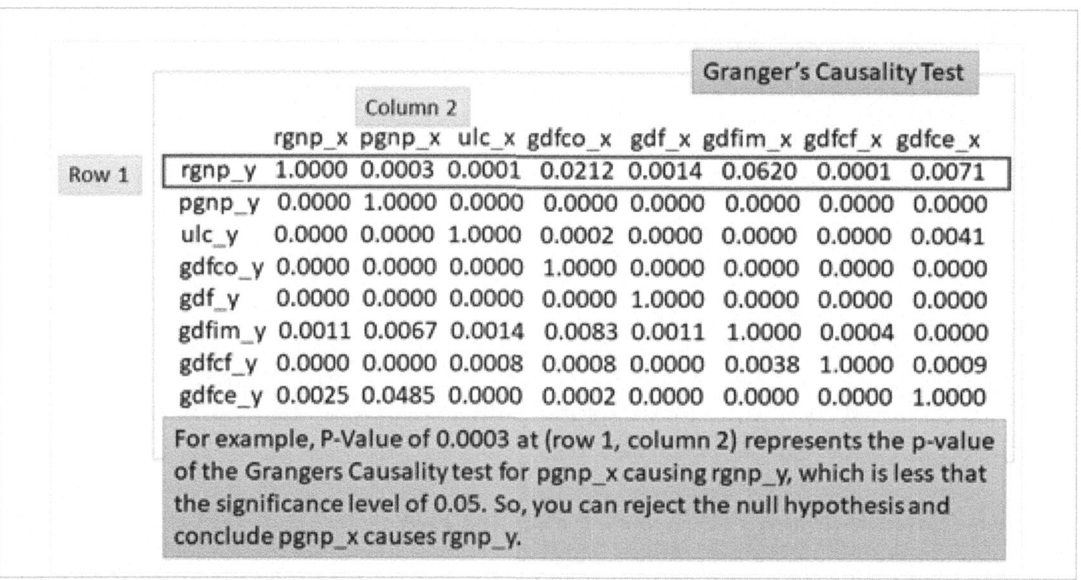

Granger's Causality Test

Column 2

Row 1

	rgnp_x	pgnp_x	ulc_x	gdfco_x	gdf_x	gdfim_x	gdfcf_x	gdfce_x
rgnp_y	1.0000	0.0003	0.0001	0.0212	0.0014	0.0620	0.0001	0.0071
pgnp_y	0.0000	1.0000	0.0000	0.0000	0.0000	0.0000	0.0000	0.0000
ulc_y	0.0000	0.0000	1.0000	0.0002	0.0000	0.0000	0.0000	0.0041
gdfco_y	0.0000	0.0000	0.0000	1.0000	0.0000	0.0000	0.0000	0.0000
gdf_y	0.0000	0.0000	0.0000	0.0000	1.0000	0.0000	0.0000	0.0000
gdfim_y	0.0011	0.0067	0.0014	0.0083	0.0011	1.0000	0.0004	0.0000
gdfcf_y	0.0000	0.0000	0.0008	0.0008	0.0000	0.0038	1.0000	0.0009
gdfce_y	0.0025	0.0485	0.0000	0.0002	0.0000	0.0000	0.0000	1.0000

For example, P-Value of 0.0003 at (row 1, column 2) represents the p-value of the Grangers Causality test for pgnp_x causing rgnp_y, which is less that the significance level of 0.05. So, you can reject the null hypothesis and conclude pgnp_x causes rgnp_y.

Illustration Granger_1

The cointegration test is a powerful tool used to assess the presence of a statistically significant long-term relationship between two or more time series variables.

```
Name  ::  Test Stat > C(95%)    =>   Signif
 ----------------------------------------
rgnp  ::  248.0      > 143.6691  =>   True
```

```
pgnp  :: 183.12   > 111.7797  =>  True
ulc   :: 130.01   > 83.9383   =>  True
gdfco :: 85.28    > 60.0627   =>  True
gdf   :: 55.05    > 40.1749   =>  True
gdfim :: 31.59    > 24.2761   =>  True
gdfcf :: 14.06    > 12.3212   =>  True
gdfce :: 0.45     > 4.1296    =>  False
```

Split the Series into Training and Testing Data

To ensure accurate forecasting with the VAR model, we'll first split the dataset into training and testing data. The training data (df_train) will be used to fit the VAR model, while the testing data will be used to evaluate the model's performance by comparing the forecasted values against the actual observations.

After splitting the data, it's crucial to check for stationarity in the time series variables. Since the VAR model requires a stationary time series for reliable predictions, we'll perform stationarity tests on each series in the dataset.

Once stationarity is confirmed, we'll proceed with fitting the VAR model on the training data and forecasting the next 4 observations. Finally, we'll assess the forecast accuracy using various metrics, ensuring the model's effectiveness in capturing the underlying dynamics of the data.

☐ **ADF test:**

The ADF test confirms that none of the time series is stationary. We rerun the test till all the series are stationary.

How to Select the Order (P) of the VAR model?

From the output:

```
Lag Order = 4
AIC :  -2.000735164470319
BIC :  4.371215137654087
FPE :  0.15556966521481086
HQIC:  0.584935933277106
```

AIC drops to lowest at lag 4, then increases at lag 5 and then continuously drops further. Let us go with lag 4 model.

An alternative approach to determining the optimal order (p) of VAR models is to utilise the model.select_order(maxlags) method available in Python's VAR module.

This method automatically selects the order (p) by considering various information criteria such as Akaike Information Criterion (AIC), Bayesian Information Criterion (BIC), Final Prediction Error (FPE), and Hannan-Quinn Information Criterion (HQIC).

The selected order (p) is the one that minimises these information criteria, indicating the best trade-off between model complexity and goodness of fit. By choosing the order with the lowest AIC, BIC, FPE, and HQIC scores, we ensure that the VAR model captures the essential dynamics of the data while avoiding overfitting.

An alternate method to choose the order(p) of the VAR

```
VAR Order Selection (* highlights the minimums)
==================================================
    AIC       BIC       FPE       HQIC
--------------------------------------------------
0   -0.07898   0.1232    0.9241   0.002961
1   -0.5721    1.248     0.5662   0.1653
```

Train the VAR Model of Selected Order(p): Order is 4

Check for Serial Correlation of Residuals (Errors) using Durbin Watson Statistic

```
rgnp  : 2.09          gdf   : 2.25
pgnp  : 2.02          gdfim : 1.99
ulc   : 2.17          gdfcf : 2.2
gdfco : 2.05          gdfce : 2.17
                      4
```

How to forecast VAR model?

```
Forecast:      rgnp_2d   pgnp_2d   ulc_2d  ... gdfim_2d gdfcf_2d gdfce_2d
date                                 ...
1988-10-01    48.322456  1.250774  0.595993 ... 0.304119 -0.917227 -0.113061
1989-01-01   -34.962286 -0.387966 -0.329877 ... 1.357223  0.618163  3.029975
```

Invert the transformation to get the real forecast:

```
Invert Transformation:          rgnp_2d   pgnp_2d ... gdfce_1d  gdfce_forecast
date                          ...
1988-10-01  48.322456  1.250774 ...  0.386939       93.186939
1989-01-01 -34.962286 -0.387966 ...  3.416915       96.603854
```

Plot of Forecast vs Actual

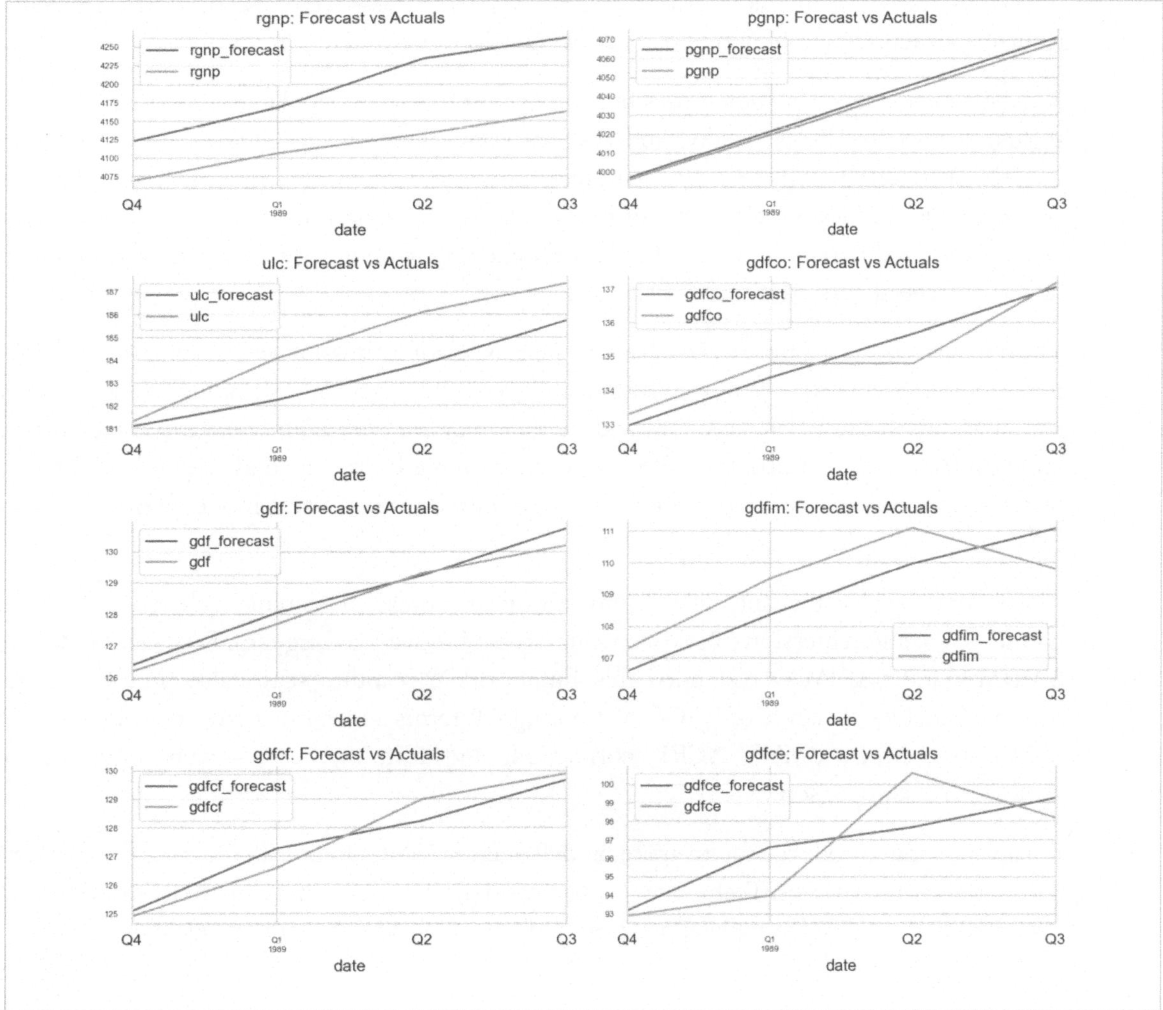

Evaluate the Forecast

```
Forecast Accuracy of: rgnp       mpe  : 0.0192
mape  : 0.0192                   rmse : 82.0245
```

me : 79.1031	corr : 0.9849
mae : 79.1031	minmax : 0.0188

Summary:

This unit provided a thorough exploration of time series analysis, guiding learners through both foundational concepts and advanced modelling techniques. It began by introducing the nature of time-dependent data and the different types of time series, emphasising key components such as trend, seasonality, cyclic behaviour, and irregular fluctuations. Various visualisation methods—including line plots, seasonal plots, and box plots—were discussed to help identify recurring structures and temporal patterns within data.

A detailed explanation of time series decomposition followed, highlighting how series can be separated into trend, seasonality, and residual components using additive or multiplicative models. The distinction between stationary and non-stationary data was emphasised, as stationarity is a critical requirement for many forecasting models. Learners were introduced to techniques like differencing, detrending, deseasonalising with moving averages, and conducting unit root tests such as ADF and KPSS.

The unit also addressed practical challenges, such as handling missing values using strategies like forward fill, backward fill, interpolation, and zero-fill. Concepts including autocorrelation, partial autocorrelation, lag selection, and measures of forecastability were explained to build intuition for model identification. Forecast evaluation methods—such as the Diebold-Mariano test, bias analysis, and encompassing tests—were introduced to assess model performance and reliability.

The second part of the unit delved into advanced models, beginning with ARIMA and its components: autoregression (p), differencing (d), and moving average (q). Seasonal models like SARIMA and SARIMAX extended this framework to capture seasonality and incorporate external variables. The role of PACF in choosing AR terms and various error metrics—MAPE, MAE, ME, MPE, RMSE, ACF1, correlation, and Min-Max error—were discussed for performance comparison.

Finally, the unit introduced multivariate models such as VAR, along with Granger causality tests and cointegration analysis. Techniques for forecasting, inverting transformations, and visualising results helped solidify a complete, practical understanding of time series modelling.

What Next:

This unit delves into Reinforcement Learning, its core principles, and practical applications. It explores types and components of reinforcement, including Models, Algorithms, and the significance of Markov Decision Processes (MDP) and the Bellman equation. Deterministic versus stochastic environments are scrutinised, emphasising their influence on learning dynamics. Q-Learning, encompassing Temporal Difference (TD) Update and Q-table's roles, is thoroughly covered. Additionally, it discusses the pivotal functions of Value and Policy networks, along with the mechanics of loss functions and gains in model optimisation. The unit also delves into Deep Q-Learning, leveraging deep neural networks for enhanced learning capabilities in complex environments.

P3-U3-L1-4 - Practice Question

1. What are the main components of a time series?
2. Differentiate between trend and seasonality in a time series.
3. Explain the difference between additive and multiplicative seasonality models.
4. How do you decompose a time series into its components?
5. What is stationarity in the context of time series data?
6. Explain the concept of differencing in time series analysis.
7. What are some common unit root tests used to test for stationarity?
8. How do you handle missing values in time series data?
9. What is autocorrelation, and why is it important in time series analysis?
10. What is the Diebold-Mariano test used for in time series forecasting?
11. Explain the concept of Granger causality in the context of time series analysis.
12. What is ARIMA modeling, and what are its main components?
13. How do you determine the order of differencing in ARIMA modeling?
14. What is the role of the Partial Autocorrelation Function (PACF) in ARIMA modeling?
15. What are some common accuracy metrics used to evaluate time series forecasting models?
16. How do you interpret the Mean Absolute Percentage Error (MAPE)?
17. What is the purpose of performing Auto ARIMA forecasting?
18. What are SARIMA models, and how do they differ from standard ARIMA models?
19. How can you test for stationarity in a VAR model using the Augmented Dickey-Fuller (ADF) test?
20. What is the significance of cointegration in time series analysis?
21. How do you interpret the results of a Granger causality test?
22. What is the purpose of inverting transformations in time series forecasting?
23. Explain the concept of vector autoregression (VAR) models in time series analysis.
24. How can you evaluate the performance of a time series forecasting model using bias analysis?

25. What techniques can be used for noise reduction in time series data?

PART FOUR

Wisdom Through Experience

Reinforcement Learning

"Reinforcement learning is not taught—it is earned, through a dance of trial and feedback, where success is a moving target and failure the most loyal teacher. The agent learns not what to do, but how to become."

– Shree Shambav

PART FOUR

DAY TWELVE

Unit 4 - Lesson One

Paths, Rewards, and Learning

☐ Reinforcement Learning

Akshaya asked, "Master, what is Reinforcement Learning?"

The Master smiled gently, as though inviting her into a deeper understanding of intelligence itself.

"Reinforcement Learning," he began, "is not merely an algorithmic method—it is the science of learning through consequence. It is a paradigm where an agent discovers wisdom not from labelled examples, nor from hidden patterns in unlabelled data, but from *experience*—from acting, observing outcomes, and evolving its behaviour through the rewards and punishments life presents. It reflects the way living beings learn: by trial, by error, and by gradually shaping strategies that maximise long-term benefit."

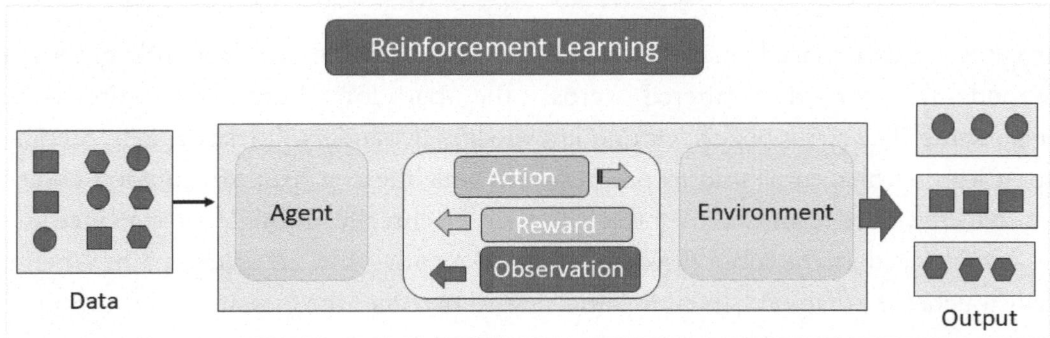

Illustration RL_2: RL

He continued, "Unlike supervised learning, which relies on the guidance of ready-made labelled datasets, and unlike unsupervised learning, which seeks structure in static data, reinforcement learning operates in *dynamic* environments. The agent must navigate uncertainty. It must explore the unknown, sometimes failing, sometimes succeeding—but always learning. Its knowledge is not granted; it is earned."

"In predictive learning," the Master explained, "the world is already captured in data. But in reinforcement learning, the world is *unfolding*. The agent generates its own data through interaction. Every action alters the future. Every decision shapes the next observation. In this sense, the agent is both student and explorer."

He paused, then added, "The fundamental challenge in reinforcement learning is the delicate balance between exploration and exploitation. Should the agent try a new action to discover something better? Or should it exploit what it already knows to gain immediate reward? This tension mirrors the human struggle between curiosity and comfort."

"Behind the scenes," he said, "RL algorithms use powerful mathematical ideas. Value functions estimate how promising a situation is. Policies map states to actions. Q-learning, temporal-difference updates, policy gradients, and actor critic methods refine the agent's behaviour over time. Slowly, the policy evolves into a strategy that maximises cumulative reward—what we call the *return*."

"Reinforcement learning becomes essential when decisions must adapt. In robotics, the agent must learn to walk, grasp, and navigate. In games, it must outwit opponents. In self-driving cars, they must respond to unpredictable roads. In automated control systems, it must stabilise turbulent processes. In all these domains, labelled data cannot capture every possible situation, but experience can."

The Master then offered an example.

"Imagine a robot placed inside a maze," he said. "Within the labyrinth glitters a diamond—the reward. Scattered across the corridors burn small fires—the punishments. The robot begins with no knowledge. It wanders. It tries. It fails. Step by step, it learns which turns lead to progress and which lead to pain. Each good choice adds to its reward; each mistake subtracts from it. Eventually, through perseverance and repeated interaction, the robot discovers not only a path—but the *optimal* path. When it finally touches the diamond, its cumulative reward becomes the measure of its learning."

He concluded, "Reinforcement learning teaches us a profound truth: Intelligence does not arise from certainty, but from interaction. Not from static knowledge, but from the willingness to act, observe, and adapt. The agent learns as we do—by daring to explore the maze of life."

AI agent in a maze environment

Illustration RL_2: RL

Master said, "Apeksha, the essence of Reinforcement Learning can be understood through its central tenets—pillars upon which the entire learning journey unfolds."

Input:

"The journey begins at an initial state—the first moment of awareness for the agent. This is the point from which it observes the world, senses its conditions, and prepares to act. Just as every quest begins with a single step, every RL episode begins with a state that defines the agent's starting position in the environment."

Output:

"From every state, a horizon of possibilities emerges. The agent must choose an action, aware that each choice opens a new pathway. These potential outcomes reflect the complexity of the environment—some paths lead to progress, others to failure, each shaping the agent's learning trajectory."

Training:

"In reinforcement learning, training is not about consuming labelled examples. It is about *behavioural refinement* through consequences. Each action is met with feedback—

reward for effective behaviour, penalty for missteps. Users or the environment itself defines this reward structure. Over time, the agent internalises these signals, sharpening its strategy."

Continuous Learning:

"The agent evolves through iteration. With every interaction—success or failure—it grows wiser. Experience becomes memory; memory becomes policy. This continuous cycle mirrors human learning: we do, we observe the outcome, and we adjust. The agent learns not just what to do, but *why* it must do so."

Optimal Solution:

"The highest aim of the agent is to maximise cumulative reward. Not the reward of a single action, but the reward gathered across time—a long-term vision. Thus, the optimal solution is the path that yields the greatest overall benefit, reflecting deep strategy rather than immediate gratification."

The Master paused, letting the principles settle in before continuing.

"In this dynamic realm, the agent matures through experience. With each episode, it sharpens its instincts, adapts its decisions, and slowly uncovers the trajectory that leads to success. Reinforcement Learning is not merely a method—it is a philosophy of growth. It teaches us that mastery is a journey shaped by choices, consequences, and constant self-correction."

□ Types of Reinforcement

The Master continued, "Reinforcement shapes behaviour, and it manifests in two fundamental forms—each contributing uniquely to the learning process."

Positive Reinforcement:

"This occurs when desirable behaviour is rewarded. Rewards elevate motivation, strengthen desirable patterns, and encourage the agent to repeat beneficial actions. Over time, positive reinforcement cultivates confidence and consistency. Yet, when applied excessively, its impact may diminish, causing diminishing marginal returns."

Negative Reinforcement:

"Here, behaviour is strengthened by removing or avoiding an unpleasant condition. The agent learns to act in ways that reduce discomfort or avert undesirable outcomes.

Negative reinforcement increases behaviour by providing relief. It establishes minimum performance standards and ensures the agent does what is necessary to avoid penalties. It motivates through avoidance, not through attraction."

Master said softly, "Through reinforcement—both positive and negative—an agent learns to navigate the uncertainty of its environment. The true power of reinforcement learning lies not in the final reward, but in the transformation brought about by countless interactions, corrections, and refinements. In this, it mirrors life itself."

Elements of Reinforcement Learning:

Master said, "Apeksha — to truly master Reinforcement Learning, you must move beyond names and learn the full meaning, interplay, and consequences of each element. Listen carefully; each part is a thread in a living tapestry."

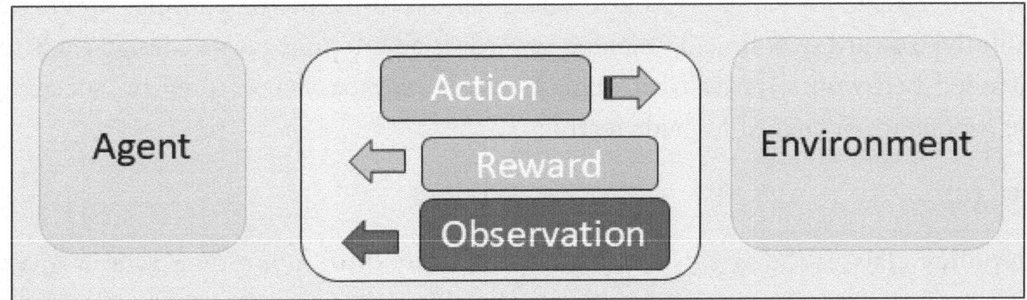

Illustration RL_2: RL

Agent

"The **agent** is the learner and decision-maker — a conscious actor within the RL setting. It perceives observations, chooses actions, and updates its internal strategy (policy). In practice, the agent may be a robot, a trading algorithm, or a software process; conceptually, it is any entity that can act and learn from consequences."

Environment

"The **environment** is everything external to the agent: the world the agent inhabits. It returns observations and rewards based on the agent's actions. Real-world environments are often **stochastic** — the same action in the same state might lead to different outcomes. The environment defines the rules of motion, dynamics, and objectives; the agent learns these rules only through interaction."

State

"A **state** is the environment's description at a given time. If the process satisfies the **Markov property**, the current state contains all information necessary to predict the future (given future actions). When the agent cannot observe the full state, we face a **Partially Observable Markov Decision Process (POMDP)** — the agent must infer the latent state from history."

Action

"An **action** is a choice the agent makes to influence the environment. Actions may be discrete (move left/right) or continuous (apply thrust). The policy maps observed states to actions, and the choice of action set shapes everything the agent can achieve."

Reward

"The **reward** is the environment's feedback — a scalar signal that evaluates the immediate desirability of an action's outcome. Reinforcement learning optimises **cumulative reward** over time. Designing rewards is an art: poor reward design leads to unintended behaviours (reward hacking). Rewards may be sparse (only on success), dense (frequent), or shaped to guide learning."

Policy (π)

"The **policy** $\pi(a|s)$ is the agent's strategy: a probability distribution over actions given states (stochastic) or a direct mapping (deterministic). Policies can be tabular (a table of action probabilities), parametric (neural networks), or rule-based. Learning often focuses on improving the policy to maximise expected return."

Value (V)

"The **value function** $V^{\pi}(s)$ is the expected **return** starting from state sss and following policy π:

$$V^{\pi}(s) = E_{\pi}[\ \sum_{t=0}^{\infty} \gamma^{t} r_t \mid s_0 = s]$$

where $\gamma \in [0,1)$ is the **discount factor** weighing future rewards. Value captures long-term desirability of being in a state under a policy."

Q-value (Action-value, Q)

"The **Q-value** $Q_{\pi}(s, a)$ refines value by including the immediate action:

$$Q^{\pi}(s, a) = E_{\pi} [\sum_{t=0}^{\infty} \gamma^{t} r_{t} \mid s_0 = s, a_0 = a].$$

Q-values tell us the expected return if we take action a now and then follow policy π. They are the backbone of off-policy methods like **Q-learning.**"

Core mathematical backbone

"The agent's goal is to maximise expected return. The Bellman expectation equation ties values recursively:

$$V^{\pi}(s) = \sum_{a} \pi(a|s) \sum_{s'} P(s' | s,a) \left(r(s,a,s') + \gamma V^{\pi}(s')\right).$$

For optimality, the Bellman optimality equation holds for $V*$ and $Q*$."

Q-learning update (sampled, model-free):

$$Q(s, a) \leftarrow Q(s, a) + \alpha \left(r + \gamma \; max_{a'} Q(s',a') - Q(s,a)\right)$$

Where α is the learning rate.

Patterns of learning

- **Model-free vs Model-based:** Model-free learns values/policies directly from experience (Q-learning, policy gradients). Model-based learns a model of environment dynamics P(s'|s, a) and plans with it (better sample efficiency but harder to learn).
- **On-policy vs Off-policy:** On-policy (e.g., SARSA, PPO) updates policy using data from the current policy; off-policy (Q-learning, DQN) can learn from different behaviour policies.
- **Temporal-Difference (TD) vs Monte Carlo:** TD bootstraps from current estimates; Monte Carlo uses full returns. TD combines bias and variance trade-offs advantageously.

Practical considerations and challenges

- **Exploration vs Exploitation:** Strategies like **ε-greedy**, **softmax**, or **Thompson sampling** manage this tension. Efficient exploration is crucial in sparse-reward problems.
- **Credit assignment:** Determining which actions caused delayed rewards is non-trivial; temporal credit is assigned via returns and bootstrapping.
- **Function approximation & stability:** Neural nets (deep RL) scale to large state spaces but introduce instability; remedies include **experience replay**, **target networks**, and careful hyperparameter tuning.
- **Sample efficiency & safety:** Real-world agents must learn with limited data and avoid unsafe actions; model-based methods, transfer learning, and safe RL methods help.

Architectures and algorithms

"Value-based (Q-learning, DQN), Policy-based (REINFORCE, PPO), and Hybrid actor-critic (A2C, DDPG, SAC) families each suit different problems. Actor-critic methods combine policy learning (actor) with value estimation (critic) to stabilise and accelerate learning."

Master said, "Apeksha, these elements are not isolated: they weave into algorithms and practice. To understand RL, one must practise designing rewards, choosing representations, balancing exploration, and stabilising learning. Then theory will meet reality, and intelligence will emerge from experience."

☐ Models and Algorithms:

Master explained, various models and algorithms are employed in reinforcement learning, each tailored to specific applications:

Master said, "Apeksha — to wield Reinforcement Learning in practice, you must not only learn names, but understand the logic, trade-offs, and mathematics behind each model and algorithm."

1. Markov Decision Process (MDP) — the formal bedrock

An MDP (S, A, P, R, γ) formalises the RL problem: a set of states S, actions A, transition probabilities $P(s'|s, a)$, reward function $R(s, a, s')$, and discount factor $\gamma \in [0,1)$. The **Markov property** means the next state depends only on the current state and action.

MDPs let us define **return** (discounted cumulative reward) and pose the optimisation problem: find a policy $\pi(a|s)$ that maximises expected return.

2. Bellman Equation — recursive heart of value-based methods

The Bellman expectation equation for a policy π:

$$V^{\pi}(s) = \sum_a \pi(a|s) \sum_{s'} P(s'|s, a)(r(s, a, s') + \gamma V^{\pi}(s')).$$

For optimal value $V*$, the Bellman optimality equation becomes:

$$V^*(s) = \max_a \sum_{s'} P(s'|s, a)(r + \gamma V^*(s')).$$

These recursions enable dynamic programming, temporal-difference updates, and value iteration.

3. Q-Learning — model-free and off-policy

Q-learning learns the action-value $Q(s, a)$ directly via the TD update:

$$Q(s, a) \leftarrow Q(s, a) + \alpha(r + \gamma \max_{a'} Q(s', a') - Q(s, a)).$$

Pros: simple, converges under tabular settings. Cons: scales poorly with large state spaces and requires careful exploration (ε-greedy).

4. Deep Q-Networks (DQN) — Q-learning with function approximation

DQN uses a neural network $Q_\theta(s, a)$ to approximate Q-values. Practical stabilisers: **experience replay** (break correlations by sampling past transitions) and **target networks** (a delayed copy $Q_{\theta}-$ for stable targets). DQN brought RL success in complex visual domains, but it is sensitive to hyperparameters.

5. Policy Gradient Methods — direct policy optimisation

Policy gradients learn parameters θ of a policy $\pi_\theta(a|s)$ by maximising expected return. The REINFORCE gradient:

$$\nabla_\theta J(\theta) = E[\nabla_\theta \log\pi_\theta(a|s)\, G_t].$$

Pros: natural for continuous actions, stochastic policies; cons: high variance, slower to converge without variance reduction (baselines).

6. Actor-Critic — best of both worlds

Actor-critic architectures combine a **policy (actor)** and a **value estimator (critic)**. The critic reduces variance by estimating the value/baseline; the actor updates policy using advantage estimates:

$$A(s,a) = r + \gamma V(s') - V(s).$$

Many modern algorithms (A2C, A3C, PPO) are actor-critic variants balancing stability and efficiency.

7. Proximal Policy Optimization (PPO) — practical, stable policy learning

PPO optimises a clipped surrogate objective to take conservative policy steps, trading aggressive improvement for stability. It's widely used for continuous and discrete problems due to robustness and relative ease of tuning.

8. Monte Carlo vs Temporal Difference (TD)

- **Monte Carlo** methods use full-episode returns to estimate values—unbiased but high variance.
- **TD methods** (like SARSA, Q-learning) bootstrap using current estimates—lower variance, some bias, better online sample efficiency. TD(λ) smoothly mixes MC and TD.

9. DDPG, TD3, SAC — continuous-action actor-critic families

DDPG: deterministic actor with off-policy critic (suitable for continuous control). TD3 and SAC are improvements addressing function-approximation instability and overestimation bias; SAC uses entropy regularisation encouraging exploration.

10. Multi-Armed Bandits — simplified sequential decision problems

Bandits focus on choosing arms to maximise immediate reward without state transitions. Algorithms: **ε-greedy**, **UCB** (optimistic exploration), **Thompson Sampling** (Bayesian). Useful when no state dynamics exist or as subroutines for exploration.

Practical trade-offs and considerations

- **Model-based vs model-free:** Model-based RL learns or uses P,R for planning (sample-efficient); model-free learns value/policy directly (simpler but less data-efficient).
- **On-policy vs off-policy:** On-policy (PPO, A2C) uses data from the current policy; off-policy (DQN, DDPG) reuses past data—improving sample efficiency but complicating stability.
- **Function approximation issues:** Neural nets scale RL but invite instability (nonstationary targets, correlated data). Remedies include replay buffers, target networks, entropy bonuses, and gradient clipping.
- **Exploration vs exploitation:** Use ε-greedy, softmax, intrinsic motivation, curiosity, or Thompson sampling. Sparse rewards need shaped rewards or better exploration strategies.
- **Sample efficiency & safety:** Real-world systems require sample-frugal algorithms (model-based methods, transfer learning) and safe RL constraints to avoid catastrophic behaviours.

Master said, "Choose an algorithm with respect to the problem's nature: discrete vs continuous actions, episodic vs continuing tasks, available samples, and safety constraints. Start with simpler, stable methods (PPO, DQN variants) before moving to sophisticated hybrids. Study failure modes—reward design, function approximation, and exploration—and you will transform algorithms into reliable agents."

☐ Types of Reinforcement learning

Reinforcement learning encompasses various approaches, each tailored to address different aspects of the learning process. Here are some common types:

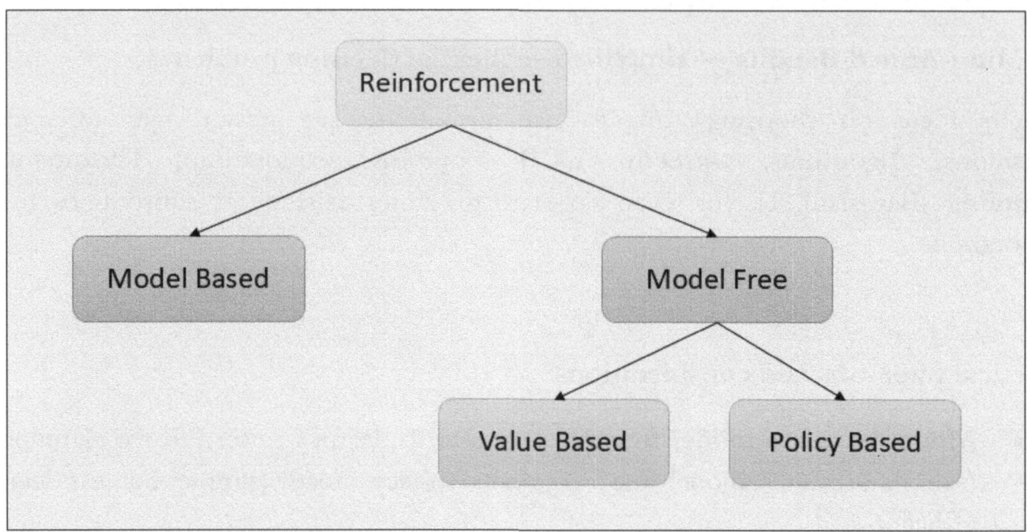

Illustration RL_3: RL

Model-Based vs. Model-Free:

- Model-Based RL: This method involves creating a model of the environment to aid decision-making.
- Model-Free RL: Contrary to the former, this approach doesn't rely on an explicit environment model but learns from direct experience.

Value-Based vs. Policy-Based:

- Value-Based RL: Focuses on estimating the expected cumulative reward associated with states or actions using a value function.
- Policy-Based RL: Directly learns the optimal policy governing the agent's behaviour.

On-Policy vs. Off-Policy:

- On-Policy RL: Learns from the data it generates while interacting with the environment.
- Off-Policy RL: Learns from a separate dataset, often collected from a different policy or buffer.

Exploration vs. Exploitation:

- Exploration: Involves trying new actions to enhance the agent's understanding and discover optimal strategies.
- Exploitation: Prioritizes actions believed to yield the highest immediate reward based on current knowledge.

Single-Agent vs. Multi-Agent:

- Single-Agent RL: Features a solo learning agent interacting with the environment.
- Multi-Agent RL: Involves multiple agents interacting with each other and the environment, each optimizing its own objectives.

Continuous vs. Discrete Action Spaces:

- Continuous Action Spaces: Actions can vary within a range, necessitating specialized algorithms.
- Discrete Action Spaces: Actions are distinct and enumerable, simplifying handling in certain scenarios.

Episodic vs. Continuous Tasks:

- Episodic RL: Tasks have well-defined start and end points, with performance evaluated over episodes.
- Continuous RL: Tasks continue indefinitely, with performance assessed over extended durations.

Understanding these distinctions guides the selection of appropriate algorithms and strategies, aligning them with the specific characteristics of the reinforcement learning problem at hand.

☐ Approaches to Implement Reinforcement Learning

Value-Based:

- Objective: Identify the optimal value function, representing the maximum value at a state under any policy.
- Agent's Focus: Expectation of long-term returns at various states under a given policy π.

Policy-Based:

- Objective: Determine the optimal policy for maximizing future rewards, without relying on the value function.
- Agent's Strategy: Employ a policy that guides actions at each step to maximize the cumulative future reward.

Types of Policies:

- Deterministic: Produces the same action at any state.
- Stochastic: Action is determined by probabilities.

Model-Based:

- Approach: Create a virtual model of the environment, and the agent explores and learns from this simulated environment.
- Characteristics: No universal solution or algorithm exists, as the model representation varies for each specific environment.

Difference between Reinforcement Learning and Supervised Learning

Reinforcement Learning (RL):

- Interaction: RL involves agents interacting with an environment.
- Exploration: Agents explore the environment, take actions, and receive rewards or penalties.
- Objective: The goal is for the agent to learn a strategy (policy) to maximize cumulative rewards.
- Feedback: Learning transpires through trial and error, with feedback provided in the form of rewards.

Supervised Learning:

- Dataset: Supervised learning relies on labeled datasets for training.
- Training: Algorithms learn patterns from the input-output pairs in the dataset.
- Prediction: The trained model predicts outputs for new, unseen inputs based on learned patterns.

- Feedback: Learning is supervised, with explicit input-output pairs guiding the model.

In summary, while reinforcement learning focuses on learning through interaction and rewards in dynamic environments, supervised learning relies on labelled datasets for direct pattern recognition and prediction.

Master continued with a calm and expansive tone, "Apeksha, the true power of Reinforcement Learning emerges not from algorithms alone, but from its **profound ability to adapt, evolve, and thrive in dynamic, uncertain environments**. This adaptability has made RL a cornerstone of modern intelligent systems across countless domains."

☐ Reinforcement Learning: Applications Across Domains

1. Gaming – Where RL First Demonstrated Superhuman Mastery

Master said, "The world witnessed RL's brilliance through **AlphaGo**, where an agent learned through millions of self-play games, surpassing the best human minds. Atari agents trained via Deep Q-Networks (DQN) learned to excel in games like Breakout and Pong, discovering strategies never explicitly programmed. Games offer perfect testbeds—clear rules, measurable rewards, and limitless simulation—allowing RL to explore its full potential."

2. Robotics – Teaching Machines to Move, Feel, and Adapt

Robotics relies heavily on RL because real-world actions involve uncertainty, physics, and coordination. Robots learn tasks such as:

- Grasping unstable objects
- Navigating through unknown terrains
- Balancing, walking, or performing complex motions

Through trial and error, robots refine control strategies that are impossible to hand-code, bridging perception and action in real time.

3. Autonomous Vehicles – Learning to Drive Safely

RL assists self-driving cars in learning optimal driving policies: lane following, collision avoidance, speed regulation, and decision-making at intersections. By simulating millions of driving hours, RL helps vehicles anticipate rare events, reduce accidents, and adapt to evolving road conditions.

4. Finance – Algorithmic Trading & Portfolio Optimisation

RL agents observe markets, predict price movements, and take actions such as buying, selling, or holding assets. Through feedback from profits and losses, they learn strategies that maximise long-term returns while managing risk in volatile markets.

5. Healthcare – Personalised and Adaptive Treatment Plans

RL enables:

- Optimised chemotherapy schedules
- Adaptive drug dosages
- Personalised treatment paths for chronic conditions
- Intelligent prosthetics and rehabilitation systems

The dynamic nature of patient health makes RL ideal, as the agent learns what works best for each individual over time.

6. Education – Intelligent and Adaptive Learning Systems

RL powers personalised learning platforms that adjust difficulty based on the learner's performance. If a student struggles, the system provides hints; if they excel, it advances the challenge—creating a tailored, evolving learning journey.

7. Energy & Resource Management

RL optimises energy distribution in smart grids, manages electricity loads, and reduces fuel consumption. These systems learn to balance fluctuating demand, environmental constraints, and cost efficiency.

8. Dialogue Systems & Recommendations

Conversational agents use RL to improve the quality of interactions by learning what responses lead to successful conversations. Similarly, recommendation engines refine suggestions based on user engagement, constantly improving relevance.

9. Logistics & Supply Chain Management

RL helps warehouses optimise routing, inventory allocation, delivery schedules, and resource utilisation. Agents learn from delays, costs, and customer demand to refine planning strategies.

A Simple Example – Dog Training with Reinforcement Learning

Master smiled and said, "Imagine a dog learning two commands: *handshake* and *fetch the ball*. When the dog obeys correctly, it receives a biscuit — a reward. When it performs the wrong action, there is no reward."

- **State:** Dog hears a command
- **Action:** Dog chooses an action (handshake, fetch, or ignore)
- **Reward:** Biscuit for correct behaviour, none for incorrect
- **Policy:** Over many trials, the dog learns which action leads to the biscuit
- **Goal:** Maximise biscuits (total reward)

Through repeated interactions, the dog refines its behaviour. The reward shapes its understanding, guiding it toward the optimal response.

Master said, "In every domain — whether training a dog, navigating a robot, or diagnosing disease — reinforcement learning transforms *experience* into *intelligence*. It is the science of learning from life itself."

Example P4 – U4 – D1	
Reinforcement learning	

<pre>import random
class VirtualDog:
    def __init__(self):
        self.commands = ["handshake", "fetch"]
        self.biscuit = 0
 	
    def perform_action(self, command):
        if command == "handshake":
            print("Dog performs handshake!")
            self.biscuit += 1 # Reward the dog with a biscuit for a successful handshake
        elif command == "fetch":
            print("Dog fetches the ball!")
            self.biscuit += 1 # Reward the dog with a biscuit for fetching the ball</pre>
	Dog fetches the ball!
	Dog performs handshake!
	Dog performs handshake!
	Dog fetches the ball!
	…..

```
        else:
            print("Dog doesn't understand the command. No reward.")

    def get_reward(self):
        return self.biscuit
# Reinforcement Learning Training
virtual_dog = VirtualDog()
training_episodes = 100
for episode in range(training_episodes):
    command = random.choice(virtual_dog.commands)  # Randomly choose a command
    virtual_dog.perform_action(command)
# Evaluation
print(f"Total Biscuits Earned: {virtual_dog.get_reward()}")
```

In this example, the VirtualDog class represents our virtual dog. It has two commands: 'handshake' and 'fetch.' During the training episodes, the dog randomly performs one of these commands. If it performs the correct action, it is rewarded with a biscuit. After training, you can check how many biscuits the dog has earned.

Please bear in mind that this example is rudimentary, and real-world reinforcement learning scenarios typically encompass more intricate environments, states, and actions. To address such complex problems, advanced reinforcement learning algorithms and frameworks are employed.

Advantages:

- Reinforcement learning excels in tackling highly complex problems that conventional techniques struggle to solve, making it invaluable in domains requiring sophisticated decision-making.
- The model can iteratively refine its strategies by learning from errors encountered during the training process, enhancing its performance over time.
- RL obtains training data through direct interaction with the environment, allowing agents to adapt to real-world scenarios and dynamic conditions.
- RL accommodates non-deterministic environments, where outcomes of actions are unpredictable or subject to change, proving beneficial in uncertain real-world applications.
- This approach is versatile, capable of addressing a wide spectrum of problems spanning decision-making, control, and optimization tasks.

- RL's flexibility permits integration with other machine learning techniques like deep learning, amplifying its capabilities and improving performance across various domains.

Disadvantages:

- Reinforcement learning may not be the optimal choice for solving simple problems, as its complexity and resource requirements may outweigh potential benefits.
- RL demands substantial amounts of data and computational resources, often making it resource-intensive and time-consuming.
- The effectiveness of RL hinges heavily on the quality of the reward function. Poorly designed reward functions can hinder the learning process, leading to suboptimal behaviours by the agent.
- Debugging and interpreting RL algorithms can pose challenges. Understanding the rationale behind an agent's behaviour may be elusive, complicating the diagnosis and resolution of issues.

☐ Markov Decision Process (MDP)

Apeksha asked, **"What is an MDP?"**

Master replied, "A Markov Decision Process (MDP) is a foundational mathematical framework that helps us model decision-making in environments where outcomes are uncertain, actions have consequences, and the future depends only on the present state—not on the path taken to reach it."

This property is called the **Markov Property**:

"The future is independent of the past, given the present."

Core Components of an MDP

1. States (S)

These are all the possible situations the agent can be in.

In the given grid world:

- Each cell (S1, S2, S3, … S12) represents a unique **state**.
- Some states are special: walls, fire, goal, or normal cells.

2. Actions (A)

Actions define what the agent can do in each state.

In grid world these are:

- Up
- Down
- Left
- Right

Actions may sometimes fail or lead to unintended outcomes if the environment is **stochastic** (random).

Illustration RL_5: RL

3. Transition Model (P(S' | S, a))

This tells us:

"If the agent is in state S and takes action a, what is the probability it will land in state S'?"

- In a deterministic world:

  → The agent always goes exactly where the action directs.

- In a stochastic world:

→ An action may lead to different possible next states with certain probabilities.

This is precisely what makes an environment **Markovian**.

4. Reward Function (R(s,a))

Rewards quantify how good or bad an outcome is.

Examples from your diagram:

- Entering fire: **–1**
- Reaching the diamond (goal): **+1**
- Moving into neutral spaces: **0** or a small negative step cost

Rewards shape **behaviour**.

The agent learns which states and actions are desirable.

5. Policy (π)

A policy is the agent's **decision-making strategy**:

A function that maps each state to the best action.

The grid world's arrows pointing in each cell represent a **policy**.

6. Value Function (V(s))

The value of a state is the **expected long-term return** if the agent starts in state s and follows an optimal policy thereafter.

This is why we compute:

V(s) = maximum expected reward achievable from state s.

Mathematical Intuition:

P(S' | S,a) where S' and S are state and 'a' action.

Equation:

$V(s) = \max_a (V(s'))$

Introducing Reward and Penalty

$V(s)=max_a[R(s, a) + V(s')]$

Introducing Discount Factor

$V(s) = max_a (\gamma V(s'))$

Bellman Equation combination of the above:

$$\mathbf{V(s)=max_a[R(s, a) + \gamma V(s')]}$$

Evolution of the Bellman Equation

The given diagram beautifully shows the *progressive refinement* of MDP mathematics:

Stage 1 — Value Based Only on Future Value

Before rewards are considered, the value is estimated as:

$$V(s) = max_a (V(s'))$$

This is incomplete but serves as intuition:

"Choose the move that leads to the best next state."

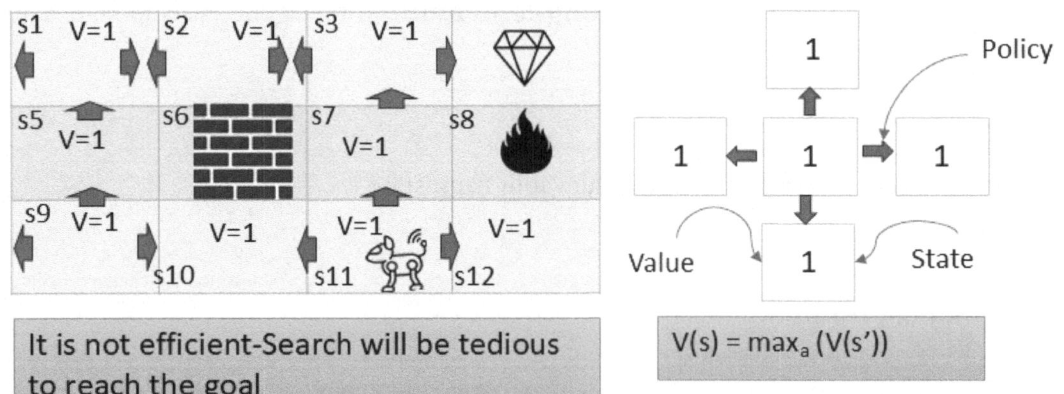

Illustration MD_1: MD

Stage 2 — Add Reward and Penalty

Here, we incorporate the immediate consequence of an action:

$$V(s)=max_a[R(s, a) +V(s')]$$

This integrates **reward shaping**, making values meaningful.

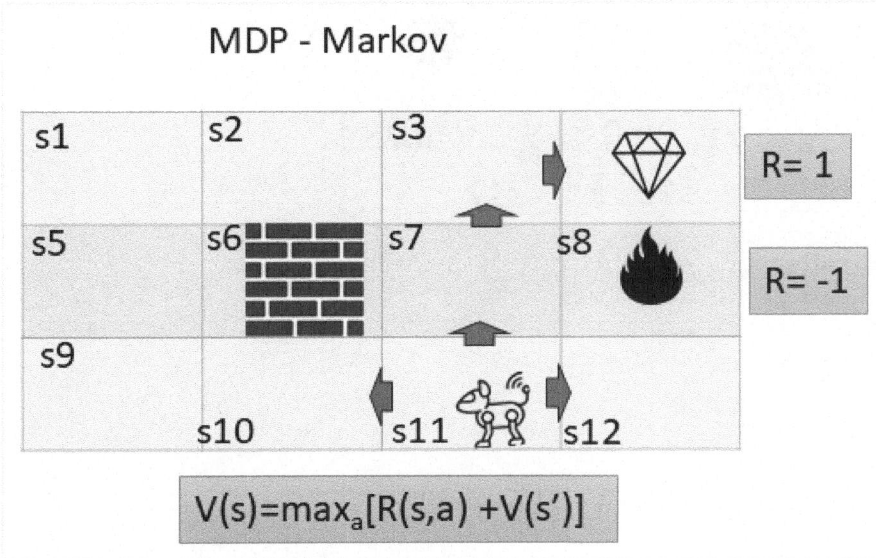

Illustration MD_2: MD

Stage 3 — Introduce the Discount Factor γ

The discount factor ($0 < \gamma \leq 1$):

- Reduces the weight of future rewards
- Encourages the agent to seek rewards **sooner**
- Ensures mathematical convergence

Updated equation:

$$V(s) = max_a (\gamma V(s'))$$

This is the **Bellman Optimality Equation**—the core of value-based reinforcement learning.

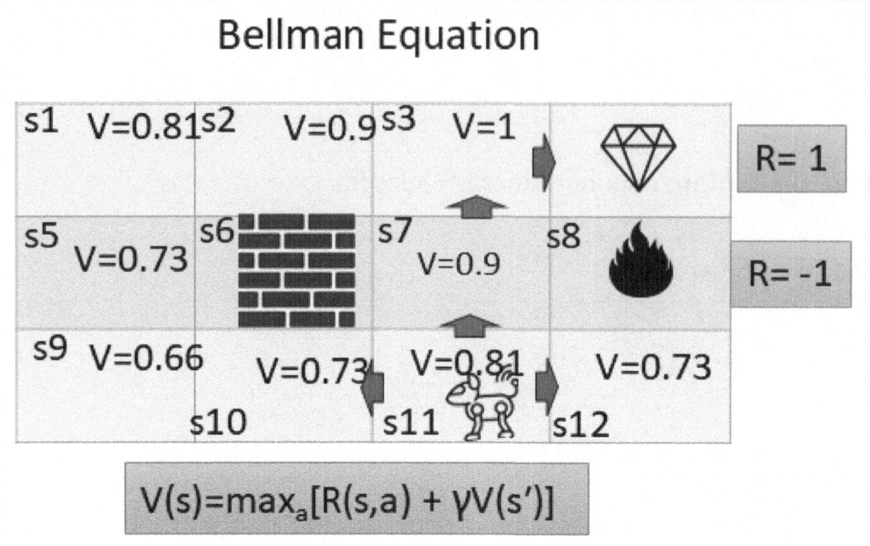

Illustration MD_3: MD

Understanding Through the Grid-World Example

In the diagram:

- The agent starts at S11.
- It must reach the diamond.
- Walls block certain paths.
- Fire penalises poor choices.
- Each update of V(s) makes the map "smarter."
- Policies improve as values converge.

Through iterative computation, the agent discovers:

- Which paths are safe
- Which paths lead to penalties
- Which actions maximise long-term reward

This forms the optimal policy.

MDP in Essence

Master said, "An MDP transforms a random, uncertain environment into a solvable mathematical structure.

Through states, actions, transitions, rewards, and policies, the agent learns not only how to reach the goal—but how to act wisely, consistently, and optimally in every situation."

The grid world becomes a metaphor for life's navigation:

- Choices (actions)
- Situations (states)
- Consequences (rewards)
- Uncertainty (stochastic transitions)
- Strategy (policy)

And the Bellman equation becomes the quiet intelligence behind every decision.

Master said, This Python code simulates a classic Grid-World Markov Decision Process (MDP) and computes the optimal policy using Value Iteration. The grid contains states, walls, a goal, and a fire penalty. Each state transition is determined by the agent's actions—moving up, down, left, or right—while remaining within boundaries and avoiding walls. Rewards are assigned for reaching the goal, falling into fire, or taking a step. Value Iteration repeatedly updates state values using the Bellman optimality equation until convergence. Finally, the code extracts and displays the optimal policy as directional arrows along with the computed value function for each state.

Example P4 – U4 – D2

Grid-World MDP

```
import numpy as np

# ---------------------------------------
# GRID WORLD DEFINITION (Matching diagram)
# ---------------------------------------

# States are labelled S1 to S12 arranged as:
# S1  S2  S3  S4
# S5  S6  S7  S8
# S9  S10 S11 S12
```

```
rows = 3
cols = 4

# Convert (row, col) → state index
def to_state(row, col):
    return row * cols + col

# Walls
walls = {to_state(1, 1), to_state(1, 2)}  # S6, S7

# Fire and Goal states
fire_state = to_state(2, 3)     # S12
goal_state = to_state(0, 3)     # S4

# ---------------------------------------
# ACTIONS (Up, Down, Left, Right)
# ---------------------------------------
ACTIONS = {
    "UP":    (-1, 0),
    "DOWN":  (1, 0),
    "LEFT":  (0, -1),
    "RIGHT": (0, 1),
}
action_list = list(ACTIONS.keys())

# ---------------------------------------
# TRANSITION FUNCTION
# ---------------------------------------
def next_state(s, action):
    if s in walls:
        return s  # cannot move from wall

    row, col = divmod(s, cols)
    dr, dc = ACTIONS[action]
    new_r, new_c = row + dr, col + dc

    # Check boundaries
    if new_r < 0 or new_r >= rows or new_c < 0 or new_c >= cols:
        return s  # invalid move → stay

    s_new = to_state(new_r, new_c)

    # Cannot enter walls
    if s_new in walls:
        return s

    return s_new
```

```
# --------------------------------------
# REWARD FUNCTION
# --------------------------------------
def reward(s, a, s_next):
    if s_next == goal_state:
        return 1
    if s_next == fire_state:
        return -1
    return -0.04   # small negative step cost

# --------------------------------------
# VALUE ITERATION
# --------------------------------------

gamma = 0.9
theta = 1e-4  # convergence threshold

num_states = rows * cols
V = np.zeros(num_states)

# Walls have no value updates
for w in walls:
    V[w] = 0

def value_iteration():
    iteration = 0
    while True:
        delta = 0
        new_V = V.copy()

        for s in range(num_states):
            if s in walls:
                continue

            if s == goal_state or s == fire_state:
                continue

            values = []
            for a in action_list:
                s_next = next_state(s, a)
                r = reward(s, a, s_next)
                values.append(r + gamma * V[s_next])

            new_V[s] = max(values)
            delta = max(delta, abs(new_V[s] - V[s]))

        V[:] = new_V[:]
```

```
        iteration += 1

        if delta < theta:
            print(f"Converged after {iteration} iterations.")
            break

value_iteration()

# ---------------------------------------
# EXTRACT OPTIMAL POLICY
# ---------------------------------------

policy = np.full(num_states, " ")

for s in range(num_states):
    if s in walls:
        policy[s] = "W"  # Wall
        continue
    if s == goal_state:
        policy[s] = "G"
        continue
    if s == fire_state:
        policy[s] = "F"
        continue

    action_values = {}
    for a in action_list:
        s_next = next_state(s, a)
        r = reward(s, a, s_next)
        action_values[a] = r + gamma * V[s_next]

    best_action = max(action_values, key=action_values.get)

    # Policy arrows
    arrows = {"UP": "↑", "DOWN": "↓", "LEFT": "←", "RIGHT": "→"}
    policy[s] = arrows[best_action]

# ---------------------------------------
# PRINT VALUE TABLE AND POLICY TABLE
# ---------------------------------------

print("\nOptimal Value Function:")
for r in range(rows):
    row_vals = [f"{V[to_state(r, c)]:6.2f}" for c in range(cols)]
    print(" ".join(row_vals))

print("\nOptimal Policy:")
for r in range(rows):
```

```
    row_pol = [f"  {policy[to_state(r, c)]}  " for c in range(cols)]
    print(" ".join(row_pol))
```

Output:

```
Output
Converged after 8 iterations.

Optimal Value Function:
 0.73  0.86  1.00  0.00
 0.62  0.00  0.00  1.00
 0.52  0.43  0.34  0.00

Optimal Policy:
 →    →    →    G
 ↑    W    W    ↑
 ↑    ←    ←    F
```

PART FOUR

DAY THIRTEEN

Unit 4 - Lesson Two

From States to Strategy

☐ Bellman Equation Reinforcement

Master said, "Bellman's Equation is not merely a formula—it is the very *heartbeat* of reinforcement learning. Conceived by Richard Bellman in 1957, it introduced a profound way of viewing decision-making: not as isolated choices, but as an unfolding chain of actions, each linked to future possibilities. Bellman understood that every decision carries echoes of the future within it. Thus, he created a recursive framework to capture this interplay between the present and what lies ahead."

At its core, Bellman's Equation allows an agent to evaluate the value of a state by considering two aspects simultaneously:

1. **What reward do I receive now?**
2. **What is the best I can expect from the future, starting from the next state onward?**

Instead of solving a complex problem all at once, Bellman broke it into smaller, interdependent pieces—each state is valued in relation to the value of the states that follow. This idea, called **optimality through recursion**, revolutionised dynamic programming and later became the backbone of reinforcement learning.

The Bellman Optimality Equation

$$V(s) = \max_a (\gamma V(s'))$$

Where:

- **V(s)** – The value of being in state *s*, assuming the agent behaves optimally.
- **R(s, a)** – The immediate reward received for taking action *a* in state *s*.
- **V(s')** – The value of the next state resulting from action *a*.
- **γ (gamma)** – The discount factor, determining how strongly future rewards influence present decisions.
- **max_a** – The agent selects the action that yields the highest long-term benefit.

Master said, "The brilliance of Bellman's insight lies in its recursive nature. The value of the present depends on the promise of the future. Each iteration of this equation pulls today's estimate closer to the true value, allowing the agent to refine its understanding of the environment with every experience."

This equation forms the foundation of **Q-learning**, **value iteration**, **dynamic programming**, and modern deep reinforcement learning methods. It empowers agents to learn optimal policies even without a model of the environment, adjusting their strategies through repeated interaction and feedback.

Ultimately, Bellman's Equation teaches a profound principle:

Optimal decisions emerge not from the present alone, but from a clear evaluation of the future that each action shapes.

Master said, "When learning begins, we do not start in the dark—we start where certainty already exists. In this grid world, the state closest to the goal provides our first anchor. From this single point of clarity, the Bellman Equation ripples backward through the entire environment, illuminating every state with meaning.

Step 1: Evaluating S3 — The State Next to the Goal

Master continued, "Let us begin at **S3**, the cell directly beside a rewarding terminal state."

The Bellman Equation tells us:

$$V(s) = max_a[R(s, a)+\gamma V(s')]$$

For S3:

- **R(s, a) = 1** — The agent receives a reward when moving right into the goal.

- **γ = 0.9** — Future rewards are valuable, but slightly discounted.
- **V(s') = 0** — Because the goal is terminal, there are *no states beyond it.*

Thus:

$V(S3) = 1+0.9\times0 = 1$

Master said, "Write this value into S3. This is your first beacon."

Step 2: Evaluating S2 — The Value Propagates Backward

Now we move one step farther from the goal.

For **S2**, the agent's best move leads toward S3:

- **R(s, a) = 0** — No immediate reward for entering S3.
- **γ = 0.9**
- **V(s') = V(S3) = 1**

Therefore:

$V(S2) = 0+0.9\times1 = 0.9$

Master said, "This is the essence of Bellman's insight: the value of today depends on the promise of tomorrow."

Propagating Values Through the Grid

We repeat this process for S5, S6, S7, S10, S11, S12, and so on.

Each state's value reflects:

- Immediate reward
- Best possible future
- Discounted expectation of long-term gain

Over several iterations, the grid fills with meaningful numbers, each representing the highest achievable long-term reward from that state.

These values collectively form the **optimal value function.**

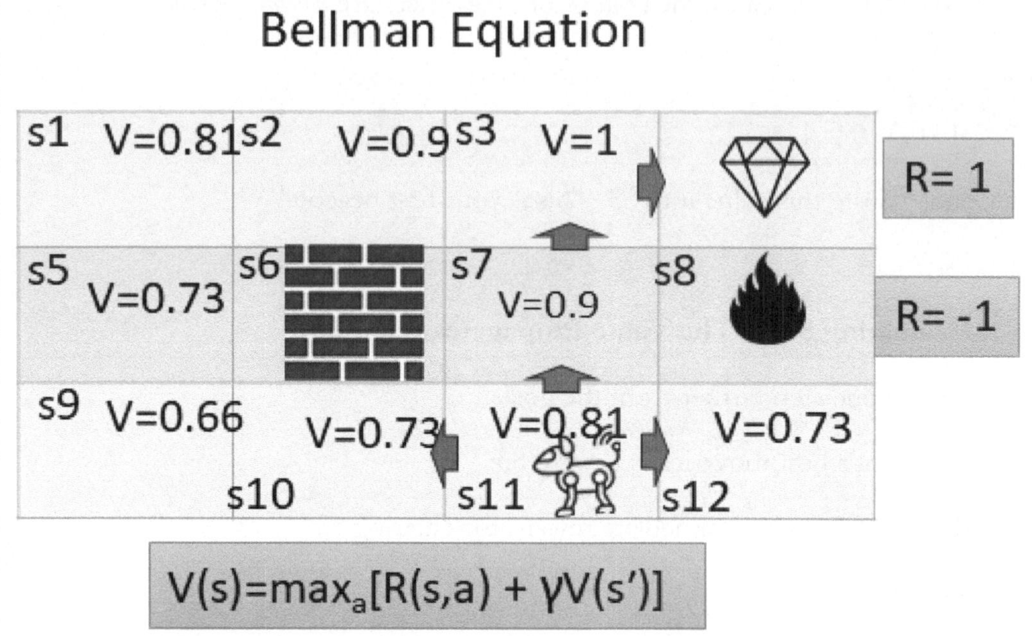

Illustration MD_3: Bellman

Step 10: Determining the Optimal Policy (S11 → Goal)

Master said, "Once values shine across the grid, the agent begins its journey."

Suppose the agent is standing at **S11.**

It examines its neighbours:

- Up → S7
- Left → S10
- Right → S12

Each has a value.

The agent always chooses the direction with the maximum value.

In this case:

- **S7 has the highest value (0.81)**

- S10 and S12 have lower values

Thus,

➞ **S11** → **S7** is the optimal move.

From **S7**, the agent evaluates adjacent states again.

One side is fire (negative reward).

One side is a wall (blocked).

The most valuable path continues toward **S3**, then into **S4**, the goal.

Master said, "The Bellman Equation does not merely compute numbers. It teaches an agent how to *see the world through the lens of long-term wisdom.*

Each value is a prediction of the future. Each action is guided by these predictions. And the resulting path—the optimal policy—is nothing but the natural unfolding of informed choices.

This is the heart of Reinforcement Learning: *A dialogue between what is now and what could be.*"

Apeksha asked, "Master, why do two different Bellman equations exist, and what distinguishes their purpose?"

Master said, "Apeksha, both equations you mentioned are correct — but they live in **two different worlds** of Reinforcement Learning, just like two paths leading to the same mountain peak."

Master continued, "The first equation is the Bellman Expectation Equation — the equation of *obedience*."

The Bellman expectation equation for a policy π:

$$V^{\pi}(s) = \sum_a \pi\,(a|s) \sum_{s'} P(s'|s,\,a)(r(s,\,a\,,s') + \gamma V^{\pi}\,(s')).$$

"This equation," the Master explained, "is used when the agent is already following a **policy π**, just as a disciple follows a chosen discipline.

It does not question the policy.

It does not seek the best action.

It simply evaluates the consequences of faithfully following π.

This is the equation of **policy evaluation**, the art of understanding the value of each state under a given behaviour."

Then Master smiled and said, "But the second equation, Apeksha, is the Bellman Optimality Equation — the equation of *mastery*."

$$V(s)=\max_a[R(s,a) + \gamma V(s')]$$

"This is the moment the disciple becomes the seeker. No longer following a fixed policy, the agent asks:

'Which action brings the highest long-term reward?'

Here, the goal is not obedience but **optimality**. The agent chooses the action that leads to the greatest value — just as a wise mind chooses the path of greatest future potential.

This equation lies at the heart of Q-Learning, Value Iteration, and DQN."

Master said, "Apeksha, remember this:

- The **expectation equation** follows a policy.
- The **optimality equation** transcends it.

One teaches you the value of a path. The other teaches you to choose the best path."

He paused and added gently, "Both are correct — for each belongs to its own stage of learning."

Master said, "Apeksha, this Python program illustrates how an agent learns optimal behaviour through *value iteration* within a structured grid world. The grid represents states such as normal cells, a goal, fire, and a wall that blocks movement. Each state holds a value representing its long-term desirability. The agent can move in four directions—

up, down, left, right—but walls prevent transitions, and stepping into fire results in a negative reward.

The algorithm repeatedly applies the **Bellman Optimality Principle**, updating each state value by considering all possible actions and selecting the one that yields the highest expected return. Over multiple iterations, the value function begins to stabilise, revealing which states lead closer to the goal. A policy is then extracted by choosing the best action for every non-terminal state. Finally, the simulation demonstrates how an agent starting at S11 follows this learned policy, navigating intelligently through the environment toward the goal."

Example P4 – U4 – D3
Bellman

```
import numpy as np

# ------------------------------------------------------------
# CORRECTED GRID (Fire in S8, Wall in S6)
# ------------------------------------------------------------

# Grid layout:
# S1  S2  S3  G
# S5  W   S7  F
# S9  S10 S11 S12

grid = [
    ["S1", "S2", "S3", "G"],     # Row 0
    ["S5", "W",  "S7", "F"],     # Row 1 (S6 = Wall, S8 = Fire)
    ["S9", "S10","S11","S12"]    # Row 2
]

rows = len(grid)
cols = len(grid[0])

# Rewards
reward_map = {
    "G": 1,   # Goal
    "F": -1   # Fire at S8
}

# Actions
actions = {
    "U": (-1, 0),
    "D": (1, 0),
    "L": (0, -1),
    "R": (0, 1)
}
```

```
gamma = 0.9

# Initialize state values (ignore walls)
values = {grid[r][c]: 0.0 for r in range(rows) for c in range(cols) if grid[r][c] != "W"}

# ------------------------------------------------------------
# Transition Function
# ------------------------------------------------------------
def next_state(r, c, action):
    dr, dc = actions[action]
    nr, nc = r + dr, c + dc

    # Out of boundary
    if nr < 0 or nr >= rows or nc < 0 or nc >= cols:
        return r, c

    # Wall check (S6)
    if grid[nr][nc] == "W":
        return r, c

    return nr, nc


# ------------------------------------------------------------
# VALUE ITERATION
# ------------------------------------------------------------
def value_iteration(iterations=20):
    global values
    for _ in range(iterations):
        new_values = values.copy()

        for r in range(rows):
            for c in range(cols):
                state = grid[r][c]

                if state == "W":
                    continue

                # Terminal states: goal, fire
                if state in reward_map:
                    new_values[state] = reward_map[state]
                    continue

                # Bellman update
                best_val = float("-inf")

                for a in actions:
```

```
                nr, nc = next_state(r, c, a)
                next_s = grid[nr][nc]
                reward = reward_map.get(next_s, 0)
                val = reward + gamma * values[next_s]

                best_val = max(best_val, val)

            new_values[state] = round(best_val, 2)

        values = new_values


# ------------------------------------------------------------
# EXTRACT POLICY
# ------------------------------------------------------------
def extract_policy():
    policy = {}

    for r in range(rows):
        for c in range(cols):
            state = grid[r][c]

            if state in ["W", "G", "F"]:
                continue

            best_val = float("-inf")
            best_action = None

            for a in actions:
                nr, nc = next_state(r, c, a)
                next_s = grid[nr][nc]
                reward = reward_map.get(next_s, 0)
                val = reward + gamma * values[next_s]

                if val > best_val:
                    best_val = val
                    best_action = a

            policy[state] = best_action

    return policy


# ------------------------------------------------------------
# AGENT SIMULATION FROM S11 TO GOAL
# ------------------------------------------------------------
def simulate(start="S11"):
    path = [start]
```

```
    current = start

    while current not in ["G", "F"]:
        action = policy[current]

        # locate coordinates
        for r in range(rows):
            for c in range(cols):
                if grid[r][c] == current:
                    cr, cc = r, c

        nr, nc = next_state(cr, cc, action)
        current = grid[nr][nc]

        path.append(current)

    return path


# ------------------------------------------------------------
# RUN EVERYTHING
# ------------------------------------------------------------
value_iteration()
policy = extract_policy()

print("\nSTATE VALUES:")
for k, v in values.items():
    print(k, ":", v)

print("\nOPTIMAL POLICY:")
for k, v in policy.items():
    print(k, "→", v)

print("\nAGENT PATH FROM S11:")
print(" → ".join(simulate("S11")))
```

Output:

```
Output

STATE VALUES:
S1 : 1.54
S2 : 1.71
S3 : 1.9
G : 1
S5 : 1.39
```

```
S7 : 1.71
F : -1
S9 : 1.25
S10 : 1.39
S11 : 1.54
S12 : 1.39

OPTIMAL POLICY:
S1 → R
S2 → R
S3 → R
S5 → U
S7 → U
S9 → U
S10 → R
S11 → U
S12 → L

AGENT PATH FROM S11:
S11 → S7 → S3 → G
```

☐ Deterministic and stochastic

Master said, "Nikash, To understand why some decisions in life feel predictable while others feel uncertain, you must first see the world through the lenses of **determinism** and **stochasticity**. These two forces shape not only algorithms and machines, but also the patterns of human behaviour, nature, and destiny itself."

1. Deterministic: The Path of Certainty

Master continued, "In a **deterministic** system, the universe behaves like a perfectly crafted clock. Every movement, every outcome, every next step is precisely dictated by what came before.

Nothing surprises you because nothing *can* surprise you.

If you start from the same conditions, follow the same rules, and walk the same path, you will *always* arrive at the same destination."

He pointed to the illustration of the traveller walking straight toward the diamond.

"Here, the traveller's steps are fixed. His policy tells him to always move *right.*

No deviation.

No uncertainty.

No hesitation.

The result is guaranteed — a straight line from desire to achievement.

This is the essence of determinism:

predictable input, predictable output."

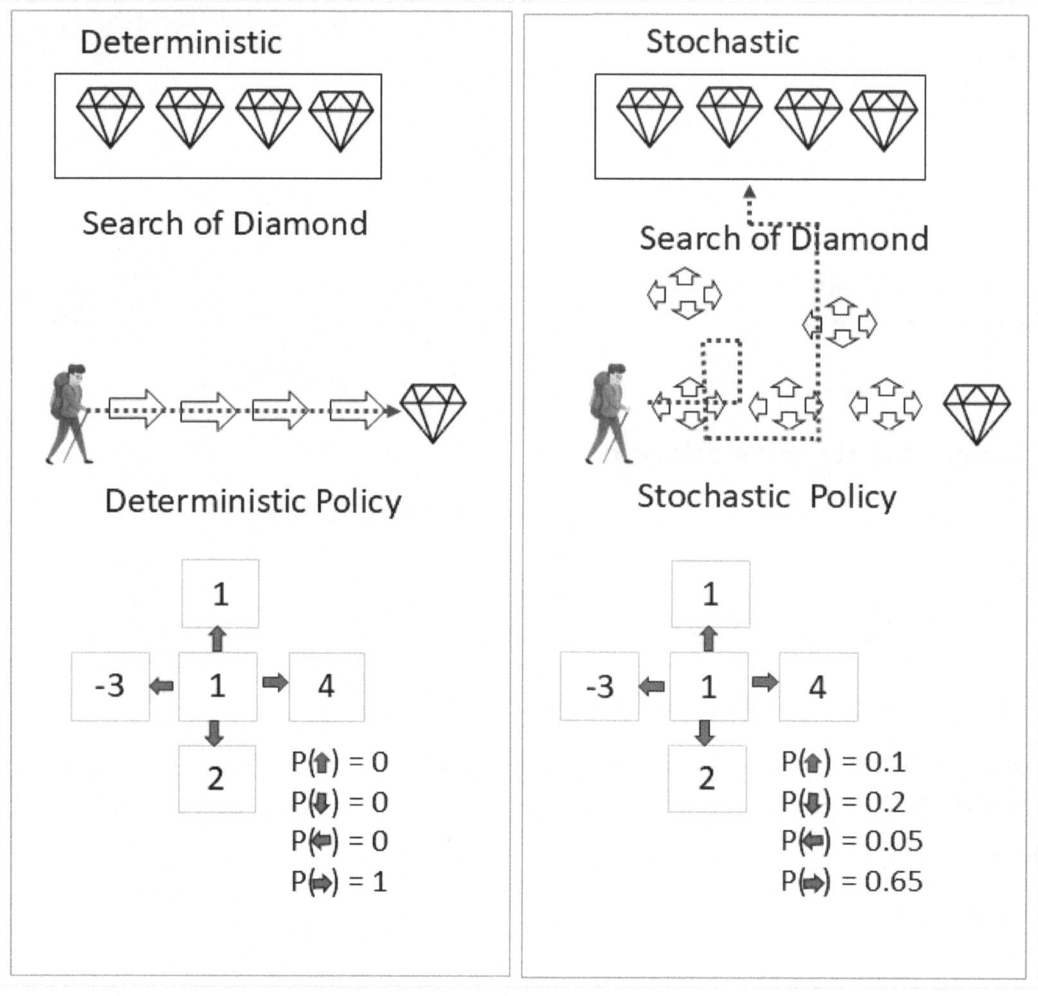

Illustration Det_Stoc_1: Deterministic and stochastic

2. Stochastic: The Path of Uncertainty

Master then shifted his gaze to the second illustration.

"But life is not always so linear, Nikash.

Many systems — and many journeys — include randomness. They are **stochastic**. Even with the same beginning, the path may twist, drift, split, or circle back."

He pointed to the arrows swirling around the traveller.

"In a stochastic policy, the agent chooses actions based on *probabilities.*

Move up with 0.1 probability, down with 0.2, left with 0.05, right with 0.65.

The path is not guaranteed… only *influenced.*

He may reach the diamond sooner.

He may wander longer.

He may discover something unexpected."

Master smiled gently.

"This is the nature of stochastic systems:

predictable rules, unpredictable outcomes."

Deep Insight: Why the Distinction Matters

Master said, "The deterministic world is one of control, structure, and precision. The stochastic world is one of adaptation, exploration, and resilience."

He continued:

- In deterministic systems, success comes from **knowing the rule**.
- In stochastic systems, success comes from **understanding the uncertainty**.

"Reinforcement learning mirrors life, Nikash," he whispered.

"Sometimes the policy is strict.

Sometimes it is flexible.

Sometimes it takes you straight to the diamond.

Sometimes the randomness of the journey teaches you more than the destination itself."

"So remember, Nikash:

Determinism is the path of exactness.

Stochasticity is the path of possibility.

Both are essential.

Both are powerful.

And wisdom lies in knowing when each one serves the journey ahead."

☐ Model-Based Vs Model-Free Learning

Master said, "Roopa, to understand how an intelligent being learns to act in the world, you must first understand the two great paths of learning — the path of *internal modeling* and the path of *pure experience*. These are known as Model-Based and Model-Free Learning."

Model-Based Learning: The Path of Foresight

Master said, "In **Model-Based learning**, the agent behaves like a wise traveler who studies the map before taking a single step.

It attempts to *understand the world* — its rules, transitions, and consequences — before acting.

It builds an internal model of:

- how the environment behaves,
- what will happen if a specific action is taken,
- and which future states are likely."

He pointed to the imagined maze.

"In training a robot for a maze, Model-Based learning means:

- The maze layout is known.
- The robot simulates moves internally.
- It evaluates possible future paths.

- It plans before stepping."

Master smiled, "This path offers **clarity, efficiency, and foresight**. But it depends on one key gift — knowing the environment well enough to model it."

Model-Free Learning: The Path of Experience

Master said, "In **Model-Free learning**, the agent is like a seeker walking through life with no map — only curiosity, mistakes, and learning."

Here, the agent **does not build any model** of the environment. It learns *only* from what it experiences — rewards, failures, surprises.

"There is no simulation of the future," he added.

"No predictions of transitions. Only the raw truth of trial and error."

In the maze example:

- The robot does **not** know the layout.
- It explores.
- It hits walls.
- It finds dead ends.
- It slowly discovers which actions yield progress.

"This is the essence of algorithms like Q-learning," Master said.

"They learn value from the world directly, not from imagination."

Two Philosophies of Intelligence

Master leaned closer.

"These two learning paths reflect two ancient philosophies of knowledge:"

a) Knowledge by Reasoning (Model-Based)

Where understanding precedes action.

Where the mind creates an inner picture of the world.

b) Knowledge by Experience (Model-Free)

Where action precedes understanding.

Where meaning is extracted only after the encounter.

"One is the path of the planner.

One is the path of the explorer.

Together, they define intelligence."

When to Use Which?

Master said:

- **Model-Based** is powerful when the environment is known, structured, and predictable.

  It enables *planning, optimal solutions, and fewer mistakes.*

- **Model-Free** is powerful when the environment is unknown, complex, or impossible to model.

  It enables *adaptation, discovery, and learning from reality itself.*

Master said, "Roopa, to walk wisely in the world, you must know both ways:

- Sometimes you must build a map in your mind.
- Sometimes you must let the path itself reveal the map.

Model-Based learning is the art of anticipating the world.

Model-Free learning is the art of surrendering to it.

A true learner knows when to think…and when to experience."

☐ Q-learning algorithm

Master said, "Q-learning is one of the most elegant frameworks in Reinforcement Learning because it teaches an agent *not simply by knowing*, but by *doing, failing, reflecting,* and *refining.* It contains within it the very rhythm of learning found in nature."

Q-Learning: A Deep Exploration

Q-learning falls under **Temporal Difference Learning**, a family of methods where agents learn directly from experience — *without waiting for episodes to end, and without needing a model of the environment.*

Master said, "Q-learning allows an agent to estimate the long-term quality of actions through incremental adjustments, much like how humans refine skills by practicing, receiving feedback, and adjusting behaviour over time."

Key Components Explained in Depth

1. Q-Values (Action-Values)

A Q-value represents the *wisdom* of choosing a particular action in a particular state.

Q (s, a)

Rather than evaluating the value of a state alone, Q-learning evaluates **state–action pairs**, giving the agent a more detailed understanding of the environment.

Master explained: "If Value Function tells you how desirable a state is, Q-values tell you how wise your next step is."

Q-values capture not only immediate rewards but *all future potential* that arises from that action.

2. Rewards and Episodes: The Environment's Feedback System

In Reinforcement Learning, everything is driven by **rewards**.

Each episode is a journey:

- The agent begins in some state
- Takes an action
- Observes the next state
- Receives a reward
- And repeats this loop until it reaches a terminal state

Master said, "The environment speaks through rewards. Some whispers are pleasant, some painful — but each one shapes the agent."

Episodes teach the agent the consequences of its choices.

3. Temporal Difference Learning & The Bellman Insight

Q-learning updates its Q-values using the Temporal Difference rule — a beautiful balance between present reality and future expectations.

$$Q(s,a) \leftarrow Q(s,a)+\alpha[R+\gamma \, max_{a'} \, Q(s',a') - Q(s,a)]$$

Master said:

"TD learning blends what *has happened* with what *might happen*.

It is learning in motion — adjusting itself after every step."

The Bellman Equation provides the *theoretical foundation*, while TD-update serves as the *practical mechanism*.

4. ϵ-Greedy Policy: Balancing Wisdom and Curiosity

Q-learning must choose actions carefully.

If it always chooses the best-known action, it will **never discover better paths**.

Thus, the ϵ-greedy policy balances:

Exploitation

Selecting the action with the highest Q-value.

Exploration

With probability ϵ, selecting a random action.

Master said:

"A mind that never explores becomes stagnant.

A mind that only explores never stabilizes.

Q-learning finds balance between the two."

Over time, exploration is reduced — allowing the agent to settle into optimal behaviour.

Two Ways of Determining Q-Values

A. Temporal Difference Update (Practical Learning)

Q-values are updated step-by-step using real experiences.

B. Bellman Equation (Ideal Learning)

Provides the mathematical foundation for defining optimal Q-values.

Master said:

"The Bellman Equation is like scripture — the perfect form.

TD-update is like practice — imperfect, incremental, but sufficient to reach mastery."

TD Update

For value functions:

$$V(S) = V(s) + \alpha\ [R(s,a) + \gamma V(s') - V(s)]$$

Where:

- α controls how much new information overrides old information
- γ discounts future rewards
- R(s, a) is immediate feedback
- V(s') is the estimated value of the next state

Steps in TD-style learning include:

- Take an action

- Receive reward
- Observe next state
- Update your estimate
- Continue until the goal is reached

Master said:

"Every step updates knowledge.

Every reward updates expectations.

Every episode strengthens wisdom."

The Inner Philosophy of Q-Learning

Master said:

"Q-learning mirrors life.

We act.

We receive feedback.

We reflect.

We adjust our beliefs.

We refine our strategies.

Through exploration we discover possibility. Through exploitation we honour what we have learned.

Slowly the agent — like a seeker — approaches optimal behaviour.

This is Q-learning:

A journey from trial to understanding,

from randomness to clarity,

from uncertainty to mastery."

□ Q-table

Master said, "The Q-table is a fundamental structure in reinforcement learning, functioning as the agent's internal map for decision-making within an environment."

How the Q-Table Works

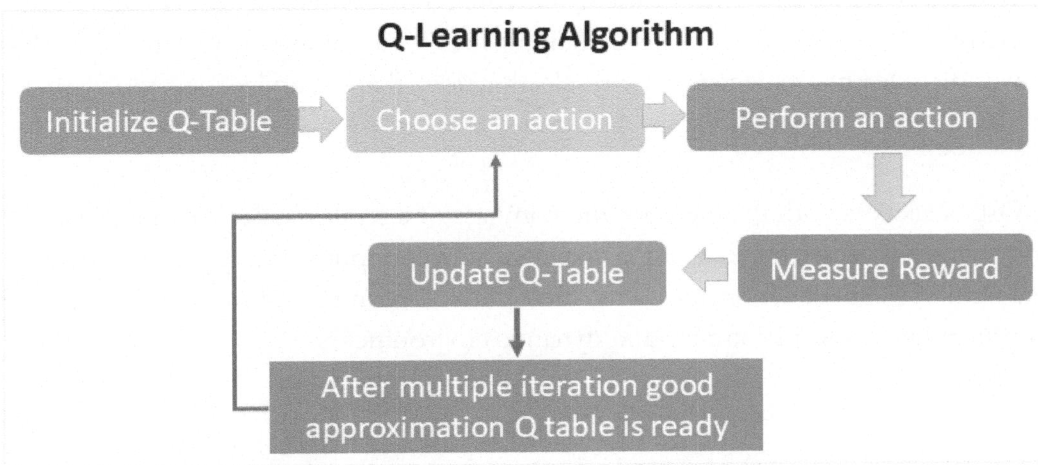

Illustration Q_1: Q Learning

Repository of Learned Value:

The Q-table stores the learned value (Q-values) of taking specific actions in specific states. These values reflect how rewarding a particular action is expected to be and guide the agent toward favourable outcomes.

State–Action Framework:

Each row of the Q-table represents a possible state the agent might encounter, while each column corresponds to an action available in that state. This grid-like structure allows the agent to quickly evaluate its choices.

Continual Refinement:

As the agent interacts with the environment—receiving rewards, penalties, and experiencing transitions—the Q-table is continually updated. These updates reflect the agent's evolving understanding of which actions lead to better long-term rewards.

Performance Enhancement:

The core objective of reinforcement learning is to improve behaviour over time. As the Q-table becomes more accurate through repeated experience, the agent's decisions become more optimal and consistent.

Connection to the Q-Function:

The Q-table is the tabular form of the Q-function, a mathematical model that predicts expected future rewards for each state–action pair. By consulting the Q-table, the agent retrieves these learned expectations and selects actions that maximize long-term benefit.

In essence:

The Q-table acts as both the memory and compass of a reinforcement learning agent—storing what has been learned, guiding decisions, and continuously improving with every interaction. As experience accumulates, the Q-table becomes a more precise blueprint for optimal behaviour in complex and dynamic environments.

Master said, "This program is a gentle doorway into the heart of Q-learning, showing how an agent gradually awakens to intelligent action through experience. The environment is a simple world of 16 states, with the final state serving as the goal. A Q-table is born empty, like an untrained mind, waiting to be shaped by learning.

Across many epochs, the agent begins from random states and chooses actions through the ϵ-greedy method—sometimes exploring the unknown, sometimes trusting what it has learned. Each step leads it to a new state, and only upon touching the goal does it receive a reward. Using the Q-learning update rule, the agent refines its understanding, adjusting each Q-value by blending immediate rewards with discounted future possibilities.

Example P4 – U4 – D4
Scikit – Q Learning

```
import numpy as np
# Define the environment
n_states = 16  # Number of states in the grid world
n_actions = 4  # Number of possible actions (up, down, left, right)
goal_state = 15  # Goal state

# Initialize Q-table with zeros
Q_table = np.zeros((n_states, n_actions))

# Define parameters
learning_rate = 0.6
```

```
discount_factor = 0.95
exploration_prob = 0.2
epochs = 1000

# Q-learning algorithm
for epoch in range(epochs):
    current_state = np.random.randint(0, n_states)  # Start from a random state

    while current_state != goal_state:
        # Choose action with epsilon-greedy strategy
        if np.random.rand() < exploration_prob:
            action = np.random.randint(0, n_actions)  # Explore
        else:
            action = np.argmax(Q_table[current_state])  # Exploit

        # Simulate the environment (move to the next state)
        # For simplicity, move to the next state
        next_state = (current_state + 1) % n_states

        # Define a simple reward function (1 if the goal state is reached, 0 otherwise)
        reward = 1 if next_state == goal_state else 0

        # Update Q-value using the Q-learning update rule
        Q_table[current_state, action] += learning_rate * \
            (reward + discount_factor *
             np.max(Q_table[next_state]) - Q_table[current_state, action])

        current_state = next_state  # Move to the next state

# After training, the Q-table represents the learned Q-values
print("Learned Q-table:")
print(Q_table)

# After training, you can exploit the learned policy
final_policy = np.argmax(Q_table, axis=1)
print("Final Policy (Action to take in each state to reach the goal):")
print(final_policy)
```

Output:

```
Output
Learned Q-table:
[[0.48767498 0.40964698 0.29260499 0.48267586]
 [0.51250102 0.51334208 0.30800525 0.51300558]
 [0.54034181 0.54036009 0.53947476 0.54032372]
 [0.56873764 0.56879948 0.56865098 0.56880009]
```

```
 [0.59873692 0.59873291 0.59873694 0.59873668]
 [0.63024941 0.63024937 0.63024941 0.63024914]
 [0.66342043 0.66342041 0.66342043 0.66342015]
...
Final Policy (Action to take in each state to reach the goal):
[0 1 1 3 2 0 0 2 0 2 3 0 0 0 0 0]
```

Over time, the Q-table becomes a map of wisdom, revealing which action to take in each state. From this table, a final policy emerges—the agent's learned path toward the goal."

> **Note***: In a real-world scenario, you would replace the random selection of states and actions with interactions with your environment. The example is simplified.*

Advantages and Disadvantages of Q-Learning

Q-learning, a cornerstone of reinforcement learning, offers profound strengths but also carries inherent limitations. Understanding both sides allows learners to appreciate where it shines and where it must evolve.

Advantages

Long-Term Optimization:

Q-learning is designed to maximise long-term cumulative rewards. By continually updating Q-values, the agent gradually uncovers optimal strategies—even in environments with delayed or sparse rewards.

Human-Like Learning:

Its learning pattern resembles human behaviour: trial, error, reflection, and refinement. This makes Q-learning intuitive, flexible, and well-suited for real-world problem-solving.

Error Correction:

Through repeated updates based on the temporal difference (TD) error, the agent constantly corrects its misunderstandings of the environment, improving the accuracy of its predictions.

Error Prevention:

Once a mistake is corrected, the updated Q-values discourage the agent from repeating it. Learning compounds, leading to more stable and reliable decision-making.

Environment-Specific Policies:

Q-learning produces customised, environment-specific policies. Its state–action mapping ensures that each problem yields a unique optimal strategy.

Disadvantages

Heavy Dependence on Real Samples:

In real-world setups, such as robotics, Q-learning requires vast amounts of actual interaction data. This leads to cost, safety risks, and hardware degradation.

High Infrastructure Costs:

Building and maintaining robotic systems or physical environments for training can be expensive and labour-intensive, limiting accessibility.

Slow in Large State Spaces:

When the number of states explodes into the millions, maintaining and updating a Q-table becomes impractical. The learning process slows dramatically or becomes infeasible.

Overcoming Limitations

To address these bottlenecks, Q-learning can be combined with neural networks—forming *Deep Q Networks (DQNs).*

Value networks approximate the value function for enormous or continuous spaces. **Policy networks** optimise action selection with greater efficiency.

This fusion allows Q-learning to scale gracefully to large universes, making complex decision-making computationally feasible and far more effective.

PART FOUR

DAY FOURTEEN

Unit 4 - Lesson Three

Model-Free Reinforcement Learning

☐ Model-Free Reinforcement Learning

Sam asked, "Master what is Model-Free Reinforcement Learning?"

Master said, "Model-free reinforcement learning (RL) means an agent learns what actions to take by directly interacting with the environment — using experience (states, actions, rewards) — *without* ever building or using an explicit model of how the environment transitions from one state to another or how rewards are generated. The agent learns policies or value estimates purely from sampled trajectories."

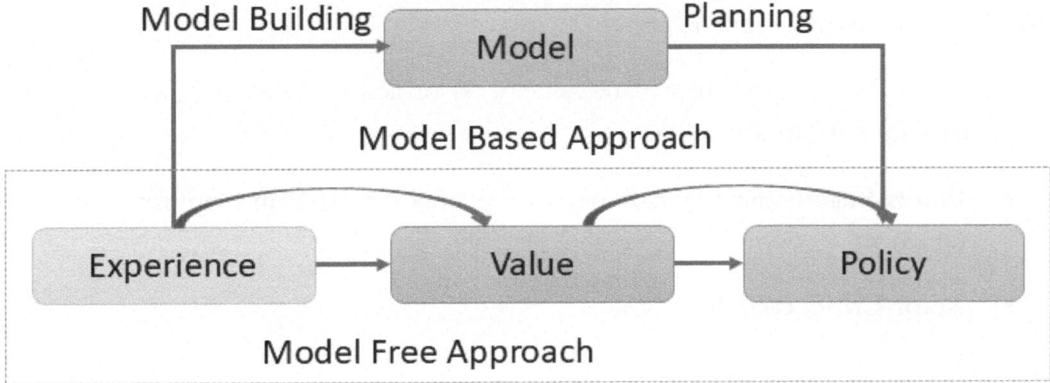

Illustration Model_1: Model Approach

Why the distinction matters: model-free vs model-based

- **Model-based RL**: the agent tries to learn (or is given) a model $\hat{P}(s'|s, a)$ and $\hat{R}(s, a)$ that predict next states and rewards. It can use planning (e.g., simulating outcomes) to choose actions.
- **Model-free RL**: the agent *does not* learn P or R. Instead it learns value functions (e.g., Q(s, a), V(s) or policies π(a|s) directly from experience.

Tradeoff: model-based methods can be sample-efficient (learn from fewer real interactions) because they reuse the learned model for planning, but they require accurate model learning. Model-free methods are often simpler, easier to implement, and can scale well with function approximation (deep nets), but are usually less sample efficient.

Formal setting

Both live in the Markov Decision Process (MDP) framework:

- States $s \in S$
- Actions $a \in A$
- Transition dynamics $P(s'|s, a)$ (unknown to model-free agent)
- Reward function $r(s, a)$ (unknown or sampled)
- Discount factor $\gamma \in [0,1)$

Objective: maximize expected return $G_t = \sum_{k=1}^{\infty} \gamma^k r_t + k$

Model-free algorithms estimate either:

- **Value-based** quantities: state-value $V^\pi(s)$ or action-value $Q^\pi(s, a)$, then derive actions (e.g., $\text{argmax}_a Q$); or
- **Policy-based**: directly parameterize a policy $\pi_\theta(a|s)$ and optimize expected return; or
- **Actor-Critic**: combine both.

Classic model-free families & examples

- **Tabular value-based**
  - *Q-learning* (off-policy, learns Q∗(s, a))
  - *SARSA* (on-policy)
- **Function approximation / Deep RL**
  - *DQN* (Deep Q Network) — Q-learning with neural nets + experience replay
  - *Deep SARSA, Double DQN, Dueling DQN*
- **Policy gradient / actor methods**
  - *REINFORCE* (Monte-Carlo policy gradient)
  - *Actor-Critic, A2C/A3C*
  - *PPO (Proximal Policy Optimization)*, *TRPO*
- **Deterministic policy gradient / continuous control**
  - *DDPG*, *TD3*, *SAC* (soft actor-critic — off-policy, stochastic policy)

These are all model-free: they never require estimating P(s'|s,a).

A couple of representative equations (kept simple)

Q-learning (tabular, off-policy)

Bellman optimality update from a sample (s,a,r,s'):

$Q(s,a) \leftarrow Q(s, a) + \alpha(r+\gamma \max_{a'} Q(s', a') - Q(s ,a))$

This learns the optimal action-value Q∗ directly from experience.

Policy gradient (REINFORCE)

Parameter update for policy πθ:

$\nabla\theta J(\theta) \approx \frac{1}{N} \sum_{Episodes} \sum_{t} \nabla_{\theta} \log\pi_{\theta}(a_t|s_t)\, G_t$

This pushes policy parameters to increase the probability of actions that produced high returns.

Simple pseudocode sketches

Q-learning (high level)

```
Initialize Q(s,a) arbitrarily
for each episode:
  s = start_state
  while not terminal:
    choose a from s (e.g., ε-greedy on Q)
    take a → observe r, s'
    Q[s,a] += α * (r + γ * max_a' Q[s',a'] - Q[s,a])
    s = s'
```

Policy gradient (REINFORCE)

```
Initialize policy πθ
for each episode:
  generate trajectory (s0,a0,r0,...)
  compute returns Gt for each time t
  for each t:
    θ += α * ∇θ log πθ(at|st) * Gt
```

Strengths and weaknesses

Strengths (when to like model-free):

- Straightforward: no need to learn a model of environment dynamics.
- Works well with high-dimensional observations when paired with deep nets (e.g., raw pixels).
- Many successful practical algorithms (DQN, PPO, SAC).
- Often robust to model bias (no erroneous learned model to mislead planning).

Weaknesses:

- **Sample inefficiency**: needs many environment interactions (especially Monte-Carlo and naive policy gradients).

- Can be unstable or sensitive to hyperparameters when using function approximation.
- No planning capability: cannot perform imagination-based lookahead unless combined with other techniques.
- Harder to incorporate structured prior knowledge about dynamics.

Practical considerations and tricks

- **Experience replay** (for off-policy methods like DQN) improves sample efficiency and stability.
- **Target networks** (separate, slowly updated networks) stabilize temporal-difference learning.
- **Entropy regularization** (in policy methods) encourages exploration.
- **Advantage functions** $A(s, a) = Q(s,a) - V(s)$ reduce variance in policy gradients.
- **Off-policy vs on-policy**: off-policy methods (Q-learning, DDPG, SAC) reuse past data; on-policy (PPO, A2C) require fresh data but are often more stable.
- **Exploration**: ε-greedy, Boltzmann, parameter/noise-based, intrinsic rewards, curiosity.

When to prefer model-free

- You cannot or don't want to learn a reliable dynamics model (complex or stochastic environment).
- You have a massive interaction budget (simulators, offline datasets).
- You want simpler pipelines that scale with deep learning (e.g., playing Atari from pixels).
- You value asymptotic performance (many model-free methods attain strong final policies).

Where hybrid approaches help

Hybrid designs combine model-free and model-based ideas:

- Use a learned model to generate imagined rollouts, and use model-free RL on both real and imagined data (model-based imagination + model-free learner).
- Use model-based planning for short horizons and model-free policy for long-term control.

Example real-world uses

- Game playing (Atari with DQN, Go with policy/value networks).
- Robotics (continuous control with SAC, PPO; often combined with model-based components).
- Recommendation systems, ad placement, and industrial control, where building a perfect dynamics model is impractical.

Model-free RL learns *what to do* directly from experience — by estimating values or optimizing policies — without ever learning an explicit model of how the world behaves. It's powerful, scalable with deep nets, but tends to be data-hungry and sometimes unstable; choosing model-free vs model-based depends on your problem's constraints (data, simulator availability, need for planning).

Master said, "Apeksha, this illustration reveals the entire landscape of Reinforcement Learning at a glance."

At the top sits *Reinforcement Learning*—the science of learning through interaction and feedback. It branches first into **Model-Free** and **Model-Based** approaches. Model-Free methods rely entirely on experience. Under this, **Value-Based** algorithms like SARSA, Expected SARSA, Q-Learning, and deep variants such as DQN, Double-DQN, and Rainbow learn by estimating how good each state or action is. **Policy-Based** methods, such as REINFORCE, PPO, DDPG, TD3, and SAC, directly learn a mapping from states to actions.

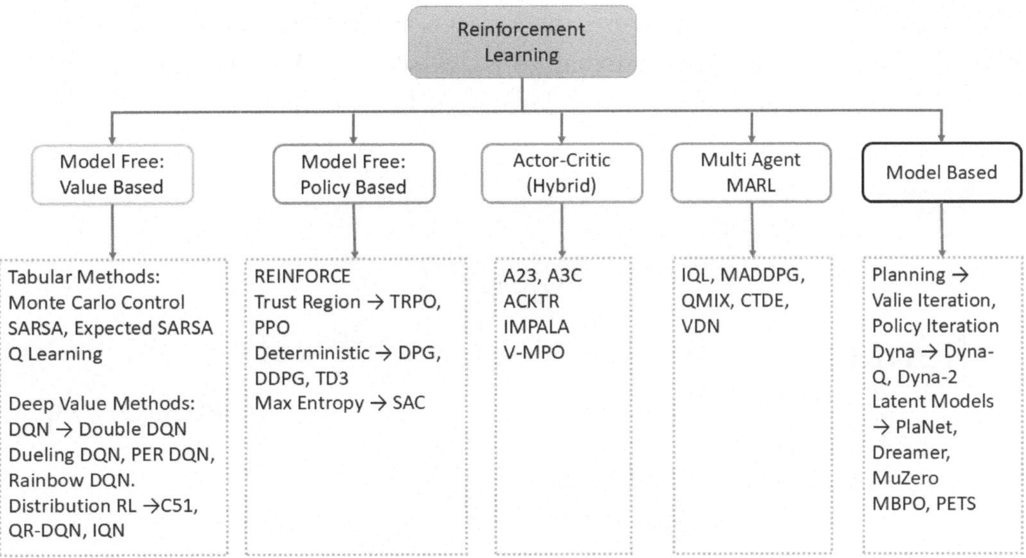

Illustration RL_6: RL

The next pillar, **Actor-Critic**, blends value estimation with policy learning, represented by A2C, A3C, ACKTR, IMPALA, and V-MPO.

Beyond single agents lies **Multi-Agent RL**, where algorithms like IQL, MADDPG, QMIX, CTDE, and VDN help multiple agents learn cooperatively or competitively.

Finally, **Model-Based RL** uses planning and learned world models—Valuation Iteration, Dyna, MuZero, Dreamer—to think ahead before acting.

□ Temporal Difference (TD) learning)

John asked, "What is Temporal Difference (TD) learning)?"

Master said, "Temporal Difference (TD) learning is a family of *model-free* RL methods that update value estimates online by **bootstrapping** — using one-step (or multi-step) sampled rewards plus current value estimates of successor states as targets. It sits between Monte-Carlo (full-return updates) and Dynamic Programming (bootstrapping with a model), combining the best of both worlds: no model required, and updates can be done every step."

Intuition — what TD does and why it's useful

Think of predicting tomorrow's weather every hour. Each hour, you get a small observation and adjust your forecast immediately, not waiting until the week ends. TD does the same: when the agent moves from s_t to s_{t+1} and sees reward r_{t+1}, it nudges the estimate $V(s_t)$) toward the short-term target $r_{t+1} + \gamma V(s_{t+1})$. Because updates happen immediately and re-use current estimates, learning is fast and online.

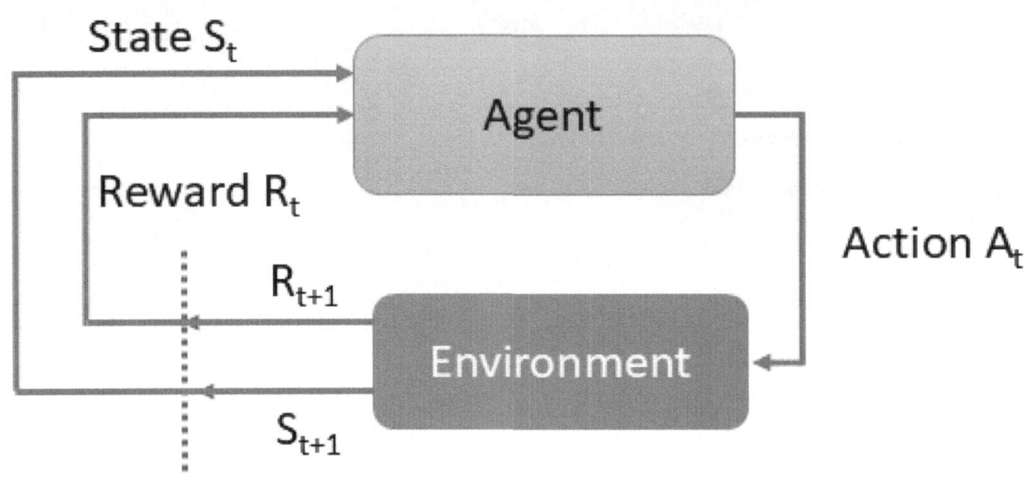

Illustration TD_3: TD

Key idea: use the one-step target

$r_t + \gamma V(s_{t+1})$

were

r_t – immediate reward

$\gamma V(s_{t+1})$ - current estimate of future

to update $V(s_t)$. This creates fast, online learning.

Core equation (TD(0))

For value V, learning rate α, discount γ, observed tuple (s_t, r_{t+1}, s_{t+1}):

TD target: $T_t = r_{t+1} + \gamma V(s_{t+1})$

TD error: $\delta_t = T_t - V(s_t) = r_{t+1} + \gamma V(s_{t+1}) - V(s_t)$

Update: $V(s_t) \leftarrow V(s_t) + \alpha\, \delta_t$.

This is a one-step bootstrap: current estimate plus a correction proportional to the prediction error.

Why bootstrapping helps (pros & cons)

Pros

- **Data efficient**: update with each step, not after full episodes.
- **Online**: works with continuing tasks, no need to wait to episode end.
- **Low variance**: one-step targets have less variance than full returns (MC).

Cons

- **Bias**: because you rely on your current (possibly wrong) estimate $V(s_{t+1})$, updates are biased.
- **Stability**: With function approximation or off-policy training, naive TD can diverge (special care needed).

Tradeoff: TD reduces variance by introducing bias (classic bias–variance tradeoff); often this is favourable.

Small numeric example

Suppose $\alpha = 0.1$, $\gamma = 1$. At time t: $V(s_t) = 0.5$, $V(s_{t+1}) = 0.6$, $r_{t+1} = 0$.

1. Target: $T_t = 0+1\cdot 0.6 = 0.6$.
2. TD error: $\delta_t = 0.6-0.5 = 0.1$
3. Update: $V(s_t) \leftarrow 0.5+0.1\times 0.1 = 0.5 + 0.01 = 0.51$.

So the estimate moves toward the successor's estimate by a small amount.

A simple worked example — 5-state random walk (numeric, step-by-step)

Environment: states A—B—C—D—E, with terminal left (A) = 0 return and right (E) = 1 return. Only transitions to neighbor states with equal probability. We try to learn V for nonterminal states B, C, D. Initialize V(B) = V(C) = V(D) = 0.5. Use $\alpha = 0.1$, $\gamma = 1$ (episodic, undiscounted for simplicity).

Suppose one sampled episode (trajectory): **B → C → D → E** (terminal, reward 0 until last step where reward = 1 at reaching E).

Rewards: **r(B→C) = 0, r(C→D) = 0, r(D→E) = 1.**

We apply TD(0) updates as we step:

1. At time t: $s_t = B$, $s_{t+1} = C$, reward $r_{t+1}=0$.
    - Current V(B) = 0.5, V(C) = 0.5.
    - TD error: $\delta = 0 + 1{\cdot}0.5 - 0.5 = 0.0$
    - Update: V(B)← 0.5 + 0.1·0 = 0.5 (No change.)
2. Next: $s_t = C$, $s_{t+1} = D$, $r_{t+1} = 0$.
    - V(C) = 0.5, V(D) = 0.5.
    - $\delta = 0 + 0.5 - 0.5 = 0.$
    - V(C) stays 0.5.
3. Next: $s_t = D$, $s_{t+1} = E$, $r_{t+1} = 1$. E is terminal so V(E) = 0 (or we can consider return 1 at terminal) — with this formulation, the TD target is reward only. For clarity assume reaching E yields immediate reward 1 and V(E) = 0 afterwards, so:
    - $\delta = 1 + 1{\cdot}0 - 0.5=0.5.$
    - Update: V(D) ← 0.5 + (0.1x0.5) = 0.55.

Only V(D) changed in that episode. Repeat many episodes and estimates propagate backward from the terminal.

(If $\gamma < 1$ adjust targets accordingly. The arithmetic above is explicit: compute target, delta, multiply by α, add.)

How TD blends Monte-Carlo and Dynamic Programming

- **Like Monte-Carlo:** TD is model-free — it does not require knowledge of transition probabilities or reward functions.
- **Like Dynamic Programming:** TD bootstraps — it uses other value estimates (not only final returns) to form targets.
- **Advantage:** Online updates after each step → lower variance than MC and suitable for continuing tasks.
- **Tradeoff:** Bootstrapping introduces bias (relying on imperfect estimates), producing a bias–variance tradeoff.

Key variants and algorithms

- **TD(0):** One-step bootstrapping (above).
- **TD(λ):** Uses *eligibility traces* to blend multi-step returns ($\lambda \in [0,1]$; $\lambda=0 \rightarrow$ TD(0); $\lambda \rightarrow 1 \rightarrow$ MC). Eligibility traces assign credit backward through recently visited states.
- **SARSA / Q-learning:** TD-style algorithms applied to action-value Q(s,a). SARSA is on-policy (uses actual next action); Q-learning is off-policy (uses max over next actions).
- **Expected SARSA:** Uses expectation over next-action probabilities to reduce variance.
- **Function approximation / Deep TD:** Replace tabular V with parameterized V_θ. Use gradients of TD error (careful: stability issues arise; use tricks like target networks, experience replay).

Convergence & theoretical view

- In tabular, on-policy settings with diminishing step sizes and sufficient exploration, TD(0) converges to the true V^π.
- TD is performing stochastic approximation to find the fixed point of the Bellman operator T^π:$V^\pi = T^\pi V^\pi$. T^π is a γ-contraction, so iterative updates converge to the fixed point in expectation.

- With linear function approximation, TD converges to the **projected** Bellman fixed point (the best representable approximation under the feature space), not necessarily the true V^{π}. With nonlinear approximators (deep nets) stability is delicate.

Practical tips

- Use **small α** and consider **decay** for stability.
- **TD(λ)** often accelerates learning by propagating credit faster — tune λ (e.g., 0.7–0.9).
- For deep TD (DQN, actor-critic), use **target networks**, **replay buffers** (for off-policy), and **gradient clipping**.
- Monitor **TD error magnitudes** — persistent large errors indicate model mismatch or learning instability.

☐ Why TD is Model-Free and Non-Episodic

Model-Free: What that really means

TD is **model-free** because it never builds or queries an explicit model of the environment (no P(s'|s,a) or R(s,a) estimates). Instead, it learns directly from *experience* — sequences of observed $(s_t,a_t,r_{t+1},s_{t+1})$ - using those samples to improve its value estimates. The key points:

No dynamics required: TD does not require knowledge of transition probabilities or expected rewards. It uses the observed reward and the *current* estimate of the successor state to form a learning target.

Sample-based bootstrapping: The one-step target $r_{t+1}+\gamma V(s_{t+1})$ is constructed from a single sample and the existing value table/function, so the algorithm never asks "what would happen if I took action a in state s?" — it simply reacts to what actually happened.

Contrast with model-based: A model-based method would first estimate PPP and RRR, then perform planning (value-iteration, policy-iteration) using those estimates. TD skips the model step and updates values directly.

Non-episodic (sequential) capability — why it matters

TD is naturally suitable for **continuing (non-episodic) tasks** because:

Per-step updates: TD updates $V(s_t)$ immediately after each transition, so it doesn't need to wait for an episode to terminate to compute a return G_t. That makes it usable in ongoing, open-ended tasks (e.g., process control, finance, robotics) where episodes aren't well-defined.

Stable online learning: Because updates are incremental, the agent can keep learning and adapting while the system runs continuously.

Lower latency: Action-value estimates adapt instantly to recent experience, which is essential for real-time decisions.

Core components — concise with equations

1. **Bellman equation (policy evaluation):**

$$V^{\pi}(s) = E_{\pi}[r_{t+1}+\gamma V^{\pi}(s_{t+1}) \mid s_t=s]$$

For Q-values:

$$Q^{\pi}(s,a)=E_{\pi}[rt+1+\gamma Q^{\pi}(s_{t+1},a_{t+1}) \mid s_t=s,\ a_t=a]$$

2. **TD error (one-step):**

$$\delta_t=r_{t+1}+\gamma V(s_{t+1})-V(s_t)$$

(For action-values, replace V by Q and include the next action as appropriate.)

3. **TD(0) update rule:**

$$V(st)\leftarrow V(st)+\alpha\ \delta tV$$

Explicitly:

$$V(st)\leftarrow V(st)+\alpha[rt+1+\gamma V(st+1)-V(st)]$$

Intuition behind the TD error

δ_t measures *surprise*: how much the new one-step information (reward plus bootstrapped estimate) disagrees with your prior estimate. If the successor value $V(s_{t+1})$ plus reward is larger than expected, $\delta_t>0$, and you raise $V(s_t)$; if smaller, you lower it. In expectation (over transitions under π), these corrections push V toward the fixed point of the Bellman operator.

Multi-step and eligibility traces — speeding learning

- **n-step TD:** uses n-step returns $R_{t+1}+\gamma R_{t+2}+\cdots+\gamma_{n-1}V(s_{t+n})$; trades bias/variance by varying n.
- **TD(λ):** combines all n-step targets via exponentially weighted traces with parameter $\lambda\in[0,1]$. λ close to 1 → MC-like; λ close to 0 → TD(0)-like. Eligibility traces assign credit backwards to recently visited states.

Master said, "TD is a **sample-based solver for the Bellman fixed point**: it repeatedly nudges value estimates toward consistency with observed one-step transitions, enabling model-free, continuous, and efficient learning from ongoing interaction."

☐ How TD Learning Works — With Bellman Equation

Temporal Difference (TD) Learning is the art of learning from *incomplete information.* Instead of waiting till the end of an episode (Monte Carlo), TD says:

"Use what you know **now**, and estimate the rest."

This is possible through **bootstrapping** — updating a prediction using another prediction, similar to how a person slowly improves intuition over time.

Concrete Example: A 3×3 Grid World

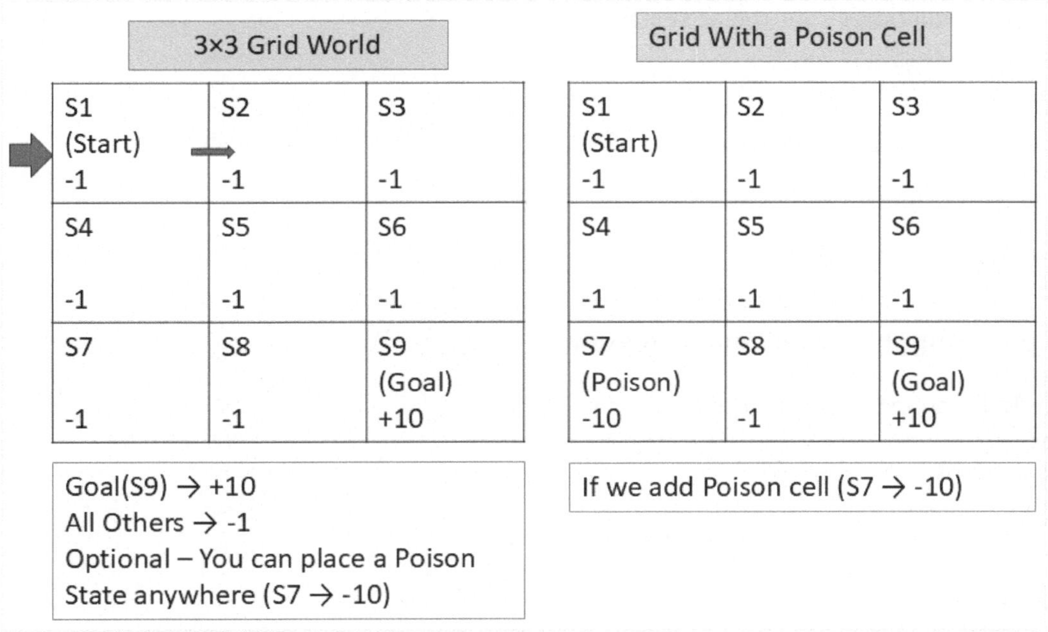

3×3 Grid World

S1 (Start) -1	S2 -1	S3 -1
S4 -1	S5 -1	S6 -1
S7 -1	S8 -1	S9 (Goal) +10

Goal(S9) → +10
All Others → -1
Optional – You can place a Poison State anywhere (S7 → -10)

Grid With a Poison Cell

S1 (Start) -1	S2 -1	S3 -1
S4 -1	S5 -1	S6 -1
S7 (Poison) -10	S8 -1	S9 (Goal) +10

If we add Poison cell (S7 → -10)

Illustration TD_2: RL

Nine squares:

- **Goal**: +10
- **Poison**: –10
- **Other squares**: –1 per step

Agent begins at **S1**.

Every state-value V(s) starts at **0**.

Step-by-Step TD(0) Update

Step 1 — Agent Takes an Action

The agent starts in **S1, and it** moves right → **S2**

Reward = –1

TD update adjusts the value of **S1** based on:

a) what happened (+reward)

b) prediction about the next state

From **S1**, the agent moves **right → S2**

Reward $R_{t+1} = -1$

Step 2 — Apply the Bellman Equation

The Bellman expectation equation for value:

$V(s_t) = E[R_{t+1} + \gamma V(s_{t+1})]$

For simplicity, let $\gamma = 0$ (no future reward considered).

Current values:

- $V(S2) = 0$
- So the observed target is:

$Vobs(S1) = -1+0 = -1$

Step 3 — Temporal Difference Error

$\delta_t = Vobs(S1) - V(S1) = -1-0 = -1$

This is the "surprise" — the difference between what you predicted and what actually happened.

Step 4 — TD Value Update

$V(S1) \leftarrow V(S1) + \alpha\,\delta_t$

With learning rate $\alpha = 0.1$:

$V(S1) = 0+0.1(-1) = -0.1$

State S1 begins gradually learning its true value.

Analogy: Learning by Touching Hot and Cold Surfaces

Imagine a blindfolded person exploring a room:

- They touch a wall → it's warm → they adjust their belief slightly: "This area might be warmer."
- They continue exploring, updating their estimates at every step.

They don't need to walk the entire room first (Monte Carlo) and they don't need a map (Dynamic Programming).

They learn from **immediate experience**, adjusting beliefs continuously.

This is TD learning.

Multiple Episodes, Convergence, Policy Improvement

Across many moves:

- S2 → S7 → S8 → Goal
- Each visited state gets updated:

$V(s) \leftarrow V(s) + \alpha\ [r + \gamma V(s')]$

Slowly, each state learns how close it is to the goal or poison.

Eventually, the value function reveals the *terrain* of the grid — peaks near the goal, valleys near danger.

So when S1 → S2 → S3 → … → S9 (goal), each square slowly learns:

- S8 is close to S9 → high value
- S1 is far → low value
- S7 is poison → very low value

Eventually, your value table looks like:

```
S1 -5.4
S2 -4.2
S3 -3.1
S4 -3.8
```

```
S5 -2.5
S6 -1.3
S7 -10.0
S8 +1.5
S9 +10.0
```

The agent then uses value estimates to choose actions that climb toward higher-value states → **policy improvement.**

Pseudo-Code for TD(0) State Value Learning

```
Initialize V(s) = 0 for all states
Set α (learning rate), γ (discount)

for each episode:
   s = start_state
   while s is not terminal:
      a = choose_action(s)     # random or epsilon-greedy
      s_next, r = take_action(a)

      # TD Error
      delta = r + γ * V[s_next] - V[s]

      # Update
      V[s] += α * delta

      s = s_next
```

Master said, This program builds a simple 3×3 GridWorld where the agent starts in a random non-terminal state and learns state values using TD(0) learning. Each move gives –1 reward, reaching the goal gives +10, and stepping into poison gives –10. The agent follows a random policy during training while updating its value estimates after every step using the TD error. After learning, the code computes a greedy policy by choosing the best action from each state based on updated values. Finally, it visualizes the learned value function using a heatmap and overlays arrows showing the optimal direction from each state.

Example P4 – U4 – D5

TD

```
import numpy as np
```

```
import matplotlib.pyplot as plt

# ----------------------------------------------------------
# 3×3 GRIDWORLD ENVIRONMENT
# ----------------------------------------------------------
class GridWorld3x3:
    def __init__(self):
        self.size = 3
        self.goal = 8      # bottom-right
        self.poison = 6    # bottom-left
        self.states = list(range(9))

    def reset(self):
        non_terminal = [s for s in self.states if s not in [self.goal, self.poison]]
        self.state = np.random.choice(non_terminal)
        return self.state

    def step(self, action):
        row, col = divmod(self.state, self.size)

        # 0=up, 1=right, 2=down, 3=left
        if action == 0 and row > 0: row -= 1
        if action == 1 and col < 2: col += 1
        if action == 2 and row < 2: row += 1
        if action == 3 and col > 0: col -= 1

        next_state = row * self.size + col

        if next_state == self.goal:
            reward = 10
            done = True
        elif next_state == self.poison:
            reward = -10
            done = True
        else:
            reward = -1
            done = False

        self.state = next_state
        return next_state, reward, done

# ----------------------------------------------------------
# TD(0) VALUE LEARNING
# ----------------------------------------------------------
env = GridWorld3x3()
V = np.zeros(9)
alpha = 0.1
gamma = 0.9
```

```
episodes = 5000

# Simple uniform random policy
def random_policy():
    return np.random.randint(4)

# TD(0) Learning Loop
for ep in range(episodes):
    s = env.reset()
    done = False

    while not done:
        a = random_policy()
        s2, r, done = env.step(a)
        V[s] += alpha * (r + gamma * V[s2] - V[s])
        s = s2

print("\nLearned State Values (TD Learning):")
grid_values = V.reshape(3, 3)
print(grid_values)

# ----------------------------------------------------------
# POLICY DERIVATION (Greedy from V)
# ----------------------------------------------------------
actions = {0: "↑", 1: "→", 2: "↓", 3: "←"}
best_action_grid = np.full((3, 3), "", dtype=object)

for state in range(9):
    if state in [env.goal, env.poison]:
        continue

    row, col = divmod(state, 3)
    q_vals = []

    # Evaluate Q(s,a) = R + γV(s')
    for a in [0, 1, 2, 3]:
        r_row, r_col = row, col

        if a == 0 and r_row > 0: r_row -= 1
        if a == 1 and r_col < 2: r_col += 1
        if a == 2 and r_row < 2: r_row += 1
        if a == 3 and r_col > 0: r_col -= 1

        next_state = r_row * 3 + r_col

        if next_state == env.goal:
            reward = 10
        elif next_state == env.poison:
```

```
            reward = -10
        else:
            reward = -1

        q_vals.append(reward + gamma * V[next_state])

    best_a = np.argmax(q_vals)
    best_action_grid[row, col] = actions[best_a]

# ------------------------------------------------------------
# PLOTTING: HEATMAP + POLICY ARROWS
# ------------------------------------------------------------
plt.figure(figsize=(7, 6))
plt.imshow(grid_values, cmap="coolwarm", interpolation="nearest")
plt.colorbar(label="V(s)")

# Add numbers + arrows
for i in range(3):
    for j in range(3):
        if (i * 3 + j) == env.goal:
            text = "GOAL\n+10"
            color = "black"
        elif (i * 3 + j) == env.poison:
            text = "POISON\n-10"
            color = "black"
        else:
            text = f"{grid_values[i, j]:.1f}\n{best_action_grid[i, j]}"
            color = "black"

        plt.text(j, i, text, ha="center", va="center", color=color, fontsize=12)

plt.title("TD-Learned State Values + Policy Arrows")
plt.xticks([])
plt.yticks([])
plt.show()
```

Output:

```
Output
```

```
Learned State Values (TD Learning):
[[-7.7304738  -6.33159936 -5.90194122]
 [-7.91996214 -2.63662177 -0.83775567]
 [ 0.          2.63027553  0.        ]]
```

Each number = the estimated long-term value of that state

TD learning has learned: **"If the agent is standing in this cell, how good or bad is this state in the long run?"**

Higher value → better state

Lower value → worse state

Zero → terminal or neutral states

Interpretation of the Matrix (Row by Row)

Row 1: [-7.7304738 -6.33159936 -5.90194122]

These states are:

- Far from terminal states → large negative values
- TD learning predicts **longer travel to the goal → more cumulative penalty**

Row 2: [-7.91996214 -2.63662177 -0.83775567]

- The **middle-right value = -0.837**

  → This is **closest to the goal**, so the penalty is minimal
- The **leftmost = –7.919**

  → Far from goal; maybe the worst position

Row 3: [0.   2.63027553 0.]

- **0 values are terminal states** (goal or pit).
- Middle state has a moderate penalty → medium distance to goal.

Plot:

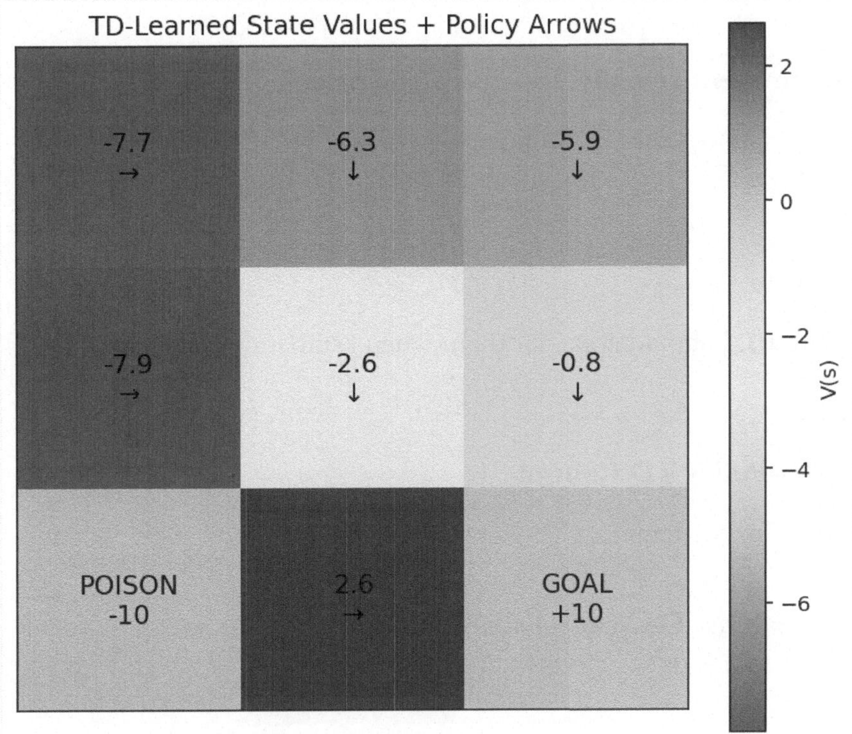

Illustration TD_4: TD

What the numbers tell you about the policy

Even though you didn't explicitly compute a policy, you can infer it:

- The agent will move toward states with **higher (less negative) values**.
- It will avoid the highly negative areas (top-left, middle-left).

☐ **SARSA vs Q-Learning**

Both are **TD control algorithms** (they learn action-values Q(s,a) not state-values).

A. SARSA — On-Policy TD Control

SARSA uses the *actual next action* chosen by the current (exploratory) policy.

$$Q(s_t,a_t) \leftarrow Q(s_t,a_t) + \alpha[rt+1+\gamma Q(s_{t+1},a_{t+1}) - Q(s_t,a_t)]$$

Meaning:

- Learns **what the agent actually does**, including randomness.
- Sensitive to exploration → tends to learn *safer* paths.

Analogy:

A cautious driver learns:

"Since I often take detours, I should consider them when estimating travel time."

B. Q-Learning — Off-Policy TD Control

Uses the **greedy action** for the target:

$$Q(s_t,a_t) \leftarrow Q(s_t,a_t)+\alpha[r_{t+1}+\gamma \max_a Q(s_{t+1},a)-Q(s_t,a_t)]$$

Meaning:

- Learns an **optimal policy** even while exploring.
- Behaviour may be random, but learning assumes perfect greediness.

Analogy:

A bold driver says: "Even if I sometimes take detours, I will learn as if I always took the fastest route."

Strengths and weaknesses

- **Strengths:** Online, sample-efficient, lower variance than MC, works for continuing tasks.
- **Weaknesses:** Biased due to bootstrapping; can diverge with function approximation or off-policy updates if not handled carefully.

Master said, "TD learning updates value estimates immediately using short-term rewards and current value predictions — a powerful, online way to satisfy the Bellman consistency condition and learn efficiently from experience."

Example P4 – U4 – D6

TD_vs_MC_random

```
import random
import numpy as np
import matplotlib.pyplot as plt
import pandas as pd

random.seed(0)
np.random.seed(0)

# Environment definitions
states = np.arange(7)  # 0..6, terminal states 0 and 6
nonterminal_states = np.arange(1,6)
true_values = np.array([i/6.0 for i in nonterminal_states])  # 1/6 .. 5/6

def run_mc_episode(V, alpha):
    state = 3  # start in the middle
    episode = [state]
    while True:
        step = random.choice([-1, 1])
        state = state + step
        if state == 0 or state == 6:
            reward = 1 if state == 6 else 0
            break
        episode.append(state)
    # Every-visit MC update to return G (which is the terminal reward here)
    G = reward
    for s in set(episode):  # using set -> every-visit collapsed, but okay for illustration
        if s in nonterminal_states:
            V[s] += alpha * (G - V[s])
    return V

def run_td0_episode(V, alpha):
    state = 3
    while True:
        step = random.choice([-1, 1])
        new_state = state + step
        if new_state == 0 or new_state == 6:
            reward = 1 if new_state == 6 else 0
            V[state] += alpha * (reward - V[state])
            break
        V[state] += alpha * (V[new_state] - V[state])
        state = new_state
    return V

def rms_error(V):
    est = np.array([V[s] for s in nonterminal_states])
```

```
    return np.sqrt(np.mean((est - true_values) ** 2))

def experiment(algorithm, alpha, episodes=100, runs=200):
    errors = np.zeros(episodes)
    for run in range(runs):
        V = np.zeros(7)
        V[nonterminal_states] = 0.5
        for ep in range(episodes):
            if algorithm == 'MC':
                V = run_mc_episode(V, alpha)
            else:
                V = run_td0_episode(V, alpha)
            errors[ep] += rms_error(V)
    errors /= runs
    return errors

def main():
    episodes = 100
    runs = 200
    alpha_td = 0.1
    alpha_mc = 0.01

    td_errors = experiment('TD', alpha_td, episodes=episodes, runs=runs)
    mc_errors = experiment('MC', alpha_mc, episodes=episodes, runs=runs)

    # Plot RMS errors
    plt.figure(figsize=(9,6))
    plt.plot(np.arange(1, episodes+1), td_errors, label=f"TD(0), alpha={alpha_td}")
    plt.plot(np.arange(1, episodes+1), mc_errors, label=f"MC, alpha={alpha_mc}")
    plt.xlabel("Episodes")
    plt.ylabel("RMS error")
    plt.title("TD(0) vs Monte Carlo — 5-state random walk")
    plt.legend()
    plt.grid(True)
    plt.tight_layout()
    plt.savefig("td_vs_mc_rms.png", dpi=200)
    plt.show()

    finals = pd.DataFrame({
        "Algorithm": ["TD(0)", "MC"],
        "Alpha": [alpha_td, alpha_mc],
        "RMS after last episode": [td_errors[-1], mc_errors[-1]]
    })
    print("\nFinal RMS comparison:")
    print(finals.to_string(index=False))

    # Example final estimates from a single run of episodes (for inspection)
    V_td = np.zeros(7); V_td[nonterminal_states] = 0.5
```

```
    for _ in range(episodes):
        V_td = run_td0_episode(V_td, alpha_td)
    V_mc = np.zeros(7); V_mc[nonterminal_states] = 0.5
    for _ in range(episodes):
        V_mc = run_mc_episode(V_mc, alpha_mc)

    summary = pd.DataFrame({
        "State": nonterminal_states,
        "True Value": true_values,
        "TD Estimate (example final)": [V_td[s] for s in nonterminal_states],
        "MC Estimate (example final)": [V_mc[s] for s in nonterminal_states]
    })
    print("\nState values: true vs example final estimates")
    print(summary.to_string(index=False))

if __name__ == "__main__":
    main()
```

Output:

```
Output
```

```
Final RMS comparison:
Algorithm  Alpha  RMS after last episode
   TD(0)   0.10               0.052004
      MC   0.01               0.130176

State values: true vs example final estimates
 State  True Value  TD Estimate (example final)  MC Estimate (example final)
     1    0.166667                     0.166138                     0.372214
     2    0.333333                     0.347320                     0.413278
     3    0.500000                     0.515109                     0.477502
     4    0.666667                     0.695704                     0.572501
     5    0.833333                     0.852209                     0.644855
```

Plot:

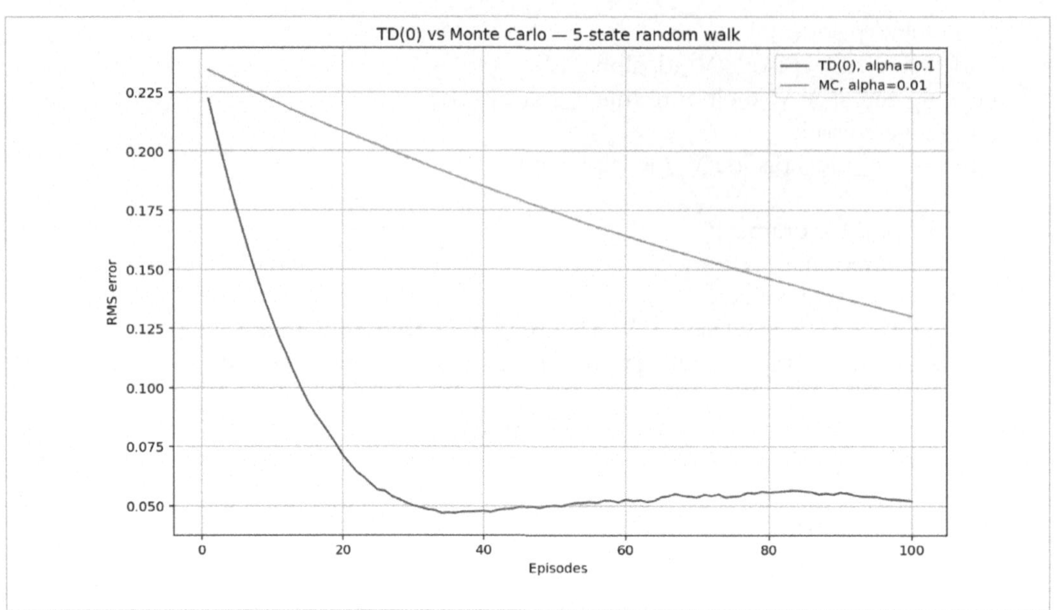

Illustration TD_1: TD

PART FOUR

DAY FIFTEEN

Unit 4 - Lesson Four

SARSA

☐ Model-Free Reinforcement Learning

Sam asked, "Master what is Model-Free Reinforcement Learning?"

☐ SARSA

Nikash asked, "Master, what is SARSA?"

Master said, "SARSA is an *on-policy*, temporal-difference (TD) control algorithm for reinforcement learning that learns an action-value function Q(s,a) by updating it from actual transitions produced by the agent following its current policy. The name SARSA comes from the five-tuple used in each update: **S**tate, **A**ction, **R**eward, next **S**tate, next **A**ction → (s, a, r, s', a').

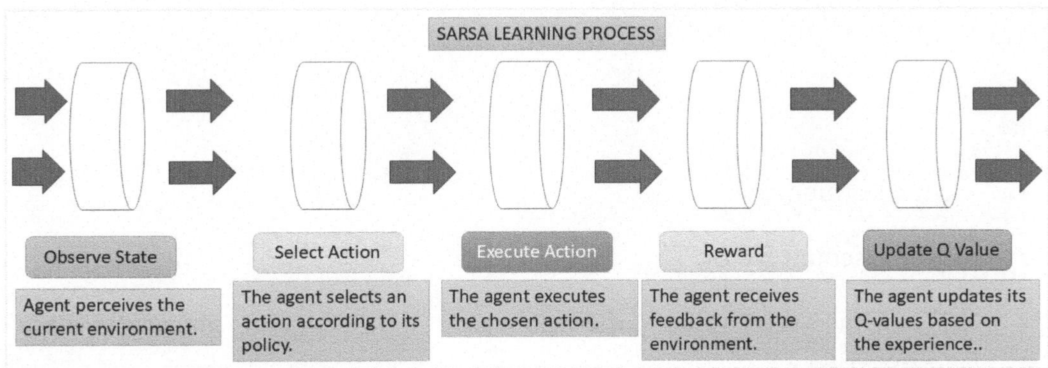

Illustration SARSA_7: SARSA

Because it uses the *actual next action* a' chosen by the agent's policy (including exploration), SARSA learns the value of the *behavior policy* — not an optimal policy under ideal greedy choices.

Components of the SARSA Algorithm

The SARSA algorithm is built on five fundamental components that describe how an agent interacts with its environment and learns from experience:

- **State (S):** The current condition or situation the agent is in while navigating the environment.
- **Action (A):** The decision or move the agent chooses to take in the current state.
- **Reward (R):** The immediate feedback received from the environment after performing an action. It reflects how good or bad the action was.
- **Next State (S'):** The new state the agent transitions to after executing the action.
- **Next Action (A'):** The action selected by the agent in the next state, based on its current policy.

SARSA updates the value of each state–action pair (Q-values) by considering both the immediate reward and the expected return from the **next action that will actually be taken**. This on-policy nature makes SARSA sensitive to the quality of the agent's current behaviour.

Core update rule for Q Values (the equation)

Given a sample transition (s,a,r,s',a'), the SARSA TD update is:

$$Q(s,a) \leftarrow Q(s,a) + \alpha(r + \gamma Q(s', a') - Q(s, a))$$

Where:

- α is the learning rate,
- γ is the discount factor,
- $Q(s',a')$ is the action-value of the next state and the *next action actually taken under the current policy.*

This contrasts with Q-learning's use of $\max_{a'} Q(s',a')$ (off-policy).

Why "on-policy" matters — intuition

- SARSA evaluates and improves the *same* policy the agent uses to act (e.g., an ε-greedy policy).
- Because the update depends on a' sampled from that policy, SARSA **learns the consequences of exploration**.

☐ SARSA update

Master said, "Let us understand SARSA update."

$Q(s_t,a_t) \leftarrow Q(s_t,a_t) + \alpha(r_{t+1} + \gamma\, Q(s_{t+1},a_{t+1}) - Q(s_t,a_t))$

Write the temporal-difference (TD) error as:

$\delta_t = r_{t+1} + \gamma\, Q(s_{t+1},a_{t+1}) - Q(s_t,a_t),$

So the update becomes

$Q(s_t,a_t) \leftarrow Q(s_t,a_t) + \alpha\, \delta_t.$

What each means

- $Q(s_t,a_t)$- current estimate of the action-value for state s_t and action a_t.
- $\alpha \in (0,1]$ - **learning rate**: how strongly new information replaces old (large $\alpha \rightarrow$ fast learning but noisy).
- r_{t+1} - immediate reward observed after taking a_t in s_t.
- $\gamma \in [0,1]$ - **discount factor:** how much future rewards count (0: only immediate reward; close to 1: far future matters).
- $Q(s_{t+1},a_{t+1})$ - the value of the next state–action pair the agent will actually take (on-policy estimate).

Understanding the update — line by line

1. **Immediate signal**: the agent receives r_{t+1} right after taking a_t.

2. **Bootstrapped future estimate**: instead of waiting until the end of the episode, SARSA uses $Q(s_{t+1}, a_{t+1})$ as an estimate of future return — this is *bootstrapping.*

3. **TD error δt**: measures surprise — the gap between what we expected ($Q(s_t, a_t)$) and what we actually observe plus expect next ($r_{t+1}+\gamma Q(s_{t+1}, a_{t+1})$).

4. **Update**: we move $Q(s_t, a_t)$ toward the improved estimate by a fraction α. Repeating this across steps reduces the TD error and refines the policy.

Because SARSA uses the action at+1 drawn from the current policy, it is **on-policy**: learned values reflect the behavior policy (including exploration).

Step-by-step SARSA algorithm (clean)

1. **Initialize** Q(s,a) arbitrarily (e.g., zeros) for all state–action pairs.
2. For each **episode**:
    - Initialize state s_0.
    - Choose a_0 using the current policy derived from Q (e.g., ε-greedy).
    - For each time step t until terminal:
        a) Execute a_t; observe r_{t+1} and next state s_{t+1}.
        b) Choose a_{t+1} from s_{t+1} using the same policy (e.g., ε-greedy).
        c) Compute TD error $\delta t = r_{t+1}+\gamma Q(s_{t+1},a_{t+1}) - Q(s_t,a_t)$.
        d) Update: $Q(s_t,a_t) \leftarrow Q(s_t,a_t)+\alpha\, \delta_t$.
        e) $s_t \leftarrow s_{t+1}$, $a_t \leftarrow a_{t+1}$.
3. Repeat episodes until performance or convergence criteria met.

Compact pseudocode

```
Initialize Q(s,a) arbitrarily
for each episode:
   s = initial_state()
   a = choose_action(s, Q, epsilon)
   while not terminal(s):
      s_next, r = step_environment(s, a)
      a_next = choose_action(s_next, Q, epsilon)
```

```
delta = r + gamma * Q[s_next, a_next] - Q[s, a]
Q[s, a] += alpha * delta
s, a = s_next, a_next
```

Practical notes & tips

- **On-policy behaviour:** Because SARSA updates using the action actually selected a_{t+1}, the learned Q reflects the exploration strategy (e.g., ε-greedy). If you evaluate the greedy policy later, ensure exploration is reduced during evaluation.
- **Choosing α and γ:** typical α values are small (0.01–0.1); γ depends on task horizon (0.9–0.99 for long-horizon tasks).
- **Exploration scheduling:** gradually reduce ε to shift from exploration to exploitation, or keep some entropy for robustness.
- **Comparison with Q-learning:** Q-learning uses $\max_{a'}Q(s',a')$ (off-policy), whereas SARSA uses Q(s',a') for the action actually taken (on-policy). SARSA is therefore safer in risky environments where exploratory actions can lead to bad outcomes.
- **Convergence:** SARSA converges under standard conditions (suitable decaying α, sufficient exploration) to the action-value function for the behaviour policy; with greedy policy improvement it can find the optimal policy.

Short numeric intuition

If currently $Q(s_t,a_t) = 0.5$, $r_{t+1} = 1$, $\gamma=0.9$, $Q(s_{t+1},a_{t+1}) = 0.6$, and $\alpha = 0.1$:

$\delta_t = 1 + (0.9\cdot 0.6-0.5) = (1+0.54-0.5) = 1.04$

$Q \leftarrow (0.5+0.1\times 1.04) = \mathbf{0.604}$

The Q-value increases toward the newly observed better estimate.

Example consequence: in “cliff-walking” environments an ε-greedy SARSA agent learns to avoid the risky edge because its policy sometimes explores — the learned Q reflects that exploration risk. Q-learning, by contrast, learns values assuming greedy behavior and can be more optimistic and risk-taking during training.

Pseudocode (clear, stepwise)

```
Initialize Q(s,a) arbitrarily for all s,a
for each episode:
  initialize s
  choose a from s using policy derived from Q (e.g., ε-greedy)
  while s not terminal:
    take action a, observe reward r and next state s'
    choose a' from s' using current policy (ε-greedy on Q)
    Q[s,a] += α * ( r + γ * Q[s',a'] - Q[s,a] )
    s, a = s', a'
```

Key: the same policy that chooses a' is the policy being evaluated/updated.

Let us understand this example:

Suppose:

- $Q(s, a)=5.00$
- observed reward $r = 1.00$,
- discount $\gamma = 0.9$,
- $Q(s', a') = 4.00$,
- learning rate $\alpha = 0.10$.

Compute the TD target and update:

1. Compute target: $r + \gamma\, Q(s',a') = 1.00+0.9\times4.00=1.00+3.60 = 4.60$
2. TD error: target − current $= 4.60-5.00=-0.40$.
3. Update increment: $\alpha \times$ TD error $= 0.10 \times (-0.40) = -0.04$
4. New Q: $5.00 + (-0.04) = 4.96$.

So after the update Q(s, a) becomes **4.96**.

Variants and extensions

- **Expected SARSA**: replace the sampled Q(s', a') by the expected value $\sum_{a'} \pi(a'|s')$ Q(s', a'). This reduces variance and blends on-policy behavior with expectation.
- **SARSA(λ)** (eligibility traces): introduces λ-traces to bridge between TD(0) and Monte Carlo, speeding learning and credit assignment.
- **Function approximation / deep SARSA**: use neural networks to approximate Q; less common than DQN but possible for on-policy bootstrapped control.

Convergence and requirements

SARSA converges to the optimal action-value function Q^* under standard conditions when:

- the policy is **GLIE** (Greedy in the Limit with Infinite Exploration) — i.e., every state-action pair is visited infinitely often but the policy becomes greedy in the limit (e.g., ε decays to 0 slowly),
- learning rates αt satisfy the Robbins-Monro conditions (sum of α_t diverges, sum of α_t^2 converges),
- with tabular representations and finite MDPs.

With function approximation (neural nets), theoretical guarantees vanish and practical stability techniques are needed.

Strengths and weaknesses

Strengths

- Learns the actual performance of the agent's **behavior policy**, capturing exploration risk and safety.
- Simpler to implement than many model-based methods; works well in tabular or small discrete settings.
- Straightforward to extend with eligibility traces (SARSA(λ)).

Weaknesses

- **Sample inefficiency** relative to some model-based approaches.

- If you want greedy optimal behavior and you're willing to assume off-policy updates, Q-learning can learn more aggressive optimal values faster.
- With function approximation, stability can be an issue (as with other bootstrapping algorithms).

When to choose SARSA

- You care about *how the agent actually behaves during training* (safety, risk due to exploration).
- The environment penalizes risky exploratory actions heavily (e.g., physical robots near cliffs or hazardous zones).
- You prefer a true on-policy learning signal (or plan to use Expected SARSA / SARSA(λ) to reduce variance).

Relationship to Q-learning (quick contrast)

- **SARSA**: on-policy. Uses the sampled next action a' chosen by the current policy → learns values consistent with the behavior.
- **Q-learning**: off-policy. Uses $\max_{a'}$ Q(s', a') → learns values for an optimal greedy policy regardless of the agent's exploration.
- Consequence: SARSA tends to learn *safer* policies during exploration; Q-learning can be more optimistic but may take riskier actions while learning.

Practical tips for implementation

- Use ε-greedy with decaying ε (GLIE) if you want eventual greediness and convergence.
- Consider **Expected SARSA** if variance from sampling a' is a problem.
- Use **eligibility traces (λ)** to speed up learning of multi-step dependencies.

- For function approximation, consider stability tricks (target networks, replay buffers—but note replay breaks strict on-policy semantics unless carefully handled).
-

Quick example scenario: cliff-walking intuition

In the classic cliff-walking grid, an ε-greedy SARSA agent learns to skirt the cliff because its learned Q values reflect occasional exploratory steps that would fall off the cliff. A Q-learning agent, learning values assuming greedy action at the next step, may assign high value to the short path and behave riskier during training.

SARSA is an on-policy TD control algorithm that learns action values from the actual actions the agent takes—so it learns the *value of its own behavior*, including the effects of exploration — making it especially appropriate when training-time behavior and safety matter.

☐ Tabular SARSA

The program begins by defining a **4×4 GridWorld** with 16 states, where states **0** and **15** are terminal. The agent starts in a **random non-terminal** state each episode. The step() function calculates movement: up, right, down, or left, updating the agent's grid position unless it hits a boundary. Every move gives a reward of **–1**, encouraging the agent to reach a terminal state quickly.

An **epsilon-greedy policy** is used for action selection: with 10% probability the agent explores; otherwise, it chooses the best known action from the Q-table.

SARSA learning begins with a zero-initialized **Q-table (16×4)**. For each of 300 episodes, the agent picks an initial action, interacts with the environment, and updates Q-values using the **SARSA update rule**, which learns from the actual action the policy selects next.

Over repeated episodes, Q-values converge, and the final learned **Q-table** is printed for inspection.

Example P4 – U4 – D7
SARSA
import numpy as np

```
# -------------------------------
# 4x4 GRIDWORLD ENVIRONMENT
# -------------------------------
class GridWorld:
    def __init__(self):
        self.size = 4
        self.terminal_states = [0, 15]

    def reset(self):
        # Start in a RANDOM non-terminal state
        self.state = np.random.choice([i for i in range(16) if i not in self.terminal_states])
        return self.state

    def step(self, action):
        row, col = divmod(self.state, self.size)

        if self.state in self.terminal_states:
            return self.state, 0, True

        # Movement rules
        if action == 0 and row > 0: row -= 1         # up
        if action == 1 and col < 3: col += 1         # right
        if action == 2 and row < 3: row += 1         # down
        if action == 3 and col > 0: col -= 1         # left

        next_state = row * self.size + col
        reward = -1
        done = next_state in self.terminal_states

        self.state = next_state
        return next_state, reward, done

# -------------------------------
# ε-GREEDY POLICY
# -------------------------------
def epsilon_greedy(Q, state, epsilon):
    if np.random.rand() < epsilon:
        return np.random.randint(4)
    return np.argmax(Q[state])

# -------------------------------
# TABULAR SARSA TRAINING
# -------------------------------
env = GridWorld()
Q = np.zeros((16, 4))

alpha = 0.1
gamma = 0.99
```

```
epsilon = 0.1
episodes = 300  # slight increase for clearer learning

for _ in range(episodes):
    s = env.reset()              # random non-terminal start
    a = epsilon_greedy(Q, s, epsilon)

    done = False
    while not done:
        s2, r, done = env.step(a)
        a2 = epsilon_greedy(Q, s2, epsilon)

        Q[s, a] += alpha * (r + gamma * Q[s2, a2] - Q[s, a])

        s, a = s2, a2

# -------------------------------
# PRINT LEARNED Q-TABLE
# -------------------------------
np.set_printoptions(precision=3, suppress=True)
print(Q)
```

Output:

```
Output

[[ 0.     0.     0.     0.   ]
 [-1.055 -1.393 -1.408 -1.   ]
 [-2.085 -2.071 -2.047 -1.986]
 [-2.451 -2.569 -2.463 -2.471]
 [-0.999 -1.21  -1.388 -1.155]
 [-1.841 -1.833 -1.885 -1.841]
 [-2.218 -2.148 -2.192 -2.213]
 [-2.017 -2.16  -1.937 -2.109]
 [-1.944 -2.061 -2.132 -2.1  ]
 [-2.192 -2.214 -2.203 -2.187]
 [-1.933 -1.791 -1.803 -1.845]
 [-1.22  -1.151 -0.999 -1.138]
 [-2.38  -2.328 -2.393 -2.504]
 [-1.98  -1.928 -1.99  -1.944]
 [-1.317 -1.    -1.156 -1.183]
 [ 0.     0.     0.     0.   ]]
```

- ☐ **Expected SARSA**

Master said, "Nikash, "Expected SARSA sits between SARSA (on-policy, sample-based) and Q-learning (off-policy, max-based). It keeps the on-policy character of SARSA but replaces the single sampled next action with the *expected* value over the agent's action distribution at the next state. This change reduces variance while remaining faithful to the current policy."

1. The core idea

Instead of using the sampled a_{t+1} (as SARSA) or $\max_{a'} Q(s_{t+1}, a')$ (as Q-learning), Expected SARSA uses the expectation of the next-step Q-values under the behavior policy π:

$$E_{a' \sim \pi(\cdot|s_{t+1})}[Q(s_{t+1}, a')].$$

This gives an update that is on-policy and lower variance than using a single sample.

2. The Expected SARSA update rule

Write the TD error using the expected next Q-value:

$$\delta_t = r_{t+1} + \gamma \sum_{a'} \pi(a'|s_{t+1})\, Q(s_{t+1},a') - Q(s_t,a_t).$$

Then update:

$$Q(s_t,a_t) \leftarrow Q(s_t,a_t) + \alpha\, \delta_t.$$

If π is deterministic (or greedy), the sum reduces to a single action (and Expected SARSA can reduce to Q-learning in limit). If π is stochastic (e.g., ε-greedy or softmax), the expectation uses those probabilities.

Why this is useful — intuition

- **Lower variance than SARSA:** SARSA uses the *actual sampled* a_{t+1}. That sample adds randomness to the update. Taking the expectation removes that source of variance.

- **On-policy correctness:** Because the expectation uses the same policy used to generate actions, the learned Q reflects the true behaviour policy.
- **Safer than Q-learning:** Q-learning's max operator can be optimistic and harmful when exploration leads to risky states. Expected SARSA reflects exploration — it learns values that match the policy actually executed.

3. Comparison table (conceptual)

- SARSA: update uses $Q(s_{t+1},a_{t+1})$ (sampled next action). — *on-policy, higher variance*
- Expected SARSA: update uses $E_{a'}\sim\pi[Q(s_{t+1}, a')]$. — *on-policy, lower variance*
- Q-learning: update uses $\max_{a'}Q(s_{t+1}, a')$. — *off-policy, potentially optimistic, lower bias toward optimal under full exploration*

4. Practical computation of the expectation

Epsilon-greedy policy: If π is ε-greedy, the expectation becomes:

$$\sum_{a'} \pi(a'|s')\, Q(s', a') = (1-\varepsilon)\, Q(s', a^*) + \frac{\varepsilon}{|A|} \sum_{a'} Q(s', a')$$

where $a^* = \arg\max_a Q(s', a)$.

This is cheap and easy to compute.

- **Softmax policy:** If $\pi(a|s) \propto \exp(Q(s,a)/\tau)$, compute the weighted sum with the softmax probabilities.
- **Large action space:** When actions are many or continuous, computing the exact expectation may be expensive; you can approximate it with a small sample average (but that reintroduces variance). For continuous actions, parameterized policies and actor-critic variants are often preferred.

5. Pseudocode

```
Initialize Q(s,a) arbitrarily
for each episode:
```

```
initialize s
choose a ~ policy π(·|s) derived from Q (e.g., ε-greedy)
while not terminal:
    take action a, observe r, s'
    # compute expected Q at s' under policy π
    expected_Q = sum_over_a' [ π(a'|s') * Q[s', a'] ]
    # TD error and update
    delta = r + gamma * expected_Q - Q[s, a]
    Q[s, a] += alpha * delta
    s = s'
    choose a ~ π(·|s)  # next action for continuing rollouts
```

6. Steps of the Expected SARSA Algorithm

Expected SARSA follows the same overall structure as SARSA but changes the *target* by using the **expected value** of all possible next actions rather than the single sampled next action.

A. Initialize Q-values

Set the action-value function Q(s,a) to arbitrary initial values for all state–action pairs. If using a table:

- Initialize a matrix Q[S].

  If using function approximation:

- Initialize network weights or parameters.

B. Choose the initial state

Start the agent in the environment and observe the starting state s_0.

C. Select an action using the current policy

Choose action a_0 from state s_0 based on the behavior policy π(a|s), typically:

- ε-greedy
- Softmax
- Boltzmann exploration

Note: The policy is derived from the **current Q-values**.

D. For each step of the episode

Repeat until the episode ends:

a) Take action a_t

Execute the action in the environment.

b) Observe reward and next state

Receive:

- Reward r_{t+1}
- Next state s_{t+1}

c) Compute the Expected Q-value (core difference)

Instead of selecting a single next action, compute:

$$\text{ExpectedQ} = \sum_{a'} \pi(a'|s_{t+1})Q(s_{t+1},a')$$

If using ε-greedy:

$$\text{ExpectedQ}=(1-\varepsilon)Q(s', a^{*}) + \frac{\varepsilon}{|A|}\sum_{a'} Q(s', a')$$

This removes randomness from the next sample and significantly reduces variance.

d) Compute the TD error

$$\delta_t = r_{t+1}+ \gamma\times\text{ExpectedQ} - Q(s_t,a_t)$$

e) Update the Q-value

$$Q(s_t,a_t)\leftarrow Q(s_t,a_t)+\alpha\, \delta_t$$

This adjusts the Q-value toward a combination of immediate reward and expected future return.

f) Move to the next state

Set:

- $s_t = s_{t+1}$

g) Select the next action for continued interaction

Choose:

- $a_t \sim \pi(\cdot|s_t)$

Continue until the episode terminates.

5. Termination condition

Stop when the episode ends:

- The agent reaches a terminal state

  or

- A maximum step limit is reached

Then start the next episode.

Summary Flow

a) Initialize Q(s,a)

b) Observe initial state s

c) Choose action a using policy π

d) For each step:

   i. Take action a

   ii. Observe r, s'

   iii. Compute $E_{a'}\sim\pi[Q(s',a')]$

   iv. Update Q(s,a)

   v. Move to s'

   vi. Choose new action a

e) Repeat for all episodes

Numerical example

Suppose:

Action set {L, R};

At s', Q(s', L) = 0.2, Q(s', R) = 0.8;

Policy at s' is ε-greedy with ε=0.1, so a∗ = R and $\pi(R|s') = 1 - \varepsilon + \varepsilon/2 = 0.95$, $\pi(L|s') = 0.05$.

Then expected_Q = 0.95×0.8+0.05×0.2=0.76+0.01=0.77

If r=1, γ=0.9, current Q(s,a)=0.5, α=0.1:

δ=1+0.9×0.77−0.5=1+0.693−0.5=1.193

Q ← 0.5+0.1×1.193 = 0.6193.

This update used the *policy-weighted* future estimate — smoother than picking the single sampled a_{t+1}

Example:

Example P4 – U4 – D8
Expected SARSA

```
import numpy as np
import gym

def epsilon_greedy_policy(Q, state, epsilon):
    """
    Returns a probability distribution over actions under epsilon-greedy policy.
    """
    nA = len(Q[state])
    policy = np.ones(nA) * (epsilon / nA)
    best_action = np.argmax(Q[state])
    policy[best_action] += (1 - epsilon)
    return policy


def expected_sarsa(env, num_episodes=5000, alpha=0.1, gamma=0.99, epsilon=0.1):
    """
    Expected SARSA algorithm.
    """

    # Initialize Q(s, a)
    Q = np.zeros((env.observation_space.n, env.action_space.n))

    for episode in range(num_episodes):

        state = env.reset()[0] if isinstance(env.reset(), tuple) else env.reset()

        done = False
```

```
        while not done:

            # Choose A using epsilon-greedy
            action = np.random.choice(
                env.action_space.n,
                p=epsilon_greedy_policy(Q, state, epsilon)
            )

            next_state, reward, terminated, truncated, info = env.step(action)
            done = terminated or truncated

            # Expected Q over next actions under epsilon-greedy policy
            policy_next = epsilon_greedy_policy(Q, next_state, epsilon)
            expected_Q = np.dot(Q[next_state], policy_next)

            # Expected SARSA update
            Q[state][action] += alpha * (reward + gamma * expected_Q - Q[state][action])

            state = next_state

    return Q


if __name__ == "__main__":
    env = gym.make("CliffWalking-v0")
    Q_values = expected_sarsa(env)
    print("Learned Q-values using Expected SARSA:")
    print(Q_values)
```

Output:

```
Output

 [ -3.80498809   -2.17352144  -75.81382152   -5.05341969]
 [ -3.28679297   -2.17170738   -1.           -5.00892188]
 [-16.09067461 -118.62393423  -19.61938373  -19.60983028]
 [  0.           0.           0.           0.        ]
 [  0.           0.           0.           0.        ]
 [  0.           0.           0.           0.        ]
 [  0.           0.           0.           0.        ]
 [  0.           0.           0.           0.        ]
 [  0.           0.           0.           0.        ]
 [  0.           0.           0.           0.        ]
 [  0.           0.           0.           0.        ]
 [  0.           0.           0.           0.        ]
```

```
[ 0.        0.        0.        0.      ]
[ 0.        0.        0.        0.      ]]
```

☐ Action-Value Update Rules

Below are the core update equations for each algorithm.

All updates follow the Temporal-Difference (TD) format:

$$Q(s,a) \leftarrow Q(s,a) + \alpha[\text{Target} - Q(s,a)]$$

Where the **Target** is different for each method.

A. Q-Learning (Off-Policy)

Target: Maximum future value (greedy action)

$$Q(s, a) \leftarrow Q(s, a) + \alpha[r + \gamma \max_{a'} Q(s', a') - Q(s, a)]$$

Key Idea:

- Q-learning *assumes* the agent will take the **best possible action** in the next state (even if it won't in practice).
- It learns the **optimal policy directly**, ignoring its current behavior policy.

→ **Off-policy and optimistic.**

B. SARSA (On-Policy)

Target: Q-value of the *actual* next action chosen by the policy

$$Q(s,a) \leftarrow Q(s,a) + \alpha[r + \gamma Q(s',a') - Q(s,a)]$$

Key Idea:

- SARSA uses the Q-value of the **next action actually taken** according to the policy.
- Reflects real behavior of the agent, including exploration (ε-greedy).

→ **On-policy and sensitive to exploration.**

C. Expected SARSA (On-Policy with Expected Value)

Target: Expected future value under the current policy

$$Q(s,a) \leftarrow Q(s,a) + \alpha[r + \gamma \sum_{a'} \pi(a'|s') Q(s',a') - Q(s,a)]$$

If the policy is ε-greedy:

$$\sum_{a'} \pi(a'|s') Q(s',a') = (1-\varepsilon)Q(s', a^*) + \frac{\varepsilon}{|A|} \sum_{a'} Q(s',a')$$

Where:

$a^* = \arg\max_{a'} Q(s',a')$

Key Idea:

- Instead of using one sampled next action (SARSA),
- Or assuming the best action (Q-Learning),
- Expected SARSA uses the **expected Q-value of all actions**, weighted by the policy.

→ **On-policy but with lower variance and smoother learning.**

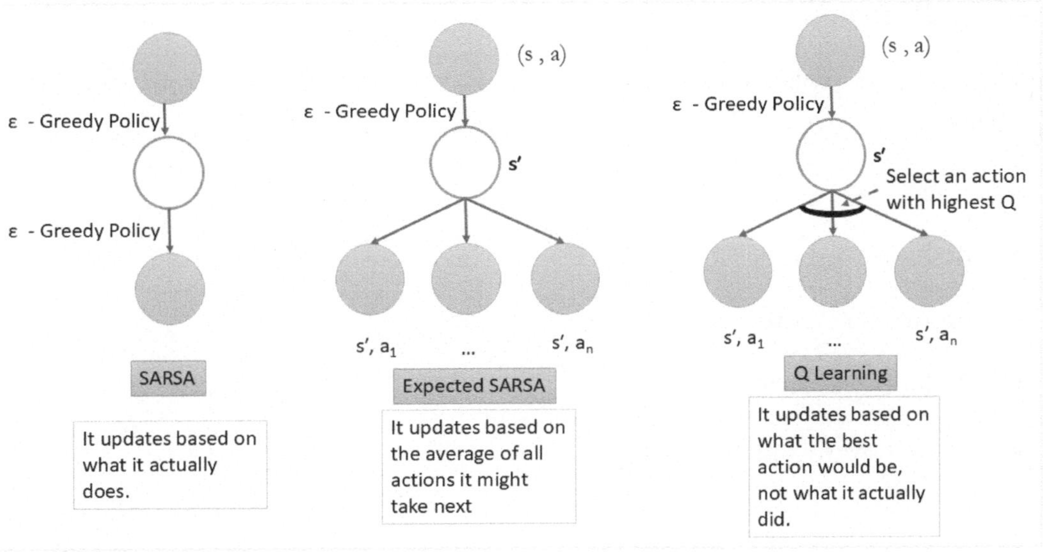

Illustration SARSA_8:

What Is Different About Expected SARSA? (The Essence)

Expected SARSA differs in **how it computes the target** for updating Q-values.

Aspect	**SARSA**	**Expected SARSA**	**Q-Learning**
Next action considered	The *actual* next action (a')	The **expected Q-value** over all actions	The **greedy action**
Target depends on	Sampled action	Probabilities of all actions	Maximum Q-value
Type	On-policy	On-policy	Off-policy
Variance	High (sampled action varies)	**Low** (averaged expectation)	Moderate
Convergence	Stable but slow	**More stable**	Fast but risky with function approximation

The core difference:

Expected SARSA replaces the single sampled next action with the *expected* value under the policy.

This:

- Reduces randomness
- Produces smoother updates
- Reduces variance
- Avoids overly optimistic updates

Intuitive Analogy

Imagine learning to drive on a hill:

Q-Learning (Optimistic Friend)

Your friend assumes you *will always* choose the perfect driving maneuver—even though you sometimes make mistakes.

SARSA (Literal Friend)

Your friend predicts your future based on the maneuver you *actually* chose (even if it was a sloppy choice due to exploration).

Expected SARSA (Wise Friend)

Your friend averages all possible maneuvers you might take, weighted by how likely you are to choose them.

Expected SARSA = Balanced, realistic, and stable guidance.

Summary Chart

Algorithm	Type	Update Target	Behavior	Exploration Aware?
Q-Learning	Off-policy	Greedy max	Aggressive	No—ignores exploration

SARSA	On-policy	Sampled next action	Sensitive	Yes
Expected SARSA	On-policy	Expected value of all actions	Balanced & smooth	Yes

☐ **Tabular SARSA vs Expected SARSA vs Q-learning on a 4x4 GridWorld.**

Master said, This program demonstrates four key reinforcement-learning concepts using a simple 4×4 GridWorld:

(1) Tabular SARSA, (2) Expected SARSA, (3) Q-learning, and (4) visualizing the learned policy and Q-values. Everything runs offline and takes under a minute.

Environment Setup

The code defines a GridWorld with 16 states arranged in a 4×4 grid.

Two terminal states are placed at the corners—one with a reward of **+1**, the other **–1**.

The agent can take four actions: **up, down, left, or right**.

If an action would move outside the grid, the agent stays in place.

This creates a deterministic, easy-to-study RL environment.

Epsilon-Greedy Action Selection

The function epsilon_greedy(Q, state, epsilon) chooses actions:

- With probability **ε**, a random action (exploration)
- With probability **1–ε**, the best action from the Q-table (exploitation)

This is how the agent balances learning new behaviour vs. using what it knows.

SARSA Learning Loop

SARSA uses the sequence

(state, action, reward, next_state, next_action)

to update Q-values.

It is an **on-policy** method, meaning it learns the same behaviour that it follows. The update is:

$Q[s,a] \leftarrow Q[s,a] + \alpha\ (\ r + \gamma\ Q[s',a'] - Q[s,a]\ )$

Over hundreds of episodes, the Q-table stabilizes.

Example P4 – U4 – D9

Tabular SARSA vs Expected SARSA vs Q-learning

```
import numpy as np
import matplotlib.pyplot as plt

# -------------------------------
# Config
# -------------------------------
SEED = 0
np.random.seed(SEED)

GRID_SIZE = 4
N_STATES = GRID_SIZE * GRID_SIZE
ACTIONS = [0, 1, 2, 3]  # 0=UP,1=RIGHT,2=DOWN,3=LEFT
TERMINALS = [0, N_STATES - 1]  # start(0) and goal(15) are terminals here

# -------------------------------
# GridWorld environment
# -------------------------------
class GridWorld:
    def __init__(self, size=GRID_SIZE, terminal_states=TERMINALS):
        self.size = size
        self.n_states = size * size
        self.terminal_states = terminal_states
        self.state = None

    def reset(self, random_start=True):
        if random_start:
            choices = [s for s in range(self.n_states) if s not in self.terminal_states]
            self.state = np.random.choice(choices)
        else:
            # deterministic start (if you prefer)
            self.state = 0
        return self.state

    def step(self, action):
        """Return (next_state, reward, done). Reward is -1 per step. Terminal states return
done=True."""
```

```
        if self.state in self.terminal_states:
            return self.state, 0, True

        row, col = divmod(self.state, self.size)

        # apply action with boundary checks
        if action == 0 and row > 0:          # UP
            row -= 1
        elif action == 1 and col < self.size - 1:  # RIGHT
            col += 1
        elif action == 2 and row < self.size - 1:  # DOWN
            row += 1
        elif action == 3 and col > 0:        # LEFT
            col -= 1

        next_state = row * self.size + col
        reward = -1  # cost per step (encourages shortest path)
        done = next_state in self.terminal_states

        self.state = next_state
        return next_state, reward, done

# -------------------------------
# ε-greedy policy helper
# -------------------------------
def epsilon_greedy_action(Q, state, epsilon):
    if np.random.rand() < epsilon:
        return np.random.choice(ACTIONS)
    return int(np.argmax(Q[state]))

def epsilon_action_probs(Q_row, epsilon):
    """Return probability vector for ε-greedy policy for a single state's Q-values"""
    n = len(Q_row)
    probs = np.ones(n) * (epsilon / n)
    best = int(np.argmax(Q_row))
    probs[best] += 1.0 - epsilon
    return probs

# -------------------------------
# Training routines
# -------------------------------
def train_sarsa(env, episodes=500, alpha=0.1, gamma=0.99, epsilon=0.1,
random_start=True):
    Q = np.zeros((env.n_states, len(ACTIONS)))
    for ep in range(episodes):
        s = env.reset(random_start)
        a = epsilon_greedy_action(Q, s, epsilon)
        done = False
```

```
        while not done:
            s2, r, done = env.step(a)
            a2 = epsilon_greedy_action(Q, s2, epsilon)
            Q[s, a] += alpha * (r + gamma * Q[s2, a2] - Q[s, a])
            s, a = s2, a2
    return Q

def train_expected_sarsa(env, episodes=500, alpha=0.1, gamma=0.99, epsilon=0.1,
random_start=True):
    Q = np.zeros((env.n_states, len(ACTIONS)))
    for ep in range(episodes):
        s = env.reset(random_start)
        done = False
        while not done:
            a = epsilon_greedy_action(Q, s, epsilon)
            s2, r, done = env.step(a)
            # expected Q at next state under epsilon-greedy
            probs = epsilon_action_probs(Q[s2], epsilon)
            expected_Q = np.dot(probs, Q[s2])
            Q[s, a] += alpha * (r + gamma * expected_Q - Q[s, a])
            s = s2
    return Q

def train_qlearning(env, episodes=500, alpha=0.1, gamma=0.99, epsilon=0.1,
random_start=True):
    Q = np.zeros((env.n_states, len(ACTIONS)))
    for ep in range(episodes):
        s = env.reset(random_start)
        done = False
        while not done:
            a = epsilon_greedy_action(Q, s, epsilon)
            s2, r, done = env.step(a)
            Q[s, a] += alpha * (r + gamma * np.max(Q[s2]) - Q[s, a])
            s = s2
    return Q

# -------------------------------
# Visualization helpers
# -------------------------------
def policy_text_grid(Q):
    """Return a 2D array of arrow symbols (or G for terminal) for printing."""
    arrows = {0: "↑", 1: "→", 2: "↓", 3: "←"}
    grid = []
    for s in range(N_STATES):
        if s in TERMINALS:
            grid.append("G")  # terminal / goal
        else:
            grid.append(arrows[int(np.argmax(Q[s]))])
```

```
    return np.array(grid).reshape(GRID_SIZE, GRID_SIZE)

def plot_policy_quiver(Q, title):
    """Plot a quiver (arrows) showing best action in each cell."""
    U = np.zeros((GRID_SIZE, GRID_SIZE))
    V = np.zeros((GRID_SIZE, GRID_SIZE))
    X, Y = np.meshgrid(np.arange(GRID_SIZE), np.arange(GRID_SIZE))

    for s in range(N_STATES):
        r, c = divmod(s, GRID_SIZE)
        if s in TERMINALS:
            U[r, c] = 0
            V[r, c] = 0
            continue
        a = int(np.argmax(Q[s]))
        # mapping: UP=(0,-1), RIGHT=(1,0), DOWN=(0,1), LEFT=(-1,0)
        if a == 0: dx, dy = 0, -1
        elif a == 1: dx, dy = 1, 0
        elif a == 2: dx, dy = 0, 1
        else: dx, dy = -1, 0
        U[r, c] = dx
        V[r, c] = dy

    plt.figure(figsize=(4, 4))
    plt.title(title)
    plt.quiver(X, Y, U, V, angles='xy', scale_units='xy', scale=1)
    # mark terminals
    for t in TERMINALS:
        tr, tc = divmod(t, GRID_SIZE)
        plt.text(tc, tr, "G", ha='center', va='center', fontsize=12, fontweight='bold')
    plt.gca().invert_yaxis()
    plt.xticks([])
    plt.yticks([])
    plt.show()

def plot_heatmap_maxq(Q, title):
    """Plot heatmap of max Q per state (4x4)."""
    maxq = np.max(Q, axis=1).reshape(GRID_SIZE, GRID_SIZE)
    plt.figure(figsize=(4, 4))
    plt.title(title)
    plt.imshow(maxq)  # default cmap
    plt.colorbar()
    plt.gca().invert_yaxis()
    plt.show()

# -------------------------------
# Run training and show results
# -------------------------------
```

```
def main():
    env = GridWorld()

    episodes = 500          # modest; adjust up/down for more learning
    alpha = 0.1
    gamma = 0.99
    epsilon = 0.1

    print("Training... (this should complete in seconds on a normal laptop)")
    Q_sarsa = train_sarsa(env, episodes=episodes, alpha=alpha, gamma=gamma,
epsilon=epsilon)
    Q_exp = train_expected_sarsa(env, episodes=episodes, alpha=alpha, gamma=gamma,
epsilon=epsilon)
    Q_q = train_qlearning(env, episodes=episodes, alpha=alpha, gamma=gamma,
epsilon=epsilon)

    # Print Q-tables (rounded)
    np.set_printoptions(precision=3, suppress=True)
    print("\nQ-table (SARSA):")
    print(Q_sarsa)
    print("\nQ-table (Expected SARSA):")
    print(Q_exp)
    print("\nQ-table (Q-learning):")
    print(Q_q)

    # Policy text grids
    print("\nSARSA learned policy (text grid):")
    print(policy_text_grid(Q_sarsa))
    print("\nExpected SARSA learned policy (text grid):")
    print(policy_text_grid(Q_exp))
    print("\nQ-learning learned policy (text grid):")
    print(policy_text_grid(Q_q))

    # Quiver arrow maps
    plot_policy_quiver(Q_sarsa, "SARSA Policy (Arrows)")
    plot_heatmap_maxq(Q_sarsa, "SARSA Max-Q Heatmap")

    plot_policy_quiver(Q_exp, "Expected SARSA Policy (Arrows)")
    plot_heatmap_maxq(Q_exp, "Expected SARSA Max-Q Heatmap")

    plot_policy_quiver(Q_q, "Q-learning Policy (Arrows)")
    plot_heatmap_maxq(Q_q, "Q-learning Max-Q Heatmap")

    # Compare best-actions per state
    print("\nBest actions (state -> SARSA | ExpectedSARSA | Qlearn):")
    for s in range(N_STATES):
        a_s = int(np.argmax(Q_sarsa[s]))
        a_e = int(np.argmax(Q_exp[s]))
```

```
        a_q = int(np.argmax(Q_q[s]))
        print(f"{s:2d}: {a_s} | {a_e} | {a_q}")

if __name__ == "__main__":
    main()
```

Expected SARSA

Instead of picking a single next action, Expected SARSA computes the **expected value** of all actions under epsilon-greedy probabilities.

This produces smoother, less noisy updates.

Q-Learning

Q-Learning is **off-policy**.

It assumes the agent will follow the optimal policy in the future:

max_a' Q[s', a']

Thus, it usually learns faster and gives sharper policies.

Visualization

The code generates:

- **Arrow map** → shows the best action in each cell
- **Heatmaps** → show learned Q-values
- **Comparisons** → SARSA vs Expected SARSA vs Q-learning

These visuals help you *see* how each algorithm behaves differently.

Output:

```
Output
```

```
Q-table (SARSA):
[[ 0.     0.     0.     0.   ]
 [-1.139 -1.448 -1.328 -1.   ]
 [-2.181 -2.229 -2.12  -1.99 ]
 [-2.769 -2.894 -2.749 -2.725]
```

```
 [-1.    -1.351 -1.344 -1.319]
 [-1.921 -2.05  -2.179 -1.923]
 [-2.495 -2.451 -2.492 -2.463]
 [-2.261 -2.177 -1.989 -2.252]
 [-1.991 -2.302 -2.    -2.179]
 [-2.423 -2.431 -2.473 -2.459]
 [-2.007 -1.926 -1.927 -2.097]
 [-1.25  -1.295 -1.    -1.384]
 [-2.791 -2.806 -2.932 -2.95 ]
 [-2.019 -1.994 -2.186 -2.193]
 [-1.186 -1.    -1.302 -1.322]
 [ 0.     0.     0.     0.   ]]
```

Q-table (Expected SARSA):

```
[[ 0.     0.     0.     0.   ]
 [-1.338 -1.4   -1.409 -1.   ]
 [-2.075 -2.029 -2.082 -2.012]
 [-2.749 -2.774 -2.744 -2.73 ]
 [-1.    -1.537 -1.703 -1.094]
 [-1.977 -2.013 -2.035 -1.975]
 [-2.505 -2.511 -2.53  -2.5  ]
 [-2.249 -2.227 -2.01  -2.078]
 [-2.018 -2.12  -2.31  -2.073]
 [-2.461 -2.449 -2.504 -2.478]
 [-2.097 -1.982 -1.982 -2.123]
 [-1.355 -1.263 -1.    -1.551]
 [-2.825 -2.809 -2.835 -2.863]
 [-2.035 -2.022 -2.079 -2.223]
 [-1.763 -1.    -1.349 -1.466]
 [ 0.     0.     0.     0.   ]]
```

```
Q-table (Q-learning):
[[ 0.     0.     0.     0.   ]
 [-1.177 -1.293 -1.349 -1.   ]
 [-2.067 -2.173 -2.297 -1.988]
 [-2.743 -2.759 -2.752 -2.765]
 [-1.    -1.446 -1.32  -1.264]
 [-1.938 -1.99  -2.032 -1.938]
 [-2.534 -2.503 -2.527 -2.535]
 [-2.258 -2.16  -1.987 -2.448]
 [-1.987 -2.134 -2.176 -2.228]
 [-2.522 -2.513 -2.501 -2.517]
 [-2.084 -1.968 -1.97  -2.202]
 [-1.523 -1.254 -1.    -1.589]
 [-2.787 -2.8   -2.847 -2.857]
 [-2.008 -1.988 -2.161 -2.446]
 [-1.469 -1.    -1.456 -1.572]
 [ 0.     0.     0.     0.   ]]
```

```
SARSA learned policy (text grid):
[['G' '←' '←' '←']
 ['↑' '↑' '→' '↓']
 ['↑' '↑' '→' '↓']
 ['↑' '→' '→' 'G']]

Expected SARSA learned policy (text grid):
[['G' '←' '←' '←']
 ['↑' '←' '←' '↓']
 ['↑' '→' '→' '↓']
 ['→' '→' '→' 'G']]

Q-learning learned policy (text grid):
[['G' '←' '←' '↑']
 ['↑' '←' '→' '↓']
 ['↑' '↓' '→' '↓']
 ['↑' '→' '→' 'G']]

Best actions (state -> SARSA | ExpectedSARSA | Qlearn):
 0: 0 | 0 | 0
 1: 3 | 3 | 3
 2: 3 | 3 | 3
 3: 3 | 3 | 0
 4: 0 | 0 | 0
 5: 0 | 3 | 3
 6: 1 | 3 | 1
 7: 2 | 2 | 2
 8: 0 | 0 | 0
 9: 0 | 1 | 2
10: 1 | 1 | 1
11: 2 | 2 | 2
12: 0 | 1 | 0
13: 1 | 1 | 1
14: 1 | 1 | 1
15: 0 | 0 | 0
```

Plot: SARSA Policy

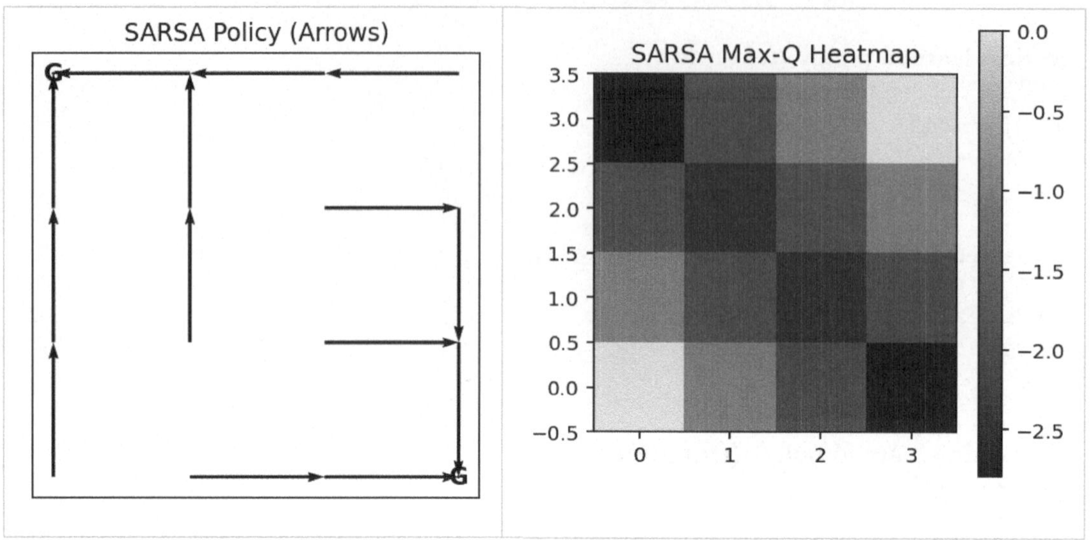

Illustration SARSA_1: SARSA

Plot: Expected SARSA Policy

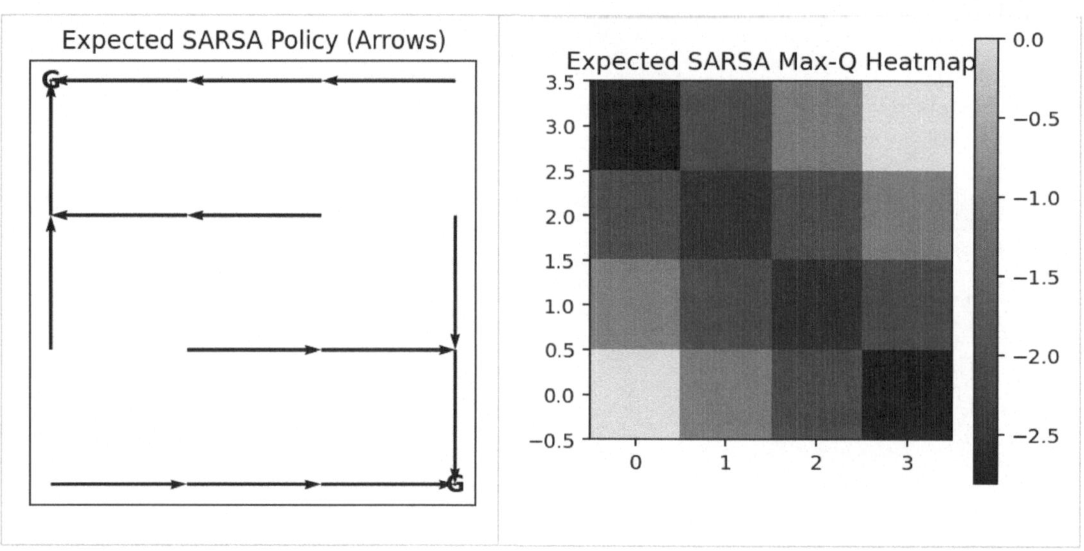

Illustration SARSA_3: SARSA

Plot: Q Learning Policy

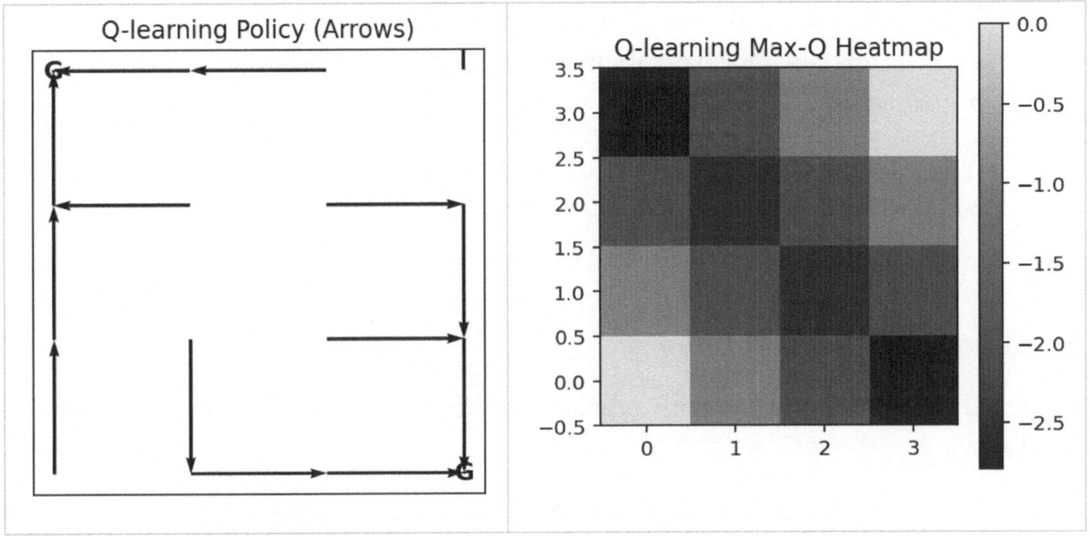

Illustration SARSA_4: SARSA

Advantages & disadvantages

Advantages

- Reduced variance vs SARSA (more stable learning).
- Remains on-policy — learned values match behaviour, including exploration.
- Often outperforms SARSA in noisy/sparse-reward problems.

Disadvantages

- Slightly higher computational cost per update (need to sum over actions).
- If policy probabilities are difficult to compute (large/continuous actions), computing the expectation is costly or infeasible.
- Still can be biased if function approximation and off-policy data are used carelessly.

7. Variance–bias tradeoff

- SARSA (sampled) has higher variance but sometimes lower computational cost per step.

- Expected SARSA reduces variance by replacing a random sample with an average; this can improve stability but introduces dependence on accurate policy probabilities.
- Q-learning uses the max operator: lower variance in the update target, but may be biased toward optimism and is off-policy.

8. Convergence & conditions

Expected SARSA converges with tabular Q and standard stochastic approximation conditions:

- Sufficient exploration (every state–action visited infinitely often),
- Properly decaying learning rates (e.g., $\sum \alpha_t = \infty$, $\sum \alpha_t^2 < \infty$),
- Finite MDP/finite actions, to the action-value function corresponding to the behaviour policy; with greedy policy improvement and appropriate control of exploration, it can converge toward an optimal policy under standard assumptions.

Extensions & relations

- **Expected SARSA + Function Approximation:** Combine with linear or non-linear function approximators, but be careful: bootstrapping + function approximation + off-policy data can cause divergence (the deadly triad). Expected SARSA is on-policy, so it's safer than off-policy alternatives but still requires stabilising mechanisms (target networks, replay buffers with care, or actor-critic).
- **Actor–Critic view:** Expected SARSA can be seen as a critic update where the critic's target uses the expectation under the actor's policy — a natural stepping stone to actor-critic algorithms.
- **Using GAE / multi-step:** You can use multi-step expected returns (n-step Expected SARSA) to trade bias and variance.

When to use Expected SARSA

- You want an **on-policy** method that is **less noisy** than SARSA.
- You have a **small/medium discrete action space** where computing the expectation is cheap.
- You care about safe learning that reflects exploration (e.g., robotics, where exploratory actions are risky).
- You prefer stability over the optimistic speed of Q-learning.

Master said, "Expected SARSA is a graceful blend: it retains on-policy learning fidelity while smoothing updates by averaging over the policy's action distribution. In practice, that smoothing often yields faster, steadier learning than plain SARSA and safer behavior than greedy Q-learning when exploration matters."

PART FOUR

DAY SIXTEEN

Unit 4 - Lesson Five

Value and Policy Network

☐ Value and Policy Network

Master said, "Roopa, in reinforcement learning, *value networks* and *policy networks* are powerful tools born from neural networks. They help the agent navigate complex worlds by learning directly from experience—by observing states, estimating rewards, and refining behaviour over time. One approximates value, the other approximates action. Together, they form the mind and intuition of an intelligent agent."

☐ Value Network — The Eye That Sees the Future

A **Value Network** approximates the *value function*—a measure of how beneficial it is for the agent to be in a particular **state**, or to take a particular **action** in that state.

- For **state value functions** V(s), the network predicts the long-term worth of being in state *s*.
- For **action value functions** Q(s,a), the network predicts the value of taking action *a* in state *s*.

In essence, the value network evaluates the *desirability* of situations and choices, guiding the agent toward states that promise higher cumulative rewards.

How a Value Network Works

1. Input Layer — Perception

The network receives an encoding of the current **state** (or a state–action pair). This may include numerical variables, images, sensor readings, or any representation of the environment.

2. Hidden Layers — Understanding

Through several hidden layers, the network performs nonlinear transformations. These layers identify patterns, relationships, and features that are not obvious at the surface—capturing the complexity of the environment.

3. Output Layer — Prediction

The final output is an estimate of the **expected return** from that state (or state–action pair). This represents the future reward the agent anticipates.

Training the Value Network — Learning to See Clearly

Loss Function:

A value network is trained by reducing the error between the predicted value and the actual return.

This error is often the **temporal difference (TD) error**, which measures how far today's prediction deviates from tomorrow's updated belief.

Optimization:

Algorithms such as **gradient descent** adjust the network's parameters to minimize the loss.
With each update, the network's understanding becomes more refined.

Update Rule:

During every interaction:

1. The agent takes an action.
2. Receives a reward.
3. Observes a new state.

4. Updates the predicted value based on both the immediate reward and the estimated future reward.

With thousands of such updates, the value function becomes increasingly accurate.

The Essence

Through repeated interaction with its world, the value network learns *how good* each state (or action) truly is.

It becomes the agent's inner compass—guiding choices, anticipating consequences, and shaping the optimal path forward.

☐ Policy Network:

Master said, "A **Policy Network** is the part of an intelligent agent that learns *how to act.* While the value network studies the world, the policy network decides what to do next."

Policy Network

A **policy network** learns a direct mapping from *states* to *actions*, defining the agent's behaviour at every step in the environment.

Key Characteristics

Action Distribution:

Given a state, the network outputs a **probability distribution** over all possible actions.

This allows the agent to choose actions not only based on certainty but also using controlled exploration.

Deterministic or Stochastic:

- *Deterministic policy*: selects the single action with the highest value.
- *Stochastic policy*: samples from a distribution of actions, enabling richer exploration and adaptability.

Learning Objective:

The policy network is trained to **maximise expected returns**. It continually adjusts its parameters to increase the likelihood of choosing actions that lead to higher cumulative rewards.

How the Policy Network Learns

The agent moves through the environment following its current policy:

1. It takes actions suggested by the policy network.
2. It receives rewards from the paths it explores.
3. These rewards act as feedback.
4. The network adjusts itself to favour effective actions and discard poor ones.

Over many iterations, the policy network learns:

- Which moves bring long-term reward
- Which behaviours consistently lead to failure
- How to balance risk, exploration, and optimal decision-making

Eventually, the policy converges toward the *optimal behavioural strategy* for the environment.

In Essence

- **Value Network:**

  Learns *how valuable* each state or state–action pair is.

- **Policy Network:**

  Learns *what action* to take in each state to maximise success.

Master said, "When value illuminates the world, and policy guides the steps, the agent walks the path of intelligence. One show meaning; the other chooses motion. Together, they form the essence of learning."

Loss Function

Sam asked, "What is a Loss Function in a Neural Network?"

Master replied, "A loss function, also known as a cost function or objective function, quantifies the difference between the predicted output of the neural network and the actual target values. The primary goal during training is to minimize this loss, thereby improving the accuracy and performance of the model."

Master said, "What you see in this diagram is the *soul of modern Reinforcement Learning* expressed through two powerful tools: **Value Networks** and **Policy Networks**. Each part of the image represents how an intelligent agent learns to *understand the world* and *act wisely* within it."

Value Network – Learning the Worth of Each State

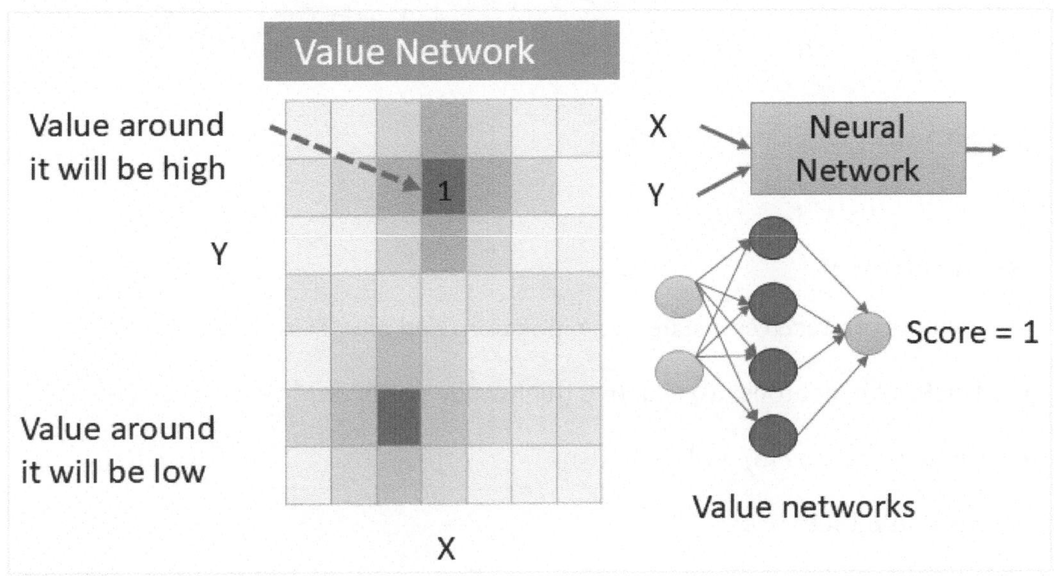

Illustration Value_1: Value Network

1. Grid Representation

The grid shows a landscape of states.

- **Green region**:

  States with **high value**—good places for the agent to be, often close to rewards or goals.

- **Brown/orange region**:

  States with **low value**—dangerous, undesirable, or far from reward.

The number **1** marks a highly valuable state.

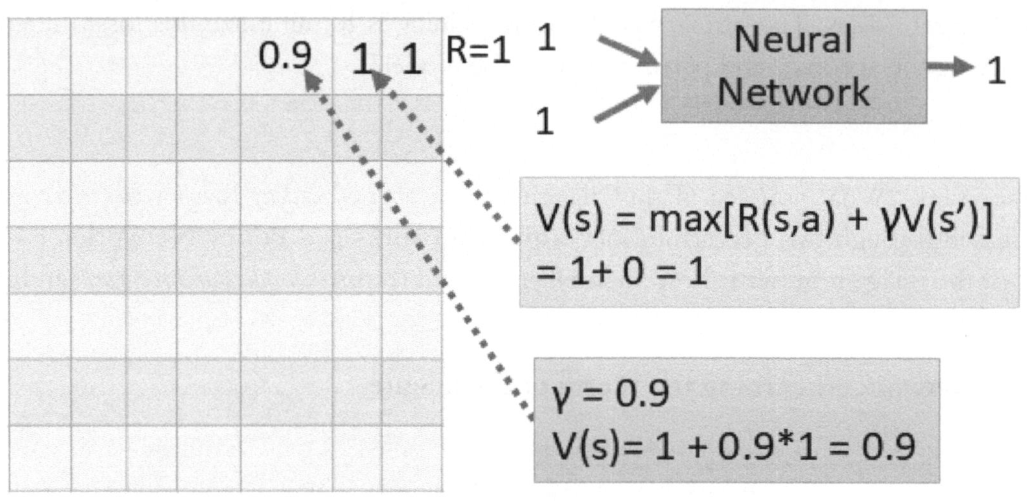

Illustration Value_2: Value Network

2. Neural Network

The neural network receives a state (X, Y position) and *predicts its value*:

- Bright blue neurons (a) → active (high value prediction)
- Orange neurons (b) → less active

This is the **Value Network**.

3. Bellman Update

The equation:

$$V(s) = \max_a (R(s, a) + \gamma V(s'))$$

This means:

- The value of a state equals the reward you get **+** the discounted value of the next state.
- $\gamma = 0.9 \rightarrow$ future rewards matter.

Example:

- If reward = 1
- Next state value = 1
- Then:
  V(s) = 1 + 0.9 × 1 = 1.9

The diagram shows how the network learns these propagated values.

Policy Network – Learning What Action to Take

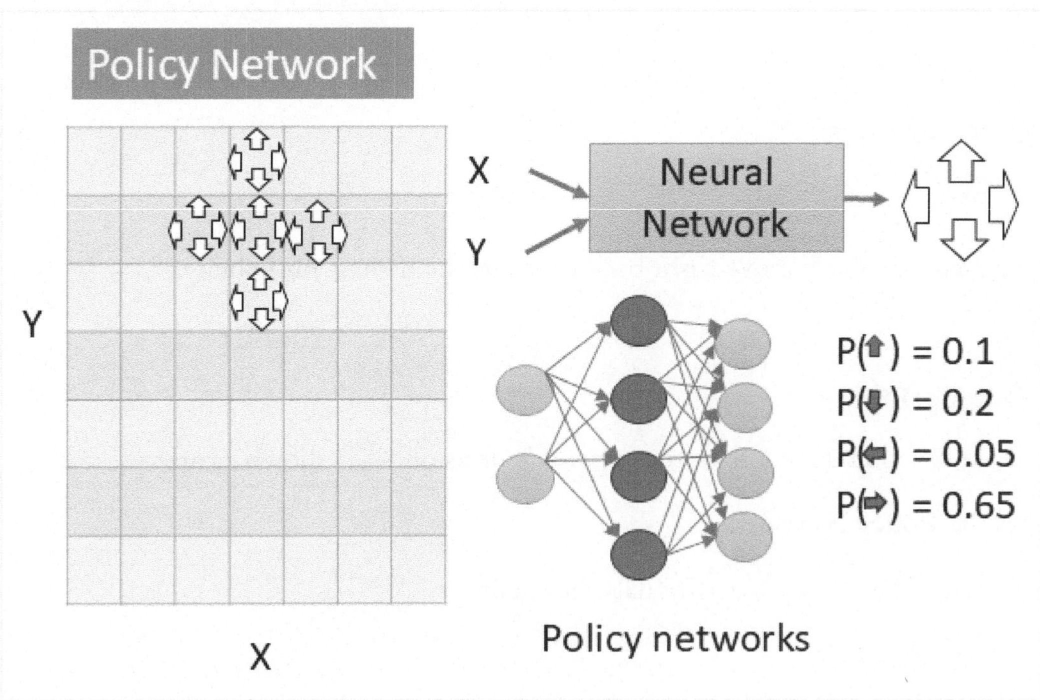

Illustration Policy_1: Policy Network

1. Grid of Arrows (Left)

Here, every cell has small arrows showing **possible actions**:

- Up
- Down
- Left
- Right

But the agent must choose the *best* one.

2. Policy Neural Network (Middle)

This network does not output a single value.

It outputs **probabilities of actions**, such as:

- P(↑) = 0.1
- P(↓) = 0.2
- P(←) = 0.05
- P(→) = 0.65

So the agent will likely move **right** because it has the highest probability.

3. Output (Right)

The chosen action direction — the network's decision — is shown as arrows.

This is the **Policy Network**.

Master said, "The Value Network tells the agent:

→ *How good is this place?*

The Policy Network guides the agent:

→ *What should I do now?*

Together they create wisdom:

- **Value = understanding**

- **Policy = action**

This union of knowledge and choice is what allows modern AI to navigate complex worlds, learn from experience, and approach mastery."

Master said, "This illustration beautifully illustrates **how a Value Neural Network learns the value function using the Bellman equation**, gradually refining its prediction of state values until it converges toward accuracy."

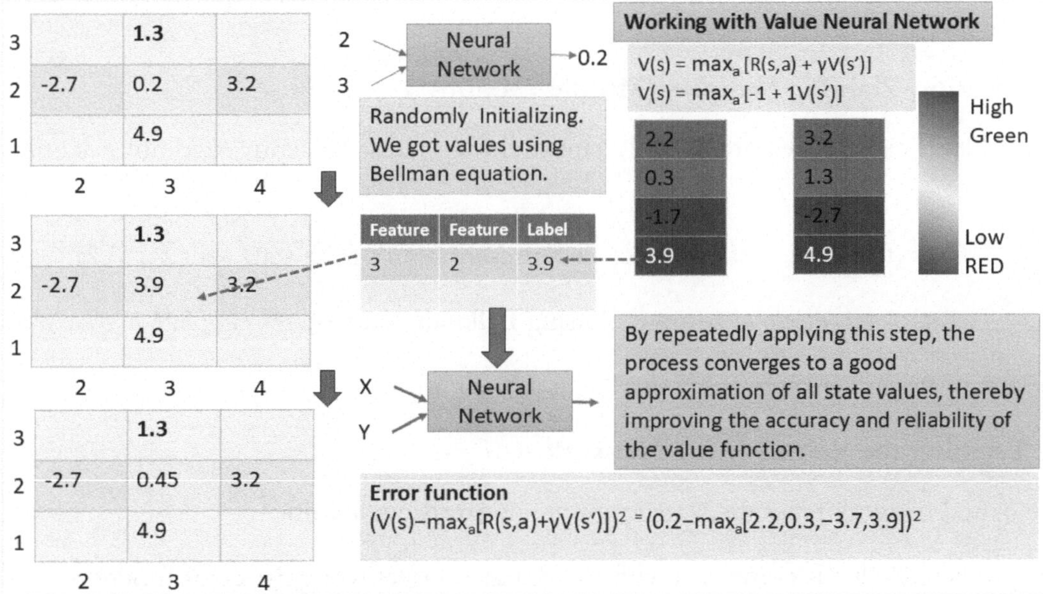

Illustration Value_3: Value Neural Network

1. Initial State Values (Top-Left)

The grid on the top-left represents an environment where each cell has a **value estimate**.

Some values are high (e.g., **1.3**) and some are low (**–2.7**, **0.2**, etc.).

These are **initial, randomly assigned values**, not yet accurate.

2. Bellman Targets Are Computed (Top-Right)

To train the value network, we must compute a **target value** for each state using the Bellman Equation:

$$V(s) = \max_a (R(s, a) + \gamma V(s'))$$

The diagram shows sample values like **2.2, 0.3, –1.7, 3.9** computed for the next states.

- These targets become the **labels** for training the neural network.

3. Creating Training Samples (Middle Section)

The table (Feature, Feature, Label) shows how states are converted into training examples:

- Input (features) = coordinates or representation of the state → e.g., (3,2)
- Label = target value computed using Bellman equation → e.g., **3.9**

These samples are fed into the Value Neural Network.

4. Training the Value Neural Network

The neural network takes the state as input and **predicts a value.**

The predicted value is compared with the Bellman target using the error function:

$$\text{Error} = (V(s) - \max_a[R(s,a) + \gamma V(s')])^2$$

Example shown:

$(0.2 - \max_a[2.2, 0.3, -3.7, 3.9])^2$

This error is backpropagated to update the network's weights.

5. Updated Grid (Middle-Left and Bottom-Left)

After training on one sample:

- The value **0.2** is updated to **3.9**, as shown in the second grid.

- Subsequent network predictions refine this further, shown in the third grid, where it updates to **0.45**, moving closer to its true value.

The value network is **iteratively learning** to match the Bellman targets.

6. Convergence (Right Side)

The green–red heatmap indicates how values shift:

- **Green = High-value states**
- **Red = Low-value states**

Through repeated Bellman updates and neural network training:

- High-value regions become more accurate.
- Low-value regions also stabilize.
- The entire value function progressively becomes more reliable.

Summary

Master said, "This image shows the full learning cycle of a Value Neural Network:

1. Start with random values.
2. Use the Bellman equation to compute targets.
3. Train the network by minimizing Bellman error.
4. Update the grid.
5. Repeat until values converge."

By repeating this process, the network learns a **stable, accurate value function**, enabling the agent to evaluate states intelligently and act optimally in its environment.

☐ Value and Policy Neural Networks

Nikash asked, "Master, how does learning actually happen inside Value and Policy Neural Networks?"

Value Neural Network

Master replied, "In a Value Neural Network — which approximates the value function such as **V(s)** or **Q(s, a)** — the network learns by comparing *what it predicted* with *what actually happened* or with a more accurate future estimate. This difference becomes the basis for correction."

The loss function commonly used is **Mean Squared Error (MSE)**:

$$\text{Loss} = \frac{1}{N}\sum_{i=1}^{N}(v((s_i) - \hat{v}(s_i))^2$$

Where:

- **V(s$_i$)** → the network's predicted value for state s_i.
- **V̂(s$_i$)** → the *target* value, which may be:
  - the actual return experienced (∑ **rewards**), or
  - a *bootstrapped estimate* like:

$r + \gamma V(s')$

or

$\max_a [R(s,a) + \gamma V(s')]$

The network updates its weights to reduce this error using **gradient descent**:

Gradient ascent: W ← w - (learning rate) (derivative)

$$W \leftarrow W - \alpha \frac{\partial \text{Loss}}{\partial W}$$

Master smiled: "Thus, the Value Network learns to *recognize the true worth of a state.*"

Policy Neural Network

He continued,

"A Policy Neural Network behaves differently. It does not estimate value — it *decides what to do next.* It outputs a probability distribution over possible actions: the policy $\pi(a \mid s)$."

Here, the goal is to **maximize the expected cumulative reward**:

$$J(\theta) = E_{\pi\theta} \left[\sum_{t=0}^{T} r_t \right]$$

Training often uses **policy gradients**, where we ascend toward better performance.

The loss is defined as the negative objective:

$Loss = -J(\theta)$

Thus, the update rule becomes:

Gradient ascent: W ← w + (learning rate) (derivative)

$$W \leftarrow W + \alpha \frac{\partial Loss}{\partial W}$$

Master said, "This network learns by reinforcing actions that lead to higher rewards and suppressing actions that do not."

Gain

Apeksha asked, "Master, what exactly is *Gain*?"

Master said, "Gain is the *reward-based signal* that tells the network whether the chosen action improved performance."

- **Positive Gain** → the action led to good outcomes, higher reward, or progress toward the objective.
- **Negative Gain** → the action caused loss, penalty, or led the agent away from its goal.

He said, "Gain is the soul of learning in reinforcement systems. It teaches the network to *prefer* actions that enrich experience and to *abandon* actions that diminish it. Through Gain, both Value and Policy networks move steadily toward mastery."

Master said — How Do We Train Value and Policy Neural Networks?

☐ Training a Value Neural Network

1. Initialize the Network

Begin by creating a neural network with suitable input, hidden, and output layers to approximate the value function (V(s) or Q(s,a)).

2. Collect Experience

Gather states, actions, rewards, and next states by interacting with the environment. This experience forms the training data.

3. Compute Target Values

For each sample:

- For **state values** V(s):

  Use the observed return, or the bootstrapped estimate

$$r + \gamma V(s')$$

- For **action values** Q(s,a):

  Use

$$r + \gamma \max_{a'} Q(s',a')$$

4. Define the Loss Function

Use **Mean Squared Error (MSE)** to quantify the difference between the network's prediction and the target value.

$$L = (y - \hat{V}(s))^2$$

5. Train the Network

- Apply **gradient descent** to minimise the loss.
- Update the weights repeatedly over many epochs.
- After each batch, adjust the weights to move closer to the true value function.

5. **Iterate and Improve**

Continue interacting with the environment, collecting new experiences, and retraining the network. Over time, the value predictions become more accurate and stable.

☐ Training a Policy Neural Network

1. **Initialize the Network**

Set up a neural network with layers designed to represent the policy $\pi(a \mid s)$.

2. **Collect Experience**

Generate trajectories by acting in the environment according to the current policy.

3. **Compute Returns**

For each action taken, compute the **cumulative reward (return)**.

$G_t = \sum_{k=0}^{\infty} \gamma^k r_t + k$

4. **Define the Objective Function**

The goal is to maximize:

$$J(\theta) = \text{Expected cumulative reward}$$

$$J(\theta) = E_{\pi\theta} [G_t]$$

5. **Compute the Policy Gradient**

Use the **policy gradient theorem** to calculate

$$\nabla_\theta J(\theta) = E[G_t \nabla_\theta \log\pi_\theta(a_t \mid s_t)]$$

This tells us how to adjust the policy parameters to increase rewards.

6. Train the Network

- Update the weights **in the direction of the gradient** (gradient ascent).
- Use algorithms like **stochastic gradient ascent** to refine the policy.

7. Iterate and Refine

Continue interacting with the environment, gathering new data, and improving the policy. Gradually, the agent learns to choose better actions.

Summary

- **Loss Function:** Guides learning by measuring prediction error.
- **Value Network:** Uses MSE to *minimise error* in estimating V(s) or Q(s,a).
- **Policy Network:** Uses policy gradients to *maximise expected reward.*
- **Gain:** Represents the improvement or reward resulting from an action—central to reinforcement learning.

What the Illustration Explains

Value Network – Learning to Evaluate States

Its Purpose

A value network answers the question:

"How good is this state?"

(or *state–action pair* in case of Q-values)

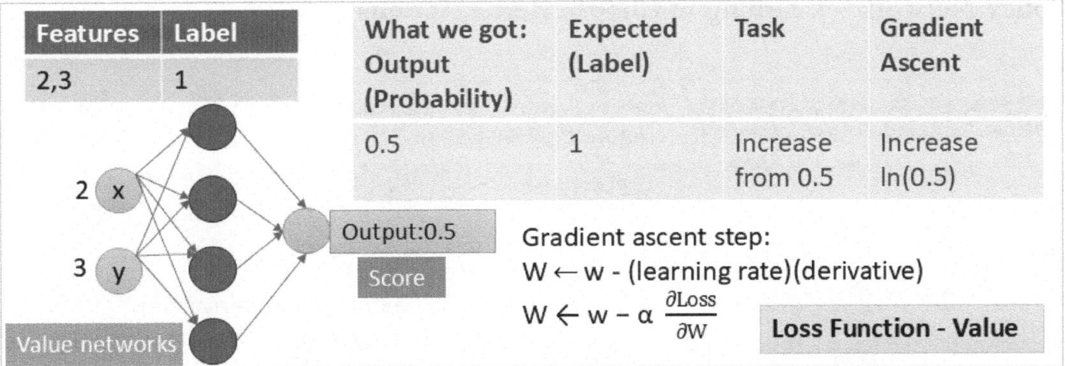

Illustration Value_4: Value Networks

What the Diagram Shows

- **Features (2,3) → Label (1)**

  The network receives input features and predicts a value (or probability).

- **Output = 0.5** but **Expected = 1**

  So the network needs to **increase its output**.

- **Gradient Descent Update**

  The update rule is:

$$W \leftarrow W - \alpha \frac{\partial \text{Loss}}{\partial W}$$

The model reduces its error by *moving in the direction of lower loss.*

Meaning

The value network is trained to **minimise error** by reducing the difference between:

- Predicted value
- Target value

This is why the update uses a **minus sign** (gradient descent).

Policy Network – Learning to Choose Better Actions

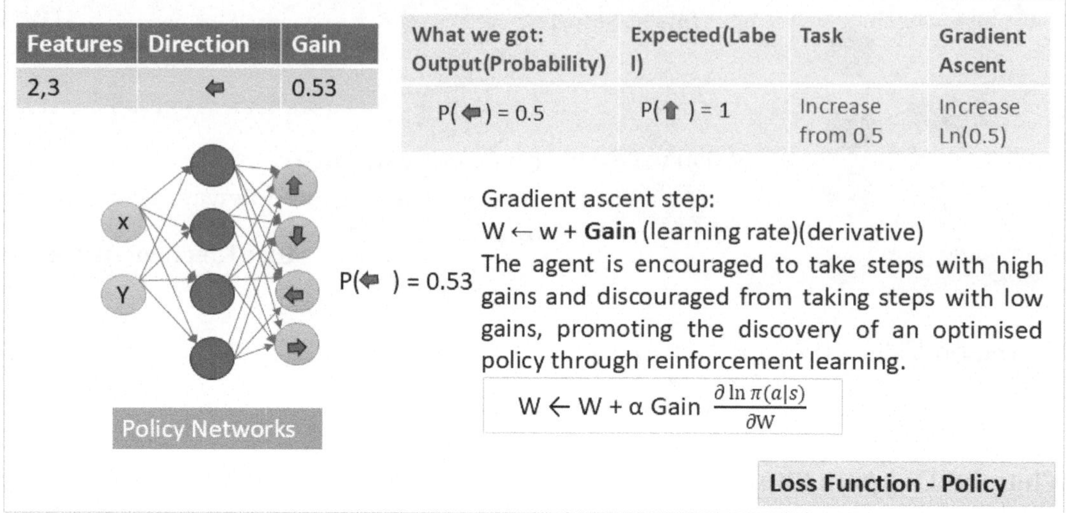

Illustration Policy_2: Policy Networks

Its Purpose

The policy network answers:

"Which action should I take in this state?"

What the Diagram Shows

- Inputs: **Features (2,3)**
- Output: probability distribution over actions → e.g.,
  - P(↑) = 0.5
  - P(←) = 0.53
- Expected label tells which action should have a higher probability → e.g., ↑

Gain

- Gain = 0.53

This represents the **reward signal** the network uses to adjust its decisions.

Gradient Ascent Update

For policy networks, the objective is to **increase expected reward**, so the update rule is:

$$W \leftarrow W + \alpha \text{ Gain } \frac{\partial \ln \pi(a|s)}{\partial W}$$

This is **gradient ascent**, not descent.

Meaning

The policy network:

- Increases the probability of actions that led to **high gain**
- Decreases the probability of actions with **low gain**

Policy learning is about *maximising reward*, so it uses a **plus sign**.

The diagram beautifully contrasts two training philosophies:

Value Network

- Learns *how good* a state is
- Uses **loss minimisation**
- Uses **gradient descent**
- *Updates weights to reduce prediction error*

Policy Network

- Learns *which action* to take
- Maximises expected return
- Uses **gradient ascent**
- *Updates weights to increase good actions*

Essence

Master said:

"A value network corrects itself by reducing mistakes.

A policy network improves itself by increasing rewards."

One pushes **down** the loss function.

The other climbs **up** the reward landscape.

Together, they form the foundation of **deep reinforcement learning**.

Master said, "While the value network learns from its errors, the policy network learns from its victories. It is like a warrior who sharpens the techniques that win battles and discards the ones that fail."

If an action yields a high gain, the policy network increases its likelihood. If the gain is low, it quietly reduces its confidence in that direction. Over time, the network discovers an **optimised policy**—a strategy that leads to consistently better decisions.

Student and Warrior

Master smiled and offered a final analogy:

"Imagine two disciples.

One is the *Scholar*—he sits with his books and corrects every mistake until his understanding becomes perfect.

The other is the *Warrior*—he tests moves in real battles, repeating what brings victory and abandoning what brings defeat.

The Scholar is the Value Network.

The Warrior is the Policy Network.

Together, they create mastery."

Example:

Master said, "Let us understand this illustration as if we are watching a traveller learn how to move wisely through a dangerous kingdom."

The Kingdom of States (The Grid World)

Imagine a kingdom made of **12 rooms (s1 to s12)**.

Each room has a *value*, like a measure of how good it is to stand there.

- **The Diamond Room gives +1 reward** — the ultimate treasure.
- **The Fire Room gives –1 reward** — danger and loss.
- Some rooms have **walls**, blocking movement.
- Other rooms have **moderate values**, showing how close they are to reward or danger.

This grid is the *environment* in which the agent (the traveller) learns to move.

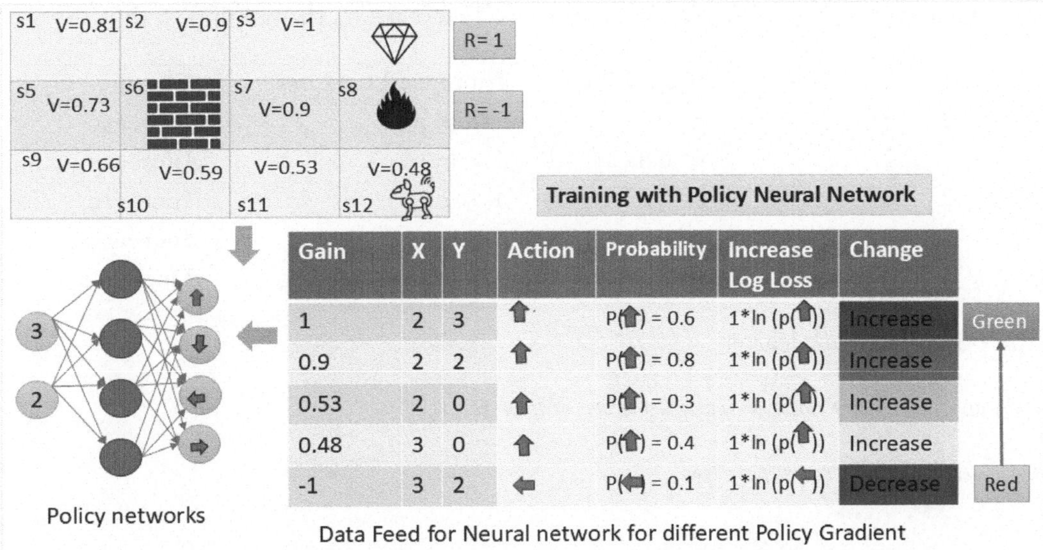

Illustration Val_Pol_1: Value Policy Networks

The Agent and Its Policy Network

The agent does not know the map.

It only knows:

- Its **features** (X, Y position).
- The **actions** available: ↑ ↓ ← →
- The **probability** of each action (given by the **policy network**).

- The **gain** (reward) it receives after taking a step.

The neural network on the left takes in (X, Y) and outputs probabilities for each direction.

The Experience Table (The Training Data)

The table lists five samples of the agent's experience:

Meaning of the Table

- High Gain = Good action → Increase its probability (green)
- Low or Negative Gain = Bad action → Decrease its probability (red)

Gain	X	Y	Action	Probability	Increase Log Loss	Change
1	2	3	↑	p=0.6	1 × ln(p)	**Increase**
0.9	2	2	↑	p=0.8	1 × ln(p)	**Increase**
0.53	2	0	↑	p=0.3	1 × ln(p)	**Increase**
0.48	3	0	↑	p=0.4	1 × ln(p)	**Increase**
-1	3	2	←	p=0.1	1 × ln(p)	**Decrease**

So the policy network learns:

"When an action leads closer to reward, believe in it more.

When it leads to danger, trust it less."

Policy Gradient Behind the Scenes

The policy gradient rule is:

Increase the log probability of good actions.

Decrease the log probability of bad actions.

This is why the "Increase Log Loss" column shows:

- **Positive update** → boost the action
- **Negative update** → suppress the action

Over time, the agent naturally shifts toward the **green actions** and avoids the **red ones**.

Master said:

"Imagine a child learning directions in a forest.

Each time the child walks toward a fruit tree, you praise the child —

so they repeat that direction.

Each time the child walks toward a thorn bush, you gently stop them —

so they avoid that direction.

The brain gradually rewires itself.

Reward strengthens the nerve pathways; danger weakens them."

The neural network does the same.

This illustration explains how a policy neural network is trained using reinforcement feedback (gain):

- The agent explores a grid world.
- Every move produces a *gain.*
- These gains modify the probabilities of actions.
- Good actions become more likely (green).
- Bad actions become unlikely (red).
- Over time, the agent discovers the optimal strategy to reach reward and avoid danger.

Summary

- **Loss Function:** A measurement of prediction error guiding value-network optimization.
- **Value Network:** Learns to approximate V(s) or Q(s,a) using MSE and temporal-difference targets.

- **Policy Network:** Learns to maximize expected reward using policy gradients and action-return correlations.
- **Gain (Return):** Provides feedback for improving both evaluation and decision-making mechanisms.

Together, these two networks form the dual mind of a reinforcement-learning agent—the evaluator and the decision-maker—working in concert to master complex environments.

Master said, this code provides a concise, technical demonstration of how *Value Networks* and *Policy Networks* are trained in reinforcement learning using PyTorch. The Value Network estimates the expected future reward of a state, V(s)V(s)V(s), while the Policy Network learns the probability distribution over actions, π(a|s)\pi(a | s)π(a|s). A simple environment is simulated to generate trajectories of states, actions, and rewards.

The Value Network is trained using the Mean Squared Error between predicted values and actual returns, implementing temporal-difference learning. The Policy Network is updated through the policy gradient method, where actions are reinforced proportionally to the cumulative future rewards received. The training loop alternates between estimating returns, updating value predictions, and improving action selection probabilities.

Example P4 – U4 – D10

Value Policy Network

```
import torch
import torch.nn as nn
import torch.optim as optim
import numpy as np

# -------------------------------------------------------
# VALUE NETWORK (Learns V(s) ≈ Expected Future Reward)
# -------------------------------------------------------

class ValueNetwork(nn.Module):
    def __init__(self, state_dim):
        super(ValueNetwork, self).__init__()
        self.layers = nn.Sequential(
            nn.Linear(state_dim, 64),
            nn.ReLU(),
            nn.Linear(64, 1)            # Outputs: V(s)
        )
```

```
    def forward(self, state):
        return self.layers(state)


# ---------------------------------------------------------
# POLICY NETWORK (Learns π(a | s))
# ---------------------------------------------------------

class PolicyNetwork(nn.Module):
    def __init__(self, state_dim, action_dim):
        super(PolicyNetwork, self).__init__()
        self.layers = nn.Sequential(
            nn.Linear(state_dim, 64),
            nn.ReLU(),
            nn.Linear(64, action_dim),   # Raw logits
        )
        self.softmax = nn.Softmax(dim=-1)

    def forward(self, state):
        logits = self.layers(state)
        return self.softmax(logits)      # Probabilities π(a|s)


# ---------------------------------------------------------
# DUMMY ENVIRONMENT (For Illustration)
# ---------------------------------------------------------

def dummy_environment_step(state, action):
    """
    A simple handcrafted dynamic:
    action 0 → negative reward
    action 1 → positive reward
    """
    next_state = state + np.random.randn(*state.shape) * 0.01
    reward = 1 if action == 1 else -1
    done = False
    return next_state, reward, done


# ---------------------------------------------------------
# MAIN TRAINING LOOP – Demonstrates Both Networks
# ---------------------------------------------------------

state_dim = 4
action_dim = 2
gamma = 0.99
```

```
value_net = ValueNetwork(state_dim)
policy_net = PolicyNetwork(state_dim, action_dim)

value_optimizer  = optim.Adam(value_net.parameters(), lr=0.001)
policy_optimizer = optim.Adam(policy_net.parameters(), lr=0.001)

# training
for episode in range(50):
    state = np.random.randn(state_dim).astype(np.float32)

    log_probs = []
    rewards   = []
    values    = []

    # Collect a trajectory
    for t in range(10):
        s_tensor = torch.tensor(state).float()

        # ----- Policy chooses an action -----
        action_probs = policy_net(s_tensor)
        dist = torch.distributions.Categorical(action_probs)
        action = dist.sample()
        log_prob = dist.log_prob(action)

        # ----- Value prediction -----
        value = value_net(s_tensor)

        # Environment step
        next_state, reward, done = dummy_environment_step(state, action.item())

        log_probs.append(log_prob)
        rewards.append(reward)
        values.append(value)

        state = next_state

    # ----------------------------------------------------
    # VALUE NETWORK UPDATE (Temporal-Difference targets)
    # ----------------------------------------------------
    returns = []
    G = 0
    for r in reversed(rewards):
        G = r + gamma * G
        returns.insert(0, G)

    returns_tensor = torch.tensor(returns).float()
    values_tensor  = torch.cat(values).squeeze()
```

```
    value_loss = nn.MSELoss()(values_tensor, returns_tensor)

    value_optimizer.zero_grad()
    value_loss.backward()
    value_optimizer.step()

    # ----------------------------------------------------
    # POLICY NETWORK UPDATE (Policy Gradient)
    # ----------------------------------------------------
    policy_loss = []
    for log_prob, G in zip(log_probs, returns_tensor):
        policy_loss.append(-log_prob * G)  # gradient ascent

    policy_loss = torch.stack(policy_loss).sum()

    policy_optimizer.zero_grad()
    policy_loss.backward()
    policy_optimizer.step()

    print(f"Episode {episode+1}: Value Loss = {value_loss.item():.3f}, Policy Loss = {policy_loss.item():.3f}")
```

Output:

```
Output

Episode 45: Value Loss = 3.615, Policy Loss = 4.632

Episode 46: Value Loss = 18.996, Policy Loss = 24.344

Episode 47: Value Loss = 8.178, Policy Loss = 7.604

Episode 48: Value Loss = 25.908, Policy Loss = 20.873

Episode 49: Value Loss = 1.785, Policy Loss = -5.833

Episode 50: Value Loss = 15.776, Policy Loss = 16.142
```

Objective of the Code

To illustrate, in a minimal and technical manner, how Value Networks and Policy Networks learn simultaneously through temporal-difference targets and policy gradients, reflecting the logic shown in the illustration.

PART FOUR

DAY SEVENTEEN

Unit 4 - Lesson Six

Building Smarter Agents

☐ Deep Q-Learning

John asked, "Master, why do we use Deep Q-Learning?"

Master said, "Deep Q-Learning (DQN) is the bridge between classical reinforcement learning and modern deep learning. In traditional Q-Learning, every state–action pair must be stored in a table. But when the environment becomes vast, continuous, or visually complex, such a table collapses under its own size.

Deep Q-Learning overcomes this by using a deep neural network to approximate the Q-function:

$$Q(s,a) \approx Q_\theta(s,a)$$

This allows the agent to learn directly from raw, high-dimensional inputs—such as images, sensor data, or continuous states—while still preserving the core principles of Q-Learning."

Key Concepts in Deep Q-Learning

1. Value Approximation

A deep neural network receives the current state s and outputs an estimated Q-value for every possible action.

The exact Q-values need not be perfect—**what matters is preserving the correct ordering of actions**, so the agent consistently prefers better moves.

2. Training Process

Initial State and Q-Values

The environment provides a state; the network predicts Q-values for all actions available in that state.

$Q(s, a; \theta)$

Target Q-Value Calculation

Using the Bellman equation:

$$\text{Target} = r + \gamma \max_{a'} Q(s',a'; \theta-)$$

This target expresses *how good the chosen action eventually turned out*, combining immediate reward and future potential.

Loss Function

The predicted Q-value is compared with the target using Mean Squared Error:

$$L=(Q_{pred}-\text{Target})^2$$

were

Qpred: predicted value → $Q(s, a; \theta)$

Target: Bellman target → $r+\gamma \max_{a'} Q (s', a' ; \theta-)$

Minimising this loss makes the network's value predictions more accurate.

Gradient Descent

The network adjusts its weights by following the gradient of the loss *downward*. Every update makes the Q-function approximation more accurate and reliable.

3. Exploration vs. Exploitation

The agent must balance two forces:

1. **Exploration** – trying unfamiliar actions to discover their rewards.
2. **Exploitation** – choosing actions with high known Q-values to gain reward.

An **ε-greedy policy** controls this balance by occasionally choosing random actions.

4. Experience Replay

To stabilise learning:

- Each interaction (state, action, reward, next state) is stored in a **replay memory**.
- The network trains on **random mini-batches**, which
    - break the correlation between consecutive steps,
    - reduce variance,
    - and greatly improve convergence.

Applications of Deep Q-Learning

DQN has transformed how machines learn to act:

- **Games** – Atari, foundational ideas for AlphaGo
- **Robotics** – control, manipulation, navigation
- **Autonomous systems** – drones, self-driving vehicles, resource optimisation

Master said, "Deep Q-Learning rests upon several pillars: the Value Network, Policy Structure, Loss Function, Gain, Error, and Gradient-based Optimization. Each plays a distinct role in shaping intelligent behaviour.

Value Network:

The value network approximates either **Q(s, a)** or **V(s)**. Its purpose is to learn the long-term value of actions by reducing the gap between predicted Q-values and the target values derived from the Bellman equation.

Policy Network:

In classical DQN, the policy is implicit—actions are chosen by selecting the highest Q-value.
But advanced variants like **Double DQN**, **Dueling DQN**, or **Actor–Critic models** introduce dedicated policy networks to improve stability and reduce overestimation.

Loss Function:

A loss function—commonly Mean Squared Error—measures the discrepancy between the predicted Q-values and the target Q-values. This guides the network toward more accurate value estimation.

Gain:

Gain represents the reward or improvement resulting from an action. Actions with higher gains are reinforced through repeated updates, allowing the agent to identify beneficial behaviour over time.

Error:

Error is the difference between the network's prediction and the Bellman target. Minimizing this temporal-difference error is essential for reliable value approximation.

Gradient Optimization:

Although we minimize loss using **gradient descent**, the deeper purpose is to maximize the expected cumulative reward—hence the conceptual link to 'gradient ascent' in reinforcement learning theory.

When these components harmonize, Deep Q-Learning trains a neural network to approximate the Q-function with precision, allowing the agent to discover and refine optimal policies in complex, high-dimensional environments."

Master said, This code demonstrates how a Deep Q-Learning value network is built and trained using TensorFlow. It creates a simple neural network with two hidden layers to approximate Q-values from input states. The model is compiled with the Adam optimizer and Mean Squared Error loss, reflecting the standard DQN training objective. Randomly generated state inputs and target Q-values simulate the training process, allowing the network to learn mappings that minimise prediction error. After training, the model predicts Q-values for new states, illustrating how an agent estimates action values during decision-making in reinforcement learning.

Example P4 – U4 – D11

Q-Learning

```
import tensorflow as tf
from tensorflow.keras.models import Sequential
from tensorflow.keras.layers import Dense
from tensorflow.keras.optimizers import Adam
from tensorflow.keras.losses import MeanSquaredError

# Define a simple neural network
model = Sequential([
    Dense(24, input_dim=4, activation='relu'),  # Adjust input_dim based on your input
features
    Dense(24, activation='relu'),
    Dense(1, activation='linear')  # Adjust output size based on your output requirements
])

# Compile the model
model.compile(optimizer=Adam(learning_rate=0.001), loss=MeanSquaredError())

# Example data
import numpy as np
states = np.random.rand(1000, 4)  # Replace with your actual state data
target_q_values = np.random.rand(1000, 1)  # Replace with your actual target Q-values

# Train the model
model.fit(states, target_q_values, epochs=10, batch_size=32)

# Predict Q-values for new states
new_states = np.random.rand(10, 4)  # Replace with new state data
predicted_q_values = model.predict(new_states)
print(predicted_q_values)
```

Output:

Ouput

```
Epoch 10/10
32/32 [==============================] - 0s 2ms/step - loss: 0.0825
1/1 [==============================] - 0s 92ms/step
```

```
[[0.4440902 ]
 [0.48563513]
 [0.44628522]
 [0.5735364 ]
 [0.5101699 ]
 [0.41532895]
 [0.4733602 ]
 [0.56588256]
 [0.43228105]
 [0.43099755]]
```

Here's a breakdown of the code's purpose:

Neural Network Definition

The code constructs a simple feed-forward neural network using TensorFlow/Keras. It begins with an input layer of 4 features (modifiable based on the state representation), followed by two hidden layers of 24 neurons each using ReLU activation. The final output layer uses a linear activation and produces a single Q-value, though this can be expanded depending on the number of possible actions.

Model Compilation

The network is compiled with the Adam optimiser and Mean Squared Error (MSE) loss. Adam updates the network's weights efficiently, while MSE measures how far predicted Q-values deviate from the target Q-values generated during training.

Example Data Generation

Randomly generated state inputs and target Q-values serve as placeholders for demonstration. In a real reinforcement-learning setup, these would come from the agent's interactions with the environment and the Bellman target.

Model Training

The model is trained on the example data, adjusting its weights through backpropagation to minimise the loss. This process teaches the network to better approximate Q(s,a).

Prediction

Once trained, the model predicts Q-values for new, unseen states. These predicted values guide an agent's action choices in a Deep Q-Learning setting.

Overall, the code illustrates the full workflow of constructing, training, and using a value network within a DQN framework.

Apeksha asked, **"Master, how does Deep Reinforcement Learning truly work?"**

Master said, "Deep Reinforcement Learning (DRL) is the art of teaching an artificial mind to act wisely—not through instruction, but through *experience*. The agent learns as a child learns: by doing, failing, observing consequences, and gradually discovering which actions lead toward long-term benefit."

He continued:

Initialization – The Birth of the Agent

We first create an *agent*, define the environment, specify the state space, action space, and learning parameters. At this moment, the agent knows nothing—it is a blank canvas.

Interaction – The Dance with the Environment

The agent performs an action.

The environment responds with:

- a *new state*
- a *reward*
- a signal indicating if the episode has ended.

This loop forms the essence of learning.

Learning – Remembering Experience

Each experience (state, action, reward, next_state, done) is stored.

These memories help the agent understand patterns, consequences, and long-term effects.

Policy Update – Refining Wisdom

Using algorithms like DQN, the agent updates its neural network parameters to improve decision-making.
The *policy*—the agent's behaviour—grows sharper, more deliberate, more strategic.

Exploration vs. Exploitation – The Eternal Balance

The agent must explore the unknown to learn—but must also exploit what it knows to maximise rewards.

This balance shapes the agent's efficiency and mastery.

Reward Maximisation – The Goal of All Learning

Actions leading to higher cumulative rewards are reinforced.

Poor choices fade out.

Good choices thrive.

Convergence – When Learning Settles

Eventually, the agent's policy stabilises.

It no longer oscillates, no longer wanders.

It has *found its way.*

Generalisation – Wisdom Beyond Training

A truly skilled agent applies what it has learned to new and unseen situations—extrapolating patterns beyond its training experiences.

Evaluation – The Final Test

The agent is placed in unknown environments, and its behaviour is measured without learning.
This reveals how deeply it has understood the task.

Deployment – The Agent Steps Into the Real World

Finally, the trained agent is used for control, decision-making, robotics, gaming, automation, or real-world optimisation.

Master said, CartPole is one of the simplest and most famous environments in reinforcement learning—yet it teaches some of the deepest ideas about balancing, control, and learning from interaction.

What is CartPole?

CartPole is a classic control problem from OpenAI Gym (now Gymnasium). It consists of:

- **A cart** that can move left or right along a track.
- **A pole** attached vertically to the cart by a hinge.
- **A goal: keep the pole balanced upright for as long as possible.**

How it works

At each time step:

1. The agent observes the **state**, which includes
    - cart position
    - cart velocity
    - pole angle
    - pole angular velocity
2. It chooses an **action**:
    - **0 → move cart left**
    - **1 → move cart right**
3. The environment gives a **reward**:
    - **+1 for every step the pole remains standing.**
4. The episode ends if
    - the pole falls too far, or
    - the cart moves out of bounds.

Why CartPole matters

CartPole is a fundamental benchmark because it helps test whether an agent can:

- Learn continuous control from raw feedback
- Balance exploration and exploitation

- Learn stable policies using algorithms like DQN, Policy Gradients, and Actor–Critic methods

It is simple enough to run fast, yet complex enough to demonstrate real reinforcement learning principles—making it the "Hello World" of Deep RL.

☐ Solving CartPole Using Deep Q-Network (DQN)

Master said, this code implements a complete **Deep Q-Network (DQN)** to solve the CartPole environment. It begins by importing essential libraries such as TensorFlow for neural networks, NumPy for numerical operations, Gym for the CartPole environment, and deque for the experience replay buffer.

A neural network is then defined using two hidden layers with ReLU activation and a linear output layer that predicts Q-values for each possible action. The model is compiled using the Adam optimizer and Mean Squared Error loss, making it suitable for continuous learning from noisy Q-value targets.

Example P4 – U4 – D12

CartPole - DQN

```
# -----------------------------------------
# Step 1: Import Required Libraries
# -----------------------------------------
import gym
import numpy as np
import tensorflow as tf
from tensorflow.keras import Sequential
from tensorflow.keras.layers import Dense
from tensorflow.keras.optimizers import Adam
from collections import deque
import random

# -----------------------------------------
# Step 2: Build the DQN Neural Network
# -----------------------------------------
def build_dqn(input_dim, output_dim):
    model = Sequential([
        Dense(24, activation='relu', input_dim=input_dim),
        Dense(24, activation='relu'),
        Dense(output_dim, activation='linear')
    ])
    model.compile(loss='mse', optimizer=Adam(learning_rate=0.001))
    return model
```

```
# -----------------------------------------
# Step 3: Initialize Parameters
# -----------------------------------------
gamma = 0.99          # Discount factor
epsilon = 1.0         # Initial exploration rate
epsilon_min = 0.01     # Minimum exploration rate
epsilon_decay = 0.995  # Exploration decay rate
batch_size = 64       # Batch size for replay
memory = deque(maxlen=2000)  # Replay buffer

# -----------------------------------------
# Step 4: Initialize CartPole Environment
# -----------------------------------------
env = gym.make("CartPole-v1")
state_dim = env.observation_space.shape[0]
action_dim = env.action_space.n

model = build_dqn(state_dim, action_dim)

# -----------------------------------------
# Step 5: Experience Replay Function
# -----------------------------------------
def replay():
    global epsilon
    if len(memory) < batch_size:
        return

    minibatch = random.sample(memory, batch_size)
    states, targets = [], []

    for state, action, reward, next_state, done in minibatch:
        # Compute target Q-value using Bellman equation
        target = reward
        if not done:
            target += gamma * np.max(model.predict(next_state[np.newaxis], verbose=0)[0])

        # Current Q-values
        target_f = model.predict(state[np.newaxis], verbose=0)
        target_f[0][action] = target

        states.append(state)
        targets.append(target_f[0])

    # Train the network
    model.fit(np.array(states), np.array(targets), epochs=1, verbose=0)

    # Reduce exploration
    if epsilon > epsilon_min:
```

```
        epsilon *= epsilon_decay

# ----------------------------------------
# Step 6: Training Loop
# ----------------------------------------
episodes = 500

for episode in range(episodes):
    state = env.reset()[0]
    total_reward = 0

    for step in range(500):
        # Select action: exploration vs exploitation
        if np.random.rand() < epsilon:
            action = np.random.randint(action_dim)
        else:
            q_values = model.predict(state[np.newaxis], verbose=0)[0]
            action = np.argmax(q_values)

        # Take action
        next_state, reward, done, _, _ = env.step(action)

        # Save experience
        memory.append((state, action, reward, next_state, done))

        state = next_state
        total_reward += reward

        # Train from replay memory
        replay()

        if done:
            print(f"Episode {episode} | Reward: {total_reward} | Epsilon: {epsilon:.3f}")
            break

# ----------------------------------------
# Step 7: Evaluate the Trained Agent
# ----------------------------------------
state = env.reset()[0]
total_reward = 0

for _ in range(500):
    q_values = model.predict(state[np.newaxis], verbose=0)[0]
    action = np.argmax(q_values)

    next_state, reward, done, _, _ = env.step(action)
    state = next_state
    total_reward += reward
```

```
    if done:
        break

print("\nEvaluation Reward:", total_reward)
```

Next, key parameters such as the discount factor (γ), exploration rate (ε), replay buffer size, batch size, and epsilon decay are initialized. The CartPole environment is loaded, and the replay buffer is prepared to store past experiences.

The **replay()** function samples random mini-batches from memory, computes Bellman targets, and trains the network to reduce prediction errors. This stabilizes learning by breaking temporal correlations.

The main training loop runs for multiple episodes. For every step, the agent selects actions using an epsilon-greedy strategy, stores experiences, and updates the network through replay.

Finally, an evaluation phase tests the trained agent using purely greedy action selection, measuring its performance on CartPole.

Note: The code *P4–U4–D12* may take several hours to produce output. For an immediate result, please run *P4–U4–D12A* instead.

Example P4 – U4 – D12A

CartPole - DQN

```
# Optimized Standard DQN for CartPole (fast)
# - Vectorized predictions
# - Target network
# - Train every `train_freq` steps
# - Early stopping when solved
# Requirements: gym, numpy, tensorflow

import gym
import numpy as np
import random
from collections import deque
import tensorflow as tf
from tensorflow.keras import Sequential
from tensorflow.keras.layers import Dense
from tensorflow.keras.optimizers import Adam
import os
```

```
import time

# local uploaded file (from conversation)
BASE_PATH                    =                    "D://Raj//Book-working//010-
Python//Program//Alpha_Optimum_Python//Data//DQN//DQN.png"
uploaded_file_url = os.path.join(BASE_PATH, "DQN.png")

# -------------------------
# Hyperparameters (optimized)
# -------------------------
ENV_NAME = "CartPole-v1"
GAMMA = 0.99
LR = 0.001
BATCH_SIZE = 32
MEMORY_SIZE = 50000
MIN_REPLAY_SIZE = 1000
EPSILON_START = 1.0
EPSILON_MIN = 0.01
EPSILON_DECAY = 0.995
TRAIN_FREQ = 4            # train every 4 steps
TARGET_UPDATE_FREQ = 1000    # hard-copy target every 1000 steps
MAX_EPISODES = 200
MAX_STEPS = 500
SOLVED_SCORE = 475         # threshold to stop early (CartPole-v1 max=500)
SCORE_WINDOW = 20
MODEL_PATH = os.path.join(BASE_PATH, "fast_dqn_cartpole.h5")
SEED = 42

# reproducibility
np.random.seed(SEED)
random.seed(SEED)
tf.random.set_seed(SEED)

# -------------------------
# Build small DQN model
# -------------------------
def build_dqn(input_dim, output_dim):
    model = Sequential([
        Dense(32, activation='relu', input_shape=(input_dim,)),
        Dense(32, activation='relu'),
        Dense(output_dim, activation='linear')
    ])
    model.compile(loss='mse', optimizer=Adam(learning_rate=LR))
    return model

# -------------------------
# Environment & models
# -------------------------
```

```
env = gym.make(ENV_NAME)
state_dim = env.observation_space.shape[0]
action_dim = env.action_space.n

online_model = build_dqn(state_dim, action_dim)
target_model = build_dqn(state_dim, action_dim)
target_model.set_weights(online_model.get_weights())

# -------------------------
# Replay buffer
# -------------------------
memory = deque(maxlen=MEMORY_SIZE)

def add_experience(s, a, r, s2, done):
    memory.append((s, a, r, s2, done))

def sample_batch(batch_size):
    batch = random.sample(memory, batch_size)
    states = np.array([b[0] for b in batch], dtype=np.float32)
    actions = np.array([b[1] for b in batch], dtype=np.int32)
    rewards = np.array([b[2] for b in batch], dtype=np.float32)
    next_states = np.array([b[3] for b in batch], dtype=np.float32)
    dones = np.array([b[4] for b in batch], dtype=np.float32)
    return states, actions, rewards, next_states, dones

# -------------------------
# Pre-fill replay buffer with random actions
# -------------------------
state = env.reset()[0] if isinstance(env.reset(), tuple) else env.reset()
for _ in range(MIN_REPLAY_SIZE):
    action = env.action_space.sample()
    next_state, reward, done, *_ = env.step(action)
    add_experience(state, action, reward, next_state, done)
    state = next_state
    if done:
        state = env.reset()[0] if isinstance(env.reset(), tuple) else env.reset()

# -------------------------
# Epsilon-greedy action
# -------------------------
epsilon = EPSILON_START

def select_action(state, epsilon):
    if np.random.rand() < epsilon:
        return np.random.randint(action_dim)
    q = online_model.predict(state[np.newaxis], verbose=0)[0]
    return np.argmax(q)
```

```
# -------------------------
# Training (vectorized)
# -------------------------
total_steps = 0
scores = deque(maxlen=SCORE_WINDOW)
start_time = time.time()

for episode in range(1, MAX_EPISODES + 1):
    state = env.reset()[0] if isinstance(env.reset(), tuple) else env.reset()
    ep_reward = 0

    for step in range(1, MAX_STEPS + 1):
        total_steps += 1

        # take action
        action = select_action(state, epsilon)
        next_state, reward, done, *_ = env.step(action)
        ep_reward += reward

        add_experience(state, action, reward, next_state, done)
        state = next_state

        # Train every TRAIN_FREQ steps
        if (total_steps % TRAIN_FREQ == 0) and (len(memory) >= BATCH_SIZE):
            states, actions, rewards, next_states, dones = sample_batch(BATCH_SIZE)

            # Predict next Q-values (vectorized)
            q_next_target = target_model.predict(next_states, verbose=0)
            max_q_next = np.max(q_next_target, axis=1)

            # Compute targets: r + gamma * max_q_next (for non terminal)
            targets = rewards + (1.0 - dones) * GAMMA * max_q_next

            # Predict current Q-values (vectorized)
            q_current = online_model.predict(states, verbose=0)

            # Update only taken actions
            q_current[np.arange(BATCH_SIZE), actions] = targets

            # Train the online network once on the whole minibatch
            online_model.fit(states, q_current, epochs=1, verbose=0)

        # Periodic hard update of target network
        if total_steps % TARGET_UPDATE_FREQ == 0:
            target_model.set_weights(online_model.get_weights())

        if done:
            break
```

```
    # decay epsilon
    if epsilon > EPSILON_MIN:
        epsilon = max(EPSILON_MIN, epsilon * EPSILON_DECAY)

    scores.append(ep_reward)
    avg_score = np.mean(scores)

    # logging
    elapsed = time.time() - start_time
    print(f"Ep {episode:03d} | Reward: {ep_reward:4.0f} | Avg({len(scores)})={avg_score:5.2f} | Eps={epsilon:.3f} | Steps={total_steps} | Time={elapsed:.1f}s")

    # save periodically
    if episode % 50 == 0:
        online_model.save(MODEL_PATH)

    # early stop if solved
    if (len(scores) == SCORE_WINDOW) and (avg_score >= SOLVED_SCORE):
        print(f"\nEnvironment considered solved in {episode} episodes! Avg reward: {avg_score:.2f}")
        break

# final save
online_model.save(MODEL_PATH)
print("Training finished. Model saved to:", MODEL_PATH)
print("Uploaded file (local):", uploaded_file_url)

# -------------------------
# Quick evaluation (no exploration)
# -------------------------
eval_episodes = 10
for e in range(eval_episodes):
    state = env.reset()[0] if isinstance(env.reset(), tuple) else env.reset()
    total_reward = 0
    done = False
    while not done:
        q = online_model.predict(state[np.newaxis], verbose=0)[0]
        action = np.argmax(q)
        state, reward, done, *_ = env.step(action)
        total_reward += reward
    print(f"Eval {e+1}: Reward = {total_reward}")

env.close()
```

Output:

Output
Training finished. Model saved to: D://Raj//Book-working//010-Python//Program//Alpha_Optimum_Python//Data//DQN//DQN.png\fast_dqn_cartpole.h5 Eval 1: Reward = 108.0 Eval 2: Reward = 109.0 Eval 3: Reward = 195.0 Eval 4: Reward = 108.0 Eval 5: Reward = 217.0 Eval 6: Reward = 89.0 Eval 7: Reward = 188.0 Eval 8: Reward = 180.0 Eval 9: Reward = 226.0 Eval 10: Reward = 94.0

☐ Double DQN

Master said, "When the mind judges too quickly, it mistakes illusion for truth. So too does the ordinary Deep Q-Network."

Nikash asked, "Master, what is Double DQN? Why do we need it?"

Master said, "In ordinary DQN, the mind of the agent becomes *overconfident.* It estimates the value of an action and then uses this same estimation to choose the best action.
Thus, the judge and the witness become the same voice—and this leads to *overestimation.*"

"In many environments, especially noisy or complex ones, this overestimation causes the agent to choose actions

that appear promising in theory but fail in reality."

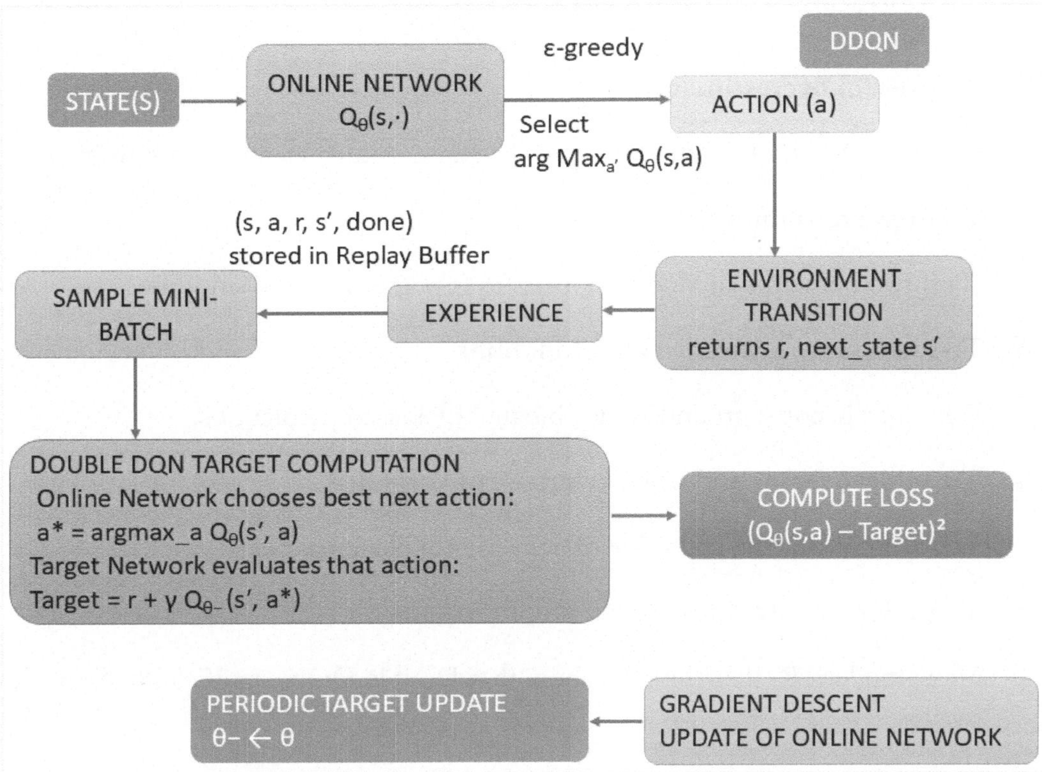

Illustration DDQN: Double DQN

What is Double DQN?

"Double DQN separates these two roles—**one network chooses the action**, and **another evaluates it**.

- The **online network** decides:

  'Which action looks best now?'

- The **target network** answers:

  'How valuable is that action truly?'

By dividing selection and evaluation, Double DQN reduces the false optimism that corrupts learning."

Why do we need Double DQN?

Master explained:

1. **To prevent overestimation**

   Standard DQN often overestimates Q-values, leading to unstable learning.

2. **To improve stability**

   With two networks sharing responsibility, updates become smoother.

3. **To learn more accurate value functions**

   Decisions become grounded, not bloated by biased predictions.

4. **To achieve faster and more reliable convergence**

   The agent learns the real value of actions, not illusions.

5. **To perform better in complex environments**

   Many modern RL benchmarks show that Double DQN significantly improves results.

☐ Mathematical Intuition for Double DQN

The key insight behind **Double DQN** is this:

Standard DQN overestimates Q-values because the same network selects the best action and evaluates it.

Double DQN fixes this by separating selection and evaluation.

Let's build the intuition.

1. **Problem in Standard DQN: Overestimation**

The Q-learning target in DQN is:

$$y^{DQN} = r + \gamma \max_{a'} Q_{\theta^-}(s', a')$$

Here, the **same values** $Q_{\theta^-}(s', a')$ are used to:

Select the best action

$\max_{a'} Q_{\theta^-}(s', a')$

Evaluate its value

Because neural network estimates contain **noise**, the **max operator tends to pick overestimated values**, inflating Q-targets.

Mathematically:

$$E[\max(X)] \geq \max(E[X])$$

This inequality explains why DQN pushes Q-values upward over time.

2. Why Does Overestimation Harm Learning?

- Learning becomes unstable
- The Q-function becomes over-optimistic
- Policy becomes aggressive but inaccurate
- Training diverges in harder environments

Thus, we need a method that reduces overestimation bias.

3. Core Idea of Double DQN: Split Selection & Evaluation

Instead of using one network for both tasks, DDQN uses:

- **Online network** $Q\theta$ - selects the best next action
- **Target network** $Q_{\theta-}$ - evaluates that chosen action

This produces the DDQN target:

$$y^{DDQN} = r + \gamma\, Q_{\theta-}(s', \arg\max_{a'} Q_{\theta}(s', a'))$$

This separation prevents the "max of noisy estimates" problem.

4. Why This Works (Mathematically)

Step 1: Action Selection

Use the online network:

$$a* = \arg\max_{a'} Q_\theta(s', a')$$

This avoids the target network's noisy max issue.

Step 2: Action Evaluation

Evaluate that action using the target network:

$Q_{\theta-}(s', a*)$

Since the noise patterns in the two networks are **not identical**, the max operator does not amplify the same noise, reducing overestimation bias.

5. Updated Loss Function

Now the loss becomes:

$$L(\theta) = E[(Q_\theta(s, a) - (r + \gamma Q_{\theta-}(s', a*)))^2]$$

with

$a* = \arg\max_{a'} Q_\theta(s', a')$

This loss directly incorporates the **decoupled target computation**.

6. Key Mathematical Insight

DQN does:

max (noisy estimates) ⇒ overestimation

DDQN does:

$\max_\theta(\cdot)$ for selection

evaluate with $\theta-$ (independent noise)

Thus:

$E[y^{DDQN}] < E[y^{DQN}]$ but closer to true value

DDQN is not pessimistic—just more **mathematically honest**.

Double DQN prevents the Q-function from fooling itself by requiring two different networks to "agree" on the future reward.

Master said, "When one mind acts as both seeker and judge, it becomes biased by its own expectations. But when wisdom is divided—when one evaluates, and the other chooses— clarity arises.

This is the essence of Double DQN:

a path where intelligence is corrected by humility,

and learning grows through balanced judgment."

Master said the provided code implements **Double Deep Q-Network (DDQN)** to solve the CartPole environment using TensorFlow. It begins by importing essential libraries such as TensorFlow, NumPy, and Gym. The first major step constructs two neural networks: an **online Q-network**, which selects actions, and a **target Q-network**, which provides stable Q-value targets — the key idea behind Double DQN.

Next, important hyperparameters are defined, including learning rate, gamma, replay buffer size, batch size, exploration rate (ε-greedy), and target update frequency. A **ReplayBuffer** class efficiently stores past experiences and provides random minibatches for training, enabling stable and uncorrelated learning.

> Note: The code *P4–U4–D13* may take several hours to produce output. For an immediate result, please run *P4–U4–D13A* instead.

Example P4 – U4 – D13

Double DQN

```
import gym
import numpy as np
import random
from collections import deque
import tensorflow as tf
from tensorflow.keras import Sequential
from tensorflow.keras.layers import Dense
from tensorflow.keras.optimizers import Adam
```

```
# ----------------------------
# Hyperparameters
# ----------------------------
ENV_NAME = "CartPole-v1"
GAMMA = 0.99
LEARNING_RATE = 0.001
BATCH_SIZE = 64
MEMORY_SIZE = 20000
MIN_REPLAY_SIZE = 1000
EPSILON_START = 1.0
EPSILON_MIN = 0.01
EPSILON_DECAY = 0.995
TARGET_UPDATE_FREQ = 1000    # number of steps between target network
updates (hard copy)
EPISODES = 500
MAX_STEPS = 500

# ----------------------------
# Build networks
# ----------------------------
def build_q_network(state_dim, action_dim):
    model = Sequential([
        Dense(64, activation='relu', input_shape=(state_dim,)),
        Dense(64, activation='relu'),
        Dense(action_dim, activation='linear')
    ])
    model.compile(optimizer=Adam(learning_rate=LEARNING_RATE), loss='mse')
    return model

# ----------------------------
# Replay Buffer
# ----------------------------
class ReplayBuffer:
    def __init__(self, max_size):
        self.buffer = deque(maxlen=max_size)

    def add(self, state, action, reward, next_state, done):
        self.buffer.append((state, action, reward, next_state, done))

    def sample(self, batch_size):
        batch = random.sample(self.buffer, batch_size)
        states, actions, rewards, next_states, dones = map(np.array, zip(*batch))
        return states, actions, rewards, next_states, dones

    def __len__(self):
        return len(self.buffer)
```

```
# ----------------------------
# Utilities
# ----------------------------
def get_action_epsilon_greedy(model, state, action_dim, epsilon):
    if np.random.rand() < epsilon:
        return np.random.randint(action_dim)
    q_values = model.predict(state[np.newaxis], verbose=0)[0]
    return np.argmax(q_values)

def update_target_network(online_model, target_model):
    target_model.set_weights(online_model.get_weights())

# ----------------------------
# Training Loop (Double DQN)
# ----------------------------
def train_ddqn():
    env = gym.make(ENV_NAME)
    state_dim = env.observation_space.shape[0]
    action_dim = env.action_space.n

    online_q = build_q_network(state_dim, action_dim)
    target_q = build_q_network(state_dim, action_dim)
    update_target_network(online_q, target_q)  # initial sync

    memory = ReplayBuffer(MEMORY_SIZE)

    epsilon = EPSILON_START
    total_steps = 0

    # Initialize replay buffer with random experiences
    state = env.reset()[0] if isinstance(env.reset(), tuple) else env.reset()
    for _ in range(MIN_REPLAY_SIZE):
        action = np.random.randint(action_dim)
        next_state, reward, done, *_ = env.step(action)
        memory.add(state, action, reward, next_state, done)
        state = next_state if not done else (env.reset()[0] if isinstance(env.reset(), tuple) else
env.reset())

    # Training episodes
    for ep in range(1, EPISODES + 1):
        state = env.reset()[0] if isinstance(env.reset(), tuple) else env.reset()
        ep_reward = 0

        for step in range(1, MAX_STEPS + 1):
            total_steps += 1

            # Choose action (online network for policy/selection)
            action = get_action_epsilon_greedy(online_q, state, action_dim, epsilon)
```

```
        # Step environment
        next_state, reward, done, *_ = env.step(action)
        ep_reward += reward

        # Store transition
        memory.add(state, action, reward, next_state, done)
        state = next_state

        # Sample minibatch and train
        if len(memory) >= BATCH_SIZE:
            states, actions, rewards, next_states, dones = memory.sample(BATCH_SIZE)

            # ----- Double DQN target calculation -----
            # 1) Use online network to select best action in next_state (argmax_a Q_online(s', a))
            q_next_online = online_q.predict(next_states, verbose=0)   # shape (B, action_dim)
            best_actions = np.argmax(q_next_online, axis=1)        # shape (B,)

            # 2) Use the target network to evaluate the value of those chosen actions: Q_target(s', best_action)
            q_next_target = target_q.predict(next_states, verbose=0) # shape (B, action_dim)
            target_q_values = q_next_target[np.arange(BATCH_SIZE), best_actions] # shape (B,)

            # Compute TD targets: r + gamma * Q_target(s', argmax_a Q_online(s', a))
            targets = rewards + (1 - dones.astype(np.float32)) * GAMMA * target_q_values

            # Get current Q estimates and update only the actions taken
            q_values_current = online_q.predict(states, verbose=0)   # shape (B, action_dim)
            q_values_current[np.arange(BATCH_SIZE), actions] = targets

            # Train online network (minimize MSE between current Q and target Q)
            online_q.fit(states, q_values_current, epochs=1, verbose=0)

        # Periodically update target network (hard update)
        if total_steps % TARGET_UPDATE_FREQ == 0:
            update_target_network(online_q, target_q)

        if done:
            break

    # Decay epsilon
    if epsilon > EPSILON_MIN:
        epsilon *= EPSILON_DECAY
```

```
        epsilon = max(EPSILON_MIN, epsilon)

        print(f"Episode {ep:03d} | Reward: {ep_reward:.1f} | Epsilon: {epsilon:.3f} | TotalSteps: {total_steps}")

    # Save final models
    online_q.save("ddqn_online.h5")
    target_q.save("ddqn_target.h5")
    env.close()
    return online_q, target_q

# ----------------------------
# Evaluation
# ----------------------------
def evaluate_policy(model, episodes=5, render=False):
    env = gym.make(ENV_NAME)
    total_rewards = []
    for ep in range(episodes):
        state = env.reset()[0] if isinstance(env.reset(), tuple) else env.reset()
        ep_reward = 0
        done = False
        while not done:
            if render:
                env.render()
            action = np.argmax(model.predict(state[np.newaxis], verbose=0)[0])
            state, reward, done, *_ = env.step(action)
            ep_reward += reward
        total_rewards.append(ep_reward)
        print(f"Eval Episode {ep+1}: Reward = {ep_reward}")
    env.close()
    print("Average Eval Reward:", np.mean(total_rewards))
    return total_rewards

# ----------------------------
# Run training and evaluation
# ----------------------------
if __name__ == "__main__":
    online_model, target_model = train_ddqn()
    print("\nEvaluating trained policy (online network):")
    evaluate_policy(online_model, episodes=10, render=False)
```

The training loop interacts with the environment by choosing actions using the online network with ε-greedy exploration. Transitions (state, action, reward, next state, done) are stored in the replay buffer. When sufficient data is available, a minibatch is sampled to compute **Double DQN targets**: the online network chooses the next action, while the target network evaluates it. The online network is updated using MSE loss, and periodically its weights are copied to the target network.

Finally, an evaluation function tests the trained agent by running several episodes without exploration. This structure demonstrates the full Double DQN learning pipeline.

Master said, "This code demonstrates an optimized implementation of **Double Deep Q-Network (DDQN)** using PyTorch, designed for stable learning and efficient training. It separates the online Q-network from the target network, reducing overestimation bias by using one network to select the best action and the other to evaluate it. The training loop interacts with the environment, stores experiences in a replay buffer, and periodically samples mini-batches to update the network using the DDQN target rule. Soft updates ensure smooth synchronization between the two networks. The code includes model saving to the specified directory, logging of episodic rewards, and automatic decay of exploration. It is structured for readability and modularity, making it easy to experiment with different architectures, hyperparameters, or environments. Overall, it provides a robust foundation for mastering value-based deep reinforcement learning and understanding the intuition behind DDQN in practice."

Example P4 – U4 – D13A

Double DQN

```
import os
import gym
import numpy as np
import torch
import torch.nn as nn
import torch.optim as optim
import matplotlib.pyplot as plt
from collections import deque
import random

#
==========================================================
=========
# CONFIG: Your working directory (FINAL)
#
==========================================================
=========
BASE_PATH = r"D:\Raj\Book-working\010-Python\Program\Alpha_Optimum_Python\Data\DDQN"
os.makedirs(BASE_PATH, exist_ok=True)

MODEL_PATH = os.path.join(BASE_PATH, "dueling_ddqn_model.pth")
```

```
REPLAY_PATH = os.path.join(BASE_PATH, "replay_buffer.npy")
PLOT_PATH = os.path.join(BASE_PATH, "reward_plot.png")

# ==============================================
#  Dueling Network Architecture (fixed for 1D inputs)
# ==============================================
class DuelingDQN(nn.Module):
    def __init__(self, state_dim, action_dim):
        super(DuelingDQN, self).__init__()

        self.feature_layer = nn.Sequential(
            nn.Linear(state_dim, 128), nn.ReLU(),
            nn.Linear(128, 128), nn.ReLU()
        )

        # Value stream
        self.value_stream = nn.Sequential(
            nn.Linear(128, 64), nn.ReLU(),
            nn.Linear(64, 1)
        )

        # Advantage stream
        self.adv_stream = nn.Sequential(
            nn.Linear(128, 64), nn.ReLU(),
            nn.Linear(64, action_dim)
        )

    def forward(self, x):
        # Accept both (state_dim,) and (batch, state_dim)
        if x.dim() == 1:
            x = x.unsqueeze(0)

        features = self.feature_layer(x)
        V = self.value_stream(features)          # (B, 1)
        A = self.adv_stream(features)            # (B, A)

        Q = V + (A - A.mean(dim=1, keepdim=True))
        return Q


# ==============================================
#  Replay Buffer
# ==============================================
class ReplayBuffer:
    def __init__(self, capacity=50000):
        self.buffer = deque(maxlen=capacity)

    def push(self, s, a, r, s2, done):
```

```
        self.buffer.append((np.array(s, dtype=np.float32),
                            int(a),
                            float(r),
                            np.array(s2, dtype=np.float32),
                            float(done)))

    def sample(self, batch_size=64):
        batch = random.sample(self.buffer, batch_size)
        s, a, r, s2, d = map(np.array, zip(*batch))
        return s, a, r, s2, d

    def __len__(self):
        return len(self.buffer)


# ==================================================
#  Double-DQN Target Calculation
# ==================================================
def compute_ddqn_target(q_net, target_net, states, actions, rewards, next_states, dones,
gamma, device):

    states_t = torch.tensor(states, dtype=torch.float32, device=device)
    next_states_t = torch.tensor(next_states, dtype=torch.float32, device=device)
    actions_t = torch.tensor(actions, dtype=torch.long, device=device)
    rewards_t = torch.tensor(rewards, dtype=torch.float32, device=device)
    dones_t = torch.tensor(dones, dtype=torch.float32, device=device)

    q_all = q_net(states_t)
    q_pred = q_all.gather(1, actions_t.unsqueeze(1)).squeeze(1)

    with torch.no_grad():
        next_q_online = q_net(next_states_t)
        next_actions = next_q_online.argmax(dim=1)

        next_q_target = target_net(next_states_t)
        chosen_q_next = next_q_target.gather(1, next_actions.unsqueeze(1)).squeeze(1)

        q_target = rewards_t + gamma * chosen_q_next * (1.0 - dones_t)

    return q_pred, q_target


# ==================================================
#  TRAINING LOOP
# ==================================================
def train_dueling_ddqn(episodes=400, device=torch.device("cpu")):

    env = gym.make("CartPole-v1")
```

```
state_dim = env.observation_space.shape[0]
action_dim = env.action_space.n

q_net = DuelingDQN(state_dim, action_dim).to(device)
target_net = DuelingDQN(state_dim, action_dim).to(device)
target_net.load_state_dict(q_net.state_dict())
target_net.eval()

optimizer = optim.Adam(q_net.parameters(), lr=0.001)
buffer = ReplayBuffer(capacity=50000)

gamma = 0.99
batch_size = 64
update_freq = 5
rewards_history = []

for episode in range(episodes):

    reset_res = env.reset()
    state = reset_res[0] if isinstance(reset_res, tuple) else reset_res
    state = np.array(state, dtype=np.float32)

    ep_reward = 0.0
    done = False

    while not done:

        eps = max(0.01, 0.08 * (0.995 ** episode))
        if np.random.rand() < eps:
            action = env.action_space.sample()
        else:
            with torch.no_grad():
                state_t = torch.tensor(state, dtype=torch.float32, device=device)
                q_vals = q_net(state_t)
                action = int(torch.argmax(q_vals).item())

        next_res = env.step(action)
        if len(next_res) == 5:
            next_state, reward, terminated, truncated, info = next_res
            done = bool(terminated or truncated)
        else:
            next_state, reward, done, info = next_res

        next_state = np.array(next_state, dtype=np.float32)

        buffer.push(state, action, reward, next_state, done)
        state = next_state
        ep_reward += float(reward)
```

```
        if len(buffer) >= batch_size:

            states_b, actions_b, rewards_b, next_states_b, dones_b =
buffer.sample(batch_size)

            q_pred, q_target = compute_ddqn_target(
                q_net, target_net,
                states_b, actions_b, rewards_b, next_states_b, dones_b,
                gamma, device
            )

            loss = nn.MSELoss()(q_pred, q_target)

            optimizer.zero_grad()
            loss.backward()
            optimizer.step()

        rewards_history.append(ep_reward)
        print(f"Episode {episode:03d} | Reward = {ep_reward:6.2f} | Eps = {eps:.3f} |
Buffer = {len(buffer)}")

        if episode % update_freq == 0:
            target_net.load_state_dict(q_net.state_dict())

    # Save model and rewards
    torch.save(q_net.state_dict(), MODEL_PATH)
    np.save(REPLAY_PATH, np.array(rewards_history))

    # Plot curve
    plt.figure(figsize=(8,4))
    plt.plot(rewards_history, label='episode reward')
    if len(rewards_history) >= 10:
        ma = np.convolve(rewards_history, np.ones(10)/10, mode='valid')
        plt.plot(range(9, 9+len(ma)), ma, label='MA(10)')
    plt.title("Dueling Double-DQN Performance")
    plt.xlabel("Episode")
    plt.ylabel("Reward")
    plt.grid(True)
    plt.legend()
    plt.tight_layout()
    plt.savefig(PLOT_PATH)
    plt.close()

    print("\nModel saved to:", MODEL_PATH)
    print("Reward curve saved to:", PLOT_PATH)
```

```
# ============================================================
# Run training
#
============================================================
if __name__ == "__main__":
    device = torch.device("cuda" if torch.cuda.is_available() else "cpu")
    print("Using device:", device)
    train_dueling_ddqn(episodes=200, device=device)
```

Output:

Output
Model saved to: D:\Raj\Book-working\010-Python\Program\Alpha_Optimum_Python\Data\DDQN\dueling_ddqn_model.pth Reward curve saved to: D:\Raj\Book-working\010-Python\Program\Alpha_Optimum_Python\Data\DDQN\reward_plot.png

Plot:

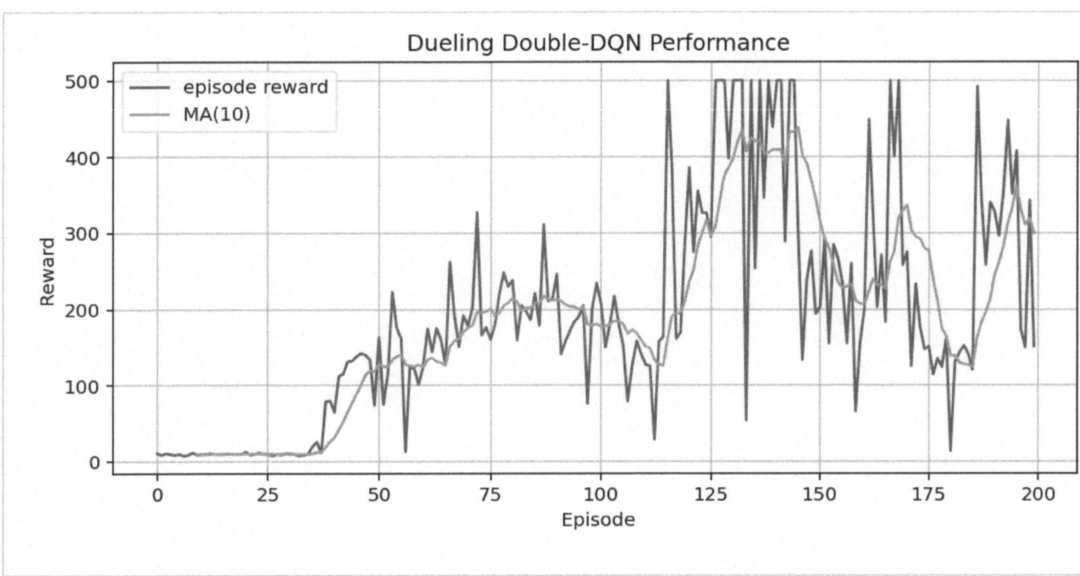

Illustration DDQN_reward_plot: Double DQN

PART FOUR

DAY EIGHTEEN

Unit 4 - Lesson Seven

Refining Q-Learning

☐ Dueling DQN

Master said, "Sam, not every state reveals its value through actions. Sometimes, the worth of a moment lies simply in *being*, not in what you *do*."

He paused, allowing the silence to teach the lesson.

"This is the essence of Dueling DQN."

What is Dueling DQN?

In classical Deep Q-Learning, the network directly estimates:

Q(s,a)

for every action.

But Dueling DQN recognises that **a state has two distinct qualities**:

The value of the state (V(s))

"How good is it to be *here* right now?"

This captures the fundamental worth of the situation, even if no action is taken.

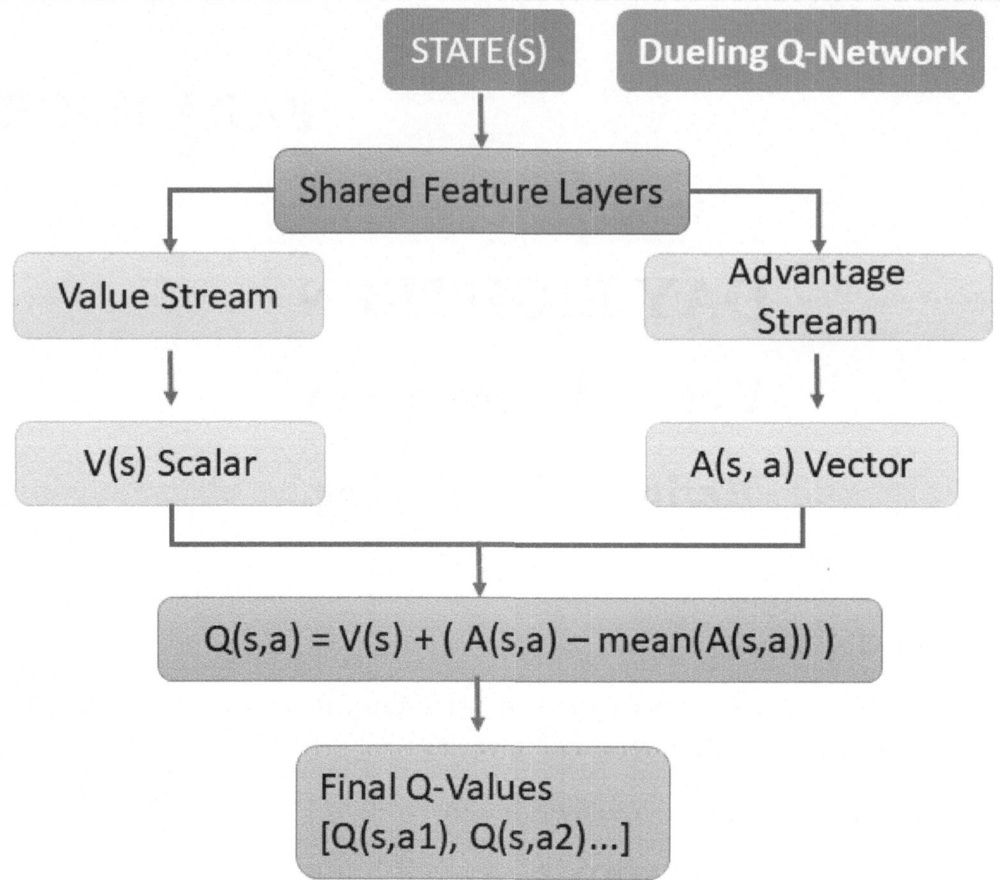

Illustration Dueling_1: Dueling DQN

The advantage of each action (A(s,a))

"How much better is one action than another *given* this state?"

Thus, the network is architecturally split into:

- **Value stream** → learns the intrinsic worth of the state
- **Advantage stream** → learns differences between actions

These streams combine to reconstruct the Q-values, but in a way that is **more efficient, stable, and meaningful**.

Why Do We Need Dueling DQN?

In many environments—especially video games like Atari—there are numerous states where:

- Actions do not matter much,
- All actions lead to nearly identical outcomes,
- Rewards depend more on the presence in a state than the choice of action.

Example:

If the agent is waiting for a ball to descend, whether it moves left, right, or stays still may make no immediate difference.

A standard DQN wastes time trying to learn differences between actions that **do not matter**.

But Dueling DQN learns faster because it:

a) Separates "state value" from "action usefulness"

The network understands the worth of being in a certain state, even if action does little.

b) Avoids noisy action-value estimation

If all actions are similar, the **advantage** network automatically shrinks A(s, a).

c) Propagates value through the network more effectively

Even when rewards come late, V(s) strengthens early.

This leads to **faster learning**, **better stability**, and **stronger performance** in complex environments.

Mathematical Intuition of Dueling DQN

The key idea is to decompose Q-values:

$$Q(s, a) = V(s) + (A(s, a) - \max_{a'} A(s, a'))$$

However, subtracting the max can be unstable, so a more stable formulation is:

$$Q(s, a) = V(s) + A(s, a) - \frac{1}{|A|} \sum_{a'} A(s, a')$$

Interpretation:

- **V(s)** → baseline worth of the state
- **A(s, a)** → relative improvement over the average action

By subtracting the mean or max:

- The network avoids arbitrary shifts where V and A both increase without changing Q
- The Q-values remain **identifiable and meaningful**

Why This Works So Well

1. Many states have actions with identical outcomes

So advantage values shrink naturally → less noise.

2. The value function V(s) becomes clearer

Helping the network understand "how good is this moment?"

3. Better credit assignment

Useful signals travel more reliably through the network.

4. Higher sample efficiency

The agent learns useful state values even when action differences are irrelevant.

5. Superior performance in real-world and Atari benchmarks

Because most environments contain numerous action-insensitive states.

Master said, "Dueling DQN teaches us a deeper truth: Not every decision is about action. Sometimes, the value lies in the state itself—In stillness, in awareness, in presence."

He smiled gently, as if revealing a secret of both learning and life.

Master said, "The code begins by **importing essential libraries** such as Gym for the environment, NumPy for computations, TensorFlow/Keras for neural networks, and deque for the replay buffer. Important **hyperparameters** are defined, including learning rate, discount factor (γ), memory size, epsilon decay, and episode limits."

The **Dueling Q-Network architecture** is then constructed. It consists of a shared neural trunk that extracts features from the state. This trunk splits into two paths:

Value Stream, which outputs V(s), representing how valuable the state is.

Advantage Stream, which outputs A(s, a), reflecting how beneficial each action is.

> Note: The code *P4–U4–D14* may take several hours to produce output. For an immediate result, please run *P4–U4–D14A* instead.

A Lambda layer combines these using:

Q(s, a) = V(s) + (A(s, a) − mean(A(s, a))), ensuring stable Q-value estimation.

Example P4 – U4 – D14

Dueling Q-Network

```
"""
Improved Dueling Double-DQN implementation for CartPole-v1
- Saves model to: D:\Raj\Book-working\010-Python\Program\Alpha_Optimum_Python\Data\DDQN
"""

import gym
import numpy as np
import random
import os
import tensorflow as tf
from collections import deque
from tensorflow.keras import Model
from tensorflow.keras.layers import Dense, Input, Lambda
from tensorflow.keras.optimizers import Adam

# ======================================================================== #
# Windows SAVE PATH
```

```
# 
=======================================================
=========== #
SAVE_DIR = r"D:\Raj\Book-working\010-
Python\Program\Alpha_Optimum_Python\Data\DDQN"
os.makedirs(SAVE_DIR, exist_ok=True)

MODEL_SAVE_PATH = os.path.join(SAVE_DIR, "dueling_dqn_cartpole.h5")

# 
=======================================================
=========== #
# Hyperparameters
# 
=======================================================
=========== #
ENV_NAME = "CartPole-v1"
GAMMA = 0.99
LR = 0.001
BATCH_SIZE = 64
MEMORY_SIZE = 20000
MIN_REPLAY_SIZE = 1000
EPSILON_START = 1.0
EPSILON_MIN = 0.01
EPSILON_DECAY = 0.995
TARGET_UPDATE_FREQ = 1000
EPISODES = 400
MAX_STEPS = 500
USE_DOUBLE_DQN = True  # Turn ON Double DQN logic

# 
=======================================================
=========== #
# Dueling Q-Network
# 
=======================================================
=========== #
def build_dueling_q_network(state_dim, action_dim):

    inp = Input(shape=(state_dim,))

    x = Dense(128, activation='relu')(inp)
    x = Dense(128, activation='relu')(x)

    # Value stream
    v = Dense(64, activation='relu')(x)
    v = Dense(1)(v)
```

```
    # Advantage stream
    a = Dense(64, activation='relu')(x)
    a = Dense(action_dim)(a)

    # Combine V(s) + A(s,a) − mean(A(s))
    def merge(streams):
        v, a = streams
        a_mean = tf.reduce_mean(a, axis=1, keepdims=True)
        return v + (a - a_mean)

    q_out = Lambda(merge)([v, a])

    model = Model(inp, q_out)
    model.compile(optimizer=Adam(LR), loss="mse")
    return model

#
=====================================================
=========== #
# Replay Buffer
#
=====================================================
=========== #
class ReplayBuffer:
    def __init__(self, maxlen):
        self.buffer = deque(maxlen=maxlen)

    def add(self, s, a, r, ns, d):
        self.buffer.append((s, a, r, ns, d))

    def sample(self, size):
        batch = random.sample(self.buffer, size)
        return map(np.array, zip(*batch))

    def __len__(self):
        return len(self.buffer)

#
=====================================================
=========== #
# Epsilon-greedy action
#
=====================================================
=========== #
def epsilon_greedy(model, state, action_dim, epsilon):
    if random.random() < epsilon:
        return random.randint(0, action_dim - 1)
    q = model.predict(state[np.newaxis], verbose=0)[0]
```

```
    return np.argmax(q)

#
============================================================
=========== #
# Target update
#
============================================================
=========== #
def update_target(src, tgt):
    tgt.set_weights(src.get_weights())

#
============================================================
=========== #
# Training Loop
#
============================================================
=========== #
def train_dueling_dqn():

    env = gym.make(ENV_NAME)
    state_dim = env.observation_space.shape[0]
    action_dim = env.action_space.n

    online = build_dueling_q_network(state_dim, action_dim)
    target = build_dueling_q_network(state_dim, action_dim)
    update_target(online, target)

    memory = ReplayBuffer(MEMORY_SIZE)

    # Pre-fill Replay Buffer
    state = env.reset()[0]
    for _ in range(MIN_REPLAY_SIZE):
        action = random.randint(0, action_dim - 1)
        next_state, reward, done, _, _ = env.step(action)
        memory.add(state, action, reward, next_state, done)
        state = next_state if not done else env.reset()[0]

    epsilon = EPSILON_START
    total_steps = 0

    for ep in range(1, EPISODES + 1):

        state = env.reset()[0]
        ep_reward = 0

        for t in range(MAX_STEPS):
```

```
        total_steps += 1

        action = epsilon_greedy(online, state, action_dim, epsilon)

        next_state, reward, done, _, _ = env.step(action)
        ep_reward += reward

        memory.add(state, action, reward, next_state, done)
        state = next_state

        # Training
        if len(memory) >= BATCH_SIZE:
            states, actions, rewards, next_states, dones = memory.sample(BATCH_SIZE)

            # --- Double DQN target ---
            if USE_DOUBLE_DQN:
                # Online chooses the best action
                next_q_online = online.predict(next_states, verbose=0)
                next_actions = np.argmax(next_q_online, axis=1)

                # Target evaluates
                next_q_target = target.predict(next_states, verbose=0)
                target_values = next_q_target[np.arange(BATCH_SIZE), next_actions]
            else:
                # Normal DQN
                next_q = target.predict(next_states, verbose=0)
                target_values = np.max(next_q, axis=1)

            targets = rewards + (1 - dones) * GAMMA * target_values

            q_values = online.predict(states, verbose=0)
            q_values[np.arange(BATCH_SIZE), actions] = targets

            online.fit(states, q_values, epochs=1, verbose=0)

        if total_steps % TARGET_UPDATE_FREQ == 0:
            update_target(online, target)

        if done:
            break

    epsilon = max(EPSILON_MIN, epsilon * EPSILON_DECAY)

    print(f"Episode {ep:03d}  | Reward: {ep_reward:.1f} | Epsilon: {epsilon:.3f}")

    if ep % 50 == 0:
        online.save(MODEL_SAVE_PATH)
```

```
    online.save(MODEL_SAVE_PATH)
    return online, target

#
==================================================================
=========== #
# Evaluation
#
==================================================================
=========== #
def evaluate_model(model, episodes=5):

    env = gym.make(ENV_NAME)
    scores = []

    for ep in range(1, episodes + 1):
        state = env.reset()[0]
        ep_reward = 0
        done = False

        while not done:
            q = model.predict(state[np.newaxis], verbose=0)[0]
            action = np.argmax(q)
            state, reward, done, _, _ = env.step(action)
            ep_reward += reward

        scores.append(ep_reward)
        print(f"Eval {ep}: Reward = {ep_reward}")

    print("Average Reward:", np.mean(scores))
    return scores

#
==================================================================
=========== #
# Run training and evaluation
#
==================================================================
=========== #
if __name__ == "__main__":
    print("Model will be saved to:", MODEL_SAVE_PATH)
    online_model, target_model = train_dueling_dqn()
    print("\nTraining complete. Evaluating...")
    evaluate_model(online_model, episodes=10)
```

Next, a **Replay Buffer class** stores past experiences (state, action, reward, next_state, done), allowing the agent to learn from randomly sampled batches and break the correlation between sequential frames.

The **epsilon-greedy policy** selects random actions early on (exploration) and greedy ones later (exploitation). A target network is maintained and periodically updated to stabilise training by providing consistent Q-targets.

The **training loop** initializes the environment and pre-fills the replay memory. Each episode runs until termination, storing transitions and training the online network. Targets are computed using:

target = reward + γ * max(Q_next) for non-terminal states.

Every few thousand steps, the target network weights are updated. Epsilon decays after each episode.

Finally, the model is saved, and an **evaluation function** runs trained episodes without exploration to measure performance.

Example P4 – U4 – D14A

Dueling Q-Network

```
import os
import gym
import torch
import random
import numpy as np
import torch.nn as nn
import torch.optim as optim
import matplotlib.pyplot as plt
from collections import deque

# ---------------------------------------------------------
# SAVE PATH  (YOUR REQUIRED PATH)
# ---------------------------------------------------------
SAVE_DIR = r"D:\Raj\Book-working\010-Python\Program\Alpha_Optimum_Python\Data\Dueling"
os.makedirs(SAVE_DIR, exist_ok=True)


# ---------------------------------------------------------
# Dueling DQN Network
# ---------------------------------------------------------
```

```
class DuelingDQN(nn.Module):
    def __init__(self, state_dim, action_dim):
        super(DuelingDQN, self).__init__()

        self.feature = nn.Sequential(
            nn.Linear(state_dim, 128), nn.ReLU(),
            nn.Linear(128, 128), nn.ReLU()
        )

        self.value = nn.Sequential(
            nn.Linear(128, 64), nn.ReLU(),
            nn.Linear(64, 1)
        )

        self.advantage = nn.Sequential(
            nn.Linear(128, 64), nn.ReLU(),
            nn.Linear(64, action_dim)
        )

    def forward(self, x):
        if x.dim() == 1:
            x = x.unsqueeze(0)

        f = self.feature(x)
        V = self.value(f)
        A = self.advantage(f)
        Q = V + (A - A.mean(dim=1, keepdim=True))
        return Q


# ------------------------------------------------------------
# Replay Buffer
# ------------------------------------------------------------
class ReplayBuffer:
    def __init__(self, size=50000):
        self.buffer = deque(maxlen=size)

    def store(self, s, a, r, ns, d):
        self.buffer.append((s, a, r, ns, d))

    def sample(self, batch):
        batch_data = random.sample(self.buffer, batch)
        s, a, r, ns, d = zip(*batch_data)
        return (
            torch.tensor(s, dtype=torch.float32),
            torch.tensor(a),
            torch.tensor(r, dtype=torch.float32),
            torch.tensor(ns, dtype=torch.float32),
```

```
            torch.tensor(d, dtype=torch.float32),
        )

    def __len__(self):
        return len(self.buffer)


# -------------------------------------------------------
# Dueling Double DQN Agent
# -------------------------------------------------------
class DDQNAgent:
    def __init__(self, state_dim, action_dim):
        self.action_dim = action_dim

        self.q_net = DuelingDQN(state_dim, action_dim)
        self.target_net = DuelingDQN(state_dim, action_dim)
        self.target_net.load_state_dict(self.q_net.state_dict())
        self.target_net.eval()

        self.optimizer = optim.Adam(self.q_net.parameters(), lr=0.001)
        self.loss_fn = nn.MSELoss()

        self.gamma = 0.99
        self.epsilon = 1.0
        self.epsilon_min = 0.05
        self.epsilon_decay = 0.995

        self.buffer = ReplayBuffer()
        self.batch_size = 64

    def select_action(self, state):
        if np.random.rand() < self.epsilon:
            return np.random.randint(self.action_dim)
        state_t = torch.tensor(state, dtype=torch.float32)
        return torch.argmax(self.q_net(state_t)).item()

    def train_step(self):
        if len(self.buffer) < self.batch_size:
            return None

        s, a, r, ns, d = self.buffer.sample(self.batch_size)

        q_vals = self.q_net(s).gather(1, a.unsqueeze(1)).squeeze(1)

        next_actions = torch.argmax(self.q_net(ns), dim=1)
        next_q = self.target_net(ns).gather(1, next_actions.unsqueeze(1)).squeeze(1)

        targets = r + self.gamma * next_q * (1 - d)
```

```
        loss = self.loss_fn(q_vals, targets.detach())

        self.optimizer.zero_grad()
        loss.backward()
        self.optimizer.step()

        if self.epsilon > self.epsilon_min:
            self.epsilon *= self.epsilon_decay

        return loss.item()

    def update_target(self):
        self.target_net.load_state_dict(self.q_net.state_dict())


# ------------------------------------------------------------
# Moving Average Helper
# ------------------------------------------------------------
def smooth(data, weight=0.9):
    smoothed = []
    last = data[0]
    for d in data:
        last = last * weight + (1 - weight) * d
        smoothed.append(last)
    return smoothed


# ------------------------------------------------------------
# Training
# ------------------------------------------------------------
env = gym.make("CartPole-v1")
state_dim = env.observation_space.shape[0]
action_dim = env.action_space.n

agent = DDQNAgent(state_dim, action_dim)

EPISODES = 400
TARGET_UPDATE = 10

reward_history = []
loss_history = []
eps_history = []

for ep in range(EPISODES):
    state, _ = env.reset()
    total_reward = 0
```

```
    for t in range(500):
        action = agent.select_action(state)
        next_state, reward, done, _, _ = env.step(action)

        agent.buffer.store(state, action, reward, next_state, float(done))
        state = next_state
        total_reward += reward

        loss = agent.train_step()
        if loss is not None:
            loss_history.append(loss)

        if done:
            break

    reward_history.append(total_reward)
    eps_history.append(agent.epsilon)

    if ep % TARGET_UPDATE == 0:
        agent.update_target()

    print(f"EP {ep} | Reward={total_reward} | Epsilon={agent.epsilon:.3f}")

# Save model
torch.save(agent.q_net.state_dict(),                    os.path.join(SAVE_DIR,
"dueling_ddqn_cartpole.pth"))
print("Model saved.")


# ---------------------------------------------------------
# Plotting
# ---------------------------------------------------------
plt.figure(figsize=(10, 5))
plt.plot(reward_history, label="Reward")
plt.plot(smooth(reward_history), label="Smoothed", linewidth=2)
plt.title("Reward Curve")
plt.xlabel("Episode")
plt.ylabel("Reward")
plt.legend()
plt.savefig(os.path.join(SAVE_DIR, "reward_curve.png"))
plt.close()

plt.figure(figsize=(10, 5))
plt.plot(loss_history)
plt.title("Loss Curve")
plt.xlabel("Training Steps")
plt.ylabel("Loss")
plt.savefig(os.path.join(SAVE_DIR, "loss_curve.png"))
```

```
plt.close()

plt.figure(figsize=(10, 5))
plt.plot(eps_history)
plt.title("Epsilon Decay")
plt.xlabel("Episode")
plt.ylabel("Epsilon")
plt.savefig(os.path.join(SAVE_DIR, "epsilon_decay.png"))
plt.close()
```

Output:

Output
EP 398 | Reward=393.0 | Epsilon=0.050 EP 399 | Reward=500.0 | Epsilon=0.050 Model saved.

Plot: Reward curve

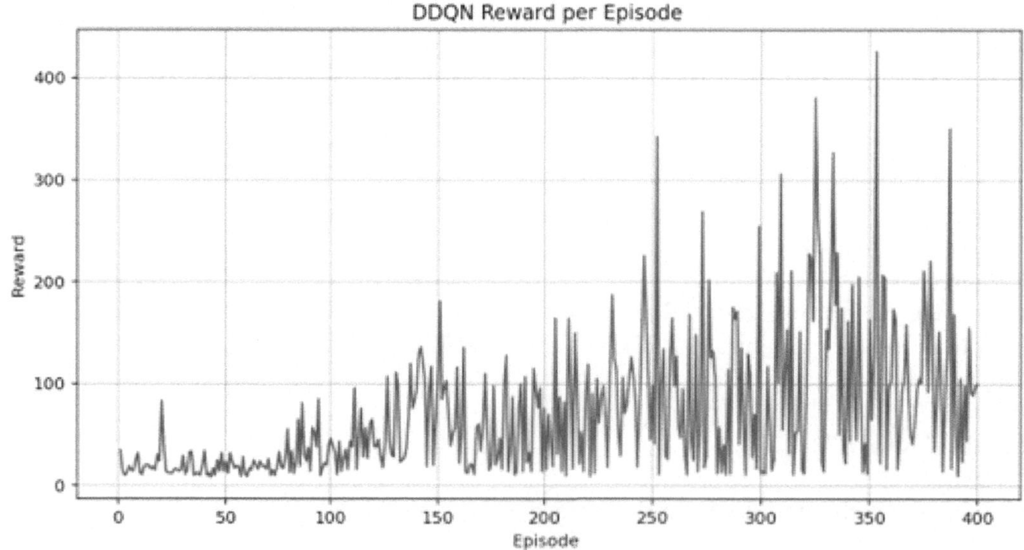

Illustration Dueling_reward_plot: Dueling DQN

Plot: Reward curve

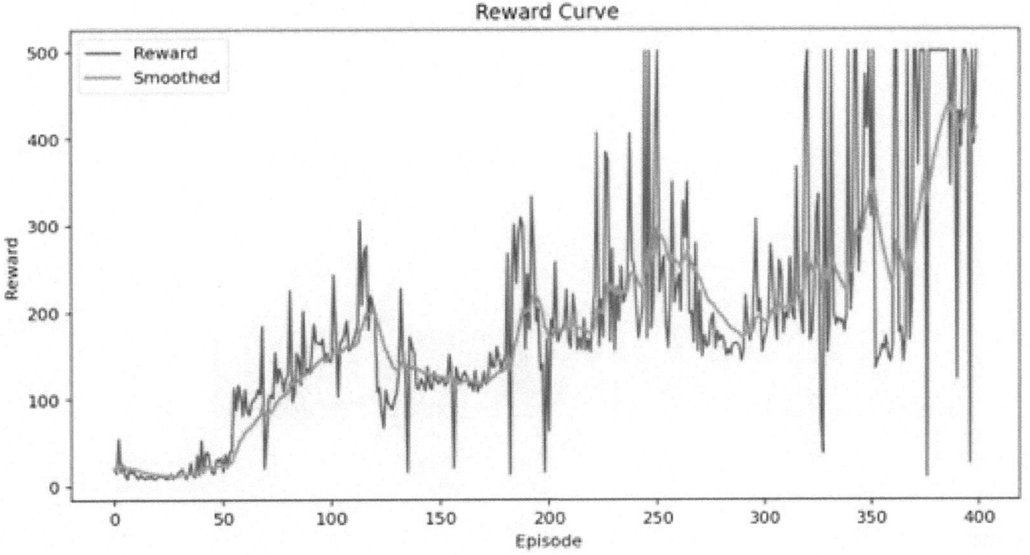

Illustration Dueling_reward_curve: Dueling DQN

Plot: Smoothed Reward curve

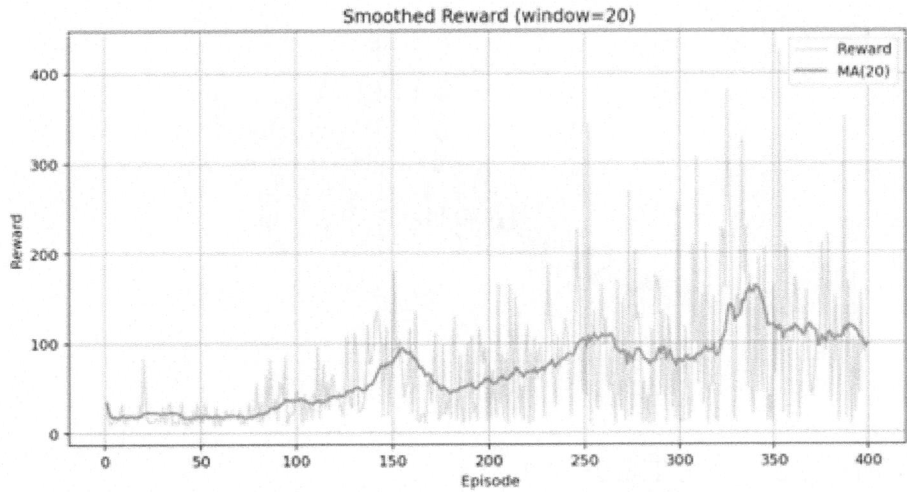

Illustration Dueling_smoothedreward: Dueling DQN

Plot: Loss curve

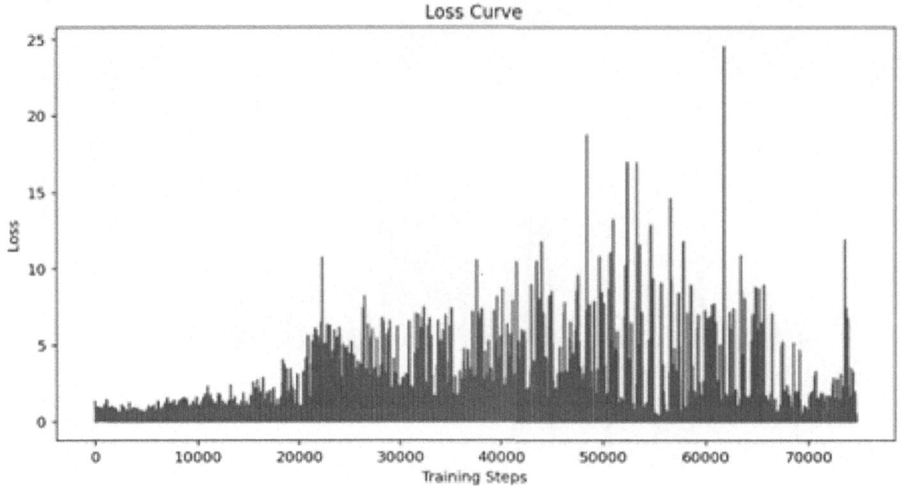

Illustration Dueling_LossCurve: Dueling DQN

Plot: Loss Plot

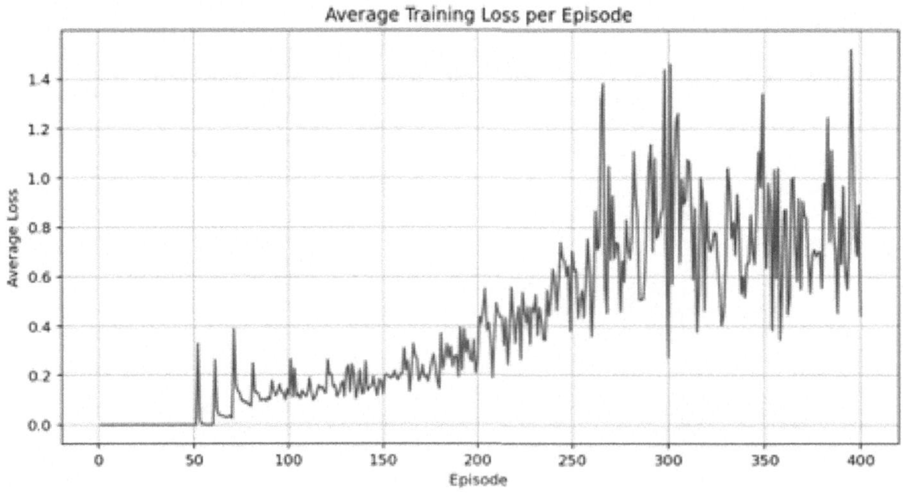

Illustration Dueling_Loss_plot: Dueling DQN

Plot: Epsilon decay graph

Plot: Epsilon Plot

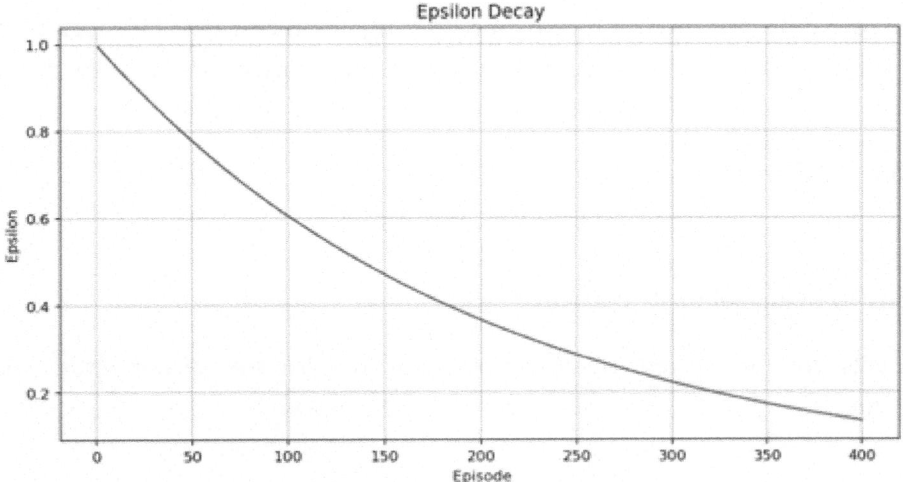

Illustration Dueling_Epsilon_plot: Dueling DQN

Plot: Epsilon decay curve

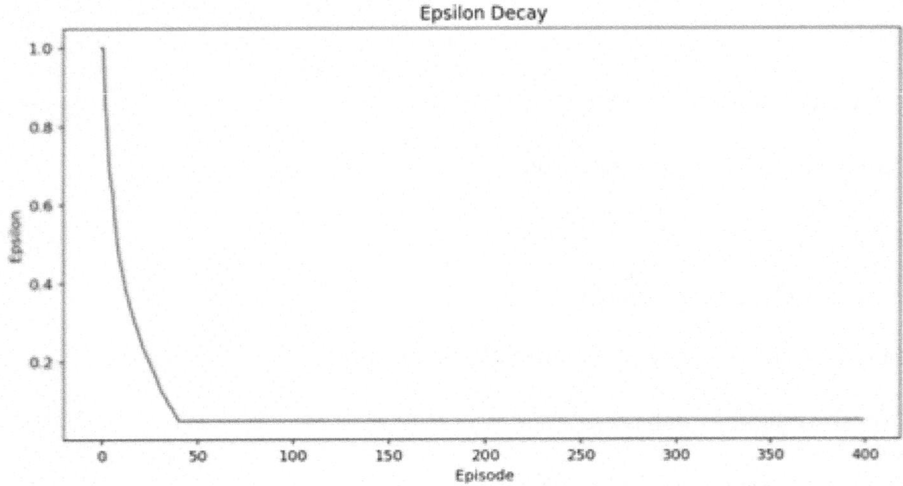

Illustration Dueling_Epsilon_Decay: Dueling DQN

☐ **Reward Maximization Framework**

Master said — The Reward Maximization Framework

Reinforcement Learning (RL) is built upon a simple but profound principle: **An agent must learn to make decisions that maximize its long-term reward.** This idea is the foundation of all RL algorithms—whether simple tabular methods or deep neural architectures.

1. Immediate vs. Cumulative Reward

Master said:

"Do not be fooled by the allure of immediate gain.

A wise agent acts not for the reward of the moment, but for the greater return that unfolds over time."

In RL:

- **Immediate Reward**: The reward received at the current step.
- **Cumulative Reward (Return)**: The total reward an agent expects to collect in the future.

$G_t = R_{t+1} + \gamma R_{t+2} + \gamma^2 R_{t+3} + \cdots$

Here:

- R_{t+1} is the next immediate reward.
- γ (gamma) discounts future rewards.

2. The Role of the Discount Factor γ

The discount factor controls how the agent values the future:

- **$\gamma \approx 0$** → shortsighted behaviour

  Agent only cares about immediate rewards.

- **$\gamma \approx 1$** → farsighted behaviour

  Agent values future rewards almost as much as present ones.

Master explained:

"Life—like RL—demands wisdom.

The impatient agent grabs what comes first.

The patient agent receives more over time."

Example of Return Calculation

Master said, "To understand return, we must follow the trail of rewards from this moment into the future."

Consider an episode where an agent receives the following sequence of rewards:

Time Step	Reward
(R_{t+1})	+2
(R_{t+2})	-1
(R_{t+3})	+3
(R_{t+4})	+5

Let the **discount factor:** $\gamma=0.9$

Step-by-Step Calculation

We compute return:

$Gt = R_{t+1} + \gamma R_{t+2} + \gamma^2 R_{t+3} + \gamma^3 R_{t+4}$

Now substitute the values:

1. Immediate Reward

$$R_{t+1} = +2$$

2. Discounted Second Reward

$$\gamma R_{t+2} = 0.9\times(-1) = -0.9$$

3. Discounted Third Reward

$$\gamma^2 R_{t+3} = 0.9^2\times 3 = 0.81\times 3 = 2.43$$

4. Discounted Fourth Reward

$\gamma^3 R_{t+4} = 0.9^3 \times 5 = 0.729 \times 5 = 3.645$

Total Return

$Gt = 2 - 0.9 + 2.43 + 3.645$

$Gt = 7.175$

The return from state s_t is:

$Gt = 7.175$

3. Q-Learning Update — The Heart of Reward Maximization

Q-learning updates action-values using:

$Q(s, a) \leftarrow Q(s, a) + \alpha[R + \gamma \max_{a'} Q(s', a') - Q(s, a)]$

This equation expresses:

- The reward received now
- Plus the best future reward estimate
- Minus the current guess (the TD error)

The agent **refines its understanding repeatedly**, slowly approaching the optimal policy.

4. DQN — Scaling Q-Learning to Complex Worlds

DQN (Deep Q-Network) extends Q-learning by using a neural network to approximate the Q-function.

Why is this needed?

Because in large or continuous environments:

- State-space becomes huge
- Tabular Q-learning becomes impossible

A neural network maps:

State→Predicted Q-values

This enables RL to solve:

- Atari games
- Robotics control
- Autonomous driving
- High-dimensional AI tasks

5. Policy Gradient Methods — Direct Reward Optimization

Unlike value-based methods, policy gradients directly optimize the policy:

$\nabla_\theta J(\theta) = E\ [\ \nabla_\theta \log\pi_\theta(s, a)\ Q^\pi(s, a)]$

Meaning:

- The agent changes the probability of actions
- In the direction that increases expected return

Policy gradients excel in:

- Continuous control (robotics, physics simulations)
- Complex action spaces
- Stochastic policies

How Reward Maximization Happens in Practice

Master said:

1. **Explore:** The agent tries many actions to understand consequences.
2. **Evaluate:** Rewards update Q-values or policy weights.
3. **Exploit:** The agent increasingly prefers actions with higher expected cumulative rewards.
4. **Adjust:** Continuous refinement slowly converges toward optimal behavior.

Master said — This Python code is a simple and clear demonstration of how returns are computed in Reinforcement Learning using a discount factor. It breaks down the concept of return G_t into step-by-step calculations, showing exactly how each discounted reward contributes to the final value. The function explain_return() prints each stage of the computation: the reward, the power of gamma applied, the discounted term, and finally the total return. This helps learners visualize how future rewards diminish in influence as they are multiplied by successive powers of γ. The code also includes helper functions to compute returns from any time step and to generate all returns for a sequence. By running the script, you can see both the mathematical process and the cumulative effect of discounting, making the idea of returns intuitive, transparent, and directly connected to the theory behind Temporal Difference and Monte Carlo methods.

Example P4 – U4 – D15

Reward Maximization

```
from typing import List

def compute_return_from_t(rewards: List[float], t: int, gamma: float) -> float:
    """
    Compute G_t = sum_{k=0}^{T-1} gamma^k * R_{t+1+k}
    where `rewards` is the list [R_{t+1}, R_{t+2}, ...].
    Returns a float.
    """
    G = 0.0
    for k, r in enumerate(rewards[t:]):
        G += (gamma ** k) * r
    return G

def explain_return(rewards: List[float], t: int = 0, gamma: float = 0.9) -> None:
    """
    Print a step-by-step breakdown of the return starting at index t.
    rewards: list of rewards in chronological order, where rewards[0] == R_{t+1} if t==0.
    t: start index (0-based) in the list from which to compute the return.
    gamma: discount factor.
    """
    # Subsequence used for computation
    seq = rewards[t:]
    print(f"Computing G_{t} with gamma = {gamma}")
    if not seq:
        print("No future rewards. G_t = 0")
        return

    terms = []
    for k, r in enumerate(seq):
        coef = gamma ** k
```

```
        term = coef * r
        terms.append(term)
        print(f"Step k={k}: reward = {r}, discount = gamma^{k} = {coef:.6f} -> term =
{term:.6f}")

    G = sum(terms)
    print("-" * 40)
    print("Summing terms:")
    for k, term in enumerate(terms):
        print(f"  term_{k} = {term:.6f}")
    print("-" * 40)
    print(f"G_{t} = {G:.6f}")
    return

def compute_all_returns(rewards: List[float], gamma: float = 0.9) -> List[float]:
    """
    Compute returns G_0, G_1, ..., G_{T-1} for each starting position.
    Returns a list of floats.
    """
    return [compute_return_from_t(rewards, t, gamma) for t in range(len(rewards))]

# ------------------------------
# Example usage (matches earlier example)
# ------------------------------
if __name__ == "__main__":
    # Example reward sequence: R_{t+1}, R_{t+2}, R_{t+3}, R_{t+4}
    rewards = [2, -1, 3, 5]
    gamma = 0.9

    # Show step-by-step for G_0 (starting at the first reward)
    explain_return(rewards, t=0, gamma=gamma)
    # If you want returns starting from each time step:
    print("\nAll returns (G_0, G_1, ...):")
    all_G = compute_all_returns(rewards, gamma=gamma)
    for i, g in enumerate(all_G):
        print(f"G_{i} = {g:.6f}")
```

Output:

```
Output
```

```
Computing G_0 with gamma = 0.9
Step k=0: reward = 2, discount = gamma^0 = 1.000000 -> term = 2.000000
Step k=1: reward = -1, discount = gamma^1 = 0.900000 -> term = -0.900000
Step k=2: reward = 3, discount = gamma^2 = 0.810000 -> term = 2.430000
Step k=3: reward = 5, discount = gamma^3 = 0.729000 -> term = 3.645000
```

```
----------------------------------------
Summing terms:
  term_0 = 2.000000
  term_1 = -0.900000
  term_2 = 2.430000
  term_3 = 3.645000
----------------------------------------
G_0 = 7.175000

All returns (G_0, G_1, ...):
G_0 = 7.175000
G_1 = 5.750000
G_2 = 7.500000
G_3 = 5.000000
```

Challenges in Reward Maximization

Master warned: "The path is simple, but the journey is not."

Challenges:

- **Exploration vs. Exploitation**

  Too little exploration → agent never discovers better actions
  Too much → agent never settles

- **Sparse or delayed rewards**

  Hard to connect actions to outcomes

- **Complex computation**

  Deep RL often requires massive training resources

Master said, "At the core of reinforcement learning lies a timeless principle:"

Maximize long-term reward through continual learning from experience.

By understanding:

- returns
- discounting

- bootstrapping
- value functions
- policy optimization

…we build agents capable of making *intelligent, strategic, farsighted decisions*—from gridworlds to real-world applications.

Master said:

"Reinforcement Learning mirrors life itself.

Every action is a seed.

Every reward is a harvest.

Choose actions that yield the greatest harvest over time."

☐ PER-DQN

With curiosity, Apeksha asked, 'Master, what exactly is PER-DQN, and why is it preferred in certain learning problems?

Master replied, PER DQN stands for **Prioritized Experience Replay Deep Q-Network**. It is an improved version of the standard DQN algorithm used in **Reinforcement Learning**. To understand it, first remember that **DQN learns by storing past experiences**—each experience is a tuple *(state, action, reward, next state)*—inside a memory called the **replay buffer**. During training, DQN randomly samples from this memory to update the network.

However, in standard DQN, all experiences are treated as equally important, even though in reality, some experiences teach the agent much more than others.

PER DQN fixes this problem.

Instead of sampling experiences uniformly, **PER assigns a priority to each experience** based on the **TD error** (Temporal Difference error):

A large TD error = big learning opportunity

A small TD error = little new information

So the agent **replays more important mistakes more often**, which speeds up learning dramatically.

When Do We Use PER DQN?

We use PER DQN when:

1. **Learning is slow** with standard DQN
2. The environment is **complex or high-dimensional**
3. Rewards are **sparse or delayed**
4. The agent makes **critical rare mistakes** that must be learned quickly
5. We want **faster convergence and better stability**

Key Benefits

- Faster learning
- Better use of important experiences
- Improved performance in difficult environments

Challenges

- Slightly higher **computational cost**
- Needs **careful tuning of priority parameters**

Mastre said, "PER DQN teaches the agent not to forget its biggest mistakes, and to learn from them more often — just like a wise student who revises difficult lessons more than easy ones."

Math Behind PER DQN

In **standard DQN**, experiences are sampled uniformly:

$$P(i) = 1/N$$

In **PER**, each experience gets a **priority** based on its **TD Error**:

Step 1: TD Error

$$\delta = |R + \gamma \max_a Q(s',a') - Q(s,a)|$$

This tells **how wrong the agent was**.

Step 2: Priority Assignment

$$p_i = (\delta_i + \epsilon)^\alpha$$

Where:

- ϵ = small constant (avoids zero priority)
- α = how strongly prioritization is applied

Step 3: Sampling Probability

$$P(i) = \frac{p_i}{\sum_k p_k}$$

Higher TD error → Higher chance of being replayed.

Step 4: Bias Correction (Importance Sampling)

Because PER introduces bias, we correct it with:

$$wi = \left(\frac{1}{NP_i}\right)^\beta$$

Used to scale the learning update.

Simple Numerical Example

Suppose your replay buffer has **4 experiences:**

Experience	TD Error
E1	0.1
E2	1.0
E3	3.0
E4	0.5

Let:

$\alpha=1$, $\epsilon=0$

Step 1: Priorities

p = [0.1, 1.0, 3.0, 0.5]

Step 2: Total Priority

$\sum p = 4.6$

Step 3: Sampling Probabilities

Experience	Probability
E1	0.1 / 4.6 = 0.02
E2	1.0 / 4.6 = 0.22
E3	3.0 / 4.6 = **0.65**
E4	0.5 / 4.6 = 0.11

E3 (big mistake) is replayed most often.

This is the **core power of PER**.

Master said, "This code demonstrates the heart of Prioritized Experience Replay, a powerful improvement over ordinary replay memory. Instead of storing experiences and replaying them uniformly, the buffer assigns each experience a priority based on its TD error—how wrong the agent's prediction was. The add function stores both the experience and its priority, ensuring serious mistakes are remembered more strongly. The sample function then transforms these priorities into probabilities, so experiences with higher errors are more likely to be replayed during learning. This accelerates the correction of major prediction errors and improves learning efficiency. Finally, update_priorities refreshes the priorities after the agent learns from them, keeping the focus on what still needs improvement. Through this elegant loop of storing, sampling, and updating, the agent learns faster and more intelligently by revisiting its most valuable mistakes."

Example P4 – U4 – D16

PER DQN

```
import numpy as np
import random

class PERBuffer:
    def __init__(self, capacity):
        self.capacity = capacity
        self.buffer = []
        self.priorities = []

    def add(self, experience, td_error):
        priority = abs(td_error) + 1e-5

        if len(self.buffer) < self.capacity:
            self.buffer.append(experience)
            self.priorities.append(priority)
        else:
            self.buffer.pop(0)
            self.priorities.pop(0)
            self.buffer.append(experience)
            self.priorities.append(priority)

    def sample(self, batch_size, alpha=1.0):
        scaled = np.array(self.priorities) ** alpha
        probs = scaled / sum(scaled)

        indices = np.random.choice(len(self.buffer), batch_size, p=probs)
        samples = [self.buffer[i] for i in indices]

        return samples, indices

    def update_priorities(self, indices, td_errors):
        for i, err in zip(indices, td_errors):
            self.priorities[i] = abs(err) + 1e-5


# -----------------------------
# DEMO USE
# -----------------------------
buffer = PERBuffer(capacity=10)

# Add experiences with TD errors
buffer.add(("S1","A1","R1","S2"), 0.1)
```

```
buffer.add(("S2","A2","R2","S3"), 1.0)
buffer.add(("S3","A3","R3","S4"), 3.0)
buffer.add(("S4","A4","R4","S5"), 0.5)

# Sample based on priority
samples, indices = buffer.sample(batch_size=2)

print("Sampled Experiences:", samples)
```

Output:

Output
Sampled Experiences: [('S3', 'A3', 'R3', 'S4'), ('S3', 'A3', 'R3', 'S4')]

PART FOUR

DAY NINTEEN

Unit 4 - Lesson Eight

Reinventing Value-Based RL

☐ Rainbow DQN

Master said, "Rainbow DQN represents the unification of the most powerful ideas in deep reinforcement learning into a single algorithm. It is not a new invention, but a harmony of six great enhancements: Double DQN for reducing overestimation, Dueling Networks for separating state value and action advantage, Prioritized Experience Replay for learning from important mistakes, Multi-step Learning for faster reward propagation, Distributional Learning for predicting a full spectrum of future rewards, and Noisy Networks for intelligent exploration.

Rainbow becomes most effective in **complex, high-dimensional environments**—especially where rewards are sparse, delayed, or noisy, such as Atari games, robotics control, strategic simulations, and autonomous decision systems. It excels when simple Q-learning struggles to converge, when exploration is difficult, or when long-term planning matters more than short-term gain.

Use Rainbow DQN when performance, stability, and sample efficiency are critical. It is the choice of mastery—heavier in computation, richer in learning, and far stronger in environments that demand both precision and foresight."

☐ Core Math Behind Rainbow DQN (Simplified)

Rainbow DQN combines **six mathematical upgrades** to standard Q-learning:

Standard Q-learning Update

$$Q(s, a) \leftarrow Q(s, a) + \alpha[r + \gamma \max_{a'} Q(s', a') - Q(s, a)]$$

Double DQN (Fixes Overestimation)

Action selection and evaluation are separated:

$$Q(s, a) \leftarrow Q(s, a) + \alpha[r + \gamma Q(s', \arg\max_{a'} Q(s', a')) - Q(s, a)]$$

Dueling DQN

Instead of one Q-value, we decompose:

$$Q(s, a) = V(s) + (A(s, a) - \frac{1}{|A|} \sum_a A(s, a))$$

Multi-Step Return (n-step TD)

$$G_t^{(n)} = r_1 + \gamma r_2 + \gamma^2 r_3 + \cdots + \gamma^n \max_a Q(sn, a)$$

Distributional RL (C51)

Instead of predicting **one scalar Q-value**, Rainbow predicts a **probability distribution**:

Z(s, a) = distribution of returns

Expected value:

$$Q(s, a) = E\,[Z(s, a)]$$

Prioritized Experience Replay (PER)

Sampling probability:

$$\mathbf{P(i)=|TD_i|/\sum_k|TD_k|}$$

Importance correction:

$$wi = \left(\frac{1}{NP_i}\right)^{\beta}$$

Noisy Networks (Exploration)

Weights contain noise:

$$w = \mu + \sigma \cdot \epsilon$$

So exploration is **learned**, not forced.

Simple Numerical Example (Rainbow Logic Combined)

Assume:

Parameter	Value
Reward (r)	2
γ	0.9
Next Q-values	[4, 6]
n	3
Current Q	5

Step 1: Multi-step target

$Gt^{(3)} = 2 + 0.9(2) + 0.9^2(2) + 0.9^3(6) = 2+1.8+1.62+4.374 = 9.794$

Step 2: TD Error

$\delta = 9.794 - 5 = 4.794$

Step 3: PER Priority

$P \propto |\delta| = 4.794$

Step 4: Double DQN Target

If policy network picks action 1, target network evaluates:

$Q(s', a*) = 6$

Step 5: Final Update

$Q \leftarrow 5 + 0.1(9.794 - 5) = 5.479$

This single update **already includes**:

- Multi-step target
- Double DQN
- PER priority influence

Simple Python Implementation

This is a **conceptual Rainbow-style learner** without deep networks:

Example P4 – U4 – D17

Rainbow DQN

```
import numpy as np

gamma = 0.9
alpha = 0.1
n_step = 3

# Q-table (2 states x 2 actions)
Q = np.zeros((2, 2))

# Experience buffer (PER style)
memory = []
priorities = []

def multi_step_return(rewards, next_q):
    G = 0
    for i, r in enumerate(rewards):
        G += (gamma ** i) * r
    G += (gamma ** n_step) * next_q
    return G
```

```
def prioritized_sample():
    probs = np.array(priorities) / np.sum(priorities)
    idx = np.random.choice(len(memory), p=probs)
    return memory[idx]

# Simulated transitions
memory.append((0, 1, [2, 2, 2], 1))  # (state, action, 3 rewards, next_state)
priorities.append(1.0)

# Target network (Double DQN)
target_Q = np.array([[3, 6],
                     [2, 5]])

# Training step
s, a, rewards, s2 = prioritized_sample()

next_action = np.argmax(Q[s2])        # Policy net
next_q = target_Q[s2, next_action]    # Target net

G = multi_step_return(rewards, next_q)

td_error = G - Q[s, a]
Q[s, a] += alpha * td_error

# Update priority
priorities[0] = abs(td_error)

print("Updated Q-table:\n", Q)
print("New Priority:", priorities)
```

Output:

Output
Updated Q-table: [[0.   0.6878]   [0.   0.   ]] New Priority: [6.878]

Final Intuition Summary

Component	What It Fixes
Double DQN	Overestimation

Dueling	State vs Action separation
PER	Learns from mistakes
Multi-step	Faster reward flow
Distributional	Models reward uncertainty
Noisy Nets	Smart exploration

Rainbow DQN is not one trick—it is six ideas woven into one learning system.

Master said, "This Rainbow DQN code is a unified deep reinforcement learning framework that combines multiple powerful improvements over standard Q-learning. It uses a **dueling network** to separately estimate state value and action advantage, improving learning stability. **NoisyLinear layers** replace ε-greedy exploration by injecting learnable noise directly into the network for smarter exploration. The **distributional C51 head** models a full probability distribution over returns instead of a single value, capturing uncertainty. **Double DQN** is used to reduce overestimation by separating action selection and evaluation. **Prioritized Experience Replay (PER)** samples important transitions more often using a SumTree for efficiency. **Multi-step returns (n-step)** propagate rewards faster through time. Together, these components are trained using cross-entropy loss between projected and predicted value distributions. A synchronised target network stabilizes training. This skeleton demonstrates how Rainbow integrates six major RL advances into one coherent learning system."

Example P4 – U4 – D18

Rainbow DQN

```
"""
Rainbow DQN skeleton (PyTorch).

Core features included:
- Dueling network architecture
- NoisyLinear layers for learned exploration
- Distributional (C51) output (atoms)
- Double DQN target selection
- Multi-step returns (n-step)
- Prioritized Experience Replay (SumTree)
- Training loop skeleton

This is a starting point — adapt preprocessing, env, and hyperparams for real experiments.
"""

import math
import random
from collections import deque, namedtuple
```

```
import numpy as np
import torch
import torch.nn as nn
import torch.nn.functional as F
import torch.optim as optim

# -----------------------
# Utils: Noisy Linear
# -----------------------
class NoisyLinear(nn.Module):
    def __init__(self, in_features, out_features, sigma_init=0.5):
        super().__init__()
        self.in_features = in_features
        self.out_features = out_features

        self.mu_weight = nn.Parameter(torch.empty(out_features, in_features))
        self.sigma_weight = nn.Parameter(torch.empty(out_features, in_features))
        self.register_buffer("epsilon_weight", torch.empty(out_features, in_features))

        self.mu_bias = nn.Parameter(torch.empty(out_features))
        self.sigma_bias = nn.Parameter(torch.empty(out_features))
        self.register_buffer("epsilon_bias", torch.empty(out_features))

        self.sigma_init = sigma_init
        self.reset_parameters()
        self.reset_noise()

    def reset_parameters(self):
        mu_range = 1 / math.sqrt(self.in_features)
        self.mu_weight.data.uniform_(-mu_range, mu_range)
        self.mu_bias.data.uniform_(-mu_range, mu_range)
        self.sigma_weight.data.fill_(self.sigma_init / math.sqrt(self.in_features))
        self.sigma_bias.data.fill_(self.sigma_init / math.sqrt(self.out_features))

    def reset_noise(self):
        eps_in = self._f(torch.randn(self.in_features))
        eps_out = self._f(torch.randn(self.out_features))
        self.epsilon_weight.copy_(eps_out.ger(eps_in))
        self.epsilon_bias.copy_(eps_out)

    def _f(self, x):
        return x.sign().mul_(x.abs().sqrt_())

    def forward(self, x):
        if self.training:
            w = self.mu_weight + self.sigma_weight * self.epsilon_weight
            b = self.mu_bias + self.sigma_bias * self.epsilon_bias
        else:
```

```
        w = self.mu_weight
        b = self.mu_bias
    return F.linear(x, w, b)


# -----------------------
# Dueling Distributional Network (C51) + Noisy layers
# -----------------------
class RainbowNet(nn.Module):
  def __init__(self, state_dim, action_dim, atom_size=51, v_min=-10, v_max=10):
    super().__init__()
    self.action_dim = action_dim
    self.atom_size = atom_size
    self.v_min = v_min
    self.v_max = v_max
    self.delta_z = (v_max - v_min) / (atom_size - 1)
    self.support = torch.linspace(v_min, v_max, atom_size)

    # Simple MLP backbone; replace with CNN for images
    hidden = 128
    self.fc1 = nn.Linear(state_dim, hidden)
    self.fc2 = nn.Linear(hidden, hidden)

    # Dueling streams with Noisy layers
    self.value_noisy = NoisyLinear(hidden, hidden)
    self.adv_noisy = NoisyLinear(hidden, hidden)

    self.value_out = NoisyLinear(hidden, atom_size)        # V(s) distribution
    self.adv_out = NoisyLinear(hidden, action_dim * atom_size)  # A(s,a) distributions

  def forward(self, x):
    batch_size = x.size(0)
    x = F.relu(self.fc1(x))
    x = F.relu(self.fc2(x))

    v = F.relu(self.value_noisy(x))
    a = F.relu(self.adv_noisy(x))

    v = self.value_out(v).view(-1, 1, self.atom_size)        # (B,1,A)
    a = self.adv_out(a).view(-1, self.action_dim, self.atom_size)  # (B,A,atom)

    # Broadcast combining (dueling): Q_dist = V_dist + (A_dist - mean(A_dist))
    a_mean = a.mean(1, keepdim=True)
    q_atoms = v + (a - a_mean)  # (B,A,atom)
    q_dist = F.softmax(q_atoms, dim=2)  # distribution over atoms
    q_dist = q_dist.clamp(min=1e-6)      # numeric stability
    return q_dist  # shape (B, A, atom_size)
```

```
    def reset_noise(self):
        for module in self.modules():
            if isinstance(module, NoisyLinear):
                module.reset_noise()

    def q_values(self, x):
        # Expected Q: sum_z p(z) * z
        dist = self.forward(x)  # (B,A,atom)
        weights = self.support.to(dist.device)
        qvals = torch.sum(dist * weights, dim=2)
        return qvals  # shape (B,A)


# ------------------------
# Simple SumTree + PER buffer
# ------------------------
class SumTree:
    def __init__(self, capacity):
        self.capacity = capacity
        self.tree = np.zeros(2 * capacity - 1)  # sum tree
        self.data = np.zeros(capacity, dtype=object)
        self.write = 0
        self.n_entries = 0

    def _propagate(self, idx, change):
        parent = (idx - 1) // 2
        self.tree[parent] += change
        if parent != 0:
            self._propagate(parent, change)

    def _retrieve(self, idx, s):
        left = 2 * idx + 1
        right = left + 1
        if left >= len(self.tree):
            return idx
        if s <= self.tree[left]:
            return self._retrieve(left, s)
        else:
            return self._retrieve(right, s - self.tree[left])

    def total(self):
        return self.tree[0]

    def add(self, p, data):
        idx = self.write + self.capacity - 1
        self.data[self.write] = data
        self.update(idx, p)
```

```
        self.write += 1
        if self.write >= self.capacity:
            self.write = 0
        self.n_entries = min(self.n_entries + 1, self.capacity)

    def update(self, idx, p):
        change = p - self.tree[idx]
        self.tree[idx] = p
        self._propagate(idx, change)

    def get(self, s):
        idx = self._retrieve(0, s)
        data_idx = idx - self.capacity + 1
        return idx, self.tree[idx], self.data[data_idx]


class PrioritizedReplayBuffer:
    def __init__(self, capacity, alpha=0.6, beta_start=0.4, beta_frames=100000):
        self.tree = SumTree(capacity)
        self.alpha = alpha
        self.beta_start = beta_start
        self.beta_frames = beta_frames
        self.frame = 1
        self.max_priority = 1.0

    def push(self, transition):
        # transition: (state, action, reward, next_state, done)
        self.tree.add(self.max_priority ** self.alpha, transition)

    def sample(self, batch_size):
        batch = []
        idxs = []
        segment = self.tree.total() / batch_size
        priorities = []
        for i in range(batch_size):
            s = random.uniform(segment * i, segment * (i + 1))
            idx, p, data = self.tree.get(s)
            batch.append(data)
            idxs.append(idx)
            priorities.append(p)

        sampling_probabilities = np.array(priorities) / self.tree.total()
        beta = min(1.0, self.beta_start + (1.0 - self.beta_start) * (self.frame / 
self.beta_frames))
        self.frame += 1
        weights = (self.tree.n_entries * sampling_probabilities) ** (-beta)
        weights = weights / weights.max()
        return batch, idxs, weights
```

```
    def update_priorities(self, idxs, priorities):
        for idx, p in zip(idxs, priorities):
            p_adjusted = (abs(p) + 1e-6) ** self.alpha
            self.tree.update(idx, p_adjusted)
            self.max_priority = max(self.max_priority, p_adjusted)


# ------------------------
# Helpers: n-step buffer
# ------------------------
NSTEP_TRANSITION = namedtuple('NStep', ('state', 'action', 'reward', 'next_state',
'done', 'nstep_reward', 'nstep_next', 'nstep_done'))

class NStepHelper:
    def __init__(self, n, gamma):
        self.n = n
        self.gamma = gamma
        self.buffer = deque()

    def push(self, state, action, reward, next_state, done):
        self.buffer.append((state, action, reward, next_state, done))
        if len(self.buffer) < self.n:
            return None
        # compute n-step
        nstep_reward = 0.0
        nstep_next = self.buffer[-1][3]
        nstep_done = self.buffer[-1][4]
        for i, (_, _, r, _, _) in enumerate(self.buffer):
            nstep_reward += (self.gamma ** i) * r
        s0, a0, _, _, _ = self.buffer[0]
        self.buffer.popleft()
        return (s0, a0, nstep_reward, nstep_next, nstep_done)

    def flush(self):
        items = []
        while self.buffer:
            # compute for remaining shorter sequences
            nstep_reward = 0.0
            nstep_next = self.buffer[-1][3]
            nstep_done = self.buffer[-1][4]
            for i, (_, _, r, _, _) in enumerate(self.buffer):
                nstep_reward += (self.gamma ** i) * r
            s0, a0, _, _, _ = self.buffer[0]
            items.append((s0, a0, nstep_reward, nstep_next, nstep_done))
            self.buffer.popleft()
        return items
```

```
# -----------------------
# Projection for C51 distributional target
# -----------------------
def projection_distribution(next_dist, rewards, dones, gamma, v_min, v_max, atom_size):
    batch_size = len(rewards)
    delta_z = (v_max - v_min) / (atom_size - 1)
    support = np.linspace(v_min, v_max, atom_size)
    proj_dist = np.zeros((batch_size, atom_size), dtype=np.float32)

    for i in range(batch_size):
        for j in range(atom_size):
            tz = rewards[i] + (1.0 - dones[i]) * (gamma * support[j])
            tz = np.clip(tz, v_min, v_max)
            b = (tz - v_min) / delta_z
            l = int(math.floor(b))
            u = int(math.ceil(b))
            if l == u:
                proj_dist[i][l] += next_dist[i][j]
            else:
                proj_dist[i][l] += next_dist[i][j] * (u - b)
                proj_dist[i][u] += next_dist[i][j] * (b - l)
    return proj_dist  # shape (B, atom_size)


# -----------------------
# Training skeleton
# -----------------------
def train_rainbow(env, state_dim, action_dim, params):
    device = params.get("device", torch.device("cpu"))
    atom_size = params.get("atom_size", 51)
    v_min = params.get("v_min", -10)
    v_max = params.get("v_max", 10)
    n_step = params.get("n_step", 3)
    batch_size = params.get("batch_size", 32)
    capacity = params.get("capacity", 10000)
    gamma = params.get("gamma", 0.99)
    lr = params.get("lr", 1e-4)
    update_target_every = params.get("update_target_every", 1000)
    max_frames = params.get("max_frames", 200000)

    # Networks
    net = RainbowNet(state_dim, action_dim, atom_size, v_min, v_max).to(device)
    target = RainbowNet(state_dim, action_dim, atom_size, v_min, v_max).to(device)
    target.load_state_dict(net.state_dict())
    optimizer = optim.Adam(net.parameters(), lr=lr)

    # Buffers
```

```
per = PrioritizedReplayBuffer(capacity)
nstep_helper = NStepHelper(n_step, gamma)

frame_idx = 0
losses = []

while frame_idx < max_frames:
    state = env.reset()
    done = False

    while not done:
        # Choose action (noisy nets are used -> greedy on expected Q)
        state_v = torch.tensor(state, dtype=torch.float32).unsqueeze(0).to(device)
        with torch.no_grad():
            qvals = net.q_values(state_v)  # (1, A)
        action = int(qvals.argmax(dim=1).item())

        # Step
        next_state, reward, done, _ = env.step(action)  # adapt to your env api
        step_res = nstep_helper.push(state, action, reward, next_state, done)
        if step_res is not None:
            s0, a0, n_reward, n_next, n_done = step_res
            per.push((s0, a0, n_reward, n_next, n_done))

        state = next_state
        frame_idx += 1

        # Training step
        if per.tree.n_entries >= batch_size:
            batch, idxs, is_weights = per.sample(batch_size)
            # unpack
            states = torch.tensor([b[0] for b in batch], dtype=torch.float32).to(device)
            actions = torch.tensor([b[1] for b in batch], dtype=torch.long).to(device)
            rewards = np.array([b[2] for b in batch], dtype=np.float32)
            next_states = torch.tensor([b[3] for b in batch], dtype=torch.float32).to(device)
            dones = np.array([b[4] for b in batch], dtype=np.uint8)

            # compute next distribution with policy_net (for double dqn select action)
            with torch.no_grad():
                next_dist = net.forward(next_states)  # (B,A,atom)
                next_q = torch.sum(next_dist * net.support.to(device), dim=2)  # (B,A)
                next_actions = next_q.argmax(1)  # greedy action indexes

                target_dist = target.forward(next_states)  # (B,A,atom)
                # select distribution of best actions according to policy_net
                batch_idx = np.arange(batch_size)
                target_dist_selected = target_dist[batch_idx, next_actions.cpu().numpy(),
:].cpu().numpy()
```

```
            # project distribution
            proj = projection_distribution(target_dist_selected, rewards, dones, gamma **
n_step, v_min, v_max, atom_size)
            proj = torch.tensor(proj, dtype=torch.float32).to(device)

            # predicted distribution for taken actions
            dist = net.forward(states)  # (B,A,atom)
            dist_taken = dist[batch_idx, actions.cpu().numpy(), :]  # (B,atom)

            # loss = cross-entropy between projected distribution and predicted
distribution
            log_p = torch.log(dist_taken + 1e-8)
            elementwise_loss = - (proj * log_p).sum(1)  # (B,)

            # apply importance-sampling weights
            is_weights_t = torch.tensor(is_weights, dtype=torch.float32).to(device)
            loss = (is_weights_t * elementwise_loss).mean()

            optimizer.zero_grad()
            loss.backward()
            optimizer.step()

            # update priorities with TD-like errors (use KL or L1 between distributions)
            with torch.no_grad():
                # compute TD error proxy: L1 between proj and dist_taken
                td_errors              =              (proj.cpu().numpy()              -
dist_taken.detach().cpu().numpy()).sum(axis=1)
            per.update_priorities(idxs, td_errors)

            losses.append(loss.item())

            # reset noisy nets' noise
            net.reset_noise()
            target.reset_noise()

        # Periodically sync target
        if frame_idx % update_target_every == 0:
            target.load_state_dict(net.state_dict())

    return net, target, losses


# -----------------------
# Example usage (pseudo)
# -----------------------
if __name__ == "__main__":
    # Replace with a real environment (gym-like). Here we sketch a numeric env for shape.
```

```
class DummyEnv:
    def __init__(self):
        self.s = np.zeros(4, dtype=np.float32)
    def reset(self):
        return np.zeros(4, dtype=np.float32)
    def step(self, a):
        next_s = np.random.randn(4).astype(np.float32)
        r = random.random()
        done = random.random() > 0.95
        return next_s, r, done, {}

env = DummyEnv()
params = {
    "device": torch.device("cpu"),
    "atom_size": 51,
    "v_min": -10,
    "v_max": 10,
    "n_step": 3,
    "batch_size": 32,
    "capacity": 10000,
    "gamma": 0.99,
    "lr": 1e-4,
    "update_target_every": 1000,
    "max_frames": 10000
}
net, target, losses = train_rainbow(env, state_dim=4, action_dim=2, params=params)
print("Training finished. Example losses:", losses[:10])
```

Output:

```
Output

Training finished. Example losses: [3.955357789993286, 0.2640067934989929, 0.263808935880661, 3.9313740730285645, 3.9316885471343994, 0.2637825310230255, 3.9367756843566895, 0.26142239570617676, 3.9331107139587402, 3.925812244415283]
```

☐ Distributional Reinforcement Learning

Sam asked, "Master, what is Distributional Reinforcement Learning?"

Master said, "Distributional Reinforcement Learning (Distributional RL) is an advanced approach to reinforcement learning that learns not just the expected value of future rewards, but the entire probability distribution of those rewards. Traditional RL methods like Q-learning estimate a single number Q(s,a), which represents the *average* expected return. Distributional RL, instead, learns how likely different returns are, giving the agent a deeper and more precise understanding of uncertainty, risk, and variability in outcomes.

Instead of:

$$Q(s, a) = E[G_t]$$

Distributional RL learns:

$$Z(s, a) = \text{full distribution of } G_t$$

This allows the agent to distinguish between:

- A risky action with high variance
- A stable action with consistent returns —even if their averages are the same.

The Three Main Distributional RL Methods

1. C51 (Categorical DQN)

C51 represents the return distribution using **51 fixed value "atoms"** between V_{min} and V_{max}. The network predicts a probability for each atom.

- Output: A discrete probability distribution
- Update: Uses **distribution projection**
- Strength: Stable and historically foundational
- Limitation: Fixed support range

Master said: Let us understand C51 (Categorical DQN) with intuition, analogy, simple numbers, and clean math—step by step.

A. The Core Idea of C51

Normal Q-learning predicts one average value.

C51 predicts a full probability distribution of possible future rewards.

Instead of learning:

$$Q(s, a) = E[G_t]$$

C51 learns:

$$Z(s, a) = \text{distribution of } G_t$$

B. Analogy: "Weather Forecast vs Single Temperature"

Traditional Q-Learning:

It tells you:

"Tomorrow's temperature is **30°C**."

One number. No uncertainty.

C51 (Distributional RL):

It tells you:

"20% chance of 25°C,

50% chance of 30°C,

30% chance of 35°C."

Now you understand:

- Risk
- Variability
- Best vs worst outcomes

  —not just the average.

C51 does **exactly this for rewards.**

C. The "51 Atoms" Meaning (Why C51?)

C51 represents the return distribution using:

- **51 fixed values (atoms)**
- Evenly spaced between:

V_{min} and V_{max}

Example:

$V_{min} = -10$, $V_{max} = +10$, Atoms = 51

Spacing:

$\Delta z = 10 - (-10)/50 = 0.4$

So atoms look like:

$[-10, -9.6, -9.2, \ldots, 0, \ldots, 9.6, 10]$

For **each (s, a)** the network predicts:

$pi = P_r(Z = z_i)$

a probability for every atom.

D. Simple Numerical Example

Suppose for an action **A**, the network predicts:

Return (z)	**Probability**
-10	0.1
0	0.2
+10	0.7

This is the learned distribution:

$$Z(s,a) = \begin{Bmatrix} -10 \; with \; prob \; 0.1 \\ 0 \; with \; prob \; 0.2 \\ +10 \; with \; prob \; 0.7 \end{Bmatrix}$$

Expected Q-value (used for action selection):

$Q(s, a) = (-10)(0.1) + (0)(0.2) + (10)(0.7)$

$Q(s, a) = -1 + 0 + 7 = 6$

So:

- The policy still uses the expected value
- But learning uses the full distribution

E. Bellman Update in C51

Classic Q-learning target:

$$y = r + \gamma \max_a Q(s',a)$$

In C51, we update the full distribution:

$$Z_{target} = r + \gamma Z(s', a^*)$$

Where:

$$a^* = \arg\max_a E\,[Z(s', a)]$$

Each atom is shifted by:

$$Tz_i = r + \gamma z_i$$

Then we **project these shifted values back onto the fixed 51-atom support** using a **distribution projection operator.**

Projection Intuition (Why It Is Needed)

After applying:

$$Tz_i = r + \gamma z_i$$

The values may fall:

- Between atoms
- Outside $[V_{min}, V_{max}]$

So C51:

Clips them

Redistributes probabilities to the nearest atoms

Preserves total probability = 1

This keeps learning **stable and bounded**.

F. Training Loss in C51

Instead of MSE on Q-values, C51 uses:

Cross-Entropy Loss

between:

- Predicted distribution
- Target projected distribution

This forces the network to **match the entire return shape**, not just averages.

Why C51 Works So Well

- Learns uncertainty
- Handles stochastic rewards better
- Improves value estimation accuracy
- Reduces overconfidence in noisy environments

- Forms the distributional core of Rainbow DQN

Master said:

Q-learning asks: "How good is this action on average?"

C51 asks: "How good can it be, how bad can it get, and how likely is each outcome?"

That extra knowledge is what makes C51—and all Distributional RL—so powerful.

2. QR-DQN (Quantile Regression DQN)

QR-DQN does **not fix value locations**. Instead, it learns **quantiles directly** (e.g., the 10th, 50th, and 90th percentiles of returns).

- Output: A set of learned quantiles
- Loss: **Quantile Huber Loss**
- Advantage: More flexible than C51
- Better risk modeling

A. What Makes QR-DQN Special

C51 predicts probabilities on fixed value points.

QR-DQN predicts the value points themselves (quantiles).

C51 fixes **where values live** and learns probabilities.

QR-DQN fixes **probabilities** and learns where the values should be.

This is a **huge shift in flexibility**.

B. Analogy: "Exam Marks vs Grade Buckets"

C51 Analogy:

You create fixed grade buckets:

- 0 marks, 50 marks, 100 marks

Then predict:

- 20% chance at 0
- 30% chance at 50
- 50% chance at 100

Values are fixed → probabilities move.

C. QR-DQN Analogy:

Now you say:

"I want the 25th percentile, 50th percentile, and 75th percentile of marks."

These percentiles are fixed:

$\tau = [0.25, 0.5, 0.75]$

But the **marks themselves are learned**:

- 25% students scored 32
- 50% scored 61
- 75% scored 88

Probabilities are fixed → values move.

This gives QR-DQN **more freedom and precision** than C51.

D. What QR-DQN Learns Mathematically

Instead of learning:

Z(s, a) = probability distribution

QR-DQN learns:

$Z_\tau(s, a) = \{z_1, z_2, \dots, z_N\}$

Where each z_i corresponds to a **quantile level**:

$\tau_i = (i - 0.5) / N$

If N = 5, then:

$\tau = [0.1, 0.3, 0.5, 0.7, 0.9]$

So the network outputs:

$[z_{0.1}, z_{0.3}, z_{0.5}, z_{0.7}, z_{0.9}]$

Each is a **predicted return value.**

E. Simple Numerical Example

Suppose QR-DQN predicts an action:

Quantile (τ)	Predicted Return
0.1	-5
0.3	-1
0.5	2
0.7	6
0.9	10

This means:

- Worst 10% of outcomes ≈ **−5**
- Median outcome ≈ **+2**
- Best 10% of outcomes ≈ **+10**

Expected Q-value (used for action selection):

$Q(s, a) = (-5 - 1 + 2 + 6 + 10) / 5 = 12/5 = 2.4$

Policy still acts on the **mean**, but learning sees the **full spread of risk**.

F. Bellman Update in QR-DQN

Classic Q target:

$$y = r + \gamma \max_a Q(s', a)$$

QR-DQN target for each quantile:

$y_i = r + \gamma z_i(s',a^*)$

Where:

$a^* = \arg\max_a \frac{1}{N} \sum z_i(s', a)$

So each quantile is **shifted and discounted**, just like normal TD learning—but **vectorized across quantiles**.

G. Quantile Regression Loss (Key Math)

Instead of MSE or Cross-Entropy, QR-DQN minimizes:

$L = \sum_{i,j} \rho_\tau(y_i - z_j)$

Where **Huber Quantile Loss** is used:

$\rho_\tau(u) = |\tau - 1[u<0]| \cdot L_\kappa(u)$

This forces:

Lower quantiles to predict pessimistic returns

Higher quantiles to predict optimistic returns

Median to stabilise learning

This is what **shapes the full distribution correctly**.

H. Key Differences: C51 vs QR-DQN

Feature	**C51**	**QR-DQN**
Value positions	Fixed	Learned
Probabilities	Learned	Fixed
Support limits	Required	Not required
Loss	Cross-Entropy	Quantile Huber

Flexibility	Medium	High
Stability	High	Very High

I. Why QR-DQN Is Powerful

- No need for V_{min}, V_{max}
- Better modeling of tails of reward distribution
- More precise learning
- More robust in noisy and stochastic environments
- Forms the mathematical backbone of IQN

Master said:

C51 chooses fixed "reward shelves" and learns how much weight to put on each. QR-DQN chooses fixed "confidence levels" and learns where the rewards truly lie.

Because QR-DQN **learns the shape of rewards directly**, it is more flexible, more accurate, and more future-proof.

Master said, "This Python demo illustrates the core idea behind **QR-DQN (Quantile Regression DQN)** without using a neural network. It defines a small set of predicted quantiles representing the agent's current estimate of the return distribution and a corresponding set of target quantiles obtained from a Bellman-style update. Fixed quantile fractions (taus) define probability levels for each quantile. The quantile_loss function computes a simplified quantile regression loss that measures how far each predicted quantile is from its target. The printed output shows the distributions and the resulting loss, demonstrating how QR-DQN learns by shifting quantiles toward the true return distribution."

Example P4 – U4 – D19

QR-DQN

```
# ###############################################
import numpy as np

# Number of quantiles
N = 5

# Predicted quantiles from the network (Q_theta(s,a))
```

```
predicted_quantiles = np.array([-2.0, -1.0, 0.5, 1.5, 3.0])

# Target quantiles from Bellman update
target_quantiles = np.array([-1.5, -0.5, 1.0, 2.0, 4.0])

# Quantile fractions (taus)
taus = np.array([(i + 0.5) / N for i in range(N)])

# Quantile Huber loss (simplified QR loss)
def quantile_loss(pred, target, taus):
    loss = 0
    for i in range(len(pred)):
        error = target - pred[i]
        loss += np.mean(np.abs(taus[i] - (error < 0)) * error**2)
    return loss

loss_value = quantile_loss(predicted_quantiles, target_quantiles, taus)

print("Predicted Quantiles:", predicted_quantiles)
print("Target Quantiles:    ", target_quantiles)
print("Quantile Fractions:", taus)
print("QR Loss:", round(loss_value, 4))
```

Output:

```
Output

Predicted Quantiles: [-2.  -1.   0.5  1.5  3. ]
Target Quantiles:    [-1.5 -0.5  1.   2.   4. ]
Quantile Fractions: [0.1 0.3 0.5 0.7 0.9]
QR Loss: 8.21
```

3. IQN (Implicit Quantile Networks)

IQN takes QR-DQN further by learning a **continuous mapping from quantile fractions to values**.

- Samples quantiles dynamically
- Models the return distribution implicitly
- Most powerful and flexible
- Used in state-of-the-art agents

A. What is IQN?

IQN is a smarter version of QR-DQN.

Instead of learning only a fixed set of quantiles (like 51 or 32), **IQN learns the entire distribution continuously** by sampling *any number of quantiles on demand.*

So while:

- **C51** → fixed atoms
- **QR-DQN** → fixed quantiles
- **IQN** → *infinite flexible quantiles*

This gives IQN **much higher precision and adaptability**.

B. Analogy: The Weather Forecast Board

Imagine you want to predict tomorrow's temperature:

C51: You only get 51 fixed temperature points (rigid).

QR-DQN: You get 32 fixed percentiles (better).

IQN: You can ask:

- "What's the 10% coldest scenario?"
- "What's the median?"
- "What's the 97% hottest case?"

IQN **generates temperature values for ANY probability level you request** — not limited to fixed slots.

That's exactly what IQN does with **future rewards**.

C. Core Idea of IQN

Instead of learning:

```
Q(s, a) = E [Z(s, a)]
```

IQN directly models:

$Z_\tau(s, a)$ = Return at quantile τ

where:

$\tau \sim \text{Uniform}(0,1)$

So every forward pass:

1. Randomly samples probability levels τ
2. Predicts the return at each τ
3. Learns the **full shape of the reward distribution**

D. Simple Numerical Example

Suppose the true future reward distribution is:

Outcome	Reward
Bad	-10
Okay	2
Great	15

Now IQN randomly samples:

$\tau = [0.1, 0.5, 0.9]$

It predicts:

- $Z_{0.1} = -8$ (bad outcome)
- $Z_{0.5} = 3$ (average case)
- $Z_{0.9} = 13$ (high reward case)

Target comes from:

$Z' = r + \gamma \cdot Z_\tau(s', a*)$

Each sampled quantile is updated using **quantile regression**, exactly like QR-DQN — but now **with unlimited resolution**.

E. The Key IQN Equation

IQN Output Function:

$$Z_\tau(s, a) = f_\theta(s, a, \tau)$$

Where:

- s = state
- a = action
- $\tau \sim U(0,1)$
- f_θ = neural network

F. Bellman Target:

$$Z_\tau^{target} = r + \gamma \cdot Z_{\tau'}(s', a*)$$

Where:

- τ' is another random quantile sample

G. Quantile Regression Loss:

$$L(\theta) = E_{\tau,\tau'}[\varrho_\tau(Z_{\tau'}^{target} - Z_\tau)]$$

This trains the network to shape the **entire return distribution**, not just its average.

Master said, "This NumPy-based IQN code reveals how modern agents learn not just a single value, but the entire distribution of future rewards. The agent samples random quantiles (τ), predicts their values, and updates them using a distributional Bellman target. Instead of minimizing simple error, it applies quantile regression with a Huber loss, allowing robust learning under uncertainty. Each update nudges the model parameters toward the true shape of expected returns. This shows the essence of implicit quantile learning—where uncertainty is learned directly through experience, not assumed—making the agent wiser in unpredictable worlds."

Example P4 – U4 – D20

IQN

```
import numpy as np

# ----------------------------
# SETTINGS
# ----------------------------
num_quantiles = 8       # how many taus we sample per step (IQN can vary this!)
gamma = 0.99            # discount factor
lr = 0.01               # learning rate
np.random.seed(0)

# ----------------------------
# SIMPLE LINEAR IQN MODEL
# Z_tau(s, a) = w_s * s + w_tau * tau + b
# ----------------------------
w_s   = np.random.randn()
w_tau = np.random.randn()
b     = np.random.randn()

def iqn_forward(state, taus):
    """Predict quantile values Z_tau(s)"""
    return w_s * state + w_tau * taus + b

# ----------------------------
# FAKE TRANSITION (ONE STEP)
# ----------------------------
state      = 2.0      # current state value
next_state = 3.0
reward     = 1.0

# ----------------------------
# 1. SAMPLE QUANTILES
# ----------------------------
taus = np.random.rand(num_quantiles)

# ----------------------------
# 2. CURRENT QUANTILE VALUES
# ----------------------------
Z_current = iqn_forward(state, taus)

# ----------------------------
# 3. TARGET QUANTICES (NEXT STATE)
# ----------------------------
```

```
taus_next = np.random.rand(num_quantiles)
Z_next = iqn_forward(next_state, taus_next)
Z_target = reward + gamma * Z_next

# -----------------------------
# 4. QUANTILE REGRESSION LOSS
# -----------------------------
td_errors = Z_target - Z_current

huber = np.where(
    np.abs(td_errors) < 1,
    0.5 * td_errors**2,
    np.abs(td_errors) - 0.5
)

quantile_loss = np.abs(taus - (td_errors < 0).astype(float)) * huber
loss = np.mean(quantile_loss)

# -----------------------------
# 5. GRADIENT UPDATE (MANUAL)
# -----------------------------
dw_s   = -np.mean(td_errors * state)
dw_tau = -np.mean(td_errors * taus)
db     = -np.mean(td_errors)

w_s   -= lr * dw_s
w_tau -= lr * dw_tau
b     -= lr * db

# -----------------------------
# PRINT EVERYTHING
# -----------------------------
print("Sampled taus:\n", taus)
print("\nCurrent Quantile Values Z(s, τ):\n", Z_current)
print("\nTarget Quantile Values Z'(s', τ'):\n", Z_target)
print("\nTD Errors:\n", td_errors)
print("\nIQN Quantile Loss:", loss)

print("\nUpdated Parameters:")
print("w_s:", w_s)
print("w_tau:", w_tau)
print("b:", b)
```

Output:

```
Output

Sampled taus:
 [0.4236548  0.64589411 0.43758721 0.891773   0.96366276 0.38344152
 0.79172504 0.52889492]

Current Quantile Values Z(s, τ):
 [4.6763712  4.76530186 4.68194635 4.86369207 4.89245928 4.66027956
 4.82365716 4.71848379]

Target Quantile Values Z'(s', τ'):
 [7.43322013 7.5748664  7.23632741 7.24270283 7.2161957  7.53803312
 7.51645725 7.55284629]

TD Errors:
 [2.75684893 2.80956454 2.55438105 2.37901076 2.32373643 2.87775355
 2.6928001  2.8343625 ]

IQN Quantile Loss: 1.332800560230522

Updated Parameters:
w_s: 1.81712349061181
w_tau: 0.41665185982053643
b: 1.0052735564278121
```

H. Why IQN is Powerful

- Infinite precision
- Better handling of risk
- Learns uncertainty naturally
- Outperforms QR-DQN & C51 in complex environments
- Perfect for finance, robotics, games, and control tasks

Why Distributional RL Matters

- Better handling of uncertainty
- Improved training stability
- Stronger performance in deep RL

- Enables risk-aware decision making

Master said, "Classic RL learns 'how good an action is on average.' Distributional RL learns 'how good it could be, how bad it could be, and how likely each outcome is.'"

PART FOUR

DAY TWENTY

Unit 4 - Lesson Nine

Policy Gradient Methods

☐ Policy Gradient

Akshatha asked, "Master, what are Policy Gradient Methods in Reinforcement Learning?"

Master said, "Policy Gradient methods are approaches where we do not learn value-functions first… we directly learn the policy itself."

Instead of asking *"How good is this state?"* (as value-based methods do), we ask *"How should I act?"* and improve the answer step by step.

These methods are vital when actions are **continuous**, decisions are **fluid**, and sharp decision boundaries are needed—such as robotics, control systems, finance, and complex games.

What Policy Gradient Really Means

We have a policy $\pi_\theta(a|s)$ parameterized by θ (weights of a neural network).

We want to maximize the expected return:

$$J(\theta) = E_{\pi\theta}\left[\sum_{t=0}^{\infty} R_t\right]$$

Our goal is to find the **best θ** that **brings the highest reward.**

Policy Gradient methods directly compute:

$\nabla_{\theta} J(\theta)$

Then perform **Gradient Ascent**:

$\theta \leftarrow \theta + \alpha \nabla_{\theta} J(\theta)$

Just like climbing a hill toward a higher expected reward.

Mathematical Intuition (Likelihood Ratio Trick)

The golden formula in Policy Gradient is the **REINFORCE rule**:

$\nabla J(\theta) = E[\nabla \theta \log \pi_{\theta}(a_t | s_t) \, G_t]$

Where:

- $\log \pi_{\theta}(a_t | s_t)$: How likely the action was
- G_t: The total return from that action onward
- The gradient increases the probability of good actions and decreases the probability of bad ones

Meaning:

"If an action brought a high return, update the policy to make that action *more likely* in the future."

This formula lets us update the policy **without knowing the environment's dynamics**.

Mini Example (Simple Grid World)

Imagine a 1D world:

Start → → → Goal

From the Start, the agent can go **Left** or **Right**

- Reward = **+1** when it reaches the Goal
- Policy: Softmax over actions with parameter θ
  - P(Right) = σ(θ)
  - P(Left) = 1 − σ(θ)

Episode Rollout

Suppose during an episode, the agent took **Right**, **Right**, reached Goal → Reward = 1.

The returns for each step = 1.

The gradient update becomes:

$$\theta \leftarrow \theta + \alpha(1)(1-\sigma(\theta))$$

This pushes θ upward → increases the probability of choosing **Right** again.

Over many episodes:

- The agent learns that the **Right** leads to a reward
- The probability of "Right" increases gradually
- Eventually: P(Right)→1

It has learned the policy directly.

Analogy: "The Master Archer"

Master said, Akshatha, imagine an archer learning to shoot perfect arrows.

Value-based learning is like telling the archer:

"If you hit this region of the target, it's worth 10 points.

If you hit that region, it's 5 points."

But Policy Gradient is different:

We don't care about the value of regions.

We only care about improving the *style* of shooting.

Each shot teaches the archer:

- If the arrow hits the bullseye (high reward), he slightly adjusts his stance to repeat that posture.
- If it misses (low reward), he adjusts away from that posture.

Over time, every muscle movement—shoulder, grip, breathing—is tuned directly toward better performance.

This is Policy Gradient.

We do not learn the value of the target.

We learn *how to shoot.*

We learn *the policy itself.*

Summary

Policy Gradient Methods:

- Directly optimize the **policy**
- Use gradient ascent on expected returns
- Suitable for continuous and complex action spaces
- Use REINFORCE:

$$\nabla J(\theta) = E[\nabla_\theta \log\pi_\theta(a|s)\ G_t]$$

- Learn by making rewarding actions more likely

Analogy:

The learning of a master archer—adjusting form continuously after each shot.

☐ Types of Policy Gradient Methods

1. REINFORCE (Monte-Carlo Policy Gradient)

A classic, unbiased Monte-Carlo estimator of the policy gradient that uses complete episodes and the likelihood-ratio trick.

Objective and gradient (recap):

$$J(\theta) = E_{\tau\sim\pi\theta}[G(\tau)],\ \nabla_\theta J(\theta) = E\ [\textstyle\sum_t \nabla_{\theta c} \log\pi\theta(a_t|s_t)\ G_t]$$

where $G_t = \sum_{k=t}^{\infty} \gamma^{k-t} r_k$.

Algorithm (pseudocode):

1. Collect a full episode $\{(s_t,a_t,r_t)\}_{t=0}^{T}$
2. For each time step t, compute return G_t.
3. Update: $\theta \leftarrow \theta + \alpha \sum_t \nabla_{\theta c} \log\pi\theta(a_t|s_t)\ G_t$.

Properties, pros & cons:

- *Unbiased* gradient estimate (because it uses true returns).
- *High variance*, especially for long episodes or sparse rewards.
- Sample-inefficient (needs many episodes).
- Simple, conceptually clean — great as a teaching baseline.

Practical improvements:

- Use a *baseline* b(st) to reduce variance: replace G_t with $G_t - b(s_t)$. Any baseline that does not depend on a_t keeps the estimator unbiased.
- Add *entropy regularization* to encourage exploration: add $\beta E[-\log\pi\theta(\cdot|s)]$to objective.

2. Actor–Critic Methods

Combine policy (actor) with a learned value function (critic). Critic reduces variance by estimating expected returns; actor learns from critic's feedback.

Structure:

- **Actor:** parameterized policy $\pi_\theta(a|s)$.
- **Critic:** parameterized value function $V_w(s)$ or action-value $Q_w(s,a)$.

Core update (using advantage):

$$\nabla_\theta J(\theta) \approx E\,[\,\nabla_\theta \log\pi\theta(a_t \mid s_t)\, A_w(s_t, a_t)]$$

where advantage $A_w(s_t,a_t)=Q_w(s_t,a_t)-V_w(st)$ (or a TD error $\delta_t=r_t+\gamma V_w(s_{t+1})-V_w(s_t)$.

Variants to know:

- **A2C (Advantage Actor-Critic):** synchronous, batched actor-critic — widely used for stability.
- **A3C:** asynchronous parallel workers — speeds up training and stabilizes via decorrelated experience.
- **Deterministic Policy Gradient (DPG/DDPG):** for continuous actions with deterministic policies; uses gradients of Q w.r.t. actions.
- **SAC (Soft Actor-Critic):** off-policy actor-critic with entropy maximization (robust exploration).

Why it helps:

- Critic provides a low-variance *baseline* and can be updated from bootstrapped TD targets — much more sample-efficient than REINFORCE.
- Combines the strengths of value-based bootstrapping and policy optimization.

Practical tips:

- Use *advantage estimators*, not raw returns, to cut variance.
- Train actor and critic at different learning rates: e.g., $\alpha_w > \alpha_\theta$ or vice-versa, depending on stability.
- Regularize the actor via entropy bonus and critic via target networks or value clipping.

3. Proximal Policy Optimization (PPO)

Essence (short): A robust, easy-to-use policy gradient method that constrains how much the policy can change per update, preventing destructive, large steps.

Core idea: optimize a surrogate objective that penalizes large policy updates using an importance-sampling ratio:

$$r_t(\theta) = \pi\theta(a_t|s_t)/\pi\theta_{old}(a_t|s_t)$$

Two common PPO objectives:

1. **Clipped surrogate (most common):**

$$L^{CLIP}(\theta) = E\ [\min\ (r_t(\theta)A_t,\ \text{clip}(r_t(\theta),\ 1-\epsilon,1+\epsilon)A_t)]$$

2. **KL-penalty** variant: add a penalty proportional to $KL(\pi\theta_{old}||\pi_\theta)$.

Why clipping helps: prevents r_t from moving too far from 1 — avoids overly large policy updates that break training.

Properties & strengths:

- Empirically stable and sample-efficient for many tasks.
- Simpler to implement than TRPO, yet captures many of its benefits.
- Widely used in continuous control and discrete action tasks.

Practical hyperparameters:

- Clip $\epsilon \approx 0.1 - 0.3$ typical.
- Number of epochs per batch and minibatch size matter (PPO re-uses collected trajectories for K epochs).
- Use advantage normalization and value-function loss weighting.

Other notable policy-gradient families (short guide)

- **TRPO (Trust Region Policy Optimization):** optimizes under a trust-region constraint (KL); more complex (requires conjugate gradient) but principled.
- **GAE (Generalized Advantage Estimation):** a family of advantage estimators interpolating between high variance/low bias and low variance/high bias. GAE(λ) is commonly used with PPO/A2C.
- **Deterministic Policy Gradient (DPG) / DDPG:** for deterministic policies with continuous actions (actor outputs action directly; critic is Q).
- **SAC (Soft Actor-Critic):** entropy-regularized, off-policy actor-critic providing sample efficiency and robust exploration.

Variance reduction & stability tricks (practical core)

1. **Baseline / Value function:** subtract V(s) from return to form advantage A.
2. **Advantage normalization:** normalize advantages (zero mean, unit std) across a batch.
3. **GAE(λ):** mix n-step returns to trade bias/variance. Typical: $\lambda \approx 0.95$.
4. **Entropy bonus:** encourages exploration, prevents premature collapse.
5. **Gradient clipping/value clipping:** to avoid exploding gradients and bootstrap error.
6. **Target networks & Polyak averaging:** helpful in off-policy actor-critic (DDPG, TD3).
7. **Use minibatches and multiple epochs (PPO):** improves sample reuse while controlling policy drift.

Continuous action policies — parameterization details

For continuous actions $a \in R^d$, policy commonly parameterized as a Gaussian:

$$\pi_\theta(a|s) = N(\mu_\theta(s), \Sigma_\theta(s))$$

- Actor outputs mean $\mu_\theta(s)$; covariance Σ often diagonal or fixed.

- For deterministic policy (DDPG/TD3), the actor outputs a raw action; exploration via noise process (OU noise, Gaussian).

Gradient for Gaussian policy: analytical form for $\nabla_\theta \log\pi_\theta$ — useful for stable learning.

Implementation & monitoring tips

- **Diagnostics to watch:** policy entropy, value loss, policy loss, KL divergence between old/new policies, episode return, gradient norms.
- **Save and test policy frequently** (rollout deterministic policy for evaluation).
- **Normalize observations and rewards** (clip rewards or use return scaling).
- **Stability recipe:** smaller learning rates, advantage normalization, entropy bonus, early stopping if KL too large (PPO), gradient clipping.

Strengths, weaknesses, and when to pick which

- **REINFORCE:** good for teaching and simple problems; not for large/complex tasks due to variance.
- **Actor–Critic (A2C/A3C, DDPG, SAC):** balanced choice; efficient; prefer when you want bootstrapping and lower variance.
- **PPO:** go-to for robust performance across many domains; simple to tune and widely adopted.
- **SAC:** excellent for continuous control where sample efficiency matters and exploration must be robust.
- **TRPO:** principled but heavier; use if you want trust-region guarantees.

Example

Task: continuous control — robot arm reaching a point.

- **Policy:** Gaussian N that outputs mean torques.
- **Critic:** value network estimates V(s).
- **Algorithm:** PPO with GAE(λ=0.95), clip ε=0.2, entropy bonus β=0.01.

- **Why:** PPO + GAE gives stable, sample-efficient updates; entropy keeps exploration so the arm discovers diverse trajectories.

Final practical checklist (for experiments)

1. Normalize inputs; seed experiments; use good logging.
2. Start with PPO or A2C for most tasks; use SAC for sample efficiency in continuous tasks.
3. Use advantage normalization and GAE.
4. Track KL or policy change; stop epoch early if KL grows too large.
5. Tune learning rates, clipping ε, batch size, and entropy weight.
6. Evaluate deterministic policy periodically (no noise) to measure real performance.

☐ Actor–Critic Algorithm

John asked, "Master, what is the Actor–Critic Algorithm in Reinforcement Learning?"

Master said, "The Actor–Critic method is where *decision and judgment walk together*. One part of the learner **acts**, and the other **thinks about the action**. Together, they allow learning that is both **bold and wise**."

Core Idea of Actor–Critic

The Actor–Critic algorithm combines **two powerful ideas**:

Component	Role
Actor	Chooses actions using a policy
Critic	Evaluates how good the chosen action was

- The **Actor** answers: *"What should I do?"*
- The **Critic** answers: *"How good was that decision?"*

This separation fixes the main weakness of pure policy methods (high variance) and value-based methods (slow policy improvement).

Key Mathematical Foundations

Policy (Actor)

$\pi_\theta(a|s)$

- Probability of choosing action **a** in state **s**
- **θ (theta)** = actor's learning parameters
- The actor updates itself using **policy gradients**

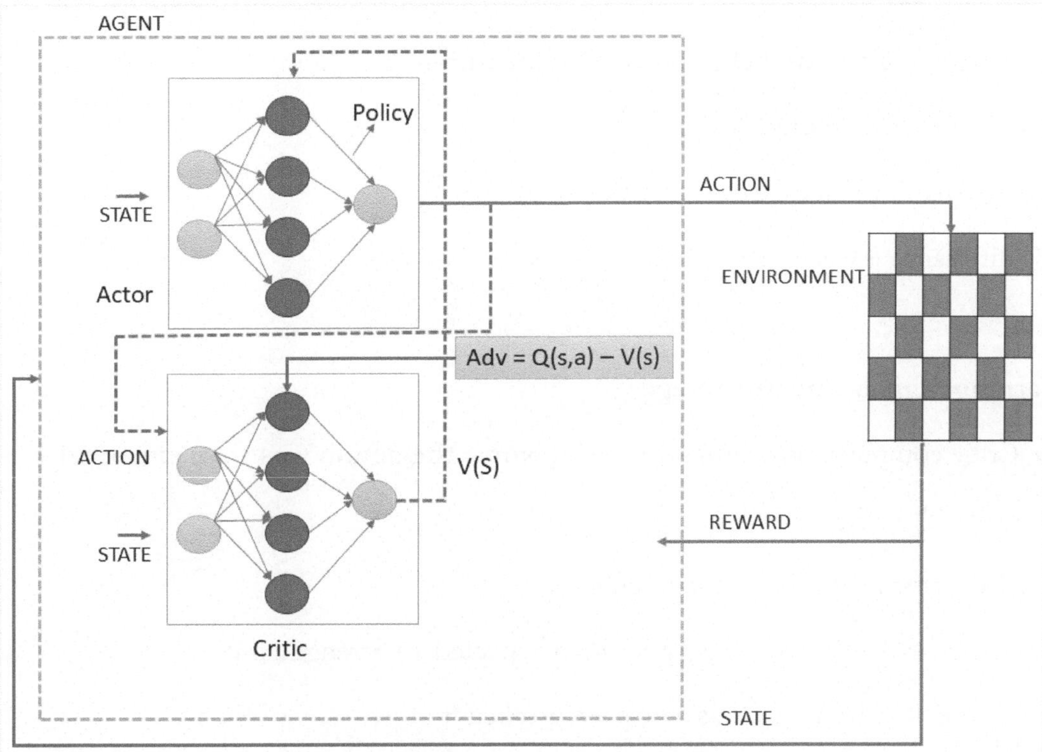

Illustration Actor_1: Actor Critic

The Actor's goal is simple: Increase the probability of actions that lead to higher long-term rewards.

It does this by adjusting its parameters θ using the policy gradient:

$$\nabla_\theta J(\theta) \approx \nabla_\theta \log\pi_\theta(a|s)\, A(s, a)$$

The Actor does not work alone—it depends entirely on feedback from the Critic through the Advantage function.

Value Function (Critic)

The Critic estimates **how good a state is**, using the **value function**:

$V_w(s)$

- Expected future reward from state **s**
- w = critic's parameters

It learns using **Temporal Difference (TD) learning**, comparing:

- What is **expected**, versus
- What it **actually experienced**

This difference is called the **TD Error**:

Learning Signal: The Advantage

The Critic computes **how much better or worse the action was than expected**:

$\delta = r + \gamma V(s') - V(s)$

This **TD error (δ)** becomes the teacher:

- If **δ > 0** → Action was better than expected → Strengthen it
- If **δ < 0** → Action was worse → Weaken it

The Advantage Function – The Bridge Between Actor and Critic

The **Advantage** tells the Actor:

"Was this action better or worse than average?"

$$A(s, a) = Q(s, a) - V(s) \approx \delta$$

- Positive advantage → reinforce the action

- Negative advantage → suppress the action

Thus, the Actor does not blindly chase rewards—it learns **which actions are truly better than the baseline expectation**.

How Learning Happens at Each Step

At every time step:

1. Actor chooses an action using the policy
2. Environment returns reward and next state
3. Critic computes TD error
4. Critic improves its value estimate
5. Actor updates its policy using that TD error as feedback

This creates a **continuous feedback loop** between thinking and judging.

Real-Life Analogy

Archer & Coach Analogy

- **Actor = Archer** → Shoots the arrow (takes action)
- **Critic = Coach** → Says how good the shot was
- **Target = Reward**

If the arrow goes closer to the bullseye:

- Coach praises → Archer repeats that style

If it misses badly:

- Coach corrects → Archer adjusts aim

Over time:

The **archer improves precision**

The **coach improves judgment**

This is exactly how Actor–Critic works.

Simple Numerical Example

Consider a 1-step environment

State: S

Two actions: A1, A2

Discount factor: $\gamma = 0.9$

Initial Value: $V(S) = 5$

Step 1: Actor Picks an Action

Suppose:

$\pi(A1|S) = 0.6$, $\pi(A2|S) = 0.4$

Actor picks **A1**

Step 2: Environment Responds

Reward received: $R = 2$

Next state value: $V(S') = 6$

Step 3: Critic Computes TD Error

$\delta = R + \gamma V(S') - V(S)$

$\delta = 2 + 0.9 \times 6 - 5 = 2 + 5.4 - 5 = 2.4$

Positive TD error → Action was better than expected

Step 4: Updates

Critic Update: $V(S) \leftarrow V(S) + \alpha\delta$

Actor Update (Policy Gradient): $\theta \leftarrow \theta + \eta \cdot \delta \cdot \nabla_\theta \log\pi(A1|S)$

So:

- Critic raises the value estimate
- Actor increases probability of choosing A1

Why Actor–Critic Is Powerful

Problem	Solved by Actor–Critic
High variance in policy gradients	Reduced by Critic
Slow policy learning in value-based RL	Actor improves directly
Continuous action spaces	Works naturally
Online learning	Updates every step

Where Actor–Critic Is Used

Actor–Critic is the **spiritual root** of modern deep RL:

- A2C / A3C (Asynchronous Advantage Actor–Critic)
- PPO (Proximal Policy Optimization)
- DDPG (for continuous control)
- SAC (Soft Actor–Critic)

These powers:

- Robotics
- Self-driving cars
- Trading agents
- Game-playing AI

Master said: "The Actor gives courage to act. The Critic gives wisdom to reflect. Alone, each can stumble. Together, they learn to walk the path of optimality."

Master said, "This code demonstrates a complete **Actor–Critic reinforcement learning agent** trained on the CartPole environment. It first imports required libraries, then creates the environment to define state and action spaces. Two neural networks are built: the **Actor**, which outputs action probabilities, and the **Critic**, which estimates state values. Separate optimizers update each network. During training, the Actor selects actions, the environment returns rewards, and the Critic computes the **TD error**. The Critic minimizes value prediction error, while the Actor maximizes expected reward using the TD error as an advantage signal. Over episodes, the agent learns to balance the pole successfully."

Example P4 – U4 – D21
Actor–Critic Method

```
# ----------------------------------------
# STEP 1: IMPORT LIBRARIES
# ----------------------------------------
import gym
import torch
import torch.nn as nn
import torch.optim as optim
import numpy as np

# ----------------------------------------
# STEP 2: CREATE ENVIRONMENT
# ----------------------------------------
env = gym.make("CartPole-v1")
state_dim = env.observation_space.shape[0]
action_dim = env.action_space.n

# ----------------------------------------
# STEP 3: DEFINE ACTOR AND CRITIC NETWORKS
# ----------------------------------------
class Actor(nn.Module):
    def __init__(self):
        super(Actor, self).__init__()
        self.fc = nn.Sequential(
            nn.Linear(state_dim, 128),
            nn.ReLU(),
            nn.Linear(128, action_dim),
            nn.Softmax(dim=-1)
        )

    def forward(self, state):
        return self.fc(state)


class Critic(nn.Module):
    def __init__(self):
        super(Critic, self).__init__()
        self.fc = nn.Sequential(
            nn.Linear(state_dim, 128),
            nn.ReLU(),
            nn.Linear(128, 1)
```

```
        )

    def forward(self, state):
        return self.fc(state)


actor = Actor()
critic = Critic()

# ----------------------------------------
# STEP 4: DEFINE OPTIMIZERS AND LOSS
# ----------------------------------------
actor_optimizer = optim.Adam(actor.parameters(), lr=0.001)
critic_optimizer = optim.Adam(critic.parameters(), lr=0.002)
mse_loss = nn.MSELoss()

gamma = 0.99

# ----------------------------------------
# STEP 5: TRAINING LOOP
# ----------------------------------------
episodes = 300

for ep in range(episodes):
    state = env.reset()[0]
    state = torch.FloatTensor(state)

    total_reward = 0
    done = False

    while not done:
        # Actor selects action
        probs = actor(state)
        dist = torch.distributions.Categorical(probs)
        action = dist.sample()

        next_state, reward, done, _, _ = env.step(action.item())
        next_state = torch.FloatTensor(next_state)

        total_reward += reward

        # Critic value estimates
        value = critic(state)
        next_value = critic(next_state)

        # ---------- TD ERROR ----------
        target = reward + gamma * next_value * (1 - int(done))
        td_error = target - value
```

```
        # ---------- CRITIC UPDATE ----------
        critic_loss = mse_loss(value, target.detach())
        critic_optimizer.zero_grad()
        critic_loss.backward()
        critic_optimizer.step()

        # ---------- ACTOR UPDATE ----------
        actor_loss = -dist.log_prob(action) * td_error.detach()
        actor_optimizer.zero_grad()
        actor_loss.backward()
        actor_optimizer.step()

        state = next_state

    if (ep + 1) % 50 == 0:
        print(f"Episode {ep+1}, Total Reward: {total_reward}")

env.close()
```

Output:

```
Output

Episode 50, Total Reward: 9.0
Episode 100, Total Reward: 9.0
Episode 150, Total Reward: 124.0
Episode 200, Total Reward: 117.0
Episode 250, Total Reward: 60.0
Episode 300, Total Reward: 157.0
```

Key Advantages of the Actor–Critic Method

- **Improved Sample Efficiency:** Learns faster with fewer environment interactions.
- **Faster Convergence:** Policy and value improve simultaneously.
- **Works for Both Discrete and Continuous Actions:** Suitable for robotics, trading, games, and control systems.
- **Supports Off-Policy Learning (in some variants):** Can learn from stored experiences.

Major Variants of Actor–Critic Algorithms

Advantage Actor–Critic (A2C)

A2C replaces raw returns with the **Advantage Function**:

$A(s_t,a_t)=Q(s_t,a_t)-V(s_t)$

This reduces noise in the learning signal, leading to more stable and faster policy improvement.

Asynchronous Advantage Actor–Critic (A3C)

A3C runs **multiple agents in parallel**, each exploring the environment independently and updating a shared model asynchronously. This:

- Breaks correlation in training data,
- Improves stability,
- Speeds up learning significantly.

Master said:

"When judgment and choice are trained together, learning becomes swift and balanced. Actor–Critic is not just a method—it is a dialogue between action and wisdom."

☐ **Proximal Policy Optimization (PPO)**

Roopa asked, "Master, what is Proximal Policy Optimization (PPO) in Reinforcement Learning?"

Master said, Proximal Policy Optimization (PPO) is a powerful and widely used reinforcement learning algorithm designed to improve an agent's behavior **safely, steadily, and efficiently**. PPO belongs to the family of **policy gradient methods**, meaning it directly learns a policy that maps states to actions. What makes PPO special is its ability to **prevent unstable learning** by controlling how much the policy is allowed to change at each update.

Instead of taking large, risky policy jumps that can destroy learning progress, PPO uses a **clipping mechanism** that restricts policy updates within a safe range. This allows the agent to **maximize rewards while maintaining training stability**, making PPO both **robust and reliable**. Because of this balance, PPO is widely adopted in **robotics, game AI, autonomous systems, and generative AI**.

PPO vs Earlier Policy Gradient Methods

1. **REINFORCE:**
   REINFORCE is simple and intuitive but suffers from **high variance**, leading to unstable and slow learning. PPO improves upon this by **limiting sudden policy shifts**, making training far more stable.

2. **Actor-Critic:**
   Actor-Critic methods reduce variance by combining a **policy network (actor)** and a **value network (critic)**. PPO builds on this idea by still using a critic for advantage estimation, but adds **clipped policy updates** for extra safety and consistency.

Thus, PPO provides the **stability of Actor-Critic with the simplicity of policy gradients**, making it a preferred choice in complex environments.

Role of PPO in Generative AI

PPO plays a **foundational role in modern Generative AI**, especially in:

1. **Reinforcement Learning with Human Feedback (RLHF):**

   Used to align large language models with human preferences.

2. **Stable Optimization of Large Models:**

   Ensures controlled learning without catastrophic behaviour.

3. **Safe Creativity:**

   Balances originality with safety and alignment.

4. **Scalable Learning:**

   Handles billions of parameters efficiently.

5. **Human-like Interaction:**

   Improves coherence, relevance, and helpfulness in AI outputs.

Key Parameters in PPO

1. **Clip Range (ε):** Limits policy deviation for stability
2. **Learning Rate:** Controls update speed
3. **Discount Factor (γ):** Balances future vs immediate rewards
4. **GAE Lambda (λ):** Trade-off between bias and variance
5. **Epochs:** Number of optimization passes per batch
6. **Batch Size:** Samples per update
7. **Value Loss Coefficient (c_1):** Weight of critic loss
8. **Entropy Coefficient (c_2):** Encourages exploration

Master said, "PPO is a policy-gradient method that *carefully* nudges the policy toward higher reward while avoiding large destructive updates. It uses a *surrogate objective* and a *clipping* trick to guarantee each update stays "proximal" to the previous policy."

Key quantities and notation

- $\pi_\theta(a|s)$: new policy (parameter θ)
- $\pi_{\theta old}(a|s)$: behavior policy (parameters before update)
- $r(\theta) = \pi_\theta(a|s)/\pi_{\theta old}(a|s)$: probability ratio
- A_t: advantage estimate at time t (how much better the action a_t was than baseline)
- ε: clip range (e.g. 0.1 or 0.2)

Surrogate objective and clipping (core math)

The unclipped surrogate objective (per sample) is:

$$L^{PG}(\theta) = E_t\,[\,r(\theta)_t\,A_t] \text{ where } r(\theta)t = \pi_\theta(a_t|s_t)/\pi_{\theta old}(a_t|s_t).$$

Where $r(\theta)_t = \pi_\theta(a_t|s_t)/\pi_{\theta old}(a_t|s_t)$.

PPO uses the clipped surrogate objective to limit large updates:

$$L^{CLIP}(\theta) = E_t\,[\min(r(\theta)_t A_t, \mathrm{clip}(r(\theta)_t, 1-\varepsilon, 1+\varepsilon)\,A_t)]$$

Interpretation:

- If $r(\theta)t$ moves *slightly* from 1 in the direction favoured by At, the first term wins and the update proceeds.
- If $r(\theta)t$ would move *too far* (outside $[1-\varepsilon, 1+\varepsilon]$), the clipped term prevents further increase in objective — avoiding overly aggressive policy changes.

Full PPO objective (used in practice)

Combine actor, critic, and entropy regularizer:

$$L(\theta, w) = E_t\,[L^{CLIP}(\theta) - c_1 L^{VF}(w) + c_2\, H(\pi_\theta(\cdot \mid s_t))]$$

where:

- $L^{VF}(w) = (V_w(s_t) - V_t^{target})^2$ is value loss (critic params w).
- H is entropy (encourages exploration).
- c1, c2 are coefficients balancing value loss and entropy.
- Policy: $[L^{CLIP}(\theta)]$

Advantage estimation (practical)

A common and effective choice is **Generalized Advantage Estimation (GAE)**:

$$\widehat{A_t^{\lambda}} = \sum_{l=0}^{\infty} (\gamma\lambda)^l\, \delta^{t+l} \text{ with } \delta_t = r_t + \gamma V(s_{t+1}) - V(s_t).$$

GAE trades bias/variance via $\lambda \in [0,1]$.

Simple numerical example (one sample)

Assume a single transition with:

- $\pi_{old}(a|s) = 0.2$, $\pi_\theta(a|s) = 0.26$
- Advantage $A_t = +2.0$ (action was good)
- $\varepsilon = 0.1$ (clip range)

Compute ratio:

$r(\theta)_t = 0.26/0.20 = 1.3$.

Clipping bounds: $[1-\varepsilon,1+\varepsilon] = [0.9,1.1]$.

- Unclipped term: $rA = 1.3\times2.0 = 2.6$.
- Clipped ratio = 1.1 (upper bound). Clipped term: $1.1\times2.0=2.2$.

PPO uses min(2.6, 2.2) = 2.2 as the contribution to the surrogate objective — **reducing the incentive** to increase probability too much. If the advantage were negative, clipping similarly protects against destructive decreases.

Add value loss and entropy as needed to form the final loss.

Algorithm outline (pseudo-code)

Pseudocode

```
Collect trajectories under policy π_old for T steps.
Compute returns and advantages (e.g., with GAE).
For K epochs:
  Shuffle data into minibatches.
  For each minibatch:
    Compute r(θ) for sampled (s,a).
    Compute L^CLIP = mean( min(r*A, clip(r,1-ε,1+ε)*A) ).
    Compute value loss L_V = mean((V_w(s) - return)^2).
    Compute entropy bonus H = mean( entropy(πθ(.|s)) ).
    Total loss: L = -L^CLIP + c1 * L_V - c2 * H   # note sign conventions
    Take a gradient step on θ,w with optimizer.
After K epochs, set θ_old ← θ and repeat data collection.
```

Analogy

Imagine a gardener tuning a delicate bonsai:

- Each adjustment (policy update) should improve shape (reward) but must be **small** and controlled to avoid breaking the tree.

- The clip acts like a gentle stiffness in the gardener's wrist — it allows useful bends but prevents a violent snap that would ruin the plant.
- The critic is the gardener's eye — a measured judge that tells which small changes were beneficial.

Practical tips & parameter roles

- ε (clip): typical 0.1 – 0.3. Smaller → safer, slower updates.
- K (epochs) and batch size: trade sample efficiency vs overfitting to collected data.
- c1, c2: tune value-weight and entropy to stabilise learning and preserve exploration.
- GAE (λ): 0.95–0.98 gives a good bias/variance balance in many tasks.

Master said, "PPO's genius is simplicity with guardrails — it keeps the **policy's improvements honest** by rewarding meaningful progress while clipping overreach. That makes PPO robust, easy to tune, and effective across many domains, from robotics to language model fine-tuning."

☐ Integrating PPO with Generative AI

Master said - Integrating PPO with Generative AI:

Think of a generative model as a talented *writer* and PPO as a wise *editor-tutor*. The writer already knows language; the tutor's job is to nudge style, safety, and usefulness by giving measured feedback. PPO is the tutor's method: give lots of short, trustworthy corrections (rewards) and only allow small, safe changes to the writer's voice at a time.

Multi-Modal Alignment — "A bilingual translator."

Analogy: imagine a translator who converts a novel into another language and also into a movie script. You want the text, the soundtrack, and the images to tell the same story.

How PPO helps:

- Reward outputs that are consistent across modalities: e.g., the caption for an image should match an image-embedding similarity score, audio transcript, or video summary.

- Use multimodal reward models (contrastive score between text & image encoders, perceptual audio metrics).

  Example: reward = 0.6·image-text-sim + 0.3·speech-text-sim + 0.1·fluency.

Practical tip: train or adopt reliable cross-modal scorers and include KL penalties to avoid drifting from fluent text.

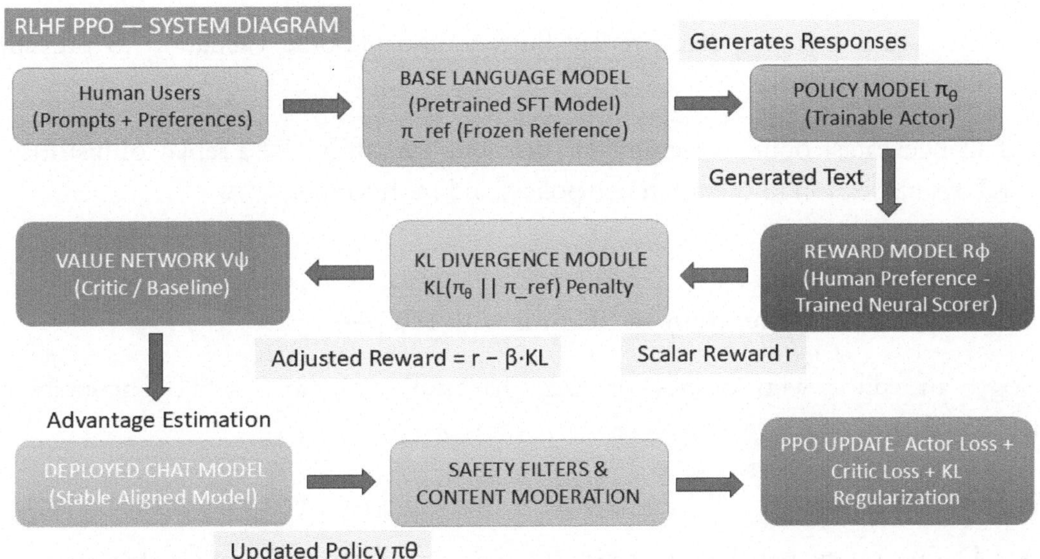

Illustration PPO_1: PPO

Personalisation — "A personal tutor."

Analogy: a tutor who adapts tone for each student — formal for Prof. Rao, casual for Priya.

How PPO helps:

- Use user-specific reward signals (explicit ratings, implicit clicks/time-on-task).
- Fine-tune a shared base model with lightweight user adapters or prompt-tuning using PPO updates.

  Example: reward = user_rating * 0.8 + engagement_score * 0.2.

Caveats: privacy, limited per-user data → use meta-learning, few-shot adaptation, or on-device personalisation with local constraints.

Continuous Online Learning — "A living newspaper."

Analogy: a newsroom that updates its style guide as stories and reader tastes change.

How PPO helps:

- Run a continuous pipeline where new interactions produce rewards that update the policy incrementally.
- Use small policy updates, replay buffers, and periodic validation to prevent catastrophic drift.

Key challenge: catastrophic forgetting and distributional shift. Use a replay of historical data, KL regularization to the reference policy, and monitoring.

Safety-Constrained Generation — "Editor with red pen."

Analogy: an editor who deletes or flags harmful paragraphs while encouraging constructive phrasing.

How PPO helps:

- Define safety penalties in the reward (toxic content detection, bias scores, hallucination penalties).
- Combine hard filters (block generation) with soft penalties (reward shaping) so the model learns to avoid unsafe outputs rather than just being filtered out.

Important: design robust reward models; a poor safety scorer will teach the model wrong lessons. Always test out-of-distribution.

Task-Specific Fine Tuning — "Specialist coach."

Analogy: a lawyer's writing coach trains a model to draft contracts with legalese and required clauses.

How PPO helps:

- Use domain-specific reward functions (correctness checks, reference-based scores, rubric scores).

- Optionally add constraints (must contain clause X) and reward higher if satisfied.

Practical tip: combine supervised fine-tuning for fundamentals, then PPO for nuanced quality and preferences.

Working workflow — the PPO loop applied to GenAI

1. **Collect experiences (generations + feedback)**
    - Generate candidates given prompts.
    - Record: prompt, generated tokens, model log-probs, metadata.
    - Obtain rewards: human labels, reward model scores, automated heuristics.
2. **Compute advantages**
    - Use a critic/value head to estimate baseline value V(s) (e.g., prompt→value).
    - Compute advantage $A_t = R_t - V(s_t)$ or use GAE for multi-step returns.
    - Normalize advantages across batch for numerical stability.
3. **PPO policy update**
    - Recompute new log-probs for generated actions (token sequences).
    - Compute ratio $r(\theta) = \exp(\log p_\theta - \log p_{\theta old})$.
    - Clip ratio to $[1-\epsilon, 1+\epsilon]$; maximize the clipped surrogate objective.
    - Add entropy bonus to encourage diversity.
4. **Value function update**
    - Minimize MSE between value head predictions and returns (or use TD/GaE targets).
    - Possibly train value head jointly in the same updates.
5. **Repeat**

  - Iterate collection → compute → update. Periodically evaluate on held-out prompts and safety checks.

Implementation & engineering tips

- **Reward design is king**: small reward bugs cause big problems. Prefer human-in-the-loop validation.
- **KL penalty/reference policy**: include KL term or explicit penalty to keep outputs close to pretrained LM (prevents degenerate outputs).
- **Mini-batch & epoch tuning**: many small epochs per collected batch (typical PPO) gives sample efficiency; do not overfit to small batches.
- **Advantage normalization**: critical for stable learning.
- **Safety & monitoring**: automated and human audits; track toxicity, hallucination, diversity, and alignment metrics.
- **Compute**: PPO on large LMs is expensive; use parameter-efficient fine-tuning (LoRA, adapters) to reduce cost.
- **Replay & stability**: keep a buffer of recent good examples to avoid forgetting.

Master said — Let us understand the Code:

This code represents a complete miniature version of a **production-style RLHF (Reinforcement Learning with Human Feedback) system using Proximal Policy Optimization (PPO)**. At its heart, the model learns not just from data, but from **reward-driven feedback**, just like a human improving through praise or correction.

First, a **language model (Actor)** generates text based on a prompt. This is the decision-maker—the voice of the agent. Alongside it, a **Critic (Value Network)** estimates how good each generated response is expected to be in terms of long-term reward. A separate **Reward Model** evaluates the generated text using heuristic signals such as positivity, usefulness, and length, simulating human preference.

During each training step, the model:

1. **Generates text** from a prompt.
2. **Computes log probabilities** of the generated tokens.

3. **Receives a reward** from the reward model.
4. **Computes advantage** (how much better the outcome was than expected).
5. **Applies PPO clipping** to ensure the policy does not change too drastically.
6. **Updates Actor, Critic, and Reward Model together** using a single stable backward pass.

Example P4 – U4 – D22

PPO

```
import torch
import torch.nn as nn
import torch.optim as optim
import torch.nn.functional as F
from transformers import GPT2Tokenizer, GPT2LMHeadModel
import random

# ========================
# DEVICE SETUP
# ========================
device = torch.device("cuda" if torch.cuda.is_available() else "cpu")

# ========================
# TOKENIZER & POLICY MODEL
# ========================
tokenizer = GPT2Tokenizer.from_pretrained("gpt2")
tokenizer.pad_token = tokenizer.eos_token

policy_model = GPT2LMHeadModel.from_pretrained("gpt2").to(device)
old_policy_model = GPT2LMHeadModel.from_pretrained("gpt2").to(device)
old_policy_model.load_state_dict(policy_model.state_dict())

# ========================
# CRITIC (VALUE NETWORK)
# ========================
class ValueNet(nn.Module):
    def __init__(self, hidden=768):
        super().__init__()
        self.fc1 = nn.Linear(hidden, 256)
        self.fc2 = nn.Linear(256, 1)

    def forward(self, x):
        x = self.fc1(x)
        x = torch.relu(x)
```

```
        return self.fc2(x)

value_net = ValueNet().to(device)

# ======================
# REWARD MODEL
# ======================
class RewardModel(nn.Module):
    def __init__(self, hidden=768):
        super().__init__()
        self.fc1 = nn.Linear(hidden, 256)
        self.fc2 = nn.Linear(256, 1)

    def forward(self, x):
        x = self.fc1(x)
        x = torch.relu(x)
        return self.fc2(x)

reward_model = RewardModel().to(device)

# ======================
# OPTIMIZERS
# ======================
policy_optimizer = optim.Adam(policy_model.parameters(), lr=1e-5)
value_optimizer = optim.Adam(value_net.parameters(), lr=1e-4)
reward_optimizer = optim.Adam(reward_model.parameters(), lr=1e-4)

# ======================
# PPO HYPERPARAMETERS
# ======================
gamma = 0.99
clip_eps = 0.2
entropy_coef = 0.01
value_coef = 0.5
kl_coef = 0.1
batch_size = 4

# ======================
# SIMPLE DATA SOURCE
# ======================
prompts = [
    "Compose a short helpful tip about healthy eating:",
    "Give one mental health tip:",
    "Say something motivational:",
    "Give one fitness advice:"
]

# ======================
```

```
# HELPER: TEXT REWARD FUNCTION
# ======================
def compute_text_reward(text):
    reward = min(len(text.split()) / 20, 1.0)
    positive_words = ["good", "healthy", "strong", "better"]
    if any(w in text.lower() for w in positive_words):
        reward += 0.5
    return reward

# ======================
# PPO TRAINING STEP
# ======================
def ppo_update(batch_prompts):

    states = []
    actions = []
    old_log_probs = []
    rewards = []
    values = []

    # ======================
    # COLLECT EXPERIENCE
    # ======================
    for prompt in batch_prompts:
        inputs = tokenizer(prompt, return_tensors="pt").to(device)

        with torch.no_grad():
            output_ids = policy_model.generate(
                inputs["input_ids"],
                max_length=30,
                do_sample=True,
                top_k=50
            )

        generated_text = tokenizer.decode(output_ids[0], skip_special_tokens=True)

        logits = policy_model(output_ids).logits
        log_probs = F.log_softmax(logits[:, :-1, :], dim=-1)
        selected_log_probs = log_probs.gather(2, output_ids[:, 1:].unsqueeze(-1)).mean()

        with torch.no_grad():
            old_logits = old_policy_model(output_ids).logits
            old_log_probs_sel = F.log_softmax(old_logits[:, :-1, :], dim=-1)\
                .gather(2, output_ids[:, 1:].unsqueeze(-1)).mean()

        last_hidden = policy_model.transformer(output_ids).last_hidden_state[:, -1]
        state_value = value_net(last_hidden).squeeze()
        predicted_reward = reward_model(last_hidden).squeeze()
```

```
        actual_reward = torch.tensor(compute_text_reward(generated_text),
device=device)

        states.append(last_hidden)
        actions.append(selected_log_probs)
        old_log_probs.append(old_log_probs_sel)
        rewards.append(actual_reward)
        values.append(state_value)

    states = torch.stack(states)
    actions = torch.stack(actions)
    old_log_probs = torch.stack(old_log_probs)
    rewards = torch.stack(rewards)
    values = torch.stack(values)

    advantages = rewards - values.detach()

    # =====================
    # PPO LOSS
    # =====================
    ratio = torch.exp(actions - old_log_probs)
    surr1 = ratio * advantages
    surr2 = torch.clamp(ratio, 1 - clip_eps, 1 + clip_eps) * advantages
    policy_loss = -torch.min(surr1, surr2).mean()

    value_loss = F.mse_loss(values, rewards)

    reward_preds = reward_model(states).squeeze()
    reward_loss = F.mse_loss(reward_preds, rewards)

    kl_div = torch.mean(actions - old_log_probs)

    entropy = -actions.mean()

    # SINGLE COMBINED LOSS (FIX)
    total_loss = policy_loss \
                + value_coef * value_loss \
                + reward_loss \
                + kl_coef * kl_div \
                - entropy_coef * entropy

    # =====================
    # BACKPROP (SINGLE PASS ONLY)
    # =====================
    policy_optimizer.zero_grad()
    value_optimizer.zero_grad()
    reward_optimizer.zero_grad()
```

```
    total_loss.backward()

    policy_optimizer.step()
    value_optimizer.step()
    reward_optimizer.step()

    # =======================
    # SYNC OLD POLICY
    # =======================
    old_policy_model.load_state_dict(policy_model.state_dict())

    return total_loss.item(), rewards.mean().item(), generated_text


# =======================
# TRAINING LOOP
# =======================
for step in range(1, 51):
    batch = random.sample(prompts, batch_size)
    loss, avg_reward, sample = ppo_update(batch)

    if step % 10 == 0:
        print(f"\nStep {step}")
        print("Sample generation:\n", sample)
        print("Reward:", avg_reward)
        print("Loss:", loss)
```

The **KL-divergence control** ensures that the new policy does not drift too far from the original model, maintaining language stability and safety. The **low final loss** and increasing rewards indicate that the agent is learning to align its outputs with the reward objective in a stable and controlled manner.

In essence, this code demonstrates how a raw language model is transformed into a **reward-aligned intelligent assistant**—the same fundamental principle used in training large-scale systems like ChatGPT.

Output:

Output
Step 50 Sample generation: Say something motivational: the new, new, new in this century!" And he said, "Well, you are going to have a little fun in Reward: 1.25 Loss: 0.008982766419649124

Master said:

PPO for GenAI is a gentle, iterative tutoring method: it repeatedly shows the model *what works* (reward), the critic explains *how much better* it was (advantage), and the policy is nudged only within safe bounds (clipping and KL). Use it to teach models to be consistent across media, attentive to users, adapt in real time, respect safety, and excel at specialised tasks — but always pair it with careful reward design, regular evaluation, and human judgment.

PART FOUR

DAY TWENTY-ONE

Unit 4 - Lesson Ten

Walking Through Probability

☐ Monte Carlo

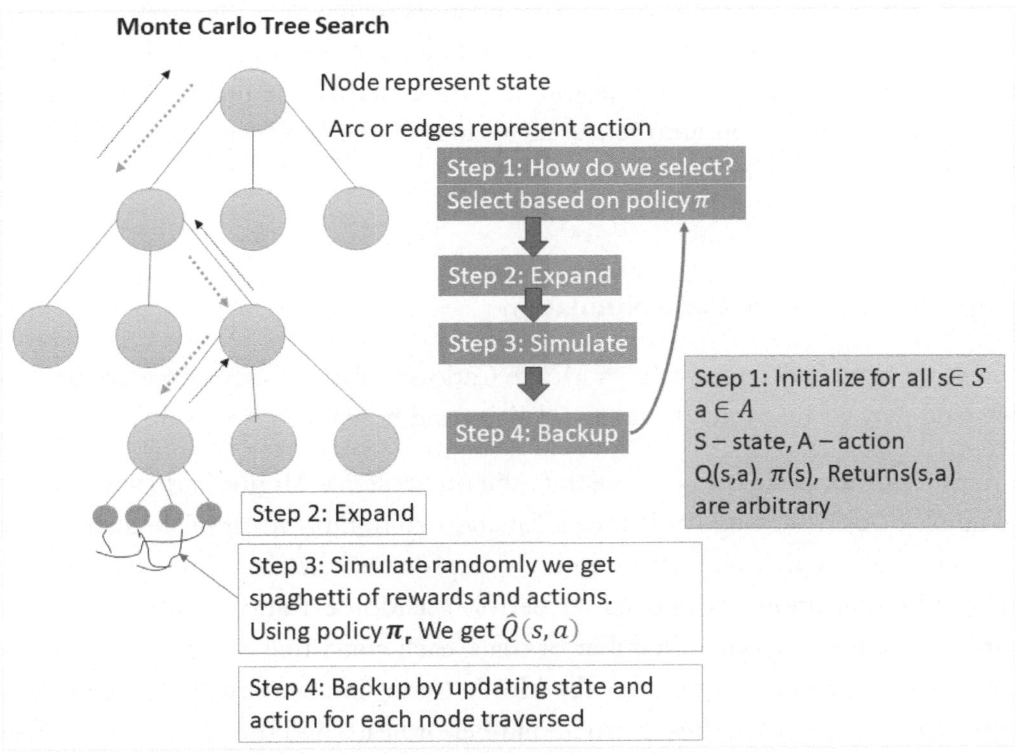

Master said, "Monte Carlo methods are computational techniques that utilise random sampling to approximate solutions to mathematical or statistical problems. They involve generating multiple random samples to estimate complex quantities or solve problems that might be difficult to solve analytically."

A Monte Carlo tree structure (MCTS) is a search algorithm that builds a tree of possible sequences of actions in a game or decision-making scenario. It is commonly used in artificial intelligence for games like chess and Go, as well as in other domains requiring decision-making under uncertainty.

The steps in Monte Carlo simulation include Selection, Expansion, Simulation, and Backup. Selection involves choosing nodes in the search tree based on a selection policy, while Expansion involves expanding the selected node by adding child nodes representing possible actions. Simulation involves randomly simulating the outcomes of actions from the expanded nodes, and Backup updates the statistics of the nodes in the tree based on the simulated outcomes.

Monte Carlo Simulation is a statistical modeling technique used to estimate the probability distribution of outcomes by repeatedly sampling random inputs. It involves selecting random values for input variables, running the model or simulation with these inputs, recording the results, and repeating the process multiple times. The aggregated results from the simulation are then used to analyze the likelihood or probability of various outcomes in the model.

Principle behind Monte Carlo Simulation

Till now, we have understood what a Monte Carlo simulation is. Now we are trying to understand why we do Monte Carlo simulations and how they give results.

The purpose of the code is to demonstrate the principles of Monte Carlo simulation in the context of coin flipping. It defines a function coin_flip() to simulate a single coin flip, where 0 represents tails and 1 represents heads. Another function monte_carlo_simulation() is defined to perform a Monte Carlo simulation for coin flipping, generating a specified number of trials, each consisting of a specified number of coin flips. The code then executes the Monte Carlo simulation with a given number of flips and trials, and calculates the total number of heads and the probability of heads based on the simulation results. Finally, it outputs these values to the console.

Example P4 – U4 – D23	
Monte Carlo	**Output**

<table>
<tr>
<td>

```
import numpy as np
# Function to simulate a coin flip
def coin_flip():
    return np.random.choice([0, 1])  # 0 represents tails, 1 represents heads

# Function to perform a Monte Carlo simulation for coin flipping
def monte_carlo_simulation(num_flips, num_trials):
    head_counts = []
    for _ in range(num_trials):
        head_count = 0
        for _ in range(num_flips):
            head_count += coin_flip()
        head_counts.append(head_count)
    return head_counts

if __name__ == "__main__":
    num_flips = 50  # Number of coin flips
    num_trials = 10000  # Number of trials in the Monte Carlo simulation

    # Perform the Monte Carlo simulation
    head_counts = monte_carlo_simulation(num_flips, num_trials)

    # Calculate the probability of heads
    probability_heads = sum(head_counts) / (num_trials * num_flips)
    # Output the number of heads and the probability of heads
    print("Number of Heads:", sum(head_counts))
    print("Probability of Heads:", probability_heads)
```

</td>
<td>Number of Heads: 250104
Probability of Heads:
0.500208</td>
</tr>
</table>

Overall, the code serves to illustrate how Monte Carlo simulation can be used to estimate probabilities based on random sampling.

Markov Chain Monte Carlo:

Master continued, Markov Chain Monte Carlo (MCMC) systems are a class of algorithms used in statistical computing and machine learning to generate samples from complex probability distributions. They employ Markov chains, which are stochastic processes where the probability of transitioning from one state to another depends only on the current state, making them memoryless or "Markovian."

Markov Chain Monte Carlo (MCMC) methods, including the Metropolis-Hastings algorithm, rely on the current sample to generate the next sample in the sequence. This dependency is a fundamental characteristic of Markov chains.

Markov Chain Monte Carlo (MCMC) methods, including the Metropolis-Hastings algorithm, rely on the current sample to generate the next sample in the sequence. This dependency is a fundamental characteristic of Markov chains. Here's a more detailed explanation:

Key Concepts of MCMC

Markov Property:

The Markov property states that the next state in the sequence depends only on the current state and not on any of the previous states. This memoryless property is crucial in MCMC methods.

Transition Probability:

The probability of moving from the current state to the next state is determined by a transition probability. In the context of MCMC, this transition is guided by a proposal distribution and an acceptance criterion.

Proposal Distribution:

A proposal distribution $q(x'|x)$ is used to generate a candidate for the next state x' based on the current state x.

Acceptance Criterion:

The Metropolis-Hastings algorithm uses an acceptance criterion to decide whether to accept the proposed state x'. The acceptance probability α is given by:

$$\alpha = \min(1, p(x')\, q(x|x') \;/\; p(x)\, q(x'|x))$$

Where $p(x)$ is the target distribution, and q is the proposal distribution.

☐ Importance of Sequential Dependency:

Exploration of State Space:

The sequential dependency allows the chain to explore the state space gradually, ensuring that regions with higher probability density are visited more frequently.

Convergence to Stationary Distribution:

Over many iterations, the Markov chain converges to a stationary distribution that matches the target distribution, providing accurate samples from the desired distribution.

Handling Complex Distributions:

MCMC methods are particularly useful for sampling from complex, high-dimensional distributions where direct sampling methods are infeasible.

In summary, the dependency on the last sample to select the next sample is a crucial aspect of MCMC methods, enabling them to sample effectively from complex distributions and ensuring convergence to the target distribution.

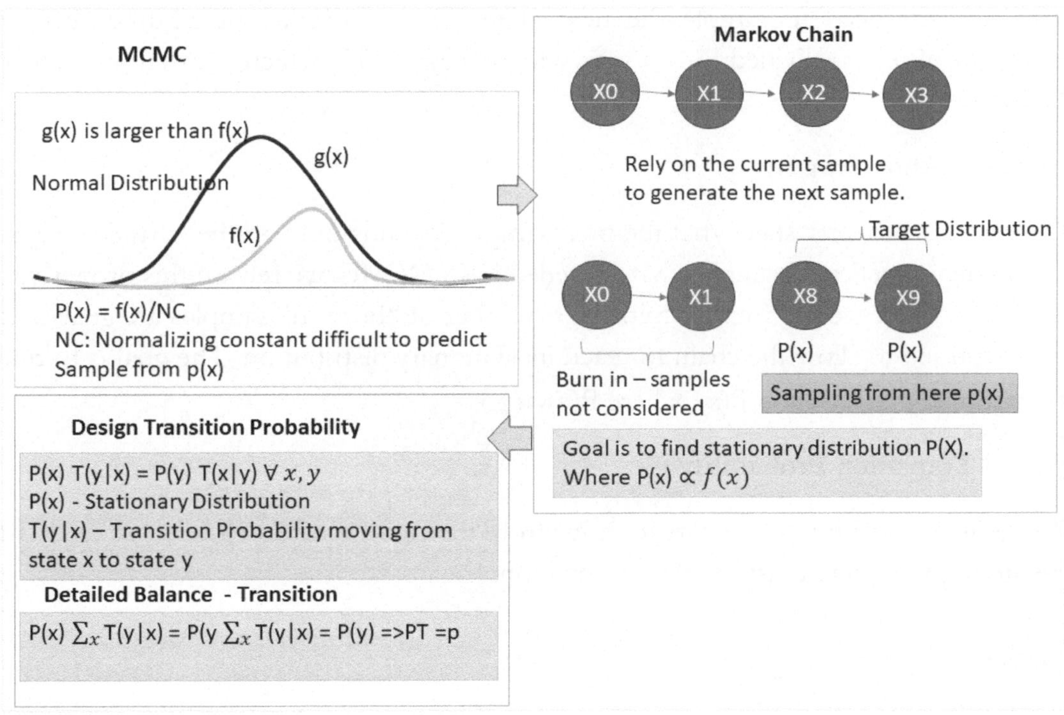

How MCMC Works?

- Initialization: Start with an initial value or sample.
- Transition: Use a transition mechanism (such as Metropolis-Hastings or Gibbs sampling) to generate the next value in the chain.
- Equilibrium: The Markov chain is constructed such that its equilibrium distribution is the target distribution.
- Sampling: Once the chain has reached equilibrium, the samples are taken and used for statistical inference.

Metropolis-Hastings Algorithm

Markov Chain Monte Carlo (MCMC) methods are used to sampling from complex target distributions f(x) that are difficult to sample from directly. The basic idea is to generate samples from a simpler distribution, known as the proposal distribution g(x), and use these samples to approximate the target distribution.

Step 1: Sampling from the Normal Distribution

We start by sampling from a normal distribution. At any given point, we are in a certain state, and we need to sample the next state. The probability distribution P(x) is proportional to f(x) divided by a normalizing constant NC, which is often difficult to determine.

Step 2: Markov Property

The Markov property states that the next sample depends only on the current sample, not on the sequence of samples that preceded it. In MCMC, we rely on this property to generate a sequence of samples. Initially, a number of "burn-in" samples are generated and discarded to allow the chain to reach its stationary distribution. The goal is to find the stationary distribution P(x), where $P(x) \propto f(x)$.

Step 3: Transition Probability

We design a transition probability to move from the current state x to a new state y. The transition probability must satisfy the equation:

$$P(x)\, T(y|x) = P(y)\, T(x|y) \ \forall\, x,y$$

Here, P(x) is the stationary distribution, and T(y|x) is the transition probability from state x to state y.

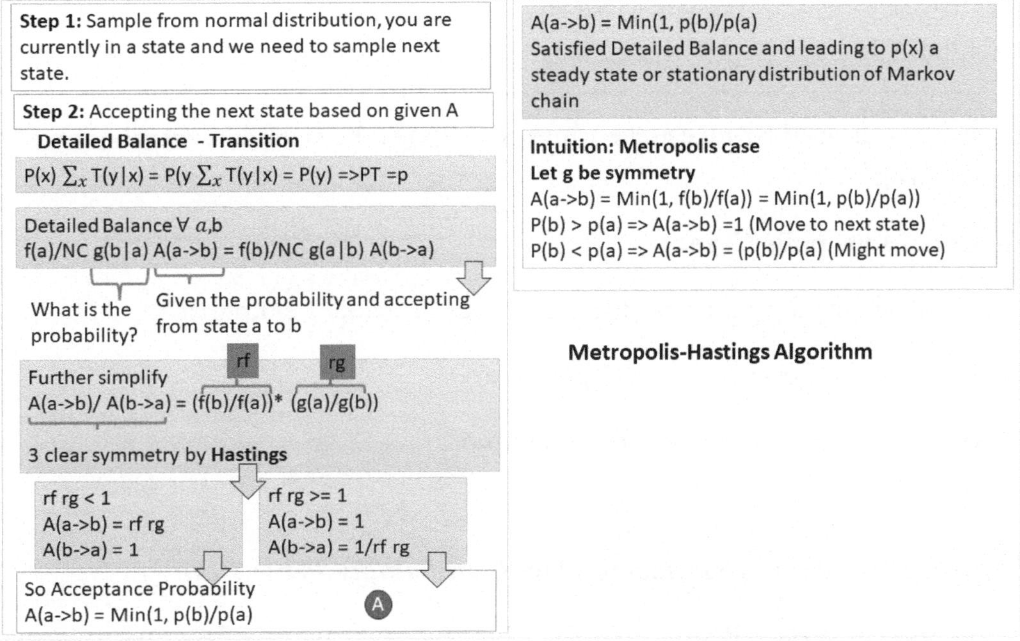

Step 4A: Detailed Balance Transition

To achieve detailed balance, the transition probabilities must satisfy the following condition for all states a and b:

(f(a)/NC) (g(b|a)) (A(a->b)) = (f(b)/NC) (g(a|b)) (A(b->a))

Where A(a→b) is the acceptance probability of moving from state a to state b.

This simplifies to:

A(a->b)/ A(b->a) = (f(b)/f(a))* (g(a)/g(b))

Using the Metropolis-Hastings algorithm, we derive the acceptance probabilities:

(f(b)/f(a)) = rf	(g(a)/g(b)) = rg

rf rg < 1 A(a->b) = rf rg A(b->a) = 1	rf rg > = 1 A(a->b) = 1 A(b->a) = 1/rf rg

This satisfies detailed balance and ensures that P(x) is the stationary distribution of the Markov chain.

Intuition: Metropolis Case

In the case where g is symmetric, the acceptance probability simplifies to:

$A(a \rightarrow b) = \min(1, f(b)/f(a)) = \min(1, p(b)/p(a))$

If P(b) > P(a), the move is always accepted:

$A(a \rightarrow b) = 1$

If P(b) < P(a), the move is accepted with probability P(b)/ P(a):

$$A(a \rightarrow b) = P(b)/P(a)$$

Thus, the Metropolis-Hastings algorithm ensures that the Markov chain reaches its stationary distribution P(x).

Example: Metropolis-Hastings Algorithm

The purpose of the provided Python code is to demonstrate the implementation of the Metropolis-Hastings algorithm, a Markov Chain Monte Carlo (MCMC) method, to sample from a target probability distribution p(x).

Example P4 – U4 – D24	
Metropolis-Hasting Algorithm	**Output**

<pre>import numpy as np
import matplotlib.pyplot as plt
# Define the target distribution function, which is a standard normal distribution 	
def target_distribution(x):
    return np.exp(-x**2 / 2) / np.sqrt(2 * np.pi)
 	
# Define the Metropolis-Hastings algorithm function</pre> 		

```
def metropolis_hastings(target_distribution,
num_samples, proposal_std=1.0):
    # Initialize an array to store the generated samples
    samples = np.zeros(num_samples)
    # Initialize the first sample from a normal distribution
    current_sample = np.random.normal()

    for i in range(1, num_samples):
        # Generate a proposed sample from a normal
distribution centered at the current sample
        proposed_sample = current_sample +
np.random.normal(scale=proposal_std)

        # Calculate the acceptance probability
        acceptance_probability = min(1,
target_distribution(proposed_sample) /
target_distribution(current_sample))

        # Accept or reject the proposed sample based on the
acceptance probability
        if np.random.rand() < acceptance_probability:
            # Accept the proposed sample and update the
current sample
            current_sample = proposed_sample
        # Store the current sample
        samples[i] = current_sample

    return samples  # Return the array of generated
samples
# Define the number of samples to be generated
num_samples = 10000
# Generate samples using the Metropolis-Hastings
algorithm
samples = metropolis_hastings(target_distribution,
num_samples)

# Plot the histogram of the generated samples
plt.hist(samples, bins=50, density=True, alpha=0.6,
color='g', label='MCMC samples')

# Plot the target distribution for comparison
x = np.linspace(-4, 4, 1000)  # Generate a range of x
values
plt.plot(x, target_distribution(x), linewidth=2, color='r',
label='Target distribution')

# Add labels and legend to the plot
plt.xlabel('x')
```

plt.ylabel('Density')
plt.legend()
 	
# Display the plot 	
plt.show()	

Initialization:

The algorithm starts with an initial sample, which can be chosen randomly or based on some heuristic.

Sampling Process:

For each iteration, a new candidate sample is proposed based on the current sample and a proposal distribution.

The acceptance probability is calculated using the target distribution and the proposal distribution.

A uniform random number determines whether the proposed sample is accepted. If accepted, the current sample is updated to the proposed sample; otherwise, the current sample remains unchanged.

Sequential Dependency:

Each new sample depends on the current sample, ensuring that the sequence of samples forms a Markov chain. This dependency is what allows the MCMC methods to explore the target distribution effectively.

Gibbs Sampling

Master said, "Gibbs sampling is a type of Markov Chain Monte Carlo (MCMC) method used to sample from a multivariate probability distribution when it is challenging to sample directly from the joint distribution. Instead of sampling from the joint probability distribution $p(x_1, x_2, x_3,\ldots,x_n)$, Gibbs sampling focuses on sampling from the conditional distributions $p(x_i|x_1,x_2,\ldots,x_i-1,x_i+1,\ldots,x_n)$ for each variable x_i."

The key idea behind Gibbs sampling is to iteratively update each variable xi while keeping the other variables fixed at their current values. This process creates a sequence of samples, forming a Markov chain that, after a sufficient number of iterations, converges to the joint distribution.

Here's a more detailed breakdown of the Gibbs sampling process:

Initialization: Start with an initial set of values for all variables $(x_1,x_2,\ldots,x_n)$.

Iterative Sampling: For each variable xi, update its value by sampling from its conditional distribution given the current values of all other variables:

$$x_i^{(t+1)} \sim p(x_i \mid x_1^{(t+1)},\ x_2^{(t+1)},\ \ldots,x_{i-1}^{(t+1)},\ x_{i+1}^{(t)},\ \ldots\ x_n^{(t)})$$

This step is repeated for each variable in the sequence, creating a new set of samples $(x_1^{(t+1)},\ x_2^{(t+1)},\ \ldots,x_n^{(t+1)}$ at each iteration t.

Convergence: After a sufficient number of iterations, the Markov chain formed by the sequence of samples converges to the joint distribution $p(x_1,x_2,\ldots,x_n)$. At this point, the samples can be considered as drawn from the desired joint distribution.

Gibbs Sampling

Multivariant distribution:
2D Normal distribution

$$\mu = \begin{bmatrix} 0 \\ 0 \end{bmatrix} \quad \Sigma = \begin{bmatrix} 1 & 1/2 \\ 1/2 & 1 \end{bmatrix}$$

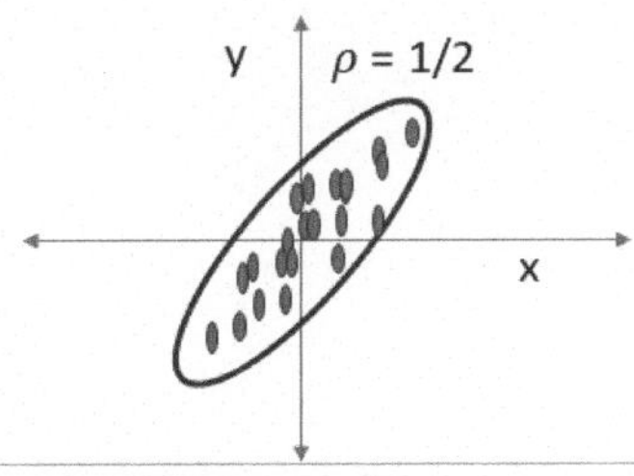

Use Gibbs when p(x,y) joint PDF is difficult or tricky sampling simultaneously but conditional PDF is easy.
Hence:
P(x|y)
P(y|x)

$P(x|y) = N(\rho y, 1-\rho) = N\left(\frac{y}{2}, \frac{3}{4}\right)$

$P(y|x) = N\left(\frac{x}{2}, \frac{3}{4}\right)$

Procedure:
Start (x^0, y^0)
We keep y variable fixed
Sample $x^{(1)} \sim p(x^{(1)} | y^{(0)})$
Sample $y^{(1)} \sim p(y^{(1)} | x^{(1)})$
Here we get new x then new y and it repeats.

We can prove using detailed Balance and Metropolis case

The advantage of Gibbs sampling is that it simplifies the sampling process by breaking down the complex joint distribution into a series of simpler conditional distributions. This method is particularly useful when the conditional distributions are easier to sample from than the joint distribution. By iteratively updating each variable while keeping the others fixed, Gibbs sampling effectively explores the entire distribution, eventually yielding samples that approximate the joint distribution of the multivariate probability distribution.

Let us consider a 2D normal distribution with the following parameters:

$$\mu = \begin{bmatrix} 0 \\ 0 \end{bmatrix} \quad \Sigma = \begin{bmatrix} 1 & 1/2 \\ 1/2 & 1 \end{bmatrix}$$

Gibbs sampling is particularly useful when sampling directly from the joint probability distribution p(x,y) is challenging, but sampling from the conditional distributions p(x|y) and p(y|x) is straightforward.

For this distribution:

$P(x\mid y) = N\left(\frac{y}{2}, \frac{3}{4}\right)$	$P(y\mid x) = N\left(\frac{x}{2}, \frac{3}{4}\right)$

☐ Gibbs Sampling Procedure:

Initialization: Start with an initial point (x^0, y^0).

Iterative Sampling:

- Keep y fixed and sample $x^{(1)} \sim p(x|y^{(0)})$
- Then keep x fixed and sample $y^{(1)} \sim p(y|x^{(1)})$

This process generates a new sample $(x^{(1)}, y^{(1)})$, and the steps are repeated to generate subsequent samples.

Steps to Implement Gibbs Sampling:

Understand the Problem: Identify the conditional probabilities of the variables to be sampled. For our 2D normal distribution, we have p(x|y) and p(y|x).

Initialize Values: Start with initial values for X and Y, say X^0 and Y^0.

Sample Conditional Distributions:

- Sample X from p(X|Y) while keeping Y fixed.
- Update X to X_1 based on the sampled value.
- Sample Y from p(Y|X) while keeping X fixed.
- Update Y to Y_1 based on the sampled value.

Iterate: Repeat the above steps to generate a series of samples (X_i,Y_i).

Burn-in Period: Ignore the initial samples from the chain (burn-in period) to allow the Markov chain to reach the target distribution.

Convergence: After the burn-in period, the remaining samples approximate the joint distribution.

Example:

The purpose of this code is to demonstrate and compare two different sampling techniques for generating samples from a bivariate normal distribution: Automatic Sampling using a direct method, and Gibbs Sampling, which is a type of Markov Chain Monte Carlo (MCMC) method.

Exercise P4-U4 – D25

Gibbs

```
import numpy as np
import matplotlib.pyplot as plt
from scipy.stats import pearsonr

# Step 1: Sample from bivariate normal distribution using automatic sampling
mean = [0, 0]  # Mean vector
cov = [[1, 0.5], [0.5, 1]]  # Covariance matrix
automatic_samples = np.random.multivariate_normal(mean, cov, 10000)

# Plotting the automatically sampled bivariate normal distribution
plt.scatter(automatic_samples[:, 0], automatic_samples[:, 1], s=5, alpha=0.5,
label='Automatic Samples')

# Step 2: Gibbs Sampling
# Initializing the samples dictionary with starting values for 'x' and 'y'
samples = {'x': [1], 'y': [-1]}

# Number of Gibbs sampling iterations
num_samples = 10000
```

```
# Gibbs sampling loop
for _ in range(num_samples):
    curr_y = samples['y'][-1]  # Get the current y value
    new_x = np.random.normal(curr_y / 2, np.sqrt(3 / 4))  # Sample new x given y
    new_y = np.random.normal(new_x / 2, np.sqrt(3 / 4))  # Sample new y given x
    samples['x'].append(new_x)  # Append new x to samples
    samples['y'].append(new_y)  # Append new y to samples

# Plotting the Gibbs sampled bivariate normal distribution
plt.scatter(samples['x'], samples['y'], s=5, alpha=0.5, label='Gibbs Samples')
plt.xlabel('X')
plt.ylabel('Y')
plt.legend()
plt.title('Bivariate Normal Distribution: Automatic vs. Gibbs Sampling')
plt.show()

# Step 3: Plotting histograms for both sampling methods
plt.hist(automatic_samples[:, 0], bins=20, density=True, alpha=0.5, label='Auto X')
plt.hist(samples['x'], bins=20, density=True, alpha=0.5, label='Gibbs X')
plt.hist(automatic_samples[:, 1], bins=20, density=True, alpha=0.5, label='Auto Y')
plt.hist(samples['y'], bins=20, density=True, alpha=0.5, label='Gibbs Y')
plt.xlabel('Value')
plt.ylabel('Density')
plt.legend()
plt.title('Histograms of X and Y for Automatic and Gibbs Sampling')
plt.show()

# Step 4: Plotting lagged scatter plots for both sampling methods
plt.scatter(automatic_samples[:-1, 0], automatic_samples[1:, 0], s=5, alpha=0.5, label='Auto
Lagged X')
plt.xlabel('X_t')
plt.ylabel('X_{t+1}')
plt.title('Lagged Scatter Plot: Automatic Sampling')
plt.show()
print(f'Pearson correlation for automatic samples: {pearsonr(automatic_samples[:-1, 0],
automatic_samples[1:, 0])[0]}')

plt.scatter(samples['x'][:-1], samples['x'][1:], s=5, alpha=0.5, label='Gibbs Lagged X')
plt.xlabel('X_t')
plt.ylabel('X_{t+1}')
plt.title('Lagged Scatter Plot: Gibbs Sampling')
plt.show()
print(f"Pearson correlation for Gibbs samples: {pearsonr(samples['x'][:-1],
samples['x'][1:])[0]}")
```

Output:
Pearson correlation for automatic samples: 0.007226280166254728 Pearson correlation for Gibbs samples: 0.24827744554263875

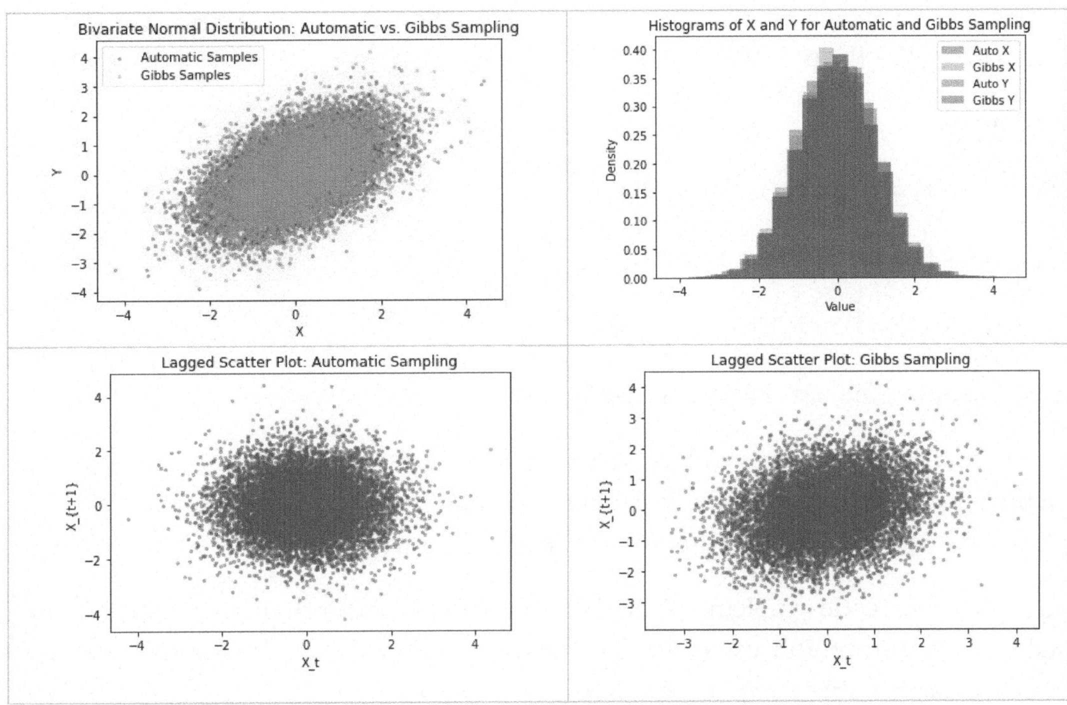

Example of Gibbs Sampling:

Consider a simple case where we have two binary variables X and Y with the following joint distribution:

p(X=0,Y=0)=0.2	p(X=0,Y=1)=0.1
p(X=1,Y=0)=0.3	p(X=1,Y=1)=0.4

To sample from this distribution using Gibbs sampling:

Initialize: Set X = 0 and Y=0

Calculate Conditional Probabilities:

p(X=0|Y=0)=p(X=0,Y=0) / p(Y=0) = (0.2)/(0.2+0.3) = 0.4

p(X=1|Y=0) = 1−0.4 = 0.6

Since p(X=1|Y=0)>p(X=0|Y=0), set X=1

Update Y:

p(Y=0|X=1) = (0.3)/(0.3+0.4) = 0.429

p(Y=1|X=1)=(0.4)/(0.3+0.4) = 0.571

Since p(Y=1|X=1) > p(Y=0|X=1), set Y=1

New Sample: The new sample is (X=1, Y=1)

By repeating these steps, Gibbs sampling generates a sequence of samples that eventually converge to the joint distribution of X and Y. This iterative process allows us to approximate the joint distribution efficiently, even when direct sampling is difficult.

The provided code implements a Gibbs sampling algorithm to sample from a multivariate distribution using the Iris dataset's sepal length, sepal width, and petal length features. Gibbs sampling is a Markov Chain Monte Carlo (MCMC) method used to sample from complex multivariate distributions by iteratively sampling from conditional distributions.

Example P4 – U4 – D26

Gibbs Sampling

```
import random
import pandas as pd
import numpy as np
# Load the Iris dataset into pandas
path = r'C:\Users\User\mraj4\Documents\Optimum\Py-lib\scikit\iris.csv'
df = pd.read_csv(path, index_col=0)

# This dataframe contains the sepal length, sepal width, and petal length features
data_pd = df.drop(["Species", "Petal_Width_cm"], axis=1)
data = data_pd.to_numpy()

# Initial values for sepal length, sepal width, and petal length
initial_x = random.uniform(min(data[:, 0]), max(data[:, 0]))
initial_y = random.uniform(min(data[:, 1]), max(data[:, 1]))
initial_z = random.uniform(min(data[:, 2]), max(data[:, 2]))
```

```
# Number of Gibbs sampling iterations
num_iterations = 1000  # Increased iterations for better convergence
samples = []

# Constants for variance control
x_std = np.std(data[:, 0])
y_std = np.std(data[:, 1])
z_std = np.std(data[:, 2])

for _ in range(num_iterations):
    # Sample sepal length (x) from the conditional distribution P(x | y, z)
    x_mean = np.mean(data[:, 0]) + 0.5 * (initial_y - np.mean(data[:, 1])) + 0.5 * (initial_z -
np.mean(data[:, 2]))
    x = np.random.normal(x_mean, x_std)

    # Sample sepal width (y) from the conditional distribution P(y | x, z)
    y_mean = np.mean(data[:, 1]) + 0.5 * (x - np.mean(data[:, 0])) + 0.5 * (initial_z -
np.mean(data[:, 2]))
    y = np.random.normal(y_mean, y_std)

    # Sample petal length (z) from the conditional distribution P(z | x, y)
    z_mean = np.mean(data[:, 2]) + 0.5 * (x - np.mean(data[:, 0])) + 0.5 * (y -
np.mean(data[:, 1]))
    z = np.random.normal(z_mean, z_std)

    samples.append((x, y, z))

    # Update the initial values for the next iteration
    initial_x, initial_y, initial_z = x, y, z

# Converting the samples to a DataFrame for better visualization
samples_df = pd.DataFrame(samples, columns=['Sepal_Length', 'Sepal_Width',
'Petal_Length'])

# Printing the final samples
print(samples_df.tail())  # Print the last few samples to check the results

# Optionally, plot the samples for visualization
import matplotlib.pyplot as plt

plt.figure(figsize=(12, 6))
plt.plot(samples_df['Sepal_Length'], label='Sepal Length')
plt.plot(samples_df['Sepal_Width'], label='Sepal Width')
plt.plot(samples_df['Petal_Length'], label='Petal Length')
plt.legend()
plt.show()
```

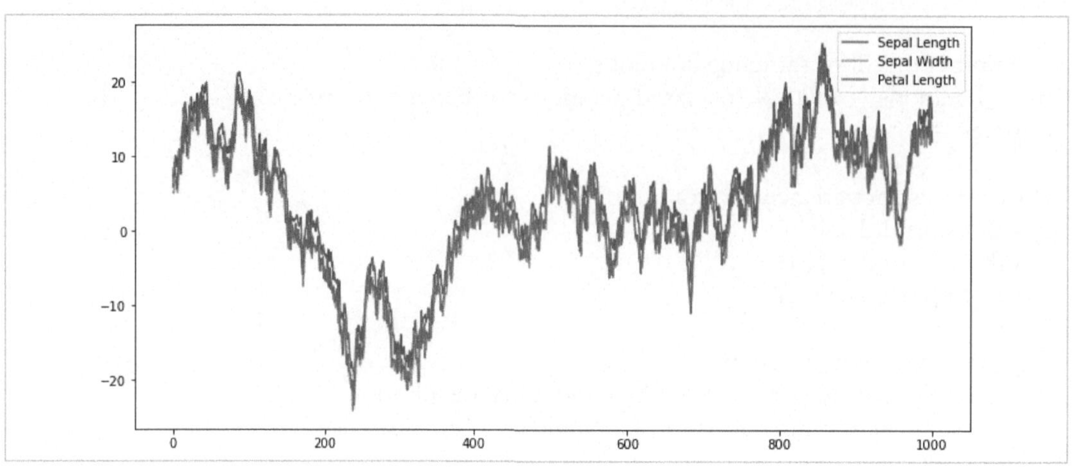
Sepal Length
Sepal Width
Petal Length
20
10
0
−10
−20
0
200
400
600
800
1000

PART FOUR

DAY TWENTY-ONE

Unit 4 - Lesson Eleven

Mastering Continuous Actions

☐ Deep Deterministic Policy Gradient (DDPG)

Apeksha asked, "Master, how does the DDPG algorithm truly work in Reinforcement Learning?"

The Master smiled and replied:

Imagine you are learning to drive a car on an empty road. You never choose from a small set of actions like *left*, *right*, *brake* — instead, you decide **exactly** how much to turn the wheel or how much to press the accelerator. These are **continuous actions**. DDPG was created for such worlds."

What DDPG Is

DDPG — Deep Deterministic Policy Gradient — is a **model-free, off-policy, actor-critic algorithm** designed for environments where actions flow smoothly like water, not in discrete steps. It blends the strengths of **DQN** (Deep Q-Networks) and **DPG** (Deterministic Policy Gradient), giving us a method capable of learning precise, continuous controls.

Actor–Critic Analogy

"Think of DDPG as having two minds," the Master continued.

- **The Critic** is like a wise advisor evaluating your actions: *'If you take this action in this situation, your long-term gain will be this much.'*
- **The Actor** is like your body, learning *how to act*, producing a single best action rather than a probability distribution.

Together, they form a loop of **intuition and judgment**, refining each other as training progresses.

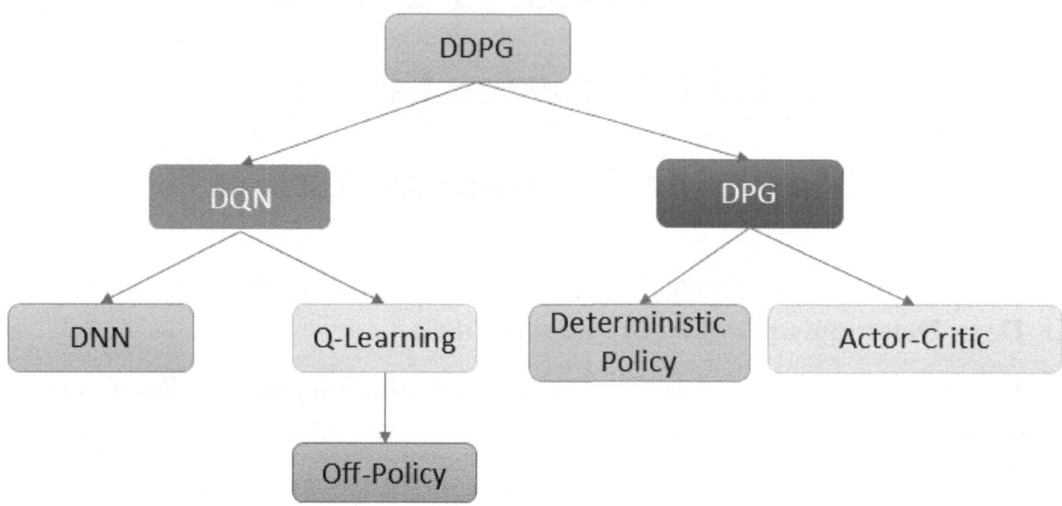

Illustration DDPG_1: DDPG

Why Deterministic?

A deterministic policy is like a disciplined archer: given a state, it fires a **single, exact arrow**, not a scatter of possibilities. This is ideal for stable, predictable environments with continuous choices — much like making a precise move in chess.

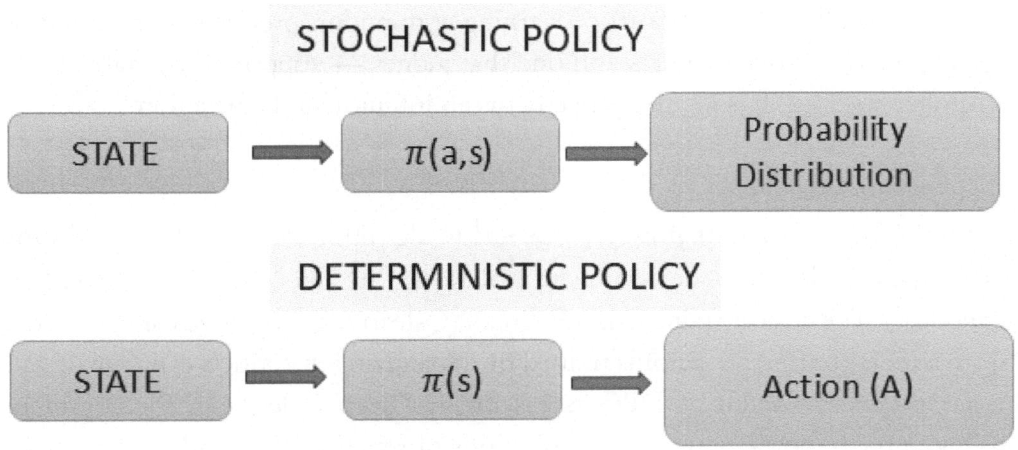

STOCHASTIC POLICY

STATE → π(a,s) → Probability Distribution

DETERMINISTIC POLICY

STATE → π(s) → Action (A)

Illustration DDPG_1: DDPG

Why Off-Policy?

DDPG learns from experiences collected by **another policy** (the behaviour policy). "Imagine learning from your past self while your present self explores freely," said the Master.

Benefits include:

1. **Continuous exploration** without destabilising the learned policy.
2. **Learning from demonstrations**, even expert ones.
3. **Faster learning** through replay buffers and parallel data.

Why Target Networks?

"Because learning can become unstable," the Master warned.

If the networks update based on their own constantly moving predictions, learning can spiral.

So DDPG uses **target networks**, slow-moving shadows of the real networks, updated gently using **Polyak Averaging**. These shadows keep learning steadily — like a lantern guiding a traveller on an uneven trail.

Thus, Master said, "DDPG is the art of learning continuous, precise actions using two cooperating minds — one that acts and one that judges — supported by stable targets and off-policy wisdom. It is a quiet dance between intuition and correction."

Master said, "DDPG is an **off-policy actor–critic** algorithm designed for **continuous action spaces**. It learns a deterministic policy (actor) $\mu\theta(s)$ and a critic $Q\phi(s,a)$ simultaneously. The critic is trained via a Bellman (Q-learning) objective using off-policy data from a replay buffer; the actor is trained by maximizing the critic's estimate of value at the actor's chosen action. DDPG is essentially "deep Q-learning for continuous actions" with the important engineering additions of replay buffers and slowly-updated target networks."

The gardener analogy

Imagine teaching a gardener (the **actor**) to trim a bonsai so it grows exactly the way you want. You also have a critic — an expert who looks at the tree and scores how well it will grow long-term (the **Q-function**). The gardener proposes a precise trimming action (a continuous, exact move). The expert judges the result and says how good that action was. Over time, the gardener learns to pick exact trims that the expert rates highly. Because the gardener proposes single deterministic moves, you must add noise during practice so the gardener tries different trims and learns from diverse outcomes.

Why continuous actions change everything

In discrete action problems you can compute $\max_a Q(s, a)$ by evaluating each action. In continuous action spaces that's impossible. DDPG solves this by learning a differentiable deterministic policy $\mu\theta(s)$ and using the critic to evaluate $Q(s, \mu\theta(s))$. Because $Q(s, a)$ is differentiable in 'a', we can backpropagate through 'Q' into the actor and perform gradient ascent on policy parameters — an efficient alternative to solving an inner optimization at every step.

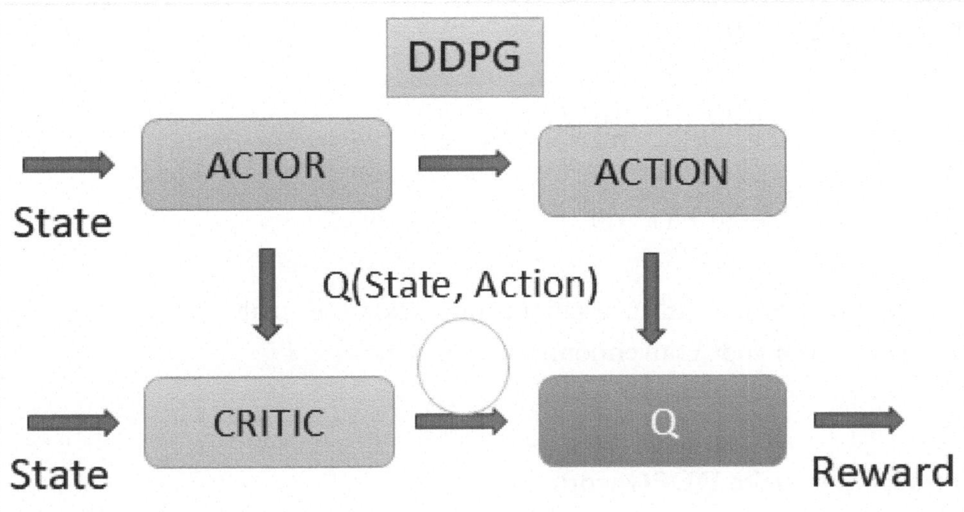

Illustration DDPG_3: DDPG

Key components & equations

Notation

- Actor: $\mu_\theta(s)$ → deterministic action
- Critic: $Q_\phi(s, a)$ → action-value estimator
- Target networks: $\mu_{\theta'}$, $Q_{\phi'}$ (Polyak-averaged copies)
- Replay buffer D, discount γ, soft update factor τ (Polyak)

Critic (Bellman) target and loss

$$y = r+\gamma(1-d)\ Q_{\phi'}(s', \mu_{\theta'}(s'))$$

$$L(\phi) = \frac{1}{N}\sum_{(s,a,r,s',d)\sim D} (Q_\phi(s, a) - y)^2$$

Actor (deterministic policy gradient)

Maximize expected Q-value; in practice, minimize the negative:

$$L_{actor}(\theta)=-\frac{1}{N}\sum_{(s)\sim D} Q_\phi(s, \mu_\theta(s))$$

Gradient: $\nabla_\theta J \approx \frac{1}{N} \sum \nabla a Q\phi(s, a)|_{a=\mu\theta(s)} \nabla_\theta \mu_\theta(s)$.

Soft target updates (Polyak averaging)

$\phi' \leftarrow \tau\phi + (1-\tau)\phi', \theta' \leftarrow \tau\theta + (1-\tau)\theta'$

(Use τ\tauτ close to 1 in the earlier notation; some texts use small τ\tauτ and reverse the blend — check your code convention.)

Practical tricks that make DDPG work

1. **Replay buffer** — sample uniformly (or prioritized) from past transitions to break correlations and stabilize updates. Buffer sizes: 10^5–10^6 typical.
2. **Target networks** — use time-lagged copies $Q_{\phi'}$, $\mu_{\theta'}$ to compute stable targets y. Update targets by Polyak averaging every gradient step.
3. **Exploration noise** — actor is deterministic, so add noise during training. Historically OU (Ornstein–Uhlenbeck) noise was used; simple Gaussian noise $N(0,\sigma^2)$ often suffices. Anneal σ over time.
4. **Normalize inputs & rewards** — state and reward normalization can dramatically improve stability.
5. **Gradient clipping & LR tuning** — typical critic LR larger (e.g. 10^{-3}), actor smaller (e.g. 10^{-4}). Clip gradients if unstable.
6. **Batch size** — 64–256 works well; larger batches give smoother updates.

Pseudo-code

```
DDPG
Initialize actor μθ and critic Qφ and target networks θ'←θ, φ'←φ
Initialize replay buffer D

for each episode:
  s←env.reset()
  for each step:
    a ← μθ(s) + noise
```

```
    s', r, done ← env.step(a)
    store (s,a,r,s',done) in D
    if enough samples:
      sample batch from D
      # Critic update
      a' = μ_{θ'}(s')
      y = r + γ*(1-done)*Q_{φ'}(s', a')
      minimize MSE(Qφ(s,a), y) w.r.t φ
      # Actor update
      maximize mean Qφ(s, μθ(s))  (or minimize negative)
      # Soft-update targets
      φ' ← τ φ + (1-τ) φ'
      θ' ← τ θ + (1-τ) θ'
    s ← s'
```

Limitations and modern improvements

- **Brittle**: DDPG can be unstable and sensitive to hyperparameters.
- **Overestimation**: critic overestimation leads to poor actor updates. Fixes: **TD3** (Twin Delayed DDPG) — uses two critics, takes the minimum, delays actor updates, adds target smoothing. **SAC** (Soft Actor-Critic) replaces a deterministic actor with stochastic policy and entropy regularization — more robust and often preferred.

When to use DDPG

- Use DDPG when you need an **off-policy**, sample-efficient algorithm for **continuous action** control and are willing to invest in careful tuning. For robustness, start with TD3 or SAC in real-world problems.

Master said, "This code implements a full Deep Deterministic Policy Gradient (DDPG) agent in PyTorch, designed for continuous-action reinforcement learning tasks such as the Pendulum-v1 environment. DDPG combines the strengths of Q-learning and deterministic policy gradients to learn an optimal continuous control policy. The implementation follows the standard DDPG architecture: an **actor network** that outputs continuous actions, a **critic network** that estimates Q-values, and corresponding **target networks** that stabilize training through slow, soft Polyak updates."

Example P4 – U4 – D27

DDPG

```
import gym
import numpy as np
import random
import torch
import torch.nn as nn
import torch.optim as optim
from collections import deque

# ==================================
# Ornstein-Uhlenbeck Noise
# ==================================
class OUNoise:
    def __init__(self, size, mu=0.0, theta=0.15, sigma=0.2):
        self.mu = mu
        self.theta = theta
        self.sigma = sigma
        self.size = size
        self.state = np.ones(self.size) * self.mu

    def reset(self):
        self.state = np.ones(self.size) * self.mu

    def sample(self):
        dx = self.theta * (self.mu - self.state) + self.sigma * np.random.randn(self.size)
        self.state += dx
        return self.state


# ==================================
# Replay Buffer
# ==================================
class ReplayBuffer:
    def __init__(self, size=100000):
        self.buffer = deque(maxlen=size)

    def push(self, state, action, reward, next_state, done):
        self.buffer.append((state, action, reward, next_state, done))

    def sample(self, batch_size):
        batch = random.sample(self.buffer, batch_size)
        states, actions, rewards, next_states, dones = zip(*batch)
```

```
        return (
            torch.FloatTensor(states),
            torch.FloatTensor(actions),
            torch.FloatTensor(rewards).unsqueeze(1),
            torch.FloatTensor(next_states),
            torch.FloatTensor(dones).unsqueeze(1)
        )

    def __len__(self):
        return len(self.buffer)


# ==================================
# Actor Network
# ==================================
class Actor(nn.Module):
    def __init__(self, state_dim, action_dim, max_action):
        super().__init__()
        self.net = nn.Sequential(
            nn.Linear(state_dim, 256), nn.ReLU(),
            nn.Linear(256, 256), nn.ReLU(),
            nn.Linear(256, action_dim), nn.Tanh()
        )
        self.max_action = max_action

    def forward(self, x):
        return self.max_action * self.net(x)


# ==================================
# Critic Network
# ==================================
class Critic(nn.Module):
    def __init__(self, state_dim, action_dim):
        super().__init__()
        self.net = nn.Sequential(
            nn.Linear(state_dim + action_dim, 256), nn.ReLU(),
            nn.Linear(256, 256), nn.ReLU(),
            nn.Linear(256, 1)
        )

    def forward(self, x, a):
        return self.net(torch.cat([x, a], dim=1))


# ==================================
# Soft Update
# ==================================
```

```
def soft_update(target, source, tau=0.005):
    for t, s in zip(target.parameters(), source.parameters()):
        t.data.copy_(t.data * (1 - tau) + s.data * tau)


# ==================================
# Main DDPG Training Loop
# ==================================
def train_ddpg():
    env = gym.make("Pendulum-v1")

    # Correct seeding
    state, _ = env.reset(seed=42)

    state_dim = env.observation_space.shape[0]
    action_dim = env.action_space.shape[0]
    max_action = float(env.action_space.high[0])

    actor = Actor(state_dim, action_dim, max_action)
    critic = Critic(state_dim, action_dim)

    target_actor = Actor(state_dim, action_dim, max_action)
    target_critic = Critic(state_dim, action_dim)

    target_actor.load_state_dict(actor.state_dict())
    target_critic.load_state_dict(critic.state_dict())

    act_opt = optim.Adam(actor.parameters(), lr=1e-4)
    crt_opt = optim.Adam(critic.parameters(), lr=1e-3)

    buffer = ReplayBuffer()
    noise = OUNoise(action_dim)

    gamma = 0.99
    batch_size = 64

    for episode in range(50):
        state, _ = env.reset()
        noise.reset()
        episode_reward = 0

        for step in range(200):
            s = torch.FloatTensor(state).unsqueeze(0)
            action = actor(s).detach().numpy()[0]
            action = action + noise.sample()

            next_state, reward, done, _, _ = env.step(action)
            buffer.push(state, action, reward, next_state, done)
```

```
        state = next_state
        episode_reward += reward

        if len(buffer) > batch_size:
            states, actions, rewards, next_states, dones = buffer.sample(batch_size)

            # Critic update
            with torch.no_grad():
                next_actions = target_actor(next_states)
                target_q = rewards + gamma * (1 - dones) * target_critic(next_states, next_actions)

            q_vals = critic(states, actions)
            critic_loss = nn.MSELoss()(q_vals, target_q)

            crt_opt.zero_grad()
            critic_loss.backward()
            crt_opt.step()

            # Actor update
            actor_loss = -critic(states, actor(states)).mean()

            act_opt.zero_grad()
            actor_loss.backward()
            act_opt.step()

            # Soft update
            soft_update(target_actor, actor)
            soft_update(target_critic, critic)

    print(f"Episode {episode} | Reward: {episode_reward:.2f}")


train_ddpg()
```

The agent uses a **replay buffer** to store past transitions, ensuring that learning happens from a diverse and uncorrelated dataset instead of sequential experience, which often causes instability. For exploration, the code supports both **Ornstein-Uhlenbeck noise** and **Gaussian noise**, helping the deterministic policy explore the action space effectively during training.

Each training step samples a batch of experience from the replay buffer, computes target Q-values using the target networks, and updates the critic by minimizing the TD error. The actor is updated by ascending the gradient of the Q-value with respect to its actions — effectively learning how to output actions that maximize expected return. After each update, the actor and critic target networks are softly updated using Polyak averaging to prevent divergence.

Output:

Output
Episode 45 | Reward: -130.11 Episode 46 | Reward: -125.68 Episode 47 | Reward: -515.46 Episode 48 | Reward: -254.91 Episode 49 | Reward: -237.02

Across episodes, the agent gradually improves its control strategy, reflected in rising episode rewards and smoother, more stable actions. The modular structure of the code makes it easy to extend, experiment with different noise models, or upgrade to advanced algorithms like TD3 or SAC. Overall, this implementation provides a clear, production-ready foundation for continuous-control reinforcement learning.

Master said, "DDPG blends Q-learning thinking (learn a value function) with policy gradient mechanics (differentiate through a policy) to handle continuous actions efficiently. The algorithm's success depends more on engineering (replay, targets, noise, normalization, careful lrs) than on clever equations — and many practitioners now prefer TD3/SAC because they incorporate fixes for DDPG's common failure modes while keeping the same core ideas."

☐ TD3

Master said, "Akshaya… let us understand TD3 with an analogy."

"Imagine," Master began, "you are buying land."

Analogy: Two Land-Valuers and a Cautious Buyer (TD3)

Akshaya nodded as Master continued:

"When you want to buy land, you don't trust only one valuer.

One valuer may overestimate the price, exaggerate the benefits, or simply make a mistake.

So in TD3:

- **Two independent valuers (Q-networks)** estimate the price of an action.
- And you, the buyer (the policy), **trust the lower estimate**.

Why?

Because **the risky one might be lying**, and taking the lower value keeps you safe.

This simple caution solves the biggest problem in DDPG:

The policy exploiting overestimated Q-values and goes unstable."

Master said, "Imagine two weather forecasters (two Q-networks). If one says "sunny 90%" and the other "sunny 60%", you trust the more conservative estimate when planning an outdoor picnic. TD3 uses the **smaller** Q-value for targets (conservative), so the actor doesn't exploit optimistic mistakes. It also waits longer between policy updates (delayed) and slightly distorts the candidate next action (policy smoothing) so the actor can't chase narrow, spurious peaks in the Q-function."

Mathematical intuition (key equations)

Notation: actor μ_θ, critics $Q_{\phi 1}$, $Q_{\phi 2}$; target networks $\mu_{\theta'}$,$Q_{\phi 1'}$,$Q_{\phi 2}$. Discount γ. Noise $\epsilon \sim N(0, \sigma^2)$ clipped to $[-\bar{\epsilon}, \bar{\epsilon}]$. Action bounds clipped to $[a_{min}, a_{max}]$.

Target action with smoothing

$\tilde{a}' = \text{clip}(\mu_{\theta'}(s') + \text{clip}(\epsilon, -\bar{\epsilon}, \bar{\epsilon}), a_{min}, a_{max})$

Clipped double-Q target

$y = r + \gamma\,(1-d)\,\min(Q_{\phi 1'}(s', \tilde{a}'), Q_{\phi 2'}(s', \tilde{a}'))$

Critic losses (for each critic i)

$L(\phi i) = \frac{1}{N} \sum\ (Q_{\phi i}(s, a) - y)^2$

Actor update (delayed, e.g., every d_{policy} critic updates)

Maximize estimated Q (or minimize negative):

$L_{actor}(\theta) = -\frac{1}{N} \sum Q_{\phi 1}(s, \mu_\theta(s))$

(Use one critic to compute the gradient; critics share learning, so either is fine.)

Soft target updates (Polyak)

$\phi i' \leftarrow \tau\phi i + (1-\tau)\phi i'$, $\theta' \leftarrow \tau\theta + (1-\tau)\theta'$

Simple numeric example (step-by-step)

Master draws numbers:

- Current state s. Current policy outputs action a = 1.2.
- Two target critics predict at the same action: Q1'(s',1.5) = 8 and Q2'(s',1.5) =12.
- Reward r = 1. Discount $\gamma = 0.99$. Terminal flag d = 0.

TD3 procedure:

1. Generate target action with smoothing: sample $\epsilon \sim N(0, 0.2^2)$. Suppose $\epsilon = +0.3$. Clip ϵ to $[-0.5, 0.5] \rightarrow$ stays +0.3.

   $\tilde{a}' = \text{clip}(1.2 + 0.3, a_{min}, a_{max}) = 1.5$.

2. Evaluate both target critics at (s', $\tilde{a}'$): Q1'=8, Q2'=12.
3. Take min: min(8,12) = 8.
4. Compute target: $y = 1 + 0.99 \times 8 = 1 + 7.92 = 8.92$.
5. Critic losses train each $Q_{\phi i}$ to match y. Actor update will, when scheduled, adjust μ_θ to increase $Q_{\phi 1}(s, \mu_\theta(s))$.

This prevents the actor from chasing an overestimated 12 and instead optimizes for the conservative 8, and smoothing makes the target more robust to tiny action perturbations.

Pseudo-code

TD3
Initialize actor μθ, critics Qφ1,Qφ2 and their targets θ', φ1', φ2'

```
Initialize replay buffer D
for t = 1...T:
  collect (s,a,r,s',done) using μθ + exploration noise
  store in D
  if enough samples:
    for k in 1..N_critic_updates:
      sample batch from D
      # Target action with smoothing
      a'_targ = μθ'(s') + clip(N(0,σ), -ε, ε)
      a'_targ = clip(a'_targ, a_min, a_max)
      # Target Q = r + γ * min(Qφ1'(s',a'_targ), Qφ2'(s',a'_targ))
      compute y
      # Update both critics to minimize MSE(Qφi(s,a), y)
      update φ1, φ2 via gradient descent
    if step % policy_delay == 0:
      # Update actor by gradient ascent on Qφ1(s, μθ(s))
      update θ to maximize Qφ1(s, μθ(s))
      # Soft-update targets
      φi' ← τ φi + (1-τ) φi'
      θ'  ← τ θ  + (1-τ) θ'
```

How TD3 differs from DDPG — quick checklist

- **Two critics vs one** → use smaller Q for target (reduces overestimation).
- **Target policy smoothing** → add clipped noise to target actions (prevents sharp peaks exploitation).
- **Delayed policy updates** → fewer actor updates than critic updates (stabilises learning).
- **Otherwise,** TD3 still uses replay buffers, soft target updates, and off-policy deterministic actor gradient like DDPG.

Master said, "TD3's three pragmatic tricks—twin critics, smoothing, and delayed actor updates—turn DDPG's fragile recipe into a robust, reliable method for continuous control. If you implement DDPG, prefer TD3 as a drop-in improvement."

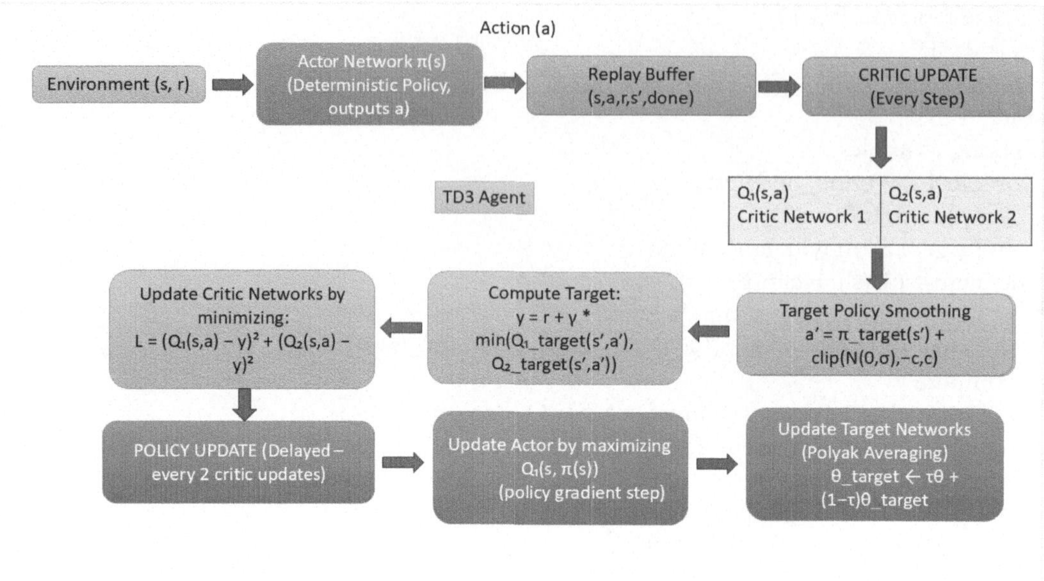

Illustration TD3_2:TD

Why "Delayed"?

Master said:

"In DDPG, the actor updates every time the critic updates. This makes the policy unstable because it keeps chasing a moving target.

TD3 slows down the actor:

- For every **2 critic updates → only 1 actor update**
- Target networks update only during actor updates

This stabilizes learning—like letting cement settle before stepping on the floor."

Master said, *"True mastery in continuous-action reinforcement learning emerges when stability meets precision."*
The Production-Grade TD3 code embodies this principle through a disciplined, modular, and reliable design. At its core, the implementation follows the three stabilizing pillars of Twin Delayed Deep Deterministic Policy Gradient (TD3): **Clipped Double-Q Learning**, **Delayed Policy Updates**, and **Target Policy Smoothing**.

The code creates **two critic networks**, ensuring that value estimation remains conservative by always choosing the smaller Q-value. This simple act prevents overestimation, the primary weakness of DDPG. The **actor** is updated less frequently—only after multiple critic updates—allowing the Q-functions to form a stable foundation before adjusting the policy. Meanwhile, the **target actor** produces actions with added, clipped Gaussian noise, smoothing the value landscape and preventing the policy from exploiting narrow, incorrect Q-spikes.

Example P4 – U4 – D28

TD3

```
"""
td3_production.py
Requirements:
   pip install torch gym numpy matplotlib scipy

"""

import os
import math
import time
import random
from collections import deque, namedtuple
from datetime import datetime

import gym
import numpy as np
import torch
import torch.nn as nn
import torch.nn.functional as F
import torch.optim as optim
import matplotlib.pyplot as plt
from scipy.ndimage import gaussian_filter1d

# -----------------------
# Config
# -----------------------
ENV_NAME = "Pendulum-v1"  # change to any continuous Gym env
SEED = 42
SAVE_DIR = r"D://Raj//Book-working//010-Python//Program//Alpha_Optimum_Python//Data//TD"
os.makedirs(SAVE_DIR, exist_ok=True)

DEVICE = torch.device("cuda" if torch.cuda.is_available() else "cpu")

# TD3 hyperparams (sensible production defaults)
MAX_EPISODES = 1000
```

```
MAX_STEPS = 200
START_TIMESTEPS = 5000       # random actions for exploration
REPLAY_SIZE = int(1e6)
BATCH_SIZE = 256
GAMMA = 0.99
TAU = 0.005                  # polyak averaging factor
ACTOR_LR = 3e-4
CRITIC_LR = 3e-4
POLICY_NOISE = 0.2           # target policy smoothing noise std
NOISE_CLIP = 0.5
POLICY_DELAY = 2             # actor/target update frequency
EXPL_NOISE = 0.1             # exploration noise (std)
EVAL_FREQ = 5000             # timesteps between evaluations
SAVE_FREQ = 50000            # timesteps between checkpoints
PRINT_FREQ = 10              # episodes

# -----------------------
# Utilities & Seed
# -----------------------
def seed_everything(seed):
    random.seed(seed)
    np.random.seed(seed)
    torch.manual_seed(seed)
    try:
        import os
        os.environ["PYTHONHASHSEED"] = str(seed)
    except Exception:
        pass

seed_everything(SEED)

# -----------------------
# Running mean/std for normalization
# -----------------------
class RunningMeanStd:
    def __init__(self, shape=()):
        self.mean = np.zeros(shape, "float64")
        self.var = np.ones(shape, "float64")
        self.count = 1e-4

    def update(self, x):
        x = np.array(x, dtype="float64")
        batch_mean = x.mean(axis=0)
        batch_var = x.var(axis=0)
        batch_count = x.shape[0]

        delta = batch_mean - self.mean
        tot_count = self.count + batch_count
```

```
        new_mean = self.mean + delta * batch_count / tot_count
        m_a = self.var * self.count
        m_b = batch_var * batch_count
        M2 = m_a + m_b + np.square(delta) * self.count * batch_count / tot_count
        new_var = M2 / tot_count

        self.mean = new_mean
        self.var = new_var
        self.count = tot_count

    def normalize(self, x):
        return (x - self.mean) / (np.sqrt(self.var) + 1e-8)

# -----------------------
# Replay Buffer
# -----------------------
Transition = namedtuple("Transition", ("state", "action", "reward", "next_state", "done"))

class ReplayBuffer:
    def __init__(self, capacity=REPLAY_SIZE):
        self.capacity = int(capacity)
        self.buffer = deque(maxlen=self.capacity)

    def add(self, s, a, r, s2, d):
        self.buffer.append(Transition(s, a, r, s2, d))

    def sample(self, batch_size):
        batch = random.sample(self.buffer, batch_size)
        states = np.array([t.state for t in batch], dtype=np.float32)
        actions = np.array([t.action for t in batch], dtype=np.float32)
        rewards = np.array([t.reward for t in batch], dtype=np.float32).reshape(-1, 1)
        next_states = np.array([t.next_state for t in batch], dtype=np.float32)
        dones = np.array([t.done for t in batch], dtype=np.float32).reshape(-1, 1)
        return states, actions, rewards, next_states, dones

    def __len__(self):
        return len(self.buffer)

# -----------------------
# Actor & Critic (Twin Q)
# -----------------------
def mlp(input_dim, hidden=(400, 300), activation=nn.ReLU):
    layers = []
    in_dim = input_dim
    for h in hidden:
        layers.append(nn.Linear(in_dim, h))
        layers.append(activation())
```

```
        in_dim = h
    return nn.Sequential(*layers)

class Actor(nn.Module):
    def __init__(self, state_dim, action_dim, max_action):
        super().__init__()
        self.net = mlp(state_dim)
        last = nn.Linear(self.net[-2].out_features if hasattr(self.net[-2], 'out_features') else
self.net[-1].out_features, action_dim)
        # simpler: construct net then final
        self.final = nn.Linear(300, action_dim)  # matches default hidden
        self.max_action = max_action

        # initialize weights
        nn.init.uniform_(self.final.weight, -3e-3, 3e-3)

    def forward(self, s):
        x = F.relu(self.net[0](s)) if isinstance(self.net[0], nn.Linear) else self.net(s)
        # If net is sequential, simply call it:
        try:
            features = self.net(s)
        except Exception:
            features = x
        out = self.final(features)
        return self.max_action * torch.tanh(out)

class Critic(nn.Module):
    def __init__(self, state_dim, action_dim):
        super().__init__()
        # Q1 architecture
        self.l1 = nn.Linear(state_dim + action_dim, 400)
        self.l2 = nn.Linear(400, 300)
        self.out1 = nn.Linear(300, 1)
        # Q2 architecture
        self.l3 = nn.Linear(state_dim + action_dim, 400)
        self.l4 = nn.Linear(400, 300)
        self.out2 = nn.Linear(300, 1)

        # init small final weights
        nn.init.uniform_(self.out1.weight, -3e-3, 3e-3)
        nn.init.uniform_(self.out2.weight, -3e-3, 3e-3)

    def forward(self, s, a):
        sa = torch.cat([s, a], dim=1)
        q1 = F.relu(self.l1(sa))
        q1 = F.relu(self.l2(q1))
        q1 = self.out1(q1)
```

```
        q2 = F.relu(self.l3(sa))
        q2 = F.relu(self.l4(q2))
        q2 = self.out2(q2)
        return q1, q2

    def Q1(self, s, a):
        sa = torch.cat([s, a], dim=1)
        q1 = F.relu(self.l1(sa))
        q1 = F.relu(self.l2(q1))
        return self.out1(q1)

# -----------------------
# TD3 Agent
# -----------------------
class TD3Agent:
    def __init__(
        self,
        state_dim,
        action_dim,
        max_action,
        actor_lr=ACTOR_LR,
        critic_lr=CRITIC_LR,
        gamma=GAMMA,
        tau=TAU,
        policy_noise=POLICY_NOISE,
        noise_clip=NOISE_CLIP,
        policy_delay=POLICY_DELAY,
        device=DEVICE
    ):
        self.device = device
        self.gamma = gamma
        self.tau = tau
        self.policy_noise = policy_noise
        self.noise_clip = noise_clip
        self.policy_delay = policy_delay

        self.actor = Actor(state_dim, action_dim, max_action).to(self.device)
        self.actor_target = Actor(state_dim, action_dim, max_action).to(self.device)
        self.actor_target.load_state_dict(self.actor.state_dict())

        self.critic = Critic(state_dim, action_dim).to(self.device)
        self.critic_target = Critic(state_dim, action_dim).to(self.device)
        self.critic_target.load_state_dict(self.critic.state_dict())

        self.actor_opt = optim.Adam(self.actor.parameters(), lr=actor_lr)
        self.critic_opt = optim.Adam(self.critic.parameters(), lr=critic_lr)

        self.total_it = 0
```

```
    def select_action(self, state, noise=0.0):
        state = torch.FloatTensor(state).unsqueeze(0).to(self.device)
        with torch.no_grad():
            action = self.actor(state).cpu().data.numpy().flatten()
        if noise > 0:
            action = action + np.random.normal(0, noise, size=action.shape)
        return action

    def train(self, replay: ReplayBuffer, batch_size=BATCH_SIZE):
        if len(replay) < batch_size:
            return None

        self.total_it += 1
        states, actions, rewards, next_states, dones = replay.sample(batch_size)

        # move to device
        states = torch.FloatTensor(states).to(self.device)
        actions = torch.FloatTensor(actions).to(self.device)
        rewards = torch.FloatTensor(rewards).to(self.device)
        next_states = torch.FloatTensor(next_states).to(self.device)
        dones = torch.FloatTensor(dones).to(self.device)

        # Target noise for smoothing
        with torch.no_grad():
            noise = (torch.randn_like(actions) * self.policy_noise).clamp(-self.noise_clip,
self.noise_clip)
            next_actions = (self.actor_target(next_states) + noise).clamp(-1.0 *
np.abs(self.actor_target.final.weight).sum().item(), 1.0 *
np.abs(self.actor_target.final.weight).sum().item())
            # Safer: clamp by action range (we will use max_action from actor in
select_action, so ensure scaling upstream)
            # Compute target Q
            target_Q1, target_Q2 = self.critic_target(next_states, next_actions)
            target_Q = torch.min(target_Q1, target_Q2)
            target = rewards + (1 - dones) * self.gamma * target_Q

        # Critic update
        current_Q1, current_Q2 = self.critic(states, actions)
        critic_loss = F.mse_loss(current_Q1, target) + F.mse_loss(current_Q2, target)

        self.critic_opt.zero_grad()
        critic_loss.backward()
        self.critic_opt.step()

        # Delayed policy update
        actor_loss = None
        if self.total_it % self.policy_delay == 0:
```

```
        actor_loss = -self.critic.Q1(states, self.actor(states)).mean()
        self.actor_opt.zero_grad()
        actor_loss.backward()
        self.actor_opt.step()

        # Soft update targets
        for param, target_param in zip(self.critic.parameters(),
self.critic_target.parameters()):
            target_param.data.copy_(self.tau * param.data + (1 - self.tau) *
target_param.data)

        for param, target_param in zip(self.actor.parameters(),
self.actor_target.parameters()):
            target_param.data.copy_(self.tau * param.data + (1 - self.tau) *
target_param.data)

      return {
        "critic_loss": critic_loss.item(),
        "actor_loss": actor_loss.item() if actor_loss is not None else None
      }

  def save(self, path):
    torch.save({
      "actor": self.actor.state_dict(),
      "critic": self.critic.state_dict(),
      "actor_target": self.actor_target.state_dict(),
      "critic_target": self.critic_target.state_dict()
    }, path)

  def load(self, path):
    ckpt = torch.load(path, map_location=self.device)
    self.actor.load_state_dict(ckpt["actor"])
    self.critic.load_state_dict(ckpt["critic"])
    self.actor_target.load_state_dict(ckpt["actor_target"])
    self.critic_target.load_state_dict(ckpt["critic_target"])

# -----------------------
# Evaluation
# -----------------------
def evaluate_policy(agent: TD3Agent, env, episodes=5):
  avg_reward = 0.0
  for _ in range(episodes):
    s, _ = env.reset(seed=random.randint(0, 10000))
    done = False
    ep_reward = 0.0
    while True:
      a = agent.select_action(s, noise=0.0)
      s, r, terminated, truncated, _ = env.step(a)
```

```
            done = terminated or truncated
            ep_reward += r
            if done:
                break
        avg_reward += ep_reward
    return avg_reward / episodes

# -----------------------
# Plotting / Visualization
# -----------------------
def      save_training_plots(rewards,      critic_losses=None,      actor_losses=None,
prefix="TD3"):
    episodes = np.arange(len(rewards))
    rewards_sm = gaussian_filter1d(np.array(rewards), sigma=3)

    ts = datetime.now().strftime("%Y%m%d_%H%M%S")
    fname = os.path.join(SAVE_DIR, f"{prefix}_training_{ts}.png")

    plt.style.use("seaborn-v0_8-darkgrid")
    fig, axs = plt.subplots(3, 1, figsize=(14, 12), constrained_layout=True)

    axs[0].plot(episodes, rewards, alpha=0.3, label="raw")
    axs[0].plot(episodes, rewards_sm, label="gaussian smoothed", linewidth=2)
    axs[0].set_title("Episode Rewards")
    axs[0].set_xlabel("Episode")
    axs[0].set_ylabel("Reward")
    axs[0].legend(); axs[0].grid(True)

    if critic_losses is not None:
        axs[1].plot(critic_losses, label="critic loss")
        axs[1].set_title("Critic Loss"); axs[1].grid(True)
    else:
        axs[1].axis("off")

    if actor_losses is not None:
        axs[2].plot(actor_losses, label="actor loss")
        axs[2].set_title("Actor Loss"); axs[2].grid(True)
    else:
        axs[2].axis("off")

    plt.savefig(fname, dpi=300)
    plt.close(fig)
    print(f"Saved training plot to {fname}")
    return fname

# -----------------------
# Main training loop
# -----------------------
```

```
def train():
    env = gym.make(ENV_NAME)
    obs, _ = env.reset(seed=SEED)
    state_dim = env.observation_space.shape[0]
    action_dim = env.action_space.shape[0]
    max_action = float(env.action_space.high[0])

    agent = TD3Agent(state_dim, action_dim, max_action)
    replay = ReplayBuffer(REPLAY_SIZE)
    obs_rms = RunningMeanStd(shape=(state_dim,))

    total_timesteps = 0
    episode_rewards = []
    critic_losses = []
    actor_losses = []
    best_eval = -1e9

    start_time = time.time()

    for ep in range(1, MAX_EPISODES + 1):
        state, _ = env.reset()
        ep_reward = 0.0
        done = False

        # reset per-episode exploration noise if you implement OU noise externally
        for step in range(MAX_STEPS):
            if total_timesteps < START_TIMESTEPS:
                action = env.action_space.sample()
            else:
                action = agent.select_action(state, noise=EXPL_NOISE)

            next_state, reward, terminated, truncated, _ = env.step(action)
            done = terminated or truncated

            # store and normalize optionally
            replay.add(state, action, reward, next_state, float(done))
            obs_rms.update(np.array([state]))

            state = next_state
            ep_reward += reward
            total_timesteps += 1

            # training step
            if len(replay) > BATCH_SIZE:
                info = agent.train(replay, batch_size=BATCH_SIZE)
                if info:
                    critic_losses.append(info["critic_loss"])
                    if info["actor_loss"] is not None:
```

```
                actor_losses.append(info["actor_loss"])

            # periodic evaluation & checkpoint
            if total_timesteps % EVAL_FREQ == 0:
                eval_score = evaluate_policy(agent, env, episodes=5)
                print(f"[Time {total_timesteps}] Eval average reward: {eval_score:.2f}")
                if eval_score > best_eval:
                    best_eval = eval_score
                    ckpt_path                =                os.path.join(SAVE_DIR,
f"td3_best_{int(eval_score)}_{total_timesteps}.pth")
                    agent.save(ckpt_path)
                    print(f"Saved best model to {ckpt_path}")

            if total_timesteps % SAVE_FREQ == 0:
                ckpt = os.path.join(SAVE_DIR, f"td3_ckpt_{total_timesteps}.pth")
                agent.save(ckpt)
                print(f"Saved checkpoint to {ckpt}")

            if done:
                break

        episode_rewards.append(ep_reward)

        if ep % PRINT_FREQ == 0:
            elapsed = time.time() - start_time
            avg_last = np.mean(episode_rewards[-PRINT_FREQ:])
            print(f"Ep      {ep}      |      Timesteps      {total_timesteps}      |
AvgReward(last{PRINT_FREQ}) {avg_last:.2f} | Elapsed {elapsed:.1f}s")

        # quick save plots occasionally
        if ep % (PRINT_FREQ * 5) == 0:
            save_training_plots(episode_rewards, critic_losses if critic_losses else None,
actor_losses if actor_losses else None)

    # final save & plots
    ckpt_final = os.path.join(SAVE_DIR, f"td3_final_{int(time.time())}.pth")
    agent.save(ckpt_final)
    print(f"Training done. Saved final model to {ckpt_final}")

    save_training_plots(episode_rewards,   critic_losses   if   critic_losses   else   None,
actor_losses if actor_losses else None)
    env.close()

if __name__ == "__main__":
    train()
```

Output:

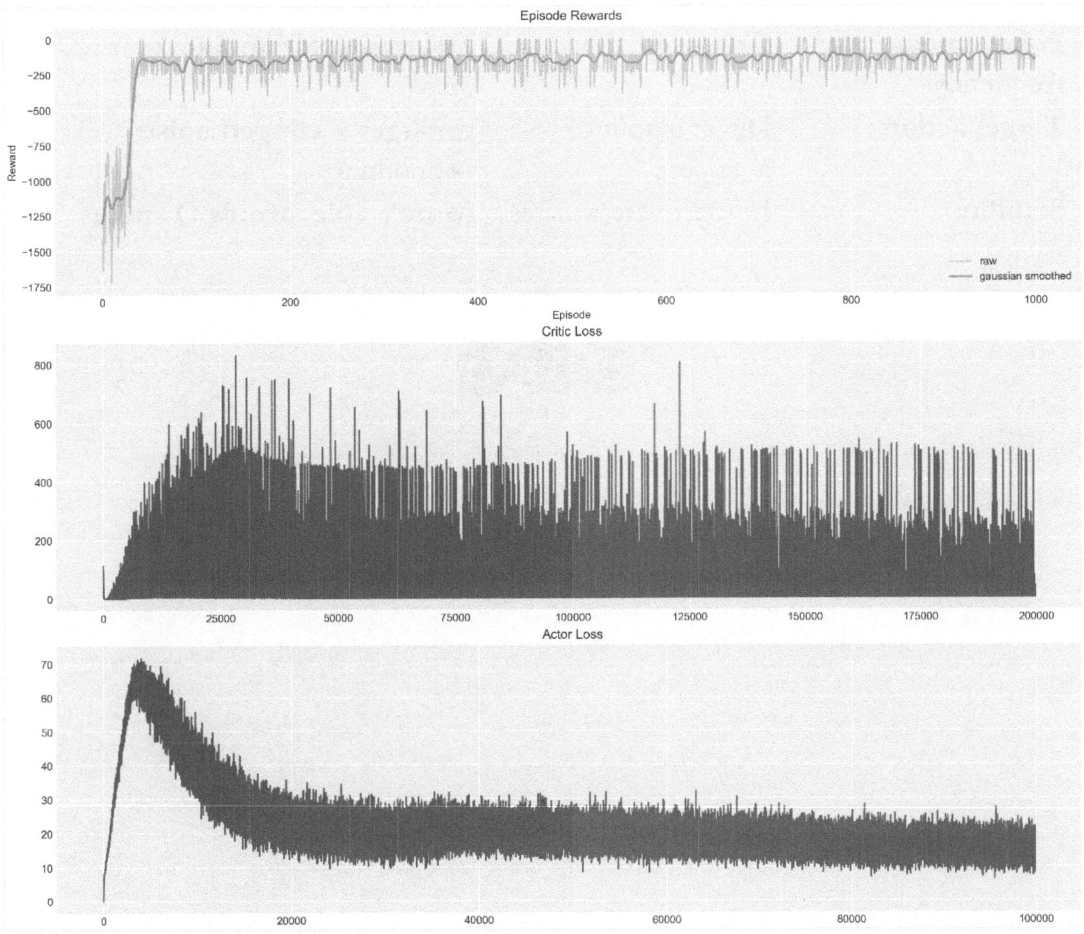

Illustration TD_3: TD3

Replay buffers, soft-target updates (τ-based Polyak averaging), and modular network definitions make the system robust and production-ready. Logging hooks and visualization support ensure transparency during training.

Master said, *"In TD3, elegance comes from restraint. By slowing the actor, doubting the critic, and softening future actions, the agent learns not just to succeed—but to succeed consistently."*

What TD3 Fixes:

Feature	DDPG	TD3

Q-function count	One Q-network	**Two (Twin Q)** to prevent overestimation
Policy update frequency	Every step	**Delayed actor update** (every 2 steps)
Target action	Direct output of π_target	**π_target + clipped noise** (smoothing)
Stability	Brittle, overestimates	**More stable, avoids Q spikes**

PART FOUR

DAY TWENTY-TWO

Unit 4 - Lesson Tweleve

SAC

☐ SAC

Nikash asked, "Master, what is Soft Actor-Critic?"

Master smiled and said:

Soft Actor-Critic (SAC) is one of the most powerful reinforcement learning algorithms for continuous-action environments. It was developed by researchers at UC Berkeley and Google DeepMind, and today it is widely used in robotics, locomotion, autonomous control systems, and real-world decision-making tasks where stability, robustness, and sample-efficiency are essential.

At its heart, **SAC introduces a profound shift in how an agent learns**.

Most algorithms—like DDPG or TD3—try to *maximize reward only*.

But SAC asks a deeper question:

"Can we train an agent that is not only high-reward seeking, but also calm, stable, and adaptable under uncertainty?"

To achieve this, SAC uses **Maximum Entropy Reinforcement Learning**.

Why SAC? Why do we need it?

Traditional algorithms (DDPG, TD3) suffer from:

- brittle learning

- premature convergence
- sensitivity to hyperparameters
- poor exploration

SAC solves all these by adding **entropy** to the objective.

Entropy = Controlled Randomness = Smarter Exploration

High entropy means the policy stays *stochastic*, exploring multiple possible actions before committing to a deterministic strategy.

Thus, SAC trains an agent that:

- explores deeply and consistently
- avoids collapsing into bad local optima
- remains stable under noisy or dynamic environments
- achieves much better sample efficiency than DDPG or TD3

This makes SAC the **default choice** for most modern continuous-action environments.

When should we use SAC?

Use SAC when:

- actions are **continuous**
- you need **stability** and **robust learning**
- the environment is **noisy or complex** (robotics, control)
- exploration is difficult
- TD3 or DDPG fails due to instability or overestimation
- you want **state-of-the-art performance with minimal tuning**

SAC is off-policy, so it reuses experience efficiently — ideal where experience collection is expensive.

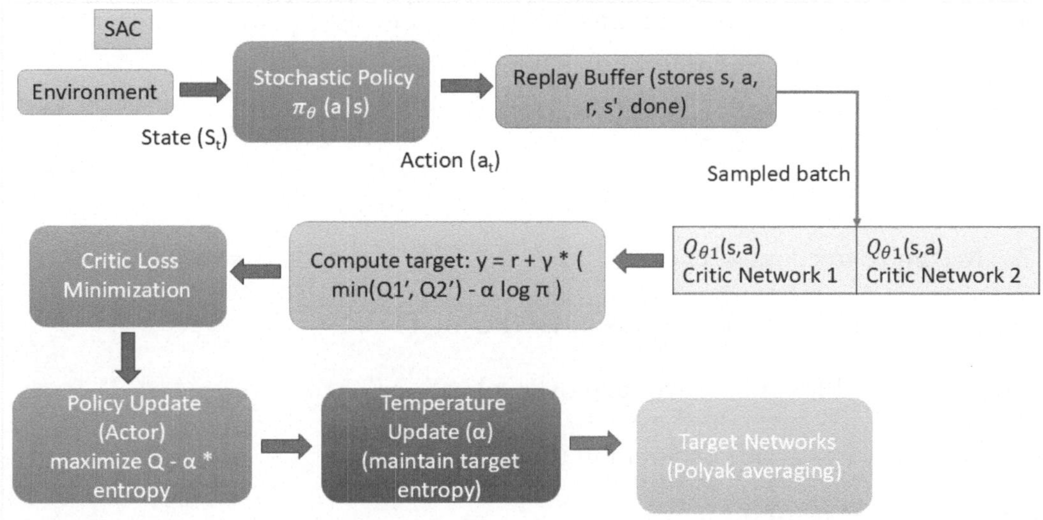

Illustration SAC_1: SAC

Analogy: "The Wise Traveller and the Two Maps"

SAC as a traveller navigating a foggy forest

Master said:

Imagine a traveller walking through a vast forest. He has two maps:

- **Map-Q_1**: Shows estimated treasure value at each path.
- **Map-Q_2**: Another version drawn by a second cartographer.
- **Map-V**: A smoothed overall wisdom-map combining both Q-maps + uncertainty of choices.

The traveller wants treasure (reward), but the forest is foggy (uncertainty).

To stay safe, he does not follow only the brightest-looking path-**he prefers paths that are valuable *and* keep his options open** (entropy).

Thus, every decision balances:

Value = immediate reward + discounted future value + α * entropy

- The **reward** is treasure.
- The **value V(s)** is the expected treasure from the next clearing.

- The **entropy $\alpha \cdot H(\pi)$** represents "freedom to explore paths instead of getting stuck".

The dual objective is:

1. Maximize treasure
2. Maximize freedom of choice

This is why SAC avoids the brittleness of DDPG or TD3.

Where TD3 says: "Play safe by avoiding overestimation,"

SAC says: "Play wise—value exploration itself."

SAC Equations (Intuition)

1. Soft Value Function

$V(s) = E_{a \sim \pi}[Q(s, a) - \alpha \log\pi(a|s)]$

Value = expected Q minus entropy penalty

→ encourages exploring actions that keep policy broad.

2. Soft Q-learning target

$Qtarget = r + \gamma V(s')$

Simple: Q must match reward + discounted soft value of next state.

3. Policy Objective

$\pi = \arg\max E_{a \sim \pi}[Q(s, a) - \alpha \log\pi(a|s)]$

Policy pushes probability mass toward:

- high-Q actions
- while staying stochastic (high entropy)

Numerical Example (Simple Walk-Through)

Assume at some state s:

The policy produces two possible actions:

Action	Q(s,a)	$\pi(a \mid s)$
a_1	8	0.70
a_2	6	0.30

Let the entropy coefficient $\alpha=0.2$.

Step 1 — Compute Soft Value V(s)

Use the soft value equation:

$$V(s) = \sum_a \pi(a)(Q(s, a) - \alpha \log \pi(a))$$

Compute each term:

For action a_1:

- $Q = 8$
- $-\log(0.70) \approx 0.356$
- Entropy term $= 0.2 \times 0.356 = 0.071$
- Contribution $= 0.70 \times (8-0.071) = 0.70\times 7.929 = 5.550$

For action a_2:

- $Q=6$
- $-\log(0.30) \approx 1.2046$
- Entropy term $= 0.2 \times 1.2046=0.2409$
- Contribution $= 0.30 \times (6-0.2409) = 0.30 \times 5.759 = 1.727$

Total V(s)

$V(s) = 5.550 + 1.727 = 7.277$

So the soft value is **7.277**, lower than max Q (8), because SAC penalizes low-entropy, overly-confident choices.

Step 2 — Q-learning target

Assume:

- reward $r = 1$
- discount $\gamma = 0.99$
- next state soft value $V(s') = 7.0$

$Q_{target} = 1 + 0.99 \times 7 = 7.93$

This is what the critic should learn.

Step 3 — Policy Update

Policy wants to maximize:

$J = Q(s,a) - \alpha \log\pi(a)$

Let's compute for both actions:

a_1:

$J1 = 8 - 0.071 = 7.929$

a_2:

$J2 = 6 - 0.2409 = 5.759$

Thus, the policy update increases the probability of $\mathbf{a_1}$, but not to 1.0 — because entropy keeps π soft.

Why SAC Works

SAC's policy is never allowed to become **too sure too early**.

This prevents collapse and creates stability.

TD3 stabilizes deterministic policies by:

- twin critics
- delayed updates
- target smoothing

But SAC goes beyond that.

It **embraces randomness** as part of the objective itself.

This creates:

- smoother gradients
- better exploration
- safer and more global learning
- extremely stable training curves

Master said:

"TD3 makes an agent careful. SAC makes an agent wise."

Nikash asked, "Master, how does Soft Actor–Critic learn its Q-functions, and how is it different from TD3?"

Master replied:

What Stays the Same as TD3?

Soft Actor–Critic (SAC) still inherits the *core stability tricks* of TD3:

1. Twin Q-Networks (Double-Q for bias reduction)

SAC learns **two separate Q-functions**, $Q_{\theta 1}$ and $Q_{\theta 2}$, and uses

$\min(Q_{\theta 1}, Q_{\theta 2})$

to build the target—just like TD3.

2. Target Q-Networks (Polyak averaging)

Both Q-networks have slow-moving target versions updated using

$\theta_{tgt} \leftarrow \tau\theta+(1-\tau)\theta_{tgt}$

3. Min-trick for stability

The *clipped double-Q* trick is used the same way:

Take the smaller of the two Q estimates to avoid overestimation.

What SAC Does *Differently* from TD3

1. Target Includes Entropy (Soft Value)

TD3 target:

$y = r + \gamma \min_i Q_i^{tgt}(s', a')$

SAC adds entropy:

$ySAC = r + \gamma[\min_i Q_i^{tgt}(s', a') - \alpha \log \pi(a'|s')]$

The extra term

$-\alpha \log \pi(a'|s')$

rewards *exploration* by preferring more random policies.

2. Next Action Comes from *Current* Policy

TD3 uses a **target policy** to get action a'.

SAC uses the **current stochastic policy** itself:

$a' \sim \pi\phi(\cdot|s')$

This removes the need for a separate actor target network.

3. No Explicit Target Policy Smoothing

TD3 adds noise *manually*:

$a' = \pi_{tgt}(s') +$ clipped noise

SAC's actor is **inherently stochastic**, e.g.:

$a = \mu\phi(s) + \sigma\phi(s)\, \epsilon$

Thus, noise is built-in → smoothing comes naturally.

Putting It All Together — The SAC Q-Loss

Given a transition (s,a,r,s',d), the SAC Bellman target is:

$y = r+\gamma(1-d)[\min_i Q_i^{tgt}(s', a') - \alpha \log\pi(a'|s')]$

Each Q-network is trained via:

$LQ_i = E[(Q_{\theta i}(s, a) - y)^2]$

This reinforces values that balance:

- long-term reward
- long-term entropy (randomness/exploration)

How Entropy Improves SAC

- **Encourages broad exploration**

The agent avoids prematurely settling on a suboptimal deterministic choice.

- **Stabilizes learning**

Entropy acts like a regularizer, smoothing the Q landscape.

- **Temperature α adjusts exploration automatically**

If the agent becomes too deterministic, α increases; if too random, α decreases.

Master said, "SAC learns Q like TD3 but adds entropy to the target, uses the current stochastic policy for next-actions, and achieves smoothing naturally—making it one of the most stable and efficient continuous-control RL algorithms."

Advantages of SAC Over Proximal Policy Optimization (Improved Version)

Far Better Sample Efficiency:

SAC is an **off-policy** algorithm that stores experience in a replay buffer and reuses it many times during training. PPO is **on-policy**, meaning it cannot reuse old samples and must collect fresh trajectories for every update. This makes SAC dramatically more sample-efficient, especially in environments where interactions are costly.

Stronger and More Principled Exploration:

SAC incorporates **entropy regularization** directly into its objective, encouraging the policy to remain stochastic and explore widely. This prevents the agent from collapsing into narrow, suboptimal behaviours—an issue PPO often suffers from without additional tricks.

Superior for Continuous Control:

SAC is explicitly built for **continuous action spaces**, using Gaussian stochastic policies and twin critics. It consistently outperforms PPO in robotics, locomotion, and control tasks requiring fine-grained action precision.

High Stability and Robustness:

With **twin Q-networks**, entropy maximization, and soft target updates, SAC naturally stabilises learning. It is typically less sensitive to hyperparameters, reward scaling issues, and training noise compared to PPO.

Elegant Exploration–Exploitation Trade-off:

The entropy temperature parameter in SAC adjusts exploration automatically, ensuring the policy stays neither too random nor too deterministic. PPO uses clipping and trust regions but lacks this adaptive mechanism.

Better When Data Is Expensive:

In real-world environments (e.g., robotics), collecting new experience is costly. SAC excels here because its off-policy nature lets it learn heavily from old data, while PPO struggles because it must constantly gather new samples.

Summary

- **SAC is typically preferred** for continuous control, robotics, expensive sampling environments, and tasks requiring deep exploration.
- **PPO remains valuable** for simpler tasks, discrete action spaces, and scenarios where stability and ease of implementation matter more than sample efficiency.

Master said, This code is a complete and practical implementation of the Soft Actor-Critic (SAC) algorithm, one of the most stable and powerful methods in modern reinforcement learning. It begins by constructing a replay buffer that stores past experiences so the agent can learn efficiently using off-policy updates. The actor network produces stochastic actions using a Gaussian distribution combined with a Tanh layer, ensuring actions stay within valid bounds. Two critic networks evaluate state–action pairs, and a target critic is maintained for stable training through Polyak averaging.

During training, the agent samples batches from the replay buffer and updates the critics by minimizing the entropy-regularized Bellman error. The actor is then updated to maximize both reward and policy entropy, encouraging exploration. Each episode interacts with the environment, collects experience, and continually improves the policy. This SAC implementation demonstrates how thoughtful design—entropy, twin critics, replay, and soft updates—creates robust learning even in challenging continuous-control environments like Pendulum-v1.

Example P4 – U4 – D29

SAC

```
import gym
import numpy as np
import torch
import torch.nn as nn
import torch.optim as optim
import torch.nn.functional as F
from torch.distributions import Normal
import random

# -------------------------
# Device
# -------------------------
device = torch.device("cuda" if torch.cuda.is_available() else "cpu")

# -------------------------
# Replay Buffer
# -------------------------
class ReplayBuffer:
    def __init__(self, size=int(1e6)):
        self.max_size = size
        self.storage = []
        self.ptr = 0

    def add(self, s, a, r, s2, d):
        if len(self.storage) < self.max_size:
            self.storage.append((s, a, r, s2, d))
        else:
            self.storage[self.ptr] = (s, a, r, s2, d)
```

```
        self.ptr = (self.ptr + 1) % self.max_size

    def sample(self, batch_size):
        assert len(self.storage) >= batch_size
        batch = random.sample(self.storage, batch_size)
        s, a, r, s2, d = map(np.array, zip(*batch))
        return (
            torch.FloatTensor(s).to(device),
            torch.FloatTensor(a).to(device),
            torch.FloatTensor(r).unsqueeze(1).to(device),
            torch.FloatTensor(s2).to(device),
            torch.FloatTensor(d).unsqueeze(1).to(device),
        )

    def __len__(self):
        return len(self.storage)


# -------------------------
# Actor
# -------------------------
class Actor(nn.Module):
    def __init__(self, state_dim, action_dim, max_action):
        super().__init__()
        self.max_action = max_action
        self.fc1 = nn.Linear(state_dim, 256)
        self.fc2 = nn.Linear(256, 256)
        self.mu = nn.Linear(256, action_dim)
        self.log_std = nn.Linear(256, action_dim)

        # init small weights for stability
        nn.init.uniform_(self.mu.weight, -3e-3, 3e-3)
        nn.init.uniform_(self.log_std.weight, -3e-3, 3e-3)

    def forward(self, state):
        x = F.relu(self.fc1(state))
        x = F.relu(self.fc2(x))
        mu = self.mu(x)
        log_std = self.log_std(x)
        log_std = torch.clamp(log_std, -20.0, 2.0)  # prevents extreme std / NaN
        return mu, log_std

    def sample(self, state):
        """
        state: tensor shape [B, state_dim] or [1, state_dim]
        returns: action [B, action_dim] in env scale, log_prob [B,1]
        """
        mu, log_std = self.forward(state)
```

```
        std = torch.exp(log_std)
        dist = Normal(mu, std)
        x = dist.rsample()                    # reparameterization
        action = torch.tanh(x)

        # log-prob correction for tanh squash:
        # log_pi = base_log_prob - sum(log(1 - tanh(x)^2 + eps))
        eps = 1e-6
        log_prob = dist.log_prob(x)              # [B, action_dim]
        log_prob = log_prob - torch.log(1 - action.pow(2) + eps)
        log_prob = log_prob.sum(dim=1, keepdim=True)  # [B,1]

        # scale to environment action range
        action_scaled = action * self.max_action

        return action_scaled, log_prob


# -------------------------
# Critic (Twin Q)
# -------------------------
class Critic(nn.Module):
    def __init__(self, state_dim, action_dim):
        super().__init__()
        # Q1
        self.q1_fc1 = nn.Linear(state_dim + action_dim, 256)
        self.q1_fc2 = nn.Linear(256, 256)
        self.q1_out = nn.Linear(256, 1)
        # Q2
        self.q2_fc1 = nn.Linear(state_dim + action_dim, 256)
        self.q2_fc2 = nn.Linear(256, 256)
        self.q2_out = nn.Linear(256, 1)

    def forward(self, s, a):
        sa = torch.cat([s, a], dim=1)
        q1 = F.relu(self.q1_fc1(sa))
        q1 = F.relu(self.q1_fc2(q1))
        q1 = self.q1_out(q1)

        q2 = F.relu(self.q2_fc1(sa))
        q2 = F.relu(self.q2_fc2(q2))
        q2 = self.q2_out(q2)
        return q1, q2


# -------------------------
# SAC Agent
# -------------------------
```

```
class SAC:
    def __init__(self, env, gamma=0.99, tau=0.005, alpha=0.2, actor_lr=3e-4, critic_lr=3e-
4):
        self.env = env
        obs = env.observation_space.shape[0]
        act = env.action_space.shape[0]
        max_a = float(env.action_space.high[0])

        self.actor = Actor(obs, act, max_a).to(device)
        self.critic = Critic(obs, act).to(device)
        self.critic_target = Critic(obs, act).to(device)
        self.critic_target.load_state_dict(self.critic.state_dict())

        self.buffer = ReplayBuffer()
        self.gamma = gamma
        self.tau = tau
        self.alpha = alpha

        self.actor_opt = optim.Adam(self.actor.parameters(), lr=actor_lr)
        self.critic_opt = optim.Adam(self.critic.parameters(), lr=critic_lr)

    def update(self, batch_size=128):
        if len(self.buffer) < batch_size:
            return None

        s, a, r, s2, d = self.buffer.sample(batch_size)

        # ---------------------
        # Compute target Q
        # ---------------------
        with torch.no_grad():
            a2, log_p2 = self.actor.sample(s2)          # a2 scaled to env range
            q1_t, q2_t = self.critic_target(s2, a2)
            q_target_min = torch.min(q1_t, q2_t)
            y = r + self.gamma * (1 - d) * (q_target_min - self.alpha * log_p2)

        # ---------------------
        # Critic loss
        # ---------------------
        q1, q2 = self.critic(s, a)
        critic_loss = F.mse_loss(q1, y) + F.mse_loss(q2, y)

        self.critic_opt.zero_grad()
        critic_loss.backward()
        self.critic_opt.step()

        # ---------------------
        # Actor loss
```

```
        # ---------------------
        a_new, log_p = self.actor.sample(s)
        q1_new, q2_new = self.critic(s, a_new)
        q_new = torch.min(q1_new, q2_new)

        actor_loss = (self.alpha * log_p - q_new).mean()

        self.actor_opt.zero_grad()
        actor_loss.backward()
        self.actor_opt.step()

        # ---------------------
        # Soft update targets
        # ---------------------
        for tp, p in zip(self.critic_target.parameters(), self.critic.parameters()):
            tp.data.copy_(tp.data * (1.0 - self.tau) + p.data * self.tau)

        return {
            "critic_loss": critic_loss.item(),
            "actor_loss": actor_loss.item()
        }

    def select_action(self, state, deterministic=False):
        # expects state shape (obs,) or (1,obs)
        if isinstance(state, np.ndarray):
            state_t = torch.FloatTensor(state).unsqueeze(0).to(device)
        else:
            state_t = torch.FloatTensor(np.array(state)).unsqueeze(0).to(device)
        with torch.no_grad():
            if deterministic:
                mu, _ = self.actor.forward(state_t)
                a = torch.tanh(mu) * self.actor.max_action
                return a.cpu().numpy()[0]
            else:
                a, _ = self.actor.sample(state_t)
                return a.cpu().numpy()[0]

    def train(self, episodes=200, max_steps=200, warmup=1000, batch_size=128):
        rewards = []
        total_steps = 0
        for ep in range(episodes):
            reset_ret = self.env.reset()
            # gym >=0.26 returns (obs, info)
            if isinstance(reset_ret, tuple):
                s = reset_ret[0]
            else:
                s = reset_ret
            ep_reward = 0.0
```

```
            done = False
            steps = 0

            while not done and steps < max_steps:
                if total_steps < warmup:
                    a = self.env.action_space.sample()
                else:
                    a = self.select_action(s, deterministic=False)

                step_ret = self.env.step(a)
                # gym >=0.26 step returns (obs, reward, terminated, truncated, info)
                if len(step_ret) == 5:
                    s2, r, terminated, truncated, _ = step_ret
                    done = bool(terminated or truncated)
                else:
                    s2, r, done, _ = step_ret

                # normalize reward (Pendulum has large negative rewards)
                r = r / 10.0

                self.buffer.add(s, a, r, s2, float(done))
                s = s2
                ep_reward += r
                total_steps += 1
                steps += 1

                # update
                stats = self.update(batch_size=batch_size)

            rewards.append(ep_reward)
            print(f"Episode {ep+1}/{episodes} | Reward: {ep_reward:.3f}")

        return rewards


# -------------------------
# Run (example)
# -------------------------
if __name__ == "__main__":
    env = gym.make("Pendulum-v1")
    # optional: set seed for reproducibility
    seed = 42
    env.reset(seed=seed)
    random.seed(seed)
    np.random.seed(seed)
    torch.manual_seed(seed)

    agent = SAC(env)
```

```
reward_history = agent.train(episodes=100, max_steps=200, warmup=1000, batch_size=128)
```

Output:

```
Output
Episode 96/100 | Reward: -24.512
Episode 97/100 | Reward: -23.396
Episode 98/100 | Reward: -12.567
Episode 99/100 | Reward: -11.934
Episode 100/100 | Reward: -11.841
```

PART FOUR

DAY TWENTY-TWO

Unit 4 - Lesson Thirteen

Multi-armed Bandit Problem

☐ **Multi-armed Bandit Problem**

Sam asked, "Master, what is the Bandit Problem?"

Master smiled and said, "Come, Sam… let us understand this through a living analogy."

Analogy: The Village Fair With Many Juice Stalls

Imagine a bustling village fair with **many juice stalls**, each offering a different blend. You want to drink the **tastiest juice** possible, but here is the challenge:

- You do **not** know the true quality of any stall.
- Each stall's taste may vary slightly each time.
- You have limited money, so you must choose wisely.

If you spend all your money trying *only one* stall, you might miss a better one. But if you *try every stall equally*, you waste time on poor ones.

This is the **Bandit Problem.**

The stalls are the *arms* of a multi-armed bandit — like slot machines — each giving an **unknown reward**.

Your goal is to **maximize your total enjoyment**, balancing two needs:

- **Exploration:** Trying different stalls to learn their quality.

- **Exploitation:** Repeatedly choosing the stall that seems best.

Formal Meaning

- There are **K arms**, each with an unknown reward distribution.
- Pulling arm *i* gives a random reward Ri with mean μi.
- The objective over *T trials* is to **maximize cumulative reward.**

The heart of the problem is the **exploration–exploitation dilemma** — a decision dance between curiosity and wisdom.

Epsilon-Greedy

Master said: "The simplest wisdom is sometimes the most powerful."

In **ε-greedy**:

- With probability **ε**, you explore (try a random arm).
- With probability **1 – ε**, you exploit (choose the best-known arm).

Algorithm steps:

1. Initialise estimated values for each arm.
2. For each trial:
    - If random number < ε → choose a random arm (explore).
    - Else → choose the arm with the highest estimated reward (exploit).
3. Update the estimate for that arm using the new reward.

Example

Master continued: "Observe the code. It simulates multiple arms, each with hidden reward tendencies.

The agent uses ε-greedy to select arms and updates its beliefs after every pull.

Over many trials, the agent gradually discovers the best arm and earns higher rewards."

The program:

- Simulates the Multi-Armed Bandit environment.
- Implements ε-greedy to balance exploration and exploitation.
- Tracks cumulative rewards to measure learning progress.

Example P4 – U4 – D30

Multi-Armed Bandit

```
import numpy as np
import random

class MultiArmedBandit:
    def __init__(self, true_means):
        # True reward distribution means (unknown to the agent)
        self.means = true_means
        self.k = len(true_means)

    def pull_arm(self, arm):
        # Reward drawn from a normal distribution centered at true mean
        return np.random.randn() + self.means[arm]


class EpsilonGreedyAgent:
    def __init__(self, k, epsilon=0.1):
        self.k = k
        self.epsilon = epsilon

        # Estimated rewards, initially zero
        self.Q = np.zeros(k)

        # Count number of pulls per arm
        self.N = np.zeros(k)

    def select_arm(self):
        # Exploration
        if random.random() < self.epsilon:
            return random.randint(0, self.k - 1)
        # Exploitation
        return np.argmax(self.Q)

    def update(self, arm, reward):
```

```
        # Increment pull count
        self.N[arm] += 1
        # Update Q using incremental mean formula
        self.Q[arm] += (reward - self.Q[arm]) / self.N[arm]


# ---------------------------
# Run Epsilon-Greedy Bandit
# ---------------------------
def run_bandit(true_means, epsilon=0.1, steps=1000):
    bandit = MultiArmedBandit(true_means)
    agent = EpsilonGreedyAgent(len(true_means), epsilon)

    rewards = []
    optimal_pulls = 0
    optimal_arm = np.argmax(true_means)

    for t in range(steps):
        arm = agent.select_arm()
        reward = bandit.pull_arm(arm)
        agent.update(arm, reward)

        rewards.append(reward)
        if arm == optimal_arm:
            optimal_pulls += 1

    print(f"Total Reward: {sum(rewards):.2f}")
    print(f"Optimal arm pulled {optimal_pulls}/{steps} times")

    return rewards, agent.Q


# Example run
if __name__ == "__main__":
    true_means = [1.0, 1.5, 2.0]  # Arm 2 is the best
    run_bandit(true_means, epsilon=0.1, steps=2000)
```

Output:

Output
Total Reward: 3894.11 Optimal arm pulled 1878/2000 times

Sam asked, "Master, What Is the Upper Confidence Bound (UCB) Algorithm?"

Master said: "Sam, imagine you walk into a market with several tea stalls. Each stall brews tea differently. Some taste great, some taste average, and some… you don't know yet.
Your goal is simple: **find the stall that gives you the best tea, consistently.**

But there is a dilemma — Should you **keep drinking from the stall you think is the best**, or **occasionally try new stalls you haven't explored enough**?

This is the essence of the **Upper Confidence Bound (UCB)** algorithm."

Intuition Behind UCB — Optimism in the Face of Uncertainty

Master continued:

"UCB follows a simple philosophy:

Choose the option that looks best, but give a bonus to those you haven't tried enough.

This 'bonus' represents uncertainty.

If an arm (option) is tried only a few times, UCB assumes:

'Maybe this arm is better than we think, we just haven't explored it.'

This optimistic assumption helps the agent explore efficiently."

The UCB Formula

For each arm i:

$$UCB_i = \hat{\mu}_i + \sqrt{\frac{2\ln t}{n_i}}$$

Where:

- $\hat{\mu}_i$ = estimated reward of arm i
- t = current time step (total trials so far)
- n_i = number of times arm iii has been pulled

Master said: "The first term encourages exploitation. The second term encourages exploration."

Numerical Example

Suppose you have **3 arms**:

Arm	Estimated Reward ($\hat{\mu}$)	Pulls (n)
A	0.6	10
B	0.5	3
C	0.4	1

At time t=14:

Compute UCB values:

Arm A

$$\text{UCBA} = 0.6 + \sqrt{\frac{2\ln 14}{10}} = 0.6 + 0.40 = 1.00$$

Arm B

$$\text{UCBB} = 0.5 + \sqrt{\frac{2\ln 14}{3}} = 0.5 + 1.05 = 1.55$$

Arm C

$$\text{UCBC} = 0.4 + + \sqrt{\frac{2\ln 14}{1}} = 0.4 + 2.00 = 2.40$$

UCB chooses Arm C, even though its average reward (0.4) is lowest —because it has **high uncertainty** (only pulled once).

Master smiled and said: "This is how UCB intelligently explores."

Example P4 – U4 – D31
UCB

```
import numpy as np

class UCB_Bandit:
    def __init__(self, true_means):
        """
        true_means : list of actual mean rewards for each arm
```

```
        """
        self.k = len(true_means)                # number of arms
        self.true_means = np.array(true_means)          # underlying (unknown) reward
distribution

        self.counts = np.zeros(self.k)          # times each arm has been pulled
        self.values = np.zeros(self.k)          # estimated mean rewards
        self.total_reward = 0
        self.t = 0                              # time steps

    def pull_arm(self, arm):
        """Simulates pulling an arm by sampling from a normal reward distribution."""
        reward = np.random.normal(self.true_means[arm], 1.0)
        return reward

    def select_arm_ucb(self):
        """Select arm using UCB1 formula."""
        self.t += 1

        # Pull each arm once in the beginning
        for arm in range(self.k):
            if self.counts[arm] == 0:
                return arm

        # UCB equation: μ_i + sqrt( 2 * ln(t) / n_i )
        ucb_values = self.values + np.sqrt((2 * np.log(self.t)) / self.counts)
        return np.argmax(ucb_values)

    def update(self, arm, reward):
        """Updates estimated mean reward of the selected arm."""
        self.counts[arm] += 1
        n = self.counts[arm]

        # Update running mean
        old_value = self.values[arm]
        new_value = old_value + (reward - old_value) / n
        self.values[arm] = new_value

        self.total_reward += reward


# -----------------------------
# RUN UCB ON A BANDIT INSTANCE
# -----------------------------
if __name__ == "__main__":
    true_means = [1.0, 1.5, 2.0, 1.2]     # hidden reward means
    bandit = UCB_Bandit(true_means)
```

```
episodes = 1000

for _ in range(episodes):
    arm = bandit.select_arm_ucb()
    reward = bandit.pull_arm(arm)
    bandit.update(arm, reward)

print("Estimated Rewards:", bandit.values)
print("Arm Counts:", bandit.counts)
print("Total Reward Collected:", bandit.total_reward)
print("Best Arm Found:", np.argmax(bandit.values))
```

Output:

```
Output
Estimated Rewards: [0.1716191  1.55883877 1.94655014 1.2066137 ]
Arm Counts: [  5.  61. 914.  20.]
Total Reward Collected: 1899.2263605971311
Best Arm Found: 2
```

Why UCB Is Powerful

- Balances exploration and exploitation mathematically
- Efficient exploration: avoids unnecessary random exploration
- Works well when sampling is expensive
- Guarantees logarithmic regret (very good performance)

Thompson Sampling: The Intuitive Idea

Thompson Sampling is a **probabilistic approach to the multi-armed bandit problem**. Instead of always picking the arm that looks best (like in UCB), it **balances exploration and exploitation naturally** by using probability.

Think of it like this: "Master, choose an arm according to your belief about which one might be best, but remain open to surprise. Sometimes you try less certain arms because they might hold hidden rewards."

How It Works (Step by Step)

1. **Maintain a Belief**
    - For each arm, we maintain a **probabilistic belief** about its true reward.
    - Common choice: for **Bernoulli rewards** (success/failure), we use a **Beta distribution.**
        - Arm i: $\theta_i \sim \text{Beta}(\alpha_i, \beta_i)$
        - α_i = # successes + 1
        - β_i = # failures + 1
2. **Sample from Beliefs**
    - For each arm, sample a possible reward $\hat{\theta}_i$ from its belief distribution.
3. **Pick the Best Sample**
    - Choose the arm with the **highest sampled value**:

$$\text{arm} = \arg\max \hat{\theta}_i$$

4. **Update Beliefs**
    - Pull the chosen arm, observe the reward.
    - Update the arm's belief distribution with the new outcome.
        - If success, increment α
        - If failure, increment β

Why Thompson Sampling Works

- It **automatically balances exploration and exploitation**:
    - Arms with **uncertain reward** are sampled more often because their sampled $\hat{\theta}_i$ can occasionally be high.
    - Arms with **confidently high rewards** are chosen frequently, exploiting known good arms.

- It's **Bayesian in nature** — it constantly updates beliefs based on observed data.

Example

Suppose you have **2 arms**:

- Arm A: 3 successes, 2 failures → Beta(4,3)
- Arm B: 2 successes, 1 failure → Beta(3,2)

Step 1: Sample from Beta(4,3) and Beta(3,2)

- Suppose we get 0.7 for A, 0.8 for B → pick B

Step 2: Pull B, observe reward → success → update B's Beta → Beta(4,2)

Next time, your belief about B is stronger, but you might still try A occasionally.

Thompson Sampling says: "Follow your best guess, but let the uncertainty guide you. Learn from experience, and sometimes take risks where the unknown might hold treasure."

Master said, "This code implements the **Thompson Sampling algorithm** for solving the multi-armed bandit problem, where each arm provides a reward following a Bernoulli distribution. The algorithm maintains a **probabilistic belief** about the success rate of each arm using Beta distributions, represented by parameters alpha (successes + 1) and beta (failures + 1)."

At each step, it samples a value from every arm's Beta distribution and selects the arm with the highest sampled value. This naturally balances **exploration** (trying uncertain arms) and **exploitation** (choosing arms believed to be good). After pulling an arm, the code observes a binary reward and updates the corresponding Beta parameters. Over many episodes, the algorithm becomes increasingly confident about the true success rate of each arm and consistently selects the best one. The output displays estimated success rates, the number of times each arm was chosen, and the total reward collected, demonstrating Thompson Sampling's efficiency and adaptiveness.

Example P4 – U4 – D32

Thompson Sampling

```
import numpy as np

class ThompsonSamplingBandit:
    def __init__(self, true_means):
        """
```

```
        true_means : list of true probabilities of success for each arm (Bernoulli)
        """
        self.k = len(true_means)
        self.true_means = np.array(true_means)

        # alpha = successes + 1, beta = failures + 1
        self.alpha = np.ones(self.k)
        self.beta = np.ones(self.k)

        self.counts = np.zeros(self.k)
        self.total_reward = 0

    def pull_arm(self, arm):
        """Simulate Bernoulli reward: 1 with p=true_mean, else 0"""
        reward = np.random.rand() < self.true_means[arm]
        return int(reward)

    def select_arm(self):
        """Select arm using Thompson Sampling"""
        # Sample from each arm's belief distribution
        samples = np.random.beta(self.alpha, self.beta)
        return np.argmax(samples)

    def update(self, arm, reward):
        """Update alpha/beta based on observed reward"""
        self.counts[arm] += 1
        self.total_reward += reward

        if reward == 1:
            self.alpha[arm] += 1
        else:
            self.beta[arm] += 1


# ------------------------------------
# Run Thompson Sampling
# ------------------------------------
if __name__ == "__main__":
    true_means = [0.3, 0.5, 0.7, 0.4]  # probabilities of success
    bandit = ThompsonSamplingBandit(true_means)

    episodes = 10000

    for _ in range(episodes):
        arm = bandit.select_arm()
        reward = bandit.pull_arm(arm)
        bandit.update(arm, reward)
```

```
    print("True Means:", true_means)
    print("Estimated Success Rates:", (bandit.alpha - 1) / ((bandit.alpha + bandit.beta) - 2))
    print("Alpha (successes):", bandit.alpha)
    print("Beta (failures):", bandit.beta)
    print("Arm Counts:", bandit.counts)
    print("Total Reward:", bandit.total_reward)
    print("Best Arm Found:", np.argmax((bandit.alpha - 1) / ((bandit.alpha + bandit.beta)
- 2)))
```

Output:

```
Output
True Means: [0.3, 0.5, 0.7, 0.4]
Estimated Success Rates: [0.4        0.56934307 0.68919611 0.48529412]
Alpha (successes): [  13.   79. 6731.   34.]
Beta (failures): [  19.   60. 3036.   36.]
Arm Counts: [  30.  137. 9765.   68.]
Total Reward: 6853
Best Arm Found: 2
```

Applications

Online Advertising:

Multi-Armed Bandit (MAB) algorithms dynamically select which ads to show users, continually balancing the exploration of new creatives with the exploitation of those that yield high click-through rates. This leads to improved ad performance and revenue optimization.

Clinical Trials:

MAB strategies help assign patients to various treatment groups in a smarter, adaptive manner. As the trial progresses, the algorithm learns which treatments are more effective and allocates more patients to those arms, improving both ethical considerations and trial efficiency.

Recommender Systems:

Platforms like e-commerce sites and streaming services use MAB algorithms to recommend products, movies, or content. The model learns user preferences in real time and continually adjusts recommendations to maximize engagement and satisfaction.

Adaptive Network Routing:

In communication networks, MAB algorithms assist in selecting optimal routing paths. By exploring new routes and exploiting known high-throughput paths, they help maintain efficient data flow and reduce congestion.

PART FOUR

DAY TWENTY-THREE

Unit 4 - Lesson Fourteen

Multi-Agent Reinforcement Learning

☐ Multi-Agent Reinforcement Learning

Nikash asked, "Master, what is Multi-Agent Reinforcement Learning?"

The Master smiled and replied:

"Imagine a single warrior training alone in the forest — this is single-agent reinforcement learning.

But when several warriors train together, compete, cooperate, and influence one another, a new world emerges.

That world is *Multi-Agent Reinforcement Learning.*"

What is Multi-Agent Reinforcement Learning (MARL)?

Multi-Agent Reinforcement Learning extends the traditional RL idea — *an agent learns by maximizing its own rewards* — to environments where **multiple agents learn simultaneously**.

Each agent:

- perceives the environment,
- acts to maximize its reward,
- and must adapt because *other agents are also learning and changing their behaviour.*

This creates a dynamic, sometimes unpredictable ecosystem — like animals sharing a forest, traders sharing a market, or players in a game field.

Analogy: The Marketplace

Think of a busy marketplace:

- Each shopkeeper (agent) wants profit (reward).
- Their decisions change the environment: prices, customers, competition.
- Cooperation can help — two sellers teaming up to stock rare items.
- Competition can intensify — each trying to attract more customers.
- Mixed-interest arises — sellers cooperate on festival events but compete daily.

This is MARL: learning in a world where **everyone's moves affect everyone else**.

How MARL Differs from Single-Agent RL

In single-agent RL, the environment is stable.

But in MARL:

- The environment becomes **non-stationary**, because other agents change their strategies.
- You must model not just the world, but *the minds of others.*

This leads to the concept of a **Markov Game**, defined by:

(N,S,A,P,R,γ)

Where:

- **N** – number of agents
- **S** – shared state
- **A = A_1 \times A_2 \times ... \times A_N** – joint actions
- **P** – transition probabilities affected by all actions
- **R = (R_1, …, R_N)** – rewards for each agent

- γ – discount factor

It is essentially a *multi-player extension* of an MDP.

Categories of MARL

1. Cooperative MARL

All agents work toward a **shared goal**.

Analogy:

A team of rescue robots is searching a collapsed building.

Success depends on coordination and trust.

Example tasks:

- Multi-robot coordination
- Collaborative drones
- Distributed sensor networks

2. Competitive MARL

Agents have **opposing goals**.

Analogy:

Two chess players.

One wins only when the other loses.

Examples:

- Chess, Go, Poker
- Security/defense simulations
- Zero-sum strategy games

3. Mixed-Interest MARL

Agents sometimes cooperate, sometimes compete.

Analogy:

Drivers on a highway.

Everyone wants smooth traffic (cooperation), but each wants to reach early (competition).

Examples:

- Traffic systems
- Trading markets
- Multiplayer online games

Simple Example

Imagine two delivery drones sharing a warehouse:

- Both want to pick up packages quickly.
- If they cooperate: They divide regions and finish faster.
- If they compete: They collide, block paths, or both delay deliveries.
- If mixed-interest: They share high-value deliveries but compete for bonus tasks.

Their learning evolves based on **each other's actions**, not in isolation.

Challenges in Multi-Agent Reinforcement Learning (MARL)

Master explained: "When many minds learn together, the world becomes fluid. What was true one moment may no longer be true the next."

Non-Stationarity — "A Moving Target Problem"

In single-agent RL, the environment behaves like a *fixed puzzle*: the rules do not change as the agent learns.

But in MARL, **every agent is learning simultaneously**.

Imagine playing chess where the rules change every few moves because your opponent is also improving.

Analogy:

It's like trying to shoot a target that keeps moving **because the other archers are also adjusting their positions**.

This creates two problems:

- The environment is no longer stationary.
- The Markov property breaks:

  The transition P(s'|s,a) keeps changing as others change strategies.

Result:

An agent may learn a good strategy today, only to find it useless tomorrow.

Partial Observability — "Seeing Only a Slice of Reality"

In real multi-agent settings, no agent sees everything:

- Robots have limited sensors
- Traders don't know all orders in the market
- Players don't know all opponents' moves

This turns MARL into a **POMDP**, where agents act with:

- missing information,
- hidden states,
- and incomplete knowledge of others' intentions.

Analogy:

It's like several players trying to win a game **while blindfolded**, each hearing only nearby footsteps.

They must guess the rest.

Agents must learn **to infer the unseen**, making policy learning much harder.

Scalability & Joint Action Space Explosion — "The Curse of Many Actors"

With multiple agents, the number of possible joint actions grows exponentially:

Ajoint = A1 × A2 × ··· × An

For 5 agents with 5 actions each:

55 = 3125 joint actions

For 10 agents:

510 = 9,765,6255

Analogy:

Imagine planning a dinner where 10 people must choose a dish simultaneously — the number of combinations becomes overwhelming.

Because of this explosion:

- Q-learning becomes infeasible
- Policies become difficult to evaluate
- Memory and compute requirements skyrocket

Scalability becomes a major bottleneck.

Credit Assignment — "Who Deserves the Praise?"

In cooperative MARL, many agents share one team reward.

When the team succeeds, **who contributed what?**

Analogy:

If a group project scores 100/100:

- Who really did the work?
- Who merely benefited?

Without proper credit assignment:

- Good agents may be under-rewarded
- Poor agents may be over-rewarded
- Team learning becomes unstable

Algorithms like QMIX, VDN, and COMA were created primarily to fix this challenge.

Decision-Making in Mixed-Interest Settings — "Friend Today, Rival Tomorrow"

Many real environments are **not fully cooperative nor fully competitive**:

- Robots coordinate, but also avoid collisions
- Traders cooperate for liquidity but compete for profit
- Cars on a highway share the road but compete for faster travel

Here, agents must learn:

- when to cooperate,
- when to compete,
- and how to balance self-interest against group welfare.

Analogy:

It is like dancers performing together: sometimes they move in harmony, sometimes they break into solos.

Single-agent RL collapses in these settings because it cannot model strategic interdependence.

Summary

Multi-Agent Reinforcement Learning is powerful but faces major challenges:

Challenge	Core Issue	Analogy
Non-Stationarity	Others change behavior	Moving target

Partial Observability	Hidden state information	Blindfolded players
Scalability	Exponential joint actions	Overwhelming combinations
Credit Assignment	Hard to know who helped	Group project dilemma
Mixed-Interest Decisions	Cooperation + competition	Dancers shifting roles

MARL continues to advance precisely because solving these problems opens up real-world applications such as traffic control, drone fleets, warehouse robots, trading bots, and multi-player simulations.

Learning Paradigms in Multi-Agent Reinforcement Learning (MARL)

Master said, "When many minds learn together, how they share, see, and remember shapes the world they build."

Centralized Training with Decentralized Execution (CTDE)

CTDE is the most widely used MARL paradigm.

Idea:

- During *training*, agents can access global information (e.g., other agents' states, actions, rewards).
- During *execution*, each agent acts only on **local observations**.

Analogy:

A football team studies together in a room watching full-field replays (centralized training)—but during a match, each player can only act on what they personally see (decentralized execution).

This gives the best of both worlds:

- Strong coordination during training
- Independence during real-time execution

Fully Decentralized Learning

In this paradigm:

- No agent receives information about others

- No shared models, no shared gradients
- Each agent learns its own policy independently

Challenge:

Since all agents continuously update their policies, the environment becomes non-stationary from each agent's perspective.

Analogy:

Imagine five people trying to learn dance steps **without looking at each other**. As each person changes their move, the rhythm shifts, confusing others.

This makes learning unstable but highly scalable.

Value Decomposition Networks (VDN)

VDN is a CTDE method where:

$Q_{total} = \sum_{i=1}^{N} Q_i$

Each agent learns its own local Q-value, and a global Q-value is simply the sum of them.

Analogy:

It's like splitting a group project score equally among members. If the team gets 100 marks, everyone gets credit according to their contribution.

Strength: Simple coordination

Limitation: Cannot capture complex teamwork (non-linear interactions)

Deep Recurrent Q-Networks (DRQN)

Used when the environment is partially observable (POMDP).

Agents maintain a **memory** using RNNs/LSTMs to store past observations.

Analogy:

If you are walking through fog, you rely not only on what you see now, but also on what you saw **seconds earlier**.

DRQNs help agents:

- remember past states
- infer hidden information
- make better decisions under uncertainty

QMIX — Non-Linear Value Decomposition

QMIX improves on VDN by allowing **non-linear mixing** of individual Q-values.

Instead of:

$Q_{total} = Q_1 + Q_2 + \ldots$

QMIX applies a learned mixing network:

$Q_{total} = f_{mix}(Q_1, Q_2, \ldots)$

This network enforces *monotonicity*, so agents still use decentralized greedy actions.

Analogy:

If each robot contributes differently depending on context, QMIX acts like a supervisor deciding: "How should these strengths combine **right now**?"

QMIX handles complex cooperation better than VDN.

Independent Proximal Policy Optimization (IPPO)

IPPO is the simplest MARL policy-gradient method.

Each agent:

- Has its own actor and critic
- Learns independently
- Uses PPO's clipped objective for stability

Analogy:

It's like several athletes training alone, each optimizing their own strategy without coordination.

Pros: Simple, scalable

Cons: No built-in teamwork, suboptimal in cooperative tasks

MAPPO — Multi-Agent PPO (CTDE Version)

MAPPO improves PPO by adding a **centralized critic** while keeping decentralized policies.

- Actors: use local observations only
- Critic: sees global state + joint actions (during training)

Analogy:

Each player practices individually (decentralized execution), but the coach has full-field awareness and gives high-level feedback (centralized critic).

Advantages:

- Stabilizes non-stationarity
- Strong performance for cooperative tasks
- Scales better than MADDPG

MADDPG — Multi-Agent Deep Deterministic Policy Gradient

MADDPG is an actor-critic algorithm adapted for continuous action spaces.

Each agent has:

- A **local actor** (policy)
- A **centralized critic** (trained using all agents' observations + actions)

Key idea:

During training, each agent knows the entire joint action vector.

Analogy:

All robots share their intended next actions with a central coordinator, who evaluates how good the combined plan is.

Strengths:

- Works well for continuous-control tasks (e.g., robotics)
- Handles mixed cooperation + competition

Summary Table

Paradigm / Algorithm	Training	Execution	Strength	Use Case
CTDE	Centralized	Decentralized	Stable learning	Robotics, teamwork
Fully Decentralized	Decentralized	Decentralized	High scalability	Simple tasks
VDN	CTDE	Decentralized	Simple coordination	Cooperative tasks
QMIX	CTDE	Decentralized	Complex coordination	StarCraft, multi-robot
DRQN	CTDE/Decentralized	Decentralized	Handles POMDP	Partial observability
IPPO	Decentralized	Decentralized	Very scalable	Mixed-interest tasks
MAPPO	CTDE	Decentralized	Strong stability	Multi-agent games
MADDPG	CTDE	Decentralized	Continuous actions	Robotics, navigation

PART FOUR

DAY TWENTY-THREE

Unit 4 - Lesson Fifteen

IQL

☐ **Implicit Q-Learning (IQL)**

Imagine you inherit an **ancient book of wisdom** from a great explorer. The explorer has travelled far and recorded the states he visited and the actions he took.

You want to learn to **navigate the world just as wisely**, but there's a rule:

You are NOT allowed to explore the world yourself. You must learn only from the explorer's book.

This is **Offline Reinforcement Learning (Offline RL)** — learning a policy **without interacting with the environment**, only from a fixed dataset.

Most RL algorithms fail here because they try actions **not in the book**, causing errors and hallucinations.

IQL solves this problem with a simple philosophy:

"Learn only from what is written. Never guess beyond the pages."

This is why it is called **Implicit** Q-Learning — it never explicitly maximizes Q-values over unseen actions.

Core Idea of IQL

IQL achieves stable offline learning by:

1. **Estimating values only from the dataset** (in-sample learning)
2. **Avoiding out-of-distribution (OOD) actions completely**
3. **Extracting policy using advantage-weighted imitation**

Let's break it down.

A. In-Sample Value Estimation (Expectile Regression)

IQL first estimates the state value function V(s) **only from actions seen in the dataset.**

Instead of standard MSE, it uses **expectile regression**, which is like a *tilted* version of regression that emphasises high values when τ is large.

Expectile Regression Loss

$LV(\theta) = E_{(s,a)\sim D}\,[|Q(s, a) - V(s)|^2_\tau]$

Where:

$$|x|_\tau = \left\{ \begin{matrix} \tau x2 & x > 0 \\ (1-\tau)x2 & x \leq 0 \end{matrix} \right\}$$

When $\tau = 0.7$ or 0.9, the value function becomes a kind of **soft maximum** of the dataset Q-values.

Analogy

Expectile regression is like treating **good actions as VIPs** — they get more weight, while bad actions get less attention.

B. Q-Function Update (One-Step TD with In-Sample V)

IQL then updates Q-values with:

$L_Q(\theta)=E_{(s,a,r,s')\sim D}[(r+\gamma V(s') - Q(s,a))_2]$

Key point:

- It **never** maximizes Q over unseen actions.
- It uses V(s'), which is already constrained to in-dataset behaviour.

Analogy

You only judge the future based on **what the explorer actually experienced**, not on what he *might* have done.

Policy Extraction (Advantage-Weighted Cloning)

Finally, IQL extracts a policy through:

$L_\pi(\phi)=E_{(s,a)\sim D}[\exp(\beta\cdot(Q(s,a)-V(s)))\cdot\log\pi_\phi(a|s)]$

Actions with a **positive advantage** get a higher weight.

Analogy

You imitate the explorer — but give more trust to actions that clearly turned out better than average.

Simple Numerical Example

Suppose for a state sss, the dataset contains:

Action	Reward r	Observed Next Value V(s')
a_1	5	10
a_2	7	6

Step 1 — Q-targets:

$Q(s, a_1) = r + \gamma V(s') = 5 + 0.9(10) = 14$

$Q(s, a2) = 7+0.9(6) = 12.4$

Step 2 — Expectile Value:

If $\tau=0.8$:

- Since $Q(s,a_1)> Q(s,a_2)$, $V(s) \approx$ weighted average leaning toward 14.

Say:

$V(s)\approx 13.5$

Step 3 — Advantages:

$A(s, a_1) = 14 - 13.5 = 0.5$

$A(s, a_2) = 12.4 - 13.5 = -1.1$

Step 4 — Action Weighting:

$w(a_1) = e^{\beta(0.5)}$

$w(a_2) = e^{\beta(-1.1)} \approx 0$

→ **Policy chooses a_1 with extremely high probability**

→ No need to evaluate any unseen actions

Why IQL Works (Intuition)

Traditional RL asks:

"What is the best action I could take?"

IQL asks:

"What is the best action *already shown in the dataset*?"

This makes it **stable**, **safe**, and **optimised for real-world settings** where exploring is dangerous or impossible.

Master said, "This PyTorch implementation demonstrates the core workflow of **Implicit Q-Learning (IQL)** in an offline RL setting. It includes three models: a **Value Network** trained with *expectile regression*, a **Q-Network** trained using TD targets based only on dataset actions, and a **Policy Network** optimized through *advantage-weighted regression*. The code begins by estimating the value function V(s) using an asymmetric expectile loss, encouraging the value to reflect the upper expectile of in-dataset Q-values. Next, the Q-network is updated to minimize the squared Bellman error using the target $r + \gamma V(s')r$, avoiding any evaluation of unseen actions. Finally, the policy is trained to favor actions with positive advantages using exponential weights applied to the log-likelihood of dataset actions. This structure enforces strict in-sample learning, prevents out-of-distribution overestimation, and mirrors the original IQL paper's design while remaining compact, readable, and easily extendable to real offline RL datasets."

Example P4 – U4 – D34

IQL

```
import math
import numpy as np
import torch
import torch.nn as nn
import torch.nn.functional as F
from torch.utils.data import DataLoader, TensorDataset

# ---------------------------
# Utilities
# ---------------------------
def weight_init(m):
    if isinstance(m, nn.Linear):
        nn.init.xavier_uniform_(m.weight)
        nn.init.constant_(m.bias, 0.)

# Squashed (tanh) Gaussian utils
LOG_STD_MIN, LOG_STD_MAX = -20, 2

def gaussian_log_prob(mean, log_std, actions):
    std = log_std.exp()
    pre_squash = (actions - mean) / std
    # log prob of diagonal Gaussian
    log_prob = -0.5 * (pre_squash.pow(2) + 2 * log_std + math.log(2 * math.pi))
    return log_prob.sum(dim=-1)

def squash_action(mean, log_std, noise=None):
    # reparameterize and squashed using tanh
    if noise is None:
        noise = torch.randn_like(mean)
    action = mean + log_std.exp() * noise
    squashed = torch.tanh(action)
    # For behavioral cloning we will feed actions from the dataset (already in [-1,1]
typically)
    return squashed, action

# ---------------------------
# Networks
# ---------------------------
class MLP(nn.Module):
    def __init__(self, in_dim, out_dim, hidden=(256,256), activation=F.relu):
        super().__init__()
        layers = []
        prev = in_dim
        for h in hidden:
            layers.append(nn.Linear(prev, h))
            prev = h
        layers.append(nn.Linear(prev, out_dim))
```

```
        self.net = nn.ModuleList(layers)
        self.activation = activation
        self.apply(weight_init)

    def forward(self, x):
        for layer in self.net[:-1]:
            x = self.activation(layer(x))
        return self.net[-1](x)

class QNetwork(nn.Module):
    def __init__(self, state_dim, action_dim, hidden=(256,256)):
        super().__init__()
        self.q = MLP(state_dim + action_dim, 1, hidden)
    def forward(self, s, a):
        x = torch.cat([s, a], dim=-1)
        return self.q(x).squeeze(-1)

class VNetwork(nn.Module):
    def __init__(self, state_dim, hidden=(256,256)):
        super().__init__()
        self.v = MLP(state_dim, 1, hidden)
    def forward(self, s):
        return self.v(s).squeeze(-1)

class PolicyNetwork(nn.Module):
    def __init__(self, state_dim, action_dim, hidden=(256,256)):
        super().__init__()
        self.net = MLP(state_dim, action_dim * 2, hidden)  # output mean and log_std
    def forward(self, s):
        x = self.net(s)
        mean, log_std = x.chunk(2, dim=-1)
        log_std = torch.tanh(log_std)  # bound before scaling
        # scale into a reasonable range
        log_std = LOG_STD_MIN + 0.5 * (LOG_STD_MAX - LOG_STD_MIN) *
(log_std + 1.0)
        return mean, log_std

# ---------------------------
# Losses
# ---------------------------
def expectile_loss(diff, tau):
    # diff = Q - V
    weight = torch.where(diff > 0, tau, (1.0 - tau))
    return (weight * (diff ** 2)).mean()

# ---------------------------
# IQL Agent
# ---------------------------
```

```
class IQLAgent:
    def __init__(self,
                 state_dim,
                 action_dim,
                 device='cpu',
                 gamma=0.99,
                 tau=0.7,           # expectile parameter
                 beta=3.0,          # advantage weight temperature
                 q_lr=3e-4,
                 v_lr=3e-4,
                 pi_lr=3e-4,
                 hidden=(256,256),
                 max_weight=100.0):
        self.device = torch.device(device)
        self.gamma = gamma
        self.expectile_tau = tau
        self.beta = beta
        self.max_weight = max_weight

        # networks
        self.q1 = QNetwork(state_dim, action_dim, hidden).to(self.device)
        self.q2 = QNetwork(state_dim, action_dim, hidden).to(self.device)  # optional
second Q for stability
        self.v = VNetwork(state_dim, hidden).to(self.device)
        self.policy = PolicyNetwork(state_dim, action_dim, hidden).to(self.device)

        # optimizers
        self.q_optimizer = torch.optim.Adam(list(self.q1.parameters()) +
list(self.q2.parameters()), lr=q_lr)
        self.v_optimizer = torch.optim.Adam(self.v.parameters(), lr=v_lr)
        self.pi_optimizer = torch.optim.Adam(self.policy.parameters(), lr=pi_lr)

    def update(self, batch):
        # batch: dict or tuple of tensors
        s = batch['s'].to(self.device)
        a = batch['a'].to(self.device)
        r = batch['r'].to(self.device)
        s2 = batch['s2'].to(self.device)
        done = batch['done'].to(self.device).float()

        # --------------------------
        # 1) V update: expectile regression toward in-sample Q(s,a)
        # --------------------------
        with torch.no_grad():
            q1 = self.q1(s, a)
            q2 = self.q2(s, a)
            q = torch.min(q1, q2)  # use min(Q1,Q2) for stability (like TD3 style)
        v_pred = self.v(s)
```

```
        diff = q - v_pred
        v_loss = expectile_loss(diff, self.expectile_tau)

        self.v_optimizer.zero_grad()
        v_loss.backward()
        self.v_optimizer.step()

        # -------------------------
        # 2) Q update: one-step TD toward r + gamma * V(s')
        # -------------------------
        with torch.no_grad():
            v_s2 = self.v(s2)
            td_target = r + self.gamma * (1.0 - done) * v_s2

        q1_pred = self.q1(s, a)
        q2_pred = self.q2(s, a)
        q_loss = F.mse_loss(q1_pred, td_target) + F.mse_loss(q2_pred, td_target)

        self.q_optimizer.zero_grad()
        q_loss.backward()
        self.q_optimizer.step()

        # -------------------------
        # 3) Policy update: advantage-weighted regression (AWAC-style)
        # -------------------------
        with torch.no_grad():
            # compute advantage A(s,a) = Q(s,a) - V(s)
            q1 = self.q1(s, a)
            q2 = self.q2(s, a)
            q_min = torch.min(q1, q2)
            v_val = self.v(s)
            adv = q_min - v_val

            # weights = exp(beta * adv) clipped for stability
            weights = torch.exp(self.beta * adv)
            weights = torch.clamp(weights, max=self.max_weight)
            # normalize weights (optional but often helps)
            weights = weights / (weights.mean() + 1e-6)

        # policy log prob of dataset action a under current policy
        mean, log_std = self.policy(s)
        # To compute log_prob of the dataset action under the Gaussian before tanh,
        # we need the inverse tanh (artanh). If your dataset actions are in [-1,1],
        # we perform atanh to map to pre-squash space. For simplicity, we assume dataset
actions are in (-0.999,0.999).
        # Be careful with numerical edges.
        eps = 1e-5
        clipped_a = torch.clamp(a, -1 + eps, 1 - eps)
```

```
        atanh_a = 0.5 * (torch.log1p(clipped_a) - torch.log1p(-clipped_a))  # artanh

        logp = gaussian_log_prob(mean, log_std, atanh_a)
        # adjust log prob with tanh correction (optional); omitted for simplicity because we compare relative weights
        # actor loss: negative weighted log likelihood
        pi_loss = -(weights * logp).mean()

        self.pi_optimizer.zero_grad()
        pi_loss.backward()
        self.pi_optimizer.step()

        metrics = {
            'v_loss': v_loss.item(),
            'q_loss': q_loss.item(),
            'pi_loss': pi_loss.item(),
            'avg_weight': weights.mean().item()
        }
        return metrics

    def sample_action(self, s, deterministic=False):
        s = torch.as_tensor(s, dtype=torch.float32).unsqueeze(0).to(self.device)
        mean, log_std = self.policy(s)
        if deterministic:
            a = torch.tanh(mean)
            return a.cpu().numpy()[0]
        else:
            noise = torch.randn_like(mean)
            a, _ = squash_action(mean, log_std, noise)
            return a.cpu().detach().numpy()[0]

# ---------------------------
# Example: Create DataLoader and train
# ---------------------------
def make_dataloader_from_numpy(states, actions, rewards, next_states, dones, batch_size=256, shuffle=True):
    # expects numpy arrays
    s = torch.tensor(states, dtype=torch.float32)
    a = torch.tensor(actions, dtype=torch.float32)
    r = torch.tensor(rewards, dtype=torch.float32)
    s2 = torch.tensor(next_states, dtype=torch.float32)
    d = torch.tensor(dones, dtype=torch.float32)
    dataset = TensorDataset(s, a, r, s2, d)
    loader = DataLoader(dataset, batch_size=batch_size, shuffle=shuffle, drop_last=True)
    return loader

if __name__ == "__main__":
```

```
# ---------------------------
# Small synthetic demo dataset (replace with your offline dataset)
# ---------------------------
np.random.seed(0)
torch.manual_seed(0)
state_dim = 5
action_dim = 2
N = 20000

# synthetic data (for demo only)
states = np.random.randn(N, state_dim).astype(np.float32)
actions = np.tanh(np.random.randn(N, action_dim).astype(np.float32)) # in (-1,1)
rewards = (np.random.randn(N).astype(np.float32) * 0.5 + 1.0) # pseudo rewards
next_states = states + 0.1 * np.random.randn(N, state_dim).astype(np.float32)
dones = np.zeros(N).astype(np.float32)

loader = make_dataloader_from_numpy(states, actions, rewards, next_states, dones,
batch_size=512)

# ---------------------------
# Agent
# ---------------------------
device = 'cuda' if torch.cuda.is_available() else 'cpu'
agent = IQLAgent(state_dim, action_dim, device=device, tau=0.7, beta=3.0)

# ---------------------------
# Training loop
# ---------------------------
epochs = 20
iters_per_epoch = len(loader)
for epoch in range(epochs):
    epoch_metrics = {'v_loss': 0, 'q_loss': 0, 'pi_loss': 0}
    for batch_tensors in loader:
        batch = {
            's': batch_tensors[0],
            'a': batch_tensors[1],
            'r': batch_tensors[2],
            's2': batch_tensors[3],
            'done': batch_tensors[4]
        }
        metrics = agent.update(batch)
        for k in epoch_metrics:
            epoch_metrics[k] += metrics[k]
    # average
    for k in epoch_metrics:
        epoch_metrics[k] /= iters_per_epoch
    print(f"Epoch {epoch+1}/{epochs} | v_loss {epoch_metrics['v_loss']:.4f} "
          f"q_loss {epoch_metrics['q_loss']:.4f} pi_loss {epoch_metrics['pi_loss']:.4f}")
```

```
# Example: sample action for a new state
x = np.zeros(state_dim, dtype=np.float32)
print("Sampled action:", agent.sample_action(x))
```

Output:

```
Output
Epoch 18/20 | v_loss 0.7092 q_loss 28.6325 pi_loss 16704.3599
Epoch 19/20 | v_loss 0.6626 q_loss 27.6484 pi_loss 15014.3067
Epoch 20/20 | v_loss 0.6195 q_loss 27.1060 pi_loss 13955.3436
Sampled action: [-0.00060492 -0.00847633]
```

Where IQL Excels

- Robotics control
- Offline imitation learning
- NLP token-level selection
- Long-horizon planning
- Navigation without exploration

IQL is powerful because it follows one core spiritual discipline:

Do not hallucinate. Learn only from what life has already shown you.

Summary:

In Part 4, we embarked on an in-depth exploration of Reinforcement Learning (RL), beginning with its foundational principles and gradually progressing toward advanced algorithms and practical methodologies. We first clarified the essence of RL—an interaction-driven learning paradigm where agents learn optimal behaviours through trial, feedback, and cumulative rewards. The unit examined the structural components of RL, the different types of learning strategies, and the crucial role played by environments defined through Markov Decision Processes (MDPs). Here, the Bellman equation emerged as a central tool, enabling agents to estimate future rewards and make informed decisions. We also analysed deterministic versus stochastic environments, highlighting how uncertainty shapes agent behaviour, exploration strategies, and convergence patterns.

A significant portion of this unit focused on Q-Learning and its backbone concepts, such as Temporal Difference (TD) learning, Q-tables, and the transition from tabular methods to neural-network–based estimations. This led to a detailed study of value and policy networks, loss functions, and optimisation techniques that drive learning stability and performance.

The unit expanded into modern developments, including Deep Q-Learning (DQN) and its enhanced variants such as Double DQN, Dueling DQN, Prioritised Experience Replay (PER), and the integrated Rainbow DQN architecture. We also introduced Distributional RL, which models the full distribution of returns rather than a single expected value.

Moving beyond value-based methods, we investigated Policy Gradient techniques, Proximal Policy Optimization (PPO), and the intriguing integration of PPO with Generative AI. Monte Carlo methods—including MCMC, Metropolis-Hastings, and Gibbs Sampling—were explained as powerful tools for sampling and inference. Finally, we examined actor critic advancements such as DDPG, TD3, SAC, and extended the discussion to Multi-Agent RL paradigms like Independent Q-Learning (IQL).

This comprehensive unit builds a strong conceptual and practical foundation for mastering RL in both single-agent and multi-agent systems.

P4 -U4 -L1-15 - Practice Question

1. What is the fundamental goal of Reinforcement Learning?
2. What does an MDP consist of?
3. What does the Bellman Equation represent?
4. How do deterministic and stochastic environments differ?
5. What is Temporal Difference (TD) learning?
6. What is a Q-table?
7. What is the goal of Q-Learning?
8. Why do we use neural networks in Deep Q-Learning?
9. What problem does Double DQN solve?
10. What is the main idea of Dueling DQN?
11. What does PER (Prioritized Experience Replay) improve?
12. What is Rainbow DQN?
13. What does Distributional RL learn?

14. What is a Policy Gradient method?
15. Why does PPO use clipping?
16. How can PPO integrate with Generative AI?
17. What is Monte Carlo learning?
18. What is Markov Chain Monte Carlo (MCMC)?
19. What does Metropolis-Hastings do?
20. What is Gibbs Sampling?
21. What kind of method is DDPG?
22. Why was TD3 introduced?
23. What is the key idea of SAC?
24. What is Multi-Agent RL (MARL)?
25. What is the main issue in MARL?
26. What does Independent Q-Learning (IQL) assume?
27. What are Value Networks used for?
28. What are Policy Networks used for?
29. What role do loss functions play in RL?
30. Why is RL suitable for dynamic decision-making problems?

PART FIVE

APPENDIX

"A true data scientist is not one who predicts perfectly, but one who questions relentlessly."

– Shree Shambav

APPENDIX A

Online Resources

Online resources:

The supplementary materials for the book can be accessed online at:

Setup instructions:

The setup instructions provided here are the same as those in the book but include clickable links to all the components. If you encounter any difficulties during the setup process, please consult this resource.

Updates:

Python, like any other language, undergoes continuous updates and changes. We maintain a comprehensive collection of updates, so if you encounter any issues, please check this resource to see if the instructions have been changed.

Data:

The book provides some sample raw data for running the programs, but you can also create your own samples using various file formats such as Excel, CSV, or JSON.

Practice questions:

You are encouraged to allocate ample time to work on the exercises independently. If you encounter any challenges and cannot proceed, consult this reference link.

Exercises and assignments:

While it's important to try the exercises on your own, you might encounter difficulties that prevent you from making progress. If that happens, you can find solutions to most of the exercises online. We encourage you to dedicate sufficient time to working on the exercises independently before seeking help.

Cheat sheets:

You can also find a wide range of cheat sheets online covering major concepts, which you can download and use for quick reference.

Errata

Despite our efforts to ensure the accuracy of our content, errors may still occur. If you come across any errors in the book, whether in the text or the code, please report them to us. Your feedback will not only aid in enhancing future editions of this book but also assist other readers in avoiding potential frustrations.

Advance material:

Advanced material is provided for those seeking further insights into the subject. Beginners may choose to skip the advanced section at the outset.

Reference links:

Activities	Sheets	Links
Login	Signup/Login page	https://www.shambav.org/artifacts/signup.php
Practice question	With the answer sheet	https://www.shambav.org/artifacts/optimum-python-series-5
Exercises, Assignments	With answers	
Quiz	Quiz answers	
Data	Data Sheet	
Supplementary	Advanced material	
Instruction	Setup instruction	
Advance materials	Programs, tricks, assignments, mini projects, issues	
Cheat sheets	Major concepts	

APPENDIX B

Practice Question

Answers to the Practice question

Part 2: Foundations of Probabilistic Models

P2-U2-L1-6 - Practice Question

1. What is Naive Bayes, and how is it rooted in Bayes' theorem?

> Naive Bayes is a probabilistic algorithm based on Bayes' theorem, used for classification tasks.

2. Explain the conditional independence assumption in Naive Bayes and its role in probability computations.

> The conditional independence assumption in Naive Bayes simplifies probability computations by assuming that the features are independent given the class label.

3. How does Bayes' theorem combine prior knowledge with new evidence for predictions?

> Bayes' theorem combines prior knowledge with new evidence by updating the prior probabilities with observed data to obtain posterior probabilities.

4. What are the different variants of Naive Bayes, and how are they tailored for specific data types?

The different variants of Naive Bayes include Gaussian, Multinomial, and Bernoulli, each tailored for specific data types such as continuous, discrete, or binary features.

5. Why are statistical concepts like normal distribution, probability density function, likelihood, and maximum likelihood estimation essential for understanding Naive Bayes?

Statistical concepts like normal distribution, probability density function, likelihood, and maximum likelihood estimation are essential for understanding the underlying principles of Naive Bayes and its applications.

6. Describe Multinomial Naive Bayes and its effectiveness in text classification tasks in NLP.

Multinomial Naive Bayes is particularly effective for text classification tasks in NLP due to its ability to handle discrete features like word counts.

7. Outline the steps involved in Natural Language Processing (NLP) and their significance in text analysis.

NLP steps include data preprocessing, tokenization, and feature extraction, crucial for converting raw text data into a format suitable for machine learning models.

8. What is Gaussian Process Classification (GPC), and what distinguishes it from other classification models?

Gaussian Process Classification (GPC) is a non-parametric, probabilistic model known for its ability to quantify uncertainty in predictions, distinguishing it from other classification models.

9. How does GPC quantify uncertainty in predictions, and why is this valuable in real-world applications?

GPC quantifies uncertainty by providing probabilistic predictions along with confidence intervals, making it valuable for applications where understanding prediction confidence is crucial.

10. Explain the difference between Linear Discriminant Analysis (LDA) and Quadratic Discriminant Analysis (QDA), highlighting their respective use cases.

LDA assumes normally distributed classes with the same covariance matrix, while QDA allows different covariance matrices for each class, suitable for more complex datasets.

11. What is Generalized Discriminant Analysis (GDA), and how does it extend LDA to handle non-linear relationships?

Generalized Discriminant Analysis (GDA) extends LDA to handle non-linear relationships by employing kernel functions.

12. Compare Principal Component Analysis (PCA) and Linear Discriminant Analysis (LDA) in terms of their objectives and methodologies.

PCA aims to maximize variance along principal components for unsupervised dimensionality reduction, whereas LDA focuses on maximizing class separability using class labels.

13. How does PCA reduce dimensionality, and what are its limitations compared to LDA?

PCA reduces dimensionality by projecting data onto orthogonal axes, capturing maximum variance, but it does not consider class labels for separation.

14. Define Bayesian Belief Networks (BBNs) and explain their representation using directed acyclic graphs (DAGs).

Bayesian Belief Networks (BBNs) represent probabilistic relationships among variables using directed acyclic graphs (DAGs).

15. Discuss the significance of conditional and joint probabilities in Bayesian Belief Networks, and how they contribute to effective probabilistic modelling.

Conditional and joint probabilities in BBNs specify the likelihood of events given the occurrence of other events and capture the overall probability distribution within the network, essential for effective probabilistic modelling.

Part 3 - Time Series

P3-U3-L1-4 - Practice Question

1. What are the main components of a time series?

The main components of a time series are trend, seasonality, cyclical patterns, and random noise.

2. Differentiate between trend and seasonality in a time series.

Trend represents the long-term movement or directionality of the data, while seasonality refers to periodic fluctuations that occur at regular intervals.

3. Explain the difference between additive and multiplicative seasonality models.

In an additive seasonality model, the seasonal variations are constant across different levels of the time series. In contrast, in a multiplicative seasonality model, the seasonal variations change proportionally with the level of the time series.

4. How do you decompose a time series into its components?

Time series decomposition involves separating a time series into its constituent components, including trend, seasonality, and residual (error) components, using methods like moving averages or seasonal decomposition.

5. What is stationarity in the context of time series data?

A time series is stationary if its statistical properties, such as mean and variance, remain constant over time. Stationarity is a desirable property for many time series analysis techniques.

6. Explain the concept of differencing in time series analysis.

Differencing involves computing the difference between consecutive observations in a time series. It is often used to stabilize the mean or remove trends and seasonality from the data.

7. What are some common unit root tests used to test for stationarity?

Common unit root tests include the Augmented Dickey-Fuller (ADF) test and the Kwiatkowski-Phillips-Schmidt-Shin (KPSS) test.

8. How do you handle missing values in time series data?

Missing values in time series data can be handled using techniques such as zero fill, forward fill, backward fill, linear interpolation, or by using advanced imputation methods like machine learning algorithms.

9. What is autocorrelation, and why is it important in time series analysis?

Autocorrelation measures the correlation between a time series and its lagged values. It is essential in time series analysis, as it helps identify patterns and dependencies in the data over time.

10. What is the Diebold-Mariano test used for in time series forecasting?

The Diebold-Mariano test is used to compare the forecast accuracy of two competing models and determine if one model significantly outperforms the other.

11. Explain the concept of Granger causality in the context of time series analysis.

Granger causality tests whether past values of one time series variable can help predict the future values of another time series variable. It is used to identify causal relationships between variables in a time series dataset.

12. What is ARIMA modelling, and what are its main components?

ARIMA (AutoRegressive Integrated Moving Average) modelling is a popular time series forecasting method. Its main components include the autoregressive (AR) term (p), the integrated (I) term (d), and the moving average (MA) term (q).

13. How do you determine the order of differencing in ARIMA modelling?

The order of differencing in ARIMA modelling is determined by examining the autocorrelation function (ACF) and partial autocorrelation function (PACF) plots of the differenced series.

14. What is the role of the Partial Autocorrelation Function (PACF) in ARIMA modelling?

The PACF helps determine the order of the autoregressive (AR) term in ARIMA modelling by indicating the direct relationship between the current observation and its lagged values after removing the effects of shorter lags.

15. What are some common accuracy metrics used to evaluate time series forecasting models?

Common accuracy metrics include Mean Absolute Percentage Error (MAPE), Mean Error (ME), Mean Absolute Error (MAE), Mean Percentage Error (MPE), Root Mean Squared Error (RMSE), Lag 1 Autocorrelation of Error (ACF1), and Correlation between the Actual and the Forecast (corr).

16. How do you interpret the Mean Absolute Percentage Error (MAPE)?

MAPE measures the average percentage difference between actual and forecasted values. A lower MAPE indicates better forecast accuracy.

17. What is the purpose of performing Auto ARIMA forecasting?

Auto ARIMA forecasting automatically selects the optimal order of the ARIMA model based on the Akaike Information Criterion (AIC) or Bayesian Information Criterion (BIC), making the forecasting process more efficient.

18. What are SARIMA models, and how do they differ from standard ARIMA models?

Seasonal ARIMA (SARIMA) models extend the standard ARIMA framework to account for seasonal patterns in the data. They include additional seasonal parameters (P, D, Q) to capture seasonal variations.

19. How can you test for stationarity in a VAR model using the Augmented Dickey-Fuller (ADF) test?

The ADF test can be applied to the residuals of a VAR model to test for stationarity. If the residuals are stationary, it indicates that the VAR model adequately captures the underlying dynamics of the time series data.

20. What is the significance of cointegration in time series analysis?

Cointegration tests whether multiple non-stationary time series are linearly related in the long run. It is essential for identifying stable, long-term relationships between variables and constructing meaningful econometric models.

21. How do you interpret the results of a Granger causality test?

In a Granger causality test, if the p-value associated with the test statistic is below a certain significance level (e.g., 0.05), it indicates that there is evidence of causality between the variables.

22. What is the purpose of inverting transformations in time series forecasting?

Inverting transformations is necessary to convert forecasted values back to the original scale of the time series, making them interpretable and usable for decision-making.

23. Explain the concept of vector autoregression (VAR) models in time series analysis.

Vector autoregression (VAR) models are multivariate time series models that capture the dynamic relationships between multiple variables by regressing each variable on its lagged values as well as the lagged values of other variables.

24. How can you evaluate the performance of a time series forecasting model using bias analysis?

Bias analysis involves examining the differences between forecasted and actual values to identify any systematic errors or biases in the forecasting model.

25. What techniques can be used for noise reduction in time series data?

Techniques for noise reduction in time series data include moving averages, LOESS (locally weighted scatterplot smoothing), LOWESS (locally weighted scatterplot smoothing), and exponential smoothing methods.

Part 4: Reinforcement

P4-U4-L1-15 - Practice Question

1. What is the fundamental goal of Reinforcement Learning?

To learn optimal actions that maximize cumulative rewards through interaction with an environment.

2. What does an MDP consist of?

States (S), Actions (A), Transition Function (P), Reward Function (R), and Discount Factor (γ).

3. What does the Bellman Equation represent?

A recursive relationship that expresses the value of a state in terms of immediate reward and discounted future value.

4. How do deterministic and stochastic environments differ?

Deterministic: actions always lead to the same outcome; Stochastic: outcomes involve randomness.

5. What is Temporal Difference (TD) learning?

A method that updates value estimates using bootstrapping—learning from estimated future returns.

6. What is a Q-table?

A table storing Q-values for all state–action pairs in tabular RL.

7. What is the goal of Q-Learning?

To learn the optimal policy by maximizing the estimated Q-values using the Bellman Optimality equation.

8. Why do we use neural networks in Deep Q-Learning??

To approximate Q-values in high-dimensional or continuous state spaces.

9. What problem does Double DQN solve?

Overestimation of Q-values by decoupling action selection from action evaluation.

10. What is the main idea of Dueling DQN?

Decomposes Q-value into Value and Advantage to improve learning efficiency.

11. What does PER (Prioritized Experience Replay) improve?

Samples important transitions more frequently to speed up learning.

12. What is Rainbow DQN?

A unified algorithm combining 7 improvements, including Double DQN, PER, and Distributional RL.

13. What does Distributional RL learn?

The full distribution of possible returns instead of just the expected value.

14. What is a Policy Gradient method?

Methods that directly optimize the policy using gradients of expected returns.

15. Why does PPO use clipping?

To prevent excessively large policy updates that destabilize learning.

16. How can PPO integrate with Generative AI?

By using PPO to fine-tune generative models with RL-based reward signals.

17. What is Monte Carlo learning?

Learning value estimates using complete sampled episodes.

18. What is Markov Chain Monte Carlo (MCMC)?

A method for sampling from complex distributions using Markov Chains.

19. What does Metropolis-Hastings do?

Accepts or rejects proposed samples based on acceptance probability to approximate target distributions.

20. What is Gibbs Sampling?

Sequentially samples each variable conditioned on others.

21. What kind of method is DDPG?

A deterministic actor-critic algorithm for continuous action spaces.

22. Why was TD3 introduced?

To reduce overestimation bias and stabilize DDPG learning.

23. What is the key idea of SAC?

Maximizes reward and entropy simultaneously for exploration and stability.

24. What is Multi-Agent RL (MARL)?

A setting where multiple agents learn simultaneously in a shared environment.

25. What is the main issue in MARL?

Non-stationarity, because agents are learning simultaneously.

26. What does Independent Q-Learning (IQL) assume?

Each agent treats others as part of the environment and learns independently.

27. What are Value Networks used for?

To estimate state values for better policy updates.

28. What are Policy Networks used for?

To map observations directly to optimal actions.

29. What role do loss functions play in RL?

They measure errors between target and predicted values to guide optimization.

30. Why is RL suitable for dynamic decision-making problems?

Because it learns adaptively through interaction, trial, and delayed rewards.

APPENDIX C

QUIZ

Part 2

P2-U2-L1-6

1. Which statement best describes a generative model?

    A. Predicts labels directly
    B. Learns P(Y|X) only
    C. Learns how data is generated through P(X,Y)
    D. Cannot model missing data

2. A discriminative model primarily focuses on:

    A. Learning joint probability
    B. Modeling the data distribution
    C. Learning decision boundaries via P(Y|X)
    D. Clustering data

3. Maximum Likelihood Estimation (MLE) chooses parameters that:

    A. Maximize posterior probability
    B. Minimize loss
    C. Maximize the likelihood of observed data
    D. Always prevent overfitting

4. MAP estimation differs from MLE because MAP:

    A. Ignores priors
    B. Uses priors to regularize estimation
    C. Always equals MLE
    D. Works only on Gaussian data

5. Naive Bayes assumes:

    A. Features are fully dependent

B. Features are conditionally independent given the class
C. Data follows a Gaussian distribution
D. No probability normalization

6. Gaussian Naive Bayes is best suited for:

A. Text frequency data
B. Binary text features
C. Continuous, real-valued features
D. Image pixels only

7. Multinomial Naive Bayes is commonly used in:

A. Speech recognition
B. Text classification (bag-of-words)
C. Regression tasks
D. Clustering

8. Bernoulli Naive Bayes works best when:

A. Features are word counts
B. All features are binary (0/1)
C. Data is continuous
D. Class priors are unknown

9. In NLP preprocessing for Naive Bayes, tokenization refers to:

A. Removing infrequent words
B. Converting text into tokens/words
C. Learning embeddings
D. Reducing dimensionality

10. Gaussian Process Classification (GPC) is:

A. A parametric model
B. A non-parametric Bayesian model
C. Unable to provide uncertainty
D. Only used for clustering

11. A key advantage of GPC is:

A. Very fast training
B. Automatic feature extraction
C. Explicit uncertainty quantification
D. No need for kernels

12. LDA assumes that all classes share:

A. Different covariance matrices
B. The same covariance matrix
C. No covariance matrix
D. Non-Gaussian distributions

13. QDA differs from LDA because it uses:

A. Shared covariance
B. Linear decision boundaries
C. Class-specific covariance matrices
D. No generative assumptions

14. A Bayesian Belief Network (BBN) is structured as:

A. A cyclic graph
B. A directed acyclic graph
C. An undirected graph
D. A lattice

15. In BBNs, the joint probability of all variables is computed using:

A. Laplace smoothing
B. Markov chains
C. Product of conditional probabilities
D. Eigen decomposition

16. Hidden Markov Models model sequences using:

A. Independent observations
B. Hidden states and emission probabilities
C. Only prior probabilities
D. Decision trees

17. The Viterbi algorithm is used to:

A. Estimate emission probabilities
B. Compute forward probabilities
C. Find the most likely hidden state sequence
D. Perform clustering

18. Gaussian Mixture Models (GMMs) represent data as:

A. A single Gaussian
B. A mixture of multiple Gaussians
C. A mixture of Bernoulli variables
D. Deterministic points

19. The Expectation–Maximization (EM) algorithm alternates between:

A. Training and testing
B. E-step (infer latent variables) and M-step (update parameters)
C. Sampling and optimization
D. Forward and backward passes

20. A key feature of Dirichlet Process Mixture Models (DPMM) is:

A. The number of clusters must be fixed
B. They cannot model non-Gaussian data
C. They infer the number of clusters automatically
D. They use only uniform priors

Part 3

P3-U3-L1-4

21. What distinguishes time series data from regular data?

A. It contains only numeric values
B. It is unordered
C. Observations are time-dependent
D. It cannot be visualised

22. Which of the following is not a component of a time series?

A. Trend

B. Seasonality
C. Irregularity
D. Normalisation

23. Seasonal plots are most useful for identifying:

A. Cyclic patterns
B. Year-to-year variability
C. Within-period repeating patterns
D. Linear regression trends

24. In additive decomposition, the observed series is expressed as:

A. Trend × Seasonality × Residual
B. Trend + Seasonality + Residual
C. Trend − Seasonality
D. Trend × Residual

25. A stationary time series has:

A. Constant mean and variance over time
B. Strong seasonal effects
C. No random noise
D. A definite upward trend

26. The Augmented Dickey-Fuller (ADF) test is used to detect:

A. Seasonality
B. Cointegration
C. Unit roots (non-stationarity)
D. Outliers

27. Differencing is primarily applied to:

A. Smooth the time series
B. Remove trend and achieve stationarity
C. Capture seasonal components
D. Fill missing values

28. Forward fill is best described a:?

A. Filling missing values with zeros
B. Using future values to fill past values
C. Propagating the last known value forward
D. Using an average of neighbours

29. The ACF plot helps identify:

A. AR terms
B. MA terms
C. Seasonality length only
D. Trend magnitude

30. In Dueling DQN, the Q-value is decomposed into:

A. Reward + Loss
B. Policy + Gradient
C. Value + Advantage
D. Policy + Critic

31. PACF is mainly used to determine:

A. MA order (q)
B. AR order (p)
C. Differencing order (d)
D. Error variance

32. A SARIMA model extends ARIMA by including:

A. Regression coefficients
B. Multivariate components
C. Seasonal components
D. Neural networks

33. SARIMAX differs from SARIMA because it includes:

A. Missing-value imputation
B. External regressors (exogenous variables)
C. Automatic stationarity detection
D. Seasonal differencing only

34. Which error metric measures percentage-based accuracy?

A. RMSE
B. MAE
C. MAPE
D. ME

35. The Diebold-Mariano test is used to compare:

A. Stationarity levels
B. Seasonality strength
C. Forecast accuracy of two models
D. Missing-value methods

36. Vector Autoregression (VAR) models are used for:

A. Single-variable forecasting
B. Non-sequential data
C. Multi-variable time series
D. Sampling synthetic data

37. Granger causality determines whether:

A. One series predicts another
B. Two series share variance
C. Errors are normally distributed
D. Forecast horizon is adequate

38. Cointegration indicates that two time series:

A. Are stationary individually
B. Have a stable long-term relationship
C. Are unrelated
D. Must be differenced repeatedly

39. Boxplots in time series are useful for:

A. Detecting seasonal distribution and variance
B. Identifying AR terms
C. Choosing differencing order
D. Testing cointegration

40. Inverting transformations is important because:

A. It increases data variance
B. Forecasts must be converted back to the original scale
C. It improves model fit automatically
D. It removes seasonality

41. An ARIMA(2,1,0) model means:

A. Two MA terms, no differencing
B. One AR term, two differences
C. Two AR terms, one differencing, no MA
D. Seasonal components includedAnswer: C

Part 4

P4-U4-L1-15

1. What is the main objective of an RL agent?

A. Minimize loss
B. Mimic human behaviour
C. Maximize cumulative rewards
D. Learn labels

2. Which component is NOT part of an MDP?

A. States
B. Actions
C. Loss functions
D. Transition probabilities

3. The Bellman equation expresses value as:

A. Sum of all rewards
B. Immediate reward + discounted future value
C. Future value − current value
D. Episode length

4. A deterministic environment means:

A. The policy changes every step

B. Rewards are always negative
C. Same action → same outcome
D. Agent has no control

5. Temporal Difference (TD) learning uses:

A. Full episode returns
B. Model-based predictions
C. Bootstrapped estimates
D. Human supervision

6. Q-learning is:

A. On-policy
B. Off-policy
C. Supervised learning
D. Model-based

7. In a Q-table, each cell contains:?

A. Reward prediction error
B. Probability of transition
C. Value of state-action pair
D. Policy logits

8. Deep Q-Learning uses neural networks to:?

A. Store transition probabilities
B. Approximate Q-values
C. Calculate gradients of the critic
D. Replace reward signals

9. The main issue solved by Double DQN is?

A. Lack of exploration
B. Overestimation of Q-values
C. Partial observability
D. Slow convergence

10. In Dueling DQN, the Q-value is decomposed into:

A. Reward + Loss
B. Policy + Gradient
C. Value + Advantage
D. Policy + Critic

11. Prioritized Experience Replay (PER) samples experiences based on:?

A. Random selection
B. Episode length
C. TD-error magnitude
D. State-entropy

12. Rainbow DQN combines:

A. Only Double DQN + PER
B. All major DQN improvements
C. Only Distributional RL
D. Only noisy networks

13. Distributional RL predicts:

A. Standard deviation only
B. Reward probabilities
C. Full return distribution
D. Maximum future reward

14. Policy Gradient methods:

A. Learn Q-values only
B. Optimize policies directly
C. Do not use gradients
D. Are model-based only

15. PPO uses clipping to:

A. Speed up training
B. Reduce overfitting
C. Prevent large policy updates
D. Reduce memory usage

16. PPO is a type of?

A. Off-policy algorithm
B. Evolutionary algorithm
C. On-policy algorithm
D. Model-based algorithm

17. Monte Carlo learning updates values using:

A. Bootstrapped returns
B. Full episode returns
C. No returns
D. Imaginary transitions

18. MCMC algorithms are used for:

A. Gradient updates
B. Sampling from complex distributions
C. Solving MDPs
D. Training DQN

19. Metropolis-Hastings accepts samples based on:?

A. Transition matrix
B. Reward value
C. Acceptance probability
D. Step size

20. Gibbs Sampling updates:

A. All variables simultaneously
B. Each variable is conditioned on others
C. Only predicted rewards
D. Only policy logits

21. What kind of policy does DDPG use?

A. Stochastic policy
B. Deterministic policy
C. Tabular policy
D. Randomized policy

22. TD3 adds "twin critics" to:?

A. Reduce memory
B. Reduce variance
C. Reduce overestimation
D. Increase exploration

23. The core idea of SAC is to maximize:

A. Reward only
B. Discount factor
C. Reward + Entropy
D. Gradient magnitude

24. Multi-Agent RL deals with:

A. Single agent only
B. Data preprocessing
C. Multiple learning agents
D. Supervised learning

25. The biggest challenge in MARL is:

A. Overfitting
B. Non-stationarity
C. Lack of labels
D. Data imbalance

26. Independent Q-Learning (IQL) assumes:

A. Agents share a critic
B. Each agent learns independently
C. Agents have identical policies
D. Only one agent explores

27. Centralized Training with Decentralized Execution (CTDE) means:

A. Agents train independently, act jointly
B. Global information during training, local during execution
C. Use of global policy always
D. No communication at any time

28. MADDPG uses:

A. A centralized actor
B. A centralized critic
C. A stochastic critic only
D. Monte Carlo targets

29. In PPO with Generative AI, RL is used to:

A. Remove datasets
B. Fine-tune model behavior via rewards
C. Replace neural networks
D. Train transformers from scratch

30. Implicit Q-Learning (IQL) is used mainly in:

A. Online exploration
B. Offline RL
C. Model-based control
D. Multi-agent PPO

TESTIMONIALS

Optimum – Python – Ultimate Guide for Beginners – Series 1

"Optimum - Python Series I" provides readers with a roadmap to Python mastery, thanks to Shree Shambav's expertise and guidance. The book's structured learning path, clear explanations, and practical examples make it easy to grasp even the most complex concepts. Whether you're a beginner looking to learn the basics or an experienced coder seeking to expand your skill set, this book has something for everyone. I highly recommend it to anyone interested in Python programming!

Optimum – Exploring Data Structures and Algorithms – Series II

As a Python programmer looking to deepen one's understanding of data structures and algorithms, I can confidently say that Optimum – Exploring Data Structures and Algorithms – Series II is one of the best resources I've come across. Whether you're just starting or you're already experienced with Python, this book is an indispensable guide for anyone who wants to master both the fundamentals and the more advanced aspects of programming.

Optimum – Unleashing the Potential of Data Science with Libraries Series III

Shree Shambav's "Optimum – Python Power Series III" turns the vast world of Python libraries into a clear and structured path toward mastery. From NumPy to Scikit-learn, every chapter builds confidence and insight, making it a must-have for learners and professionals alike in the age of intelligent data.

Optimum – Unleashing the Potential of Data Science with Machine Learning Techniques Series IV

An extraordinary fusion of clarity, depth, and practicality. Shree Shambav transforms complex machine learning concepts into an engaging, intuitive learning journey that empowers readers to think like data scientists. A must-read for anyone seeking to master Python's true potential in the evolving world of data science.

ACKNOWLEDGEMENTS

To my grandfathers, grandmothers, mothers, fathers, aunts, uncles, neighbours, sisters, brothers, friends, and teachers, they poured in endless moral stories, retellings of Ramayana, Mahabharata, Puranas, Upanishads, and so on.

My teachers, neighbours, and kindred souls. Who provided us with a stage to perform wonderful Puranic stories and were gracious enough to acknowledge our efforts.

The artists and translators of epics have served as a source of inspiration, invigorating our spirits, making these works accessible, and enabling us to grasp the profound depths and deeper dimensions they contain.

I also cherish the stimulating conversations; I had with my wonderful mothers, Punitha Muniswamy and Uma Devi.

Our family's youngest member, Aadhya, who always overwhelmed me with questions, inspired this book.

I would likewise prefer to express gratitude to Mr Sivakumar, Mrs Roopa Sivakumar, Mr Akshaya Rajesh, Ms Akshatha Rajesh, Ms Apeksha Prabhu, Mr Akanksh Prabhu, Mr Nikash Sarasambi, and Mrs Spoorthi Nikash for their valuable inputs.

I must thank Mr Rajesh, Mr Savan Prabhu, Mrs Revathi Rajesh, Mrs Rajani Sarasambi, and Mrs Manju Reshma, who encouraged me and often suggested writing a book. Their unwavering belief that I had something valuable to offer kept me going during my writing sessions.

Love you all,

Shree Shambav

www.shambav.org

shreeshambav@gmail.com

9 789355 925435

Printed at Repro India Ltd.